THE AWAKENING STORM

A Rousing Journey through Life's

Tempests and Disasters

ANNE REDELFS, MD

Printed by Mira Digital Publishing
Brentwood, MO, USA

Note to Readers

Many characters in this story have been changed to protect confidentiality. Many character traits, such as those of Rocks and Minerals, have *not* been changed to inform and protect the public. In using these character types, however, I do not wish to suggest any person in particular. Any resemblance to anyone you might know is purely coincidental. I merely offer my experiences as a listener which prompted the beliefs I've come to embrace. Please try any recommendations at your own risk, as only you, in communication with Higher Guidance, can know your unique situation and exactly what it calls for. I merely give examples of some approaches that have worked for me. I am not practicing pediatrics and psychiatry without a license (I have retired from the field of medicine) since I do not diagnose disease nor offer physical treatments. I merely note developmental ages, much like anyone would distinguish a physical baby from a child, teenager, or adult. I suggest relational tactics, similar to anyone who parents, teaches, or otherwise interacts with the young. I urge caution and advise you to seek *Professional* assistance in assessing one another and applying what you learn. I also encourage you to engage the human being within every person—someone who deserves help to develop and who, whether you realize it or not, is helping to develop you.

The Awakening Storm
A Rousing Journey through Life's Tempests and Disasters

Library of Congress Control Number: 2013901700
ISBN: 978-0-9763302-1-9
EAN:9780976330219

Illustrations by Peg Redelfs
(former Femrock)

Cover photo by Mike Hollingshead, www.extremeinstability.com
Front cover design by Dan M. Griekspoor and CreateSpace
Back cover design by Anne Redelfs and CreateSpace

Dedication

This book is dedicated to wounded children the world over,
outside and within.

This book would not exist were it not for my dear mother, Peg,
who grew to listen to her wounded child,
admit her own mistakes,
share her remorse,
and take steps to heal the wounds.

Mom, may your palpable love and courage
inspire human "parents" everywhere
to do the same.

Table of Contents

Acknowledgments

Our Rescuer (p. 67) gave me much of the information in this book, telling me what is currently most pertinent for rescuing our nation and its residents. Yet, because of my many filters, this book has required much rescuing, as has its author. I'd like to thank the following people for their rescuing efforts:

Peg and Ken—I'm grateful for your daily emotional support and your willingness to walk through an incomprehensible copy with an uncomprehending author.

Peg, Kim, and Patti—your faithful editing to the end kept me plodding along.

Peg, Ken, Joe, BJ, Ann, Alan, Kerstin, Jeff, Lisa, Jing, Clive, Robin and Tim, Trevor, Bradley, Dennis, Dan J., Mike, Dianna, Sharon, and Robin (hilarious!)—thanks for enlivening a character with your own.

Dan G.—your feedback, computer skills, poetic inspiration, and availability were a godsend!

Peg, Kim, Ken, Joan, Chris I., Dorothy, Ginger, Candy, Ann, Sue, Dan G., Jo, Dan J., Effie, Lila and Jerry, Christine, Richard, Flora, Clyde, Cat, Sarah, Amanda, Monica, Bradley, Joanie, Lea, Annie and Justin, Jo Ann, Sharon, Rebecca, Dianna, Shirley, Wilma, Clare, Bernadette, Alastair, Julie Ann, Bob and Elizabeth, Chris D., Patty, Susan, Lisa, Melvin, Naquita, Bonnie, Jane, Sherry, Sandy, and Claudia— thank you for your contributions, giving my voice strength and clarity.

Dianna, Ken, and Bunny—many thanks for remembering my body with nutritional care packages during my many reclusive months.

Joan—I so appreciate your final editing that pointed out prepositional and participial faux pas, tied up loose ends, and gave positive feedback that egged me on through the last lap.

I am beholden to the Cass County Writers' Group and all the people who have crossed my path just long enough to share their stories, wisdom, intelligence, feelings, and encouragement such that this book became what it is today. Because you have so enhanced my life and my book, you have thereby touched everyone who interacts with me or reads these pages. By this I wish to acknowledge what a profound effect we all have on one another…an effect that extends as far as we are willing.

Preface

I am a listener. I have the ability to listen deeply, to hear profound communication, instruction, and guidance in the seemingly ordinary, insignificant, or even inanimate. I wasn't born with this talent, of course. I was born with a potential, and my life has granted me the opportunities and motivation to practice. These opportunities and motivations for personal growth are in all of our lives, encouraging or urging our areas of giftedness. To recognize them, however, we must be receptive, and then we must actively make use of what we receive. Let me give you an example.

I grew up in a family where games were fiercely competitive, often involving conquest and domination (Risk and Monopoly). Lengthy discussions were largely limited to the stock market, while happiness was linked with the rise and fall of the Dow Jones. I, the youngest in my family of five, was interested in people, and my immediate family members became my first subjects of study. I couldn't understand their fascination with money and their desire to amass more and more of it. To me, attending to people, bringing them together, and studying the interactions were so much more intriguing.

In retrospect, I realize my interest in people was based on my own needs. I longed for someone who would listen to me and support my growth—someone interested in my unfolding life story, who would walk with me and shelter me in general, yet know when to step back and support from a distance. I yearned for someone I could share my feelings and thoughts with, someone to help me know myself and become who I was born to be.

Back then, though, I just felt unsettled and unhappy. So while my two older brothers learned their ABCs (Assets, Bonds, Capital, etc.), I searched for a caring and concerned human being—day after day, month after month, and year after year after year. I scrutinized each person I spoke to, trying to discern whether this was "the one"—the one who would hear my voice, validate my experiences, welcome and nurture my feelings, and reflect on my thoughts. Over and over again, though, my hopes were crushed when the person sensed my serious intent and need and quickly changed the subject *or* didn't listen to me at all—"I'm sorry, did you say something? You should speak up if you want people to hear you!"

With each failure to find what I desperately wanted and needed—human connection—I slowed my search, until one day a novel thought came to mind: *Maybe listening is something I could do!* As I considered this interesting idea, my enthusiasm returned. I started questioning everyone about anything I could think of and focused on the answers with as much attention as a young girl could muster. When a conversation got rolling, I tentatively offered something from my own life and waited to see what would happen. More often than not, the conversation continued as if I hadn't uttered a word. If I questioned my companions about this slight, I heard many painful responses: "I would listen to you if you weren't so mousy...so loud...so inarticulate...so odd...so demanding...so unassertive...so vague...so dramatic...so mental..." and so on. Saddened, I tried even harder to listen and to fathom why most people have so much difficulty truly hearing another person.

By the time I was a teenager, I had given up my goal of finding a listener. Instead I practiced my own listening skills just as diligently as my peers practiced their musical instruments, played sports, or studied foreign languages. I listened to television, conversations of strangers in restaurants, passersby wherever I walked, and, of course, friends and family. I also spent many hours listening to my dearest companions—my books—which could be refreshingly open and honest about the world and its people. My books had the added benefit of quietly communicating on any topic, and they never let me down.

Negotiating life through words and meanings temporarily fed me. In listening to others, I seemed to be listening to myself as well, and I was content to have found a listener at last.

By focusing so much on receiving, I didn't say much for many years. When I did speak, my sentences were often short and usually questions, such as, "Why?"—for which I was teased in college. I discovered that most people were pleased to do most of the talking, and they willingly answered me, sometimes at length.

Only rarely did someone deny me the opportunity to exercise my listening ear. Dominic was one such person. He was an elegantly dressed world traveler, a middle-aged relative of a friend, who occasionally took us out for meals when we were struggling Duke University students. He spoke with few words.

"Do you have any children?" I inquired.

"Yes."

"Boys or girls?"

"Yes."

Dominic was so sparing of conversation that I imagined him to be an international spy! Yet, he taught me that when words are few, there is still plenty to "listen" to.

At twenty-two, I moved to New Orleans to enter Tulane Medical School to further my studies in my research topic: human beings. The patients I encountered were an education in themselves. Listening to their life experiences and noting their bodies' communications through illness and injury, I began to catch glimpses of how the psychological body and the physical body are connected. These moments of insight led me to immerse myself in books about psychology and spirituality, gleaning from listeners who had come before me and learning to listen inside myself, as well as outside. After I was awarded my MD, I continued my personal and professional training at Tulane with two years of residency in pediatrics, followed by three years in psychiatry.

I have also traveled considerably, listening to new languages, dialects, and accents in different environments and cultures. A medical mission with Haitian migrant workers in the Dominican Republic and a work-study program on a kibbutz in Israel were just a couple of my many foreign adventures. They made tangible to me the great diversity of communications, each one rich with educational value. I also grasped the universality of need, including our human need to "listen" and be heard (Ah yes—every person desires to sense and express!). After a wide variety of professional and personal experiences, I concluded that the average person doesn't know how to listen *and* is unaware that he or she isn't listening well. I also realized that most people would rather point a finger at the speaker than admit their own hearing and comprehension need some work.

Now in middle age, I am even more cognizant of how much there is to listening—the depth communicated in every instance seems infinite. "Hearing" better, more completely, is my daily practice—listening not only to words but also to tonality, eye movements, faces, dress, body postures, muscle tension, behavior, and events. I've confirmed that every person, situation, and thing is bursting with self-expression that instructs the body, enlivens the heart, and stimulates the mind of the attentive listener. My fascination has only grown stronger as I've recognized how much I have yet to learn. I've also grown in compassion for all those people over the decades who didn't hear me, because I now comprehend why they made that choice.

I often spot the child I once was in those I'm talking to—their voices suddenly get higher, softer, and more vulnerable; their bodies loosen and take on a childlike stance; a look of sweetness or innocence appears on their faces as their eyes widen. I intuit that what they are communicating—whether it seems to be about a neighbor, the stock market, or the weather—is actually their own life story. They whisper of what is behind the masks, dress-up costumes, and playacting, wishing for me to acknowledge them: "I see you. I hear you. I feel your feelings, and I understand. Thanks for trusting me with the real you." I offer the reality check and emotional support they crave. Then the "children" go back into hiding, and the "adults" go on their way, usually not even noticing what transpired.

I've heard so much sharing in this "touch and go" manner. For instance, a man at the New Orleans Jazz Festival revealed that his spouse had recently committed suicide. He then abruptly changed the topic to his local basketball team. As he talked about a certain player who "didn't play fair" in the last season and how "my wife didn't like it," I sensed that his "inner child"[1] was remorseful because he had treated his wife unfairly. His eyes became watery, as did my own, and then, his story told, he promptly disappeared. A female leader in a far-right church community confided in me about "a friend" who was a lesbian, but "no one knows." This woman's guilt was palpable, her movements anxious. I realized she was speaking of herself and felt her "inner child" hating the hypocrisy and pretense.

People often ask why such a candid aspect of our personality is called an "inner child." When those closest to us in childhood guide us away from ourselves, particularly when at least one uses violence to dissuade us, we harbor a lot of strong, uncomfortable feelings. When our caretakers dismiss or redirect these feelings and their resulting words and behaviors to something that is "nicer," more socially acceptable, or better meets their assumed needs or wishes, we cannot mature. Wherever our developmental needs are not heard and responded to, we remain, in part, "children." Having learned that these parts of us are defective, unwanted, and unsafe, and "their" self-expressions unappreciated, we try to conceal them and may even forget they exist.

These "children" don't stay concealed, however; they are deeply involved in our lives. For example, they criticize what threatens them and put down those they feel inferior to: "They're STUPID!" They feel sick to avoid or to get something: "My stomach hurts!" They get frustrated easily and give up quickly when a task appears beyond their ability or isn't "fun": "I don't want to!" They yell in anger, burst into tears, or refuse to participate when an action is contrary to their liking. They get so wrapped up in their "toys" and "play" that they can be oblivious to their surroundings and others' needs, and they require frequent reminders about important activities and events. They never tire of playing games like hide-and-seek, catch-me-if-you-can, and tag—"you're it!" Our "inner children" (yes, we usually have more than one) also come out of hiding from time to time, searching for a listener who will hear, accept, and value them for who they are.

Moved by all the "kids" stowed away in adult bodies, I've tried to share these young ones' stories, thus encouraging more people to know about them. I have altered the details, so people will not recognize themselves or others—for instance, when I mention a "client" who has parts of his personality he has no awareness of. Much like in my childhood, I often encounter people who don't hear me. Others don't believe me, consider the "client" a rare bird, or immediately rush off to attend to something apparently more pressing. *These reactions have shown me that what we don't listen to on the inside has a huge impact on the way we negotiate our outer world.* Since the average person doesn't know about these "inner children," he or she doesn't acknowledge them or offer age-appropriate help anywhere they might be found. He or she also misses out on the exuberant contributions these "inner kids" have for our lives. Wanting to shed light on the problems that these "children" have so generously confided in me over the years, I looked for a suitable vehicle. But what was it?

I received direction in May 2005, when I sat beside an extremely soft-spoken woman from Los Angeles at a writers' conference luncheon. I leaned very close to her to hear what she was saying: "You should write a self-help book—they are selling like hotcakes right now. With your background, you could turn one over in no time, I'm sure." For a moment, my memory flashed to all the nonlistening people in my life who had told me, "You should speak up if you want people to hear you!" I smiled because I now understood the communication. For years, I'd been writing a book like this woman described, in my mind and on paper, without realizing what I was doing. "That's it!" I heard my "inner child" exclaim. "That's the way!"

In this book, I wish to honor the speakers from all walks of life who have taught me so much over the years through their willingness to express the truth about their lives, their hurts, and their hurting of others. I am amplifying and broadcasting their often-soft voices so they can be more easily acknowledged and understood. I am also sharing my studies in listening—again not just to words, which are so often rehearsed or at least designed to please, but to the deeper, hidden messages of self that are contained in every utterance, movement, and moment. In gratitude for these precious gifts of open, honest communication, these priceless jewels of genuine relationship, I'm passing on what I know in order to develop more eager, willing listeners. Hopefully, over time, these listeners will join me in reaching and teaching the great number of "children" who have yet to find a listener for their lives.

Three Months Later

I spent many years learning to listen to the heart and mind of my fellowman and myself. I still struggled, however, with the practical side of listening: receiving communication pertinent to my interactions with the external world and its people, promptly acting up this knowledge, and expressing myself in ways that were most likely to be understood and acted up. After all, hearing is just a beginning, not an end. Responding effectively to the information was a skill I still needed to develop. And, of course, we all have blind spots—facts we won't attend to no matter how clearly, loudly, or poignantly stated. Little did I know when I wrote this preface and read it to my writers' group on the afternoon of August 27, 2005, that a wake-up call was right around the corner, taking a form I never could have possibly imagined…

Introduction

Listen...

Just as I, as a child, sought someone to hear me and help me grow, people of all ages in your life need you to listen and respond so they can develop. Also, aspects of yourself of all ages need your listening and responding so they can develop. Inner and outer worlds share many features, such as both require our attention and effort to be all that they can be.

This book is the result of my three decades of experience listening to and working with "inner children," as well as the youngest parts of people—our "inner infants" and "inner embryos," my own included. Yes, the smallest of children still reside within most of us, powerfully affecting our decision making in order to meet their "needs," avoid discomforts, soothe themselves, and get "their" way. Left to their own devices, these tiny humans reflexively recoil from pain, or the threat of it, greatly interfering with our "adult" lives. When these "inner babies" are unknown to us, we are oblivious to how involved they are in our choices.

My aim in writing this book is to alert you to this self-deception so you might instead choose an older and more experienced guide—one who hears and understands these hidden parts of you. Our most experienced guide, Our Rescuer, takes you into and through "their" pain to your mature self, who has no pain, no parts, and no fear, and whose happiness and power are genuine, not fabricated or playacted.

With this book, you can learn:

- The importance of listening and why we don't do it. Each chapter contains a step for improving your listening skills and suggestions for practical applications.
- Why we prefer images and stories over the truth about our lives.
- The effects of trauma on the human psyche and methods of treatment.
- How to identify the youngest stage of psychological development (compared with the psychologically mature adult).
- Steps for transcending this earliest stage.
- What we all have in common—the ability to psychologically grow and be "grown" by others.
- The vital role each person in our lives plays in our development.
- How to contact and listen to the guide found within each of us.
- How to pay attention to the opportunities for maturation that occur throughout each day.

How to Listen to this Book

Please read the entire book. As in any course, the information I've provided is important learning material. Do our teachers allow us to select which parts of the texts to read? ("Only look at the parts that speak to your current life situation.") Do our professors tell us to pursue only those homework and test questions we feel drawn to answering? I am no different in asking you to read the whole book and to process and apply the principles as directed. I realize that when much of our world demands one thing or another from us, we crave control to compensate for what is out of our control. We must rely on professionals in many aspects of our lives, but when it comes to psychology, suddenly we want to be in charge of exactly how to remedy our particular issue. ("I know, because I saw it on a talk show!") We feel we know what treatment method is best, when to begin, when we've had enough and are ready to move on, and whether we even need psychological help at all.

Because of this tendency toward self-control, psychology is handled differently than any other branch of knowledge. Why is this? Our culture supports the belief that psychological work is optional or that by seeking psychotherapy we are *proving* we have significant problems! Strangely, we don't have the biases for external explorations that we have for internal investigations. Take aeronautics, for example. Would we presume the average person is capable of traveling to the moon just because he or she has reached physical maturity and has spent many years looking at this bright ball in the night sky? Would we trust someone who has observed many airplanes and taken numerous flights to possess an innate knowledge of aeronautical engineering? One of my objectives is to demonstrate that psychology has *much* in common with every other area of study and would be best approached with the same objective standards.

Objectivity can be difficult, however, when we're schooled in labeling the psychologically impaired as those who function outside of our societal framework: those unable to hold a job or sustain any form of relationship; those who hear disembodied voices, tear off their clothes in public, or attempt to slit their wrists. As long as we define psychological dysfunction in these extremes, we miss seeing the commonplace manifestations of people acting immaturely for their physical age. So many people have told me over the years, "If a psychological issue ever shows up, don't worry, I'll deal with it!" Yet, such problems are evident daily, in our drug and alcohol abuse, caffeine and sugar addictions, obesity, relationship challenges, and difficulties achieving our goals. But when we're stuck at a young psychological age, we're limited in our abilities to listen and perceive the issues as they are, or even notice them at all!

A few statistics illustrate my point that psychological work is *not* optional if we wish to experience safety, health, and happiness:

- We have one of the highest infant mortality rates of the "developed" nations.[2]
- Assault (homicide) is the third leading cause of death in children one to four years old.[3]
- In a national survey, 60.6 percent of children had been exposed to violence, directly or indirectly, during the previous year.[4]
- Nearly 20 percent of American children have a diagnosable mental illness.[5]
- A 2010 survey revealed that 22 percent of full-time eighteen- to twenty-year-old college students use illicit drugs.[6]
- "One in three women on the planet will be raped or beaten in her lifetime."[7]
- One in five adults are mentally ill—a significantly larger number are women and young adults.[8]
- Within a one-year study, 1.1 million adults in the United States attempted suicide.[9]
- The United States has the highest divorce rate in the world.[10]

Check out the percentages of Americans suffering from chronic or degenerative illness, poverty, unemployment, and domestic violence, including the epidemic of child abuse and neglect. Is this the American way? Certainly not! I don't believe our ultimate will is to be sick, deprived, dysfunctional, or destructive to others and ourselves. In my opinion, we cannot maintain healthy living for long if we avoid listening to and working with our minds and emotions. Our assumption that we know what's best for us—"our" way—so often causes imbalances if we don't first take the crucial step of discovering who we are.

I propose that the path leading *out* of this despairing picture of pathology is the psychological journey. When we venture into ourselves and truly listen, we realize we have been far too trained, conditioned, and otherwise constrained by reward and punishment to choose our own way. We have been led off our developmental course, and we must return and proceed...but how?

During my pediatrics residency in New Orleans, I noticed that the "adults" I was working with often acted like the kids in the wards and clinics. So, as I learned to assess the actual children in terms of growth and development, where each child resides along a continuum of abilities from birth to maturity, I also began to register these "adults" according to the same standards. I came to realize that the psychological body is similar to the physical body in terms of predictable development.

Unfortunately, our culture directs us to address and interact with a person based on his or her physical age or societal position, rather than consider the person's psychological age in any moment and respond accordingly. Yet, just as we can know what a child of a certain age is likely to show an interest in or how he or she is likely to behave, when we know about the developmental assessment of "adults," we can better anticipate what any individual is likely to attend to and do. We won't get upset when the "toddler" in our spouse forgets to take out the garbage, nor will we have expectations of an "infant" in the White House fulfilling campaign promises. (I indicate "inner children" throughout this book with quotation marks. For example, "infant" refers to a psychological baby rather than a physical one. An "adult" is someone who is merely physically mature, while an adult refers to someone who truly is psychologically grown and is yet still growing.)

This knowledge of development is *not* intended for judgment and condemnation. My purpose is to facilitate assessment and treatment so that one day all people may have their psychological needs met, thus empowering them to live fulfilling and productive *adult* lives. With this information, we're also more likely to anticipate growth in one another and see the necessity of parental figures in this achievement. With a developmental perspective, we're all capable of maturation—picking up where we left off—if we are willing.

In my experience, however, people are often *not* willing. From traumatic experiences in childhood, they have learned to associate growth with pain. ("Endeavoring toward what will hurt me is crazy!") They have been told they are already all grown up (it certainly *looks* that way!), and they haven't questioned that assumption. They may feel comfortable with themselves—like with an old, worn-out sofa—and see no need or way to change. They've also been taught that having a job that pays the bills and/or raising a family is all there is to adulthood, so why look further? I wrote this book especially with these people in mind, that they might understand the value and urgency of listening with the goal of evolving our humanity. (This evolution is not Darwinism or humanism, but pediatric growth and development.)

What exactly is our humanity anyway, and why is it *so* essential? I grew up watching *Star Trek,* in which humans are an advanced species and interact with many nonhuman species from other planets that are greedy, violent, dominating, devoid of emotion, and so on. In this book, I continue these definitions of human and nonhuman. (A glossary of terms in the back of this book will keep you abreast of some of my more unusual definitions. These glossary words will be underlined in the chapters.) I hear most people defining whatever a human being does as "human," but to me, this generality is like defining every condition of a human body as "health." Later in this book, I'll redefine many words to more directly align with our true human potential. I suggest that the "psychological human" is <u>humane</u>, and all other behaviors exhibited by Homo sapiens are an immature expression of our humanity—or perhaps not human at all. In doing so, I hope to inspire people to something bigger, better, and far more beatific and all-encompassing than we as individuals can conceive—our God-given <u>humanity</u>! We cannot comprehend medicine or mental health without studying this vital, ever-nudging-us-to-evolve human soul. *By listening, we realize that the restraint of this Divinely inspired <u>human nature</u> is our sickness, and its fulfillment is our health and cure.*

Yes, the psychological journey of <u>maturation</u> naturally leads to wellness, and we have much to explore in ourselves and our infirmities along the way. We also have many decisions to make, such as *how* to best go about these travels. Shall we acquire knowledge about ourselves through ministers, therapists, teachers, philosophers, self-help books, or our families? Shall we study psychology through our interests in drama, computers, sports and games, car mechanics, and so forth, or by just going about our day-to-day lives? Questions, learning, and inspiration abound—when we're listening!

I've included questions at the end of each chapter, and also at times within the text. Please answer them all, because together they address the contrasting aspects of your psychology from different angles. *How* you go about answering them is up to you. You could ruminate about each inquiry for a week or just until you've arrived at an apt response. You could acquire your answers through prayer, conversations with relatives, or both. (Get input from those who know you.) You might respond with words (making notes in shorthand or longhand; long-winded or brief; poetic or analytical; in English, Spanish, or French) or pictures (using crayons, magic markers, or watercolors). You might wish to act out particularly resonating queries or scenes from the book with friends or a recovery group. How about considering the content and questions while gardening, cleaning house, or brushing your teeth? Be creative, but stick with the entire curriculum to maximize your learning and growth.

My chapter headings are bookstore genres. Each heading conjures up distinct <u>imagery</u>, as do the different areas of your life, and as in your experience, the forms of education vary. You will be coaxed at times from your comfort zones to what is not so comfortable. Put brackets around the parts of the book that bother you the most. Can you identify why you are upset? Underline those sentences that move you, good or bad. Circle the words that elicit strong reactions in you. What makes you happy, angry, sad, or weary? Write these reactions in the margins, as well as any thoughts you have concerning them. Be aware that the reading may get tough, and painful feelings may arise. Allow yourself breaks and plenty of support as needed.

Observe any defensive posturing as you digest the content of these pages. Instead, practice openness to what you're studying and notice what you like or dislike—this is important information *about you!* You will find story elements and instructional sections—which do you prefer? Be alert to the time you spend on each paragraph—where do you speed-read, and where do you slow to a snail's pace? During which topic does your tennis elbow act up or your war injury beckon your attention? Mark what you harshly criticize or label as "wrong." Try to look equally for what is "right," and learn through both perspectives. If you do not initially understand something, rather than decide, "This doesn't make any sense," pause for a moment, and see if you can prayerfully discern the meaning. Where do you want to attack the writing, discount its lessons, and get rid of the book? (If you do choose to discard this book, please give it to someone you believe can benefit from it!)

Periodically review material you have already read, and pay attention to the parts you don't remember seeing before or don't remember clearly or accurately. Note which questions you've spent more time on, as well as those you've given a quick one-word answer to before going on to the next. Where in the book have you skipped over a section or a question, perhaps zoning out or judging it as irrelevant to you? I recommend journaling about your growing self-awareness. My hope is that as your ability to listen to yourself improves in one area, you'll pursue this self-knowledge in all areas of your life.

If the writing seems to occasionally leap from one subject to the next, know there is a purpose for this. I wish to jolt you out of concrete, linear thinking and away from dependence on form into a more integrated manner of perception, feeling, and thought that emphasizes meaningful content. (We're so often caught up in individualism and momentary appearances!) I jump around at times, but don't our lives as well? Every day we encounter unknown people and unexpected events, and we deal with apparently unrelated subject matter with minimal or no transition from one to another. People have various interests and are in different stages of development, so I've written each chapter with a particular focus, and certain sections will appeal more to one stage of development than another. My aim is to be holistic. If you determine that something is over your head, skim it quickly and return to it at a later date. Or you might read it slowly and prayerfully and try to glean from it what you can. Some sections overlap, just as our own life's chapters do, offering the same material in different forms. Those parts of us stuck in young psychological stages need frequent repetition to grasp material fully.

By structuring this book with short segments of my life story, followed by teaching, I'm hoping you'll get into the habit of listening to your life—pausing during or after each situation and pondering its lessons. As we learn in this way, we discover a consistency of intelligent communication wherever we are willing to perceive it. We begin to appreciate and move with the perpetual rhythm beneath the moment-to-moment changes of people, places, or events. This book can assist you with this crucial developmental step toward adulthood.

I offer this book also as a tool for differentiating the more psychologically mature from the less mature, trusting the former to guide us and extending help to the latter. I aspire to dispel the notion that some of us are only "on top" and others only "beneath" us by demonstrating that each of us has specific areas where we are developmentally ahead of, similar to, or behind our companions. One of the additional benefits of a comprehensive classification system in psychological development is understanding what a person in a particular stage is capable of and requires to progress. However, never rely on first impressions. In assessing anyone, use caution, draw from other people's experiences, pursue professional guidance, and assess in multiple settings over time. Also be willing to alter your impressions as time passes, allowing for change in others and yourself.

The assessments in this book are designed to move you beyond "how things *should* be" or how you desire them to be and closer to how things *are*. You will know, understand, accept, and care for yourself and everyone else better as a result. You may also feel a heightened sense of shared humanity, as well as an appreciation for individual differences. Enhanced health, accurate perceptions, increased efficiency, more intimate relationships, improved decision making, and deep satisfaction are natural by-products of self-knowledge. This journey is worth taking!

This book stems from my life experience. I've often changed the names and descriptions of people while retaining the gist of what they expressed to me. I pass these communications on, not so much to publish "the facts," but because I believe their experiences, feelings, and thoughts carry valuable teaching. Whether or not they are true, I can only guess.

I also use the words "he" or "she" deliberately. These pronouns represent those who have found their way into my professional and personal life. I hope you will choose to see my references to males and females as strictly *my* experience, rather than evidence of a personal grudge or gender bias. My sense of gender comes from my American culture's labeling of "male" and "female" characteristics—I do not mean to classify and label all men or all women.

Along these same lines, many children grow up hearing spirituality talked about only in terms of "He" (God) and "he" (spiritual leaders) which can lead to prejudice, rigid role assignments, and crippling of our psychological bodies—our <u>psyches</u>. Masculine and feminine qualities reside in all individuals, regardless of their physical gender. When we rear boys to be only masculine and girls to be only feminine, we hobble both, forcing them to live their lives hopping on one psychological foot! I'm trying to correct this culturally induced handicap and instability by referring to "Our Rescuer"— our inner Guide throughout the psychological journey—as "she." This most mature feminine self is in stark contrast to the "inner children" and "infants" who merely pretend to be grown up. These "young ones" have misguided us and usurped many leadership positions, acclimating us to male superiority and dominance, which has stifled both genders, curtailed healthy relationships, and harmed much of our world. I believe we greatly limit our experience of God, spiritual teachers, and each other when we acknowledge only the masculine side or only the feminine, rather than embracing wholeness, which *equally* includes both. The goal of this book is absolute equality and completion.

Because so many of us presume that our individual bodies are all that we are and our apparent wills are all that we fancy, try reading this book with new assumptions in mind. For the purpose of learning, let's assume we share a common Identity, an <u>undivided Self</u> with a collective Psychology that radiates from the Divine. (This <u>united Identity</u> will always be referenced using a capital letter.) Let's also suppose that we all have the same will to remember this shared Identity and help each other return to this awareness. However, part of our <u>mind</u> has a desire for separation that manifests in experiencing ourselves as separate persons, each having different physical parts (brain, heart, lungs, and so on) *and* psychological parts, such as our "inner children" and "infants." Just try on these ideas, and see what comes up as a result. Practicing an open stance of trying on, rather than judging and reacting, is a useful place to begin this book. Letting go of what we want this book to be, let's allow what it is to take us somewhere—so that we might then attempt this same open stance with our "inner kids" and our life story.

But first we need to practice listening…

[1] John Bradshaw, *Homecoming: Reclaiming and Championing Your Inner Child* (New York: Bantam Books, 1990).

[2] Deborah Klein Walker, "Prenatal Care: Why Is Infant Mortality Still a U.S. Problem?" *CNN Opinion,* November 2, 2011, http://www.cnn.com/2011/11/02/opinion/walker-infant-mortality/index.html.

[3] Thad King, ed., *Time Almanac Powered by Encyclopedia Britannica, 2011*(Chicago: Encyclopedia Britannica, Inc., 2010), 178.

[4] "US Department of Justice Office of Juvenile Justice and Delinquency Prevention, National Survey of Children's Exposure to Violence," in National Prevention Council, *Appendix 2: National Prevention Strategy Indicators*

(Washington, DC: US Department of Health and Human Services, Office of the Surgeon General, 2011), 60, accessed April 28, 2012, http://www.healthcare.gov/prevention/nphpphc/strategy/appendix2.pdf.

[5] Madeline Vann, "MPH, Mental Illness in Kids: The Surprising Warning Signs," *Everyday Health,* May 18, 2011, http://www.everydayhealth.com/emotional-health/mental-illness-in-kids-surprising-warning-signs.aspx.

[6] US Department of Health and Human Services, "Illicit Drug Use: College Students," *Results from the 2010 National Survey on Drug Use and Health: Summary of National Findings,* http://www.samhsa.gov/data/NSDUH/2k10NSDUH/2k10Results.htm#2.4.

[7] "About One Billion Rising," One Billion Rising website, accessed March 29, 2013, http://www.onebillionrising.org/pages/about-one-billion-rising.

[8] US Department of Health and Human Services, *Results from the 2010 National Survey on Drug Usage and Health: Mental Health Findings,* figure 2.1, http://www.samhsa.gov/data/NSDUH/2k10MH_Findings/2k10MHResults.htm.

[9] Ibid., figure 2.4

[10] "People Statistics: Divorce Rate (most recent) by Country," *NationMaster.com*, accessed April 28, 2012, http://www.nationmaster.com/graph/peo_div_rat-people-divorce-rate.

Chapter 1

TRAVEL

Why We Move Away from Listening

I adore lounging in bed. I think I'm still compensating for all those laborious years of medical school and residency when my beeper would abruptly disturb my sleep in the wee hours to attend to a sick infant or another emergency. I would also lose sleep trying to keep up with my studies. Those strenuous and stressful times have made me relish my current situation, where I have no such demands on my time and can be self-indulgent before I rise. Sometimes several hours go by as I vacillate between dozing and musing about whatever is going on in my life. This particular morning, August 27, 2005, the music of "When the Saints Go Marching In" penetrated my blissful somnolence. The digital clock read 9:11 as I reached over to the nightstand to grab my cell phone.

Jayda's anxious voice responded to my groggy hello. "Hey, girl, I bet you were sleeping. Sorry about that, but they say the storm is coming our way, and I'm freaking…"

A storm? As I shook my head vigorously to wake up, my mind flew back to the night before when I was immersed in a Scrabble competition with a group of friends until nearly two a.m. Wilma, our charming Creole hostess, had announced, "I'm really worried about Katrina."

"Who is she?" I had asked, concerned.

Wilma spoke quickly. "Katrina is the category three hurricane that is headed somewhere between New Orleans and Pearl River, Mississippi. I was living in Pensacola, Florida, last year when Ivan struck. I've never been so scared in my entire life. I was terrified that I would die at any moment, which lasted for EIGHT LONG HOURS!"

Ivan, for those who don't know the local lore, was a category three hurricane that had besieged the Gulf Coast the previous September. (Hurricanes such as Ivan, Camille, Andrew, and Betsy are referred to with proper names and are not to be confused with famous New Orleans musicians, such as Louis, Kid, Mahalia, and Sweet Emma, who are also often referred to only by first name.) Wilma, who had just moved to New Orleans, showed us a souvenir book of Ivan full of graphic pictures of the destruction left behind: demolished homes, highways, beachfront, and even an eighteen-wheeler that had been hoisted into the air and hurled into someone's backyard, landing upside down.

"Even Pookie is restless." Jayda's voice on the phone brought me back to the present moment. "I have a bad feeling about this one." She continued, "I hate to leave with this storm coming in, but I've got to go to a conference in New York tomorrow, and I have absolutely no one to leave Pookie with." Pookie is Jayda's beloved twenty-two-pound rotund black cat. I joke that she is part panther because of her size, color, and the wild look that often appears in her eyes—not to mention that when my mother once tried to pet her, Pookie promptly sank her teeth into Mom's hand!

"What about…uh…your daughter…or your husband?" My questioning mind was rousing slowly.

"Jeremie is seventeen now and needing to fly the coop, so she's evacuating to Houston with her best friend and her folks. You know how teenagers are—she thinks she's grown already. She can't take Pookie with her because Pook wouldn't do well on that long of a car trip with all the evacuation traffic. As for Austin—if I begged, he'd pour on the sugar, but even then I couldn't trust him to do what he said he'd do. Anyway, Kip, our marriage counselor, told me I shouldn't depend on Austin—I should stand on my own two feet."

"That sounds rather extreme," I retorted, my therapeutic side stirring.

"Yeah, that's my gut feeling too, but for what we're paying Kip, I should at least try to listen to his advice and…lean on my friends instead. Would it put you out if Pookie went along on your evacuation?"

"No, I'll be glad to look after Pookie," I uttered before I had even considered the idea of evacuating.

In just a few minutes, though, after I hung up the phone and tripped over the stack of books beside my bed, I shifted into the ever-so-familiar hurricane mode that was becoming automatic—this was the third hurricane in three months! I threw on old clothes, flung muesli into a bowl and doused it with milk, and then hurried into the backyard. Between mouthfuls of my breakfast, I grabbed all small objects that could become dangerous projectiles in the hurricane winds of one hundred-plus miles per hour, securing them, along with my potted plants, in the garden shed. I nailed boards onto the window frames to protect the glass. Inside the house, I placed my valuable documents in an egg crate with my favorite books and packed a spare set of clothing in my suitcase. I copied important files onto CDs, then dismantled the computer and packed the whole lot into the trunk of my car.

Throughout the day, I also answered numerous phone calls from friends and four from my mother, who resides most of the year in Saint Louis. Since I was temporarily staying in her second house, I went over all the preparations with her. My friend Emily telephoned to invite me to evacuate with her to her parents' house in central Florida. That drive normally takes twelve hours, but in evacuation traffic, the travel time could easily double or triple. I persuaded her instead to follow my itinerary: sheltering at my dear adopted "auntie's" second home a hundred miles northwest of New Orleans. Since I don't have many living relatives, I tend to adopt new "family" members from people in the community whose company I enjoy. Effie was one of these people; I'd met her through a mutual friend fifteen years ago and now called her family. She was a dear soul, always up for a nature walk and some conversation. *Her* nature was to rescue the needy and lavish them with Southern hospitality.

Late afternoon, I was one of only three aspiring authors present at our monthly writers' group— attendance was typically eight to ten. Like Jayda, our hostess, Amanda, was expressing concern about traveling with her pets.

"Do you have carriers for your cat and dog?" I asked, thinking that her tabby and terrier might not get along if they were cooped up for long hours in close quarters.

"Those aren't the pets I'm worried about," she replied with a pained look on her face. Thirty-something Amanda had a beautiful peaches-and-cream complexion with freckles in all the right places. Seeing her furrowed brow was a new experience for me. She ushered me into the courtyard of her lovely Esplanade Avenue home, where my attention was drawn to my feet lest I step on one of the dozen or so large, auburn, clucking chickens roaming on the Spanish tiles. These were no ordinary chickens either. Their dark head feathers reminded me of a young Ringo hairstyle.

"I love these guys." Amanda's voice was full of tenderness. "I can't bear the thought of leaving them here for the hurricane, but driving with them in my Prius will be a problem. Though who knows…maybe a short story will come out of this."

In the evening, Jayda stopped by briefly to drop off Pookie, her carrier, litter box, litter, litter scoop, scratching post, flea comb, brush, wet food, dry food, bowls, blanket, toys, odor spray, stress medicine, special treats, and peacock feather. In retrospect, this was probably a clue for me to evacuate with everything I owned as well, but I was too frenzied at the time to notice. Jayda was overtly angry because her husband was refusing to "abandon his roost."

"Austin is so stubborn, just like an old mule! Jeremie and I will be worried sick about him! But, you know, the only one he thinks about is Austin." I gave her a rather serious look, and she instantly corrected herself. "No, Austin doesn't think. Period. Not even about himself! Staying in New Orleans is downright stupid AND DANGEROUS!" I nodded, feeling her tension, as well as my own, yet I was too exhausted from the nonstop urgent exertion of the day to get worked up about anything.

It was almost two in the morning when I'd answered all my phone calls (friends informing me of their evacuation plans), completed preparations for myself and neighbors, and finally had time to sit for a moment. "Well, Anne, this is it," I said aloud to myself. "I'll soon be vacating this place. Should I devote the remaining time to catching a few winks—or packing up as many of my possessions as can fit into my car—since there is always the possibility that there will be nothing left when I return?" My mother had already counseled me to not worry about her belongings. Like her, I felt very strongly that these objects all around me were just things. I didn't want to take the time to salvage them. I was desperate for a couple hours of sleep before my journey of unknown length, at least time-wise. "Are you sure about this?" I beseeched myself, well aware of the weight of this decision. Nothing inside me seemed to pose an argument, so I quickly got ready for bed and fell asleep instantly.

By four that morning, I was busy whisking most of the food out of the refrigerator and freezer and stuffing it into a large cooler. The electricity usually goes out during a storm, so anything remaining would probably be spoiled by the time I returned home. I zoomed through the house, scouting for anything essential I might have forgotten. In the family room, I caught sight of my notebook lying on the glass coffee table. As I tend to be mentally hyperactive when stressed, I grabbed it on the way out. Jotting down my thoughts might help clear some of the clutter in my mind.

Speaking of clutter, I'd allowed my mom's house to become *rather* messy—I'd been too preoccupied to pay much attention. "Sorry, Mom!" I muttered, making a mental note to clean up as soon as I got back. Cat carrier in one hand and cooler in the other, I raced to my car.

Soon I was driving circuitously out of New Orleans, using back streets to avoid evacuation traffic, listening to Pookie bellowing, and smelling the results of her gastrointestinal distress. Jayda had mentioned that her cat didn't fare well on car trips, but somehow in the rush neglected to inform me of the specific details. Pookie was graphically manifesting the stress that seemed to be everywhere. Outside a Greek taverna in Metairie, I honked my horn at Emily, who was waiting in her Volvo.

Within minutes, we were traveling in tandem along the twenty-four-mile Lake Pontchartrain Causeway and beyond. Our pace was impeded by the heavy traffic, but we never slowed to a standstill.

Two and a half hours later, we rolled into one of the two gas stations in the tiny town of Greensburg, Louisiana. After a severe storm, gas stations can be closed for days, so we filled up our tanks as a precaution. As we started the last two miles of the journey to Effie's farm, I tuned into evacuation station WWNO on the radio. I was too obsessed with my situation to notice much of the rural scenery, but before long, I was turning right onto a dirt road. After another half mile, I made another right through an old wooden gate, where a stately live oak tree welcomed us to Effie's.

That magnificent tree must be at least five hundred years old, I thought as I paused for a moment to

observe its massive, Spanish-moss-draped limbs extending in all directions from an enormous bifurcated trunk. With the moss swaying gently in the breeze, the tree was vibrant. It held so many life-forms in its branches—vines, ferns, lichens, fungi, birds, squirrels, and certainly insects—a microcosm of life. I felt a deep respect for this old man who stood so nobly like a sentinel over Effie's property. Many storms had blown through, and yet he prevailed, forever growing, radiating grace and strength, and receiving all who would come into his outstretched arms.

Suddenly the newscaster's voice caught my attention: "Even the casinos along the Gulf Coast have closed. Hurricane Katrina is currently a category five and heading directly toward the city of New Orleans!" *Category five!!! Oh NO!* I thought. *Our levees won't hold in a category five hurricane! I've left almost everything I own back in New Orleans, not to mention my mother's property, and it's too late to go back!*

Listening Step One: WHY DON'T WE LISTEN?

That weekend will always be etched in my memory—the last days of taking for granted what I claimed as my home, my garden where I raised organic vegetables and herbs, my possessions accumulated over a lifetime, my neighborhood, and my city. They were also the final days of keeping my distance from the community of my fellowman. Even now, my eyes tear up and my heart winces as I reflect on that time when I was so oblivious to what was to come—not only the tempest of Mother Nature, but also the stormy forces within man.

"Why didn't I hear the warnings?" I've asked myself so many times since. I never thought much about hurricanes when I first moved to the city in 1982, but in recent years, the possibility of New Orleans being pummeled by a strong storm had been discussed more and more on the news and in day-to-day conversations around town: "If a severe hurricane ever hits head-on, the whole city will fill up like a soup bowl. It'll be all over then!" It was too horrible to think about!

I Don't Like What I'm Hearing

Three weeks earlier, I had telephoned Allison, a New Orleanian who had relocated to New Mexico only two months before. I told her I was considering changing my residence to Santa Fe, and she said,

"I'm so glad you're escaping New Orleans because all the psychics around here are buzzing about 'the Big One' striking sometime soon—like within a year."

Traveling back to the present moment, I began musing. *Allison's words were supportive of my moving but NOT what I wanted to hear since New Orleans was my home. I find we listen more to those who support our decisions or tell us what we like to hear, often tuning out those who don't. We may be so unimpressed or even offended by HOW information is presented that we don't bother to assess its validity. Is how a truth conveyed really more critical than its message? Everyone we know may be using this "questionable" form (clairvoyance), but because we call it something else (alertness, intuition, anticipation, sensitivity, community spiritedness, insight, and so on), we don't notice it as such. We may be wary of second sight, and we may not like "bad news," but in this particular case, Allison had given a valuable warning well ahead of time. I didn't recognize it as such only because I didn't appreciate where I was being channeled—to consider a frightening future!*

I Don't Respect the Source

From the many advertisements for psychic readers, to the tea-leaf-reading gypsies, stalwart Vikings, and silver-stars-on-purple-cloaked wizards in the French Quarter, psychics are part of the scenery in New Orleans. I realize many folks look down on psychics because so many "quacks" assume the title of telepath. In my experience, however, the surplus of quacks in the psychic realm is no greater than in any other field—something the "cards" soon to be dealt to New Orleans would reveal to the world at large. Psychics, like anyone professing an ability, fit within a bell curve. Most are average, a few are very bad, and a few are exceptionally good. Still, I only superficially listened to this secondhand news from the psychics in New Mexico, though I shared their premonition with my New Orleans friends.

Now at Effie's, I felt my panic, and then again became lost in my thoughts. *Sometimes we don't listen because of WHO is heralding the news. If a psychic, ex-con, or person of a certain ethnic group or alternative lifestyle offers some news, we may not pay much attention. We may perceive the speaker as younger or less knowledgeable than we are, and therefore less worthy of our interest. One bad experience may have led us to slap a quick label on one type of individual, and we haven't listened to that sort of person since. We may even be so accustomed to the "ranting" of some family members that we blend them into the scenery and don't notice vital information they may give. Meanwhile, if a world leader, a movie star, a well-trained professional, or someone with great stature in the community speaks, we may be far more likely to receive what is said. We are quite happy to listen to them even if their words have little basis in reality.*

If we were to chart the degree to which we listen in our day-to-day encounters, what would the graph look like? There may be many types of people we don't hear—women or men;, children or adults; blacks, Caucasians, or Asians; foreigners or locals; the nonreligious or the religious; the poor or the rich—the list goes on and on. Those we each discount vary, but most of us disregard certain voices or shun voices expressing certain traits, such as vulnerability. In fact, sometimes we are so convinced of other people's fallibility, stupidity, immaturity, insanity, or deviousness, we don't truly listen to anyone at all!

That News Doesn't Concern Me

The part of the New Mexico psychics' report that my mind accentuated was "within a year." In my slow Southern culture, this means two years, if not more. I had immediately placed this potential disaster in a future hurricane season, thinking I would be out of New Orleans by that time—nothing for me to worry about; not yet anyway.

My rumination again distracted me from my circumstances. *How often do we listen to news that is inconvenient or uncomfortable for us? (I wasn't quite ready to move yet.) Don't we focus on what fits well with our plans, emotional states, and belief systems, rather than allow information to move us out of these comfort zones? We interpret messages according to our preconceived notions. What we discard SEEMS to be about another time or a faraway place, or about others who have nothing to do with us. We assume that if it's OUT THERE, then it's separate and independent of what's IN HERE—within our own lives and selves. These assumptions are often invalid—a lesson I was about to learn firsthand.*

They Don't Know What They're Talking About!

Then there was Wilma's concern. Having survived Hurricane Ivan only one year before, she was keenly alert to the danger and appropriately concerned. In contrast, I heard young people—probably tourists—outside a Bourbon Street bar interviewed on the news. The reporter asked why they weren't evacuating when a hurricane was going to smack the city within hours. Hurricane glasses in hand, their alcohol-laden voices exclaimed, "We're not afraid! We're gonna ride it out. Ride 'em, cowboy! Yee haw!" On the other hand, the large number of city officials and television staff looked and sounded so composed when briefing residents about the threatening storm and recommending evacuation from New Orleans that neither Emily nor I could take them seriously. Although their words were, "Please keep yourselves safe by leaving the city," their calm tone and seemingly relaxed or bored manner conveyed something else entirely to those of us who were listening, both emotionally and viscerally.

I reflected on how the best people to consult about a given event are those who have had prior experience. However, we may not trust them if we think their experiences have made them "too sensitive" to be objective or to see clearly. There are also people whose lack of experience results in their heedlessness to true danger; yet we may listen to them because their happy-go-lucky, fun-loving, or adventurous attitudes feel a lot better than someone else's words of impending doom. Individual communications can also express a duality where the voice is saying one thing and the body another. Which one do we heed? We may choose our favorite or, in our confusion, ignore both.

That's Not MY Experience!

Jayda is a massage therapist and an earth-mother type. Her particularly green thumb, her spiritual gift of gardening, enables her to do miraculous things, such as grow gorgeous Creole tomatoes under the shade of her Crepe Myrtle tree or delicate English lavender in the middle of a sweltering New Orleans summer! She feeds and neuters the neighborhood feral cats, caring for a dozen at last count. She mothers not only plants and animals but also all the stray children her daughter, Jeremie, has brought home over the years. With teenagers coming and going, her house has that lived-in look. Her decor displays all the treasures she's ferreted out of thrift stores and garage sales—Jayda is more interested in bargains and practicality than coordinating colors or motifs. Also, she always has a little extra to share with the less fortunate.

Jayda has a tender heart and has shown great attunement with nature, and she was palpably upset by the approaching storm. While I had escaped long ago into the ethereal realm of intellect and ideas, Jayda had both feet firmly planted on the ground. If I had been listening closely and reasoning clearly, I would have relied on her feelings more than my own. *But* I rationalized that she had only resided in

New Orleans for a couple of years. She lacked the experience of decades of hurricane threats, which had been hyped up and dramatized by the media. In my twenty-three years in New Orleans, the major storms had always spun to the east instead of directly striking our city. Why would this one be any different?

We all have different abilities and levels of experience in every area. Before taking a person's words or body language as truth, we need to have experience with him or her. For example, someone who consistently creates beautiful gardens in New Orleans, with its extreme heat and humidity, would be the best person for me to learn from in my own gardening, while Northern gardeners, who deal with freezing temperatures, would be best guided by their local horticultural experts. How often are we detoured, however, from this basic common sense by well-advertised "experts?" Those whose talents and experience lie merely in acquiring impressive positions, amassing money, and looking or sounding particularly good so often distract us from those capable of cultivating our inner "landscapes."

Also, a person can be truly gifted in one area and inept in another. Someone can appear very successful in the physical world and yet be a failure in the psychological, or vice versa. How often do we trust our eyes and ears more than our "listening" through heart, mind, and spirit? Also, how often do we blindly and deafly follow someone who claims to be an expert without investigating if this is indeed the case?

Our experience of people often affects how we communicate. For instance, we may avoid saying something that's likely to upset another. We may not "step" on territory that will end up altering our mood. Then, when others change or we do ourselves, this change may not register because the past is deeply engraved in our minds. We aren't open to another experience because we already "know" what will happen—we don't pursue the multiplicity of possibilities or listen for human need. Those with natural gifts or fresh eyes can thus offer a more accurate reading than our own.

She's Crazy!

Emily said her dad warned her to get out of the city fast. "He's *never* done *that* before!" she exclaimed with an air of alarm. In my two decades of knowing Emily, she's always touted the motto "Safety first!" For example, she refers to her top-of-the-line, green Volvo as "the safest car ever made." She coddles this vehicle with frequent checkups to support its optimal performance, and she insists on biannual inspections of the heating, plumbing, and air-conditioning of her rented flat. Since she's an elementary school teacher who moves around among the different grades as need arises, her safety focus has proved useful.

Behind closed doors, this cautious, soft-spoken, forty-five-year-old brunette is a pack rat par excellence. Everything she's ever owned seems to be decorating the walls, stuffed into her many bookshelves, or protruding from the numerous boxes she has stacked floor to ceiling in the corners and closets of her two-bedroom Kenner apartment. It is also filled with indoor exercise equipment: a stationary bike, treadmill, cross-country Nordic track, rower, weights, ab toners, and bun burners. Each piece she has used for a few weeks or months before turning to something else that guaranteed quick removal of those extra pounds. She even has an entire bookshelf devoted to dieting cookbooks, from *Sugar Busters!* to *The Beverly Hills Diet,* and grapefruit eating to macrobiotics. "I wish my normal appearance would return first; then I'd be happy to exercise and eat right to maintain it!" Emily has confessed to me many times. She holds on to the clothes of her youth, expecting to fit into them sometime in the not-so-distant future. They have tremendous "sentimental value" too, like everything else in her possession.

I helped Emily move to New Orleans a few years ago and, while unpacking her many boxes (wrapped and lined in waterproof garbage bags!), uncovered ten books on surviving the end of the world in the year 2000! "As a teacher, I need to be well-informed," she retorted to my questioning look. Even before the storm, she had two air-detoxifying/antimold units adorning her family/living room, and carbon monoxide, lead, and asbestos detectors next to her fire/smoke/heat alarm. She owns two top-of-the-line professional gas masks. "In case one breaks!" she retorted to my incredulous, "Two?!" She also dons solar-protective clothing during the day and flame-resistant pajamas when she sleeps. Emily had been anticipating disaster for more than five years. Since this is the Deep South, it's not surprising that it was a "li'l slow" in coming.

A saying often repeated in New Orleans conversations is, "Just because you're paranoid doesn't mean everyone is not out to get you." In our current situation, I would add that "paranoia" may indicate that danger is indeed lurking outside your door. Sometimes truth arrives through an apparently unreliable source. However, if we've been trained by our society to judge people who act "oddly" or say "peculiar" things as "psychologically unsound," or any number of pejorative labels, we may not listen to their communication. Yet, those who don't follow our crowd may be more open to conveying valid, if not lifesaving, information that is not mainstream or "politically correct."

I'm an Individual with My Own Ideas—Why Should I Listen to You?

Even my cheerful human friend Cat (short for Cathy) had been somber and teary-eyed when she and her dog, a golden retriever named Sailor, stopped by my house briefly before their evacuation to San Antonio. As we conversed about the brewing storm, I gave the panting Sailor his customary strokes under the chin. The only time I could remember Cat's effervescence diminishing in the past was once when Sailor swallowed a frog. Today, however, some part of her clearly sensed that we were about to swallow something out of the ordinary. My heart felt her sadness, but my head would not yet absorb this reality.

Communication is ever flowing in a myriad of forms—talk, barks, facial expressions, looks, movements, and so on. We may not only hear with our ears and see with our eyes—we can also "listen" with every aspect of our being, including our physical touch, our emotional heart, and our inquisitive mind. Everyone and everything may be experienced as expressing something. However, when we are not open to the information, as I was closed to what was about to befall New Orleans, then it comes to us via alternate paths, such as through our friends, our pets, our stomachs, the news media, and even the weather.

When Didn't I Listen?

Joan is a forty-five-plus-plus-plus-year-old African American woman (no one knows her age, and she's not telling!) who was born and raised in Harlem, where she learned a colorful way of communicating. She is a nurse who established residence in New Orleans five years ago when she separated from her Caucasian husband and started life anew. To put it mildly, Joan is extremely extroverted, and when we're out on the town, both men and women approach her for a date! She exudes her "gift of community" ("You can trace that to my mom," she says proudly.) and has adopted "relatives" of various ages, religions, nationalities, and socioeconomic groups all over the country. She was instructed during prayer to invite me into her "family," so she's been Cousin Joan ever since. This diverse "family" heritage is evident at her parties, where she'll hire a butler, bartender, and band, yet serve a lovely buffet dinner on paper plates. Doctors and lawyers line up with gardeners and cleaning ladies to enjoy the feast. "The Holy Spirit is there!" is Joan's experience of these gatherings.

Cousin Joan also predicted the forthcoming wreckage. Emily informed me later that at the last Scrabble party, Joan referred to Katrina as a big black woman who was furious about four hundred years of oppression. "Don't you remember?" Emily asked. "Right before I won the game, Joan gave a severe forecast—'Katrina is going to kick ass!'" Not only did I not remember her words, I didn't even remember her saying anything on this topic!

Sometimes we're such bad listeners that we don't notice someone speaking, let alone hear what they are saying. Perhaps we have "heard it all before" or think we have. Maybe we've merely never learned to listen. We may also be so threatened by the subject matter that we don't hear the words, register the message, or retain either in our memory banks. Our minds tune out our reception. When we don't have people we trust sharing their memories—"I remember that"—we don't generally believe another's memory over our own. Sometimes even when many trustworthy people remember an incident, we still don't believe them!

How Was I Supposed to Know It Was Important?

Nathan, an uptown insight-oriented psychotherapist who specializes in domestic violence, also attended the Scrabble party. He said, "The average person who enters my office for treatment does so only after divorce papers are served. I typically pose the question, 'Didn't your partner ever express her unhappiness with the marriage?' More often than not, my client replies, 'Yes, of course, many times, but she never did anything about it! How was I supposed to know she was serious?'"

Here I was, having lived through many smaller storms, storms that had been escalating in frequency and intensity, and I hadn't been listening to Mother Nature or taking her seriously. I didn't realize she wanted something from the people of our city and was communicating through the only means she had available. Before her voice could be heard and understood, however, she had to first attract our attention.

Yes, indeed, those with physical bodies are not the only ones communicating to us. Day-to-day situations in our lives also carry important information or requests for change. The same message may come to us repeatedly, perhaps bearing down on us, but we don't take it seriously. We interpret events as random acts of nature, or we perceive relationship problems as "her/his stuff" rather than LISTENING for the lessons offered within each circumstance. We aren't REALLY listening.

Let's Be Honest—Why DON'T We Listen?

When we arrived at Effie's, I surveyed with Emily the beautiful, luminous countryside that surrounded her one-story, adobe-colored brick farmhouse. To our left, bales of hay that shone in the sun like gold ingots rested on newly harvested fields. To our right, unharvested hay swayed in the gentle breeze. The sky was a soft blue with only an occasional small, bright-white cloud interrupting the expanse.

"I'm scared to death that this storm's going to ruin everything!" Emily's voice quavered, and she began picking at her fingernails.

"It may," I said matter-of-factly, annoyed by reality's intrusion dissipating my peace. "But look at what an exquisite day it is right now. Now is perfect!" I so enjoyed that moment as the beauty of the day momentarily relieved my tension.

A few minutes later, we wandered into Effie's house after a brief knock and greeted our frail, seventy-four-year-old native Louisianan hostess, sprawled on her couch in the family room, the news blaring. She turned down the volume with the remote and welcomed us with her down-home Southern drawl. After a brief exchange of pleasantries, she asked, "When y'all walked in, did either of you happen to see my Sea Breeze (a type of air freshener)?" In my stressed condition, this struck me as particularly funny since we were expecting hurricane-force winds from the Gulf of Mexico early the next morning. I laughed out loud.

I fell asleep later that morning, after learning that the mayor of New Orleans had decreed a mandatory evacuation for all of Orleans Parish. Like many people, I find sleep a cozy escape from stress. Besides, having only slept two hours the night before, I was exhausted. I awoke midafternoon, and within a few minutes, with nothing to do and nowhere to go, the gravity of the situation started to dawn on me. Like Emily, I was frightened. *If the storm doesn't veer off to the east, as it usually does, we're doomed!*

When we're tired, intoxicated, medicated, overworked, preoccupied, or particularly in need, we are less able to take in the moment, which may be one reason why we distract ourselves in so many different ways—we don't WANT to listen! The mere idea threatens us! What's stressing us, paradoxically, yet may cause us to laugh. We may prefer smiling and riding on what's nonthreatening—the momentary outward appearance of a situation. We also make excuses for our unwillingness to hear: "I don't like what I'm hearing," "I don't respect the source," "That news doesn't concern me," and so on. At best, we casually relate to the "here and now" or perhaps sightsee only what's on the right or what's on the left. We don't want to know what might be wrapped up from the past or what's looming on the horizon.

Not listening is just one of many evacuation routes—ways we travel from our home in our humanity in an attempt to avoid disaster. We sense that if we stop meandering and pause to welcome the information coming our way, the truth might be so devastating to our preferred experience, our perceived emotional security, and our belief systems that we wouldn't survive. We are afraid! Subconsciously we're aware that this knowledge could irrevocably change us. We would be thrust on a voyage of high adventure and great discovery, the psychological journey, from which there is no return.

REST STOP: Please ask yourself the following questions, and listen carefully to ALL that comes to you. Consider writing your responses in a journal. You can then add to and refer to them as needed, the more you muse on the questions.

1. Why don't you listen? Do you feel you don't have the time, energy, interest, or talent? (If you hear a defensive inner voice saying, "I *do* listen!" reassure yourself and ask again, and again if necessary, until you are open to a deeper answer. You will be able to respond to this question more thoroughly as you progress through the chapters. At this point, we're just getting a baseline.)

2. What types of people do you tend *not* to hear? Do you ignore the uneducated, the pompous, or those "off the beaten path"?

3. Who are you discrediting because you believe their past makes them too sensitive to perceive well? Is there someone who appears easygoing and even-tempered but is really unaware of what is going on?

4. What "unreliable source" has spoken to you recently? Might he or she be mirroring something unreliable in you?

5. Does your experience with people affect how you communicate to them? Is this experience moving you to travel new avenues?

6. Is there a recurring situation in your life that you're not adequately listening to?

7. Make a list of some of the normal stress reactions mentioned in this chapter.

8. In what areas or circumstances are you a good listener? (Where, when, and with whom are you like a sponge in a puddle of water that absorbs every drop?)
   a. Do you hear your body's needs? (Do you know when your body is thirsty, hungry, tired, hurt, and so on and respond accordingly?)
   b. Are you alert to the demands of your environment? (When danger is beyond your ability to manage, do you evacuate to a safe place?)
   c. Do you listen to your spouse's, children's, and friends' wishes as much as your own?
   d. Note the percentage of conversation time you spend talking and the percentage you spend listening.

Remember, with effort, your listening ability can extend to all areas of your life. It just takes practice!

Chapter 2

DRAMA

Stories Replace Reality

I was awakened around three in the morning on August 29 by an agitated, sleepless Emily, who was pacing around our shared room. I weakly inquired what was going on (though I didn't really want to know), and she replied with intense anxiety. Her strong apprehension roused me, and my body stiffened with fear. I was listening, but I didn't hear a word she said. "What was that?" I asked.

LIGHTS! Reality or Fiction

Emily spoke in a calmer voice. "I've been listening to the news. The hurricane is *still* a category five and heading straight for our city! Good thing we're out of there. Oh, and a woman named Connie and her two cranky kids just arrived. By the looks of them, this must be their first evacuation. They'll be harboring with Effie, too." As skittish as Emily is, she's well-rehearsed in evacuations, and even at her evacuation site has difficulty sitting still. She added, "I think I'll turn on the TV to *see* the updates," and then scurried out of the room.

Now I couldn't sleep. The very real threat of annihilation of my home and community gripped me. My life in New Orleans paraded before my eyes as my whole body ached and trembled. I sought the Ear of the Omnipotent Being beyond this world, crying out silently with my inner voice, "How can this be?! I DON'T WANT THIS! THIS IS HORRIBLE!" I felt desperate. "WHY IS THIS HAPPENING?!" I demanded. I was grieving intensely, even before any aspect of the approaching hurricane entered the range of my senses. "Why?" I reverted to that one-word query for which I was known in college. "Why? Why? Why? *WHY*?!"

What came to mind was the holiday TV program *How the Grinch Stole Christmas.* As you may recall, one early Christmas morning, the sour-faced Grinch was driving his sleigh, laden and overflowing with the Christmas presents, food, and decorations he had just stolen from the Whos in Whoville. Before long, his sleigh was perched atop a precipice high above the town, and he found himself and his load dangling dangerously. In that precarious moment, he got wind of a sound. The more he strained his ears, the more melodious this sound became. To his surprise, the warmhearted Whos were joyfully singing carols, despite his best efforts to keep Christmas away. In a flash he realized that Christmas was much more than gifts, feasts, and furnishings—much, MUCH more! As his thinking expanded, so did his heart. It grew within his chest, bursting out of the rigid frame that had enclosed it. Filled with good cheer, he raced his sleigh back down the hill to Whoville and gave back all that he had stolen. Then he sang his very first Christmas carol, joining hands in a circle with the welcoming Who community. I hoped my recollection of this story meant that the storm, too, would turn around and change its nature. With this thought, my heart and mind became peaceful once again, my body relaxed, and I fell back to sleep.

***

"When you're not listening, you are evacuating from your <u>original Identity</u>, which is whole and all-inclusive." This authoritative voice in my dream jolted me, and I was confronted by an enormous middle-aged woman at a podium. She exclaimed, "You mustn't presume to know who you are or what is happening! Do you hear me?" I was one of hundreds of students in a crowded, acoustically poor lecture hall. The tapping of the chalk was loud and distracting as she rapidly scribbled on the blackboard. "You cannot block any part of you or your experience if you expect to be all that you are. You are making 'holes' in your <u>Self</u>, separating out what you *don't* identify with, calling it something else: 'not me.' Notice how often you say, 'That's not *my* style, *my* issue, *my* interest,' and so on. These exclusions then stand apart from what you *do* claim as 'me' or 'mine.'"

The speaker gazed around the room before she resumed her talk. "Suddenly you experience an environment, something apart from yourself that appears beyond your volition. Then you dismiss in judgment some aspect of this new external 'reality,' and you reject some facet of who you are. One Being thus fragments into two, three, and then before you know it, many 'others' emerge that assume the characteristics of these fabricated 'gaps' in your Identity. Don't you believe that 'I'm not an object—I'm a living, breathing, human being'? Don't you say, 'I'm a woman and you're a man—we will never be the same,' or vice versa? Your true Self remains unchanged, but individuality takes root in your mind as you label as 'other' what you neither like nor want, as with not wanting this hurricane. Meanwhile, you select more pleasing traits and circumstances for yourself: 'I own this part of me, but not that!' 'I accept this aspect of life, but not that!' 'I want sunny weather, not stormy!'" In my dream, I felt very sleepy and struggled to pay attention, while my classmate beside me, wearing a headset, seemed to be elsewhere.

Clearing her throat, the speaker drew me back to her discourse: "We create different characters—men, women, and children. We construct unique settings with the addition of the animal, vegetable, and mineral. We feel an array of ever-changing sensations which give independent life or existence to each of these disowned parts. The result is an apparent splitting of One Identity into multiple forms, each representing a part of the continuum ranging from your truly alive authentic Self to your imagined individual body. In this new realm of individual creatures and objects, the apparent 'living' perceive, act on, and react to the 'nonliving' as well as each other."

Fighting fatigue in the dream, I drifted off again for some time before my anxious mind returned to the lecturer. "To fill in the blanks produced by your sleepiness and lack of listening, you contrive a fantasy world based on your wishes. You write stories about this world that you prefer to reality. Meanwhile, the whole of you, your <u>genuine Identity</u>, *is* awake and alert beyond this world and all its stories. Aware of the truth of your existence, this Self never ceases communicating to you the differences between what you desire and what is." The speaker then peered into my eyes as she declared, "This awareness is what you are fighting. Sleepiness is your resistance and a sign that you prefer your set design. You needn't struggle with stories. Merely realize that the greatest gift you give is this awakening." She extended her pointer toward the dozing student next to me as she commanded, "WAKE HIM UP!"

CAMERA! We Prefer Drama

Hurricane Katrina began battering New Orleans at daybreak on August 29, 2005—about the time I awoke again in my new Greensburg location. I trudged to the bathroom to find that the electricity was already off. The room was lit only by the cloud-covered sun, whose light was diminishing by the minute. I washed my face with the tepid water in the basin, and I slowly registered the patter of gentle rain. The tub had also been filled, almost to the brim, with water to flush the toilet.

As I dressed, I thought about the New Orleanians like me who had found shelter inland. Those holing up in New Orleans also came to mind, such as Jayda's husband, Austin. He was born and raised in a Riverbend house that never flooded. Since relocating to low-lying New Orleans East, he has kept his family tradition of staying put no matter what. He has stayed to protect his property. He has stayed to expand his worldly education, preferring firsthand experience. He has experienced every storm that has passed through New Orleans in his fifty-five years of life, and he wasn't going to miss this one. He has also stayed because he is hardheaded and hardhearted—not listening to threats from the media or the concerned pleas of family and friends. Consistently, Austin has picked the drama of stress and chaos (often self-created) over safety and peace.

My apprehension mounted as I considered the tension that those in New Orleans must be feeling right now in the extreme weather conditions they were enduring. I then flashed back to the stress of my last hurricane experience—Hurricane Georges in 1998. Fretfully awaiting that storm while barricaded in my Irish Channel home, I concluded that I didn't like being terrorized. The utter silence of nature's creatures was alarming; they'd had the good sense to abandon the area. The ferocity of winds a hundred miles per hour or more that forced trees to bend ninety degrees was scary! I adore the gorgeous trees in my city, and witnessing them contorted and torn apart left me traumatized, even though, at the last minute, Georges veered off in an easterly direction and pummeled the Mississippi Gulf Coast, leaving New Orleans comparatively unscathed.

Some New Orleanians remarked that Georges got just close enough to read the large sign posted outside a Magazine Street antique store stating, "Go away, Georges, we don't want you here!" Religious groups pointed to the international prayer network as the key that turned Georges away from New Orleans, while the scientifically minded attributed Georges's path to water temperature and prevailing currents.

What exactly changed the storm's direction was not important to me. The storm had changed and so had I—that was enough. The thrill of experiencing a hurricane had lost its appeal, and I vowed to evacuate the city for all major storms in the future. I reasoned that if New Orleans were someday hit by the "Big One," I would rather hear the news from a close friend after the fact. In general, I prefer to *not* see or listen to the stream of minute-by-minute gory details, so I don't watch the news. Instead, I read a pleasant book during stressful events and trust that if I am to apprehend something essential, it will find its way to me. Well, news of Katrina's severity before the storm struck *did* come *to* me—over and over again. However, finding its way THROUGH me and my many mental filters to maximally MOVE me was the challenge.

Now, listening to the intensifying rain and wind, I mused over what I'd learned from the "stormy weather" in my life, seeking some light to offset this dark and foreboding day. Feeling so threatened by my home's potential ravaging by this hurricane that was quickly descending on my safe haven, I stood up and shook myself, trying to ease the muscular tension. To calm myself further, I decided to add structure and a sense of permanence to my thoughts by recording them on paper. I found my notebook among my belongings, opened it, and began to write.

ACTION! Evacuation Day Two—The Story Progresses

The characters in our life stories appear unique, yet they possess many similarities, such as the ability to evacuate in one form or another. For example, just as the frightening experience of Hurricane Georges led to my choosing to evacuate for all subsequent storms, every individual has a tendency to escape when stress, instability, and danger enter the scene (our animal nature surfacing). Some of us are fast evacuators, like Emily, who makes her exit as soon as she hears of a hurricane heading her way. Others move their bodies more slowly or not at all when threatened, but instantly "check out" from their ability to see, hear, feel, or think. One illustration is Austin, who did not evacuate from his home, yet is emotionally detached from his wife, Jayda, showing no consideration for her concerns. Evacuation in all its forms is a common theme in the drama of our daily lives. Over the years, with repeated "storms" and "evacuations," we may become increasingly distant and unavailable, losing our ability to immerse ourselves fully in each moment. Not wanting anything to touch on our strong, scary feelings, we perceive our outside world and our inner condition only superficially.

Each evacuation style molds or maintains our character types—we can't receive information when and where we're absent or inattentive. We then make subjective judgments based on our remote perspective and the limited information we've let through. One person uses scientific research to evaluate, having learned in school that science always uncovers the facts. He concludes, "The eastward shift of Hurricane Georges can be fully explained through meteorology." Another assesses through her spirit. She believes the prayerful petitions of the devout were the turning point of that storm: "My faith has been my saving grace." These are just two of many possible examples of how we evacuate from the endless ways of experiencing and assessing our lives and settle on one "special" way that suits our characters and their comfort. As we interact with those who have different ways of evaluating, difficulties occur, resolve, and then recur, and plots continually unfold.

We match our life's movie with our chosen screenplay, whether it is a comedy, tragedy, mystery, or farce. We attempt to direct our characters and story lines accordingly, contributing and encouraging only the words and actions that are consistent with "our" way—controlling or upstaging other actors as required. Inside the drama, however, we are merely dancing through the continuum of our own characters, judging them from "good" to "bad," "right" or "wrong," as we perceive our own qualities in individuals, circumstances, and events throughout our world. As we get caught up with our current scenarios, potential activities, and recurring themes (outside and within), we can't see that the vast variety of story lines that contain an apparent myriad of people, places, and things are but moving pictures. These pictures can be further condensed to a series of repeated judgments ("This is 'good' for me *or* 'bad' for me."), evacuations ("I don't want the 'bad'!"), and returns to neutrality ("I am content.")

Act One—We Listen Selectively to Hear Our Own Familiar Story

Granola bar in hand, I trekked to the garden shed, a small storage room off the left side of the garage where Pookie was confined. Cracking the door, I caught sight of the largest fur ball I'd ever seen, thrown up by our feline evacuee. "The shape of Louisiana!" I muttered to myself. The living fur ball was motionless, hiding in the least accessible corner behind some lumber and too stressed to come out for fresh food, water, or promises of loving strokes. Her withdrawal was normal under the circumstances as she was in a strange location with howling winds and intensifying rain pelting the shed window and shaking the walls of her tiny refuge. After a short amount of futile coaxing, I returned to my comforting bedroom and curled up on my corner bed in a posture similar to dear Pookie's. I instantly lost myself in my book, drawn back to reality only infrequently by the forceful wind and turbulent rain.

After a while, I became restless and decided to investigate how the human evacuees were faring. Passing by Effie's closed bedroom, I heard her battery-operated radio within. Emily was squirming in a large easy chair in the southeastern corner of the most structurally sound room of the house, the family room, using earphones to listen to her favorite radio station. In the garage, Connie and her two kids were sheltering in a white Lexus SUV, listening to their chosen radio program. I knocked on the closed window of the driver's side to get their attention. When the window opened, I introduced myself. "Hi, I'm Anne from New Orleans."

"Nice to meet you. I'm Connie, and I'm from New Orleans too." She lowered the volume of the urgent male voice on the radio. "I don't mean to be unsociable staying in the car, but I need air-conditioning! We also want to keep up with the news, and well, our car is a bit of home. These are my children, Oliver, who's ten…"

"Hi," murmured dark-haired and downcast Oliver from the backseat.

"And Felicity who's six." When the blonde girl beside her didn't respond, Connie nudged her arm. Blank-faced Felicity then waved quickly before staring off into space once again.

"Are *you* listening to the news?" Oliver asked me with a bit more animation in his voice.

"No," I replied factually. "I find it too disturbing."

Oliver perked up as he filled me in. "Well, we've heard it *all*, and the storm is over! It just fizzled out. New Orleans is safe, and the entire Gulf Coast is out of danger!"

"OLIVER! We all wish that were true—but it isn't!" Connie corrected her son firmly before explaining, "Oliver has a tendency to make up stories when he's stressed. Oliver, please apologize for lying to Ms. Anne."

"Sorry." Oliver's apology was brief.

"No problem," I said, disappointed that the hurricane still raged at home. They seemed preoccupied and very tense, and my animal instincts compelled me to retreat. "Well, nice to meet y'all," I uttered before waving good-bye and racing back to the refuge of my thoughts.

I considered what I'd found in the garden shed. *Another person would have likely seen something else in Pookie's fur ball, but engrossed in my current situation, I saw my home state of Louisiana. I shook my head, realizing how often we argue over these superficial interpretations instead of listening for each interpreter's story and noticing the state of the "creature" producing the "fur ball"—in this case a* very *stressed cat (more diarrhea in the litter box!). We don't listen because we want our characters to play the roles we've assigned them—heroes and villains, milquetoasts and martyrs, caregivers and those in need of care—so we don't look deeply into what they're saying, what they're doing, or who they are. For example, although we know that a cat cowering in a corner during a hurricane is acting from her animal nature, we often presume that a person similarly hiding in her room is revealing* human *traits. Why do our judgments differ?*

I picked up my notebook and continued writing.

When we assume the role of a human being, we often attribute the traits of less-evolved aspects of ourselves to others, interpreting the same qualities and situations differently depending on whom they involve ("me" or "not me," for instance, with "not me" being the receptacle for what I've rejected in myself). These judgments become filters by which we increasingly differentiate reality—allowing in only what supports our stories (such as human traits for me and inhuman traits for Pookie). As our listening styles set, we receive only specific "radio broadcasts." (The more rigid we are in our reception, the more "static!") Our "station" has its own perspective, a unique viewpoint of our world and ourselves—what's important or unimportant. We highlight some "news" for publicity, ignore other information, slant facts to align with our biases, and concoct what suits our needs in the moment. Our "stations" may focus on inspirational messaging, event reporting, social commentary, and so forth. "News" then varies greatly, depending on the recipient and the informant. *The younger we are psychologically, the more the "broadcast" is likely to be distorted, framed to fit our sense of well-being* (as with Oliver's relaying that New Orleans was safe).

Each Character Has a Part of the News

Periodically, someone entered my room, eager to report on the waging storm. Around eight, a more relaxed Emily came in. "I have some good news and some bad news. Part of the roof blew off the Superdome!"

"Is this the bad news or the good news?" I asked, remembering the chronic losing streak of our football team, the Saints.

"The *bad* news! There's mass hysteria, and people are getting hurt! All those poor folks with nowhere to go—getting drenched, scared out of their minds, wondering if they'll survive! You sound just like my dad!" Emily was annoyed. In my stress, I had momentarily forgotten that the Superdome was sheltering about 20,000 New Orleanians from the storm.[1]

"The good news is that Katrina's power is lessening—only a category three hurricane is trouncing New Orleans—and less than that in some areas." I inhaled deeply and felt the tension in my body subside since our levees were designed for category three hurricane protection. One of our city's great debates has been whether to simply maintain those levees or spend the extra money for an upgrade to category five protection for the yearly five-and-a-half-month hurricane season (June 1– November 15), when we live in anticipation of the "Big One."

At 9:30 a.m., Effie appeared, shadowed by Bear, her fluffy, dark-brown Pomeranian. Her announcement coaxed me from my escapist reading: "New Orleans has dodged the bullet once again, dear—the storm veered off to the east at the last minute!" Tears of relief welled up in my eyes as my heart swelled with gratitude.

"The eye is smacking the Louisiana-Mississippi border!" yelled Oliver, punching a fist into his other hand as he passed by on his way from the bathroom, "so our house is probably OK!" Connie and Felicity arrived shortly after his departure.

"Did you know Saint Burnhard? He got FLOODED!" Wide-eyed Felicity's voice trembled with anxiety, and her eyes watered.

"That's Saint Bernard Parish, honey," Connie said. "There was a storm surge early this morning. The Industrial Canal gave way, and the whole area east of it is now underwater. I wish they'd relay more details of *exactly* what's going on!" Connie's voice was tense. She stroked her daughter's long, stringy, blonde hair and added, "Felicity, sweetie, pay attention." Connie exited abruptly, followed by a clingy Felicity. I was left alone once again with my book and my writing.

People filter their experiences in different ways and draft their stories and characters accordingly, so many renditions arise from each situation—some more factual and more complete than others. For example, Emily was well-rounded in her communication, speaking of both "good news" and "bad news." Effie offered a strictly positive report but, in retrospect, one of limited content and value. Oliver's information was part fact and part belief, while his little sister confused a person with a parish, warranting a correction from her mom. Our filtering sets the stage for error or insight, the stifling or stimulation of feelings, and limitation or inspiration in action, all to varying degrees, depending on who or what we are selecting out. Hearing that Hurricane Katrina had moved eastward resulted in our household feeling more relaxed and secure ("That's *good* news!"), while those living close to the Louisiana-Mississippi state line would have reacted in the opposite way ("That's *bad* news!"). When our focus is on the preferences of our unique character, we tend to interpret, judge, and edit information accordingly. An individual "life" perspective must mask or distort whatever passes through it.

Not listening to certain people or particular topics or points of view is like removing scenes from a play and still expecting to know the whole story. The more we filter, the more we miss integral aspects of people's personalities, essential plot elements, key clues to solving a mystery, or even communication vital to our well-being. Each sentence is important to the progression of any tale, the playwright's message, and the audience's understanding. So it is with the story of our lives—each "character" and every scene expresses a vital part of our personal fiction as well as our reality. Although we evacuees in Greensburg were in the midst of a moderate version of the hurricane that was buffeting New Orleans, none of us had an eyewitness account of what was going on at home. We could only tune in to our preferred radio stations, or those listening to theirs, and imagine what it must be like. Similarly, when we're editing out the communication of others, filtering them through our mind-sets, we cannot get an accurate and complete picture of our world or ourselves. We NEED to pay attention, yet we so often don't. WHY?

Act Two—Listening Step Two: PAY ATTENTION!
Listen to the Story of Our Lives

My room was empty once again with the exception of the smiling, black-haired, freckled-face baby doll that Felicity had left. Being with a mom and her two kids carried me back to my days of working in pediatrics at New Orleans Charity Hospital, where I heard many parents admonishing their children to "pay attention." I spend a lot of time musing over people's words, milking them for every drop of meaning I can find. For example, I look up even familiar words in the dictionary to glean as full and detailed a picture as I can of what a person is communicating. "Oh, no! I forgot to bring my dictionary!" I spoke with regret, shaking my head at my absentmindedness. After a long sigh, I put pen to page and slid back to my past role as a pediatrician. I began scribbling a lecture for a hall of parents with inattentive children.

PAYING attention—a recurring theme in all of our life stories! Isn't it interesting that in our language we put a word that brings *cost* to mind right next to one that is absolutely essential for our well-being? We English-speaking people seem to think that offering attention results in a deprivation of some sort. Is PAYING attention really costly? If so, what is the expense of giving someone or something our undivided focus?

Several years ago, I attended a lecture by a psychologist who talked about the then-current research on babies. He declared that if one baby in a nursery is in distress, all the babies cry to increase the likelihood that the one baby's needs will be met. The study concluded that this basic attention to and concern for our fellows is innate, as is the mechanism to seek help. I found it fascinating that a newborn can experience and express another's discomfort when many of the "adults" I know lack this ability—including this professor. At the end of his talk, the psychologist answered questions only from the male students, adding positive feedback, such as, "Good question!" When a female spoke up, she was silenced by a wave of the hand or a "Shhh!" as he proceeded to dote on the males. I wondered how a baby with unconditional regard for others grew into a professor with conditional care for his students. "Listening" to this psychologist's words *and* behavior taught me that paying attention is part instinctive and part learned. The greatest cost I saw in this scenario was to the female students whose intellectual curiosity was neither supported nor fulfilled.

This example shows *how* we learn to pay attention—our environments shape us. We notice where we are heard and encouraged—our needs are met. We're also aware of when we're *not* heard, and where we're discouraged—our needs are *not* met. With repeated episodes, we alter ourselves accordingly—expressing ourselves confidently in the first case, and holding ourselves back in the second. We enjoy learning in the first scenario and lose interest in the second. Overall, we grow in attention where we're given attention, and when our attention needs are consistently *not* met, we remain undeveloped.

During my pediatrics residency, I worked with infants in neonatal units and well-baby clinics. There I learned that the newborn's attention span is minimal. He is most attracted to seeing faces or bold designs of black and white.[2] If we are within eight to fourteen inches of the baby's eyes, the location of maximal visual acuity, we can engage his attention, at least for a few seconds.[3] His hearing isn't fully functioning either—higher pitches and louder sounds are heard better, and he's particularly attuned to his mother's familiar voice.[4] Over time, the infant learns to develop each of his abilities as he's given attention through them.

So much happens over the years that interferes with a developing human's ability to obtain and offer this much-needed attention. We may fix our eyes on unfriendly faces. As we stare at black-and-white images, we're often told that one color is better than another. What we hear may prove harmful to us, so we stop listening. Those close to us may hurt us repeatedly, so we keep at a distance. We're also reared with a variety of people, all of whom have limitations in their ability to pay attention. See if you recognize any of the following infant characteristics in the people you know.

Scripting Our Shared Beginnings: Traits of the Psychological Newborn

Limited focus: This "inner baby" has a very short attention span (like Felicity when stressed) and narrow interests. He or she only grasps a tiny bit of what is available, perhaps hearing the noisiest person or seeing whatever sparkles most.

Unclear vision: "Infants'" perceptions are blurry and nearsighted—they notice only what is close to them, but not *too* close. Familiar faces are prioritized. Everything is delineated into patterns of black and white (good and bad, right and wrong, and so forth), missing the full spectrum of every situation. For example, Oliver separates "us" from "them" when he wants the hurricane to spare his house but doesn't care about others' homes to the east.

High-pitch and loud-sound hearing: Our "babies" listen better to excess—drama, hype, and volume.

Preference for Mom's voice:[5] Psychological "infants" relate what they perceive to their past experiences with parental figures or caretakers and react accordingly. For instance, Emily heard me communicate like her father and became upset.

Attention dependence: When the attention needs of our inner "infants" are unmet, we are forever trying to fulfill this lack. Perhaps we become a radio announcer, stage performer, or parent to achieve an adoring audience. We climb the "ladder of success" to procure the recognition we crave. We even dominate conversations to attract others' eyes and ears, often sucking the life out of relationships as a consequence. We may also avoid sharing our expertise, because if people were to grow in knowledge and capability, they might no longer depend on us, and we'd lose their attention.

Costume Change: The Adaptation

When our childhood caretakers dwell in their "infant" characteristics, they cannot give our psychological identity enough attention to develop. They are too busy listening to their own radio stations and stories to appropriately see, hear, and respond to us. Yet, as immature social creatures, babies and small children are utterly dependent on outside assistance for their nurturance, protection, and education. To get more attention, they align themselves with their caretakers' theatrics, adapting to their expectations and wishes. Maybe we secure Dad's approval by casting Mom as a complaining tyrant or him as the great provider. Perhaps Mom treats us like royalty when we emotionally respond as she does. Thus, we start to take on an identity that maximizes our survival as we perceive, feel, and understand in ways that result in having our needs met, especially our need for attention.

Of course, complications set in over time with many people making different and, at times, opposing demands on us. Our families, peers, teachers, media, and others regularly guide us to whom and what we ought to pay attention, as well as when, where, how, and why. We are also counseled regarding whom and what to ignore. Before long we've each developed many character styles to minimize friction in our relationships. Each character may possess different personality traits, values, interests, desires, and abilities. Some adaptations are healthy—yielding increased flexibility and freedom within our true nature, while others are detrimental and oppressive to that nature. If our limitations award us with more of what we need, such as attention, then we favor them. But, as time progresses, we may associate our very essence or existence with these dysfunctional adaptations— they fit into our stories better than our original functional nature. We attach to them and express their voice ("I'm a type A personality" or "I'm a spendthrift"). Meanwhile, we detach from our birthright—the human being—and this child leaves the "room" unwanted. A "doll" remains.

Felicity dashed into my room and tripped on the rug. She steadied herself, then reached for her doll with an expression of relief. "I forgot my baby!" she exclaimed before darting out of the room. I continued composing my lecture.

Inattention Leads to Mistakes

Physical babies, as opposed to psychological ones, are the most genuine group of individuals I've ever encountered. Think about it. They are never malicious. They have no bad habits. They show when they are unhappy, and they quiet down when the problem is solved. They don't hold back, and they don't deny their messes. They don't pretend they are older or wiser than they are, nor do they become offended or hostile when you notice their immaturity and offer what they need to develop. They're not afraid of closeness, and they don't use it as a means to an end. As already mentioned, they are also receptive to their fellowman.

I like babies! I intend the term "infant" to be descriptive, rather than pejorative, referring to a youthful psychological state. For example, if I call someone's newborn an infant, I'm stating the facts as I see them, not criticizing the parent or child. I apply these same principles to the inner world. Just as the drama of each of our lives involves family members of varying ages, so do the dynamics of our own psychology. Every woman and man has an "infant" in their "internal family," as well as "children," "teenagers," and adults. The psychological health and functioning of this "baby" depends on how well she or he is cared for. (And, the more babies are isolated, the less they receive adequate care!)

I realize there are people who have *physically* grown to adulthood who would *never* consider that a "baby" still lives within them—they feel this is disparaging (perhaps revealing what they were exposed to growing up). Pain can surface as we remember our vulnerability as an infant and our inability to get our needs met. Our "inner infants" so often confuse this internal pain with external events and believe these events are the problem. Denying this part of ourselves can be an attempt to avoid "problems" and suffering, as well as the possibility of being hurt yet again—all of which makes denial an understandable option. Clinging to our "adult" characters seems safer than embracing our "inner babies."

However, pretending we are *only* fully mature human beings is a BIG mistake—as erroneous as recognizing only the immature "babies" within us. Either perspective demonstrates a lack of attention and understanding. For a fuller, more comprehensive view, we need merely look at the evidence presented to us in each moment. For example, someone who literally puts a foot in his or her mouth is most likely a physical infant. Babies also babble, rather than speak clear words and sentences. Psychological infancy has similar telltale signs: people say or do what's embarrassing or causes trouble, and they go on and on about what appears irrelevant or insignificant. ("Infants" speak and act without weighing the effects or consequences.) A limited attention span in a given situation is another clear indication that a person has an "infant" in this one area.

The emotions and behaviors of psychological "babies" are honest, age-appropriate self-expressions. When they surface in us, they alert us to the "infant's" presence, cluing us in on the fact that we're more than we pretend to be. As well-versed as we may be in any particular role, the unwanted baby parts of ourselves upset our performances from time to time and, in so doing, give us glimpses of the larger picture. (We are a mixture of characters—the "adult" I identify as "me" is just a part of who I am—much like the lead character is just a part of any life's story.) Our "inner infants" also show us an inkling of our tremendous potential to grow and develop when our needs are met (not just the physical, but the emotional, mental, and spiritual needs as well). *And our greatest need is to communicate the reality beyond our stories...AND BE HEARD!*

In summary, our ability to pay attention is both innate and learned. Any COST of paying attention, however, is entirely learned. Our life experiences (good, bad, and everything in between) affect how we pay attention—to whom and to what. In those areas where we have a short attention span and don't listen, the cost has outweighed the benefits—a cost we pass on to others. You see, when we don't pay attention, we cannot offer what is needed to the "tiny beings" that occupy physical bodies large and small. As a result, these "little ones" miss out on so much, such as belonging to a human "family" and receiving care from a psychological adult. This loss then sets the stage for a lifetime of heavy drama.

When we *don't* recognize these "babies" or meet their needs, we, too, miss out: Infants, inside and outside, have a powerful ability to alter our status quo and tap into the wellspring of our original human nature, moving us to change our accustomed roles and scripts so we can best meet their needs. They also remind us of our humble, shared beginnings. Once we were all vulnerable and inexperienced, yet openly receptive and genuinely expressive—until we were taught our "adult" acts.

So, wherever we find inattentive "children," let us acknowledge their cry for help along with our mutual need for growth *and* give them our rapt attention.

Mistakes Cause STRESS

A drop of my sweat landed on the center of the page, smearing my text and drawing me out of my lecture-writing mode. As I observed the effect of the moisture on the ink, another drop fell. Without air-conditioning, the high humidity and probably hundred-degree temperature was taking its toll. I was perspiring profusely despite lying nearly motionless on my bed. I put down my pen, wiped my brow, and became aware of the terrifying wailing noises outside my dark and deluge-stained window, a window I somehow didn't dare peek through. As the house convulsed with the thrashing of the violent wind and the pounding rain, my body stiffened with fear. Periodically, a cracking sound caught my attention, and I'd freeze in expectation of a broken branch flying through the window or a tree crashing through the roof. The thump of something hitting the ground rather than the house momentarily relaxed me until another frightening noise or sudden gust jarred my senses. Writing an essay, on a page or in my head, usually helps me feel better in the most stressful of times, but on this day, I needed a higher dosage. Thus, I continued.

Concentrating on a few characters rather than our original undifferentiated Identity greatly narrows our attention, much like my focus on words diverts my attention from the storm. Our preoccupation with our individual character and its most comfortable aspects narrows our attention further, like my focusing on a drop of sweat on my page. However, as much as we might momentarily reduce our attention and what we're attending to, we cannot remove our mind's connection with our true Self. This Adult follows us, like a parent trailing after an impetuous child, as we tune into our own tiny, independent life-form, which is, in comparison, a "baby." The dichotomy between individual self and undifferentiated Self endows every person with a psychological continuum, with each member of our internal family of characters fitting somewhere between the extremes of "infant" and Adult. The "oldest" or most mature members inherit the qualities of our original Nature while the "youngest" or least mature display the primitive or undeveloped traits of the psychological "infant," including inattention.

Consider this illustration: Babies notice only the "face" or superficial appearance of any person or situation. They prefer familiar voices and pictures and expect these even when they are absent. These babes see what they want, rather than what is truly present, unaware of all that they're missing. When "adults" perceive unclearly or superficially and are attached to individual characters and their unfolding dramas, anticipating the same old story rather than investigating the fullness of any event, their "inner infants" are making themselves known.

Infants react to external cues according to biologically built-in reflexes and instincts. For instance, when a finger is placed across babies' palms, they will automatically grasp it. Anything brushed across their cheeks will cause their mouths to move toward it, and if it touches their lips, babies will suck it, whether or not the object is good for the baby. Thus, when we move without conscious thought, grab hold of whatever is given to us without questioning, or automatically turn toward or even ingest something without first sensing its quality, our "inner infants" are behind the scenes directing our actions. *And* when infants are ushering in the drama, it is bound to be recurrently climactic!

Stress Directs Our **Coping** Mechanisms

The worst of the storm had passed, although moderate rain was still beating on Effie's farmhouse, our sanctuary. I was disoriented in time because of the dim light, but my grumbling stomach had me dragging myself to the kitchen. I opened the generator-powered refrigerator and briefly perused the contents before selecting the split-pea soup I had brought from my New Orleans freezer. As the soup simmered on the gas stove, Connie and Felicity trudged in from the garage.

Since my acute stress no longer consumed my attention, I registered the physical presence of mother and daughter for the first time. Felicity, quite plump for her six years, had a nice tan and long, straggly, sun-bleached hair that ran down the back of her tight purple, green, and gold Mardi Gras T-shirt. On the front was a King Cake with a slice missing. Felicity switched from chewing on her fingernails to cautiously munching on some Cajun Crawtater potato chips. Her eyes still had that faraway look.

Connie was a fortyish, trim, well-kept version of her daughter, with brilliant blue eyes instead of Felicity's soft gray. She wore designer blue jeans and a fitted black, satin T-shirt. Her black-and-blue attire seemed to express her mood for the day. Gesturing toward her daughter, Connie explained, "Feli eats when she's upset, so the stress of our hurricane seasons has made its mark in the past few years."

"We're gonna go shopping when the store opens, soooo—what kinds of foods do you like to eat…like when you're worried?" Felicity asked me, as Connie tried to comb her fingers through her daughter's tangled hair.

"Let me think…" I smiled, realizing that I ruminate with my mind more than with my mouth. "I usually eat less when I'm stressed…" I considered how this tendency has kept me from the middle-age spread in the rich-food culture of New Orleans. "But if I'm eating, I like fruits and vegetables a lot…peaches and avocados are my favorites." Felicity frowned. I continued, "I like to snack on taco chips…" Her face let me know this was a better answer but still not what she was looking for. "And guacamole."

Felicity scowled. Having lost her patience, she redirected me. "I'm talking about chocolate, cookies, donuts, ice cream, brownies, honey buns, candy, cake—those things!" Felicity rattled off her favorites.

"Oh," I said softly. My mother had discovered health foods when I was a young teenager, and I followed in her footsteps, avoiding overly processed foods and sweets. But under the circumstances, I responded positively. "I enjoy them all occasionally, when I feel a need for a treat."

Felicity grinned excitedly. "Yeah! So if my mom buys them, then you'll eat them too." She glanced at her mom.

Connie gave Felicity a long, strong hug, full of emotion, as I pondered the potential therapeutic use of sweets to take the edge off the day's intensity.

"Remember when we made fudge with David, and we sang and danced like they used to do at the fudge store at the mall?" a smiling Felicity asked her.

"Yes, sweetie, I remember that happy time," Connie said, wincing a bit, as if to accentuate the emotional difference between that time and this time. "By the way, Anne, has anyone…called for me?" she asked weakly, abruptly changing the subject.

"No," I said, realizing this was the third time she had posed this question. "Where is Oliver?"

"He's in the car trying to become a Pokémon master," Felicity replied.

"That's his favorite video game." Connie shook her head disapprovingly. "The storm briefly diverted his attention from his fantasy world, but he's right back to it now that the worst is over."

Diverting our attention away from Self and toward one individual body, identifying it alone as "self," results in fragmentation within each human character—parts that are disowned and parts owned, with some aspects unconscious and some conscious. Traumatic experiences further fragment us as we choose separation from what on the inside is uncomfortable or unhappy and cling to what feels safe. With their limited focus and penchant for patterns of "black and white," our "inner infants" pick out the parts of us that support "their" sense of well-being and assume roles for "themselves" accordingly. ("I'm just a quiet, gentle fellow.") "Naturally," they ignore contradicting qualities.

With all of our characters so one-sided, plots thicken as conflicts abound (inside and out!), all of which threaten the comfort level of our "inner babies" (more stress!). They cope by evacuating to their imaginations—a "scene" that is more pleasant, such as a "Greensburg" or "Joy Town," perhaps "Prosperity Village" or a "City of Saints." They picture a story more to their liking. (When life doesn't hand us what we want, we can still pretend it does!) From this "safe place," our "inner infants" can happily focus on what has the most pleasing appearance in any moment—perhaps the features of their loved ones that shine or the aspects of themselves that get the most attention and care.

Scene Change: Severe Stress Causes 𝔅𝔏𝔒ℭ𝔎𝔖

Later that afternoon when the storm had passed, I walked outside to assist Emily and some neighbors who were clearing the fallen trees and branches off driveways and the country road—our access to the outside world. Shredded vegetation was everywhere. A number of huge trees had uprooted and fallen over. Large branches were torn from their trunks. Across the street, one big branch was perched precariously twenty feet aboveground in the fork of another tree. Any car driving on this road would have to travel beneath this "sword of Damocles."

"All these trees were downed by a tornado!" said Lou, the man who maintained Effie's grounds and owned the adjoining property. He was slicing a two-foot-diameter trunk using a chainsaw with the ease of a bread knife. "That birch trunk beside you is actually from a tree several miles down the highway! Amazing, huh? And you should see my yard! I have twenty-five beech trees on the ground going in every direction except toward my home. Am I blessed or what?" Rather than feeling happy for him and for all of us now that Katrina had passed, I felt numb. Too much had happened in too short a time for me to process it all. I felt strangely detached, and I was exhausted.

As I picked up broken limbs, my mind continued its narration. *As we continually cope with our drama through judgment, evacuation, and imagination, we lose consciousness of our actual experience and involved aspects of ourselves, whether body, heart, or mind. These parts of our lives and ourselves that we don't claim are dispersed around "us." With our infant vision, however, such bits and pieces seem like strewn refuse, evidence of a violent nature at work, so we keep our distance, and life's traumas escalate as a result. Our persistent distancing from what we feel is unsafe (evacuation!) is a normal survival technique. Just how far each "branch" lies from each "tree," as after a hurricane, reveals the severity of the "storm" that led to the detachment.*

We are each like a tree amid broken branches and scattered debris. Rooted in "our own" limited outlook, we are surrounded by characteristics of ourselves and depictions of our experience that seem apart from "us." Sensitive to the confusion and inadequate coping skills of our "inner infants," we cling to the well-known stories that make these "babies" feel secure, and we close our eyes, turn our heads, or focus our attention elsewhere—effectively blocking what beckons our attention. This infantile survival mechanism cannot stand up to the severe "weather" in our world.

Fallen "branches" over the years cause pileups of <u>dissociated</u> pain that barricade the psychological road back to unity. A built-in potential, such as paying attention, is now barred from within. A natural ability, as with responding to our fellowman's distress, no longer comes easily, if at all! Qualities that were once familiar, as with the ability to take in only what we need and release what we don't need, seem foreign. A tale we've made up to keep our "infants" happy feels more personable and more real. We also retreat from the perspective, skill, and knowledge that each scene potentially provides us. With each obstruction or "roadblock" in place, a passage home to our <u>undivided Self</u> becomes inaccessible. Traveling from our "safe haven" becomes more confined, stress-filled, and difficult, so we increasingly choose to stay where we are. We live more and more the life of the psychological "infant" with minimal mobility.

Sometimes a sense of numbness, bout of tiredness, feeling of stress, or strong and unexpected emotion signals a blocked route within us or an uncomfortable reality trying to break through. We may also have an impulse to get busy or somehow distract ourselves when someone "dares" to approach a lost avenue of our being. Whatever threatens to expose this painful material can seem dangerous and worthy of attack or rejection as IT appears to be malicious or fictitious. Our experiences become increasingly precarious and unpredictable, and we put up even more blocks in "self"-defense. (Babies do like to play with blocks!)

Act Three: The More Blocks, the More Stories

Lou gave me the task of clearing the road that leads to the main highway, so I began scooping up armloads of branches and dumping them to the side. Near the intersection, I met Jason, a man of obvious mixed heritage with gray-streaked hair who looked to be in his fifties. After a brief introduction and short chat, he told me he was a heroin addict.

"I started when I was a soldier in 'Nam because it was so stressful over there, and you could get it so cheap—ten cents a hit! All the guys were doing it. It helped tend our wounds, you know? I think the Viet Cong figured that one out, so they made it available to keep the GIs addicted and weak. Well, it worked—I'm a normal guy, and I never got over it. *And* I got a dishonorable discharge because of it. Now, people try to tell me that I got a choice, but I don't pay any attention to them. I am what I am." He shrugged his shoulders, rubbed his day-old stubble, then extended his arms, showing me his multiple scars. "If you notice this baby here"—he pointed to one vein—"I've never used it for shooting up. I managed to save one vein for health reasons—in case doctors need to draw blood or give me IV medicine sometime." Jason smiled proudly before taking a moment to gaze at Lou's farmhouse, miraculously untouched by all the fallen trees around it.

"Look at that!" Jason pointed in amazement. "No one can tell me that God doesn't exist, because I know He does. His Hand is everywhere! Knowing our Creator is watching, I don't see how people can go about their lives hurting each other like they do. I just don't get it! I've never hurt anyone. I would *never* do that! To pay for my habit, I just rob the rich, so no one's harmed. The people I steal from always recover everything I've taken through their insurance, so no one loses. And if I ever have any heroin left over and someone asks me for it or clearly needs it, I give it away—no questions asked! I figure what I have is for today, and I can always get more tomorrow."

Seemingly satisfied with himself and his worldview, Jason left. I was unsettled, noticing the many blocks in his thought processes. He believes he has no choice about his addiction, yet he can choose to leave a vein untouched. To him, using heroin is not hurtful, nor is robbing people to support his habit. And offering heroin is helpful! We have similar stories, though, don't we? Perhaps we think we have no choice about our characters or our current situations, yet we can choose to change our behavior at any moment. How often do our blocks become assumptions: "I've ALWAYS been this way, so this must be MY way"? We presume that our actions extend from our identity. We don't remember the fork in the road where we prioritized one path or way of being ("my way") over another ("your way") and who or what in our environment prompted this decision. We also block the realization of how harmful our choreographed responses are to ourselves and others. And we block ourselves from carrying out the original, spontaneous, and constructive choices that are always available.

We erect stories within stories to cover up our blocks, building many "logical" arguments for why we act as we do and why we "can't" behave as we once could. Consider our difficulty listening. We may conclude that our inattentiveness is because of genetics ("My dad had an attention-deficit disorder"), physiology ("The language centers in the male brain are not as developed as in the female brain"), or perhaps God-given lack of ability ("The Good Lord didn't make women able to read a flow chart!"). Our misleading explanations for our handicaps then become blocks in themselves—we can't change "who we are," can we?

We can certainly shift our soap-opera characters and their dramas, but not by directing all onlookers to the one untouched "vein" or the "house" that is miraculously still standing—those aspects of our characters and stories that appear untouched by the "storms" we've experienced. When we are so busy setting the stage—"informing" people of our characters, directing their attention to the important, valorous, or charitable things we do (or what we neglect to do)—we don't realize we're actively staging a setting that holds us to our assumptions and maintains our narrow focus. Our storytelling also blocks anything that challenges our well-defended characters or negates our long-held scripts.

Our judgments, based on our limited vision, have been faulty. Meanwhile, our other "veins" and the other "homes" in the vicinity have had other versions of the story to tell. When we've pursued only what our culture or companions have sanctioned as good or helpful, we've overlooked the times when these actions were destructive. We've chastised those who have behaved in ways that our culture terms bad or harmful, unaware that the uncomfortable conditions brought on by their behavior facilitated new growth. As we've used our story addictions to indulge our favorite characters and their story lines, enjoying our "infants'" momentary good feelings, we have convinced ourselves that "no one's harmed" or "no one loses." But we've robbed everyone of the truth and thus damaged many a human "vessel" or "domicile."

Many people have asked me over the years, "Why does it matter if we tell the truth about ourselves and our lives, as opposed to reciting stories?" Well, would you rather know the facts or some glib fiction about our current situation here in southern Louisiana? Let's compare the truth with the typical fictional rewrite of "storms" in the average family or newspaper. Fact: On August 29, 2005, Hurricane Katrina ravaged the Gulf Coast of the United States. With this information, we learn to stay alert to hurricanes and protect our families, properties, cities, and coastline from damage. Scientists study the causes and patterns of these storms to predict where, when, and how severe a storm might be so we can minimize its devastation. Fiction number one (blaming the victim): The hypersensitive and attention-seeking Gulf Coast and its residents had an exaggerated response to a benign storm. In this scenario, the overly reactive Gulf Coast and those living there are the problem, and they alone need our attention, study, and help. Fiction number two (burying one's head in the sand): There was no hurricane! Those professing a storm were merely projecting their own stormy nature outside of themselves. On the contrary, extensive research shows that the widespread destruction and scattered debris over southern Louisiana, Mississippi, and Alabama were part of a normal and natural cycle for coastal areas; so there is no need for alarm or investigation (see Cuba, July 2005;[6] Grenada, September 2004;[7] Pensacola, September 2004;[8] and so on). If we ignored hurricanes in the same manner as we bury the truth of our childhood traumas and their reenactments in the news, perceiving only the effects but not the cause, then there is no bad weather to anticipate and prepare for. The populace rests, temporarily, in blissful ignorance.

Now let's look at fact and fiction within our own homes. What if we tell people that we were the child of a military hero, when Dad was actually dishonorably discharged due to drug addiction, like Jason? What if we say we grew up in a majestic house in New Orleans's Garden District, when we and our homeless mom were actually squatting in the garage behind it? Does it matter that we refer to our happy childhood when we really grew up in a dysfunctional family with one tempest after another? Yes, it matters! The sweet stories and "little white lies" we share with others, such as our children, encourage memory blocking to minimize the disparity between what we say and personal experience. Our blocks to reality then become stumbling blocks that are potentially very harmful, as we tend to ignore or exaggerate elsewhere what we won't acknowledge about our own lives. (Remember, the more magnified, the more likely an infant is to hear it!). When we deny traumatic circumstances ("I don't want to hear about hurricanes!"), we can't anticipate their coming, so we don't prepare for them. We can't receive help for what we don't recognize as a problem. Also, when we avoid the youngest parts of ourselves, we're unaware of how they are influencing perceptions, feelings, and choices—ever guarding their comfort at the expense of what is true, healthy, or necessary for growth. In such an inattentive state, we can't guard ourselves and others from the dangers that come again…and again.

The More Stories, the More We Lose Reality…and Ourselves

I meandered homeward in a daze, gasping at one point when I noticed Effie's beloved live oak was no longer standing in its usual stately manner at the corner of her drive. I stared at the jagged, splintered wood where its majestic vertical trunk had once extended; it had fallen to the ground, leaving the angular trunk alone, surrounded by broken branches. I thought sadly about the hundreds of years that tree had graced this location. One horrible hurricane, and the scene was forever altered! The tree's capacity to give shelter and shade to flora and fauna was now greatly diminished. There was a strange stillness, with no signs of wildlife and the adorning Spanish moss and ferns gone. I went over to its massive wounded trunk and placed my hand on its rough bark, still wet from the storm. "I'm sorry," I whispered to the tree. "I am *so* sorry this happened to you."

When I returned to the house, Emily and I sat down to a dinner of leftover barbecued chicken (free-range, organic, and hormone-free) from Emily's kitchen. Felicity's doll sat in one of the chairs, as if listening to our conversation. We were debriefing about the storm and New Orleans skirting "the Big One" yet again, when we were jarred by the sudden ringing of the telephone. It was Jayda. "Thank God—I finally got through! I've been trying all day. The lines must be tied up with people wanting to find out what's going on…So *please* tell me…how is Pookie?"

In summary, when we're only listening to our favorite "radio stations" and only focusing on preferred aspects of life, we can't access the fullness of our world or its creatures. With this loss of knowledge comes a concurrent loss of ability, including our abilities to receive and respond. With each block, we become less attentive, less human, and less capable of safeguarding humanity. The more holes we have in our humanity, the more we fill them with stories and confuse the literal with the fanciful. As our once-<u>unified Self</u> fragments within our mind, characters with multiple unique points of view arise, their narratives ranging from autobiography to total fiction. The one original theme, Self, ultimately branches into a multitude of metaphors (theater, radio stations, a body releasing sweat, and so on) that, if taken at face value, lead us further into make-believe. As we become more deeply embedded in drama production, plots and subplots, and the ebb and flow of conflicts, we become ensnared in the endless discovery and implementation of temporary resolutions. We seek what yields an attractive look, a satisfying saga, or an apparently happy ending, rather than the truth. We only allow our all-inclusive, ever-versatile Self a minor supporting role in our life sketches or, more commonly, a seat in the audience. Thus, the cost of our misdirected attention is to close the curtain on what is real! (Stage lights dim—NIGHTFALL.)

I put my notebook aside and turned off the flashlight. As I do each night, I laid in bed waiting for sleep and reviewed my day to perceive new meaning in what I'd experienced. With this practice, I gain insight, and I feel each event more deeply. Following my tradition, I focused on each major scene. I couldn't remember twenty-four hours ever lasting SO LONG! So much had transpired, and I felt like a frail, exhausted old lady having lived through all the drama—the details of which were replaying in slow motion in my head.

I wonder if we replay the same scenes over and over throughout our lives because there is still more to take in and learn from these events. As our days pass, we can open to more and more of what is present, and the more we absorb, the more we develop. So it is with psychological <u>maturation</u>. As we notice our acts, we are motivated to "get our act together." In becoming mindful of all parts of our characters and stories, we are more willing to part with them and return to our origin as an original expression of the Whole. Like Connie with her kids, we must attend to our "inner infants" and "children" and their great need for parenting—a means by which we receive what we require to mature and thus progress on the psychological journey. So that's the lesson...the hidden cost of attention that I hadn't considered before. Hmmm—our placement of the heavy word "paying" in front of "attention" is valid after all. The expense is enormous! The cost of paying attention is our youth! But, what we gain is DRAMATICALLY greater...

SCREEN TEST: Answer these questions as honestly as possible, giving attention to any feelings they arouse. Please note these feelings in the margins.

1. Are you aware of the fictional, story elements in your life?
   a. Do you create drama? What role do you prefer?
   b. Do you enjoy playing the hero or heroine / the villain or villainess / someone particularly helpful or helpless? Why?

   c.   Is there anyone or anything entering a scene that makes you want to exit? What judgment are you making?

   d.   Ask friends and family about how they perceive you as out of touch with reality, and compare their observations with yours.

2. Who or what in your environment has taught you not to listen? Write a short skit about this, and include your various evacuation styles. Consider staging it with loved ones.

3. What is your favorite "radio station"? What sorts of information are you drawn to? Do you like "stations" that are upbeat and positive? Are you moved by the depressing or downtrodden reports? Do you stick to worldly facts? If so, what might this fact focus mean about your inner world? Perhaps you don't listen to words, just the "music"; then what kind of "music"—classical, oldies but goodies, pop, hip-hop, or new age? Which "stations" do you avoid?

4. How do you fortify yourself when stressed? Do you seek physical stimulation, such as sweets, sex, sports, or physical labor? Are you attracted to isolation or to emotional closeness, as with sharing feelings, affection, and intimate conversation? Do you immerse yourself in the mental activities of studying, problem solving, or intellectual achievement? Do you aspire to the spiritual?

5. Which routes to progress are blocked in you? What "storms," downed "trees," or fallen "branches" caused these blocks?

6. Spend some time holding actual babies and notice what they pay attention to and how much they miss.

7. In what areas are you like an infant—what don't you pay much attention to?
   a.   In the **physical world**:
      • Are you able to see what is before you and around you?
      • Do you hear all the noises in your environment?
      • Do you have a keen sense of smell and taste?
      • Are you aware of anything that brushes against your skin?
      • Are you attuned to physical movements and sensations, inside and outside of your body? (Comparing yourself with others may help answer these questions.)
   b.   In the **emotional realm**:
      • Do you notice the feelings expressed on people's faces and in their behavior?
      • Do you listen to emotional nuances in conversations?
      • Do you feel the emotional communication in someone's touch?
      • Do you include people's emotional needs in your decision making?
      • Are you comfortable with the full range of emotions within yourself?
   c.   In the experience of **mind**:
      • Do you perceive the mental state of others?
      • Do you hear the belief systems communicated in people's sharing?
      • Do you express the full range of your experience (the "bad" times as well as the "good," the apparently "sunny" sides of yourself and others as well as the "stormy")?

- Are you alert to your thoughts moment to moment and any judgments you might have toward them?

8. A way to clarity about psychological "infancy" is noticing how people interact with babies—doting on them, cooing, responding to them immediately, and asking nothing in return. No one ever suggests that infants work through their issues. Now, are there areas of your life where people engage you in this manner or you expect them to? Whom do you want to bend over backward to please you or support you? Where are you only praised and never challenged or confronted? When do you feel entitled to being waited on hand and foot, while offering little or nothing in return? When a person's natural reaction is to coddle you, then you may have an undeveloped "infant" inside crying out for parental involvement.

9. Where is the narrow range of your newborn "inner infant's" vision primarily directed?

10. Pay particular attention to someone you usually ignore. What is the cost of giving this person your undivided focus?

The next time you consider whether to PAY attention, think about all the babies who show us unequivocally that the greatest expense is when we DON'T pay.

---

[1] "By the evening of August 28, over 100,000 people remained in the city, with 20,000 taking shelter at the Louisiana Superdome." Evacuation Order, "Effect of Hurricane Katrina in New Orleans," *Wikipedia,* last modified April 8, 2013, http://en.wikipedia.org/wiki/Effects_of_Hurricane_Katrina_in_New_Orleans.

[2] Heidi Murkoff, Sharon Mazel, Arlene Eisenberg, and Sandee Hathaway, BSN, *What to Expect the First Year* (New York: Workman Publishing Company, Inc., 2003), 206.

[3] Ibid., 203–204.

[4] Roy Benaroch, MD, reviewer, "How Well Do Newborns Hear?", *WebMD: Health and Baby,* February 24, 2011, accessed December 3, 2012, http://www.webmd.com/parenting/baby/newborn-hearing.

[5] Linda Acredolo, PhD, and Susan Goodwyn, PhD, *Baby Minds* (New York: Bantam Books, 2000), 59.

[6] Nigel Hunt, "Hurricane Dennis," CubaHurricanes.org, accessed November 25, 2012, http://www.cubahurricanes.org/hurricane-dennis-info.php.

[7] Hunt, "Cuba Historic Hurricanes: Hurricane Ivan 2004," CubaHurricanes.org, http://www.cubahurricanes.org/history-hurricane-ivan.php.

[8] Ibid.

Chapter 3

HORROR

The Grinch stole all the presents
from the people in Whoville that day.
~ Dr. Seuss, *How the Grinch Stole Christmas*

I woke up Tuesday morning feeling more optimistic. Pookie appeared happier too, now that she was familiar with her shed, the terrifying noises outside had ceased, and the walls were no longer trembling from the storm—she ventured out of her dark corner to nibble on some food. While normally a formidable creature, she seemed needy this morning. She allowed me to pet her briefly before retreating to her place of security—her need for safety clearly greater than her need for attention. Unfortunately, Effie was extremely allergic to cats, so I had to keep Pookie apart from the main living space. I visited her periodically, as did Connie and the kids, to give her some much-needed attention. After this morning visit, as I closed the door, I glanced at the lumber propped against the far corner of the shed and was startled to see the sudden emergence of a black clawed paw.

Evacuation Day Three—
Listening Step Three: WHAT IS "CLAWING" FOR OUR ATTENTION?

Let's take a closer look at how our characters are molded by our environments and how our "roadblocks" set afoot some serious consequences. Just as I sequestered Pookie away from the rest of the household because of Effie's severe allergy, we also have isolated parts of ourselves because of prolonged or intensely traumatic exposures to people who have shown repugnance toward them. For example, some child-rearing methods overly punish or control the physical being or separate it out as special. The continual needs of a child's body ("I'm hungry!" "I'm thirsty!" "I need to go potty." "I'm cold." "I'm tired.") may seem demanding or overwhelming when the "adults'" physical needs have not been adequately met. Or the comfort-seeking characteristics of a young child may be particularly pleasing or provocative to caretakers whose own desires for physical pleasure were either unrestrained or rigidly curtailed. A small, vulnerable body may also kindle anxiety in parental figures who were harmed when they were that size. To minimize their discomfort, these caretakers often use reward and punishment to hold the child's physical self at bay, in check, or captive unless he or she channels it into an activity they approve of ("All our sons have joined the military—we're so proud!").

The Silent Scream: Our Physical Body Needs Our Attention

As long as I've known Effie, she's been strong and active in managing every aspect of farm life. Since her diagnosis of metastatic cancer, however, she's slowed down tremendously. This morning, she was sleeping restlessly on the couch in the family room, while her own personal canine physician, Dr. Bear, was positioned protectively at her feet. Effie's family bestowed the honorary title of "doctor" on Bear when they noticed his keen ability to detect Effie's physical problems. As the story goes, whenever she has a temperature, he springs onto her chest and licks her face until the fever subsides. If she has other difficulties, he barks loudly until human help arrives. Effie also says he stares at her in a certain way when she needs to remember something. Quite naturally, he expects payment for his services, of which he reminds anyone with food, whether it's Effie with her daily dinner of stewed chicken or Felicity with her treats of cake and ice cream. Bear seems to sense that he fulfills an important function, and except for hygienic purposes, he never strays from Effie's side.

A sick body calls for our attention. When we haven't been tending our physical body with the best of care, it lets us know. Our body may also take on the role of messenger—just like Dr. Bear with Effie—alerting us to psychological problems or needs through uncomfortable or debilitating symptoms. For example, when our mind is preoccupied with adapting to our life's story, our body may alert us to these malignant mutations by producing cancer cells. When we're feeling particularly "hot" or angry about something, the body may raise its temperature. Impairment of recall and memory as we age may point to our lifelong tendency to forget what doesn't fit with our images and stories. Thus, as our environments condition us to shun or constrain parts of who we are, these parts must find alternate ways for their vital needs to be noticed, much like distressed infants. Rather than listening to the messenger, however, we attempt to silence our body's "voice" by ignoring, harshly judging, or eliminating its communications ("Take this pill and your symptoms *should* go away!"). Yet, like a good doctor, the body persists in informing us again and again in multiple ways until we hear it and respond.

SLASHED: Our Voice Needs Our Attention

Emily, Oliver, Felicity, and I began a rousing game of Scrabble to pass the time and, to quote Emily, "bring us back to our old selves." My old self enjoys listening to the psychological communication in participants' word choices. A skeptic might declare that the words people put together stem merely from the letters they select. *But* the players pick their own letters and, from these letters, choose their own words. I hear a hidden, if not gagged, voice in these choices, just as I do in the specific words we all use in our day-to-day conversations. Each word carries many layers of meaning about where we've been, where we are now, and where we're headed. Although our culture teaches us to differentiate these voices according to their perceived importance, much like the scoring of Scrabble words, as a listener, I weigh them all equally. With such attention to detail, we can discover the abandoned, and often kidnapped, sides of ourselves.

When our human voice is not valued in its fullness, richness, and depth, we alter it to what is more acceptable (louder, softer, funnier, more serious, and so forth). As a result, we harbor many voices inside ourselves, and each voice draws different responses from people. A sports-oriented family, for instance, may attend primarily to the expression of the physical body. A family that fosters community welfare may emphasize concerns of the heart, while an academic family may focus on intellectual output. The voices that are best received and to which people best respond eventually drown out the voices that are given the least attention.[1] Our true voice, which normally incorporates them all, fragments under such prioritization. One fragment soon opposes another, and the preferences of parts eclipse the will of the whole.

The various aspects of our human voice that are not heard, welcomed, understood, appreciated, validated, and acted on seek shelter elsewhere. For example, the personal retreats into the impersonal. Direct communication ("I believe the abuse and neglect perpetrated by my childhood caretakers have permanently damaged my psyche!") becomes indirect, hidden, *and* frequently repeated (This person reiterates, "Hurricane Katrina has damaged New Orleans—*she'll* never be the same!"). These indirect expressions are compulsive and often accompanied by strong feelings, both in desperate hope of finding a discerning listener. These softer voices that communicate our story whisper to us through our choices—every subject we talk about or *don't* talk about and every behavior. Even every gesture hints at what we've hidden away, locked in the basement of our unconscious. These muffled cries offer details that differ from our louder, encouraged utterances, which we learned long ago were the "right things" to say (what others preferred) rather than what was genuine. When we are dissuaded from speaking with sincerity, we can forget how important and powerful this authentic voice is. Ultimately, we don't remember the extent and effects of our experiences and the voice that would have them known. Our lost human voice needs our attention.

Blindfolded: Our Inner Vision Needs Our Attention

People regularly voice their observations and experiences of physical bodies—their appearances, movement, and so on. However, mainstream society largely ignores the condition and conditioning of our psychological selves. We are expected *not* to notice the deeper psychological aspects of our being. Let me give my own experience as an example.

When I was young, I practiced my nascent psychological skills overtly. I excitedly related what I perceived in people and asked questions ("You seem upset today—what's going on?"). Instead of receiving encouragement, constructive feedback, and even applause, as I did after my piano recitals, I often incurred anger, nasty criticisms, shunning, or punishment. Many painful years passed before I realized why my psychological practicing was treated so different from other normal activities. I, like so many kids, was unknowingly touching others' sore spots—those outcast, dominated, or imprisoned parts of us that are reservoirs of great pain, guilt, and shame.

When I became a psychiatrist and announced my profession, people often asked, "Are you psychoanalyzing me?" to which I *usually* replied, "No!" I don't intentionally scrutinize the people in my personal life, but my psychological senses are attuned to what people "look like" inside and what they are doing psychologically. Occasionally, a person has instantly walked away without explanation after learning what I did for a living. I understand that not everyone wants to be "seen," but to me, psychological vision is as normal and healthy as the physical vision displayed by my Cousin Joan, who is a people watcher.

"Did you see that absolutely gorgeous, to-die-for outfit that woman had on?" Joan once asked me with large envious eyes as we strolled through the French Market.

"No, I didn't," I replied. I *had* noticed that the woman's inner preschooler was out that day (she was self-absorbed and preoccupied with the manipulation of objects), which might have been why she was playing dress-up. My visual acuity (I'm nearsighted) and awareness of the physical are well below average, but my psychological perception is well above. So when people try to convince me of their virtues, I'm able to sense that these are often "outfits" they are wearing in an attempt to act grown-up or get attention. Yet, if I question their misrepresentations, I'm frequently told I'm "probing" or "invasive." In one way or another, they let me know they prefer *my* eyes closed, as they have closed theirs.

Let's face it—sharing psychological vision makes people uncomfortable, so they discourage it. An external focus on the physical world is easier and far more socially acceptable. Our observation of clothing, hair color, height, and build is acknowledged and discussed much more frequently than people's psychological facades, defenses, developmental ages, and life stories. As a result, most people stick to observing and commenting on superficial characteristics and miss the underlying reality, which can be a horrifically contrasting debacle. Since our psychological vision affects the clarity and depth of our perception of *everything* in our world—*and* how we respond—our psychological "eyes" need our attention.

The Disembodied: Our Psychological Self Needs Our Attention

A lot of us would never dream of paying attention to one child while ignoring another, feeding the first but not the second, hugging a boy with tenderness and care yet avoiding or slapping the outstretched arms of his sister. However extensively a family restrains the physical body, it is still generally treated better than the psychological self. Hunger and thirst, for example, receive *much* faster acknowledgment and response in most households than the yearnings of heart and mind.

To "adults" who have a raft of their own unexpressed and unresolved emotions, a child's expressions of these feelings are scary. In response, they freeze, flee, or fight, at times with fury. They may consider anger a "sin," worthy of avoidance or condemnation. If sadness and fear are deemed "unmanly" and the responsibility for feeling and asserting these emotions is thrust on the females of the family, each family member's psychology will be off balance. Caretakers wrestling with their own insecurities may tackle a child's questioning mind, judging the pursuit of *human* knowledge and self-awareness as "impractical" or "a waste of time." Rather than willingly work out their own issues to nurture these different aspects of a child's growing humanity, most caretakers choose instead to control their kids in the same ways they were controlled in their childhood.

Consider how we behave with babies. Their physical needs are usually met regularly because we know what they are. Infants' psychological requirements, however, can seem complicated or incomprehensible, beckoning us into unfamiliar territory, which is uncomfortable. If we find bruises on a baby, we question, "How did *that* happen?" and take the child to the doctor. But when it comes to emotional bruising, do we investigate psychological causes and remedy them? We want to share our babies' physical space and frequently hold them close, but how often are we willing to embrace their emotional bodies and share their intense feelings? Caretakers often believe that merely rocking babies until they quit crying satisfies their needs. What about tuning in to infants' tender <u>hearts</u> that sense and express the stress in their surroundings (be they construction and traffic noises, sirens, or harsh PEOPLE and strident family dynamics)?[2]

We tend to coax upset babies to our comfort zone. We command them to "shhh" or "quiet down!" and if they persist, we label them as "fussy." We inform them, "Everything's fine," teaching them our story, when these ever-so-sensitive and receptive infants are venting their own experiences. As we continually shush babies, they learn to quiet these aspects of themselves over time or cry even harder in an attempt to be heard. As we contemplate only obvious physical problems and solutions ("Maybe she doesn't like sleeping on her tummy—from now on, she'll sleep on her back."), they grow to do the same, restricting every cause to something other than the human heart and mind. As we offer milk, change diapers, or look for other physical discomforts, babies learns that food or drink, a change of clothes, or some other physical alteration is all that's required to feel better. Meanwhile, the baby's true emotions become bottled up inside, since they are not understood, valued, or encouraged as an essential biological function—self-expression! Without proper listening and responding, the shunned psychological self remains undeveloped, earnestly needing our attention.

In the game of life, our hidden feelings and thoughts do reveal themselves. Some of Emily's word choices during our Scrabble game were HAVEN, WEIGHT, SAFE, and MOON. Emily seemed her "normal" self. Oliver chose DUNK, KILL, MAD, STORM, EXIT, JET, and ZOOS, with a triple letter score on the J and Z. Underneath his video-game preoccupation, he was clearly angry about everything that was going on. Felicity, with our help, picked such words as CANDY, BIRD, TALK, SAD, and QUIT as she chomped on black licorice twists. She also put down the word PEACH, to which Emily later added IM to form the word IMPEACH, another triple word score. Although she is generally understated, Emily does divulge her political leanings to those who are paying attention. She placed ING next to Felicity's LONG, a subtle expression of her frequent emotional state.

Throughout much of the game, Oliver tossed the letter I into the air with his right hand and caught it, while Felicity fiddled with the hourglass timer with her left hand. To me, the symbolism expressed by these two children was poignant.

Emily belongs to a Scrabble club that rents out rooms in lovely Southern plantations every other month to play Scrabble all weekend—some games lasting well into the night. She could have crushed the rest of us, but she showed compassion under the circumstances and played at a level geared to the children's abilities. With her assistance, Oliver "won," which made him momentarily happy.

After the game, Oliver and Emily wanted to play another round, but Felicity insisted on finding some "decent food" for lunch. Eager for a change of scene, the four of us, with Connie, drove around for miles in Connie's SUV, searching for an open restaurant. Every street seemed so quiet and still. All the businesses were closed, likely due to a lack of power, and very few cars busied the roads. Finally, in the small town of Amite, Louisiana (actually sizable compared with tiny Greensburg), we found a generator-run restaurant selling boxed lunches of french fries and fried chicken or catfish to a long line of hungry hurricane survivors.

Starved: Our "Nutritional" Needs Require Attention

The psychological body requires daily nutrition, just as the physical body does. Our hearts and minds feed on close, loving, and trustworthy relationships: *honestly* shared experiences, feelings, and understandings with mutual reliance and help. Storybook characters with fictional lives can momentarily delight or entertain us, but they do not sustain us. A cardboard cutout cannot warmly comfort or creatively validate a child as the unique aspect of the greater Whole that he or she is. A child cannot truly know and depend on an image or be nurtured by it in the special way that says, "I know you."

Artificial personas ("I'm a winner, and so are you!" or "Fake it until you make it!") are the junk food of the psychological diet. Just as overly processed foods are not as nutritious as fresh fruits and vegetables, denatured emotions ("We allow no hurts and resentments in our family—we only 'love' one another!") are not as healthy as a valid, constructive expression of the full emotional spectrum ("I'm feeling angry today, because after all my hard work, I didn't get the promotion!"). The mere words "I care" may *seem* sweet, but when they are insincere, they leave us feeling lied to, dissatisfied, and mistrustful. They are empty psychological "calories"—a sugary substitute for true caring. Because children are biologically programmed to imitate their caretakers, if these authorities merely show facades and playact, children learn to do the same. Their psychological bodies then become increasingly malnourished and emaciated.

As with real food, we may seek excessive amounts of inadequate psychological nutrition in an attempt to meet our needs. We may automatically offer the same "meals" to others, believing we're feeding the hungry. In futility, we may also quit "eating" entirely ("I'm just not a people person") closing our "mouths" to what has not assuaged our "hunger pangs" or has been "indigestible." Just as our palette adapts to junk food, our psyche usually adjusts over time to our intakes. We develop a taste for the substandard diet while what truly nourishes us—*human* interaction—loses its tang.

We basked in the spectacularly sunny, summer day and enjoyed a picnic under the shade of some remaining tall pine trees. The fallen trunks of those that succumbed to the storm made good seats. As we munched on Southern fried food and watched Oliver add to the pile of broken pine branches, we chatted about our plans to go back to New Orleans the next day. We "adults" were relaxing as we anticipated our return to our routines. Felicity, however, was still stressed—afraid of nature, perhaps for the first time in her life. She began sobbing when she spotted ants on the log where she was sitting.

"What's wrong, honey?" Connie sounded concerned and extended a loving arm around her daughter's shoulder.

"Ants!" Felicity whimpered.

Emily examined the tiny insects and gave a quick lesson on the types of ants in southern Louisiana, concluding with, "This kind won't hurt you." The information did not assuage Felicity's distress in the slightest. She whined, "My stomach hurts!" as she draped her upper torso onto her mother's lap and cried openly. Connie rubbed her back with soothing strokes.

Psycho: Our Reactions Need Our Attention

Psychological bodies are no different from physical bodies in expressing what they have been exposed to. For example, physical bodies manifest the excesses and deficiencies of their nutritional intakes—as with corpulence and scrawniness. Psychological bodies react similarly to what they have ingested, showing arrogance or low self-esteem when they have been overly indulged or neglected. Intense emotional reactions suggest intense trauma. If someone's home is hit by a hurricane only hours after driving away, he or she may associate the two experiences and be frightened of car trips in the future. When a small problem arises on the heels of a BIG one (ants after a hurricane), a person may unload (as Felicity did) his or her pent-up feelings about the big one in apparent reaction to the minor situation. As a result, we cannot adequately assess others based purely on the here and now. A person may appear to be reacting childishly or otherwise inappropriately when those feelings are valid, based on the past. The person's psychological body may also be registering something that others do not yet realize, such as the calm before a "storm."

Sometimes an even larger tragedy strikes just as we are beginning to relax from a previous one. If we associate the two, we'll believe "Relaxation brings disaster!" and have trouble relaxing in the future. We may also pair fried food, picnics, or pine trees with emotional pain—"Fried foods give me heartburn," or "I've *never* liked picnics," or "I'm allergic to pine trees"—and avoid them for the rest of our lives. Someone observing the immediate sunny and cheerful setting, but who's unaware of our circumstances, could easily judge Felicity's fear as pathological. ("That timid kid has a problem! Maybe she has an ant phobia or an anxiety disorder, or ants are symbolic of some unconscious fear that is tormenting her mind.") A healthy psychological body, however, fathoms that Felicity's fear is a child's valid reaction to a couple of extremely stressful days.

Paradoxically, we may also be drawn to reminders of our painful times. We run toward them, craving fried food, adoring picnics, planting pine trees all over our community, and perhaps breaking their branches in memory of that destructive hurricane. In our victimized state, we seek out, perceive, feel, and recreate elements of our disasters over and over again, unconsciously attempting to bring attention to our traumas so that we might work them through. These are symptoms of post-traumatic stress disorder (PTSD)—*compulsively* running away from or toward reminders of our traumatic experiences.

The Plague: POST-TRAUMATIC STRESS DISORDER

Let's look in more detail at some of the symptoms of PTSD.[3] The following list is partial because PTSD symptoms are as vast as the varieties of trauma, but they all fit within the categories mentioned below. Note how these symptoms correspond to aspects of "personality" in everyone you know.

I. **Physical Symptoms**
    A. Victims of violence may be **drawn toward** reminders of their pain.
        1. Physical brutality. Victims become victimizers who stalk, assault, poison, starve, "accidentally" injure, and otherwise hurt people's bodies (their own included) in a way that's reminiscent of how they were once harmed.
        2. Sexual perversions. PTSD patients act out scenes of childhood molestation as in rape, pedophilia, sadomasochism, preference for one-night stands, etc.
        3. Compulsions:
            a. Patients feel compelled to perform activities or rituals that contain some aspect of their past trauma, as with compulsively watching television when this activity helped them escape from the reality of a dysfunctional home.
            b. The PTSD patient does what leads to the same physical reactions as during the trauma. (For example, drinking coffee may initiate the rapid heart rate and feelings of anxiety that occur when stressed.)[4]
            c. When children are medicated for their reactions to traumatic experiences, they may later become addicts who turn to drugs to stifle their pain.
        4. Consistent involvement in stressful events or problems ("This is urgent!") that maintain the same traumatic physiological responses, such as stress hormones pumping through the body. For instance, the trauma survivor may put off doing taxes until April.
    B. Victims of physical abuse also may **avoid** anything physical that might bring the trauma to their attention.
        1. Ignoring body sensations. ("You say I'm sick, Doctor, but I don't feel anything.")
        2. Dreading or shunning physical closeness and/or sexuality. ("I've just never met anyone who was right for me!")
        3. Having difficulty sleeping, fearing a recurrence or acting out of late-night traumatic experiences.

4. Skittishness. These victims are quick to leave when trauma threatens (storms, floods, in-laws, ex-wives, etc.).

5. Obstinacy. This trauma survivor will *not* do whatever reminds him of his trauma. (He will not drive a car, ride in a train, or fly in a plane after a crash experience.) Not following directions is a common symptom. (His perpetrators told him what to do, and he's mad about this!)

II. Emotional Symptoms

A. Victims of violence may **perpetuate** their suffering emotionally.

1. Verbal cruelties. Victims may become victimizers who use intimidation, humiliation, mean "jokes," sordid descriptive phrases, condescension, and so forth, pushing onto others their painful experiences and feelings.

2. Baited traps. Trauma survivors orchestrate endless entrapments, difficulties, and injustices (divisive or discriminatory tactics, for example) for themselves or others.

3. Dwelling in intense emotions. A PTSD patient may have extreme emotional reactions that linger or surface long after a trauma is over, as with an intensely negative reaction to a surprise.

4. Attraction to perpetrators of abuse and neglect. PTSD patients fall in love with or otherwise esteem and support those who are consistently hurtful.

B. Victims of abuse also may **avoid or control** emotions that are reminiscent of the trauma.

1. Rejecting "positive" feelings. ("What's there to smile about?")

2. Shunning "negative" feelings. ("I stay away from anyone who makes me feel less than empowered!") Stifling anger may result in passive-aggressiveness.

3. Skirting experience or information that might lead to unwanted "positive" or "negative" feelings. ("Don't tell me what our politicians are doing—that's depressing!")

4. Perhaps not feeling, expressing, or allowing emotion at all.

5. Steering clear of emotional connections. (Relationships may be merely about sex.)

6. Experiencing numbness to exploitation and oppression.

III. Mental Symptoms

A. Victims of violence often **suffer** with intrusive thoughts. They may have obsessions or be preoccupied with various aspects of past traumas or the possible recurrence of these traumas. Disturbing images are "triggered" by external and internal events: nightmares, flashbacks, partial memories, illusions, hallucinations, etc. The survivor may also be ever-watchful, certain that another calamity is right around the corner.

B. Victims of mental abuse may **avoid** mental activities, such as decision making, thinking, or the awareness of their thoughts.

1. Attention, concentration, or comprehension problems are common, particularly with topics reminiscent of the trauma. Victims of chronic brutality may not register evil intent or what to do about it.

2. Patients deny their "negative" or "unloving" thoughts.

3. Survivors may forget the disaster or the abilities or knowledge they had before it too place. *Or* they may "remember" a distorted version of what happened, or focus merely on the "good" aspects of their life. (PTSD patients may not be able to handle the underlying truth.)

4. A poor sense of reality, space, or time may permeate their lives. (Do you know anyone who is always late?)
5. Victims often rigidly adhere to unfounded beliefs.
6. Trauma survivors may be unwilling to process the past (traumatic!) or plan for the future (potentially traumatic!)—("Let's just stay in this moment, shall we?").

This list shows that the positive and negative attention we extend, or the attention we withhold, are often more about our post-traumatic stress disorder than the needs of the person receiving our encouragements or discouragements. As a result, we don't offer others clear, life-affirming messages about their behavior. (For example, "Your gentle voice works best for me if you want to communicate something important—I can hear that. My extensive experience with a raging parent makes me tune out angry voices.") Also, as we reward children for what isn't expressing their human nature and punish or ignore them for what is, they are goaded into the ranks of people suffering from PTSD.

Most of us are a unique mixture of these two pathways of post-traumatic stress disorder (attraction to and repulsion from what has been traumatic) combined with our natural attractions to what have been pleasant experiences. Such negative and positive conditioning produces our "personalities." Yes, much of what we believe is our "genetically endowed" or "God-given" character, what we support in others, and what we defend as "self," are actually symptoms of post-traumatic stress disorder. This realization is a vital step in knowing ourselves and understanding why we are so often incapable of giving infants and children what they need to become psychologically mature human beings—we're too busy running toward or away from what terrifies us! This awareness is also essential to improving our relationships, because blindly following the apparent will of any individual isn't necessarily respectful or healthy. It may even result in a grizzly nightmare for one or both parties. For these reasons, we have to discover the difference between our genuine desires and our traumatic reactions. This discernment DEMANDS our attention!

The Hook: Our Trauma Survivors Desperately Need Our Attention

When we arrived back at the house late afternoon, Effie gently informed us, "Dears, the Seventeenth Street and London Avenue Canal levees blew, and water from Lake Pontchartrain is pouring into New Orleans. The police and firemen, Coast Guard, Wildlife and Fisheries crews, Louisiana National Guard, and citizens with boats are overwrought by the number of people needing to be hauled out of the flooded areas. They're finding folks camped on rooftops, shut up in attics, or hanging on to trees to escape the floodwaters. The conditions are unbearable! Thousands are stranded in the extreme heat and humidity with no water or food. They're stressed to the max, so the most vulnerable people are dying! Yet not everyone is willing to be rescued, particularly if it means leaving their pets behind!"

Effie had plugged the TV into the generator so we could see what was happening. I watched briefly as a policeman tried to convince a distraught family to abandon their dogs and dead relative for the authorities to pick up later. Teary-eyed Felicity dashed to the freezer to grab a bag of Hershey's Kisses, which she passed around.

As the other members of our household fixated in fear on the TV and munched on chocolate, I retreated in desperation outdoors to what remained of the day. I slid into one of the eight rocking chairs Effie had lined up along her back porch. My whole body felt stiff with dread, so I began rocking my chair back and forth. The warmth and brightness of the sun was such a comfort, as were the cheery whistles of the birds, as I beheld the golden pastures of Effie's two hundred acres. The rhythmic undulations of the rocker were calming, like the heartbeat is to an infant. My aching chest and racing mind sought escape from the pain in one of my pleasant books, but I couldn't concentrate. After a brief meditation, I heard a voice within me beseeching, "*When* will this horror *end*?" I reached for my journal, as a drowning person would a life raft, and wrote furiously.

All who have experienced life-threatening circumstances, injury, and loss desperately need attention. Whether within our homes, relationships, communities, or nation, we have *all* encountered disasters! Just as people are begging to be rescued throughout the city of New Orleans right now, traumatized parts within all individuals are pleading for help. Our abusive and neglectful interaction styles, extreme feelings, and rigid or deviant thoughts and beliefs are distress signals. Without outside assistance, our inner disaster survivors are compelled to repeatedly reenact traumatic scenes or run from anything that reminds them of these painful times. This repetition compulsion is why early listening and responding to these frantic cries is of paramount importance. I call this "rescuing"—the same term used for taking anybody out of harm's way *and* administering what they need to recover.

Although simple in theory, the rescuing process when a person is traumatized is far from simple in its practical application. For example, survivors in shock or psychologically incapacitated may refuse to leave their ruined "homes." They may cling to "trees"—activities or behavioral repertoires, particular emotional states, or belief systems that originally saved their sanity or their lives. They may become slick salespeople, unflinchingly "calm" individuals, or those who daily reiterate fanciful stories of a perfect family or heroic surmounting of extremely dysfunctional ones. Letting go of such "trees" may incite a panic attack or the fear of death, yet stiffly clenching them "roots" survivors to these spots. They may also hold on to a beloved pet, a favorite person, or a pet peeve (a grievance). They may grip the memory of a dead loved one that offers comfort or even torment. Survivors may cope like animals—attacking viciously, freezing in terror, or racing away. They may be like children who are vulnerable, needy, highly emotional, and dependent. Without proper treatment, these reactions can last for years, decades, or even a lifetime. When we're busy clutching someone, something, or a particular coping pattern, we can't assist in our own rescue, and we may greatly interfere. Rescuing trauma survivors can be fruitless, expensive, dangerous,[5] exhausting, and emotionally overwhelming.

But, what is the cost of deserting these frantic survivors? The expense is a host of needy "children," wounded "animals," and vegetative incapacities. When children "grow up" amid disasters, with no one showing them how to grow "through" these experiences, they descend the evolutionary ladder, becoming more like animals that are hyperalert to any sign of threat. For protection and provision, they learn to fend and forage for themselves. If they close their ears to the human voice and its meaning, as their own voices have been unheard or wrongly interpreted, they become like vegetables. They block the information brought by their senses to avoid experiencing those who are drowning, drowned, or are "drowning" them. They shun their hearts to end the anguish and despair. They live apart from their active minds to forget the agonizing awareness of so few people willing to help *and* to stop the obsessive, lonely query of "Why did this happen to me? What did I do wrong?

What should I have done? What if it happens again?" As they become less and less attentive to defend against both past and future disasters, their human identity becomes younger and younger, ultimately regressing to the psychological newborn...if not beyond.

Disaster Survivors Also Need Treatment (HORRORS!!!)

Stranded New Orleanians must escape from the precarious disaster site if they are to recover. They must have safe shelter where people pay attention to their needs. Their immediate physical needs are a priority—water, food, rest, and medical care. We shouldn't stop there, though. Once they are physically stabilized, their psychological needs must be addressed—someone to welcome and encourage the many voices within them, validating their truth and cradling their grief. Survivors must be supported to share their experiences of hurricane and levee breaches that caused massive flooding; tremendous destruction; and the loss of life, livelihood, and many belongings. They must express the full range of their perceptions, feelings, and thoughts, as many times and for as long as they need. To regain emotional and mental vitality, stability, and strength, they require good psychological "nutrition" from people who can be close, engaging, loving, reassuring, and consistent in their care, yet sense when to step aside and give some space.

The trauma to our city and its people is obvious. This disaster is discussed openly by media and society. Health-care professionals expect shock, followed by all the stages of grieving, as *natural* reactions. With the greater community offering a support system that sympathizes with our loss, empathizes with our suffering, fortifies our healthy coping mechanisms, and "feeds" us what we need to move on *developmentally*, we can traverse the pathway of recovery. As we survivors are accorded attention and care for each aspect of ourselves, we can evolve in our ability to attend to each in ourselves and in our fellowman.

The disaster survivors within us are similar to those in New Orleans in terms of their devastation and need. They too must leave their damaged "neighborhoods"—areas of their psyches ravaged by "storms" of abuse and subsequent years of neglect that they've "grown" accustomed to and consider "home." They must be helped to gradually unclench their grasp of people, objects, events, behaviors, feelings, and beliefs from their traumatic pasts so they can be led to safety. They must be coached in firm boundaries and therapeutic methods so the intense pent-up feelings that periodically flood forth can be released with minimal <u>acting out</u> of their abuse and neglect. They must also be prompted to stop avoiding what was "bad" in the past if it is beneficial in the present. With plenty of attention and assistance, they can discover who and what genuinely fulfills their needs and receive what facilitates healing. The needs of the trauma survivor can be *extensive*, but when consistently recognized and met, healing is inevitable.

I pondered the many abused children I worked with during my pediatric rotations: preschoolers with venereal diseases or multiple unexplained bruises, burns, cuts, or bone fractures. These children's bodies were clearly showing their traumatic experiences, but the "adults" in their lives so often didn't listen. There were also kids whose emotional bodies were communicating their trauma through angry outbursts, chronic sadness, unexplained fearfulness, bullying, or withdrawing into themselves and tuning out the world. I found many parents quick to make up excuses—"He's just like Uncle Frank— always blowing off steam," or "Self-sabotage runs in the family." They were seemingly unaware that child abuse, the unspoken truth, runs in their families as well.

Forsaken: Most Survivors' Needs Remain Unmet

Unlike many survivors of the Katrina disaster, childhood-abuse survivors' needs are usually *not* met. One reason may be that caretakers do not know of the traumas. A perpetrator of child abuse usually threaten further harm to children or their loved ones if they ever tell what happened, so they don't speak directly. If they do talk, the victimizer commonly carries out these threats. The children's caretakers may not take them seriously and promptly act on the information, or they persecute the child in some way for disturbing the status quo. Since the psychologically "young" cling to what they are accustomed to, they may not condemn Dad's use of a belt on the bare back. ("If you hadn't acted up, he wouldn't have done that!") No one may openly criticize Mom's screaming fits or her blaring raunchy music at full blast. ("Everyone has their own way of unwinding—don't let it bother you!") Perhaps no one in the child's life realizes that the church school he or she attends employs some ungodly people.

When children's painful experiences are not validated—when their natural shock and grief, fear and rage, guilt and shame are not understood as appropriate to their despairing circumstances—they have no recourse. When each abuser is *not* held accountable for each destructive behavior, the children *are* inevitably reproached for their reactions to the injustice. ("I have no respect for finger-pointers!" "What's wrong with you? Why can't you just be happy?") No one assures them, "Your family members are forcing their life stories on you, rather than providing what you need. Being upset is only natural. Please tell me about it." Instead, the children are blamed and punished for their "bad" behavior. They hear, "Stop beating up your little brother, or no dessert tonight!" Their strong emotions are given "time out," ridiculed, or diagnosed and treated with medication. Their mental confusion may be labeled a lack of intelligence, a learning disorder, or merely the result of too many soft drinks or sweets. The child is left defenseless and unprotected by these cruel and insensitive stances, and the abuse and neglect usually continue.

Children experience horror and a fear of death when their needs are so neglected. They suffer when their boundaries are violated, their perceptions are ignored or corrected ("You were born into a wealthy family, you have *nothing* to complain about!"), their pain is minimized ("You're just upset about your team losing the game. If you'd practice more, you'd play better!"), their anger is judged ("You have an attitude problem, young man!"), their sadness is handled with condescension ("Time for a pity party–1-2-3-AH!"), and their trust is betrayed. Typically, they don't have a support system equipped to remedy trauma, so they are isolated in their suffering, and they learn to isolate in response.

When defending the image, reputation, or belief systems of someone older, bigger, and more powerful is more important than protecting the young, small, and vulnerable self (including body, heart, and mind), children further relinquish their hold on reality. They separate even more from their inborn identity, objectifying it, manhandling it, and even mutilating it, to surrender to the story line and character roles that their family and community assign them. They succumb to the dreadful truth that their caretakers are more interested in upholding family myths and stereotypes than nurturing the fullness of their humanity. Not given what they need to mature, they reject these needs and the parts of themselves that sense the needs. These undeveloped humans are our stranded survivors, clinging to the <u>image</u> that was deemed more worthy than their very lives. They still exist inside us...grieving...anguishing...and waiting against all odds to be rescued.

After several hours, Emily pulled up a rocking chair alongside mine. The radiant sun setting over my journal transformed the color of the page to a soft rose. She looked at me gravely and with reddened eyes. "Connie's home was in Lakeview, right by the Seventeenth Street Canal breach. She believes it's gone, so she and the kids are crying their eyes out.

Although my apartment is usually a disaster on the inside, I'm guessing it's high and dry because it's on the second story in Kenner. The west fared a lot better than other areas of the city. I'm sure your mom's house is flooded, though. Broadmoor is in the middle of the bowl and pretty low." She paused for a moment, as if to give me a chance to say something if I needed to. Then she continued. "Loads of people are stranded and have been calling the emergency operations center in City Hall begging for help. Some people are so totally flipping out by the sudden change in their lives that they're jumping off overpasses or putting a gun to their heads! A lot are hungry, thirsty, and dehydrated, suffering from heat exhaustion and sunburned from the scorching sun. If that's not bad enough, they're being eaten alive by all the biting insects at night!" Emily squirmed—she does not like bugs and shows them no mercy.

"So many people have been found dead, floating in the floodwater. Thousands are running scared, trying to get to safety. Some are swinging baseball bats to make a way through the crowd. Those who sought shelter in the Superdome have discovered that residents there are also without food or water. Since the electricity is off and there's been no A/C, they're being cooked in all that heat and humidity! It's also dimly lit, since there are only a few generators for lights. Toilets have backed up, so it really stinks like crazy. *And,* the five hundred buses and Chinook helicopters FEMA promised on the day of the storm to evacuate the Superdome still haven't arrived.[6] People also fled in droves to the Convention Center, even though this was not an official shelter, because there was nowhere else to go. It's getting wild there, too. With fewer police available, flagrant violence is breaking out everywhere, even toward rescuers! TV crews are having a hard time filming in all that chaos. It's just plain dangerous to be in New Orleans." Emily shook her head with dismay. "Many of those who didn't evacuate for Katrina are getting the hell out of there now!"

Dismemberment: Our Trauma-induced Disintegration and Escape Needs Our Attention

How much we are affected by our disasters depends on their severity as well as our age and mental, emotional, and physical conditions. Personal experience of catastrophic circumstances causes suffering in all individuals, young and old. Minor difficulties can stress infants, who have little ability to cope on their own, and their cries for help, as mentioned, are so often misunderstood. The psychological "infants" inside us also cannot handle trauma well. They react strongly to mild provocation or not at all to a significant stressor (they don't give it attention *and* may distract you from looking as well). When we are already taxed by serious illness, bereavement, family problems, work strain, and so forth, further trauma may overwhelm us. Each unresolved traumatic experience hinders our ability to address and respond to the next one.

Location or relative proximity to a disaster is also important. Connie's property lies next to a levee breach, so her house was undoubtedly washed away. My mom's house rests farther away from the breaches, but only two feet above sea level, so it's certainly flooding. Emily's apartment is even farther away, on higher ground and on the second story, so her many possessions are surely intact.

Similarly, our psyches sustain damage according to how close we are to a traumatic incident. For example, when we have experienced childhood trauma remotely, whether watching from a distance or living with its effects, we may display some mild symptoms, such as anxiety and changes in mood, appetite, or sleep patterns. When we directly experience the same trauma, our symptoms worsen—palpable anxiety, anger, depression, overeating or undereating, sleeping too much or too little, etc. When we personally endure extreme childhood trauma, we are impacted even more severely. For instance, we may not satisfy our basic human needs, as with relaying this "news" and receiving treatment. We may wander aimlessly in our distress—unable to hold a job, enjoy a long-term relationship, or be available for our kids. We may pillage or hoard (do you know anyone with a clutter problem?) in sheer desperation to "survive." We may "fight for our lives" by provoking difficulty, confrontation, an argument, or physical aggression in every encounter. We may also be too afraid to move (out of the home of our traumatic upbringing, for example), let alone stand up for ourselves—even when we and our loved ones are hurting or in danger.

Like the New Orleans evacuees scattered in all directions away from their now-ruined homes, most of us have parts of our minds spread out in various locations relative to each disaster site, with the corresponding degree and severity of symptoms. This psychic ax murder and diaspora is the common psychological condition of twenty-first century man. Some parts of us are also still stranded at the scenes of our storms, disasters, and/or crimes, like the survivors in New Orleans. We have other aspects of ourselves living in apparent safety and security in every direction away from where the traumatic event occurred and perhaps continues. We also have aspects that are conscious of these hurting parts and are trying to help, as well as those that are shielding the hideous truth from our awareness. Multiply this scenario by the number of disasters we've experienced, and we soon realize how psychically complex, fragmented, and confused most of us are.

Chronically traumatized individuals typically exhibit a full range of stress reactions over time, but we often don't recognize these reactions because "we" are sheltered in our favorite fragments (maybe an adult, child, animal, or vegetable) while our symptoms have been dispersed across the entire map of our lives. When we adopt a smiling face, share heartwarming tales of our youth, and act the part of "Mr. Easygoing" or "Ms. Perennial Optimist," we have most people, including ourselves, believing "we" are unscathed.

"We" are willing to sacrifice these most wounded parts of ourselves because these disaster survivors are in bad shape. "They" are not concerned about keeping their hair nicely trimmed and styled or wearing the latest designer fashions with matching accessories. "They" don't care if we have the latest technology. "They" don't behave in a respectful, well-spoken, and socially acceptable manner, and "they" don't perform to the best of their ability. On the contrary, "they" are shattered—incompetent, irrational, hysterical, terrified, terrorizing, and/or stuck in the polarity of life or death—*not* like "us."

To maintain "our" image, "we" exile these frenzied and reactive parts of ourselves to our unconscious and forget "they" exist. (We construct a wall of denial for "safety!") When "we" compare the parts we claim as our identity with those we spot in others, we feel entitled to hold ourselves apart from or even above the common man, presuming "we" are superior. (When I only know a small part of myself, I only know a small part of my needs, so I appear far less needy than you!) Thus, we behold the origins of our inner "infants"—those needy parts with intense reactions when their needs aren't met—*and* those who don't notice the problem. "We" have a dual existence: the parts of ourselves that recollect a sheltered past possess no knowledge of those parts in dire straits or what "they" do, want, or need. To sustain this separation, we must continually banish to the unconscious mind whatever we reject in ourselves, unaware that the more we dam (or damn!) in our unconscious, the more <u>unconscious</u> we become.

The breached levees flooding low-lying areas of New Orleans with fetid, sewage-filled water is a powerful metaphor for the horrific memories and agonizing pain that threaten to crush our "known" identity if we do not continuously and rigorously reinforce the thick protective wall around our unconscious mind, which is brimming with our banished feelings and thoughts. Despite our best efforts, the undesirable contents do seep out periodically. (Those closest to us can attest to this.) Out of our mouths gush the angry, malevolent words we heard growing up—deriding achievements, throwing salt on tender wounds, and scoffing at the forthcoming genuine feelings. We declare the truth of someone's experience a nasty lie, a dramatic distortion, a psychotic hallucination, or grim evidence of a demonic presence, *and* punish them "accordingly." We are adamant that relatives, teachers, scout masters, and religious leaders could not possibly have hurt anyone, and that people with handicaps, heartaches, or head trips have no one to blame but themselves. As with breached levees, unresolved disasters can be tremendously damaging to our fellowman, as we momentarily purge the toxic behaviors, emotions, and belief systems we have "ingested." *Or* we fiercely reject anyone or anything that reminds us of our traumas (PTSD).

I glanced at Emily, who was rocking back and forth with her eyes closed. Her lips were curled in a soft smile as if she'd temporarily forgotten the bedlam in our city. Seeing her smile reminded me of our lovely picnic, which now seemed an eerie mockery of what was to come.

The Abomination: What We've Disowned Beckons Our Attention

Our forgotten disasters and the abandoned traumatized parts of ourselves endanger every vulnerable person in our lives as we unconsciously communicate our most harrowing experiences by reenacting them. Because of this, most children are exposed to life-threatening trauma. With repetitive traumas, these children may learn to place their need for safety above all other needs, as an infant does.[7] The biological impulse to feed their bodies what is necessary for physical, emotional, mental, and spiritual maintenance and maturation is superseded by one overriding need—to stay alive! This survival mechanism can, over the long term, become grossly disfiguring and disabling as these children contort themselves in efforts to cope with threatening environments. They alter their body shape and/or try new behaviors, such as aggression, to ease their stress. So, rather than enjoying benevolent, engaging encounters with all types of people, the chronically traumatized child angrily bolts from those who remind him of scary times, dominates them, or "needs" to control them to maximize his own feelings of "security." The most injured may even slaughter them, in one form or another, just to feel "safe."

Persistently abused or neglected children eventually acclimate to the horror. They decide, "Since I'm not getting what I need, maybe I need what I'm getting!" With this admission, their stress and desperation subside, and they no longer fight their "fate." They accept it with resignation or gratitude, or relish it, "sharing" it with others. In their wizened state, they come to "desire" unhealthy or perverse attention or the lavish compensation that follows. They "feed" themselves what they've been "force-fed," refuse what they've longed for but has not been forthcoming, and ultimately crave the same "toxins" to which they have been consistently exposed. These devastated children's innate expectations to be loved, accepted, and cared for as they are now transfer to the new identity and its ways. They now demand appreciation and respect as they impose their will on you and insist you satisfy their "needs." They also project these new "needs" onto you, "giving" or even forcing exactly what they have received, expecting gratitude or even payment in return. Because these learned deviations are so contrary to their fundamental nature, such learned "desires," "needs," and "tendencies" result in them becoming *very* needy indeed. In trying to meet their original needs through poor and even decadent surrogates, their desires become insatiable.

In summary, we all are greatly affected by adverse environments, and the dynamics of a typical childhood warp us into people with behaviors, feelings, and thoughts contrary to our Original Nature. Some parts of us are hidden away as defective ("If they are not wanted, there must be something wrong with them."), and other parts adapt by ignoring the difficulties ("Problems? What problems?"). The most damaged become changelings—going on to embrace the horror, wanting or even "needing" the very things that are ruinous and that once caused them great pain. Again, healing trauma is simple in theory. However, with so many parts of us asking for what they *don't* need and rejecting what they *do* need, as well as meting out what is contrary to human need, most of us remain deprived of what is essential to our maturation. Add to this the parts that are relentless in ravaging the human spirit and all it holds dear, believing it's the right thing to do, and we catch a glimpse of the enormity of the problem! To regain our wholeness *and* humanness, every aspect of ourselves aches for our attention!

"Anne." I looked up at Emily, who was staring at me and no longer rocking. "Our city is ruined! The news claims this is the worst natural disaster our country has ever known. The looters are using the opportunity to stage a free-for-all. People are breaking into stores all over and taking everything from alcohol to TV sets. The French Quarter stores have been hit hard, and even some police officers have been found stashing goods for their own use.[8] There is no law and order! It's also devastating to watch the footage of that nasty water rising higher and higher, rushing into the houses and businesses, drowning neighborhoods, and feeling helpless to stop it! Although the French Quarter and the Southern Crescent next to the Mississippi River, due to their elevation, haven't flooded, Lakeview, Saint Bernard Parish, the lower Ninth Ward, and New Orleans East are now immersed in many feet of water…"

I didn't hear any more of Emily's report as my mind raced back to the reading camp in New Orleans East where I had volunteered earlier that summer. Kendra, an extroverted African American six-year-old, had noticed over lunch that she and I enjoyed the same foods. "You like pizza, hamburgers, tacos, and ice cream, and so do I. You must be my twin sister!" she told me excitedly. From then on, she referred to me as her twin. One day she informed a six-year-old Vietnamese boy named Tran of our sibling relationship.

"I don't believe you!" Tran protested, after staring at me with searching eyes.

"Why not?" demanded Kendra, her hands extended dramatically toward the sky.

Tran looked at me up and down, then at Kendra, and then back at me, and finally said to Kendra, "If she were really your twin sister, *you* would be taller!"

Those dear children did not see differences of race, nationality, age, or socioeconomic status, nor did they categorize in terms of "us" and "them." I wondered where they were now.

"Anne…are you OK?" My attention was back on Emily's face, which was expressing concern.

"No, Emily," I muttered with tears streaming down my cheeks. "I'm not OK. This is not OK."

The Howling: The Genuine Needs of Our "Children" Require Our Attention

Disasters can annihilate our human development—butchering our wholeness, poisoning our bodies, strangling our voices, twisting our perceptions, suffocating our sincerity, and wasting heart and mind through lack of "nutrition." They polarize our reactions, abort our "inner babies," and even coerce us into bizarre behaviors contrary to our well-being that oblige us to parasitize others trying to satisfy our "needs"! Chronic trauma can drive us to expunge much of who we are. Large bank accounts, sunny dispositions, "positive" thinking, or endearing children's stories cannot magically repair such damage nor lift the young parts of our psyches out of the "toxic floodwaters" of "their" repressed traumatic pasts. (If they possessed such power, our inner kids would be "taller.")

Each abandoned part of us is like a terrified child without a parent, and each "child" may be a different "age" and developmental stage. The only method of rescuing these once healthy "children" who have been forced from their homes of equality, full-heartedness, and open-mindedness is to coax them to come to where we are or venture to where they are. Either way, we must lead them or carry them out of their trauma-induced, self-defeating behaviors, emotions, and mind-sets, and into a place of safety and care. (More on this later.) Leaving them alone to fend for themselves is *not* OK—it's monstrous!

The deprivations each child has braved are apparent in what he or she demands, pilfers, or cannibalizes, **or** what he or she furiously refuses. For example, desperate needs for water, food, safety, comfort, and rest are a direct result of being without them. Sometimes survivors insist on substitutes, as with alcohol, TV sets, risk taking, rewards, and busyness. In untreated cases of catastrophic trauma, survivors are only fulfilled when others are left languishing. Also, as they become familiar with their deprived state, they learn to call it "home" and reject what might lead to their safe evacuation. We can hear the ever-expressed deluge of abuse and neglect the average child has suffered, literally or metaphorically, in his or her body language…when we're listening.

By the time I moved inside, Effie, Connie, and the kids had retreated to bed. The TV was still blaring disaster news. A distraught woman was sobbing and screaming, "I've got to find my mother! She stayed for the storm in the Ninth Ward! I'VE GOT TO FIND HER!" I shut off the TV, collapsed onto the sofa where Effie customarily laid, and wept. The drama on television had become the reality of my life!

Apocalypse: Our Families and Communities Need Our Attention

Who or what needs our attention? Everyone and everything in our lives!—our selves, parents, siblings, neighbors, friends, and the people with whom we cross paths each day. If people need nothing from us or have nothing to offer us, they would not be in our experience! Parts of them may be in trouble or in need, or they are reflecting, reacting, or responding to these aspects in us. We all know there are people in our communities with an extreme form of PTSD who act out their internal dynamics in horrific and graphic ways. We're aghast when people bizarrely violate the physical body, but these same atrocities perpetrated against the psyche are rarely even acknowledged! Yes, much of the psychological body is subdued, neglected, defamed, ostracized, and/or bludgeoned in our culture. All these inattentive, untended, psychological "babies" who commit these "crimes" are unable to help themselves and are waiting expectantly for a parental figure to arrive and rescue them.

Whether the abuse and neglect has been physical or psychological, the treatment is similar— tending the victim's wounds while listening to the communication in each symptom and giving the individual the most palatable form of what all bodies need for self-healing. But the family and community also need healing, as crises don't remain isolated with an individual. Often, others must be alerted to our experiences so such storms and disasters in their lives can be averted. Further damage must be anticipated and prepared for *and* assessed and remedied when it occurs. Those harming others and covering up this harm *must* receive treatment if traumatic experience is ever to come to an end.

Our "inner infants," to maintain their sense of comfort, allow us to see such darkness only in a few faraway strangers. If we're listening, however, we know this perdition lurks in the shadows of each of our life stories, and our terrified avoidance of this truth keeps us deadlocked. To exhume this savage reality and treat all our aspects suffering from PTSD—the victims *and* victimizers—we must be responsible for watching out for one another *and* looking into one another to meet unmet needs. We must receive provision for our own unmet needs, as well, to make headway on the psychological journey. *Our* own survival, well-being, and growth depend on mutual rescuing!

Emily and I shoved a few bites of food into our mouths in silence and in the dark. Afterward, I dialed my mother's number in Saint Louis, where she lives eight months of the year. She escapes with her two cats to our subtropical city for the four coldest months. "Hello?" My mom sounded fairly calm under the circumstances.

"Hi, Mom. How are you?"

"I'm doing all right. How are YOU?!" Mom asked with that attentive, loving tone that is a hallmark of motherhood.

"I'm feeling pretty numb. It's been so overwhelming." I felt very strange. "I assume you've heard the news that the lower areas of New Orleans are flooding, including where your house is?"

"Yeah. I've been on the phone most of the past two days. Friends from all over are calling— wondering where you and I are and how we are doing. I assured them that we're safe and sound." Clearly, my mom's definitions only included our physical bodies. "I'm upset about losing my little house, though. I loved that place! I had ten wonderful winters in New Orleans, so I have no regrets…except this flooding; it was *so* avoidable! I heard from my friend Leonard. He's really mad…and sad too. He and Muriel lost their house in Lakeview. What really gets to him is that he observed the Army Corps of Engineers building the Seventeenth Street Canal levee floodwalls, because that's where they walk their dogs every day."

"He's a contractor, isn't he?" I inquired, trying to recall what I knew before this disaster.

"Yes, and Len said the Corps did a lousy job."[9] My mom's voice acquired an edge of annoyance. "In some areas, they used a light, poor-quality soil, a type of peat, instead of the heavy clay soil that abounds in the region and holds together better.[10] Their pilings didn't go deep enough into the ground.[11] They also attached the concrete panels end-to-end with rubber epoxy, rather than choosing a more secure tongue-and-groove alignment.[12] Talk about a disaster waiting to happen!"

I was stunned. "Woe! That couldn't possibly withstand the tremendous pressure of rising water in the canal!"

"Yeah! My home had never flooded in its hundred-plus years standing, and now it's probably well under water." Mom sounded wistful. "At least I have another house, so I'm fine. But Len and Muriel and so many others lost everything. What a crime! This flooding would not have happened if the corps had just done the job right. They certainly knew there were problems, because the backyards of the people on the levee had been flooding for at least a year before the storm, but the necessary repairs were never made.[13] Leonard said the story going around is that the corps didn't have enough money to build a proper levee, but Muriel remarked, 'That's like saying we can't afford to put *both* wings on the airplane!'"

What We Deny Our Attention May Become **Titanic**...and Intractable!

Our preference for superficial characters and stories creates one horrific event after another as we interact with our world and everyone in it based on our imaginations rather than who we really are and what is really happening. When we don't acknowledge the consequences of our inattention, we may be convinced that they are random events of nature beyond anyone's control ("That's just the way life is!"). They may also appear to be supernatural or perhaps expressions of Divine Wrath. When examined more closely, however, "natural" or "supernatural" events often reveal the unseen, unnatural, traumatized state of us mortals. The daily neglect and outright abuses of our psychological selves *are* TRAUMATIC; they compound over time, *and* they are enabled by our coping mechanisms that block and disown our drama and trauma. Our multiplicity of mind (conscious parts and unconscious parts) leads to a duality of morality, which explains why in one moment people can be generous, loving, or creatively helpful, and in the next moment they can be hateful, depriving, violent, or vindictive. When we accept some aspects of ourselves while rejecting others, we choose some serious consequences, such as split personalities that bellow for our attention.

I went to bed feeling absolutely dumbfounded. My heart was in agony, and my thoughts were racing. *Why would people do something so hideous? Why would they deliberately construct faulty levees that breach when stressed, killing thousands, destroying billions of dollars of property, and debilitating commerce and community for the foreseeable future? Why? Why? Why? Why?!* I couldn't think straight amid my intense emotions and muddled mind, but to my horror, a logical explanation surfaced.

When the most atrociously victimized and ostracized parts of ourselves are not *allowed to speak of what happened to them, express their pain, and demand justice from their abusers, they lose their sanity...and their humanity.* Human beings can endure only so much persecution before they revert, in defense, to an earlier, prehuman stage of development. This regression is why paying attention to these abandoned aspects of us and others is critical. The shunned parts do not disappear when we deny their existence and stifle their natural outrage at traumatic events. Like small children, they only get "louder" and more determined to be noticed, to have their voices heard, to have their experience known, and to get their genuine needs met—**NO MATTER WHAT THE COST**!

BLOODY MARY BREAK:

1. Who needs your attention?
   a. On the outside?
   b. On the inside?

2. What might your body be communicating to you through physical symptoms? For example, is the itching of your athlete's foot infection encouraging you to hurry up with some much-needed developmental steps?

3. Where can you find your *human* voice? Does it come through most clearly in your spoken or written words, your body language, the music you play or listen to, or those closest to you? Do you spend much of your time unconsciously imitating people you're attached to or repeating what you've heard or have been taught to say?

4. What are your prejudices? For instance, do you sense the physical self more than the emotional, mental, or spiritual selves? Do you believe any part of you is more spiritual than any other part? What conflicts do these hierarchies set up inside you?

5. Which unresolved traumas from your past are you reenacting or avoiding in the present? Please consider abuse and neglect of both your physical and psychological bodies.

6. Look at a person in your life who is particularly troublesome, and pay close attention to his or her symptoms of PTSD. What is he or she telling you about his or her life through these symptoms?

7. What is your current awareness of the traumas and disasters in your life?
   a. Are you unaware of any experience you would call "traumatic?" (See below.)
   b. Do you have a gnawing feeling that there may have been something significant, but you can't yet put your finger on it?
   c. Are you keeping your distance from them?
   d. Are you stuck in the midst of it all and don't see a way out?
   e. Are your wounded parts healing?

One way to identify your position is by examining your reactions to the traumatized people in your life:
   a' Are you unwilling to sit with them, listen to them, and offer loving support when they share their traumatic experiences? Are you unable to confront, set proper boundaries, and deliver consequences to those acting them out? Do you prey on disaster survivors?

b' Do you observe from afar and harshly judge those who are expressing symptoms of PTSD? Do you make excuses for your lack of involvement and criticize rescuers?

c' Is some aspect of you submerged in "toxic floodwaters," perhaps screaming for help with words and behavior, but no one hears him or her? (If you answer yes to either a' or b' above, the answer to this question is also yes.)

d' Do you feel responsible for offering assistance to wounded people?

8. Commune with one of your "inner children." If you've been acting in a way that goes against your wishes or well-being, this is a good place to start. Otherwise, just talk as you would to a child in your family: "How are you today? How would you like to spend our time together?" Again, ignoring relationships with these inner parts of us is as hurtful to them as ignoring the children in our lives. (Know that in some way or at some times, you will treat kids outside of you as you do the ones inside your own psyche.)

9. For people to have conscious awareness of all aspects of themselves and their lives, they must have someone who is willing to acknowledge these parts, talk to them, be moved by them, and help them grow. What are you most uncomfortable talking about? Who are you unwilling to be moved by, and how are you unwilling to move? Which types of people are you most reticent to help?

10. What have you missed as a result of your inattentiveness? What has this cost you?

---

[1] Margot Sunderland, *The Science of Parenting* (New York: DK Publishing Inc., 2006), 18.

[2] Ibid., 119.

[3] Glenn Schiraldi, PhD, *The Post-Traumatic Stress Disorder Sourcebook* (New York: McGraw Hill Books, 2000), 6.

[4] "Caffeine is an addictive substance that chemically stimulates the stress response system." Randy J. Paterson, PhD, *The Assertiveness Workbook* (Oakland, CA: New Harbinger Publications, 2000), 35.

[5] "'Sniper fire' was…targeted at rescue helicopters, relief workers, and police officers. One of the possible causes of the sniper fire was resistance to relocation or evacuation." Aftermath-Civil disturbances, "Effect of Hurricane Katrina in New Orleans," *Wikipedia*, modified April 16, 2013, http://en.wikipedia.org/wiki/Effects_of_Hurricane_Katrina_in_New_Orleans.

[6] FactCheck.org's staff, "Katrina: What Happened When," *FactCheck.org: Annenberg Political Fact Check*, September 16, 2005, See Thursday September 1, 2005- 3 Days After, par. 5, http://www.factcheck.org/society/katrina_what_happened_when.html.

[7] "Babies seek safety above all." John Medina, *Brain Rules for BABY* (Seattle, WA: Pear Press, 2010), 62.

[8] Rusty Shackleford, "New Orleans Police Department Looting Walmart After Hurricane Katrina," *YouTube,* Published on May 27, 2012, http://www.youtube.com/watch?v=2Nfbj7zVxkE.

[9] "Five investigations (three major and two minor) were conducted by civil engineers and other experts, in an attempt to identify the underlying reasons for the failure of the federal flood protection system. All concur that the primary cause of the flooding was inadequate design and construction by the Corps of Engineers." "2005 Levee Failures in Greater New Orleans," *Wikipedia,* modified March 12, 2013, http://www.ask.com/wiki/2005_levee_failures_in_Greater_New_Orleans.

[10] "Soil borings in the area of the 17th Street Canal breach showed a layer of peat starting at about 30 feet (9.1 m) below the surface, and ranging from about 5 feet (1.5 m) to 20 feet (6.1 m) thick." Levee investigations, ibid.

[11] "A forensic engineering team from the Louisiana State University, using sonar, showed that at one point near the 17th Street Canal breach, the piling extends just 10 feet (3.0 m) below sea level, 7 feet (2.1 m) shallower than the Corps of Engineers had maintained." Flood wall design, ibid.

[12] Ivor Van Heerden and Mike Bryan, *The Storm* (New York: Penguin Group, 2006), 218.

[13] "Homeowners along the 17th Street Canal, near the site of the breach, had been reporting their yards flooding from persistent seepage from the canal for a year prior to Hurricane Katrina." Flood wall Design, "2005 Levee Failures in Greater New Orleans," *Wikipedia.*

Chapter 4

Textbooks

Learning about Disasters and Recovery

The next morning, Effie informed me that Connie had stayed up most of the night nursing a weepy Felicity, who had a headache and upset stomach. "Felicity thinks she's dying." Effie smiled warmly as she spoke. "Oliver's pretty bummed after yesterday's ordeal. He's been camping out with his video games in the back of their SUV. As you might already know, Emily has decided to visit her folks in Fort Lauderdale and is busy packing. She figures with her school underwater, she won't be working for a while, so she might as well make the most of her vacation time. I also just heard on TV that officials are planning to evacuate to Houston's Astrodome the original Superdome residents and the thousands more who sought refuge there after the flood."

In an effort to see past the fog in my mind, I noticed Effie's body lying limply on the sofa while Dr. Bear held a more vigorous stance on the floor beside her. I nodded that I'd received her morning report and then strayed out to the garden shed, where Pookie's golden eyes peered out from her dark corner. As I opened a can of chicken and cheddar, she greeted me, purring loudly.

Evacuation Day Four—Life's Textbook / Lesson One: Disasters **HURT**!

The pain of our disasters drives us to separate more and more from our home in ourselves, so instead, we seek security in our houses and belongings. We identify with our things, and when they are damaged, destroyed, or lessened in number or worth, we feel harmed or devalued as well. If we reside in an unhealthy environment, we start to think we are unhealthy too. Substituting fictional tales may temporarily enhance our self-esteem in an unstable, often hostile world, yet the truth about our situation remains.

Just as we can absorb stress from our environment, we can pass on our tension to our surroundings. Like the babies in a nursery, distress in one place is echoed in many other locations. Others' bodies may mirror our suffering and reflect our psyches' plea for attention. Our family and friends may express their pain, verbally or behaviorally, as a way of helping us admit to our own, as did Connie's kids. A sick or hurting child may be highlighting an unhealthy or unhappy "inner child" in every family member.

I moseyed back into the house, where Connie and Felicity had just gotten up. "Cedric called," Effie announced to a weary-looking Connie. By the intensity of Connie's facial expression, I could tell Cedric was someone significant in her life. "He said he's been trying to reach you since the storm but hasn't been able to until now. He's scheduled a busy day, so he gave me a list of things for you to do about your property. He'll call again later." Connie seemed burdened by the events of the past few days, and this news only weighed her down further. As if resigned to her fate, she weakly stuck out her hand to take Cedric's list, and then shoved it into her pocket.

Oliver, who had overheard the conversation from the kitchen, flew into the family room, his arms flailing as he shouted, "Yeah, I *bet* he's been trying to get through on the phone and hasn't been able to! He probably tried *once* and then quit! That's what he *always* does! He's pathetic! He does something *once* and makes it sound like some *huge* big deal! And when he says he'll do something later, like calling us again, that may take *months* or YEARS! He's such a LOSER! I HATE HIM!" Oliver threw a sponge on the floor, just missing Dr. Bear. The boy was overtly furious, yet his eyes were full of tears.

Felicity appeared crushed and sobbed, "Did I do something wrong?"

Connie hugged her daughter and avowed tenderly, "No, honey, you didn't do anything wrong." She then placed an affirming hand on each of her children's shoulders.

"Oliver, I know you're mad. You have every right to be. You've lost the only home you've ever known and all your things. And your father is doing his brick-wall routine—just business as usual! You really need your dad right now, but he's unavailable." As if suddenly realizing her own feelings, Connie added tentatively, "I'm angry about it too." She held Oliver close, resting her cheek on his curly brown hair. His enraged face softened.

She then extended her arm around her daughter. "Felicity, sweetie...I know you're scared and wondering what else might go wrong—me too. You'd love to have your father hug you, but your dad just isn't a hugger..." Connie paused, shook her head, and then uttered under her breath, "and we can't seem to teach him." Connie looked pained and then kissed her daughter. "Sweetheart, we're well insured, so we can replace everything." She suddenly stiffened, as if remembering a loss that was not so easily replaceable. "I'll try to talk to your dad. The main thing is, we're all safe, and we'll get through this." A tear trickled down Connie's face. She wiped it away before reading the piece of paper Effie had handed her. "Now, the first thing on our to-do list is...have breakfast!"

As they slowly made their way into the kitchen, I whispered to Effie, "Cedric is the kids' biological father?"

"Yes, and Connie's husband. He had to stay in New Orleans to work."

"Wow!" I said, surprised. I had assumed Connie was a single parent since the majority of the kids in Orleans Parish are reared in single-parent homes.[1]

I thought, *Cedric must be in shock to be so insensitive to the needs of his wife and kids. Oliver is angry; Felicity is needy and afraid, always at her mother's side; and Connie appears to be using all her strength to hold herself and them together. Cedric seems to be in the emergency mode of taking care of his worldly affairs at the expense of everyone's feelings. Their home and property were destroyed, so they would need to contact insurance agents and FEMA, but activities are secondary. Close family contact, sharing the fullness of our humanity should come first—at least, that's what my psych books have taught me. Traumatic experiences, however, often teach otherwise.*

Lesson Two: We Blame Ourselves

Whether our traumas and disasters are acts of nature or manmade, they are painful. For example, children have an innate expectation that their parents will fulfill their needs. When they don't, the children experience loss and grief and are liable to take on the responsibility themselves to address the lack. Drawing from their own resources, children may tap into their own emotional reserves to make up for caretakers who are without feeling ("Since they do not love me, I will intensely 'love' [them, myself, or my fellowman] to compensate"). *Or,* when the assurance "You didn't do anything wrong!" is absent, they assume accountability.

We often blame ourselves for the disasters in our childhoods. We evacuate from the parts of ourselves involved, and we assign guilt to the character traits we possessed at the time of the trauma. "If I were a different type of person, this would not have happened"—or so we think! "If I weren't so small, dependent, or vulnerable..." or "if I had more height, independence, or power..." or "if I'd only seen it coming!" We judge as negative or problematic the human qualities natural to our being and alter them accordingly. ("Being a sensitive child is no good, so I'll be a tough guy!" or "Trying to fight him off just made him beat me harder; from now on, I won't resist in any way.") This blame also extends to our environments, as we tend to attack or reject the personality traits in others we believe to be "at fault" in ourselves. In typical PTSD fashion, we run from these reminders of our guilt, or, paradoxically, we run toward them and emphasize or support these character traits.

I joined Connie's family at the breakfast table. "I am..." My voice choked as my eyes welled up with tears. "I'm so sorry about your house." I looked at Connie and then Felicity and Oliver. "My mom's house in Broadmoor, where I was living, is sure to be flooding like most of New Orleans. I feel devastated...my brain isn't functioning right...everything seems so strange...so unreal. I feel terrible." My voice cracked again. "Do you want to talk about it?"

A teary-eyed Connie shook her head no. Oliver gave me a heartrending look with his deep-blue eyes—the same color as his mother's. He banged his fist on the table before hastening outside. Red-eyed Felicity snatched a cell phone from the table. She lifted the front, illuminating her face, dialed urgently, and then propped the phone against her ear.

"Cell phones shouldn't be held next to a child's ears because they contain a frequency of radio waves that can be detrimental to the brain!" Emily scolded Connie as she passed through the breakfast room, hauling a large suitcase. Emily looked at Connie's blank stare and realized this was not the time for her educator mode, so she escaped into the garage.

"Darn! I want to call Daddy back, but it's not working!" Felicity whimpered before she started to cry.

"Yeah, I noticed that too, Felicity, when I tried to make a call," I spoke gently, imagining how desperate she must feel. "None of our cell phones seem to work out here in the country. You might try the wall phone in the kitchen, although it'll be hard to get through because the lines are so busy." Felicity nodded sadly as she rose from the table, but instead of calling from the kitchen, she disappeared out the back door where Oliver had just gone. I glanced over at Connie and offered support. "I was impressed with how you validated your children's feelings this morning."

"Oh, thanks...David taught me that. I am feeling so crushed by all this...losing our house...and then Cedric's cold phone call just when we need him most. My husband is rather...'independent'— that's what he calls himself."

"What do you call him?" I asked, preferring the straight story.

"Me? Well, hmm...his job is number one with him, and we're down the list. He doesn't have an inkling of how to be close to another person. Not a clue! He knows perfectly well that Effie is an early bird and I don't get up before eight when the kids aren't in school. So when does he phone? At seven— that's when I heard the ring. Does he want to talk to me? No. The kids? No. He never does. I plead with him to spend time with his kids, but that always ends in a huge argument. He may finally spend an hour with them, at most, maybe watching videos of his old news broadcasts—he's a meteorologist— then he goes right back to ignoring them. When I bring it up again, he says, 'Connie, I *have* spent time with the kids. *Remember?* We enjoyed my old videos!' He'll refer back to that *one time* for months or years! Oliver is right—he's hopeless!" Connie closed her eyes for a moment. Her face was wrinkled with tension.

"Anyway, this morning I thought about David. Oh, you don't know...David is Cedric's...kind-of...adopted younger brother...although Cedric would NEVER say that. Cedric doesn't really like him. It's a long story, but David has filled in for Cedric's shortcomings, meaning...he has a close relationship with both Felicity and Oliver...and me. He's been really good about talking to the kids, being involved in their lives, and supporting their feelings...and mine too. In the past, I just ignored Oliver's and Felicity's strong emotions or told them to look at the bright side. But David said I was pushing them to where *I* was comfortable. So this time, I found myself doing what David does. He connects with the kids wherever *they* are. Hmm...I wonder where David is? I've been so preoccupied...this didn't occur to me until now."

"Where does he live?"

"He's a street minister, so he moves around to wherever he's needed in the city or neighboring parishes. He's like family, so I feel at a loss not knowing where he is." Connie paused with an agonized look on her face. "I heard on the radio that those left in New Orleans have been ordered to evacuate due to the flooding. In the scurry to herd everyone onto buses and out of town as fast as possible, parents have been separated from their children. The buses then went to different shelters, so some parents have no idea where their kids are! They must be worried sick! And the children—think of how scared they must be!" With her face contorted in pain, Connie hurried away, and I sat alone with my journal.

Lesson Three: ESCAPE!

Without adequate acknowledgment and help to work through our disasters, we end up dividing our outer world in a way that resembles our mental fragmentation. Parents distance themselves from their children, and children from their parents; marriages and other partnerships break; and people feel estranged from one another. Survivors may walk away from loved ones and disappear, or wall off their hearts and minds and become unreachable, hurting those who seek their companionship. Disasters can force those who were once close to end up miles or states apart or as strangers in the same home. Some survivors, lost in oblivion or focused on "business" or superficialities, don't recognize human need, so they cannot rescue other disaster survivors. They may squander their lives retreating from a disaster, only to find or create another and another and another.

Our internal separations are always mirrored outside us (and vice versa). We run from the parts of ourselves we feel are responsible for our traumas, wherever they may seem to be. For example, if events were physically traumatic, children may tune out their physical bodies, other bodies, or the physical world. If traumas were emotionally devastating, kids may abandon their hearts and ignore expressions of feeling. If traumas were mentally overtaxing, the survivors may no longer share their ideas, digest new information, or process outdated "knowledge" or beliefs. Sometimes people negotiate traumatic experiences by becoming particularly accomplished or active in the areas where they've been compromised (a type of overcompensation)—such as a sexually abused child later becoming promiscuous. Therefore, the parts of ourselves that were once perfectly healthy, balanced, and in a state of great developmental potential, as in a newborn, begin to differentiate and become respectively minimized or maximized.

The more that aspects of our authentic human self are traumatized, altered, and ostracized, the more we look for a substitute—a personality our caretakers might care for or one that might tolerate their lack of care. Perhaps our traumatic experiences aren't validated by anyone, or maybe they are just ignored by the people who matter most. Either way, we seek a different "reality," one that seems comparatively safe and pain-free and supports some semblance of relationship. As we increasingly abandon our humanness, we give more and more of our attention to less-developed life-forms, material items, and activity, and further adapt ourselves to fit in.

Lesson Four: PSYCHOLOGY MADE EASY—What We All Have in Common Is: Disasters—Blame—Escape

Handling trauma and stress by retreating from ourselves is a universal coping strategy. We may do this in one of the following two ways, if not both:

I. **Active Avoidance**:
    A. Absorption in achieving success, whether in academics, sports, child rearing, business, social climbing, or ascending the chain of command
    B. Preoccupation with playing, scheduling, organizing (or disorganizing), cleaning (or making messes), exercising, improving one's physical appearance, immersing oneself in other people's problems, or any other activity (writing, for example!)
    C. Withdrawal into video games, computers, TV, movies, music, or books
    D. Seeking adventure through traveling, wilderness exploration, vicariously living through someone else's exciting life, or entertaining one's own fantasies
    E. Behavioral addictions, such as excessive eating, talking, sex, spending, gambling, substance abuse, or any hyperactivity of body, heart, or mind
    F. Emotional addictions as with the need to always feel happy, successful, or innocent
    G. A focus on the body, with consecutive diets, athletic achievements, or multiple elective surgeries
    H. Risk taking or thrill seeking (evading fearful places by pretending to be fearless)
    I. Criminal activity and other abusive behavior (forcing people into the persecuted child role that one is trying to escape—becoming a victimizer is a child's attempt to evacuate from being a victim)
    J. Extremes, such as suicide

II. **Passive Avoidance:**
    A. Developing physical impairments, as with chronic health problems, excessive sleep or fatigue
    B. Emotional escape, insensitivity to feeling
    C. Mental freezing (absentmindedness, attention deficits, or the inability to think or decide)
    D. Shunning relationships with self/others, as in reclusiveness or couch-potato behaviors

Now, do these avoidance patterns cover everyone you know? We inhabit a stressful, dangerous world, and whether or not we are aware of doing so, we are reacting or responding to the trauma. We alter ourselves to minimize the pain and then run from the realization of what we've done in reaction to what's been done to us. We're all doing the same thing! Yet our "inner infants," with their preferences for "black and white," so often divide the "superior," "healthy," or "productive" avoiders from the "inferior," "dysfunctional," or "unproductive" ones. We then create many different diagnoses to explain away this latter, less-functional group ("paint by numbers [or symptoms]"). We thereby complicate the simplicity of traumatic evacuation that is illustrated so well by the current situation of us New Orleanians.

Once we discern that we're all disaster survivors, running away and hiding from our guilt and pain, we can engage one another on common ground. When we grasp this underlying reality—that all individuals have been overwhelmed by disasters, no matter how apparently "good" their lives are—we can extend compassion. We learn to accept trauma as part and parcel of our worldly experience, rather than hiding from it and pretending it's not there ("Trauma? No, not me!"). We can perceive it as one of the common denominators that unites us all. In this mutuality of traumatic experience, we can help one another seek missing loved ones (outside and inside), connect the dots of our distanced parts, and heal what alone is beyond hope. As my mother mentioned in last night's phone conversation, "Now, we're all in the same boat!"

Effie left her perch in front of the TV and shuffled over to where I was writing. "Several of New Orleans's major roadways are under water, including Interstate 610. There's also no power in much of our state, so electricians are busy with repairs. I'm about to stew some chicken for lunch—would you like any?"

"No thanks, Effie. I just finished breakfast." I responded from the full feeling in my stomach. Effie was a country girl, used to rising early to feed the animals, so she had a different circadian rhythm than us city folk. As she wandered into the kitchen, she continued her report: "President Bush ended his vacation at his ranch early to fly over Louisiana on his way back to Washington today. New Orleans shipping companies haven't been able to transport their cargoes to their destinations. Also, gas prices are going up all over the country because the oil refineries and pipelines that were hit by the storm are not operational. This disaster is impacting people all over the States!"

"Time for carpooling," Connie interjected with a hint of authority in this area. "I wish more people were open to that."

Lesson Five: Disasters Mold Us into **RIGID** Postures

After a disaster, ordinary means of psychological "transportation" can be compromised or unavailable. We may no longer possess the time, money, energy, strength, or support system to carry ourselves and others from where we are, emotionally and mentally, to where we need to be. We may give up our aspirations if the "highways" to a better life appear too difficult or truly impassable. We stick with what comes easily—escape, for example. The more we roam our known paths of "evacuation," the more comfortable and familiar they feel. These well-worn tracks soon become habits—fixed routines and inflexible behavior patterns. We become increasingly rigid and unyielding, fulfilling our "infants'" needs for constancy, stability, and security in a world where these qualities are scarce or fleeting. We become locked into one way—an excess of one personality trait and a lack of another—which soon becomes "my" way. We also lose our natural eagerness to explore new and different manners of being, preferring set rules about correct times and places for everything, including the expressions of the emotional body ("If you want to cry about something—do it at home behind closed doors!"). The more we choose accustomed behaviors over the spontaneous, creative, in-the-moment meeting of human need, the more an artificial persona (a stuffy substitute teacher!) supersedes our ever-so-vivacious and free-spirited *human* child.

Chronic experience with disasters can harden our dysfunctional behavioral patterns, which then require remedial education or medical treatment that otherwise would not have been necessary. This further need often magnifies the traumatically induced anxiety, resentment, and grief—emotional patterns that also can become fixed, as in response to offered help ("I'm tired of people always picking on me—leave me alone!"). Another possibility is to psychically separate from the aspects of ourselves that always say, "*No!*" We instead become happily agreeable and get stuck saying, "Yes!" With such automatic feelings and reactions, we lose our sensitivity and flexibility, and, like Cedric, we no longer mesh with others.

Another way to cope with stress is to evacuate into the far reaches of our minds. For example, we may figuratively "fly over" our lives, observing and offering comments, rather than being deeply engaged and responsive. Perhaps we communicate our experiences and feelings as would a stoic news reporter, not as a passionately involved and caring member of the human race. We talk *about* our lives instead of speaking *from* them. In our detachment, we allow ourselves or others to be bandied about by circumstances, while we do nothing, or from our "lofty" vantage, we try to control all of the tossing. The psychological effects of disasters can be long lasting and far reaching!

Lesson Six: Disasters Incite Our **Imaginations**

I joined Connie and the kids on the back patio. Oliver sat stiffly in a still rocking chair, immobile except for his scribbling with rainbow-colored pens. He was drawing rather graphic storm and flood pictures, many of which were spread out on the ground around him. I was glad he had progressed beyond immersing himself in video games to expressing his current situation. He drew many people dying, dead, or desperately running to keep from drowning. The bubbles above these runners contained the words, "Help! Help!" In one picture, among branches and household debris in the floodwaters, was a tiny, facedown floating body that had an arrow above it pointing at the word "Dad." Clearly, Oliver was answering my question about wanting to talk. He did. He was conversing through his artwork, and he was speaking volumes. Part of his world was devastated, he was crying for help, and his father was effectively "dead" in his ability to meet his son's needs. Also, he was disclosing his anger—wishing his dad dead for neglecting him. One of Oliver's drawings showed looters with guns breaking into a store that had radios, TV sets, computers, and video games. They were all smiling and seemingly enjoying their criminal activity. Remarkably, there were no rescuers in any of Oliver's pictures.

Meanwhile, Felicity rocked furiously in her chair, chewing gum, with her eyes fixed on Wonder Woman—the image on the paper cover of a schoolbook in her lap. *One child is still, but very expressive of his internal state; the other is physically active, yet apparently still in the expression of her internal state,* I thought. *Both are in distress.* I was also aware of my body's inactivity while my hyperactive mind made constant psychological assessments—*my* comfort zone in stress. Connie and I looked at each other understandingly, and then I plopped into one of the large wooden rockers and put pen to page myself.

When we have been overwhelmed by a disaster, we may initially freeze—our bodies stiffen, our emotions are bottled up, and our brains don't function well. We may lose the ability to express ourselves, or we psychotically reiterate a false, but more comforting, reality. After a disaster, silence in children is normal. As they start to recover, they may talk excessively, telling over and over again what happened to them or substituting something that symbolizes the event. Opposite behaviors may express similar states of mind. For instance, hyperactivity and inactivity both point to trauma and are often both represented in each disaster survivor—perhaps in different areas, as illustrated by Oliver and Felicity. The older child, Oliver, lets us know unmistakably what is on his mind—the pictures he draws are full of information. The younger child, however, offers no direct clue to what she has endured.

Creating pictures with our minds is a way of coping with trauma. In these illustrations, drawn under duress, figures are often not sketched "to scale"—a psychological "infant" may be remembered as large and menacing, while a true adult is represented as small and powerless in comparison. ("Young children" within us even denote humans as sticks!) A person who plays a lead role in our lives may be painted as dead, as Oliver has done. People who are psychologically impaired may be depicted as emotionally healthy, and criminals may appear particularly happy, even saintly or heroic. Our pictures may be devoid of rescuers, as in Oliver's drawings. They may also show traumas that didn't transpire, as a diversion from those that did. These pictures may have more to do with the desires of our hearts and preoccupations of our minds than actual outer circumstances. If they meet our needs, they are more likely to be recalled later than are the actual occurrences.

The fanciful pictures we create have a quality different from our genuine life experiences. As we deal with life's disasters by removing or altering the most painful pages and inserting our own or others' imaginings, our once rich and dynamic lives lose their essence and appeal. They stiffen and dampen until they are more like books, with many characters, words, and illustrations founded in our imaginations. The more we call our pictures "reality" and drill that into others accordingly, the more we must also avoid or silence the parts of us that threaten this historical rewrite. Such poor conduct is contrary to their developmental needs, so these parts remain frozen at the age of their traumas. These are our "inner children," who, like all young ones, desire attention for what they have experienced *and* PLENTY of support to work it through.

Every part of our psyche carries some aspect of the truth of our lives. Take the trauma of child abuse, for example. There is the truth of what actually transpired and the "truth" about what our perpetrators said did or didn't happen. There is the truth of what we wished had happened instead ("I was treated like royalty when I was a kid!"). There is the reality of how we felt about the trauma (betrayed, for example) and what "truths" we learned from the situation ("People can't be trusted."). There is also the truth about how each episode of child abuse impacted us, such as training us in dysfunctional coping mechanisms. *And* there is the truth about the consequences of our denial or minimization of this trauma and training. Our "inner children" can reveal as many truths or stories as the number of pictures children can draw. If an important "truth" remains unknown, our "inner children" continue to portray the valid details through words, actions, emotions, relationships, dreams, creative expressions, and so on. The truth of our experience must be told...and is told...in one way or another.

I looked up to see that Felicity's eyes were still glued on Wonder Woman while Oliver continued to draw disaster scenes. Connie read her Bible, pausing periodically to share what she was learning, as if she were a teacher reading out of a textbook. I stretched briefly and then returned to writing in my journal.

Lesson Seven: Disasters Impact Our Learning

To know what people have learned, listen to what they teach. We can also look at where people *aren't* learning to know what they have been taught—traumatically induced training results in blocks to new learning and can keep us from freshly experiencing and creatively expressing much of who we are and what our world has to offer. Our "inner children" seek to enjoy the wonders and avoid the woes, too wary to appreciate *both* as valuable aspects of a multivolume textbook.

Our "inner children" don't want to be challenged with problems ("Where's the fun in that?"), so these problems, when noticed, are seen as annoyances, attacks, or burdens—like homework (*blah*!). They may put off the problems until they become bigger and harder to ignore, intruding on our wonders or increasing our woes past our threshold for tolerance. Such difficulties can feed our apprehensions and mistrust and further atrophy our receptivity to education. So, when life inevitably provides new challenges or crises, offering opportunities to leap ahead with new knowledge and skills, these problems can seem unwelcome at best and malicious at worst. (Perhaps we've learned that problems are only supposed to be at the *back* of each textbook chapter and not throughout the book!) As we alter our perceptions to minimize what challenges us and associate only with those who make our life easier, our learning curves are restricted.

Learning this backward system of weights and measures (weighing what's easy or gentle as better and greatly restricting what's hard), our "inner children" curtail our challenging of others in a useful manner. For example, when people are inexperienced or in error, we often don't take the time or social risk to pass on our experience and education. We similarly fail when we give erroneous "corrections" to others' facts, dispensing wishes, beliefs, or indoctrination we have labeled "truth." We may share our "inner children's" pictures, to the detriment of ourselves and others, until someone helps us understand where these concepts come from and why we're sharing them.

Our trauma induced learning colors EVERYTHING we experience, say, and do. Cedric calling himself "independent" when he's pathologically detached is an example. (Who taught him this definition?) Another example is diverting ourselves from horrific circumstances by a Felicity-like focus on imaginary heroics. (How did we learn to cope in this way?) Just as children's classrooms have samples of pupils' work hanging on the walls, we are continually "posting" what we've learned.

Lesson Eight: Disasters Distort Our Memory

Connie began chatting, seemingly to draw Felicity out of her oblivion. "It's strange what we recall from our childhoods. Do you know that I can actually picture all of my childhood textbooks with their colorful front covers? I can flip through their pages in my mind and see the tears and scribbles and the big words that were kind of scary when I was a young girl. I remember the illustrations and the endless words."

As she spoke, I suddenly recollected some of my own schoolbook covers—not the texts themselves, but the paper covers our teachers required us to fold and wrap around our books at the beginning of each semester to protect them from damage. I shared my memory. "I covered all my books with the same heavy paper when I was in school. I can only recall the front—maroon and gray stripes, the colors of our high school football team, around a bobcat, our mascot. That's the best my visual memory can do with my schoolbooks. I remember very little about my childhood, I'm afraid."

What is so frightening about our life's "textbooks" anyway? After all, they have colorful pictures, pertinent diagrams, and lots of facts, figures, and stories, like most schoolbooks. They also have dents, stains, scribbles, and torn pages that are merely by-products of wear and tear by the young. Just as children might see big, unfamiliar words as scary or a large textbook as containing insurmountable learning material, our "inner kids" affect how we "read" our lives. These "young ones" shirk what brings up feelings of smallness, ignorance, fear, powerlessness, stupidity, pain, and so forth. They ignore irritating words and saddening sentences, and they efface paragraphs of persecution and chapters of failure, guilt, and shame. They may neglect an entire volume merely because it contains a disaster. Our memories conform to minimize the discomfort of these "kids" and maximize their feelings of self-worth and safety. We memorize their drawings rather than the real events. This cover-up can be extensive, and before we know it, we've encased the textbook of our lives in cover stories and illustrations. These "covers" can be so compelling that we don't open the "books," and the original texts within are largely forgotten.

Lesson Nine: Disasters Alter Our Claimed Identity

Our reactions to trauma—avoiding hurt, blaming ourselves, running away and hiding, adapting rigid postures, learning misinformation and disability, modifying memories, and so on—all contribute to a new, diminished identity, a mere caricature on the cover of the "textbooks" of our life. For example, when a boy receives what he "needs" by feigning deftness, he develops a facade of proficiency. A girl chastised for mature behavior ("You're trying to play grown-up, eh? I'll show you where you belong!") adopts an immature-appearing facade. Caretakers may even mold a child into a loathsome creature by stomping on warm feelings, ridiculing loving thoughts, and responding cruelly to caring gestures. Understanding that these reactions and subsequent adjustments are due to environmental factors, is it really admirable if our cover image appears particularly charming, exciting, pious, or important? Moreover, are troublesome people worthy of our disdain ("Just lock up those criminals and throw away the key!") when they have reduced themselves to an image that provides the most post-disaster provisions? If some of us were raised to go to college and pursue a lucrative career and others were raised to live on welfare, aren't we both doing what we were raised to do? Despite appearances, conditioned characters have much in common. No matter how "good" or "bad" the facades or behaviors, they indicate more about where people have been than who they are. We know their early teachers were more focused on training the image than developing the human child.

How does the average family participate in this focus on image? Perhaps one child had a premature birth, a prominent handicap, a serious illness, or a keen interest that cost the parents a lot of money, time, or effort. The front book cover on this child's life might read, "The Problem Child" or "The Needy One" or "The Attention Seeker." In comparison, another child in the same family might receive a book cover that states, "The Golden Girl" or "The Angel" or "The Child Who Was Never a Child," since she was willing to balance her sibling's "demands" with quiet acceptance and compliance. Just as New Orleanians brought their culture to wherever they evacuated, these cover titles often remain with people throughout their lives, *until* they address the elementary causes.

The covers on our "books" may be true in part. For instance, the bobcat on my schoolbook covers is a potentially dangerous wild animal—peril lurks within, whether hurricanes and floods or tempestuous people. Covers may hint at some of the material or themes in the original text, as in *school* colors implying a book of learning. They may also portray the exact opposite of the contents, as in a traumatized child seeing Wonder Woman on the cover of her life's textbook. A mythical superhero may serve as a distraction from devastating disasters, a decoy for the experience of powerlessness and vulnerability. To compensate for our weakness and deficiencies, we may, like Felicity, stare blankly at this superhero to garner feelings of strength and invincibility. Meanwhile, a more mature part of our mind, represented by older brother Oliver, may obsess about the disaster and attempt to gain some control over it by creating our own scenes. The youngest "children" within us typically prefer enjoyable stories to textbooks and fun times to working with and learning from scary or hurtful events. Not surprisingly, these "inner kids" are forever playing—exaggerating the good times and minimizing or forgetting the bad—altering our lives into something "they" find more pleasing.

Felicity kicked off her pink, orange, yellow, and white sneakers and rubbed her feet together as though they were sore. I remembered the pages of my life textbook when I was a pediatric resident at Charity Hospital in New Orleans. I saw plenty of children in the clinics who wore shoes that didn't fit properly. Their parents likely couldn't afford a new pair, so these kids wore shoes that were too small or had belonged to an older sibling and their feet hadn't quite grown into them yet. Blisters were a common result of the ill-fitting shoes chafing their skin.

Likewise, the soreness and weeping of so many kids' psychological bodies seemed to me the result of their "wearing" something that didn't fit. Perhaps a girl is treated as much younger than she is, or a boy is expected to follow in the footsteps of a sibling or parent. Just as a callus develops on a foot that is rubbed and irritated for an extended period, so do children become callous when their emotional and mental sensitivities are slighted and abused over extended periods or their psychological bodies aren't allowed space for growth. To me, this explains why many parents aren't interested in learning the true cause of their kids' illnesses, injuries, or unhappiness, and don't listen to the insights of those able to help—the wounds are not confined to the child.

One day, a well-dressed set of parents visited the clinic with their only child, twelve-year-old Erin, whom her dad described as "an imbecile—she doesn't even know her colors yet!" According to her teacher, Erin was also showing a lot of anger in her seventh-grade compositions. Upon examination, we soon learned that Erin spoke with a poetic language. For example, she communicated her depression by saying, "The sky is black." Her father, an engineer, could only hear the literal words and not the underlying meaning, so he invariably corrected her with statements like, "The sky is blue, you idiot!" The girl's writings were superb! They were angry, yes, but so superior in quality that I wondered if Shakespeare had similar writings as a child. Our care plan included teaching the parents how to encourage their gifted child and to find Erin a mentor in the field of poetry who could understand and nurture her abstract communication and develop her literary brilliance. Her parents left the clinic quickly, stunned by our assessment and refusing any follow-up. I got the impression that Dad expected a diagnosis of mental retardation, and our diagnostic team didn't meet his expectations!

Michael, a ten-year-old with asthma, was the only child of middle-aged parents who had desperately wanted children but weren't able to conceive for many years. They so cherished Michael that they gloriously praised everything he did. His normal childhood achievements were given great accolades, despite average grades and behavioral reports in public school. As I took the history in his pediatric examination, he informed me proudly, "I'm a genius!" He commanded me to question him so he could demonstrate how clever he was. I did as he asked, keeping my questions appropriate to his age, and yet he missed every one! He left the clinic no smarter than when he arrived, while I pondered what impact his grandiose delusion would have on his life.

Dennis was one of the rare fathers who brought his kids to the clinic. He told me about his own childhood, starting at age five, when he nearly died in a car crash. The ensuing years were consumed by hospitalizations and clinic visits for multiple surgeries, treatments for infections, and medication adjustments. He also spent many years in rehabilitation, where he struggled to slowly reclaim the abilities he'd had before the accident. From reading comic books while bedridden, he learned to draw cartoons. These drawings were his own creations, remarkably detailed and humorous, which he sketched with passion even after his recovery. Dennis explained that after years of being so ill, his family didn't register that their now teenage son was able to return to a normal life—they were so accustomed to looking after him.

"When Mom said, 'We need milk,' I wanted everyone to see I was OK, so I said, 'I'll go to the store!' But my father always replied, 'No, Dennis, you can't do that. I'll get the milk.' They didn't let me do *anything*!" Dennis exclaimed. He hadn't developed the life skills that his friends had in the course of their family, school, and social lives because he had spent his youth fighting to stay alive. Overwrought and exhausted by the tragedy, his parents lacked the energy to orchestrate the normal developmental experiences he had missed. It was easier for them to just do everything themselves. Dennis was assigned the book cover "The Boy Who Can't Do Anything," which was followed by the sequel "The Man Who Can't Do Anything." Luckily, he landed a job as a cartoonist and otherwise relied on his skilled-in-multitasking wife and his older children to perform all the household chores.

Tamika was a seven-year-old with a brain tumor. She appeared to be improving with chemotherapy until one night she stopped breathing and lost consciousness. Attempts to rouse her failed, and although her vital functions were stabilized with machines, more and more complications set in over time. Her parents described themselves as "religious," and they encouraged her doctors to do everything possible to prolong their daughter's life because they were sure God would heal her, no matter how apparently grim the situation. As Tamika's organ systems failed one by one, her parents eagerly agreed to more and more invasive procedures and "new, exciting developments" that "might be the cure!" Continuing to feed the parents' hopes by treating this ravaged body month after month *and* not commenting when Tamika's folks excitedly planned for her joyous future seemed immoral to the more sensitive residents. I was stressed by the conflict caused by my duty to obey orders when my heart summoned my humanity.

One morning I was among a group of doctors performing an assessment at Tamika's bedside when the ward phone rang. A maternity nurse was calling to say that Tamika's baby sister, Tamara, had been born after a difficult delivery. Both mother and baby were resting in good condition. We were in the middle of cheering when I detected an ominous sound amid our rejoicing. Tamika's life-support system was signaling that her heart had stopped. A small team of doctors and nurses raced to revive her, but after several attempts she was pronounced dead. Tamika, whose presence I had not sensed for nearly a year, seemed very conscious in the last moments of her life. She had heard the news of her replacement sibling and felt she was no longer needed, so she left. Now we were crying…in sorrow, in relief, and in awe of the immensity of her devotion to her parents—to protect their feelings, her body had survived longer than any of us thought medically possible.

In our devotion to our caretakers, we have believed what they taught us about ourselves by their words and behavior. Those unwanted and disowned parts of our caregivers' "textbooks" found homes in our books and on our book covers and, like hand-me-down shoes, often did not fit. We may have been grossly underappreciated or greatly overrated. We may have been judged as incapacitated when we were merely inexperienced, or we may have appeared on the verge of revival when, psychologically speaking, we were closer to death's door. As a result, we have areas of talent, skill, or existence that we're unaware of or that require development. We have delusions that demand dispelling, inabilities calling for instruction, and areas of morbidity that necessitate professional help.

We're all acquainted with people who don't see their own beauty, loving-kindness, or brilliance. On the other hand, there are those who are blind to their own limitations. Don't we also know those who cannot recognize how much their loved ones have matured *or* have remained the same despite years of potentially growth-producing experiences? So many miscommunications, conflicts, and crimes can be reduced to confusion between Erins and Michaels and Dennises and Tamikas. *And* so much of what we "know" comes from a "child" inside who, much like Tamika, tried to shield those unable to shelter her.

How can we make beneficial decisions when we're viewing images that distort the underlying truth? For example, when our feet are burning and blistered, we inspect the socks and shoes we've been wearing to determine their contribution to our discomfort. However, when people are psychologically raw, irritated, or inflamed, we mistakenly assume something is "wrong" with them, rather than examine their contacts, past and present. Similarly, we don't notice what our chafed feet may be revealing about our inner selves. If our goal is to stride pain-free as adult human beings, then our acceptance of image, preference for image, projection of image, and protection of image are a DISASTER!

Effie stood outside briefly. She looked so pale and thin compared with the vigorous homesteader I once knew. She collapsed into a rocking chair and, after a brief rest, offered another report: "Just before Katrina, there were hundreds of school, city, and commercial buses ready for evacuations, but no one would tell them what to do or where to go, so they did nothing. Many buses were then left on low ground, so they ended up flooding. The news about the Seventeenth Street Canal levee failing on Monday morning wasn't announced in many areas until the following day, which caused many people to wake up in a flooded bed and many more not to wake up at all. Where were all the responsible people during these mishaps?"

Lesson Ten: Disasters Obscure Our Response-Abilities

Even our smallest children show when they are unhappy or in trouble. Early on, the images we place on them rub against their vulnerable psyches, causing increased tenderness and distress, but over time, a toughness develops. Similarly, kids' voices, whether external or internal, grow louder and louder when they long to be heard—becoming urgent, demanding, or overbearing. They want to share: "This is what happened to me!" "This is what I think and feel about it." "This is what I need to work through it." But they are often ignored, misinterpreted, judged, attacked, condemned, and/or diverted into worldly activity, productive or otherwise. When expected needs are not met, over time these voices become softer and softer and softer, until they are inaudible.

When the voice of our genuine experience is shunned or punished, we learn to shun or punish it also. We instead express what *is* heard and valued, imitating those in our environments who get the most attention and care. We foster habits of imitative expression, much like Effie reporting the news she's absorbed from radio and TV. As mimicry of others' words turns into habit, we add these as captions to the images on our book covers. We may largely abandon our responsibility to deliver accurate, personal, timely, or even vital information as we no longer say what we mean, want, feel, or need. We may even forget how.

Why don't our caretakers hear our cries for help, or why do they perceive a distorted message? Why do they give but a trifle or offer the opposite of what's needed? Why isn't the distress of a child seen for what it is, rather than redirected, corrected, medicated, or given convenient substitutes? ("Have some chocolate—you'll feel better.") These poor responders have been subdued by their own disasters, so they have few reserves to share with anyone else. They may have learned that disastrous parts of life's "textbooks" are best not mentioned in polite society, so they take cover when these subjects are broached. Maybe to them, "responsibility" denotes "accountability," and they don't wish to incur blame. Tragically, the uncharted material from our past proportionally interferes with our present responsibilities. However, within the caretaker's disregard of a child's plea for help is the cry of their own hurting "child"—"I'm doing what happened to me!" (Show and Tell!)

Our developing minds imprint all of our experiences, which we communicate, sooner or later, through our words, feelings, and/or behavior. As a result, most of us have many "voices" (victims and victimizers, responders and nonresponders, adults and "children," and so on) "speaking" at varying levels of volume—the louder ones stealing attention from the softer ones. The "voices" within our behaviors are also "yelling" or "whispering" through their degree of disregard and unresponsiveness to human need. Each expressive, receptive, and responsive stance resides in different areas in the average "adult." For example, a mother may be able to hear and respond to her small children's wishes to play. But she may be incapable of listening and responding to calls for more serious pursuits, as with enjoyments that expedite their psychological development.

These differences in our ability to respond affect our internal "classrooms." We learn to respond to the parts of ourselves that have been given the most teaching, the highest marks (straight As!), or the greatest perks and recognition (gold stars in all their many forms). We assume the role of teacher, star pupil, nonthreatening average kid, or class dunce accordingly—playing *each* role in some aspect of our lives. While we may maintain only one image of ourselves in our minds, our behavior clearly expresses the full diversity of the "class" and the wide range of our schooling, including the disasters that are calling so loudly for able responders.

Lesson Eleven: Disasters Can Break Down Society

Effie continued, "There are an estimated hundred thousand people still in New Orleans[2]—but it's not safe for any of them. It's anarchy! Looting is out of control, as is the brazen violence on the streets. The police escorted senior citizens from their retirement homes all over the city and bused them to the Superdome and Convention Center to await transportation out of the city, but the Superdome is bedlam—thefts, fights, rapes, beatings, murder. Why would they do that? The thousands of people who sought refuge at the Convention Center have discovered it's also unsafe. Several dead bodies were found outside, and the police officers who tried to quell the scene were beaten back. More than two hundred police officers have abandoned their posts,[3] and those remaining, along with other rescuers, are being attacked. All this commotion is interfering with the efforts to evacuate New Orleans residents.

"However, on a positive note, the news had a special segment that focused on some of the local heroes risking their lives to save those in danger. I was delighted to hear about the ham radio operators. They're helping rescuers find survivors and helping evacuees in discovering the whereabouts of lost family members. It's nice to have some good news among all the bad."

Every life's textbook has sections of unpleasantness and pain. The nature of this world and its inhabitants has marked us all. We have all taken things that either didn't belong to us or would have met a greater need in someone else. We've argued or fought to get "our" way. We've hurt or used people for our pleasure, and we've dumped our anger on innocent parties with no concern for the consequences. We have all contributed to the deadening of the HUMAN spirit. We have blocked sources of learning and inspiration or overtly attacked them, hampering the needs of many. We've also refused to give the lessons that others were earnestly seeking, whether they knew it or not. We've acted in these prohibitive ways because of our schooling. *But,* just as we're capable of learning and perpetuating abuse and neglect, we're capable of unlearning such actions. *And* we're capable of gaining new, constructive skills, such as those that facilitate psychological growth. To do this, however, we need a teacher who can direct us in studying the shame-filled pages in our textbooks and listening to their lessons.

Lesson Twelve: We Need Help!
Listening Step Four: FOCUS on the LOCAL HEROINE: **OUR RESCUER**

When we start to recognize the disasters in our lives, we realize we are not qualified to guide ourselves on our life's journey. As we become aware of our traumatized, damaged, and abandoned parts, we KNOW we need help. Although competent in many areas, as individuals we don't have the wisdom to determine when, where, how, and with whom to assert our abilities. For example, we may have rescuing skills, but saving the life of a New Orleanian who lost everything or of a hoodlum who has acquired abundantly by robbing the local store may have very different outcomes. Alone, without higher knowledge, we are powerless to effect meaningful, lasting change in ourselves and our world. The devastation is too huge, the pain is too great, and the guilt of choosing image over the well-being of ourselves and our loved ones is too much to bear. Stepping out of denial and catching a glimpse of the suffering we have stored in our unconscious mind motivates us to seek another Life, that of Our Rescuer and Teacher—the real Superhero who is capable of helping, educating, and safeguarding us through whatever comes our way.

How do we discern this Guidance amid the babble of many voices, wishes, demands, feelings, thoughts, and needs, both inside and outside of us, at any one moment? How do we filter out what is *for* us as opposed to *against* us? How do we embrace what is true and *not* the lie? How do we recognize present reality, rather than lingering, unresolved problems from our past or the stories we've concocted to cover them? Practice, practice, practice! As with learning any skill, we need to practice persistently, see and correct our errors, *and* labor ever harder to succeed. Becoming aware of and processing the storms and floods of our lives, admitting and mourning our limitations, seeking a Mentor and depending on her to conduct our steps *is* the psychological journey.

Let's acquaint ourselves with this "local" Heroine whose role is to accompany us into the learning of our life's "textbooks" and out of the disasters we have made of our lives:

(1) She heals the hurt. Our Rescuer shows us that staring at the cover story we've exchanged for our genuine experience GREATLY limits us. She gently removes the splinter of our daydreams, and where the image once was, raw pain remains (OUCH!). She responds by drawing our attention back to the original textbook that lies between all "book" covers and within all our stories. As she holds us and our "book," she recounts these tales, and the pages of our lives suddenly fall into focus, revealing exactly what we need to grow, negotiate the world around us, and serve one another.

(2) **She takes away our shame and blame.** Our Rescuer sees we are burdened with heavy "backpacks" of guilt and grief about the wreckage we've wrought and the constructive things we've refused to do. All the smiling cartoon images dangling from their "zipper pulls" to convince everyone of our innocence and happiness have never alleviated our underlying remorse and mourning. Yet, Our Rescuer offers only comfort, not harsh judgments nor punishments (no detention!). She merely helps us differentiate reality from fantasy, who we are from what we pretend to be, just like a loving parent with small children.

When we begin to listen to Our Rescuer, some devastating things may happen. Unconscious qualities and experiences surface within us, much like catching a whiff of an uneaten fish sandwich that got lost in a school locker. These may get us into trouble, not unlike sitting in class with a puppy zippered into the front of our jacket. We may want to blame these unpleasant consequences on Our New Instructor. In fact, Our Rescuer is disclosing what has been with us all along, but we were too young and inattentive to notice. *But,* by experiencing our own guilt-ridden, grief-stricken, spurious, spoiled, and/or puppy-like states, we finally let go of *our* inadequate coping efforts, and we become willing to follow an Adult who REALLY knows what she's doing.

(3) **She ends our isolation and coaxes us out of hiding.** Like any good teacher, Our Rescuer is nonjudgmental and inclusive of everyone—adults, children, and infants (outside and within). She understands that we've been absent from our lives—hiding in our images and storybooks. She acknowledges our attachment to them and our fear of losing these beloved "companions," like young kids with their dolls, stuffed animals, and action figures. She patiently points to the differences between them and her, so our fears lessen as our trust in her grows.

(4) **She leads us through the full menagerie of our imagery**—demons, clowns, tigers, lambs, fairies, unicorns, and so on (not necessarily in that order!)—all the figures in a typical children's story. She fearlessly embraces each image, whether mythical or real, and uses them to teach her lessons. Amazingly, as we learn through them, these creatures are transformed—just like in fairy tales! They turn into aspects of our own character!

(5) **She elevates society by lifting up each member.** The more we experience the horror underlying the pleasant facade of this worldly existence, the more we loosen our attachments to imagery and its dumbing-down process. The more we experience the magnificence of Our Rescuer and her powerfully positive effect on our lives, the more we are willing to switch subjects, from us to her, branching out our lessons into every aspect of our lives. For example, Language Arts becomes the study of physical, emotional, mental, and spiritual expressions. Be warned, there *will* be tests. However, when we're diligent with her savvy, all-encompassing instruction, we ultimately learn to gaze unflinchingly at this Superhero.

BACK TO SCHOOL—Our Rescuer's curriculum includes:

a. Gym: stretching, flexibility, toning, and strength exercises for behavior, feelings, and thoughts
b. Art: interpreting our "inner kids'" drawings and then sketching with realism
c. Reading and Comprehension: perusing our life stories and grasping the lessons of "good" times and "bad" (Our Rescuer can help you understand the content of this book, for instance!)
d. Grammar, Spelling, and Punctuation: knowing where to assert rules and exceptions to rules, separations and connections, additions and deletions, emphasis and reduction, and so on

e. HIStory (and HERstory): studying the past to distinguish true memory from the pleasing tales we've been told and/or we've told ourselves

f. Science: investigation into the hypothesis of our claimed identity

g. Math: subtracting our most painful memories, our lives don't add up; our responsibilities multiply as we mend the division within our psyche

h. Social Studies: analysis of our "inner people," their "culture," and "society"

i. Literature: *War and Peace*—the psychological state of every individual

With these encyclopedic classes, Our Rescuer guides us into adopting agile, pain-free, and vigorous movements, while erasing the devastation from our traumatic pasts. She ever illuminates the learning content within our cover drawings and stories, as well as in the "textbooks" beneath. Associating all that we truly are with all that we have been (matching!), she encourages us into human achievement—well worth our every effort!

Lesson Thirteen: Embracing the Sufferer and the Suffering—a Tutorial

Our Rescuer explains that we all make the same mistake of trying to live independently of her *and* from so much of ourselves. The result is that we exist as a mere fraction of who we are. She breaks our habits of active and passive avoidance by teaching us that it is ourselves we are avoiding (how scary is that?), and as long as we're evacuating and hiding from our home in our <u>collective Self</u>, problems and the need for life lessons will continue. She reminds us that we, like she, hold all aspects of our world within us. Our segregations and discriminations only maintain our fragmentation and instability. Her individually unique, hands-on, study-while-you-play program corrects each of our unhealthy reactions to disaster (those that cause worry and unnecessary pain or keep us spellbound), while we learn how to *creatively* RESPOND to both trauma and the traumatized.

Special note: Know that unresolved victimization patterns appear repeatedly in our adult lives so that we may fully process them. Gradual acceptance of the truth of our experience usually occurs in a slow progression: We may begin with an "empathic" feeling for an oppressed people somewhere far away. Then we may know someone who has been horribly victimized, or perhaps we're professionally helping these victims. Often someone close to us struggles with persecution before we are willing to speak the vocabulary and then finally admit our own victimization. When we at last own our disasters, feel and think about them, acknowledge every role we've played in these events and why, understand their instruction, *and* learn to handle them appropriately, we no longer take a defensive posture or run when trauma threatens. Instead we can stay present and open, listen to what is called for, supply what is needed, and increase our fluency and comprehension in the process.

FUN WITH AVOIDANCE PATTERNS! Create a Step-by-step Lesson Plan

I. **Active avoidance** can be constructively applied to actively avoid habitual avoidance responses. Thus, we can *welcome* Our Rescuer and the traumatized parts of ourselves. Psychology then becomes the new technology and psychological development the new academic ladder to climb.

A. **Work** on your awareness, keenly noticing the diversity, complexity, and similarities of your outer and inner worlds. Whatever you're momentarily focused on, consider how it might relate to your psychology. Then use your preferred media (maybe construction paper, crayons, glue, and sparkles) to represent this knowledge. Build a model of who you are becoming, and hang it from a bedroom fixture when you're done.

B. **Decipher** the genuine needs your addictions symbolize. (No arguments now, all individuals have addictions *and* needs!) Then use that addictive substance (stay within the law!) to make your need obvious. For example, if you're a compulsive rum drinker, you might put your booze in a baby bottle to depict your need for nurturance, to slow down your gulps, and to bring to your awareness that "inner infant" who is controlling your life. If you're a food addict, bake a cake with icing in the shape of a castle—signifying your need for protection—then give it to someone who might benefit from it.

C. **Understand** that your accidents, injuries, illnesses, and/or crimes are often communications from your most traumatized parts and can be expressed constructively and directly. Try improvisation to act out what your illness might be saying if it had a voice. Instead of harming body cells and organs, why not say, "I'm mad!" and get to know this angry part of you. As you become more conscious of this part, consider placing angry-faced stickers in prominent positions in your surroundings or on your body to warn family members so they can take cover. If something in you is out for blood, instead of hurting yourself or others, eat a cherry-flavored snow cone, then peer into the mirror and smile (or growl, if you feel so moved!).

D. **Schedule** time each day to get to know this unhappy part of you. If you have trouble accessing this aspect directly, find an old photograph of yourself (or buy a doll, stuffed animal, or finger puppet to represent him or her), talk to it daily, and listen to what it "says" in reply. (Use your imagination!)

E. **Appeal** to your "inner kids" by including physical exertion and playtime in your psychological and spiritual pursuits (child-centered learning!). Exercise on monkey bars to remind yourself that rigid structures can be used to move and strengthen yourself. With rainbow-colored chalk, draw on your front walk pictures of your "inner family"—each in their ideal setting, with the people and things they like most. Remember, the inner world must be made tangible to "children"—something they can touch, see, hear, smell, or taste—before it will seem real to them.

F. **Be a detective and hyperactively seek Our Rescuer's lessons** in your entertainments. In video games, for example, perceive the fictitious nature of imagery. With the help of your spouse and children, make up a family game in which you playfully address the various shapes and sizes within each person's psychology. Remember—inner exploration can be just as exciting and adventurous as any family outing!

II. **Passive avoidance** can be used to neglect activities that thwart your progress. You can:
   A. **Stop** telling fictional stories about yourself and others. (Try miming to "speak" the truth [don't forget the face paint!].)
   B. **Release** your grief and all other feelings (physical and emotional) involved in your traumatic experiences within the safe parameters set by Our Rescuer. (Punching pillows or a punching bag, finger painting, singing, or imitating an emotional character from a book or TV can help. Be sure to lavish praise on yourself afterward.)

C. **Allow** your thoughts to flow without judging them, crafting them, or acting on them, and discern their teaching. (Consider psychodrama to interact with these contents of your mind.)

D. **Realize** that embracing ourselves and assimilating all parts of our "inner family" requires a lot less effort and is ultimately more enjoyable than escaping them. (You can symbolize this understanding by making gingerbread-cookie men, women, children, and infants; decorating them to match your parts; and then savoring them as you eat them.)

E. **Take a recess** from experimenting with your life and return to the developmental curriculum outlined by Our Rescuer. (With glow-in-the-dark magic markers, design flash cards to alert you to activities she's guiding you to do and *not* do. Then pencil-mark a door frame as you watch your growing self-awareness.)

Meet the Teacher—How to Practice "Hearing" Our Rescuer

1. If you are an **active person**, engage in an activity you are fond of with the purpose of discovering Our Rescuer. Try dancing to music, riding your lawnmower, or picking flowers or blueberries. Pose your question, such as, "What is the best way to handle _____ (some concerning situation)?" Proceed with your activity, listening carefully to the answer that will surely come to you through your behavior, feelings, or thoughts. Perhaps a song will enter your mind, or a memory. Something in the external world may offer the information, too. Pay attention. Everything you notice within you or around you contains important clues.

2. If you're an **introspective person**, sit quietly or lie comfortably and ask the same question internally. The answer will be given to you; it's just a matter of recognizing it. Be careful not to miss the message by placing it in familiar boxes ("I'm just hearing the summer evening cicadas"), but take whatever comes as if it were information from Our Rescuer and try to understand what she's saying (perhaps there are some bugs in you or the situation that need your attention, and so on). Whether it is a certain feeling, a voice, an image, a pulse in the body, or other sensation, receive it as a transmission of vital importance.

3. If you are a **social person**, your instructions will come through daily interactions with people. Again, pay close attention and listen. What may seem to be a routine chat with your kid's teacher may actually be guidance about your own "inner child."

Even when we are lost in our imagery, Our Rescuer is a constant companion, "speaking" in the manner in which we are most comfortable. As a listener, I hear a gentle voice throughout the day that remains with me wherever I roam. Some people are awakened in the middle of the night by "an angel" giving important information for themselves or others. Some see "an opening" when they are to perform a particular task. An acquaintance, Sissy, a mother of five, has a bustling houseful of people coming and going. She said, "I don't want another person, presence, or voice in my life; I have enough as it is! When I ask for Help, I merely sense a profound calmness with the correct answer." Whatever form our guidance takes, it is one that momentarily equates with where we are…until we are ready and willing to hear Our Rescuer communicating in all things, in all places, and at all times.

Felicity awoke from her trance and called to her mother. "*Mom*…I was wondering. What if we can't fix our house? What if my school is gone? What if they can't fix our levees? What if next year there's an even bigger storm that totally wipes out New Orleans? What if…" She took a deep breath as her eyes welled up with tears.

Connie responded with tenderness. "I've been thinking about those questions myself, Feli. Houses and schools can be rebuilt, but where we choose to live is what the four of us will need to discuss and pray about. The engineers can always repair our levees too, but if, when, and how…I'm not going to hold my breath on that one! Who knows what *next* hurricane season will bring us? Our life is pretty unstable right now, which is scary, so I imagine you must be scared. But Ms. Effie said we can stay with her as long as we like, so we have a home, and we have each other."

Felicity sat on her mother's lap, resting her head on her shoulder. Connie, crying silently, combed her fingers through Felicity's long hair, periodically pausing to detangle it. After a while, she reached out to her son, who recoiled from her touch and scribbled a sketch with increased fury. Connie then removed the book from Felicity's clutching arms, opened it, and began to read out loud.

Lesson Fourteen: Developing Skill in Self-recognition

Under the instruction of Our Rescuer, we learn that our disasters are opportunities to reclaim ourselves, as with blocked passages of behavior and walled off thoughts and emotions. As long as these passages are inaccessible, we cannot receive valuable teaching and guidance through them, nor are we able to share with those who are open to experience in only these areas. We are handicapped and in need of help, but that help must come in a form we're open to receiving. Often it doesn't. Were it not for the "bullying" of storms and disasters in our "adult" lives, we might never admit our deficiencies, set the goal of tackling our psychic blocks, seek a worthy Coach and Teacher, and follow her game plan and curriculum. Life's challenges move us to find comfort and support in a larger, more capable Body that sponsors us as we slowly regain all the *human* experiences we lost while we were fighting to keep our image "alive."

As Oliver vacated his rocker, the Tasmanian Devil grinning wildly on the front of his oversized white T-shirt caught my eye. I guess I had been too absorbed in my mental musings to notice the shirt before. As the slender, frowning boy stomped back into the house, I gaped at the backside of the Tasmanian Devil on the back of his shirt.

"How could I have missed that?" I uttered, pointing at Oliver's shirt while musing over the power of our psychology to block or otherwise alter our vision—or anything else, for that matter. As I winced at how oblivious I'd been, my thoughts drifted back to last year in New Orleans during Mardi Gras when a group of elderly women were parading—each wearing an extra-large T-shirt with front and back views of a young, buxom model in a fuchsia bikini.

Lesson Fifteen: Recognizing Image

Valuing a cover more than the underlying "textbook" of our life, with its rich contents, is like being more concerned about a T-shirt than the person in it. Just as a T-shirt may disclose something about the person wearing it, our "covers" may be similarly revealing. They may reflect who we've *wished* to be but never were, or who we once were but are no longer. Our "inner infants" may just eye the "front" of a person's "shirt" and then believe this "front" is the sum total of this person. They don't realize that every front also has a back. Someone with a stately persona exuding holiness, popularity, or heroism may have a long, dark shadow trailing behind, if we'd only *look*.

Our wholeness is the cause of such duality (the back is the opposite of the front). We cannot relinquish any part of our humanity! The qualities we subtract from our "front" are automatically added to the back. For example, if we are taught to extend only "loving-kindness," as our own individual culture defines this, all the other responses in our behavioral repertoire retreat, expressing themselves where we're blocked and not looking. If we are "informed" that happiness is the healthiest emotion, our genuine feelings of sadness, anger, fear, guilt, and shame must invent ways to illustrate what we truly feel. If we are indoctrinated into only one "correct" way of stepping ahead, our intelligence and creativity may manifest with particularly backward nonconformity. If we have only "our" one way of moving forward or backward, how can we team up with the many different people who similarly have "their" own one way?

We train our friends and family in "our" way, which includes ignoring the back of our shirt (lest they too be scorned!). In mutual "respect," we learn to only look at facades. ("If you acknowledge only the front of my shirt, I'll do the same for you!") Only the occasional person has escaped such training or grown past it to dare comment on the "devil" at our backside. However, their voices seem a murmur amid the roar of the majority. Why listen?

Lesson Sixteen: See the Difference?

As I headed into the kitchen for some food, I saw the kids' Star Wars action figures, Anakin Skywalker and Queen Amidala, on the dining table. I picked them up, noticing the unmistakable difference between images and the children who play with them. These plastic dolls were small, stiff and unchanging, hard, cold, and unexpressive of any need, thought, feeling, or want. They were motionless and unresponsive to me, yet could be manipulated by anyone. What a contrast to the living children with whom I'd occupied my day.

The "textbooks" of our lives fall into only two categories. The first is a study of evacuees, who have abandoned their disaster site and remaining survivors and have sought refuge in all forms of images. The second provides adventurous, experiential learning for "children" of all ages as taught by Our Rescuer and her trained "rescuers." (Those aspects of our psychology who follow Our Rescuer's guidance henceforth will be referred to as "rescuers.") We require Our Rescuer's first course of study to unglue our eyes from the paper covers so we can read the whole of the text. We need her second course to reclaim as our own those open-hearted and broad-minded "inner children" ("No child left behind!") from whom our disasters separated us. These willing and eager pupils are capable of absorbing our life story...imbibing its knowledge...and growing...

"It's time for me to go," Emily announced as she and I stood beside her packed car. She had managed to fill her day sorting through her belongings to decide what to bring on her trip to Florida and what she'd leave behind at Effie's. Of course, she also "needed" to inspect the car thoroughly for safety purposes, even though she had inspected it before the evacuation and hadn't driven it since we arrived. "It's been through a hurricane, hasn't it?" Emily responded, as if reading my thoughts. Being an only child, she was her father's "son" as well as daughter, so she was trained in car mechanics and maintenance. As an educator, she has shared some of this knowledge with me, just as I have counseled her somewhat in psychology.

"I realized when I was trying to keep Felicity from putting her cell phone next to her ear that I was wanting to protect her...but it didn't come out right," Emily said earnestly.

"Did you tell her that?" The question easily rolled off my tongue.

"Yes, and I apologized to Connie too. Seeing how unhappy Felicity is and her tendency to cloak it with sickness or to stuff herself with food reminds me so much of when I was her age." Emily suddenly noticed that she was hugging a sizable bag of snacks, donated by Effie, so she added sheepishly, "My age too, I guess…Strange, huh?" She paused to absorb the peaceful, partially harvested hayfields all around the house before continuing. "I could relate to Oliver's anger and desire to be alone too." Emily's eyes were glassy. "You probably would say I weathered the storm with parts of myself that I abandoned a long time ago but who are still inside me, expressing themselves in my food choices, health problems…and my living alone."

I nodded with approval.

Emily continued, "Feeling for the kids and what they must be going through has made me feel more compassion for those kids inside me, too. This is the only disaster I can remember, yet resonating with the anger, sadness, fear, and loneliness in the kids has brought to my attention these strong emotions that have always been a part of me. I enthusiastically hugged Felicity and Oliver good-bye—I was glad they magnified what was inside me so I could become aware of it. Connie with her kids also showed me how to be close with my *inner* children…no matter what course we're momentarily taking."

I smiled at Emily. "Congratulations!" I said, beaming with pride at my star pupil. "And safe trip…inside and out!"

"It's not too late to change your mind, you know. You're welcome to come with me, or if you'd like some company here—I can stay a few more days."

"Thanks, I appreciate that, but I've got a lot of reading and writing to catch up on. I'll be fine."

"Sure," she muttered as she looked at the books I was holding, seemingly in the same way I had looked at her bag of treats. "Hey—it's a good thing we bought gas when we arrived the day before the storm. I have a full tank, so with luck I should be able to make it to an open gas station beyond where the storm hit." We hugged, and then she stepped into her storm-washed green Volvo. In a moment, she was off, down Effie's lengthy driveway through the hayfields, the evening sun illuminating her car like an emerald in the straw.

STUDY HALL: Be creative with the following and listen to Our Rescuer to playfully apply the course material in your own unique way. My ideas are merely suggestions.

1. While using a hula hoop or pedaling a stationary bike, consider how disasters have altered your life:
   a. Have they affected your ability to: Focus? Perceive? Take responsibility for your actions? Know yourself and others?
   b. Have they changed: Your behavior? Your goals? Your self-esteem? Your desires? Your feelings? Your relationships?
   c. Have they warped: Your thinking? Your learning (or willingness to learn)? Your truth? Your identity?

2. Have you felt the pain of your disasters directly, indirectly through the pain you've passed on to others, or not at all? Buy or design a pillow to represent your pain, and sleep with it.

3. Whom or what do you blame for these disasters? Is this blaming one-sided?

4. Which parts of you are hiding? (Choose necessary household items that represent these hidden parts, and tuck them away in a closet and close the door. Is this helping your life?)

    a. **Physical parts:** Do you engage in enjoyable activities, regular exercise, a healthy diet, sensuality (including hearing and seeing), sexuality, and community outreach? Do you get plenty of rest and relaxation? Do you admit when you hurt others and then attempt to do better?

    b. **Emotional parts:** Do you comfortably welcome and constructively express all your feelings, whether shame, anger, fear, grief, horror, happiness, joy, love, or gratitude?

    c. **Mental parts:** Do you pursue learning about the world and its life-forms? Do you practice problem solving, introspective understanding, creative expression, and self-awareness? Do you allow yourself unbiased judgments?

    d. **Spiritual wholeness:** Do you seek knowledge of, connection with, and guidance from Our Rescuer?

    Start a monthly progress report so you can chart how you're doing as you study this book.

5. Cut out pictures that represent your escape routes or avoidance patterns. Place them in prominent places to remind you to reframe these with rescuing responses.

6. Do you observe your life from a distance, as if using binoculars to see? Are you deeply involved with each aspect of it? Are you drowning in your overinvolvement? Which parts of your life need more, or less, of your effort?

7. Are people in your life showing you candid pictures of their past with their behavior? (For example, your boss is berating you like his dad berated him.) Choose a playful way to let them know you are listening.

8. Create a scrapbook of some of the recurring "pictures" in your life. Have you inflated insignificant events like a balloon, while minimizing disasters? Have you made vivacious human beings seem barely alive? Have you turned villains into heroes or heroes into villains? Adjust your scrapbook pictures accordingly, and consider what steps you can take to adjust your life's "pictures."

9. Practice "walking" in another's "shoes." How do your feet feel? Buy a pair of shoes that you wouldn't normally purchase to remind you to have compassion for those you tend to judge harshly.

10. Stand in front of a mirror and notice the differences between your image and yourself. How are they alike? How are they different? Which do you prefer and why? Now think about the image you portray—the individual qualities you identify with and those you speak and act from. Compare the image to your true identity: How are they alike? How are they different? Which do you prefer and why?

11. Illustrate the front and back covers on your life's textbook by designing a T-shirt with the front and back revealing two opposing sides of your personality. Wear it sometimes. Remember, to see the backside of our own shirt, we have to trust another's vision *or* take off the shirt!

12. Draw a picture of an image that is different from what you're in the habit of portraying, and try putting forth this image today. Whatever you say, communicate in a new way. Whatever you usually do, do differently. (For instance, if you are accustomed to fading into the scenery, buy a wild hat, go to an outdoor café, and enjoy the attention. (Please note what Our Rescuer is teaching in what transpires.)

13. Are you sharing your knowledge with others? Did anything happen in preschool that taught you *not* to share?

14. Write your own questions that you wish to answer. Now respond to these questions in riddle or rhyme.

15. Are you ready to study and learn from your life?

Jayda phoned after dinner. "I was surfing the Internet for newspaper headlines. New Orleans has succeeded in making the front page of every newspaper in the country, seems to me. Honestly, why does it take a disaster for our third-world city to be noticed and our long-term problems to be taken seriously?"

"Yeah, it's *way* overdue…Hey, I'm sorry about your house, Jayda."

"Me too!…Though that pales in comparison with the safety of my dear Austin. All that stuff I can replace, but not him. He seems to want me to worry about him. He wears me out. I can't sense if he's dead or alive. I'm sure he'll call when he gets good and ready, but that doesn't keep me and Jeremie from worrying. I told her he's fine—I wish I were sure of that! She's enjoying her time in Houston, although with all the evacuees, the crowds and crime rate are up. Jeremie is excited about spending that upcoming insurance money on a new wardrobe *and* an up-to-date CD, DVD, and book collection."

HOMEWORK—Textbooks of Psychology: A New Book Collection!

We teach our children to recognize different parts of our physical world, and we instruct them in appropriate and inappropriate methods of interacting with them. For example, we eat vegetables but not sand. It's socially acceptable to pet a strange dog (if he's friendly!) but not a person, and so on. However, we don't instruct our kids in the recognition of each stage of psychological development, nor in healthy relationship styles when dealing with people in each stage. As a result, we needlessly suffer many hardships we could have avoided with factual information and practice under the supervision of a mature caregiver—what childhood is supposed to be about.

In our world, we are comfortable with a hierarchy of ability or the delineation of quality or competence. For instance, an experienced soprano sings higher and clearer and with greater volume, more control, and a sweeter tone than does a novice. Ports such as New Orleans are ranked by their degree of easy access, depth of water, modern equipment, good security, high efficiency, and excellent roads to transport the goods to and from the ships. We also assess our children's learning through academic standards, taking note of who excels and who is falling behind. We then assist each student and, hopefully, adjust the teaching accordingly.

However, we are typically reluctant to rank psychological development. Examining and critiquing the condition of our internal world is uncommon. Why is this? We know that technological advances, as with computers, cell phones, satellites, medical imaging techniques, and many other modern conveniences, ease our days considerably when compared with primitive living. Yet we often don't notice, let alone remedy, the uncivilized activities or chronic degenerative conditions of people (or parts of people) stuck in the younger psychological stages. Also, we don't routinely admit the benefits and relief to our lives offered by those in more developed stages.

Identifying psychological maturity levels, using qualitative benchmarks *and* measurable outcomes, is just as important as classifying levels of advancement in other areas of study, if not more so. As we mature, we each acquire "height" of awareness, clarity of thought, behavioral control, depth of feeling, newness of perception, security in being, general efficiency, and so on. We become more fully alive, psychologically speaking, and more fully human. Our pediatricians routinely make assessments of children's physical development as part of good health care, so why then are we not regularly doing these assessments of our hearts and minds? An assessment system can help us monitor our internal journeys and the "folks" we meet along the way. After all, the category of a hurricane makes a *big* difference in how we prepare and what the possible outcomes will be. The same is true for people! Sensing how trustworthy each part of us is can deliver life-saving information. Once we are familiar with those developmental stages, we are more likely to understand which part of us is operating at any given moment, what it is communicating, what its goals are, how they align with ours, and what we can do to facilitate cooperation and mutual maturation.

The Hierarchy of Psychological Development: The Transition from Image to Reality[4]

1. **Mineral Stage:** "MY" WAY!—"My individual, rigidly indoctrinated image is all that I am. There is no choice."
2. **Vegetable Stage:** "MY" path!—"I alone create my special destiny, and I select every step. I choose the 'good'—what gets me what 'I' want. I reject the 'bad'—what interferes. What I choose is *none* of YOUR business! (But YOU need to...)"
3. **Animal Stage:** "My" world—"The physical realm is my playground, which I ably explore, engage, and enjoy. Where it's uncomfortable, I try to change it or move on."
4. **Child Stage*:** "Me" and "you"—"I explore, engage, and enjoy me and thee." The psychological world becomes increasingly important to the growing Child. Self-discovery and inner development, profound feeling, and deep, heartfelt connections are the hallmarks of this stage. The Child looks inside everything and everyone to see how they work and makes adjustments for more harmonious relationships and ease of living. Increasingly aware of his limitations, the Child turns more and more to Our Rescuer for guidance.
5. **Stage of Woman*:** Ourselves (mindfulness of the whole in every part and the parts in each whole)—"I give whatever is required to grow each member of our human Family (outside and

within) as directed by Our Beloved Rescuer." Through images of the family, the Woman grows beyond imagery, and new life is created.

6. **Stage of Man*:** Our One Self, manifested by Our Rescuer, is the Way and the Destination. Having transcended imagery, the man knows no other.

*Please realize these stages have nothing to do with physical age or gender. Their range of character traits are found in both males and females. Every person must negotiate all stages if she or he is to reach maturity and become fully human. (No grade skipping allowed!) Also note that our stage differs in the various aspects of our lives. For example, a woman may be uninvolved with community events, thinking this is unnecessary for her goal of being a wife and mother, thus remaining a Mineral or a Vegetable in this particular area. She is at most in the Animal Stage if she always responds to a continually running toilet by calling a plumber. She is in the Child Stage when she honestly expresses her genuine feelings about what this plumber does. A man who is absorbed in his profession may never develop his emotional self, stuck in the Mineral or Vegetable Stage in the realm of feeling. He may be in the Child Stage in his ability to work with others to methodically plan a course of action, yet because of his emotional immaturity, he steps on many toes in the process of implementing it.

Many of us have multiple lost aspects of self we have disowned through the years that are much younger than the parts we identify with and uphold as a standard. The youngest of these lost parts is stuck in the Mineral Stage, which the remainder of this book will focus on. As you are reading, please remember—it's never too late to adjust our standards and receive instruction and care so each young pupil can catch up.

---

[1] Sheila R. Zedlewski, "Building a Better Safety Net for the *New* New Orleans," *After Katrina: Rebuilding Opportunity and Equity into the* New *New Orleans,* The Urban Institute (February 2006): 3-4, http://www.urban.org/UploadedPDF/900922_safety_net.pdf

[2] Evacuation order, "Effect of Hurricane Katrina in New Orleans," *Wikipedia,* http://en.wikipedia.org/wiki/Effects_of_Hurricane_Katrina_in_New_Orleans.

[3] Kevin Johnson, "Katrina Made Police Choose between Duty and Loved Ones," *USA Today,* February 20, 2006, http://www.usatoday.com/news/nation/2006-02-20-neworleanspolice_x.htm.

[4] Jala ad-Din Rumi, *The Masnavi, Book 3, STORY XVII, The Vakil of the Prince of Bokhara:*
"I died from minerality and became vegetable;
And from vegetativeness I died and became animal.
I died from animality and became man.
Then why fear disappearance through death?
Next time I shall die
Bringing forth wings and feathers like angels;
After that, soaring higher than angels -
What you cannot imagine,
I shall be that."

Chapter 5

Natural Science

The Nature of Image and Differentiating Inorganic Compounds from Organics

I woke up feeling happy, and then I remembered that 80 percent of New Orleans was underwater.[1] I felt sick. I didn't want to believe it. I wanted this to be a lingering memory of a bad dream, not my reality! *When I fully wake up, this will all go away, and life will return to…to…to what?* I was asking a question even in my sleepy state.

I passed through the kitchen on the way to serve Pookie breakfast. Connie was staring at the phone, looking worried. I managed a weak smile before entering the garage to assess how our smallest evacuee was doing. Pookie was fast asleep, curled under the wood pieces in her cozy corner of the garden shed.

***

Connie broke one of her husband's strict rules by calling him at the TV station. "Hello." He *sounds OK,* Connie thought.

"Hi, Ced. How are you?" Connie's voice divulged her nervousness.

"Fine, Connie, but I only have a minute. Why are you phoning me at the station?" Cedric sounded commanding as usual.

"The past couple days have been rough. I just wanted to hear your voice."

"You heard how Katrina caused a breach in the Seventeenth Street Canal and our house has washed away?" Connie noticed her husband's tendency to pose yes-or-no questions.

"Yes, the kids and I watched you announce this on the news Tuesday afternoon…Cedric, why didn't you call to tell us? Don't you feel our children would fare better if they heard this devastating news from you directly, rather than your image on TV?"

"What about me, Connie? Have you considered my situation? You have no idea how crazy everything is around here—it's sheer madness. I'm trying to keep everyone calm, levelheaded, and focused on their tasks. I've got my hands full, Connie. Besides, I know Effie's looking after you, so please don't dump any of your burdens on me."

Connie found Cedric's authoritarian voice so demeaning. Nevertheless, she backed down. "I can't imagine what it must be like in the midst of it all, Ced. I'm glad you're able to help. But we miss you…we'd love to hear from you when you have a free moment. And when you call, could you please at least speak to Oli and Feli and reassure them that everything is going to be all right, rather than just leaving a to-do list?"

"These are stressful times, Connie. Talking business supports productivity—there's a lot to be done. Have you done as I instructed?"

The rest of the conversation was just Connie answering Cedric's business questions with a yes or no, and then he "had to run." After Connie hung up the phone, she realized he hadn't even asked how Oliver and Felicity were handling the news. *This puts me in a bad situation,* she thought. *Do I lie and tell the kids that their dad asked about them so they'll feel better…or…*

"Tell them the truth!" Her dear friend David's voice was clear in her head. "They need to know the truth about their dad. Kids can't have a relationship with a fantasy father, Connie. They *need* the truth!"

"David! I forgot to ask about David!" Connie exclaimed out loud.

***

Over breakfast, Connie related her talk with Cedric, which reminded me of a conversation I'd had with Jayda about her third couples' therapist, Ryan. Jayda said, "We spent our first six months of therapy with Ryan trying to teach Austin not to butt in when I was talking and actually hear my words, even if he didn't understand them. For Austin to learn to parrot me, it took six months and six thousand dollars—and guess what? He *still* doesn't listen! Seems to me that's too much time, money, and effort to persuade a grown man just to hear me!"

"That's not the behavior of a grown man, Jayda," I corrected her gently.

"An old hound dog would learn faster, I'm sure. What on earth is he?"

"He's a Rock."

Back in the present, I began journaling.

Evacuation Day Five—Leaving the Living

Sometimes talking to a person is like trying to penetrate a stone wall. The words, feelings, or ideas we convey do not penetrate and have no effect. Remember, when human beings have experienced more suffering than they can endure, they adopt other identities to ease the pain. One possibility is an in-the-moment "animal" like Pookie, who isn't aware that a disaster has occurred and its aftermath continues back home. However, when the trauma is overwhelmingly severe and recurring, these people regress even further. To the casual observer, they appear cold, distant, insensitive, obtuse, and obstructive. A listener, however, detects the results of psychological blocks "growing" so numerous that they obscure a person's human identity—he or she *becomes* a wall!

After breakfast, I noticed that three out of the four walls of Effie's family room were covered with bookshelves *full* of books. *No wonder I chose to evacuate to Effie's country house. Under normal circumstances, I would feel like a kid in a candy store with all these books to read. But these were not normal circumstances.* After several minutes of apathetic glancing at book covers, I chose a small book called *Rocks and Minerals* and returned to the breakfast table. After flipping through a few pages, I continued my writing.

Psychology Is a Natural Science: Human Growth and Development Is Natural!

Man, woman, child, animal, vegetable, and mineral are aspects of the physical world, and this world permeates our psychology. In the psychological journey, we evolve through these different aspects of our psyche, in reverse order, ultimately embracing them all.[2] We start as a microscopic part, a "fertilized egg" without psychological awareness, and we end as undivided and undifferentiated consciousness, receiving and serving the whole. In the beginning, we develop by reaching for others, perceiving as foreign everything outside our self, and we conclude this evolutionary process with a gentle knowing of all as <u>Self</u>. When we are young, we want many things, but we grow to desire what we already have and can never truly be without—our all-inclusive Self.

Negotiating the stages of psychological development is as essential as managing the various aspects of our household. We must be familiar with these stages to handle them correctly and draw on the skills inherent in each stage when required. We must, at times, be adamant like a <u>Rock</u> so the Rocks in our world don't roll over us. We must be able to don a colorful appearance, like the <u>Vegetable</u>, to attract what we need and those who need us. Like the <u>Animal</u>, we must attend to the requirements of our physical body. We call on the <u>Child</u> for playfulness, inventiveness, genuine emotional expression, and exploration. The <u>Woman</u> and <u>Man</u> within each of us have the maturity and wisdom to care for the younger stages, moving easily among all aspects of our inner and outer worlds.

Physical development is linear—when we enter puberty, we leave childhood behind. Psychological development, however, is cumulative—every stage we transcend abides with us as part of our identity and interpersonal repertoire. The healthy Infant in us, for example, is capable of crying out when there is a problem. Our development is *not* about picking the stage we most identify with *nor* assuming that what we sense is all there is. True assessment of our stages is about *how* we function within each one. Are we stuck there, *or* are we free to use each stage as needed, to mutually evolve ourselves and others? Of course, there is a continuum between these extremes. When part of us is frozen—preventing us from easily and fluidly moving in and out of that stage and along that continuum—we have a problem. Sometimes, as with Cedric and Austin, we are oblivious to this problem. So if you're not familiar with your Dog...or your Plant...or your Rock...then they exist outside of your awareness, which sooner or later forces someone else to deal with them.

Stage 1: The Mineral Stage of Psychological Development—Surrender to Image

He is <u>Mineral</u>; he has no life. He is a simple "element" or elemental compound, containing "definite atomic structures and chemical compositions which vary within fixed limits."[3] Chronic storms and disasters have so fragmented and deadened his

psyche that he has surrendered much of his human identity and assumed an <u>inanimate</u> existence. As these rigid and frozen fragments of personality take over more and more of an individual's time, volition, and sense of self, they coalesce. He becomes a <u>Rock</u>, taking on a psychologically inert image forged by his traumatic environment. He presumes this way is HIS way and the ONLY way, or at least the only way for him. No matter what his circumstances, he stays fixed. Like any rock during a human's brief lifespan, he is immobile and utterly unyielding (psychologically speaking).

This Rock is heedless of humans—their wishes, needs, longings, and even, at times, their actions. He can reside with a person for years and not have an inkling of who she is and what her talents, strengths, and preferences are. His insensitive and unalterable method of relating is not personal—since no one is "home" at his place, he assumes your place is empty as well. His communications are limited and limiting—giving few details and asking no open-ended questions. In fact, you get the impression he "knows" the answer already—his asking is merely a formality. He often expresses himself in the third person, the neuter "it" (where his identification lies), omitting human agency from his speech—"It happened—it couldn't be helped" (translation: "I *happened* to do it because I *wouldn't* be helped."). Like the self-sufficient noble elements on the periodic table, the "Rock" needs *no one* (including himself)!

The psychological Rock is unconscious—he retains nothing of his human identity. He feels no human emotions (although he forces others to feel plenty), and to compensate, he seeks extreme physical sensations of the most perverse kinds. He has no inner life or inner awareness, so he is not bothered by anything about himself, including his extreme psychological incapacity. His thinking is dense and concrete. Without human traits, nothing can disturb his delusion of being free of psychological problems and needs. He is a mere fixture of our world and therefore bound by laws of a worldly nature, such as, "for every action, there is an equal and opposite reaction." If you confront him about his gaping incapacities, he will soon have you gaping at your own inability to ward off disaster ("What a shame that beautiful house you built burned down!").

The Rock doesn't register "information" that isn't aligned with what he "knows." The warmth of a fond embrace, the kindness of loving people, or the inspiration of timeless wisdom are meaningless to him. Much like a stone splashed with water, he cannot absorb these sentiments or be altered by them. He remains hard and impervious, unaware of the human ability to genuinely receive *and* respond to one another. At best, he offers an *impression* of life, like the imprint of a fossil, but he is incapable of true living. These Rocky traits are deeply ingrained and consistent—the Rock CANNOT move himself emotionally or mentally. If he is to venture into his heart and mind, he must be carried.

Connie sauntered into the family room where Effie was asleep on the couch, Dr. Bear resting comfortably beside her. "Effie is looking after us?" she murmured. Effie had been battling cancer for over two years, and lately she seemed to be losing the battle. She occupied most of her time sleeping, listening to the radio in her bedroom, or vacillating between dozing and watching TV while sprawled on the couch. Connie approached the breakfast table, which had become my writing desk.

"The kids and I are going to spend a few days helping some of our church members with their storm-damaged homes. They live in Mandeville, just north of Lake Pontchartrain. I don't like deserting Effie, but you're here, and she thought communing with friends from home would be a blessing."

"Sure—have a nice time," I remarked, pulling myself out of my writing trance. In a few minutes, they filed out the door, Felicity grabbing a package of Oreos from the kitchen and stuffing them into her backpack before departing.

I figured this would be a perfect time to take care of some errands, including contacting FEMA to register my loss. I dialed FEMA's number—busy signal. *With the hundreds of thousands of people who lost businesses, homes, and belongings in the disaster, this is going to take a while…*

Whatever an Image Gives Can Be Taken Away

I drove to the pharmacy to pick up some of Effie's medications. While waiting for her prescriptions to be filled, I conversed with a distraught Lorna, a young woman with two diamond studs in her upper lip, wearing faded jeans and a yellow T-shirt that read, "As the World Turns." She informed me that her landlady, Gladys, had evicted her. "That was at the end of July. I had just paid the rent the day before, so I didn't understand what she was doing! I said, 'We moved here so we could be close to my daughter's school across the street! Why are you kicking me out? I'm a good person, and I've always paid the rent on time!' I was so upset! Gladys told me my apartment had been leased to someone who could pay more. She said, 'Don't worry, Lorna, I'm a good Christian woman. You have my word that you'll get your security deposit and rent money back when you leave. I'd like you out in twenty-four hours.' So I quickly packed our belongings and left—what else could I do? I went back to my landlady's place for my refund, but she was nowhere to be found. I couldn't believe she kicked me out of my place and now she was stealing my money! She only left a note saying, 'If there is ever anything else I can do for you, please call.' So I called, and no one answered. I called her every single day for a month, each time leaving her my cell phone number, but she never called back. I couldn't believe she was doing me like this! I had to stay with a friend in Midcity, New Orleans, who I didn't even like, but I was out of money and had nowhere else to go! I moved into her <u>shotgun</u> that is now flooded—five feet!

"Since my car was underwater, I had to find someone else to take me to my old apartment, which I finally did today. I hid myself until Gladys appeared, and then I ran up to her and asked her where my rent money and my deposit were. I was really mad—I couldn't believe I had to beg somebody for money they owed me. Then I started to cry as I told her what had happened and how much I needed the cash. She said, 'Lorna, dear girl, calm down!' Her voice was dripping with sugary sweetness. '*You* seem confused. To move to New Orleans and lose everything you owned was *your* decision and has nothing to do with me, child. Besides, if you wanted your money, you should have just called!' At that point, I started screaming. A neighbor walking by stuck her nose in and mentioned how impressed she was with my landlady's kindness toward a 'hysterical young woman.' She actually yelled at me for not honoring someone who is 'the salt of the earth!' I don't know why I talked to her, 'cause it was none of her business, but I tried to explain. The woman wouldn't listen though—she said she didn't like my tone. Gladys then refused to give me *any* of my money back because I was 'disrespectful' to someone old enough to be my mother! What does that have to do with anything?!"

The <u>Mineral Stager</u> is much like an element in the periodic table regarding personal positioning—value is assigned according to weight. The more she accumulates, whether money, possessions, accolades or the like, the greater she imagines herself to be. Thus her bonding with others is always based on what she can get, like Gladys with Lorna. Since people who are used tend to react adversely, the Rock cleverly uses their reactions to make her premeditated plans seem reasonable. She leads onlookers into perceiving that her own vindictive response is what any normal person would do under the circumstances. No matter how great her victims' misfortunes, she cannot empathize with their plight, nor admit the role she or anyone else played in the suffering—"If you didn't want what happened, why did you choose to live in New Orleans?"

The Rock relates to others as if they were elements. She interacts according to "valence," with fixed, predetermined methods. For example, for the Rock to be positive, *you* must be negative—if the Rock is to be good, you must be bad; if strong, then you must be weak. If she is to appear healthy, then you must be sick; and if she is to be judged innocent, then you must be "proven" guilty (the traps she sets to hold you accountable for her downfall can be legion!). Also, the more she is to gain (+1, +2, +3, +4), the more you must lose (-1, -2, -3, -4).

To escape her interminable, emotional numbness, the Rock creates opposing poles from her innate neutrality, and she projects these charges, either the positive or the negative, on all individuals. She likes to combine people of opposing "charges" who become deadlocked in their one-sidedness, so that fruitful enterprises come to a standstill. She also forms strata of "<u>one-up</u>" and "<u>one-down</u>." The "one-uppers" are those with Rock traits. The "one-downers" are "ordinary" folks (i.e., those with human characteristics) who are critical of Rocks and their activities. To maintain the illusion of a great divide between these two strata, the Mineral Stager continually lift herself and her cronies up by pushing those with human qualities **DOWN** and using the results as evidence for the validity of her classification system. She refuses others' biological needs, attacks vulnerable bodies, ignores or squelches emotional expression, belittles ingenuity, and rejects the human spirit to fulfill her ultimate, perceived "noble" purpose of generating inertia.

The Rock employs any and every form of abuse with her victims in order to feel some sort of "charge." She thrives on convincing people just how weak, powerless, primitive, and stupid *they* are. When she brings them to their knees in unbearable grief or in terror of her brutality, or to violence themselves in reaction to her complete disregard for others' humanity, she proudly says to herself, "I knew your phony appearance was a con—I made you reveal your true colors!" She feels exonerated from every atrocity and exhilarated by her achievement—she's exposed yet another fake!

Choosing Image Over Our Human Birthright Has Consequences: Image Is Neither Stable nor Stabilizing

Minerals in our world exist in different states—solid, liquid, or gas—but their composition remains the same. A person in the Mineral Stage of development can appear solid—stalwart and steady— someone with a backbone. He may be fluid, frequently shifting positions, opinions, or loyalties. He may seem to be a windbag, full of hot air, or a real gas. He easily "alters" his form by surrounding himself with those who *are* how he himself wishes to be seen (for purposes of expediency only). Since most people assume the whole represents each part, his image is secure.

The Mineral engages in "chemical bonding." He snatches the mantle of those farther up the evolutionary (developmental) ladder by filtering in the others' more human traits, which he then diffuses as a smokescreen in his interactions with others ("I adore my family," he says in imitation of someone who actually does). He may even pilfer these people's personalities, practicing their actions until they feel like his own. He uses such people to write his letters and lectures, buy his presents, and bestow necessary excuses so they sound sincere. For balance, he deposits his crusty attributes on his adversaries, framing them as elemental or primeval—disrespectful, self-seeking, destructive, deceitful, crazy, and so forth. With these clever tactics, he designs a polar shift, tainting the motives of the most honorable of men and women, while pitching his own acidic nature as basic humanitarianism. A Rock is like the Mississippi River, the southern border of New Orleans—the often calm, serene surface conceals dangerous, life-threatening whirlpools underneath.

Image Is a Far Cry from the Original

I greeted a small, weary-looking, middle-aged man named Caleb in Greensburg's only restaurant—and a Chinese one at that! We were both eagerly anticipating a lunch of red beans and rice. He spoke about his time in New Orleans's French Quarter during the disaster and its aftermath. "Do you know whether the rumors about what happened in the Superdome are true?" I inquired.

"No, none of that's true. I got a friend who was in the 'Dome, and he told me exactly what happened. He was horrified! Women and children were raped. There were murders and thieving. If you left to use the filthy bathroom, you lost your stuff when you got back. Old folks were dead in their wheelchairs. The game boys took over the whole stadium too. They were smoking crack and pushing their drugs. There was no security—everybody was on their own. The security guards were *outside* preventing residents from *leaving* the 'Dome.[4] 'Under no circumstances will anyone be allowed to leave because they might get hurt!' That's what the so-called security guards were saying. Man—talk about disaster! Our people were captive in a closed-in space with criminals, no food, no water, no electricity, and it was hot as hell! That'd stress out anybody!"

I was intrigued by his interpretation of my question. So many people seemed to assume that the "rumors" were the horrific incidents he just relayed, when he was referring to the rumors as the whitewashing of these events.

"Downtown, those looters even cut off one person's hand to get to her jewelry. Why? Why didn't they just ask?! I don't ever want to see that again! That's why I'm getting out of here. Oh, what I seen!" Caleb's face was contorted. "That's why I'll never wear jewelry, and I don't carry more than a few bucks, *and* I don't leave without my pistol. They were robbing dead folks too, prying out gold teeth—now that's sick! Let me tell you something—it was wild. Unbelievable! That's enough though—don't want to talk about it no more. I'm here in Greensburg to pick up my nephews at the Red Cross shelter. We're off to Utah to go camping. I need a vacation!"

In nature, a rock face may be entirely different in age, composition, and form from the strata of rock beneath. Similarly, psychological Rocks may maintain a beautiful, smooth, or impressive facade, but if you attempt to lean on them, you grow increasingly uncomfortable with their hardness, coldness, and inability to accommodate your shape. Even more unpleasant is butting against a landscape reminiscent of ages past when primordial man and enormous predatory creatures roamed the earth. Mineral Stagers' artifices take people back to a primitive time by reducing or eliminating vital aspects of our world and its population: safety; clean air, water, and food; sanitation (physical and psychological); modern conveniences; factual information; and the human beings who tend these necessities or depend on them. In this manner, Rocks ramrod masses of people into the survival mode.

Our Choosing Image Results in Loss

As I exited the gas station convenience store, a thirtyish man named Adam held the door for me. He said he was from Saint Bernard Parish and was passing through Greensburg on his way to visit relatives in the country. With a stony face, he narrated his recent experience.

"Early Monday morning, I was reading a book when all of a sudden, I saw my dog Max floating outside my window. I opened it to grab him, and then my door blew open. That was a good thing—I didn't have to use an ax! I swam out with Jerome, my friend who was hanging with me. We spent the rest of the storm on the roof, holding on for dear life. We were both trying to stay put and stay warm in the fierce rain and cold wind. When the wind was unbearable, we'd jump into the floodwater, and then when we warmed up, we'd jump out again. God knows what was in there, so we didn't want to stay in too long!

"After long and desperate hours, a man in his boat rescued us and took us to the nearest shelter, a school. We spent the next two days there. The conditions were horrible! There was no electricity or running water. The toilet was an overflowing bucket. People's pets were going to the bathroom everywhere. Dead bodies were stacked behind the stage. There was no food, water, or medicine, so even more people died right there! Before we left, two thieves robbed the local store to get everyone something to eat and drink. Nice guys! Jerome and I were able to find a ride out of the chaos, but…"

Adam's countenance changed abruptly as he shouted grievously. "I LOST EVERYTHING! I hadn't been to the races for months, and I was trying to do right by my ex-wife and kids, and now this! I didn't have money for insurance. I just barely had enough for my own family. Everything I worked for, for so many years, is gone. Gone! GONE! If this is what happens when you do right, then I want no part of it!" The man was angry…at his loss…at the red tape to get assistance…at the shelter, city, and state officials…at the national government. "They deliberately blew the levees to drown the suburbs and save the best parts of the city—they were sacrificing the poor to rescue the rich! You know, my grandma said they did this when Hurricane Betsy hit, back in 1927.[5] They said at the time they didn't do nothing, but later they admitted they blew the levee. Why would this be different?! If Grandma were alive, she'd tell you. They kill off poor people and destroy their stuff—who can't afford to do nothing—to protect the rich who can! And *their* houses are insured, so they'd get back everything! This makes *no* sense—why do they do this?! I LOST EVERYTHING!—my home, my car, my things! In all the commotion, I lost Max, and I don't even know where my kids and ex-wife are! But no one cares about poor people! *No one listens to us*!"

As tears formed in Adam's eyes, he quickly blinked them away. His two friends then emerged from the store with cases of beer and bags of groceries and dumped them into the back of a large black pickup, which soon disappeared down the road.

Image Is the Reverse of the Real: Rescuers May Be Found in Robbers and Robbers in Rescuers

Glancing through Effie's *Rocks and Minerals* book, I learned that rocks form when temperature, pressure, and water impact certain elements over time. A geologist can discover the conditions that formed the rock by observing its size, color, and mineral content. The lightweight elements on the periodic table come from the earth's crust, while the heavier elements are formed deeper within the earth or in the oceans. Ground movements cause these denser rocks to surface, as do erosive weather conditions, such as hurricanes.

Psychological Rocks are also forged by environmental conditions. When young, they are consistently subjected to extreme "temperatures"—too "hot" (e.g., sexual touching, screaming) or too "cold" (no physical or verbal affection) or both. Enormous pressure to conform and repetitive, brutal blows to their psyches, not to mention blows to their physical bodies, produce tremendous pain and stunting of their hearts and minds. All the while, they register who is defended, well treated, and listened to—their perpetrators. For example, children are often chastised for *talking* about the Rocky aspects of people's personalities ("Calling Father John a pervert is a *terrible* thing to say!"), and yet those who are *behaving* in a Rocky way, as in harming them, are never chastened. These victimized children must stifle their human voices that would shout in outrage at such grave injustice, and increasingly they coat their strong feelings about being unprotected, abominably treated, and unheard with aggressive actions.

Their humanity slowly erodes and repeatedly fractures through continued exposure to Rocks' ineffable abuse and neglect. When no outside help arrives, they finally "rescue" themselves by clinging to the fragments of their personalities that are impervious to these devastating assaults. They dissociate from their hurting bodies, broken hearts, and tormented minds. As these human aspects submerge in the sludge of their unconscious, they assume a separate, opaque, pain-free, inanimate existence. Their tortured pasts are only transparent when they act out their violent histories against others. They force each prey into their suspended victim roles. As he or she expresses their unconscious pain, they feel great "antagonal" pleasure—their voices have at last been heard!

The many forms of Rocks can be placed in three categories—igneous, sedimentary, and metamorphic. "Igneous rocks crystallize from molten magma or lava."[6] The children's rage toward their persecutors has superficially cooled and solidified into very dysfunctional behaviors. Their actions display a fixed form—mindless repetition of what was done to them or what they did to survive. They never alter these actions. No matter how abrasive to their fellowman or themselves, how much destruction they cause, or how many healthy or useful alternatives are available, they are compelled to be as they've "always" been. If you probe into their motives or suggest they shift, their core of smelted anger will erupt.

Extrusive igneous rocks form when hot magma flows to the surface. Extrusive psychological Rocks are cast when children's experiences of extreme abuse and neglect are known by the family and/or greater community and are at least partially acknowledged. For example, Daddy may have been well known as a violent drunk. When these traumatized kids become "adults," they are aware of their abusive and neglectful behaviors, although they are likely to not frame them as such. To them, they seem "natural."

In contrast, when the persecution is never acknowledged or validated, these children psychically separate from these parts of themselves. Just as in the geological history of our globe in which once-connected land masses separated and differentiated, the ostracized aspects of their psyches have no contact with the parts with which they identify, and their terrains all greatly vary. Like geological formations below the earth's surface, intrusive igneous Rocks are not visible—they are latent, sinister elements, sealed deep within an individual's mind. "Earthquakes," "digging," or other sudden changes in conditions may momentarily weaken defenses and expose these submerged aspects of a person. Otherwise, these Rocky parts remain as surreptitious in a life as they are in a psyche. Like many unseen forms of energy (e.g., infrared waves), intrusive Rocks must be inferred by their effects: destruction, loss, suffering, estrangement, and death.

Our society is more comfortable with the "jagged," protruding extrusive Rock formations, although only recently have we begun to admit how common they are. In psychiatry residency, I learned about the solitary, school-dropout, young male sociopath who is palpably creepy. I find that many people think these obviously odious characters are the only type of Mineral Stager—a belief that Rocks propagate. In fact, both extrusive and intrusive igneous Rocks are as varied and numerous as people's individuality. Many are well-dressed, seemingly well-mannered, married with children, and financially successful—they even appear charming to the average person...until that person *trips*!

"Sedimentary rocks form in layers..."[7] These psychological Rocks speak of layer upon layer of possibilities or potentials that create a vision of a better tomorrow. These layers are overlaid by a series of facades to persuade us that this Rocky person or leader, company, or protocol is "the way" to achieve this vision. Meanwhile, they undermine non-Rock leadership, companies, and protocols by laying down sheets of evidence or explanations of why they won't work. ("The local firms gave a higher bid than *our* company did—the added expense will cut into educational and social programs.") When the way of the Rock is chosen and disaster ensues, the sedimentary Rock delivers tiers of excuses about why this "unfortunate" event could *not* have been foreseen or averted, strata of "evidence" of how it is not as bad as it seems, and plates of optimism or hope ("We have a great opportunity here to learn how to keep this from happening in the future!"). If confronted about their manipulation, exclusivity, and lack of ownership of their failings, these Rocks deposit impenetrable defenses ("Why would you want to perceive me in a negative light?").

Metamorphic rocks are igneous or sedimentary rocks that have been altered over time by pressure and temperature.[8] Metamorphic psychological Rocks are forever changing their appearance according to circumstance. For example, they may give the impression of concern, friendliness, or sympathy, but their motivation in any endeavor is ultimately malevolent. When ferreted out, they'll offer layers of "reasonable" excuses in an attempt to mask their malice ("I regret having to use such extreme methods, but..."). As with any Mineral Stager, this Rock type's underlying destructive tendencies always come first. Offering excuses is forced on them by the need to explain away this unrestricted, primary impulse.

An Image Shows Only a Facet of the Whole

Each person possesses masculine and feminine qualities, and every culture defines them differently. Within "male" Rock culture, children are exposed to **EXTREME** traits of "masculinity." Rather than receiving the healthy stimulation, encouragement, and personal interest they require to develop, they are devastated by an onslaught of attention of the most painful and perverse forms. Their needs for love, nurturance, and support of their growing humanity are equally throttled. Within "female" Rock culture, children's human needs are ignored, while they are impelled to believe they are receiving the best of care. As these frayed children psychically encapsulate their suffering, they vacillate between perpetrating **EXTREMES** of abuse and neglect beneath a mere gilding of respectability.

The Mascrock is any Rock, whether genetically male or female, with consistent, **EXTREME** "masculine" Rock traits. The Femrock is any Rock, whether genetically female or male, with consistent, **EXTREME** "feminine" Rock traits. While both favor the behaviors of their type, they are truly opposite sides of the same coin. Each is, at times, the tumble-down-the-hill Rock, seemingly in perpetual motion ("male" Rock or Mascrock) and, at other times, the ever-stationary monolith ("female" Rock or Femrock), whether physically, emotionally, mentally, or relationally. They both jettisoned to the unconscious the aspects of their personalities that would balance their **EXTREMES**. Both are also trying to "survive" without any sense of how to do so—in becoming Rocks, they eliminated the parts of themselves that know.

Let's look in more detail at a vulnerable male child growing up with chronic exposure to ruthless Rocks who are oblivious of his human presence and needs. He is continually disappointed and agonizingly harmed. In stark contrast to his own hopeless misery, he registers the Mascrock's one-up, apparently pain-free position, surrounded by adoring Femrocks who serve him and ask little to nothing in return. Over time, he closes his eyes to what has been a pitiful human existence, and he transforms himself into a Rock in order to be included, in control, and reveling in the "good" life. He renounces his scorned self-will, cements his worn psyche to the malevolent mold of his perpetrators, and fuses his "feelings" of self-worth with the way of the Mascrock. Underneath a mask of "manliness," he *forcefully* insists that everyone and everything go "his" way ("*or else!*"). His persecutors' aggression becomes his own and the fuel to keep his angry existence aflame and himself feeling powerful. He ultimately morphs into a carbon copy of his abusers. He becomes a silver-tongued tyrant, a chip off the old block, upholding "himself" above the masses while ever shading his use and abuse of them.

Our American culture's "masculine" traits of leadership, initiative, and physical stamina and strength become grossly twisted in the Mascrock. Instead of responsibly raising up future leaders, he dominates his followers, coercing them into positions of need, subservience, and dependency (one-downers), while providing in excess for himself and his compatriots (one-uppers). He fights only for his right to do what "he" wants exactly as "he" wants—the desires and well-being of others are irrelevant. If you insist on another way, you meet TREMENDOUS resistance—**"YOU CAN'T MAKE ME!"**

The igneous Mascrock is stuck perpetuating the persecution he has known, his violent rage having cooled into these familiar casts. Again, the extrusive form is apparent—his brutality is overt. The intrusive form is subtle. The average person has no awareness of this Rock's shrewd, secret activities that have caused obvious, debilitating effects. Sedimentary Mascrocks aggressively coat each of their detrimental actions under layer upon layer of distracting excuses that fool most people. Meanwhile, Metamorphic Mascrocks assume any mold, posture, or position where they can plaster people with their evil agendas, all the while pretending to be working for the betterment of individuals and society. All "male" Rocks cycle through these various forms, ever using a person's inherent human nature to entice her or him into the unnatural and inhumane.

I decided to take a reading and writing break in a windblown garden of the "downtown" cemetery. I parked my car outside the surrounding stone wall, which had small, sharpened rocks protruding all along the top. Walking into the cemetery, I observed two very old, bent-over men propped on a bench covered with peeling, sun-faded green paint. One clutched his cane, I'm guessing, to minimize his hand tremors. In front of them was a faux-marble statue of a shapely young woman. I relaxed on an empty bench nearby and opened my notebook.

The <u>Femrock</u> forms when a Rock caretaker uses a child's body, heart, and mind for his own wayward enjoyment, to entertain his Rock-mates, or to seduce others into his lethal traps. Only when she unquestioningly does as she's told does he toss to her what meets her most basic biological needs. In an attempt to minimize her groveling, stomach pangs, and heartaches, she becomes utterly faithful to him and him alone. As he becomes the source of what she requires to physically survive, what she **"should"** do or **"shouldn't"** do, and even what she **"should"** feel and think, her identity dissolves. As he arranges severe punishments for any divergence from "his" way, she becomes accustomed to persecution and learns to call it something else ("It's *normal* to be testy at times!"). She "grows" to be self-deflecting, self-neglecting, and self-destructive, conducting all attention, praise, and provision to her dynamic Rock. As his adornment, she tries to *look* good and say whatever makes him *appear* the electric fellow she "knows" him to be. She's "delighted" to adhere to and propagate the static way of her Rock, "loving" him above all else—it's a matter of life and death!

Anything her Rock demands of her, she will do or become. She is a chameleon who readily adapts herself—her body, behaviors, feelings, thoughts, needs, or memories—to ensure his "happiness" (i.e., assuage his volatility). A typical Femrock asserts her strengths only in service to the Rock to whom she gives all credit. She willingly accepts all blame for any erupting problems, and she compulsively cares for her Rock's every whim. She feeds *his* body, cleans *his* house, rears *his* children, warms *his* bed, assists in *his* worldly endeavors, "protects" *him* from those who expose or oppose him, and does everything she can think of to ease *"his"* way—an accomplice to every crime he commits! The Femrock has no personal will, desires, or goals of her own; her whole existence revolves around satisfying her Rock—an impossible task! When she fails, she incriminates herself unmercifully, just as he does. As a one-downer, she receives only crumbs, for which she is expected to be VERY grateful. All Mineral Stagers in her life batter her, at least verbally, if she ever hints at complaint ("What a BITCH!).

Our culture's "feminine" traits of receptivity, intuition, and generosity of feeling degenerate within the Rock. The Femrock has learned to receive solely from her Mascrock, enthusiastically absorbing his "information" without discretion ("Who am I to doubt his integrity?"). Meanwhile, she is unreceptive and unresponsive to more human offerings. Her openness and willingness are reserved only for the Rock for whom she "feels" ever so strongly and passionately, perceiving good intentions in his calculated treachery and caring in his crushing injustices. The Femrock's indoctrination by her Mascrock has ossified within her, which she experiences as "intuition" or "godly counsel." She is oblivious to any authentic intuition, inspiration, or emotions of grief, anguish, and TERROR (not to mention feelings of love and care for her fellowman!).

Extrusive and intrusive igneous Rock forms are more subtle in the Femrock. The extrusive form is, of course, more obvious. Except in relation to her cherished pet-Rock, she rarely keeps her word, honors her commitments, or pitches in for the common good. If you confront her inaction, she scolds *you* for your lack of faith in her—and why should she bend over backward for someone like that? ("Yes, I'm utterly worthless—I'll just swallow some arsenic so you can rest in peace!") With her caustic manner, she is forever exuding toxicity. Because the Femrock is incapable of addressing problems, let alone allowing them to move her, her mind creates a vista that normalizes her incapacity. "There is nothing to do as everything is exactly as it should be!" She doesn't feel inclined to answer calls or e-mails and when she isn't where she's supposed to be, you are always somehow responsible. When begged for help in an urgent situation, she responds with nebulous words, such as, "Don't worry—I *will!*" (She *never* does.)

The intrusive Femrock *appears* fluid, flexible, and agreeable in that she answers pertinent calls and mail promptly and says all the "right things," yet nothing progresses. When the day arrives for her to fulfill her promises, "Something suddenly came up," "Was it *this* Thursday, I thought it was *next* Thursday," or she "forgot all about it." She may also fly into fantasy, relaying a fabricated account of having followed through on every promise. Should you bring these contrary behaviors to her attention, *she* claims hurt by *you*! In every case, the intrusive Rock is verbally willing, while her actions show just how *un*willing she really is! Closer investigation of this intrusive Rock reveals ceremonial activity—a mere going through the motions. (She cheerily greets you with, "Hi, how are you?" and then walks away as you start to answer.) She skims the surface of problems, proffers the postures, gestures, and banter of giving or receiving help when in public view, while undermining any worthwhile outcome. (Haven't we all been on committees with "women" like this?) The intrusive Femrock may report, "When I was advised to get help, I interviewed many therapists and found one exceptional woman who I'm working with diligently. She always encourages me to go 'my' own way!"

The Femrock is devastating to children—she CANNOT respond to their human voice, all the while insisting that she can't do otherwise. Besides, kids are not entitled to much as fellow occupants of the "one-downer" position and competitors for her male's attention—not until they harden themselves into the Rocky image of this Mascrock who directs their care. She facilitates this transmutation by greeting their cries of distress with stony silence. Her "inner male," however, is as abusive in the emotional realm as her mate is in the physical. "He" throws "salt" in the children's wounds, badgering them with endless harassments and interrogations, as with, "Why can't you ever look on the bright side?" "His" cold irritation discourages their emotional expression ("We'll have to start calling you 'Little Mopey'!"), their well-founded complaints ("You're not dodging grenades on your way to school, so stop your griping!"), and their attempts to garner aid ("Seeking help outside the family—What? We're not good enough for you?!"). The Femrock insists they embrace the phantasm that she has come to call "reality"—all is well!

Not all children are willing to surrender their human lives to take on the Rocky identities of their Rock parents and caretakers. As a result, the introjected Mineral Stage parts and experiences in their psyches never coalesce into Rock formations. These aspects of themselves remain merely Minerals. Inanimate and elemental in their psychological nature, Minerals seek to join with those who might enhance their "composition." At best, a crystalline nature emerges as they reflect the humanity of those around them. However, because Minerals lack human qualities themselves, such as genuine perceptions, feelings, and thoughts, as well as psychological self-movement, these people are easily manipulated by Rocks. In their company, Minerals usually remain indistinct, simple, shattered, and/or base.

Image Is Not What It Seems

Again, the "masculine" and "feminine" Rock versions have nothing to do with chromosomes or gender. Although one is usually dominant in any individual, they both subsist in those reared by Rocks, who equally thwart the assertion of genuine masculinity and femininity in all their children. The "feminine" side of the Mascrock, for instance, is typically spineless in "her" subservience to a past Rock caretaker, a boss, or a political leader. "She" may hear no wrong about Mom or Dad, "she" slaves away for an employer, or "she" becomes a martyr for a Minerally made war—*anything* to serve the Rock—just as the Femrock does. The Mascrock is independent of people, yet his "inner female" is highly dependent on objects (electronics, money, medications, illicit drugs, and so forth) or destructive activities ("workaholism," sex addictions, gambling, and so on), which "she" may talk about with great passion. Yet, if anyone tries to help him, "she" retorts, "God created me! If there *were* a problem, it would be His!" "She" champions the most dysfunctional people while passing the buck to those more functional.

The "masculine" side of every Femrock is domineering with respect to others' beliefs and emotions. "He" relentlessly demands that everyone think and feel what would be natural if this woman's fantasies were true. Meanwhile, "his" negative thoughts and feelings are relentlessly channeled toward those "sick" or "ill-tempered" people who "pervert" her version of history. "He" isolates her from them and insists all her companions are purely "gentle" and "kind" (i.e., nonconfrontational and ineffectual) no matter how she treats them. With so many Femrocky relationships, the Femrock is free to ignore problems until they are **EXTREME.** Thus, she facilitates many disasters, yet takes no responsibility: "You can't blame me—I haven't done *anything*!"

The Femrock's "masculine" side is self-abusive, frequently persecuting her body, heart, and mind in a manner similar to how her Mascrock caretaker treated her "growing up." So many illnesses are perpetrated by this introjected Mascrock! "He" plagues her with chronic pain or incapacity, emotional upheavals, vile and vicious thoughts, and destructive decision making, all of which she feels powerless to stop. If someone mentions the availability of effective treatments, however, "he" responds with burning words: "My doctor says my injury (disease, affliction) is incurable!" or, "Feeding false hopes is *hardly* helping!" In devotion to this inner "man," the Femrock is faithful in following the often torturous recommendations of her Rock docs, screening out the counsel of everyone else or sabotaging their recommendations ("Those herbal remedies nearly killed me!").

Neither Mascrock nor Femrock have life to give. Indeed, they suck the life out of others, physically exhausting them, emotionally draining them, and mentally incapacitating them. Oddly enough, these Mineral Stage deficiencies aren't noticed by many people. Instead, the psychologically young implant human characteristics in the cold, hard Rock. While Mascrocks and Femrocks project the forms these "youths" are craving—pictures of health, holiness, success, self-esteem, or sensuality—the "young" fill in the blanks with their own fantasies.

"Get a load of that lovely lady over there!"
I glanced up, surprised to see the first old man grinning and pointing at the marble statue.

"Yeah, I got eyes. I can see her," the second old guy spoke gruffly, taking a hand off his cane to rub his bushy eyebrows.

"Well, she has the 'hots' for me. We're gonna go out tonight and have a wild time." The first man's smile broadened with anticipation.

"No she doesn't, and no you're not!" The second man scowled.

"And why would you say something like that?" The first man was now staring at his friend in irritation.

"Look, Old Man, I've known that woman a long time, so I can say with no doubt that she's just using you to get to *me*!"

Images Can Never Fulfill Our Longing

Rock relationships follow the laws of magnetic attraction. As a result, aggressive Mascrocks and passive Femrocks have strong chemistry, following a sadomasochistic model. The Mascrock angrily abuses and neglects, while the Femrock gets a charge out of the daily trauma, appraising herself by her maintenance of a "positive" attitude ("Everyone knows that difficulties are part of life!" she says with a wink and a smile.). Once married, the Femrock's gaze is on her husband, supporting his every wish, whether to work, play, eat, drink, or spend too much, or to destabilize those in his vicinity. When anyone succumbs to his brutality, she rushes to her *husband's* aid, believing his one-sided interpretation of the event. As he attacks and rejects people, including her and their children, she rebounds to continue the unwarranted approval, cheerleading, and extreme exaggeration of his merits.

Because the Mascrock MUST be on top, he sabotages his spouse's self-assertion, autonomy, and personal fulfillment, forcing her to remain beneath him. As he consistently berates and demoralizes her, she strokes his ego with flattery and encouraging words, as with, "Honey, you *always* make the wisest decisions for our family!" Right before his wife's important interview, meeting, or presentation, the Rock browbeats her with everything he can imagine to be "wrong" with her, pelts her with pent-up anger from the past week (or throughout his lifetime), or perhaps flirts with some attractive young woman that he's "always greatly admired!" When his wife doesn't perform well, he "comforts" her with, "Not everyone is meant to be employed outside the home." As her self-esteem and societal standing become dependent on her husband's "success," she extracts whatever feeds her feelings of well-being and shields him even more fiercely.

The Mascrock commands his spouse with an iron fist, seizing all assets and resources without thought of anyone else. Meanwhile, "the wife" gives and gives and gives, while eagerly awaiting those rare, glorious moments when, basking in her husband's magnanimous presence, he flips a token of approval her way. The extrusive trait of one partner so often mirrors an opposing or complementary intrusive trait in the other. For example, the emotionally extreme, extrusive screamer is often married to the "good-natured" yet physically invasive, intrusive pedophile. The overtly disturbed parent is the contour of a similar but covert dysfunction in the seemingly healthy parent. Intrusive Rocks are the missing links in many family histories, particularly those with psychiatric symptoms, while the extrusive Rocks receive the blame. Just remember, excessive emotion is magnetically drawn to the absence of feeling, and where there is minimal healthy physical touch ("I don't even change my kids' diapers!"), assaultive fondling abounds in private.

The Rocks' pathological marriage of gross inequality, rigid opposition, and utter brutality seems comfortable enough to both partners. The Femrock readily dismisses the concerns of those shocked by what they observe. While she "generously" excuses her husband's greed and "good-naturedly" sympathizes with his "temper tantrums," she suggests they "graciously" submit to his outlandish demands, and "trust" him to do right by his fellowman. She then rationalizes her Mascrock's every failure. "He's just having a bad day, poor dear. I wonder what I can do to make his hard life a bit easier. I know—I'll make his favorite dessert—Mississippi Mud bars!"

The More Polished the Rock, the More Treacherous the Climb

Well-articulated words, expressions of concern, logical reasoning, or demands for justice or mercy do not prevail upon those in the Mineral Stage. What is most likely to move them is their discomfort over an extended period of time. Because EXTREME physical and psychological traumas propelled them on their Rocky course, they require the utmost threats to their *image* to alter it. Loss of money, public humiliation, descent in status, significant hardships, and/or personal experience of the very sadism with which they persecute others, all as a DIRECT RESULT of their Rocky behaviors, are necessary for them to budge. Monumental personal consequences for their sociopathic actions are imperative for the Rock to change! Tragically, the Femrock "gives her all" to impede this evolutionary process. She shields her Rock man from the "elements" (metaphorical wind, rain, snow, and ice) that would alter him over time. In other words, she "protects" him from those who would speak of his shortcomings, "rain on his parade," extend a cold shoulder, or cause him hard times—conditions that might expose him and eventually erode his impenetrable shell. The protocol of the Femrock is igneous ignoring of problems, sedimentary sentiments toward those who acknowledge them, and metamorphic mind games in defense.

IGNEOUS IGNORING: The Rock female is frozen in her ability to receive and respond. She is blind to psychological dynamics and deaf to requests concerning them, much like a crag is to a passing babbling brook. She believes her "lofty" family has been unaffected by the inevitable traumas of this world, and she encourages those "less fortunate" to be equally "unmoved" (her directing them to Mascrocks facilitates this deadening process). She is grounded and content in her delusions until they are challenged. Then the fire that formed this Rock and is contained within the casings of her rigid beliefs and feelings will flare. She retorts, "You're wrong!"…"distorted!"…"misperceiving!"…"not understanding!"…"making a mountain out of a mole hill!"…or, "I simply don't believe you!" If she feels her back against a wall, the "masculine" side of her may surface with startling aggression.

I heard about a young New Orleans man who raped and killed a teenage girl, and just before his execution, his mother embraced him and told him what a "good boy" he was! The Femrock is utterly accepting of the most atrocious circumstances and the most gripping debasements. Her faith in her Mascrock is unshakable, so she sees no need to listen to others or turn to a Higher Source for truth. Her judgments about her man ("He's innocent!") are unalterable until overwhelming evidence is presented to her. Then she progresses to:

SEDIMENTARY SENTIMENTS: The Femrock uses multiple defenses, excuses, tall tales, pipe dreams, and so on as a cover-up for the Mascrock (outside and within her) as well as her lack of willingness to implement change in each dismal situation. Here are a few examples:

- "He didn't mean to hurt anyone!" *Reality check*: What on earth leads you to believe that?
- "*Everyone* in that generation is like that!" *Reality check*: This is simply *not* true; there are psychologically healthy men and women in every generation, if we look for them.
- "That's just the way businessmen are." *Reality check*: Profiting from other's misfortunes is the way of the Rock—*not* men.
- "I trust my husband to find himself in his own way and time." *Reality check*: Rocks are *not* trustworthy. Again, those who can find their own way are not in the Rock stage; Rocks only move when someone or something shoves them.
- "I asked him if he wanted help, and he said, 'No!' so I've done my duty." *Reality check*: Rocks use "antagonal" language—communication that is antagonistic to the truth. The antagonal "No!" actually means "Yes!" "I absolutely don't want that!" may be interpreted as "I want it desperately!"
- "If people would just leave my husband alone and not try to change him, he wouldn't react so strongly." *Reality check*: Another antagonal statement—a Rock's barbarism is not the result of people in the present *trying* to change him; his violent rage is a reaction to past Rocks who *succeeded* in changing him to such an extent that he's never recovered.
- "What you're implying about my husband is *so* extreme—it *can't* be valid!"

All these plies of protest the Femrock offers are a cover for the "I will NOT meet your needs!" motto that she experienced growing up. As she refuses to help the Mascrock regain his humanity or aid those who would curtail his abuses, the "male" within her, expelled to the depth of her unconscious, remains petrified.

METAMORPHIC MIND GAMES:
- Rock **"love"**: "I unconditionally love and accept my husband as he is, and this includes *his* own unique way of showing love and care. Asking him to change is tampering with *his will*, and that's not nice!" *Reality check*: He's bending everyone in his surroundings to "his" will! Are you really loving when you watch someone you profess to care about rusting away in the Mineral Stage?
- Rock **"support"**: "My husband does an admirable job providing for his family." *Reality check*: What the Rock provides is an image. Although he may appear to materially support those who are submissive to "him," he also dumps much dross. He is antagonistic to emotional, mental, or spiritual sustenance.
- Rock **"priorities"**: "What's important is making our interactions as pleasant as possible. I don't want to rock the boat!" *Reality check*: A boat naturally shifts with the waves and flow of water, just as humans do with changes in environmental and life conditions. A Rock's stagnancy is *never* an excuse for your own.

- Rock **"thoughtfulness"**:
  1. "So you think I should help my Rock spouse/sibling/parent/child? I don't have the time to be after him twenty-four hours a day!" ***Reality check***: No one said anything about twenty-four hours.
  2. "So does having a few minor problems mean I should kill him like a dog and put him out of his misery?" ***Reality check***: No one mentioned violence—we're talking about help here. (The Femrock pairs help with violence because this has been her personal experience.)
  3. "He's only human! You shouldn't be so hard on him!" ***Reality check***: If he were *only* human, he would *not* be so dehumanizing of others. These are _inhuman_ traits.
- Rock **"rescue"**: "Anyone who counsels my husband must be able to see what an exemplary individual he is!" Reality check: Someone so psychologically blind could not budge a Rock.
- Rock **"compassion"**: "The psychotherapy must be hurting him because he says it doesn't feel good afterward. I ache when I see my sweetie suffer!" Reality check: Before, everyone else in his life was in pain because of his deplorable treatment of them! Now he is just beginning to feel the pain he's been dumping like concrete, so he has a glimmer of self-awareness—this is a step forward.
- Rock **"sharing"**: The Femrock relates stories to move others to express her feelings for her. For example, if she's angry at a man for commenting on her Stone Age family, she'll "share" a tale from her own history throughout the community, placing this "adversary" into one of her tormentor's roles, a role she herself has subsequently continued. As her vicious rumors spread, she warms herself in the fiery fallout.

While the Rock female gives the impression of sensitivity toward the Rocks in her life, she's actually excusing her unwillingness to acknowledge problems and help. In every Femrock's past are Rocks for whom she carries blazing fury; and she unconsciously and vindictively heaps this hatred on those in her present life. She gets revenge on such malignant "males" by doing everything in her power to keep them small, undeveloped, self-deluded, and handicapped for life. Her unconscious malevolence is cloaked with affection as she says, "I love all that you are—don't ever let anyone change you!" As she "edifies" each Rock, she keeps him psychologically languishing and dependent on her to maintain the illusion of his innocence, importance, success, and/or supremacy. Beneath her congenial facade lies a radioactive core that sickens her victims and causes widespread decay. Regardless of how great her *appearance* of devotion toward the Mascrock, its foundation is scathing rancor: **"YOU CAN'T MAKE ME HELP YOU GROW!"**

A Polished Image Is Still Devoid of Life

The first old man tottered over to an engraved tombstone and then ever so slowly lowered himself to the ground so that his back was supported by it. "Now, Bertha," he said patting the lawn. "I know you probably heard that conversation about me and that young lady over there, and you're not happy about it. But I'm telling you, girl, make nothing of it. Just havin' some fun, that's all. You've always been the only one for me!"

Physical illness and psychological problems are traits of the living, not the dead, which is why the psychologically lifeless Mineral Stager may *seem* to be free of them. He may, however, be drawn to those suffering from these afflictions. He may talk at length about his close relationships with the dying or dead; a rolling Rock can *appear* quite kinetic as he holds the hand of someone comatose or visits graves. Perhaps he carries a torch and a snapshot of his dear departed spouse and tells stories of what a great marriage they once had. (One wonders *how* she died!)

Whether male or female, Rocks cannot love a living human being; too many skeletons in their closets scare them away (if the other isn't scared away first!). At best, they can perform certain rituals of companionship. At worst, intimacy is a battleground where they combat their partners at every opportunity, swift in extinguishing any flickers of emotional intimacy and often avoiding physical closeness as well (at least with their spouses). If you attempt to flesh out their skeleton by reaching toward their true identity, you will touch a deep wound whose pain echoes through the caverns of their being. You become a major threat that they must conquer expediently.

Rewards and punishments are prominent in Rock relationships—Mascrocks may reward another's compliance merely by momentary pausing from their punishments. (Remarkably, when you walk away to avoid their abuse of you, they feel *you* are punishing *them*!) Rocks have learned that someone always gets hurt, so the only question is—who? Mascrocks believe, "I must hurt you lest I be hurt." On the other hand, Femrocks assert, "I must hurt myself, or you'll hurt me even more." (One false move, and she'll hold you accountable for her self-inflicted injuries!) If you attempt to interfere with either entrenchment, you pay with projectiles of persecution or shunning that's so severe you wonder if you still exist!

To Focus on Image Is to Quash the Developing Human Being Beyond It

In a healthy family, the man protects his wife and children with his life, as does the woman selflessly safeguard her family. In a Mineral household, however, the wife and children ferociously defend the positive image of the Mascrock, all the while being brutally victimized by the negative reality, often without their awareness. All family members are trained to build up this mere *impression* of a "man," regardless of how much they are dragged down by him. Thus, role reversals are in every Mineral Stage home—the children fulfill so many of the responsibilities that are normally parental duties, while the overindulged Mascrock busily carouses with his friends. Rock parents consistently use their children for their own "needs," desires, or sense of security, holding them to adult standards while demanding appreciation for their own, at best infantile behaviors ("Why can't you be grateful!").

If these Rocks could give their children a life different from what they had, their devastated inner "children" might come out of hiding for help. *But,* the Femrock is quick in her adverse response to any rescuers: "I'm an adult—I don't need parenting!" or, "It's not *my* job to parent my husband—I'm not his mother!" On the domestic front, the Mascrock is most likely to stonewall. Both Rocks angrily foil or chase away those who are willing and capable of parenting them and their children, offended that they are "making" them look like bad parents. However, blocking all attempts to move the Rocks and Minerals

in the family condemns the children, if they receive no better guidance, to a Rocky future. Without "moisture" (exposure to fluidity), these kids' relationships will be asunder and at a standstill—stalactites and stalagmites—mirroring their parents' relationship and their own broken and frozen male/female psychology.

Because of their long history of extreme conditions and the extreme opposing fragments within their own psyches, Rocks perceive extremes that are not there. For example, they see control and manipulation where there is merely expression of need and/or want. To stop the "revolt," which exists only in their minds, Rocks are compelled to strike while the iron is hot—the Mascrock physically and the Femrock verbally. They perpetually crush children who are just doing what children do. Because they interpret a child's motives as trying to undermine their authority or to exert his or her will over theirs, they trounce each "mutinous defiance," deadening the child with each blow. The "etching" upon the emerging "gravestone," the Rock, gives testimony to how the child psychologically died. Spouses receive similar treatment.

As I drove to the grocery store, I noticed a large bus in my rearview mirror. I vividly remembered a sixtyish woman with long gray hair and a large-brimmed hat that I had met in a New Orleans bus terminal years ago. She had narrated a tragic story:

"A woman named Penny was telling her husband she was pregnant with their third child. Penny said, 'I don't understand how I got pregnant—I was taking the pill every day! I know that after Jason and Marie, we weren't going to have any more kids, but...' She sighed, concerned about how he was going to respond. Her husband hugged her and said, 'Well, I guess it's meant to be.' She was relieved at that moment, but in hindsight, realized he was putting on a front. To him, this was a power play, which he needed to stop before it got out of hand. He asked around, Penny found out later, and spiked her drink when she wasn't looking. She became violently ill and was hospitalized. She lost the baby! And her own life was nearly lost, too." The woman twisted a garnet pinkie ring as she spoke.

"After this, Penny was visibly angry at her husband, without knowing why. Their friends and family felt sorry for *him*, thinking he was coping with the loss of their baby, her 'illness,' and then her anger on top of it. They comforted *him,* instead of her. Several family members recommended that Penny find a 'good shrink' before she ruined their marriage. Taking their advice, she started seeing a popular psychiatrist, who gave a diagnosis of major depression and paranoid delusions because Penny was convinced people were trying to harm her. He prescribed medicines and then shock treatments since she wasn't getting better and wasn't taking in enough fluids. He also told her that she was confused in directing her anger about *her* sickness toward her 'innocent' husband. That was the first of many therapists over the years who eventually led Penny to put the pieces of the puzzle together. Only after solving the mystery and grieving what actually happened to her did her health return."

The woman ended her story, inhaled abruptly, patted my knee, and then whisked herself away. Before she exited the terminal, I noticed a name embroidered in gold on her large, black, woven handbag—it was "Penny."

Women often see the Mascrock as a "diamond in the rough." Perhaps he appears the ruffian outside, but they sense he has an inner beauty, like a geode. An immature woman often falls for a polished Rock, who seems smooth, lustrous, and enchanting. To her, he shines like a ruby or has colorful sparkles like an opal. Riveted by such a specter, she approaches, only to be cut deeply when she comes too close or set in stone herself. If she succumbs to the many facets of his professed brilliance, he overburdens her and her family, distracting them from some nearing precipice.

Life with a Mineral Stager is always on the rocks—consistent instability, turmoil, and danger. The Rock has "grown" to thrive on the extremes of "temperature" and "pressure" that created "him" and that he will not stop re-creating for that burst of "new life." He masterminds minefields where his victim's smallest step toward self-preservation might be her last. As a result, she may become frozen in hesitancy or unwilling to lift a finger to help herself, both of which he is quick to condemn ("What's wrong with *you*?!").

A typical relationship scenario is a Mascrock "forgetting" he has a spouse. He neglects to share his experiences and important decisions. He may not even notice her physical presence—he bumps into her or steps on her toes. He interrupts her midsentence, oblivious that she's talking. He doesn't relay messages, so his wife loses her social connections by not responding to those trying to reach her. However, he informs her contacts how forgetful *she* is, and he is the one they believe because he goes out of his way to get on their good side. His wife, on the other hand, appears preoccupied, stressed, unhappy, and needy (needing to vent her anxiety, for example). The Rock may also take his spouse's possessions and watch her hunt for them. Then he returns them to an obvious place, enjoying her perplexity over why she didn't spot them in her search. He informs everyone of his concern about her mental condition, since she "loses things a lot" or "doesn't see what's right in front of her." He similarly fashions his wife's perceptions, often arguing her into the ground that what her eyes saw, her ears heard, and her body experienced were *not* accurate. He establishes himself as the sole source of truth.

A Mascrock may slip an emetic, diarrheic, or sedative into his wife's breakfast if he's agreed to do something with her that he doesn't want to do. She'll be in the bathroom all morning or go back to bed, apologizing to him that she just can't make it today, and he'll be free to pursue "his" plans. When his wife finally visits the doctor for her recurring GI upsets, chronic fatigue, or mental/emotional instability, concerned friends and relatives are not surprised—the Rock has molded their expectations. As for the rest of the family, don't be surprised when the son develops an addiction for prescription drugs and the daughter is diagnosed with anorexia nervosa because she is afraid to eat. (Note the reenactment and avoidance patterns of PTSD.) Of course, the Mascrock is given much sympathy for having so many insoluble family problems! Remember, for the Rock to leave a positive impression, he must arrange for others to imprint negatively. Just as fires erupted after the hurricane and levee breaches, when there is a Rock in the family, one disaster follows another. Anyone with chronic exposure to treacherous Rocks may lose her marbles. Recovery takes years…decades…or a lifetime. Without professional help, most people never recover.

At the grocery store, I spoke to a young woman with long, straight hair and thick dark-rimmed glasses. She had just evacuated from New Orleans after spending the recent aftermath of Katrina on the Crescent City Connection Bridge. She unloaded: "I'll *never* get over this—it was terrible! Criminals pretended to rescue people but then robbed them in their boats, leaving them stranded, wounded, or dead! Other people brought 'problem' family members to the bridge…you know, handicapped children or old folks…and then threw them over. One woman actually recited a funeral blessing as she did this! It was shocking—I'll never forget it! I'm guessing they thought it was the perfect time to relieve themselves of a family 'burden.' People would assume they died in the flood! This disaster has brought out the absolute *worst* in people, and I can't get these horrible images out of my mind!"

To Look in the Mirror Is to See a Human Reflection on a Mineral Base

Just as rocks exist beneath the events of nature and nurture occurring on the earth's crust, Mineral Stagers disguise their doings under the *appearance* of natural calamities, benevolent undertakings, unfortunate errors, tragic accidents, sudden illnesses, or acts of God. People often don't suspect their deliberate and devious deeds. Remember, the psychological "infants" inside us only notice the face of any given situation. The myriad of surface forms deceive them, and they miss the underlying distinguishing feature of all Rock enterprise: decomposition—the rotting of life, love, growth, business, property, potential, and so forth.

Whatever the Rocky surface, underneath is an active volcano that will blow—the Rock's buried rage must erupt periodically; it's just a matter of time. When a Mineral Stager is coiled in the mesh, even the most vital, creative, or productive non-Rock enterprise will peter out or end abruptly and calamitously. The Rock's responses to complaints are then deflective rather than receptive ("Look in a mirror. If you're frowning—change *yourself*!"). He excuses himself from the rubble and rolls on to the next terrain, where the results will be the same.

Sooner or Later, Choosing Image Results in <u>DISASTER</u>

My mind drifted to my beleaguered city, which has the reputation worldwide for historic charm, delicious food, outstanding music, exciting festivals, frivolity, and fun. These attractions have drawn many tourists to New Orleans. Perhaps the "laissez les bon temps rouler" front is why so many New Orleanians have apathetically accepted her exactly as she is (Femrock trait), finding no need to remedy her flip side—abject poverty in many areas (outside and within its residents), horrific crime (extending from inner-city housing projects to public offices), and alcohol and drug abuse. For generations, she's been harmed by all forms of Rocks. Before the Levee Disaster, her appalling public educational system was recognized and decried for decades, yet renovations weren't given priority. Now that so many schools have flooded, there's no other choice. New Orleans has been grievously neglected and ill-used—"the City that care forgot."

Igneous ignoring of New Orleans's problems has been the norm among leadership and citizenry alike. For instance, some of Lake Pontchartrain's flood-protection system was known to be inadequate. The contractor for the Seventeenth Street Canal floodwall went before a Corps' Board of Contract Appeals judge in 1998 because of "major construction problems." This company asserted that "the soil and the foundation for the walls were 'not of sufficient strength, rigidity, and stability' to build on, and informed the Army Corps of Engineers of these findings."[9] (Remember, Rocks follow "their" design regardless of results.)[10] I've noticed that when someone raises these uncomfortable issues, people often choose not to listen or respond. This exemplifies the frozen feeling of the Femrock ("I'm not going to let you drag me down!").

Sedimentary sentiments: I've overheard in Effie's news programs' reporters interviewing people from around the globe about New Orleans. Some interviewees have indirectly defended those involved in constructing inadequate levees by quickly shifting the focus to the victims: "If people aren't happy living in New Orleans, they should move! Some people just have an ax to grind!" Others offer weak explanations or excuses: "If New Orleans wasn't below sea level, it wouldn't have flooded!" **Reality check**: There are many places around the world below sea level that have modern, effective levees protecting them. Lying below sea level was a contributing factor to our disaster, not the cause. Also, 51 percent of New Orleans is at or above sea level.[11]

How about this tall tale? "The levee builders couldn't get funding to do what they wanted. They had NO CHOICE but to put off essential repairs!"[12] **Reality check**: If the priority is safety, there is always a way to get needed funds. For example, if heads of households were making the decisions, we would have opted for properly constructed levees and security for our families and homes. We could have requested donations from around the globe, written grants, and had fundraisers—jazz concerts and the like—all of which are currently going on in response to what was a preventable disaster! The belief in "no choice" is the mind-set of the Rock! Also, the pipe dream of believing we can trust all authorities and corporate executives to do what is right by the people without our ACTIVE oversight and participation is itself Rock-like.

Metamorphic mind games: Some news stories morphed suggestions for the most useful course of action for our disaster into something seemingly harmful or a waste of time. Here's an example: "To investigate what happened to our city would hold us in the past, keeping us from the grand future that is ours for the taking!" **Reality check**: Actually, not investigating what happened keeps us in the past, because the truth remains unknown, problems stay unresolved, and those responsible are liable to repeat their antisocial acts again…and again…

Continuing with Femrock reasoning, what is useless or detrimental is made to appear beneficial. I heard this on the news: "We need to move on. Holding the Corps of Engineers accountable for their actions won't restore the lives lost, repair property, give jobs, or bring people home!" **Reality check**: What if our criminal justice system was founded on such nonsense? "Investigating homicides is a focus on the past, and besides, it won't revive the dead!" This thinking is lunacy and EXTREMELY dangerous to our civilization!

Another reporter said, "So the engineers made a few mistakes; we all make mistakes sometimes!" **Reality check**: Professionals don't make elementary "mistakes," nor would they ignore the resulting problems and warnings months and years before the disaster.[13]

These statements may sound like reasonable, positive priorities, but they are veiled protections of criminal activities, the hallmark of the Femrock. When these Rocks aggregate, they persuade large numbers of people to do nothing while the meteor strike of their "male" conglomerates causes wide-scale demolition, far greater than any individual Rock could do on his own. When we listen deeply, we become aware of the HUGE impact that Rocks and Minerals have on our communities and the very foundations on which we live.

The Story Within the Image

The study of Rocks is incomplete without mentioning the Rocky fragments within each of us: recollecting fictional accounts of our lives and selves, defending these images, and tagging those who would unearth the truth as "the problem." The stony parts of ourselves are sculpted images, Rocky bluffs that divert our attention from the low-lying shifting sands of our fragmented consciousness. When we, with our "infant" vision, perceive some people as treasure chests full of precious stones and others as crates of gravel, we miss the fact that *every* individual is full of rich topsoil, some heavy metals, and a gem or two, *as well as* many life-forms. When we merely survey the surface, accepting or rejecting the whole lot based on appearances, much of our human nature remains buried and unexplored.

Excavation reveals that every person is a unique amalgam that includes every stage of psychological development (yes, Rocks and Minerals too!). As long as we avoid our inner "geology," the study of these most primitive parts of ourselves, these pottery shards of our psyche must display their psychology, exhuming what we've chosen to forget. As every part of us is sharing its story within the means available for its stage, our conscious remembrance and integration of these parts becomes a matter of survival and well-being. To protect those in our care, we must be willing to look beyond the treasured tales passed down by our ancestors and perform an archeological dig to obtain our natural history and its seismic impact. Delving meticulously into the "dirt" to discover Rocks, Minerals, shards, and artifacts from the past, we can slowly begin to piece together a vessel capable of holding something of infinitely greater value. We must "leave no stone unturned" if we are to uncover our faults and discover the gold nuggets of our humanity.

In between mouthfuls of stewed chicken, Effie imparted the evening report. "The Army Corps of Engineers is lowering sandbags and sheet pilings by helicopter onto the Seventeenth Street Canal breach, but it's too little too late! The military is *finally* dropping food and water into New Orleans. People in the hovering helicopters above the Ninth Ward, however, used loudspeakers to direct the residents to 'walk' to the Superdome. They were told to 'walk' when, for most of them, the water was up to their necks—not to mention that it's polluted with oil and other toxins, city sewerage, dead bodies, and even some alligators! Some people are becoming ill from exposure to these putrid floodwaters!"

After unloading her news on my listening ears, Effie went to bed, and I was left to process the appalling scene in the Ninth Ward with my notebook, pen, flashlight, and Our Rescuer, who is able to handle and shape all Mineral Stagers such that they show their best light.

Mineral Rights

Studying the extremes of nature, including hurricanes, tornados, volcanic eruptions, and earthquakes, falls into the realm of modern science—supported with research dollars, because such knowledge is essential for saving lives and minimizing devastation. Similarly, the sciences of geology, metallurgy, chemistry, and physics are recognized as important for optimizing the usage of our physical environment and avoiding adversity. However, much of psychology is unexplored; its benefits for mankind and drawbacks when ill-used are still largely unrecognized.

Perhaps only when our keen interest in the external environment extends to our internal world (starting in the Child Stage of Development) will we begin to truly understand human nature and prioritize its nurturance. Another choice is to wait until our external world has been depleted of resources, poisoned by noxious chemicals, and made hostile to the lives of all creatures dependent on it for survival before confronting the most primeval forces within us. Rocks are expediting this worst-case scenario: Mascrocks won't stop their destruction, and Femrocks won't start renewable, life-enhancing alternatives.

Despite all their horrific reenactments of their childhood experiences, Rocks deserve to be removed from their underground (unconscious) existence and returned to their humanity. However, we must take care to protect ourselves in the process. Just as rock collectors need certain safety equipment, such as a hard hat, sturdy gloves, and safety goggles, those working with Rocks need psychological strength, healthy defenses, the ability to see beyond appearances, and GREAT caution(!). Those in the Mineral Stage vacillate between ineffable violence and unfathomable neglect (both cloaked in some "reasonable" explanation). If you choose to aid their development (their behavior is SCREAMING for it), keep every aspect of your humanity on alert and get qualified assistance. You cannot move Rocks from a stance of denial, ignorance, or outdated therapeutic techniques. A Rock is as close to pure ego as a person gets. If you're trying to aid Rocks through ego, they will likely crush you—by seeking to help, your ego is obviously not as big as theirs. You must access Our Rescuer (see chapter

4) in yourself and those you trust for EVERY step (*and* make sure you are listening to Our Rescuer and not a Mineral Stager feigning her voice!). A side benefit of tumbling with Rocks in a therapeutic manner, however, is that your corresponding Rock and Mineral parts become smooth...or even transform into gemstones!

HELPFUL INTERVENTIONS for Treating Those in the Mineral Stage

If you're waiting for your Rock to hit "rock bottom" before you render aid, please realize that, despite any lofty appearances, "it's" already "happened." Psychologically speaking, the Rock has nowhere to go but up. There are not enough competent therapists in our world to move these Rocks where they need to go, and besides, Rocks resist therapy as if "their" lives were at stake (they are!). If we are to survive as a species and evolve our world, every single one of us must participate, which includes shifting the Rocks in each of our lives.

(1) Encourage the Rock in nonthreatening arenas to divert ever so slightly from "her" or "his" way. For example, if she eats plain oatmeal with milk for breakfast every morning, toss in some nuts or raisins or offer some granola. Suggest another route for his drive to work or an activity other than watching the game on TV every weekend. Each time Rocks budge with no dire consequences and maybe even some pleasant results, they have the *experience* of trying other ways (there *is* choice!) and surviving!

(2) For lasting change, Rocks *must* experience painful consequences for their detrimental acts. They must also hear *valid* feedback so they can begin to become conscious of their rigid, lifeless words and actions. ("Your emotional life seems dead as a doornail!" or "Where is your compassion for all those suffering New Orleanians?") Many people intuitively sense the danger of the Mascrock and give him a wide berth or cajole him with sweetness, flirtation, or generosity (their inner Femrock comes out to bond). Know that he interprets silence as assent and ego strokes as positive feedback on his deplorable behavior. Do *not* placate a Rock with allowances, tenderness, support, loving words, gifts, and so on. These niceties may make you feel like a good person, but they reinforce his or her unrelenting stance. Although Rocks may convey thanks for your "kindness" and extol your virtuous nature, when you turn around, they will "stab you in the back" and prove you to be otherwise.

A stone is easier to budge than a boulder, so refrain from building up a Rock's ego. A Rock collector cannot extract rock specimens with kid gloves, but needs a hammer and chisel. Likewise, Rocks respond only to firm, deliberate hammering away at their seemingly impenetrable defenses— day after day, month after month, and year after year after year.

(3) If your direct confrontation of a Rock makes him stonewall or become aggressive, try to create a crack by speaking indirectly, referring to the problems you're having with "someone" you know. Then ask the Rock's opinion. His comments may reveal apt information about his own inner state.

(4) The Rock in your life will try to manipulate you into feeling her anger and underlying terror and grief, so guard against this. She *needs* to experience *her* emotions. Work to wear away the Rock's denial of her less than "happy" emotions by inquiring about what she feels when she behaves badly. When she snaps, "I'm fine," share your experience: "I see an angry individual who treats me poorly to make me feel her pain for her. Why not feel your own pain?" or, "You said something that made me feel angry at Chris. I think *you* are feeling angry at Chris." The Rock will likely attack or ignore you, but

don't give up. You are supporting the true feelings that are buried within her, which are bound to go against the grain.

(5) Even though the Femrocks in your life *insist* there is *nothing* wrong with the Rock you are helping, you *know* better. Step aside from the rockslide of dissension that comes your way when attempting to aid a Rock. Femrocks are quick to cry out, "It's common 'knowledge' that nobody can change another person, and only *fools* try!" Consider how you might also assist these unfortunate dissenters. Rather than be dissuaded by the persistent harsh criticism and obtuseness of Femrocks, get extra support from a professional. Choose someone who is skilled and practiced in using "stone tools"—interacting with those in the Mineral Stage in an instrumental, pertinent-to-the-moment manner.

Emily called to say she had arrived safely at her parents' retirement community in Orlando. "I was tired early, since I haven't been sleeping well, so I decided to spend the night in Pensacola. The man at the reception desk of the motel told me, 'You can stay here if you want, but the whole town evacuated, including our staff. I stuck around to ask Katrina to spare my property. It worked last year when I talked to Ivan, but this year…well…dames are different.' He sighed heavily at that point, and then continued, 'We don't have a parking lot anymore. It dropped into the ocean during the storm. But you're welcome to lodge with us if you don't mind parking in front on the street…'"

(6) People can waste a tremendous amount of time and energy, and even risk their lives, attempting to "get through" to a Rock, only to discover that he did not comprehend the message and remains unaltered. The Intrusive Rock may "understand you completely," but the following day will have no recollection of your conversation or will relay a refractive version or <u>antagonal memory</u> ("I remember you telling me that you were wrong and I was right!"). Be patient! For every speck of Rocky rigidity you wear away in one moment, he lays down more sedimentary deposits in the next, so progress can be tediously slow. To maximize efficiency, ask Our Rescuer to direct you to the specific Rocks who need your form of assistance and how you might best assist them.

(7) Again, Rocks' self-declared "my way" is *not* their way. They are acting out the <u>antagonal vengeance</u> taught by their Rock caretakers. Try to bring this to a Rock's attention. "Does retaliating against your perpetrators by tormenting those who remind you of your woundedness really help you?" Astonishingly, he's apt to reply that "it" *is* helping! (Remember—Rocks have "help" and "hurt" confused.) He also thinks he's rightfully protecting himself when he fiercely defends his Rock identity. Seek out who he is underneath his Rocky armor and bring these human qualities to his attention. In your mind and heart, you must consistently uphold the truth of the Rock's once malleable psychological being, or it will quickly plummet, much like when a person releases a stone from the hand—it falls immediately.

(8) Challenging the Mineral Stager's deeply ingrained cognitive distortions ("I haven't done anything wrong!") can be arduous. Just as the earth scientist looks for the fracture in a rock and splits it there, look for the irregularities in a Rock's thinking and point these out. Know that implying that she *may* be doing something wrong or could somehow do it better angers her ("How dare you judge me—you're not God!"). As long as no one is getting seriously hurt, sometimes the most productive way of dealing with the Rock momentarily is to walk away and then try again at another time, as led by Our Rescuer.

(9) When you suggest that Mineral Stagers seek help, their response is predictable: **"YOU CAN'T MAKE ME!"** TAKE THEM (one at a time!) to a professional in sociopathology, passive-aggressiveness, post-traumatic stress disorder, and/or substance-use disorders. (Like addicts, Rocks are in denial about the severity of their condition and need "tough love."). Because they are so proficient in giving false impressions, sabotaging aid, and then "innocently" declaring, "I tried other ways, but they don't work," your average therapist will not be able to see past, let alone *get* past, their facades. You can also try a less direct approach to bringing a therapist into their lives. (For example, you could suggest that a new "acquaintance" wants to meet this Rock over lunch.)

To regain their humanity, Rocks must have people guide them into their agonizing childhood, help them control their antisocial impulses, and rediscover *their own* thoughts, feelings, behavior, and will. If a Rock refuses all therapeutic contacts, keep the appointments for yourself. You need to delve into why this person is in your life—perhaps it would be better if he or she weren't!

(10) Survival of the fittest is a law of nature; only the most adaptive creatures survive. The immutability of Mascrocks is not favored by natural selection. They are bound to have a hard time in the absence of Femrocks who constantly champion their image, shield them, and serve them. Both Rocks' inability to adapt, grow, and move with a changing environment and the creatures therein is a real handicap. However, with tremendous effort exerted by those who care enough to impinge upon their inertia and push them down an opportune vein, Rocks may begin to inch out of their habitual behaviors (they don't "*have to*" punish those who diverge from their Rocky plans). They may become aware of a fragment of feeling (anger) and even display a particle of inspiration (an original idea!), which are the origins of psychological life.

When Rocks refuse to take a serious look at themselves, Mother Nature still has Her Way. Glaciers, rivers, rainwater, fires, hurricanes, floods, and a multitude of organisms over an extended period of time do expose and wear down the rocks in our world. Similarly, interactions with other inhuman psychological forces (those stuck in the Mineral Stage of Psychological Development) may impact and eventually break down or shatter Rocks and Minerals. Of course, there is always the choice of Our Rescuer, the greater Body, who orders the movements and weather conditions that can speed up this protracted evolutionary process, otherwise known as the psychological journey.

Images Cannot Know Themselves

Jayda called. "I finally heard from Austin—thank God he's OK! Our home is another story. It's in deep water—no surprise there! Austin finally evacuated—he's at his mom's house in Natchez. His mom actually drove *to* New Orleans the day before the storm. I guess she thought she'd take care of him while I was gone. Can you believe that? Willa said, 'A woman should stand by the man she loves!' So she weathered the hurricane with her boy rather than being safe in her own home, *and* she lost her car and almost her life. My mother-in-law is as nuts as her son!

"Anyway, around noon on Monday, she was in the garage where she discovered water running under the door. She yelled, 'Get the wet vac, Aussie. There's water in here!' Just as Austin arrived with the vacuum cleaner, the door gave way, and water flooded in. Austin and his mom wound up outside floating around the rooftop. They managed to swim over, grab hold of the gutter, and hang on throughout the storm's high winds and rain. They stayed on the second story afterward. Willa thanked the Good Lord that her son had the 'wisdom' to stash munchies and sodas under the TV in our bedroom, so they were OK for food. The next day, Austin flagged down a neighbor with a boat who took them to dry land, where they got a ride out of town.

"The good news is that Austin has changed his tune about remaining in New Orleans during severe storms. Let's see—in a matter of hours, he experienced a hurricane, a flood, watching his home ruined and losing all his possessions, a flooded city with thousands dead, and nearly losing his mother's life, as well as his own. It sure took a lot to get him to shift one of his stubborn, mulish habits!"

Listening Step Five: LISTEN TO THE VILLAINS

Just as there are fossils of plants or animals in certain rocks that offer clues to their origins, all Rocks show the imprinting of their Mineral Stage caretakers that fueled their rage. When we look at the severity of circumstances that have finally dislodged Rocks from the bedrock of their disastrous background, we get a glimpse of just how catastrophic were the traumas that forged them into Rocks in the first place. Rocky childhood caretakers thrust them into the Stone Age, forcing them to develop psychologically protective scales of armor to survive. As children, they were naturally needy and vulnerable, but their caretakers were adamant: **"YOU CAN'T MAKE ME CARE FOR YOU!"**

Although a Rock makes children commit all sorts of horrible and shameful acts against their will, children cannot alter a Rock in the slightest. With consistent exposures, they are left feeling alone, desperate, hopeless, and powerless. ("No matter what I do, my needs aren't met. I give up!") To survive, the children psychologically "die" and become the inanimate Rock or Mineral that needs and cares for no one. Their victims' intense and overwhelming sentiments are what they felt before their emotions were pressured into sediments. The Mineral Stager is the end result of that human voice crying out for help and landing on deaf ears—the call is still present...but it's no longer human.

A Rock's Dispatch

"If you read your experience of me like petroglyphs, you will understand my origins. You will know the heat and pressure that long ago formed me into what I am today. My manipulation of you to see me in a good light and to trust me was how I was manipulated when I was young. When I was not totally obedient, I suffered humiliations, rejections, and failures of the worst kind, so I've made sure you have suffered and failed in your endeavors. The rage and persecution coming from me are exactly what I experienced. Your anger and terror are just like my own. You've been powerless to stop me, just like I was powerless to stop my own perpetrators. Your difficulty in finding help or even people willing to listen to you or take you seriously is exactly what happened to me. If anybody had seen my situation, heard me, and helped me when I was a child, I would not have become this way. But there was no one...

"So when you feel I've pushed you past your threshold for tolerance, know that I too was pushed past mine. If you're considering homicide, suicide, or disappearing into insanity, know that I saw these same three options and pursued each one. Of course, it isn't safe to express these things out loud—people don't understand. So I'm forced to play the role expected of me in the light of day and release the graphic reality of my existence after the sun goes down.

"In your devastation of what I have done to you, how I have destroyed your health, your property, your job, your family, your churches, and your community or city, you have finally heard my story. Now multiply your grief by that of all the others just like you whose lives I have ruined, and you will know the extent of my misery. But you never think about me, do you? No, as long as you are comfortable, you don't look into what I might be going through. So I had to come up with a way for you to comprehend how a human being becomes a quarry that was stripped and abandoned long ago…

"Now that you know my state, will you attempt to help me…

"Will you merely help yourselves by rebuilding all that I've destroyed…

"OR, will you wait to see if I do it again?"

DOUBLE-ESPRESSO BREAK: Take a moment to commune with Our Rescuer before continuing.

1. Which Mascrock traits have Cedric and Austin portrayed in this chapter?

2. Which Femrock characteristics have Connie and Jayda's mother-in-law, Willa, displayed?

3. Who are some of the Rocks in your life, and how are they graveling you? (Would you tolerate a pebble in your shoe for as long as you've been tolerating them?) Can you read any petroglyphs of their psychology in your interactions with these people?

4. How is a Rock like a hurricane?

5. In which areas are you like a Rock? (Please pray or meditate on this question.)
   a. In your interactions with the **physical** world:
      • Do you have any rigid behaviors? (You never assist your spouse with routine chores, or you always eat dinner at six p.m.)
      • Do you have any compulsions that you are unable to stop yourself from doing? Or if you do, are you then *very* uncomfortable?
   b. In the **emotional** world, are you more enlivening or deadening?
      • Do you express your emotions in a way that validates and supports others' human feelings?
      • Are your emotional responses predictable? (You always respond to unexpected ordeals with tears, angry outbursts, or no feeling at all.)
      • Do you resist emotional exchange and growth? (You don't listen deeply to the emotional expressions of your spouse and kids. You are not cooperative in helping neighbors and colleagues with emotional problems.)
   c. Regarding your **mind**:
      • Are any of your beliefs set in stone?
      • Are you more involved in FREEING the minds of others, opening them to new ways of perceiving and thinking, or INDOCTRINATING them, hammering them with your biased opinions?

6. How are you like an **igneous Rock**?
   a. Do people tell you that despite your initial willingness to work on a project, you then become deadweight?
   b. Are there any serious problems in your life or the life of someone close to you that you are ignoring?
   c. Are you passively accepting a certain situation that really needs your wholehearted rescue?

7. How are you like a **sedimentary Rock**?
   a. Do you give others true choice (devoid of ego interference)?
   b. What sort of excuses do you make for your abusive or neglectful behaviors? ("She likes it when I beat up on her!" or "I am too busy right now to join a recovery group.")
   c. What rationalizations do you use for your ingrained habits? (You assume that because you are like the men or women you know in your culture, you must be "normal." Are you willing to grow beyond the confines of your culture?)

8. Are you at times a **metamorphic Rock** that uses multiple toxic tactics to defend against or cap the truth of your life's disasters? What mind games do you use to cover up your toxic "leaks" onto your environment? Do you experience those who see beyond your facade as violently invasive, as if they are "drilling" beneath your surface?

9. Translate the antagonal language of the Femrock's sedimentary sentiments on page 94. Ask Our Rescuer how any of these might apply to you.

10. Pick out a rock or stone that resonates with an aspect of you stuck in the Mineral Stage. If it fits in your pocket, keep it there. Otherwise, put it in a prominent and symbolic place (perhaps holding closed a door to a cluttered closet that contains junk from long ago) to remind you to work on this aspect of yourself *and* what it is blocking.

11. To whom or what are you saying, "YOU CAN'T MAKE ME!"?

---

[1] "By August 31, 2005, 80% of New Orleans was flooded, with some parts under 15 feet (4.6 m) of water." "Effect of Hurricane Katrina in New Orleans," *Wikipedia*, modified April 16, 2013, http://en.wikipedia.org/wiki/Effects_of_Hurricane_Katrina_in_New_Orleans.

[2] Jala ad-Din Rumi, *The Masnavi, Book 3, STORY XVII, The Vakil of the Prince of Bokhara.*

[3] Chris Pellant, *Rocks and Minerals: A Smithsonian Handbook* (New York: Dorling Kindersley, Inc., 2002), 16.

[4] "Superdome is Seething Scene of Last Resort," *The New York Times*, September 2, 2005, http://www.nytimes.com/2005/09/01/world/americas/01iht-scene.html?_r=1&.

[5] "…city officials during The Great Mississippi Flood of 1927…set off 30 tons of dynamite on the levee at Caernarvon, Louisiana which eased pressure on levees at New Orleans but flooded St. Bernard Parish, the Ninth Ward taking the brunt of the city's flooding during Hurricane Betsy," Conspiracy theories, "2005 Levee Failures in Greater

New Orleans," *Wikipedia,* modified March 12, 2013,
http://www.ask.com/wiki/2005_levee_failures_in_Greater_New_Orleans.

[6] Pellant, 32.

[7] Ibid., 38.

[8] Ibid., 34.

[9] Lisa Myers and the NBC Investigative Unit, "News Orleans Levee Reported Weak in the 1990s" *NBC News Investigates on NBC NEWS.com,* updated September 30, 2005,
http://www.msnbc.msn.com/id/9532037/ns/nbcnightlynews-nbc_news_investigates/t/new-orleans-levee-reported-weak-s/.

[10] "2005 Levee Failures in Greater New Orleans," *Wikipedia,*
http://www.ask.com/wiki/2005_levee_failures_in_Greater_New_Orleans.

[11] Background, "Effects of Hurricane Katrina in New Orleans," *Wikipedia,* modified April 16, 2013,
http://en.wikipedia.org/wiki/Effects_of_Hurricane_Katrina_in_New_Orleans.

[12] "NOD (New Orleans District) managers stated that 'funding levels were insufficient to complete construction at existing holes in the system that were crucial to flood protection…hence levees were below grade in quite a few areas' (IPET 2006b, II-22). The question we ask is 'Why was the public not informed?'" Team Louisiana, "Chapter Five: "Was the Level of Protection Incorporated in Designs Adequate?", *The Failure of the New Orleans Levee System during Hurricane Katrina,* accessed April 11, 2013,
http://www.dotd.louisiana.gov/administration/teamlouisiana/Team%20Louisiana%20-%20Part%20II,%20chap%205.pdf, 130.

[13] "…miscalculation was so obvious and fundamental," investigators said, they, "could not fathom how the design team of engineers from the Corps, local firm Eustis Engineering, and the national firm Modjeski and Masters could have missed what is being termed the costliest engineering mistake in American history," Flood wall Design, "2005 Levee Failures in Greater New Orleans," *Wikipedia,* modified March 12, 2013,
http://www.ask.com/wiki/2005_levee_failures_in_Greater_New_Orleans.

Chapter 6

Computer Technology

Systems Science: "Remembering" How Images Control Human Beings

(Note to the reader: Consider reading this chapter slowly, a few bytes at a time, so you may systematically process the complex yet vital information it contains.)

I was feeling the need for modern conveniences and online connection, so Effie suggested I drive to the Red Cross shelter to see if I could use their computer since hers was not operational. After calling FEMA a few times (busy signals!), I drove through the sunshine to the other side of tiny Greensburg. Once in the shelter, I engaged a friendly volunteer who informed me that a long list of evacuees was signed up to use their solitary laptop for locating lost relatives and friends, submitting FEMA applications and insurance correspondence, searching for jobs, doing e-mail, and so on. She recommended that I proceed to the vocational-technical school just a few blocks away, so I did.

I strolled through the apparently empty school building with one of Effie's books in hand, *Computers for Dummies*. I stuck my head into room after room filled with desks and desktop computers. Sensing no signs of life, I was about to leave when a lone teacher appeared and offered me the computer of my choice, which she kindly taught me how to use before busying herself at the front desk.

As I stared at all the computers around me, I thought about how the year 2005 had also been noteworthy in my decision to confront my technophobia head-on by joining the New Orleans Personal Computer Club. At one particular "new user's" meeting, standing out among the very casually dressed men, a beautifully attired woman had posed the question, "Why won't the Microsoft Publisher program let me copy the background picture of my file when it lets me copy everything else?"

The soft-spoken, gray-haired expert, wearing a faded "love me—love my laptop" T-shirt, answered with an anthropomorphic twist: "You need to find out where Publisher put the background picture, and then you'll be able to copy it. 'He' must have stored it somewhere; it's just a matter of finding out exactly where."

Because I understand little of the conversation at these meetings, my mind tends to wander. I began pondering how computers are modeled somewhat after the way we humans store and process information. *To recognize and appropriately respond to everything in our world and then later to recall, build on, or even change these details, many parts of the brain must be connected and working together. Our personal input is also crucial. We can consciously choose what to retain, relate to, and pass on, and what to reject and forget. This selection process creates a foreground and background to our memory. However, we are also making UNCONSCIOUS choices. For example, our most horrific encounters with Mineral Stagers have "programmed" us to exclude that reality from the foreground, our conscious remembrance. That information is instead stored in the background, as are the parts of ourselves that know about it. In the versions of our lives that we "send" to others, we use the words, behaviors, and aspects of ourselves that support the foreground, often automatically pressing the "backspace key" to delete what doesn't align with such imagery. For instance, right before Emily left, after the Levee Disaster, she said, "This is the only disaster I can remember," yet her long-held feelings resonated with those of the multitraumatized children Oliver and Felicity. To finally face long-forgotten truths, these truths must first be sensed. As happened with Emily, a disaster in our present lives can stir and bring to the surface similar contents in the recycle bin of our unconscious mind. Our task is then to identify the source of these feelings and understand what this recycling process is showing us about ourselves.*

Forgotten aspects of our lives are forever presenting themselves in everyday experiences, but we don't recognize them as recollections of our *pasts or* our *selves. Using the classroom setting of my computer club as an example: we may relate more to the elderly expert who ran the meeting, the elegantly dressed lady asking questions (I could relate to the asking questions part!), or the ill-clad guys who seemed to focus a lot more on their computers than their clothes. Until we relate to them all, however, what we don't identify as "self" must* show up in *"bits" and pieces throughout our lives.*

A photograph of a middle-aged woman on the desktop of my computer brought me back to my surroundings. After briefly noting our similarities—curly brown, shoulder-length hair, and a slight build—I quickly opened a blank document. The teacher then exited the classroom.

Evacuation Day Six: EVERYTHING CHANGES WHEN WE CHOOSE IMAGE

How could we possibly anticipate that by selecting only parts of our identity, experience, and memory, we would so reduce our sense of wholeness? This daily decision we make is a reenactment of our choice of an individual identity, one that is separate from our Origin within Self. Since we are *not* separate, whatever we choose must affect the Whole, at least within our experience. *Because* of our choice of individuality, Self then *appears* to differentiate into individual Aspects—an <u>unlimited Mind</u>, a <u>greater Body</u>, an <u>ever-loving Heart</u>, ad infinitum.

Let's look in detail at the effect this decision for individuality has on Mind alone, the Aspect I most identify with. Our brilliant, boundless, creative, and all-attentive Mind stiffens and fragments, deadening to the extent of becoming like a PC containing programmable parts, computer circuitry, and external components, all connected by way of a motherboard (a solidified version of our <u>Source</u>). All components represent aspects of chosen self and true Self. Our individual consciousness, identifying with the whole, then operates in a restricted manner much like a personal computer—taking in information (input), processing it, and then passing it along (output). Each "PC" has its own parts, programs, and functions, which are similar to that of every other PC.

One Mind (OM) Becomes a Central Processing Unit (CPU). When we choose what to select ("This is me!") and what to reject ("That is NOT me!"), we claim personal volition, and the tiny fragment of mind we retain to do this on/off choosing becomes like a central processing unit. This "CPU" <u>microprocesses </u>who we are. The memory trace of the OM and the appealing concept of an individual self are then respectively translated into <u>binary language</u> (1 = subject, infinite, connected, unlimited, abundant, unalterable, etc.; 0 = object, infinitesimal, separate, limited, scarce, changeable, etc.). Using the language of these two domains (1=Self and 0=self), this encoded mental chip (our "CPU") communicates instructions with other parts of our <u>"computers,"</u> which themselves contain components of these two domains. As an expression of Self, this processor is fast and powerful, but functioning becomes greatly reduced and tediously slow the more the second domain—self—dominates.

RAM!: Present Awareness of OM Is Replaced by Memory of Separation. Our "computer" temporarily stores knowledge of the OM (1) and bytes about individuality (0), filing both within whatever concepts we are individually processing. The "computer" system's calculations and conduct vary greatly, depending on how much of each type of "memory" we are using.

Graphics and Sound Cards Produce Our Existence: From Duality to Multiplicity. Within a mechanized mind, our will appears like an operating system, controlling the transmission of either Self or self. When we give priority to the individual self, corresponding information is conducted through video and audio cards that translate our choice into visual and audio clips—we see different colors and forms, and we hear different sounds. These cards create a YouTube film of individual existence that we "screen" with our minds. Imagery "demands" our attention (but only because we demanded imagery first!).

The Optical Disk Drives Us: Our Attention Frames Our "Movies." The OM is ever with us, but our "computer" system reduces our experience of "It" to something like itself, something small, separate, and hard yet symbolic of Its Original Nature—a round spinning disk that carries vast amounts of information. Our system reads this "data" and incorporates it into film footage as well. But, by selecting the parts we want and don't want and modifying the disk accordingly, we produce a pirated simulation. Now we have two options—One Master live-streaming "Movie" (#1) and a cheap copy (movie #2). The second is a "spin" on the first, but revolves around the concept of individuality. Our mind becomes like a webcam, projecting video footage adjusted to our focus—either Self or self.

Our Power Supplies the Powerless

Our One Mind is the only real power source and thus the power supply for our world. When we employ the power point of our chosen fragment of this Mind (me = minimind employment) to view imagery, we must extend the qualities of self or Self. A full range of forms, from inanimate objects to spirited human beings, then appears on our "screens." We focus on the most evolved forms with whom we most identify. We perceive ourselves as individuals and become fascinated, so much so that we decide to inhabit the images fully to experience what this individual life is all about. Image becomes our identity!

Having so contained ourselves, however, the expanse, reality, vitality, and power of our dynamic, all-encompassing Life seems harnessed by images (like holograms—the whole is in each part). Thus all imagery has a surface appearance or "image," which, when investigated, carries unbounded communication. Smell, taste, touch, and emotion cards are then added to our "computers," which heighten our sensory experience, making this "world" *seem* SO REAL and teaming with LIFE! Causes appear within the world as it and its creatures produce significant and irrevocable effects—all to be studied and understood. We allow the vicissitudes of these stimuli, the intrigue of their exploration, and the new, exciting, limitless variety ("I want this!") to distract us from the familiar presence of our OM ("I don't want that!"). However, when we dispossess Self, we "sever" ourselves from access to true expanse, reality, vitality, and power. So our new identity must experience something else, such as limitation, fantasy, weakness, and disability, which we feel powerless to stop! These are new and disturbing concepts to us!

Identity Theft: Who We Are Is Applied to What We Can Never Be

Our One Mind takes the form of an enormous globe, representing completion, in our new three-dimensional reality. Since we've projected our life into only one image, our body, this world seems an inanimate planet that is yet supportive of many life-forms. This enormous rock contains extensive resources that supply what we need. We are now dependent on what is outside of us, however, and we are prey to outside forces.

To remedy our increasingly uncomfortable predicament, we cling to the lost qualities of our OM, as if they were inherent to our new identity as a "screen" image. The qualities of the image that we disown and ignore are then automatically text-wrapped around the minimized, but still extensive, "pictures" of our OM that remain on our "screen." As a result of this exchange, a corrupting "worm" enters our "computer" and begins replicating itself. These worms extract some of the information that's producing each video (Self or self-expression) and exchange it with the other one, resulting in the corruption of both sets of "files." Corruptions now manifest in all the images on the "screen"—dysfunctions, insecurities, and errors. Meanwhile, our abandoned OM appears unknowable, unnecessary, unresponsive, ineffectual, mere energy, or even nonexistent ("Show me where it is—I don't *see* it!").

The **HARD** Drive: Fear Runs Our World

The replicating worms in our system fill up our "hard drive," giving us the experience of countless finite, disconnected life-forms that replace our One Identity. These lives are competitive or combative in their striving amid limitations and scarcity. Even the most biologically advanced forms are rejecting at times and hostile at other times, forever struggling to fulfill their needs to avoid suffering. Comparing the memory spinning of our old Life with the continuum of creatures on our world causes a new feeling—fear—which permeates our system.

Knowing our Origin within the OM or staking out our individuality creates the experiential contexts by which we interface with everything on the "screen." We approach, perceive, engage, analyze, and understand everything within the context of wholeness *or* separate parts: processing character, procuring property, negotiating connection, constructing circumstances, and sharing information. Because individuality brings fragmentation, lack, identity change, and solidification, each character now faces isolation, need, unwanted alterations, and endless obstacles, some of which seem impossible to overcome. With so much to do to surmount these problems, "life" becomes difficult. Whether we inherit or acquire our handicaps and hindrances, we are "programmed" by nature and nurture, our worldly versions of the duality of our systems. Both nature and nurture express the scenario of something small (our genes) or inconsequential (the actions of images) dominating our "lives."

Our limited mind-set extends throughout our individual body as we receive discrete input through our senses (auditory and visual information within a certain range, for example), which is then filtered through our experience and training. Thus, perceptions are confined to seeing, hearing, feeling, tasting, and smelling through the internal programming of nature and the external programming of nurture, rather than being open to the infinitely educational world inside and outside of our individual images and all that lies beyond imagery. With such programmed controls, imagery locks into solid forms that are subject to certain "fixed" patterns and "immutable" laws, as in settings of date, time, region, and climate. Life has become temporal, spatial, and serial. These premises take on the unchangeable nature of the OM, which seems increasingly far away, disinterested, and foreign (only because *we* are!).

The hard drive of our "computer" stores this static construct of our world that has become the new source by which we "live." Our senses determine what we perceive and remember, and this information is added to our storage. With this new-found "knowledge," the live-stream movie of perfectly carefree, harmonious, expansive Life emanating from the OM fades from memory as we adjust to the film of individual existence—toiling to survive, to relate effectively to a wide range of creatures, to grow in many different areas, and so on.

Our vibrant, expansive, and all-engaging Life beyond the "screen," whose information we've either relegated to permanent storage or transferred in encapsulated form to our new "lives," cannot actually be contained. This Life still holds a magnetic attraction for us, yet we tend to associate these twitters of Self-memory as coming from reminiscent (or metaphoric) aspects of our world instead— *beautiful* people (a *soul* mate!), *riveting* music, technological *genius*, and so on. We strive to be, create, or achieve that which reminds us of our old Life. *Human* nature follows this course, too: children appear taller, wider, and older as they physically mature, and people are more educated, competent, and compassionate as they psychologically mature. We grow from our experiences, care for and teach our offspring, and increasingly engage, affect, and are responsive to the life around us. Our "second edition" has enough similarities to our Original Life that if we include the ever-present "hyperlinks," we might forever stay in our computer simulation, were it not for…

The ROCK VIRUS (RV)

Our focus on this rock that is our world and our adherence to the programs of nature and nurture is like connecting our "computer" to an infected remote unit through which a virulent virus enters our system. This Rock Virus is a program that produces appalling and graphic manifestations of the contents of our minds—the idea of being separate from Self (in pieces, wounded, and in pain) is projected with repugnant imagery on our mind's "screen." Our all-inclusive and all-protective Self is now experienced as a *vast* mob of small, exclusive, unknown, individually serving "others" with violent tendencies and desperate, unmet needs.

Think about it! What if the dead, inanimate, and powerless in our world suddenly had life, volition, and power and were in the majority, while you were comparatively microscopic, weak, and on your own. Alarming, huh? The identity reversal in the RV video is experienced as PROFOUND and TERRIFYING, and this overpowering fear disseminates throughout our system. A diverse collection of TERRORIZING films are made from this RV template and projected periodically onto our "screen," demonstrating this ghastly "reality" with secondary fragmentation of psyches, acute anxiety, debilitating addictions, psychotic depression, paralyzing guilt, murderous rage, and other symptoms of PTSD. Each character has a gaping, underlying wound and is quick to lash out if anyone approaches it. Safety is fleeting in this RV movie, as people are forever telling their painful tales through atrocious acting out—a new way of communicating. In reaction to these traumas, the dynamic functions of our psychology freeze.

If we take these provocative videos literally, the smallest or most primitive of life-forms do seem to affect, harm, and even kill those who are many times larger and more evolved. Violence and horror are prevalent *and* spreading. As we are but a speck on a much, much larger screen, there is seemingly no hope! In shock at what has become of our once-perfect Reality, the conscious part of our mind "clicks" on the sleep mode and fades into the background. Another part "lives" out the preferred independent existence, unaware that there is another part and another choice. This individual-self-aware part doesn't realize that everything in our experience is but a movie, a rendition of one of the following three options, *and* we can choose which to observe and participate in:

Movie #1: This original, live-streaming footage is about our shared Life in the OM—joyful, loving, openly expressing, ever-expanding, and utterly fulfilling Consciousness.

movie #2: This simple simulation of the first Movie is experienced through the "window" of an individual life that mimics the Original. The lead character is moved by a dual nature: there is much pleasure, camaraderie, love, satisfaction, and so on, but there is also the opposite—displeasure, dissension, dislike, and dissatisfaction, as we now have choice, and we often don't choose wisely.

movie #3: This Rock Virus film is an unnatural or perverse simulation of the first Movie, manifesting extreme opposition to it. The data of this movie is "ripped" and "burned" into our images. For example, "connection" may be communicated by molestation or rape! Someone who wants to eliminate the "dark" aspects of his or her psyche may exclude those of darker skin colors. In this movie, we encounter the desolate effects of our choice to separate from the OM, effects which further fragment our psyches. We experience agonizing loss, loneliness, damage, discord, incapacity, and anticipation of degeneration and death. The lead characters are scary and/or tragic (Rocks and Minerals) as they are *driven* by the programming of this infected "computer" system.

The "natural world" and all the creatures that populate it are unique combinations of these movies, showing an infinite variety of "data" from each. In Movie #1, the OM brings ecstatic, supernatural, and magnanimous moments to each of our lives. In the worldly imitation, movie #2, we grow and strive to achieve mutually harmonious functioning and interdependency. In contrast, the RV movie #3 is RUINOUS! Also, definitions change in these films. For instance, in Movie #1, we remember the One Mind. In movie #2, memory enables productive work on our "computers" and on our "computer screens." In movie #3, memory incapacitates us with painful imagery and overwhelming, intense emotions. We tend to block it as a result.

Most computer operators have experienced their computer freezing: regardless of their actions, screen images and data remain still and unresponsive. The Rock Virus similarly immobilizes individual minds. Our thinking freezes into *read-only* files, which we wade through without correcting. Our feelings polarize, expressing themselves in extremes of large or small "fonts"—emotional and physical excesses or insensitivities. Behavior becomes fixed in mindlessly conditioned actions and "plug and play" reactions, ranging from the purposefully purposeless (helicopter pilots waving to flood-stranded residents of New Orleans's Ninth Ward) to the devastatingly destructive (poorly constructed levees that failed to protect hundreds of thousands of people). *Human* functioning comes to a near standstill. All of these incapacities generate multiple storms and disasters that befall us in our lives, manifesting the recurring theme of our powerlessness! As we shrink and harden in our shame of what we have become—the antithesis of our Original Nature—we are easy to operate, much like a computer mouse.

The ROCK VIRUS PROGRAMS

In every "computer" it infects, the Rock Virus replicates many programs (MALware) that relentlessly eliminate or alter the files of our OM, reducing the vital communications of Life beyond "computer" circuitry to comic animation that supports the overall Virus Program (the agenda of "the Program" is to keep the Virus "alive" and in the power position!). As we allow such imagery to block our awareness of the OM, these programs automatically disrupt our lives on the "screen." We also back up the greater Program of the Rock Virus and its Mineral Stage users.

We all know that computers sometimes impose controls that are contrary to what we are doing. They may share false or inadequate information. They can fail to perform an operation, such as sending or receiving e-mail. While all functioning seems normal, the computer may state there is an error, *or* during a malfunction, it may provide no warning or helpful advice. PCs may cause us stress and elicit strong emotional reactions when they suddenly rearrange or otherwise alter a document for no apparent reason or delete important material against our wishes. We learn to frequently save our work, right?

Our "computer" system under the influence of RV MALware offers an extreme form of these difficulties. It tightly controls our experiences within rigid frames. Its operating system consistently distorts, blocks, or eliminates our data, perceptions, and abilities, causing undue stress. It also inserts programming that mimics human functioning—actions, feelings, thoughts, and "inspirations" that are anything *but* human. Yet, these programs all have their origins in our choice of individuality over the OM, and a loss of aliveness ("animacy"), functioning, and power is the result. We would do well to thoroughly study these RV programs, as they are operating independently from our known self and its intentions—working in the background of all of our individual lives by plugging into the most traumatized parts (Rocks and Minerals) of our psyche. Please remember—whenever we use these programs, we are being used!

A. THE CONTROL PROGRAMS

Control programs make us fearfully control ourselves and others (people, places, and things) in the same way that the RV programs control us. They include:

(1) Control Option Program (the COP). Notice that the Labeling Lock Program (see pp. 125-6) has been used to name this program. When we abandon our united Identity by choosing image, we relinquish our Self and thereby our self-control. Despite appearances to the contrary, control is no longer an option. When we *attempt* to control our or others' lives, the Rock Virus actively polices our system through this program.

Users of this MALware have a heavy hand on the "control key." They welcome only certain types of people and activities—regimented or regimenting, for example. They esteem only particular emotional states (always cheerful) and belief systems ("my" religion, which may be *no* religion). They offer people brief windows of opportunity ("I'll give you twenty minutes two weeks from Thursday.") under inflexible circumstances (furthering "their" agenda) of which these users are in total control. For instance, a user might say, "I searched for your missing flash drive, but I couldn't find it," when in fact she looked where it was convenient, rather than where you lost it!

This program maintains that the best way to be in control of all problems is to cause them. For example, if the user has a certain belief system based on past experiences, as with "women are critical and rejecting," this program makes the user treat women abominably to bring out these "latent," but "inevitable," characteristics. If another user believes that "men are abusive," she will seek out dominating, aggressive males and assume they are merely expressing their "manhood" when they harm her.

The Control Option Program only allows assistance from Rocks and their "approved" task schedules (operating within the parameters set by the Rock Virus). This MALWare also casts anyone who comments on these control tactics as judgmental and disparaging, so users feel outrage or hurt, as well as a need for greater control over human beings, including the one hiding within themselves. This program asserts that the only reasonable course of action for managing the mayhem caused by Rocks is to exert over any population, tighter and TIGHTER and **TIGHTER CONTROL!**

IT Help Desk: Curtailing the COP—Don't allow the Rock in your life to control you. Set the limits as Our Rescuer dictates, and abide by them. Stay alert, since a Rock will feel compelled to attack you for interfering with "his" Program.

Lucien is a New Orleanian who was supportive of his wife's self-improvement program until she suggested he make some improvements himself. "That's where I drew the line," he informed me. "Only a control freak tries to change another person, so I divorced her!" Without a tear or a second thought, Lucien moved on to Emma, a top-of-the-line PC. In "her" he found a more compatible companion, and he happily shared the majority of his free time and energy with "her" or related projects. "She" had him reading *Dummies* books, joining computer clubs, conversing in chat rooms, traversing the town to get parts and programs, and staying up half the night waiting in line to get the best deals when a computer store opened for a sale. There were also many expensive trips to the Computer Emergency Room to address her frequent bouts of uncontrollable behavior. For "her," he had been willing to change quite a bit. I heard through the grapevine that Emma "died" in the flood and Lucien is busy searching for a suitable replacement.

(2) The Choice Commander. Users of this program recognize only RV protocol options, but offers them to others in a way that gives the appearance of choice. For example, I was asked in a telephone survey, "Would you prefer federal funds be used toward: (1) reconstructing vital New Orleans buildings, (2) improving the local economy, or (3) bringing tourism back?" There was no mention of what New Orleans needs to survive—modernizing its antiquated levees and restoring the protective Gulf wetlands and barrier islands. Anyone who "refuses" to pick from users' select lists are bullied by them for being obstructive or *not* exercising their right to choose. If someone insists on more choices, users may comply by adding the bizarre, the perverse, or a "drop-down list" of extensive options that would require a tremendous amount of time to evaluate each one. Shocked or overwhelmed, the average person withdraws into the simplicity of the original RV "choices."

A popular accompanying feature "enlivens" users with "feelings" of independence and pride in directing their "own" destiny when they choose the Rock Virus Program. A psychological smokescreen also keeps their past traumatic conditioning and present post-traumatic stress disorder from their awareness. This Viralware also contains many "freewill" subroutines that consistently remind users that the RV schematics are "YOUR choice" and bequeath feelings of annoyance if anyone suggests otherwise. Users also experience anger when the cursor of any networking "computer" is not selecting "their" choice. Needless to say, the choice of our OM, as manifested by Our Rescuer, is considered foreign and unwanted, or not considered at all.

IT Help Desk: Treatment for the Choice Commander—Reject the programmed "choices" the user offers you. ("I don't want to play that computer game!") Talk to him about the many safe and effective solutions that exist to any worldly problem, and allow him to see you making these choices with no dire consequences.

I thought about my Cousin Joan, who chooses not to talk to me about a certain topic. Recently I inquired, "If you don't want to talk about it, why do you bring it up so often?"

She replied, "I have *no* interest in discussing this subject, so the next time I bring it up, remind me that **I DON'T WANT TO TALK ABOUT IT!**"

(3) Circumvention Program. This program is used to step around problems or their workable solutions. (An easy way to identify this unspoken issue is by observing which topic is never mentioned, pursued, or permitted for discussion.) Users can be ingenious in their avoidance gymnastics:

(a) *Diversion:* "That reminds me of something I saw in my favorite sitcom." (By directing attention to a fictional funny TV serial, the user diverts attention away from your *facts* and very *real* concerns.)

(b) *Tangents:* Starting with a reference to the topic but then going off in another direction. "I understand you're upset about computerized voting being unreliable, but clearly the best thing we can do is urge our fellow citizens to vote—woman and minorities in particular. I remember one civil rights march..."

(c) *Digression:* Hurrying the conversation to a topic that the user insists is related. "Just be patient and listen, I'll get back to it...wait...you'll see."

(d) *Fooling "facts":* Forever leading a discussion back to "the facts," which aren't facts at all, but programming. Polls and statistics become greatly skewed when people are assumed to be honest and self-aware but are really users of the Circumvention Program.

(e) *Urgency:* "If I don't interrupt you right now to tell you what I'm thinking, I'll forget it and you'll miss out." *Or* suddenly the user *has to* use the bathroom, make a phone call, or send an e-mail, but then never returns to the thread of conversation.

Users thus avoid information foreign to their programming. They will stop a nonprogrammed conversationalist midsentence by turning on music, whistling, or even walking out of the room. Questioning is either not permitted or is limited to what the Rock Virus programs can "reasonably" answer. If a question does not fit "their" criteria, users respond as though it does. They may ask questions themselves, not to gather pertinent information but to divert attention and mislead. They also make provocative statements merely to distract from the issues at hand. With such consequences, the average person learns to NEVER pursue the forbidden topics.

IT Help Desk: Circumventing Circumvention—Bringing the user back to the forbidden topic and asking her questions will threaten her (and in turn, she may threaten you!), so do so gently. Try to get her to see her diversionary tactics. For example, when she is diverting her rage onto innocent people, attempt to discern the culprit who is *deserving* of her wrath and deflect her attention to this person.

(4) Filterware. Incoming information (input) is rigorously filtered through programmed assumptions, such as "I am a healthy adult," "I have a normal family," or "People are well-intentioned." Filters can also be negative, as with "I'm a failure!" or "It's a dog-eat-dog world!" The user cannot receive data that contradicts these basic assumptions. If his male society espouses that straight boys are *never* molested, the man user has no recollection of his childhood sexual abuse. If

her female friends condemn victimizers, the woman user doesn't retain any memory of her callousness or cruelty. In all cases, users share only the data (output) that aligns with their assumptions.

Knowledge such as "I am still growing" and "every individual has a lot to learn" is filtered out along with all evidence of these truths. Meanwhile, feelings of relaxation and comfort are filtered in with each use of this application. If perceptions that challenge users' assumptions ever permeate the filter, they have feelings of physical illness; emotional turmoil; or racing, disturbing thoughts.

IT Help Desk: Filtering Filterware—Help this user examine and filter his assumptions. "You're assuming that the actions which led to the destruction of New Orleans were well-intentioned. Let's look carefully at the facts." In this manner, you may assist him in removing the filters from his awareness, so he can perceive outside himself as well as within.

(5) Partial Program. Just as we can program computers to share only certain files, this RV program restricts users to a small portion of what is available—the "good" bits or that which supports Rock Virus programming. For instance, if you say, "There are times when we help others best by doing nothing, times when we help more through active involvement, and times for all stances in between," the Femrock user hears, "We help others best by doing nothing." She then posts "*your* philosophy" on Facebook. The user retains only one piece of any input, advice, treatment plan, or instruction and then blames others when results are less than satisfactory.

Typically, the Partial Program user executes only a part of the work he was hired for. When you bring this to his attention, he focuses on the part that he did do and is offended by your unwillingness to pay his whole bill. His self-image rests, like his attention, on the more mature, functional, or "normal" part of his being, but if distracted from his admirable qualities, he only sees parts of you that are deeply flawed.

Parent users accept only the masculine sides of their sons and the feminine aspects of their daughters, psychologically hacking each child in two. They actively engage and encourage Mascrock performances in boys and Femrock traits in girls, ignoring or discouraging "defects" that do not fit with their partiality. Children then "grow" to be users who own only a small part of themselves and who receive and express in a partial, mechanized manner. Hearing only parts of every conversation, seeing only parts of every person, and experiencing only parts of every circumstance, these users don't navigate life well, yet the program deletes this PART from memory, so they never know.

IT Help Desk: Partial Program Reprogramming—Do your best to learn the *whole* story—you'll need multiple sources. Then fill in the user's missing parts. For example, Jayda mentioned on the phone that when her mother-in-law raved about Austin saving her life during the flood, Jayda added that he was also the one who put her life at risk by refusing to evacuate.

A couple once brought their three-year-old identical twin boys, Elroy and Leroy, to Charity Hospital's pediatric clinic. During the examinations, the mother criticized Leroy severely. Her Mascrock attitude conveyed that he was defective in every way and unworthy of any care or consideration. Elroy, however, was an "absolute angel" who apparently could do no wrong. I noted that Leroy reacted to his mother's ruthless insults with gasping cries and to Elroy's praise by punching his twin, kicking the examining table, or slapping himself. Elroy was smiling, similar in appearance to his father, who stood by in silence (classic Femrock), seemingly oblivious of his wife's hostility. Any of Elroy's childish behaviors went unnoticed or were assumed to be Leroy's, since, according to Mom, "only he would do such a thing!" After the examinations, both boys received a clean bill of health. They responded age-appropriately to the overt abuse and neglect from their unhealthy parents, who were themselves victims of the Partial Program.

(6) The Closed-loop Program. This program consists of a series of dead-end beliefs or actions that straightjacket the user. For example:

User A: a. Life is suffering

b. I am suffering.

c. I am just living life like everybody else.

Another Closed-loop Program may be triggered in a user friend:

User B: a. To involve oneself in another's psychological problems is to be his or her therapist.

b. It is inappropriate to practice therapy without a license.

c. Outside of a licensed counseling session, it is never appropriate to help someone with his or her psychological problems.

User B then encourages User A to see a professional counselor, triggering another Closed-loop Program in User A:

a. If I see a psychotherapist, I will have a mental-health record.

b. Having a mental-health record will interfere with my life, as in securing jobs or being elected to public office. People will assume I'm crazy.

c. If I can't get the job, position, or respect I want, I will suffer, so professional help increases suffering...I won't go!

a. Life is suffering... (The original loop begins again.)

The Closed-loop Program always returns users to start, like the Levee Disaster forcing so many families to start life anew.

IT Help Desk: Breaking through the Closed Loop—Help the user out of each step by challenging "her" logic and reinforcing her experiences to the contrary. "If life is suffering, then is everyone you know, young and old, suffering at all times?" Point out the exceptions to her "hard" and fast rules. "Look at those children joyfully laughing as they play—they seem to be functioning through another 'operating system'!"

"CONTROLLING" THE CONTROLLER: People who use the Rock Virus programs need to be shown what they are doing and taught another way of interacting with their fellowman and themselves. When they understand they're ruled by a computer program, they may be willing to admit they're out of control and compensating by attempting to control you. When you practice the techniques above and below to minimize this control, don't be surprised when these users and their Femrock supporters retort, "*You* are sooo controlling!"

COFFEE BREAK:

1. Who are you controlling like an icon on your monitor screen (conversationally, behaviorally, dogmatically, etc.)? Is this fair to her or him?

2. Are you making your own choices, or are you following a program designed by others? (You may need to spend time talking to those close to you to honestly answer this question.)

3. Are there any topics you are unwilling to discuss? Why?

4. Print out some of your assumptions, and cut them into small pieces of paper. Then place each one on the object below that best represents the extent that this assumption filters your daily input and output:
    a. spaghetti strainer—you retain very little of what does not align with this assumption.
    b. A paper coffee filter—you hold mainly what's "solid" (what fits your criteria for "hard facts").
    c. A coffee mug—you have good retention, whether information aligns with your assumptions or not.
    d. If there is another analogy that suits you better, please use it.
    Leave these articles around the kitchen or family room where they will remind you of what you are doing. You may later want to label these articles with new assumptions that would be more instrumental to your development.

5. For whom or what have you been willing to change?

B. LIES and MANIPULATION PROGRAMS

This MALware distorts truth so users and their contacts can be more effectively utilized by the RV Program.

(1) File Decompression Program. This RV program rewrites users' history by cropping and compressing the bits where users momentarily slipped from their accustomed image, falling into victim or victimizer postures, for example. On demand, these ego-deflating files are decompressed, but in reverse (the opposite of the truth): "I've never been a victim" (or a victimizer)! Users "remember" success on occasions of failing—performing flawlessly or being the epitome of a loving and supportive spouse or parent. Users "recollect" being victimized as good times ("'Making love' with my babysitter when I was six was great! I was a stud!"). They also tell others the inverse of their brutal perpetrations, recalling that their victims were actually hurting *them*! They "remember" all mistakes having been made by the other person, so they never consider their role in any fiasco. When challenged, they return to these memory checkpoints again and again—"proof" that allegations against them are ill-founded.

This MALware is responsible for the Rock's <u>antagonal memories</u>, as it effectively reverses the threatening images from the user's past. For instance, they "recall" the most hurtful people in their childhood as the ones who were most helpful. The individuals who've honestly communicated about the psychological devastation in the family are "remembered" as most troublesome. Those who speak of this or other invasive programming are "recollected" as being particularly invasive themselves.

Vast amounts of censored life experiences can be stored in the unconscious with the File Decompression Program. Because these users' treachery is instantly zipped into a folder, they have no knowledge of their pathology, thus perceiving offers of help as unwarranted and unwelcome. If a rescuer comments on a user's need for extensive treatment for his memory distortions, this MALware draws from a ready cache of fabricated recollections ("I've already thoroughly investigated myself for unresolved issues, and there are none!").

IT Help Desk: Deprogramming File Decompressions—Antagonal memories need to be recognized for what they are and corrected: "Your parents (leaders, heroes, and so forth) are ordinary people who helped at times, hurt at times, and everything else in between. Let's collect as much data as we can from the people who knew them well." Be on the alert for the Rock playing the innocent victim when confronted about his or her brutality, and stay firm in your prayerful assertions of the truth.

I remembered meeting a young tourist couple in a New Orleans store. They mentioned spending the previous day, which had been particularly stormy, in the French Quarter. As the woman wandered off to browse, I asked the man if they had stayed inside to avoid the rain. "No indeed," he replied with a grin. "When we stepped outside, the rain stopped as if by magic, only to resume when we entered another building. This happened again and again, so no drop touched us." When his wife returned and he walked away, I inquired about their tour of the French Quarter amid such a torrential downpour. She stated simply, "We got drenched!" (Guess which person I believed.)

(2) The Delineation Drive. Users of this program separate out one particular part of a person or situation as special or important, rendering them incapable of perceiving the interconnectedness of the whole. For example, they may consistently delineate their contributions as particularly valuable. If a relative was cured of his disease through multiple remedies, the user believes the treatment *she* recommended was the effective one. If that relative dies, however, then a rival's recommendation was the killer.

This program depicts each of us as one "screen" image, highlighting its "life" as ours to enjoy, process, and defend if threatened. For instance, if a woman offers the user information to support his psychological development, this program causes him to angrily attack her because of a perceived "boundary violation" ("Anything you have is for *you*, not *me*!"). The user is compelled to figuratively "tap the space bar" if anyone emotionally comes too close. But the next moment, he may feel a biochemical surge as he "presses the backspace key" and invades her physical boundaries—*not* accepting her clear delineation of "*No!*" in response. In general, users unload their delineated rage on those who disregard the limits (or lack of them) imposed by this program.

A young woman named Kate stuck her head in my classroom to inquire about her husband, Zeke. "He's like a cover model for *Geek* magazine. Have you seen him?"

I told her I was too absorbed in my writing and hadn't noticed anyone coming or going.

She peered over my shoulder and read a bit of what I had written, and then remarked, "Speaking of boundaries…A levee has been built between Orleans Parish and Jefferson Parish to keep the Orleans floodwaters from going into Jefferson—did you hear?"

"Ah, no. So they 'couldn't' build proper levees *around* the city in the decades *before* the storm, but *now* within days, they *can* build functioning levees *within* the city?" I asked painfully.

Kate continued, "Yeah! My friends still in New Orleans say the officials won't let any Orleans Parish people cross into Jefferson—'to minimize looting.' But it's all New Orleans—one city within the same country—they can't do that—it's illegal! Borders have been set up all over the place, and armed border guards won't let people pass unless they have some documented 'official' reason, like being with medical or military teams. Yet, 'authorized personnel' are breaking into everybody's homes, looking for dead bodies and forcing anyone still living there to leave town."

The mind's ability to delineate, originally designed for protection and safety, gets reversed by the Delineation Drive Program into something that separates and isolates. This separation and isolation occurs with others ("*They* may be looters!") as well as with "alien" aspects of the user's psychology ("They" may take away the user's image!) Any part of users that is contrary to their image is walled off from their awareness. This MALware then posts Rock "border guards" to prevent access to these forbidden areas of users' minds. Angry, aggressive Mascrocks threaten harm to anyone who approaches while sickeningly "sweet" Femrocks assure that there is no need to search those sites.

The Delineation Drive Program consistently interferes with accuracy and awareness by drawing inappropriate differentiating lines and deleting appropriate delineations. Users thereby lose their capacity to distinguish the momentary or short-term circumstance from the long-term trend. For example, a user can't differentiate someone further along the psychological journey and capable of leading the way from someone who merely parrots the insights of those further along. Or, a user can't see the difference between a person's youthful folly or midlife crisis and another's lifelong habit of debauchery. When this program so separates out and misaligns our minds and detaches us from our fellow humans, the powerful abilities innate to our ever-penetrating <u>unlimited Mind</u> become harnessed and relegated to the mundane.

I once met a New Orleans woman who introduced herself as a clairvoyant housewife. I was curious: "What's that?"

She replied, "Well, I'm able to see ahead of time, like what will be on sale at the stores. Once I dreamed of exactly what draperies to buy for the spare bedroom. I was doing some online shopping the following morning, and there was the pattern of stripes and dots just like in my dream! I also foresee changes of schedule, like the postponing of PTA meetings or rescheduling of my son's football practice. I tend to stay calm with all my household chores because I'm always prepared for what is to come." *If only her ability had given her the foresight of our hurricane and flood!*

IT Help Desk: Deprogramming Delineations ("Diagnose Connection Problems!")—Assist the user in differentiating appropriate from inappropriate lines of delineation and healthy from unhealthy walls of defense. Ask questions. What makes her assume that one person alone (the Mascrock) is to be congratulated for a positive outcome? Why does she single out another to be the sole cause of any difficulty (a rescuer, for example)? Is singling out realistic?

(3) Editorial Override Program. This RV program causes users to distort incoming information, altering its form and its message to defuse any threat to "their" programming. An example is when a person gently expresses concern in a normal tone and volume, while the user hears harsh demands or even screaming. Yet the same user may consider his deafening heavy-metal music to be melodic or even worshipful. Or, a man poses questions to another user to loosen her clenched mind, and she accuses him of mind-control tactics. Users reduce important information, like poorly constructed levees, to "small type font" (if noted at all), while inconsequential, mundane, or entirely fictitious details are emphasized with "LARGE, **BOLD** type" with "<u>underlining</u>."

These users customize their life according to the drives of their unique character, interpreting, judging, and then editing information accordingly. They also constantly edit both facts and figures to align with basic assumptions, such as "Rocks are right!" They highlight these revisions and then endlessly reiterate them, making them seem real and unforgettable. Since the users of this program consider transparency bad form, they employ every means from their "toolbar" to avoid it.

IT Help Desk: Treatment for Editorial Override—Correct distortions by stating the facts to the best of your ability and reiterating these again and again and again. To ascertain the truth, you need to be clear yourself, so please get *experienced* help from both outer and inner guidance. (Just as we have internal and external programming, we have internal and external help!)

(4) The Definition Lock. When reading a dictionary, we see that most words have several definitions. This MALware hooks each user into only one "valid" definition for any word—the RV-approved definition ("their" definition). If an "unacceptable" definition is mentioned—say a woman discloses her desire for emotional "intimacy" to her user husband—this program makes each user respond according to his or her unique programmed definition. One user "understands" that "intimacy means sex," so he carries his wife into the bedroom for a quickie. Another user hears "intimacy means smothering," so he leaves the house feeling suffocated. A third user hears "intimacy means mothering," so he confronts his wife with, "You're always trying to run my life, just like my mom!" Thus, users react to the definition coming through their own "headset," rather than listening to what the speaker meant.

This definition-binding program is rampant in our society as we define all things according to our individual experience of them. We translate "goodness" as belonging to those who say or do apparently nice things (they make us feel good!), rather than those who pursue the good of transcending our mind's images and movies and who encourage us to do the same. We define "knowledge" as scientifically proven facts about this universe and our world's inhabitants, while we limit our definition of "life" and its maturation to the existence and development of *physical* bodies. When the goodness, knowledge, and life of heart, mind, and spirit are excluded in these definitions, we may easily neglect these aspects of our being; yet we don't include ourselves in the definition of "disabled." Also, when "computer"-generated imagery is defined as "reality," what is beyond seems to be mere computer game fantasy or the wishful thinking of the disgruntled.

IT Help Desk: Treatment for Definition Distortions—Be very specific in your definitions and what YOU mean. Be broad in your interpretations of what others might mean, including Our Rescuer's explanation. Don't let users manipulate you by projecting the assertions of the program onto you. Remind them that asking people what *they* mean is a first step to getting beyond programmed meanings *and* a useful way to get to know others. Be aware that users will likely hear this suggestion as insulting, as it implies they don't already know.

(5) The "Cut and Paste" Translation Matrix. This program cuts words or actions away from what is unknown, incomprehensible, and/or upsetting and pastes them into a setting that is known, understood, and comfortable, giving the user the feeling of "I understand exactly what you mean." There are multiple subroutines:

(a) *The Psychological to Physical Formula.* The emotional is translated into the physical as easily as pressing the Alternate Key

(Alt). For example, when a person mentions her pain from a Rock afflicting her and her family, a user of this program "helps" by informing her of possible physical causes for her suffering and perhaps offering palliative remedies: "Maybe you're upset because of something you ate—I have some antacid in the medicine chest." or, "Lady, I can see you're having a bad day; is it that time of the month?" Psychological upsets are transformed into physical symptoms. Chronic anger may express itself through "sore" joints or muscles; the underlying anger often surfaces when someone suggests a psychological component of these symptoms. Needs for closeness and intimacy are converted into physical drives, as with lust or hunger, while a need for justice is felt as "I wish I'd gone to law school!"

This program also functions in reverse, judging the psychological based on the physical. For instance, when the physical body has grown to maturity, the heart and mind are assumed to be mature too. Users may ask why "adults" sometimes have immature behavior, rather than question why people with immature behavior are called "adults." These users assume that if people can groom and maintain their physical body, then they *must* be caring for their psychological body as well.

(b) *The Animate to Inanimate Analogy.* An urgent problem with a human being is immediately translated to an inanimate equivalent with no urgency, making the user feel relaxed in what seems a routine situation. For example, I remember once pleading with a woman to get professional help for her child, who was showing strong Rock tendencies (unwillingness to comply with anyone else's way). Her response to me was, "You sound just like my husband wanting me to buy the latest software to do our taxes!" This program is a favorite in Rock schools, where human traits are programmed into inhuman equivalents.

(c) *The Reality to Wish Paraphrase.* A student may comment to a user classmate of the opposite sex, "I enjoyed your report on the shrinking wetlands of Louisiana. This issue has many important environmental, social, and political ramifications. Consider submitting it to the campus newspaper." Projecting his own desires, the user hears, "I want your body," and responds accordingly.

(d) *The "It Means What It Says" Interpretation Lock.* This program isolates Holy Scripture of bottomless depth and timeless wisdom, as well as pertinent-for-today historical writings, into tidy, concrete slogans and clichés that bolster the Rock Virus Program (e.g., "'Spare the rod and spoil the child'[1] translates into 'Beat the crap out of your kids, or you'll be sorry!'").

(e) *The Sure to Possible to Improbable Shunt.* A favorite of the media. Actual events are reported initially in a manner that implies vague possibility, raising doubt in the audience's mind. Words like *may, maybe, possibly,* and so on are added to all statements of fact. "*Critics questioned* whether the official *might* have spent taxpayers' money for personal matters." (There's no question—he did!) Over time, choice wording makes the event seem increasingly dubious until it is finally dismissed as spurious.

(f) *The Abstract to Concrete Translation.* This program hardens all abstract communication into strict literal interpretations. ("Adam and Eve were real people. The woman screwed up, and the man made the mistake of trusting her. I say, 'Never again!'") Psychological interpretations ("Perhaps Adam and Eve represent the masculine and feminine sides of every person") or any other deeper teaching is termed "blasphemy." The one superficial meaning dubbed by this program prevails.

(g) *The Subject/Object Switch.* If the user doesn't in this moment, experience "himself" doing what you are complaining about, then "you" must be doing it. The user may respond, "You scare me!" and/or take defensive action.

(h) *The "Only What I Know Exists" Epilogue.* Having translated everything unknown and unwelcome into familiar computer programs, the user triumphantly concludes, "I know exactly what's going on!" (or at least everything of consequence).

IT Help Desk: Cropping the Translation Matrix—Because this program moves the user to translate what you say into some other meaning entirely, be prepared with your own translations. When he throws out accusations like "You're dominating me!" or "You're trying to castrate me!" give him your interpretation, as with, "Pat programmed responses shackle your manhood. I'm merely requesting that you listen and respond in *new* ways." Encourage the user to get beyond his assumptions of understanding or knowledge by having him ask questions and then listen to the responses.

I jumped as the song on my cell phone broke the silence. It was Jayda, whom I briefed on my present environment—an empty room full of desktop computers. We started chatting about e-mail.

"Sending an e-mail through spell-check can be a help or a hazard—have you seen that?" she asked me.

"Yeah," I replied. "I e-mailed some of my writing to my mother, my current editor. The computer suggested the following corrections: 'Self-seeking' was changed to 'sight-seeing' and 'mind games' to 'mainframes.' For 'self-awareness,' I was given a choice of 'selfsameness,' 'sufferableness,' or 'spermatogenesis.'" I giggled. "'Sociopathology' was changed to 'Scientology,' 'passive-aggressiveness' to 'passiveness,' and 'pedophilic' was changed to 'basophilic.' Even my e-mail program is minimizing or ignoring the psychology-based problems rampant in our society, such as child molestation, and distracting us from our self-development!"

Jayda uttered agreement and then added, "Computers do have their taboo topics, don't they? My favorite computer change recently was when I sent an e-mail to Marta, a friend whose husband is just like Austin. I said that when it comes to romance, all I get from Austin is 'lip-service,' and my computer changed that to 'lingerie!' I *wish*!" Jayda joked.

(6) Contextual Warp. The user omits the context from his rendition of a given situation, rendering inappropriate a person's otherwise useful words, behavior, or emotions. A user may, with an innocent face and wounded air, lament that a certain fellow is cold and unresponsive to her, while she is silent about the causal circumstances—that she has hounded him for years! This program warps users' ability to experience their environment. Familiar places can seem as strange as if never before visited; users need to ask directions again and again to traverse frequently traveled routes. Conversely, strange places can feel familiar, so in those situations, users *won't* seek help when navigating. Users may also sense a false familiarity in relationships when the context of their interactions has been limited. For example, a user may say, "I've known that man for thirty years, and he's a real jewel!" when she's known him merely as her mailman. (When he's not delivering mail and is at home with his family, is he delivering physical and emotional blows?)

IT Help Desk: Resetting the Contextual Warp—Remind users of the correct context, and assist them in acknowledging that their adversary's feelings, thoughts, or actions may be appropriate under the circumstances, while the users' own may *not* be. Inform them that leaving out contextual details is misleading, and invite them to repeat their story with the context included.

(7) The Labeling Lock. Just as every PC has both hardware and software, we have the ability to be hard or soft with each other, depending on whether the person we're dealing with is particularly thick-skinned and defensive or sensitive and vulnerable. This RV program bestows <u>antagonal perceptions</u> on a user, such that she perceives harshness in the Rocks' devastated victims and those rescuing them, and as a result, feels that hardness, coldness, and roughness are their due. Meanwhile, softness is granted to fellow Rocks who are believed to be like the user—calm, gentle, and worthy souls. With this program in place, victims and victimizers receive the opposite of what they require to heal, and rescuers are consistently thwarted.

Pejorative labels such as "badgering," "battering," "belittling," "shaming," "moralizing," and "pontificating" are typed and ready to be dragged onto any "file" (human being) whose "contents" (self-expression) challenge the "authenticity," "goodwill," or "superiority" of the Virus-infected person. Questions are labeled as "prying," "meddling," "intrusive," or like "cross-examination." Communication of need is considered "selfishness," "weakness," or an attempt to dominate. An assertive woman is "unsupportive," "unwilling," "difficult," "argumentative," "ornery," "combative," or "a real crone!" A man who expresses his tenderness or woundedness is called "wimp," "fag," "girl," "milquetoast," or "loser." Those who are capable of intimacy and deep bonding are termed "codependent," "enmeshed," or "not well-differentiated." Valid experience is labeled "theory," "*your* perception," or "*your* belief." Relating in an attentive, engaged, adult manner is framed as "psychotherapy." This Rock Virus program is quick to judge genuine, healthy, human qualities as pathological and deserving of the user's rage.

This program permanently places positive labels on Rocks and their activities: "loving," "charitable," "generous," or "democratic." A Rock's severe psychological defects are even labeled favorably. "My uncle (a Rock) was a *pillar of strength* (notice the inanimate analogy) at the funeral after his sister's sudden death in the flood. Such a *brave* man—*heroic,* really—he didn't shed a tear" (a testimony, in fact, to the Rock's inability to feel or care). This labeling MALware runs in the background of every image-focused mind, applying positive labels to "files" supportive of RV programming while slapping pejorative labels on anything contrary ("lies," "boring," "silly," "incomprehensible," "garbage," "unbiblical," or "of the devil"). These labels arise so quickly in users' brains that they believe this programming is their own thoughts (<u>Rockthink!</u>).

The **Mis-association Subroutine** induces users to make inaccurate labels themselves. For example, users pair unrelated words together (e.g., Muslim terrorist). By always mentioning one with the other, their minds learn to connect the two, locking both words to <u>inappropriate associations</u>. (All Rocks cause terror, and they may use religious labels to hide their irreligious inclinations!) Users also affix double-meaning tags to further the RV cause—if an adversary is hosting a joyous celebration, the user of this program might paint the event as a "gay party," thus rattling those uncomfortable with the alternative meaning of "gay." This program's deceptive renaming results in "Dragging and Dropping." (Here I use the New Orleans French Quarter's definition of "drag"). A "file" is "dressed up" to appear the opposite of what it is. With such disturbing labels and pictures on it, users and their listeners then drop it.

IT Help Desk: Loosening the Labeling Lock—Call the user on every misapplication of labels and offer more useful descriptions: "So you think I'm a 'flaming feminist' because I, a woman, am giving you, a man, constructive feedback. In my opinion, a 'caring human being' is more accurate. I'm also *not* 'dumping my shit,' but sharing my thoughts and feelings. In every discipline, whether the training of IT technicians or Olympic athletes, aren't *both* positive and negative objective feedback essential to excel?"

(8) Thumbnail Program. This RV program zooms out on users' experiences with those in the Mineral Stage, shrinking them to "thumbnail-size" (insignificant) events. For instance, when the Rock's children react to his abuse and neglect and neighbors beg him to stop his barbarism, this program makes the user wife discount their assertions: "He's done nothing wrong! They're exaggerating, overreacting, or making it up!" (See "The Labeling Lock.") The user similarly denies or minimizes her experience of being mistreated herself. Her husband's daily persecution is reframed to, "Perhaps he doesn't always treat me to the *best* of his ability."

IT Help Desk: Thumbnail Treatments—When the user denies or minimizes atrocious behavior, zoom in on what happened. Collect evidence to prove your point (videotaping can be useful, with participants' permission), as the user is likely to ignore you otherwise. If you play back the tape to the user, you will be amazed at her inability to acknowledge the truth and her sudden anger toward you.

(9) Reality Reversal Program. This MALware rotates reality 180 degrees. What's happening is NOT happening, but what is NOT happening IS! A user who is a beautiful woman sees herself as a plain Jane. An emaciated girl maintains a strict diet for her "weight problem." And an immature male holds himself as the epitome of manhood. Users "understand" that facts are just opinions that often must be changed for the "common good" (the Program), while "their" programmed opinions are in the hard drive and "cannot" be altered. This program moves the user to revise personal memoirs, family legends, official records, and history books by inserting these alterations of reality.

Similarly, this program reverses cause and effect. Strong emotions expressed by victims suddenly become the *cause* of their victimizers' attacks. For example, a spouse desperately pleads with her Rock husband to get counseling and lists the reasons why change is essential. His response is, "Your going on and on about that for months is getting on my nerves. Talk about something else!" This program causes the user to perceive his wife's "nagging" (Labeling Lock) as the problem, so she is responsible for provoking any "less than perfect" (Thumbnail) behavior from him.

These users continually waste their time, talents, and resources on those who are incapable of being enhanced by them or who squander them, and they shun those who would employ them prudently. Users may see themselves as generous and helpful when they offer what isn't needed, but if they inadvertently provide what is needed, they beat themselves up in regret. For instance, a user may adapt every aspect of her life to cook, clean, and do secretarial work for her grown and capable children and husband. However, if she "neglects her duties" one day, requiring them to do for themselves, she may be burdened with remorse for years. Under the influence of this program, users reject realism, convinced that those who speak the truth of this world are the maladapted ones ("You think my [Rock] parent might have hurt me growing up? That idea tortures me!").

A young man with uncombed blue hair and a silver dagger dangling from his left earlobe stepped into my classroom. I introduced myself and mentioned I was from New Orleans. With slurred speech, he muttered, "Man—all that hype about New Orleans! What's the big deal? Those people saying that thousands died in the Katrina disaster are just scaring people, you know? Not *that* many people died! A lot of people lost their stuff, though—now *that's* a bummer!"

IT Help Desk: Reality Recovery Disk—Users of the Reality Reversal Program will experience unprogrammed outlooks and accompanying help as harm. You will first need to discover what techniques calm each user and then use them. To understand a user's <u>antagonal communication</u>, listen to the assertions of what did NOT happen and then remove the NOTs. (If a woman volunteers, "I was *not* molested by my church choir director, *not* by my brother, and *not* by my father!" what is she *really* saying?) Then offer a step to lead the user closer to reality, sharing websites or information from people in the community she or he respects. ("Our minister was mentioning the other day the enormous number of children who have been sexually abused in church and at home. Sexual abuse is epidemic!"[2])

(10) The Deletion Program expunges threatening data—any information that may expose the Rock Virus and its Program. In a world of imagery, anything we "have" can be eliminated as easily as pressing "delete" or "backspace" on the keyboard. This program erases not only data in the mind but also feelings in the body and of the heart. For example, users may love their spouse one day, and the next day file for divorce. Skills and talents may disappear overnight if users fail to follow the Program. They may perform flawlessly and then be unable to repeat this accomplishment thereafter. Users' strong suits, such as sympathy and concern, may be deleted, and the retention of new information may be impossible. This program can also wipe out memory files one at a time until the user ultimately loses his or her mind (or the "screen" goes black)!

IT Help Desk: Deprogramming the Deletion Program—Whatever data users delete must be given to them again...and again...and again...and again. If nothing more, they may, over time, realize how forgetful they are! Know that deleted memories, feelings, personality traits, skills, perceptual abilities, and so on are still in the system, and they will resurface and integrate when the user receives adequate professional help from deft rescuers and Our Rescuer within.

MOCHA BREAK:

1. Do you give more weight to the reality of the technological world, the physical world, the emotional realm, or the mind? How do you typically handle someone who lives in a different reality?

2. When you notice someone lying or manipulating, do you challenge them? Do you challenge yourself by asking, "Am I doing something similar?" Consider writing both of you an honest e-mail and then asking Our Rescuer where to go from there.

3. How do you use the Labeling Lock Program? Print some positive labels for people you usually judge negatively and some constructively critical labels for those you tend to praise.

4. Define the following and then compare your definitions with those in your online dictionary:
   a.   Wealth
   b.   Knowledge
   c.   Maturity
   d.   Health
   e.   Being human

5. Which RV program can be deduced from the statement "Hurricane Katrina destroyed New Orleans!"?

C. The **STRIFE** Programs

This type of MALware sabotages connection, as each program is designed to promote incompatibility, conflict, and **STRESS!**

(1) Feedback Loop. If the user receives information contrary to the RV protocol, a feedback mechanism is triggered that loops the user's attention away from this "problem." This program includes several subroutines:

(a) *The "I Can't Hear/Understand You" Program* activates automatically to unwelcome communication. No matter what you say, users cannot comprehend a word of it. ("∩ ↦⊤ ⊤↦ ↦‥ ○_!") Their response is, "If you could speak in another way, you might make sense!" They attempt to alter the speaker's word choices, grammar, or linguistic style, often aggressively, rather than realize their own inability to listen is at fault. You won't find a way to get through because the problem is with this Teflon nonstick technology. Like your computer not recognizing your printer, you may elicit no reaction from users, as if you don't exist. Your comments are like Mac software with a PC—they just won't "load." Of course, when users are confronted about their lack of response to a serious problem, they can honestly state, "I didn't hear about it."

This application can also be reversed, as in the user declaring, "You refuse to hear!" or, "You can't understand me!" Questions of "What didn't I hear?" or "What don't I understand?" are ignored or answered in a nondescript way (see "The Vaguenese Language Program" in chapter 7, p. 179).

(b) *Direct Feedback* is when users mimic what has just been told to them. For example, when a spouse exclaims, "You're not listening to me—please listen," the user counters, "You're not listening to *me*!"

(c) *Negative Feedback causes* users to criticize anyone who is critical of Rocks: "Take the log out of your own eye!" or, "You are so soft-spoken—no one will ever listen to you!" But a louder tone prompts them to say, "Now you're screaming—why can't you speak normally?—you're hurting my ears!" The user repeatedly and aggressively rejects the delivery of your message, all the while censuring *your* negativity.

Remember: Rock language is binary (1/0). Users only register "subjects" (Rocks like themselves) and "objects," and how many people spend time deciphering noises emitted by objects, such as their computer? Also, when users do *not* let others talk, don't listen when they do, are unwilling to understand, and are incessantly critical, they cannot receive vital information to counteract the Rock Virus programs. The result is an information blackout. For instance, receiving the ever-present streaming of Our Rescuer is *so* easy when we want this, but the user of the Feedback Loop only hears "himself."

IT Help Desk: Feedback for the Feedback Loop—When the user "can't hear you," "can't understand you," or throws what you've said back at you, try this approach: Put your hand on her shoulder (be careful, a Femrock might accuse you of sexual harassment!), and tell her to be quiet and listen. Then say what you need to say as simply and calmly as you can. Then ask her to repeat it back to you. Be persistent until she is able to indicate the gist of what you said. When a Rock hears something outside her program, she feels bad, and she may attack you as the cause. Stay relaxed, remind her that you are no threat, and restate your position.

Where users are most harshly critical is where they have a wound. You might be thinking, "But they criticize *everything*!" Yes, they are *very* wounded. Pay close attention to what triggers their negativity, and over time see if you can trace it back to a hidden trauma. They won't be able to hear this information directly, but you can offer it indirectly: "I once read about a person who criticized whatever reminded him of his unconscious pain. For example, he witnessed as a child his mother being brutalized by his father, and he 'grew' to be confrontational—*not* of abusive men, that felt too dangerous, but of women who had been victimized" (an <u>antagonal confrontation</u>).

(2) Program Opposition. This MALware causes the user to actively oppose *human* beings and their work. For example, if an exuberant child declares, "It's a beautiful day!" the user counters with, "It is NOT!" Or, a woman shares her feelings, and the user tells her, "You shouldn't feel that way!" If this user is challenged about how he constantly opposes everything said or done by his colleagues, his predictable response is, "No, I don't!"

Users of this program respond antagonistically to every situation. For example, when a doctor pronounces, "You must *stop* drinking alcohol and smoking cigarettes and *start* eating healthy foods and exercising!" the user patient drinks and smokes *more,* becoming a junk-food-eating couch potato (an <u>antagonal response</u>). Users perceive needs and wishes to be the opposite of what they are and act accordingly. For instance, a widow beseeches her best friend, "Please fly down for my husband's funeral. I will be so alone." Using this program, the friend hears, "I want to be alone. *Don't* come to the funeral." Thus, users isolate people when they need closeness and support (or food, water, and rescuing). Users are so antagonistic to human functioning that normal human activities are resisted. Or they are experienced and/or expressed in reverse, as in <u>antagonal language, feelings, learning, spending, giving</u>, and so on (see the glossary).

This MALware also makes users struggle with themselves. For example, they talk earnestly in favor of something while rebelling with their behavior, or vice versa. (An example is the minister who preaches against sin and yet shows no aversion to participating in it.) Self-defeating behavior is common with this program's users—spending money on luxury items when in debt, eating a double cheeseburger with fries while attempting to lose weight, or needing work but being too selective in the job search. Users consistently sabotage their true desires, whether they come from inside them or from someone else—**"YOU CAN'T MAKE ME!"** Tragically, while defending this RV program, users unknowingly reinforce the rift within their own psyches. In their thrill of victory, they are oblivious of having withstood and conquered themselves.

IT Help Desk: Opposing the Opposition—Emotions are trapped in the user's compulsive opposition, which you might tap into: "When you said, "No!" to your child's request to play, what were you feeling?" You might pose questions that direct the user to speak less antagonistically: "You know your wife really well, don't you?" With his automatic opposition, he'll be forced to admit, "No, I don't!" Each time you oppose this self-destructive program in users' minds, you show them that they can do this too.

When a user says or does the opposite of what you request, avoid overt emotional reaction (this can be challenging!). Often signed contracts are necessary to take users out of their programmed head and into their prior agreement with you. Show them the evidence, and watch their show of downloaded excuses. A lot of their verbal opposition, although obnoxious, is not harming anyone—just ignore it. It may dissipate over time if given no reinforcement. Also, you might try asking for the opposite of what you want to increase the likelihood of getting your way. However, always pass your ideas through Our Rescuer, for safety purposes and to ensure "your" way is indeed the way forward.

(3) The Confounder. In this program, users belabor activities with minutiae, superfluous "requirements," and excessive details, such that their victims can collapse in exhaustion and despair after the simplest of tasks. (The use of this MALware transforms any administration into a bureaucracy!) Inefficiency reigns, as users endlessly "organize" and reorganize, first this way, now that way, repeating a task, but never getting it "exactly right." Mired in minutiae, they never have enough time for what counts! For example, preliminaries for a short drive to the park with the kids may include filling up the gas tank, checking the tires and under the hood, cleaning the car's interior and exterior, fiddling with the GPS, and more! Family togetherness takes a backseat to these more pressing, programmed child-care "obligations."

A user boss may order employees to perform pointless actions that waste exorbitant amounts of time and energy and the company's or community's resources on what is insignificant, unproductive, or purposeless. When confronted by a frustrated employee ("You're constantly telling me to redo what I've done and done well, while my talents are underutilized, if not deprecated!"), this boss replies, "If you don't like your job, then quit." If this worker counters with, "I like my job when I'm allowed to do it, but I detest the confusing and unnecessary paperwork and other tedium," the Rock boss jumbles the message by inserting his own: "So you feel this job is not fulfilling your personal goals. Have you thought of going to a career counselor?" Users of this program feel compelled to complicate *any* situation.

Right after Hurricane Katrina, people from all over the states, including hundreds of firefighters, volunteered to help victims along the Gulf Coast. However, our authorities entangled them in training programs that delayed their arrival for days *and* postponed the rescue of those in desperate need.[3]

Confounder Program users present material beautifully when it's full of Rock misinformation that confounds human development. Brochures will have bright colors; large, bold, easy-to-read print; and eye-catching illustrations. However, if the information contradicts Rock goals, the format changes radically. There will be page after page of tiny, lackluster print; wordy prose; and complicated language with a convoluted message (perhaps it's in the final paragraph of the last page, in a sentence or two with even smaller print). Check out software license agreements, listed side effects of medications, and ingredients on processed-food labels. When the user has a legal obligation to inform the public, the wording offered by this program is unclear and indigestible!

With the Confounder Program, instructions, contracts, or other important communications are made tedious, perplexing, and incomprehensible, utilizing difficult vocabulary and grammar (triple negatives!). Legalese is a perfect example of where exceptionally long sentences cause average readers to forget the subject by the time they get to the object. This MALware keeps a lot of our professionals busy and well paid, as they are required for interpretation.

I once attended a public panel, convened for the purpose of explaining proposed amendments to our Louisiana State Constitution. Here is one sentence that even baffled the experts:

"To provide that no law, unless enacted by two thirds of the elected members of each house of the legislature, requiring increased expenditures for any purpose shall be applicable to any city, parish, or other local public school board until approved by school board resolution or until, and as long as, the legislature appropriate funds to the school board for the purpose and only to the extent and amount of such funds or until a law provides for a local source of revenue to the school board for the purpose and the school board is authorized to levy and collect such revenue and only to the extent and amount of such revenue; and to provide for exceptions to such prohibition on increasing the financial burden of city, parish and other local public school boards."[4] (You may now breathe.)

IT Help Desk: Deprogramming the Confounder—Help the confounder to confine his activities and language to what is necessary. You might say, "We have half a tank of gas in the car, and the park is five miles away, so you don't need to go to the gas station. The kids will be dirty after they play, so cleaning the car *before* we go is pointless." or, "Can you tell me again what you just said in one sentence of no more than ten easy-to-understand words?" Ask him simple questions so he learns to prioritize and to think each activity through, one step at a time. For example, before performing each task, inquire, "Which step is most important right now?"

(4) lucowdefence (Incompetence) Program. This RV program renders the user incompetent. Previously well-functioning "adults" make decisions or "mistakes" with the ineptitude of a small child. Under the influence of this program, for instance, someone who has memorized vast texts on obscure topics cannot remember his wife's birthday or their anniversary date. Or, though he procures supplies for his job with finesse, he buys moldy or expired foods when shopping for his family. When their dog leaves a mess on the floor, this user of high community standing tracks it throughout the house in the process of "cleaning it up," exponentially increasing the amount of cleaning that needs to be done (by someone else).

This program can extend to all areas of life, from activities of the world to affairs of the heart and mind. Users can be ingenious in getting what "they" want, but become clueless or useless when an activity goes against the Program. They become incapable of following instructions, learning procedures, or employing common sense. For example, a user declares, "I wiped off the kitchen countertops like you asked," when he cleaned with a filthy rag from the garage, leaving the countertops even dirtier *and* now covered in grease! A spouse or coworker ultimately decides, "It's easier to just do it myself!" Relieved of "menial" tasks, household responsibilities, or even the work they're *paid* to do, these users are then free to pursue their programmed activities.

This MALware asserts that certain people are biologically incapable of performing particular activities. For example, men "can't" openly express their feelings, "can't" listen to women ("The 'male' brain 'can't' register their sound frequency well."), or "can't" multitask (then why are males suddenly capable in Rock employment settings?). Women are "unable" to be effective leaders or excel in mechanics and technology as they are "prone" to excessive sentimentality and irrational thought. As users accept these "innate" male and female shortcomings, they don't help those conditioned in these deficits to grow past them. Also, these users judge children as generally unreliable, so when the children competently communicate—either verbally or with their behavior—the abuse and neglect they are experiencing, they are ignored.

Users claim to be "deeply hurt" when their bungling incapacities and gross inadequacies aren't accepted as "fate" or a "fact" of life ("men don't do housework" and "women are the weaker vessel"). However, no matter how grievous the damage from these users' failure to perform, they cannot grasp their contributions, and they show strong emotion toward those who hold them accountable ("Your lack of appreciation makes me feel worthless, like I should roll over and die!"). If you expect them to correct their "errors," *you* will pay for it.

Another young man, fitting the "model nerd" description, stuck his cropped haired head into the classroom, thick glasses askew on his protruding nose. "Are you Zeke?" I asked.

"Yeah, man, how'd you know?" He stepped toward me, revealing a rumpled forest-green dress shirt over hole-laden blue jeans. He was carrying an external hard drive.

"Your wife was looking for you a while back. Did she find you?"

"Yeah—Katie's always looking for me…trying to get me outside more to 'smell the roses.' That's what she says. I think she blames me for not spending more time with her, but I think my computer should take some of that blame, don't you?" Zeke shook his head decisively. "Anyway, we've been getting along better since we're talking and not just texting. Today, though, I've got to get my school project done," he said, gesturing to the flash drive hung around his neck.

During a brief chat about his research paper on modern technology, he told me, "Technology has come a long way, but in the end, which system the software is in matters most—what we're doing with what we know. Just look at what the levee builders did with their technology.[5] Then look at looters in New Orleans. They're using large trash cans and air mattresses to float their loot out of the flooded areas. Now if they can use this 'technology' to rip off guns, expensive equipment, jewelry, and other junk, why couldn't people in charge think of any way to safely float *in* food, water, and medical supplies?

"My old man was in the Army overseas. He said they could get *anything* they needed, no matter what, *anywhere* in the world, in forty-eight hours. He said ANYWHERE—in the middle of a desert or the midst of an enemy-held jungle. With all our modern technology, why did our government take so long to get the goods to the stranded survivors *in our own country* and rescue them from the Superdome, from nursing homes and hospitals, and out of the boil-your-bones heat! Even the victims of Bosnia, Afghanistan, and the Indonesian tsunami got help sooner![6] My dad said, 'In my entire military career, I've never seen anything like it. No, siree—*never*!'"

Users of the Incompetence Program can be differentiated from those who truly don't have the required abilities by their secondary gain: the users' "incompetence" is well rewarded and covered up with propaganda techniques and lies ("Trained professionals COULDN'T POSSIBLY bring in necessary supplies to New Orleans because of the flooding and armed looters!"). They receive business contracts, a promotion, or increased wealth (a whopping salary or bonus checks after leading their company or its customers into financial ruin). When genuinely incompetent people are exposed, on the other hand, they lose contracts or money and are demoted or fired.

Also noteworthy is the "CONTROL panel" involved when this program is used on a large scale. (Large populations can be affected by this program *and* rendered dependent on users or the organizations they work for.) Statistical analysis can differentiate the truly incompetent from the programmed ones. The extent of the "incompetence," as well as the number of people performing "incompetently" to further a Rock agenda, is statistically significant, as is the number of people (Femrocks) covering up for their "mistakes." When we discover this unspoken (and often ruthless and self-serving) goal and tally the numbers of people fooled by the users' "incompetence," we see proof that this program is indeed *extremely* competent!

The **"You're Never Satisfied!" Subroutine** of the Incompetence Program kicks in as nonprogrammed people inevitably complain about the users' poor workmanship or sportsmanship. Defending themselves vehemently, the users perceive "complainers" (Labeling Lock) as the cause of any problems and unload their anger on them accordingly. Other users, however, view them as "occasionally absentminded," "honestly mistaken," or "not so clever," blind to their hidden malevolence masquerading as incompetence. Rocks happily download this program into their affiliates because where incompetency prevails, they may *look* competent in contrast!

IT Help Desk: Rescuing Incompetents—If possible, avoid working with these users. If you must, tell the user *exactly* what you want him to do, as you would with a small child. Know that he's likely to alter the plan in some unexpected way. Demonstrate *how* the task is to be done. Otherwise, he is sure to do something unpredictable or bizarre. You need to keep tabs on his every step to ensure he does it correctly. Doing the project *with* him may improve his performance with the added benefit of expanding your skills. Every time he "errs" make sure you take up his time as much as your own in all corrections.

Again, written contracts and taped verbal agreements are handy for minimizing the user's abuses ("*You* weren't clear." or "I remember you asking for something else!"). Witnesses are also helpful since the user does not like public exposure. Hold him to his agreements regardless of his reasonable-sounding justifications. He often has to "try" again and again (and again) until he approximates what you want from him. (Be careful!—a per hour workman will charge you for *HIS* time, oblivious to the amount of *YOUR* time he is wasting.) Expect him to call you names like "rigid," "demanding," "obsessive-compulsive," or "slanderer"!—"You're giving people the impression that I'm not great at what I do!"). Pay him only for satisfactory work (unless directed by Our Rescuer), no matter how angry he gets, how much he insists he did a good job, or even if he threatens to sue you (be wary, he might!). Make suggestions to enhance his abilities and stand by until he implements them so he might one day choose to be truly competent. (See also "Coaxing from the Stall" on p. 137.)

(5) Arguing Analog. Those using this program argue incessantly in favor of an ill-founded position. When a speaker is knowledgeable on the topic and the arguer is not, this user still wrangles fiercely to defend her ignorant, if not ridiculous, assertions. Truth is relative or irrelevant, as "facts" are generated as needed to win a debate at any cost. Ordinary conversation feels like a life-or-death duel. And when a speaker is presenting irrefutable documentation, the user hears the speaker saying something she *can* argue with. The user pounces on the speaker with derision or wild accusations, deaf to his assertions of "but I never said that!"

IT Help Desk: Treatment for the Arguing Analog—Withdraw from the arguer until she is willing to listen. Or ask, "What does it feel like in your body when you instantly dispute people rather than first listen and understand what they have to say?" If you choose to argue, point out the user's inconsistencies, projections, conversational hijacking, and/or ignorance of the topic. If you have any fears of confrontation, you may learn to overcome them as you practice in this manner.

(6) Difference Drive. "You and I are different!" This program makes the user perceive her image as distinct from other images, perhaps SUPERIOR (or inferior). She focuses on and embellishes these differences whenever possible, feeding her feelings of specialness. Because others are "different," the user frames them as alien, disagreeable, and under suspicion—*their* perceptions, feelings, and thoughts are irrelevant to her, who considers herself a separate and unique person. When confronted with facts like, "Science has proven that human beings have 99.9% of their genetic material in common,"[7] the user defends "her" difference of opinion: "I can't respect any source that links *me* to some rigid formula! I'm different!"

The user of this program recognizes her individual experience as "different" in not being prone to the ego interference that other people are (the program includes a personal validation guarantee!). She notices others have "issues," but she doesn't consider her own fallibility or weaknesses that play into them or even cause them. Since others are "different," they aren't as smart, accomplished, or naturally gifted as she is, so they are viewed with condescension, if not suspicion. She assumes they are hardwired by their genetics and therefore unchangeable. If she experiences you trying to change "who she is," a pop-up menu appears with a selection of repugnant emotions and nasty comebacks.

Users also view people with less or alternative programming as "different," requiring another set of parameters. This MALware accentuates these differences such that the others *appear* too different to be worthy of acknowledgment, association, respect, or even the requirements for basic survival. Rather, these folks are treated like computer components, used as needed, without compensation, and then "discarded." Also, this program causes superficial "differences"—such as a man who has a cowlick or occasionally stutters or a woman who has a girlish giggle or wears an unflattering shade of lipstick—to aggravate users so much that they must shun or attack these individuals to regain their "peace." Since they feel much better, they know it was "the right thing to do."

Included in this program is the basic assumption *"Only 'I' know what is good for me."* This "logic" follows from this basic premise: "Since I am so different from you, you can't know me! You have no right to tell me what I should be doing, what you feel I'm feeling, or what you think about me!" ("The Punishing Program" [p.137] automatically activates when users are challenged by such "arrogant" attitudes [Labeling Lock].) Since they alone "know," these users are like novice programmers who attempt to install their computer programs manually—they are willing to sacrifice speed and efficiency for the feeling of "I did it all by myself!" Because this MALware causes so many relationship problems, it provides a ready-made, easy-to-use "reason" why *others* do not get along with users: "No two people are exactly alike—there will always be differences!"

I was visiting my mom's local public library in Broadmoor a few years ago when I mentioned to the sixtyish woman working the information desk that I was having some trouble with my first computer, which I had just purchased. She smiled cheerfully and offered to help. She pointed to the row of PCs and explained, "All of our computers are the same make and model, so one would think they're exactly the same, but they're not. They are *very* different!" Her voice became quiet, and she leaned closer to me so I could hear (and perhaps the computers couldn't). "Do you see that computer on the right end, number six?" she whispered. I nodded. "It's absolutely nonfunctional in the mornings…but around noon it 'wakes up' and is not a problem throughout the rest of the day. It doesn't do mornings, you know what I mean?" She glanced both ways, as if to check if anyone (or anything) was listening in on our conversation, before continuing. She leaned closer. "Do you see the next computer, number five?" I nodded again. "That computer refuses to surf the Internet! I can understand that not everyone likes surfing, but it really upsets the kids trying to do their school projects! And the next computer…" She proceeded to tell me the foibles of all the computers in the row. At the end, she concluded, "So you see, they are not the lifeless machines we are led to believe. They are more like people—strengths, weaknesses, good days, bad days, likes, dislikes, 'I will do this,' 'I won't do that!'…just like us. They are no different! I couldn't do my job if I didn't recognize the differences between our computers and know how to handle each one!"

I relayed this encounter to a friend of mine, Bob, who has studied computers extensively and services them daily. He exclaimed, "She's nuts! Computers are machines. They do what they are programmed to do—end of story!"

I communicated both sides of this ongoing conversation to another man I met who works with computers in the shipping industry in New Orleans. He replied, "Actually, computers are programmed to act like people, so both the librarian and your friend are correct."

I shared all this with my professional drummer friend, Trevor, who celebrated his sixtieth birthday this year with Katrina. He remarked, "Maybe computers are programmed differently to appear more like people, and people are indoctrinated out of their diversity to be more like computers, so one day we won't be able to tell the two apart!"

The Cubby Hole. This extra feature of the Difference Drive sorts people, places, and things in the user's life and then classifies them into neat, yet rigid, categories based on *perceived* differences. With this subroutine, users also believe they can isolate time and space in protective cubby holes. For example, a user doesn't understand what in his behavior five minutes ago could have led to his spouse's lack of affection right now. Or, if the user sprays pesticides, herbicides, and fungicides all over his yard, why would the mother of four youngsters next door complain? When she offers websites that report harmful incidents involving children exposed to these chemicals, he replies, "This is different!"

IT Help Desk: Deprogramming the Difference Drive—Point out to these users that while people are different in form, these forms still, anatomically and physiologically, have much in common. Psychology is no different. As individuals, we each have some Rock programs as well as Our Rescuer within our divided minds. Let the users know that their behavior is not unique to their individual personality. They are not being "different"—they are acting like any other Rock Virus-infected system. Those close to these users may be expressing the feelings and thoughts of some of their human parts that they have long forgotten.

(7) The Stall. If an activity goes against the Rock Virus Program, this MALware is activated to endlessly delay starting or finishing the project. It has many operations:

(a) The *Talk Block*. This program prevents users from experiencing authentic feeling, thought, or recollection. When a query is posed that might instigate any of these human responses ("How do you feel about that?" or "I'm wondering what you learned from the sermon on Sunday."), they instantly reply, "I don't know." or, "I don't remember." Pausing even for a moment to consider another answer causes users anxiety. This rapid defense eventually stalls questioners from further personal queries, and the Program endures unchallenged.

(b) The *"All's Fine" Shine*. Users of this subroutine insist that they, their project, their world, and so on are just fine the way they are (as long as users follow the Program). They rationalize, "If things were to be other than they are, they *would* be!" and sense no need to make alterations.

(c) The *Eternal Hourglass* has users taking what seems like an eternity to answer a question, respond to an e-mail, or do whatever is asked or required of them. This subroutine has many variations:

(i) The *"Saying Is the Same as Doing" Stall.* With this MALware, the user *says* what is expected, much as your computer states a document is printing when nothing is happening. Speaking is so much quicker and easier than acting, and there's no prep or cleanup! Think how much time, effort, and money you put into your college education, for example. Now imagine a high school dropout stating, "I'm a college graduate." See the difference?

(ii) The *"I'll Put That on My To-do List" Dawdle.* The user jots down any unwanted chores on the *bottom* of her daily list, where they stay.

(iii) The *"Change the Font" Formula.* The appearance of a situation is changed while the reality remains the same: "I've got a new guy in my life—I'm psyched!" (The new guy has the same old Mineral mind-set with a simple change of style!)

(iv) The *"It's Just Around the Corner" Coo.* This user assures people they and their wishes are appreciated and what the user has promised is on its way: "It's in the mail," "We're just finishing up now; you'll have it within the hour," or any number of expressions (often repeated over and over) that give people the impression that their satisfaction is guaranteed—yet never fulfilled, as time reveals.

(v) The *"Ask Me Later" Lull.* Any time you approach these users about their delays is not a good time: "I'm in the middle of something now—let's talk later." As their manner continues and your annoyance increases, the users build a strong case for *your* emotional excesses *and* lack of understanding.

(vi) The *Quick Fix.* This reset program is activated by touching certain places on users' bodies, having them touch or move in particular ways, or having them say or hear unique sounds, words, or phrases. A socially acceptable version of programming then downloads into the users' systems making them *appear* to have made a fast recovery of whatever was bothering them (or more likely bothering someone else). This is a favorite of Rock doctors, therapists, ministers, and laypersons who extol the "healing touch" of a Rock rather than the consistent *hard* work necessary for genuine psychological growth—the repossession of our lost Self.

IT Help Desk: Coaxing from the Stall—As "faster is better" with computers, remind the user that her life will be easier if she works faster (particularly on herself). Set completion expectations for projects and list consequences (deduction of payment, for example, if not done on time). Stand firm on this, despite her protests of "But I *am*!" whenever you point out what the user is *not* doing. Look for opportunities to apply leverage. ("I will do what you want when you do what I want.")

Perhaps you can arrange for the user to experience what it's like to be on the receiving end of her stalling behaviors. For instance, if she needs some work done right away, a passive-aggressive worker may help her experience some of the genuine emotion behind her own passive-aggressive behaviors. (Naturally, her behaviors anger her when *others* do them!) It may take months or years, but *eventually*, if she doesn't tire you out first, she will grow weary of this program and your unwavering response to it. (See also "Rescuing Incompetents" on p. 134)

(8) The Punishing Program (a.k.a. "Kill the Messenger"). If the words or actions of users of this program are doubted or challenged in any way, they feel their "life" is in danger and react in "self"-defense. A list box of weapons drops down for the user's selection:

- **The Shun Gun:** The doubter is stonewalled until she recants or returns to a submissive posture.

- **The Missal Missile:** A lengthy commentary of the offender's faults, mistakes, and problems (many of which are projected) is torpedoed at the offender or recited to those who know him.
- **Overexposure:** The whistleblower who causes the user's reputation to suffer is exposed to public humiliation and ostracism.
- **The Pissed-off Pistol:** The user hears nonprogrammed words as assaultive and feels justified in pelting speakers with rapid-fire aggression. Her verbal bullets berate and accuse, such as, "It's ill-tempered people like YOU that cause problems in this beautiful world!"
- **The Dump:** Decades of the user's accumulated rage is heaped on any adversary to the program. "LOOK OUT BELOW!"
- **The Martyr Moratorium:** —The user perceives himself as going to extremes to please you (actually, he's 'done the opposite), and yet YOU are not pleased. He interprets your natural inclinations to withdraw from his abuse as attempts to punish *him*, and he's '"not willing to stand by and suffer" what he considers attacks. Making you suffer is only fair play!
- **The Extinguisher:** If the above methods fail to eliminate a threat, the user may succumb to drastic methods of exterminating the culprit, often without the user's awareness.

The above subroutines manifest internally as well as externally. For example, "The Extinguisher" subroutine can cause the user to self-destruct very quickly (reckless driving resulting in an accident, drug overdoses, and other overt self-injurious behaviors) or slowly or intermittently decompensate (many illnesses). The Dump may cause the body parts involved in or representative of users' "transgressions" to exhibit pain or disease. (She spoke her mind and promptly got a sore throat. He fell in love and suffered a heart attack. Inner Rocks in these circumstances may be punishing their human strivings.) The Pissed-off Pistol can fire bitter self-criticism. The Missal Missile may torment users with everything they've ever done "wrong." The Shun Gun manifests in those who are always on the go and never pause long enough to know themselves or their genuine needs. Users carry feelings of innocence or righteous judgment, aware only of the "purest intentions" in their minds and hearts.

IT Help Desk: Deprogramming the Punishing Program—Rocks' binary language receptors only hear "reward" or "punishment." If you are not rewarding them, you must be punishing, and they will retaliate accordingly (and often tenfold). Following the instructions of Our Rescuer, show users their punishing behaviors. (Passing on programming *is* a punishing behavior to recipients as well as users!) Also, be careful *not* to give Rocks the tools with which they can victimize you. Don't open your heart to a Mascrock when he's 'going to stomp on it. Don't offer the Femrock your ideas when she ridicules them. Don't share your painful memories with Minerals since they always add to your pain. Keep a safe psychological distance, while also making contact with whom these Mineral Stagers might represent inside you. When they shut down or becomes overtly hostile, take a break. Resume at another time when they are less angry and you are better connected to Our Rescuer.

Femrocks can be particularly subtle with their passive-aggressive cruelty. For example, their self-punishment is an important consideration with any illness or injury. Always ponder what an ailment might be relaying about anyone's psychological health. If you believe you'd never punish yourself, track the changes you've made to your computer—updates, defrags, defect investigations, and so on—and compare them with how often you perform similar maintenance checks and upgrades on your psyche. No comparison? Now say "hello" to your Femrock!

(9) The CRASH. The Rock Virus anticipates users becoming aware of its tactics of control, deception, manipulation, and strife and losing their compliance (i.e., wanting their power back). Through this program, the Rock Virus is preemptive in distracting users from personal growth, and the growing awareness that comes with it, by canceling or crushing whatever or whoever is important to them—family, health, friends, work, home, and/or community. The "computer" itself may be made nonfunctional as every part of the user's "life" slowly shuts down or comes to a screeching halt. The user may even perish in the crash. Chronic users of this and all the other programs can psychologically die, becoming a mechanical man or woman person stuck in the Mineral Stage of Psychological Development. Consider how upsetting it is when your much-needed PC crashes. Now imagine that mechanism applied to you, your fellowman, and your world.

IT Help Desk: Pulling Out of the Crash—Beneath the programmed rage and secondary hostility of users is an unconscious terror that the "temp file" of their presumed identity will be altered or "killed" if they don't follow the Program. After all, images on a computer screen can be enlarged, diminished, moved, or removed at any moment. Remind users that their destructive decision to follow the RV Program is what's hurting them and *not* their attempts to free themselves. (See "The Reality Reversal Program" on p. 127.) Encourage them to find Our Rescuer in their system, the shortcut and only permanent escape from the Crash.

BREAK!

1. Review the Feedback Loop and write a one-page document about how it functions in your life.

2. What in this book have you opposed with the Program Opposition? Why? How do you feel when your computer blocks your work?

3. Which programs do you use to maintain your privacy as an image? What are some other options?

4. How does the Difference Drive operate within you? For example, do you make parts of your physical or psychological body "different" (superior or inferior, more or less lively, etc.) than other parts?

5. Who in your childhood used the Strife programs? Think, feel, draw, paint, sing, or in some other way creatively and humanly express what effect this has had on you.

A Computer Program Instead of a Parent

Imagine a human infant crying in distress and her dad doesn't hear her or register her need (Feedback Loop). Picture a toddler beginning to walk away and his mom opposes his tentative steps of independence, grabbing him and pulling him back (Program Opposition). A preschooler is learning to do basic tasks, including putting on socks and shoes or carrying out simple household chores, and an older brother or sister tells her there is only one way ("my" way!) to carry out each activity (Control Option Program). Meanwhile, teachers pass on their ignorance (e.g. poor spelling) as knowledge (Incompetence Program) to school-age children and give them low marks if they assert any other learning (Punishing Program). Some kids then ask their mom for help with their class work, only to be confused even more by her Circumvention and Confounder Programs. Meanwhile, an adolescent passionate about a career path that will lead to an average-income job is thwarted by her dad's Choice Commander Program ("This family has been and always will be about making money!").

These are everyday occurrences in the psychological lives of most kids. Mineral Stage caretakers abound, who offer children a sorry podcast of parenting—a robotic imitation that shuns, counters, or conquers spontaneous self-assertion and genuine *human* exchanges. Constant exposure to unending repetitions of insensitive, inane, maddening, and/or diabolical programming conditions these young ones to recoil from relationships, to numb their senses and sensibilities to maintain some semblance of sanity, and/or to dominate or brutalize others in an attempt to show their pain. Each programmed caretaker "plugs" children into his or her program, the approach/avoidance patterns of PTSD. As these once-robust and lively youngsters are pressed into a variety of rigid, mechanical movements, they psychologically fragment and freeze. They become machines programmed to perform: if A, then B ("If you meet someone you know, then you smile and say, 'Hello, nice to see you'" [whether you like them or not!]).

Also, interactions with electronic devices largely replace human parenting, teaching, and relationships in these children's lives. Exposed to processing rather than Our Rescuer's type of parenting, these "units of function" resize their lives to fit the Rock Virus Program and regress to the Mineral Stage of Development. The RV MALware has "proven" to the Mascrock that he is high-and-mighty and doesn't need any help. The Femrock, on the other hand, has "understood" that the viral program is all there is to her existence, so it should be cherished as is.

Listening Step Six: LISTEN TO THE DIFFERENCES BETWEEN OUR RESCUER AND THE ROCK

Differentiating viral programming (the Rock) from human experience and response (Our Rescuer) is similar to distinguishing between a lone computer screen image and the presence of a living, breathing, mature human being. Let's look first at what the desktop image and Rocks have in common. **The desktop image:**

1. Is extremely **limited in time and space.** It occupies one point in time, and it is **two-dimensional,** having height and width, but **no depth.** Unlike a living person, it has **no long-term perspective,** and it has **no real body or substance.** Rocks are similarly lacking in retrospection and foresight. They are superficial, without profundity, complexity, or diversity.

2. May have an attractive appearance and offer seemingly supportive sentiments, but it **lacks personal presence.** Even while on the screen, the computer image isn't there in any human sense—it has **no feelings and thoughts.** Both it and Rocks may use words and movements to communicate like human beings, but they remain **psychologically static,** unaltered by inputs that ask for new responses. If you install a picture of a woman reading Holy Scripture on the background of your desktop, will she ever evolve beyond imagery? Neither will a Rock.

3. Is a **caricature or simulation** of an original, **"performing"** as it has been programmed. Rocks' words and behavior are also based on indoctrination. They may mouth condolences ("I'm sorry about your loss.") or motion constructive action (such as sending disaster relief), but both are devoid of human consideration, concern, or will. As much as a desktop image may ask, "What

would you like me to do?" it can only "assist" you within the limits of its programming. Rocks also work within their programming. Their interactions reduce all fruitful human endeavors to fit the mechanized menus, programmed parameters, "fail-proof" formulas, and legalistic logs of the RV Program, all the while maintaining their glossy image.

4. May **say one thing** and yet **do the opposite**. The computer wizard icon may announce, "I'm here to help you!" and yet it works no magic. What Rocks say and what they do are usually in complete contrast, but programmed people don't notice.

5. Is **inflexible in perception.** An image cannot "look" at a situation from different angles and appreciate that every person's view may be based on some level of reality. You may be saying to yourself, "The desktop picture doesn't see!" Precisely! Its communication is not the result of its experience, but of its programming. As probability would have it, Rocks sometimes step into circumstances where their programmed words are exactly what someone wants or needs. More often, however, they fail to address wishes and *requirements*, and they are incapable of caring, just like the desktop image.

6. Is **oblivious of the world beyond the screen** or its place within that world. Likewise, Rocks are incapable of knowing their own condition or their place within the <u>OM</u>. Like the desktop image, they cannot alter themselves. They can only, at best, relay information about needed alterations to attentive human beings.

7. **Cannot negotiate irregularities, inconsistencies, or paradoxes**. Neither the image nor the Rock can grasp that humans, while very similar, are unique in their momentary wishes and needs. Spend some time expressing yourself to a favorite computer image. Tell it what a bad day you are having and what you'd like to hear from it in support. Can it alter its program or its response to you? Is it appreciative of your open communication and able to comply with your requests? *No!* So it is with the Rock.

When I was a young medical student, I arrived on the adult medicine ward at Charity Hospital early one morning. As was my routine, I picked up some yellow progress-note paper in the nursing station and strolled over to the nurse's tablet, where each patient's vital signs had just been recorded. I copied down the temperature, pulse, respiration rate, and blood pressure of my sickest patient, a very elderly Mr. Smith; they were all within normal limits. Soon, poking my head into the open door of his room, I found a phlebotomist drawing blood for his chemistry tests, so I checked another patient and returned to Mr. Smith a few minutes later. I was concerned as he did not look at all good. His coloring was a ghastly pale gray, and he seemed limp and lifeless. "Mr. Smith!" I called. "Mr. Smith, it's your medical student, Anne, here for your morning checkup. How are you today?" No response. He didn't appear to be breathing, so I listened to his lungs with my stethoscope—no breath sounds! I placed two fingers on his cool wrist—no pulse! I then palpated his carotid artery, thinking that its pulse would be impossible to miss…if it were there…nothing! "Oh, *no*! Mr. Smith!" The reality of the situation dawned on me, and I ran to find my resident, who was just down the hall. "It's Mr. Smith! Mr. Smith is…is dead! He's *dead*!" I stuttered on the import of the words. My resident, who knew Mr. Smith had DNR (do not resuscitate) status, grabbed the progress note I was clutching and looked at it. Laughing, he said, "Well, at least his vital signs are stable!"

Informed Consent

In medical school, I learned that physicians have to inform a patient ahead of time of the details of any procedure they want to perform, including the potential benefits and possible consequences.

Once fully informed, the patient has the right to agree to the procedure or refuse it. Similarly, to determine whether to accept or reject psychologically developmental procedures, we must have accurate and complete information.

We are not as we seem—individual bodies growing, reproducing, and then declining in a world of similar creatures and lesser life-forms and objects. These are but images on the "screen" of a mind that believes it can separate from its Wholeness, its Source, *and* has done so. These screen images must reflect the mind that perceives them, just as desktop images must express their programming. All our struggles with images, such as our fellowman, occur because we try to change or maintain images rather than realize that these are but "vital signs" of the "patient," the mind that believes in them. When we're listening, every aspect of our lives become like the progress notes written by medical students—they report the condition of each "patient." The *accuracy* of this information in relation to the "patient" is what's important, not the "goodness" or "badness" of the news, but do these "vital signs" truly represent his or her state of health?

Thus, the Rock's cold and callous, if not egregious, programming reveals how all of us as individuals operate: maintaining our privacy settings rather than acknowledging and serving our greater Being. We seek control. We lie and manipulate to get what "we" want. *And* we cause strife to the images on our "screen" as a result! When we experience the extreme RV programming in a Rock, we must begin to sense how detrimental our own "programs" are.

We might be more willing to submit to Our Rescuer's procedures to remove the RV programs from our minds if we knew the importance and practicality of her plans for us humans to progress in our development from imagery to Reality. Like Mr. Smith, imagery by itself is dead, so there *must* be some inanimate components (the Mineral Stage) to every individual psyche, as long as we're focused on images. Also, just as Mr. Smith could not answer my question, these inanimate components do not respond to imagery. They respond to the "programmer"—the mind that is holding them to its beliefs.

Image Will Always Be a Powerless Projection

A new PC comes with a preprogrammed desktop that is customizable with various toolbars, colorful pictures, icons, and lettering. The "computer" of the Rock Virus-infected mind is similar. The installed operating system points to an individual icon or character on the screen and says, "This is you," and the RV-infected mind "buys" it! We select properties and customize our image just enough ("I like to wear earth tones and hike in the mountains") that we are convinced of our autonomy. If we ever have doubts, the Virus directs our attention to the files of "*My* Computer," "*My* Pictures," "*My* Music," "*My* Documents," and so on, to reaffirm this "reality." Once the Virus has us convinced of "our" identity and "our" reality, we will defend it! Please spend some time observing Microsoft Publisher's Mr. Clipper or any favorite icon on your computer screen to assess how much life, wealth, power, prestige, and choice an image has.

To have informed consent for the decision before us, we must know that the purpose of desktop images is to offer information and guide us. They are constructive when this information helps with our computer work. If their offerings are irrelevant or confusing, they may be a nuisance. They may be cute, funny, or shaped like familiar objects, but like any imagery, they're neutral and will never *be* inherently good or bad, no matter how they might help and amuse us or hinder and annoy us. Our individual images are similar. Even with our very best efforts, our imagery can only inspire us to recollect what truly is instructive, good, and *alive*—our One Mind—so that we may turn to where these much-desired qualities can be found. *Given this information, would anyone really prefer to save these images and their limited work, space, and time on a "desktop" of our mind, when the OM is ever available to save our entire world?*

ENTER: OUR SCREEN SAVIOR—<u>Our Rescuer</u>:

1. Is **beyond time and space**, yet permeates both and uses both to draw our attention beyond them. She is not of this world, but is in this world only because we are.
2. Is **multifaceted** in having **unrestrained vivacity, bottomless depth, complete versatility, and endless creativity**.
3. Is an **original** who designs unique and individual development programs that **answer all questions** and **meet changing needs** over time.
4. Has perfectly **aligned words and actions to press our growth**.
5. Is **spontaneous, utterly flexible, and completely adaptable** in moving each body, heart, and mind, speaking to each part as well as our whole. She swiftly, *competently,* and HUMANLY responds to all requests for help.
6. Is **conscious in all parts, places, and times**, so she is able to slowly **direct our awareness** to the areas of our screen that we've been avoiding, thus expanding our consciousness.
7. Is the **IT expert** and *Living* search engine—only a being *fully* alive can *fully* return us to our human life. (Please understand that the Virus has used the Definition Lock Program to define itself as "<u>human</u>." To access more of our humanity, we must revert back to the original definition—made in the image of God.[8])

Security Alert!

When we truly comprehend the **STUPENDOUS** difference between an existence of image alone (the Rock) and life with Our Rescuer, our consent to Our Rescuer's interventions on our behalf makes perfect sense. Scanning for her within ourselves and on the "screen" becomes our new priority. She then directs us—from what "we" *want* to know: what happened, is happening, or will happen on the "screen," to what we *need* to know: how to enable the <u>Operating System</u> of Our Rescuer *and* monitor her operations WITHOUT interfering! She transforms our outdated, infected "HARD drive" and RV MALware using the compatibility mode—adapting our "computer's" functioning so it is compatible with and supportive of *human* life. Such modernization of our "equipment" would be quick and easy with Our user-friendly Rescuer, but her Way and her 3-D high resolution threaten our security as an image! As her presence increases the brightness of our "screen," we become transparent, and we notice the many fears lurking within us:

(1) **Our multiple traumatic experiences have taught us to rely on "our" self and "our" way** as the *only way* to survive. Depending on another and being told what to do may send us back to our abusive and neglectful childhood that we *don't* want to revisit.

(2) **We sense yet MORE "loss"**—the loss of our denial, sense of self, everything "we" have ever known or cared about, and so on. As long as memory serves us, the screen image has been our identity and contains our thoughts, feelings, and will. This "computer"-generated "reality" feels more comfortable than anything we imagine lies beyond, which *seems* foreign and SCARY! We've also

invested our lives in learning the ways of the world. To admit that the world is but imagery on the "screen" of our mind makes all of our achievements seem irrelevant or even a huge waste of our imaginary time.

(3) **We don't want to admit we've been wrong**—even duped! We've accepted the deception of the RV programs and the images they run that say, "You're a success!" or, "You're a good person!" (Partial Program—all individuals have areas where they are not "successful" or "good.") "Any 'bad guys' out there have nothing to do with you!" (Difference Drive). "Only when you isolate from them" (Delineation Drive), "control them" (COP), "or punish them for their deviance (Punishing Program) can you be free of *their* influence!" When we decrease the "contrast" on our "screen," and enlarge the picture, our differences blur. We may feel VERY wary and insecure as we realize these problematic people in our lives have been portraying aspects of our own personalities!

(4) **Our lives become *obviously* troublesome** as our awareness extends beyond its accustomed infant state. Every video game has a skill set, right? The increasing safety and ease of living when we choose Our Rescuer as game controller parallels an increasing level of difficulty and danger when we choose our images. These problems can make us even more fearfully focused on imagery (even hypervigilant!). We may seek help from the very people who are themselves immersed in the RV Program—it's hard to know whom to trust! Our Rescuer explains, however, that these increasing demands made on us are to stretch and develop us even more. And we MUST depend on her instruction to navigate them successfully. Noting her constant competence and our own *gross* incapacity reveals to us that WE DO NOT WANT "OUR" WAY!

(5) **We don't wish to feel our INTENSE emotions!** After all, we have indoctrinated the next generation with the life-damaging programs to which we have succumbed. We have thus further entrenched our mind in Rock Virus programming, drowning our heart in shame and guilt. In our pride, we've refused to admit how we've undermined our shared humanity and reduced our fellows to computerized versions of themselves or an inverted travesty (movie #3). Yet we're afraid of what the Rock Virus will "do" to us and our loved ones if we seek another server. I thought about how cheap my printer was to buy, but how costly it's been to supply with ink. Likewise, printing out imagery on the "copies" of our lives we pass around has been *grievously* EXPENSIVE!

(6) **"Audiovisuals" under the influence of the Rock Virus instill mistrust of genuine rescuers,** as they look or sound inferior, hostile, crazy, or helpless in comparison with us (Reality Reversal Program). As we seek Our Rescuer, a variety of disastrous pictures appears periodically on our "screens" to frighten us from this pursuit. These can get very personal, painful, and even potentially lethal. We may surmise that Our Rescuer is trying to harm us rather than prevent our "fatal error" of refusing this One outside the system and her "on-screen" rescuers. Our mistaking Her Window to Reality for our stored data is the source of our problems and the reason we approach her with such trepidation.

(7) **We also don't trust Our Rescuer because of past experiences**. We may have cried out for rescue many times in our lives and no *apparent* help arrived (what fit with our program). Or, as with Hurricane Katrina and then the Levee Disaster in New Orleans, our rescue was short-lived, a very slow and painful process, and/or accompanied by many casualties. These persistent, agonizing memories, unconsciously if not consciously retained, bring up seemingly unbearable feelings of abandonment, betrayal, rage, and heartache. "Where were you when I REALLY needed you?!" While valid from an "infant's" or young "child's" point of view, these tormenting memories only begin to make sense when we realize that our "lives" on the "computer screens" of our minds are not the point of our

existence. When our goal is a happy, healthy, and prosperous "desktop" image, we misinterpret the problems, traumas, and disasters that come our way. We perceive them and the *seeming* lack of help as "negative" or *against* "us" (our images) when they actually have "add-ons" *for* us. These crises alert us that when we choose imagery, we've chosen to leave our truly happy, healthy, and prosperous Life, Safety, and Help behind. In response, Our Rescuer offers a full menu of Life-sharing SOFTware.

The SOFTware of Our Rescuer: SO MUCH Gentler and Sweeter than the MALware of the Rock Virus!

From mere difficulties to outright disasters, our dilemmas can be seen as an antagonal prompt for a sane server—Our Rescuer. Here are some examples of Our Rescuer's infographic SOFTware, which is automatically launched and updated when we welcome Our Rescuer into our system:

Ad-ware Software: This software alerts us to what we are promoting with our lives: the Virus's preposterous, devastating, or terrorizing stories, which pop up continuously, or Our Rescuer's underlying call for our growth. These two choices, Rock or Rescuer, are like any other computer screen ads—something requiring our "yes" or "no" to proceed for "purchasing." The enduring advantage of "buying" Our Rescuer's survival Software is the latest and greatest in "computer" protection.

IREwall: This software restricts and ultimately extinguishes the wrath of our "inner Rocks," which are the first responders to Our Rescuer's ads within our system. This rage, which has solidified in the infuriating Virus programming, begins to shift and release in an increasingly nondestructive and then constructive manner. With the IREwall, whatever exploitation these Rock parts serve is bounced back on us, so we can personally experience our graphics-laden fortress and heavy psychological artillery and thereby learn to choose again.

Sighware: The RV's siphoning of our attention to its homepage and the many differences in the images we find there (Difference Drive) is brought to our awareness with this software. It takes our computer-generated encounters with Rocks, which our audio, video, smell, taste, touch, and *emotion* cards have made so experientially real and *PAINFUL*, to another Source. Rather than endlessly judging, reacting to, "reporting as junk," and then escaping what we perceive as unwanted, and thus separating from "them" (and parts of ourselves!), Sighware responds by making every frame inherently consistent. It is encrypted instant messaging from Our Rescuer calling us to return Home to our Wholeness. (What a relief!)

Antiviral Applications: Just as any computer virus needs another program in which to replicate itself, when we choose genuine, developmental living over RV programming, the Rock Virus must "die." This software assists in this process by slowing down or eliminating distracting and habitual "on-screen" activities and relationships, while adding those that will aid our leaving the "screen" for good. (When Virus sweeps are routine, our routines are swept away—we increasingly allow ourselves to be moved each moment by Our Rescuer!) Also, every RV program is removed by altering it into enlivening correlates that encourage flexibility, breadth, and depth in our interpretation and response to programming, whether external or internal. For example, the Editorial Override Program, which we've been using to plagiarize, distort, and defame Our Rescuer's "files," may instead reformat our characters, erase our flaws, and correct the mistakes we've made. The Translation Matrix can convert the physical realm back into psychological content, so we can perceive the workings of our minds and make necessary changes.

The Cookie Jar: "Cookies" are sweet morsels of psychological nutrition from Our Rescuer (tweets of Reality!) that make their home in our "computer" system and register what we are doing, underneath what we *appear* to be doing. These tasty and satisfying "cookies" whet our genuine appetite for truth. They turn our "computer" into a secure container that has the potential to jar us from RV mind control: our programmed perceptions, behaviors, emotions, and thoughts. We then auto-fill a Whole new way of experiencing as we maximize this moment's window full-screen to our One UNLIMITED Mind!

The Trojan Horse Corral: This "Trojan horse" is the grand image of Our Rescuer. When we run this picture on our "screens," it shapes all desktop images into rescuers that won't go away until their rescuing task is complete. Whomever or whatever we need, whether to stand against the Rock Virus or stand with us in our awakening, appears on the "screen." This transformation gives us enough confidence and trust to erase the hard drive of our individual existence, lay down our programmed weaponry, and stop fighting ourselves. With the "wild horses" of our imagination now corralled in our One Mind, we remember that everything in our world has been merely a rumination!

OUR POWER RETURNS!

The idea of having power as an image is pure fantasy, and as we wean ourselves from imagery, we lose this appearance of power. Our lives no longer work in the traditional manner, and we feel powerless! "Plugging in" to Our Rescuer, allowing her SOFTware into our system and her data in our files, is our only option if we want true power. When the enormity of her power is *known* as the energy source of our experience, the removal of the Virus and all its MALware from the computerized minds that believe it is "their" nature and "their" life becomes as simple as admitting this greater Being.

This very real threat to the Rock Virus is why someone under the influence of the RV programs is hateful to children, who are brutalized and indoctrinated into believing that the powerless Virus identity is their own. These programmed ones teach every child that certain images are DEADLY, while others are essential for life, so he or she can be threatened with death, assured sustenance, or otherwise maneuvered by those who vie for the illusion of power by controlling him or her.

Our Rescuer reMINDs us that our freedom lies in finding the Character and Characteristics of our undivided Self surging powerfully through all imagery—how energizing! Contrary to the assertions of programming, our interference with this surge (not the images themselves!) is what causes imagery to shock, injure, or kill us. Just as we can be harmed by sticking metal objects into wall outlets, so is tampering with the power of our united Identity foolhardy! However, the benign nature of Self manifests increasingly the more we surrender to it. The "surge protectors" within our "Second Life" computer fantasies are then no longer "necessary" as we flow in Our Rescuer's charge.

ENTER: The Middleman—Our Mind's Ability to Choose

With the powerful, ever-present help of Our Rescuer and her effective SOFTware programs, why is the Rock Virus within our systems? The *only* reason is that we still cherish our individual identity over our true Self ("access denied!")—our individuality *is* the Virus! Also, as with our computers, running a lot of "graphics" on our "screen" leaves us little space for anything else, such as thought. Yet, even when we *are* well informed, we continue to choose imagery over Reality. Why?

Unfortunately, our attempts to restore our system to Our Rescuer trigger the "security" alarms of the Rock Virus, which complicate her Recovery Disk's operations. The RV in our system works through memory to repeatedly remind us of "who we are" and have been as an image, the extent of which will be exposed if we continue with Our Rescuer's course. The Virus has accumulated folders of evidence to "prove" just how minuscule, worthless, problematic, and even despicable we've been at times, much of which we're not aware of! The RV enslaves us through b-mail (short for blackmail)—threatening to expose our selves to "us!" These hidden "folders" hold what we've withheld from our awareness to maintain our fantasies and sense of power, superiority, sanity, or specialness. The extensive "files" within them contain volumes of data, from unpleasantries to sheer horror: incriminating logs that don't align with our chosen images. What's been said and done to us that did align, but led to a crash in the end, are also recorded. So many times we've been fooled by appearances or have fooled others. There are "pages and pages" of what we should have said but didn't, as well as what we shouldn't have said but did. There are "CDs" and "floppy disks" (yeah—*old* stuff) containing our genuine feelings of grief, rage, terror, remorse, hatred, jealousy, and even unrealized love. (There must be no distractions from programmed feelings, behaviors, and words!) There are megabytes of our weaknesses, failures, cruelties, and shirking of our duties to our fellowman and ourselves. These EXTENSIVE "write-protected" *documents*, stored under the label "my humanity," take up tremendous amounts of space on our hard disks. The Virus sends thumbnail reports of these *human* "errors" if our loyalty to its Program wavers. Our conscious mind barely notices these RV subroutines, but we usually snap back to "our" well-beaten path of programming—the alternative *seems* too scary!

All of us Program users have ineffable self-reproach and self-loathing buried deep in our unconscious minds. Hidden among these difficult feelings is the part of our mind that has owned the Virus Identity (a <u>Rock part</u>!). This part is convinced that "it" is indeed reprehensible, and "it" has acted on this conviction with gusto, believing this is who "it" is—there is no choice (this typically unconscious belief is behind every Rocky front). Our vexation with this part of ourselves keeps us focused on image control—attacking or rejecting those who discover our condition or changing our settings to find people who will go along with our text. Rather than face the truth about ourselves and feel the devastating self-abasement, we usually return to "our" multiple-hit web page of denial and the limited but much less threatening material we've posted there.

However, we need not succumb to hopelessness and despair, as every moment of our lives and every aspect of our image, including all our lost talents and capacities, are chronicled on "rewritable DVDs"—EVERYTHING can be recovered and rewritten with Our Rescuer's help! She reminds us that our individual identities are part of a "computer" simulation that *will* change as we align with her and allow *her* picture on our user's account. The b-mail material in our mind is not a product of our inherent nature, but our choice of movie—we can choose again! When we select Movie #1, we discover that our Rock parts have had a useful purpose—getting us to troubleshoot ourselves and seek help outside our system.

Wireless Networking: Our selection of the Rock Virus (i.e., individuality and independence) is the way into the RV system. Our tendencies toward control ("MY" way), manipulation (I can *prove* "my" way works by ignoring contrary information and sabotaging other ways), and strife (You can't make me go "YOUR" way!) maintains it. Fortunately, this operation of separating from Self could not be completed. Thus, the way out of our system merely requires new choices and new ways of being with others ("OUR" Way!). Networking with other "computers" under the guidance of Our Rescuer, sharing her helpful SOFTware while avoiding further infection from the RV MALware, is how we end our imagined separation. The stored files that reveal the devastating truth about "MY" way in all our images serve to motivate us to search for her Way. Like random access memory, her Life experiences are not stored in a linear or sequential fashion. Like our own, they are found in bits and pieces throughout everyone and everything on the "screen."

Engaging the nascent rescuer in each human image creates a technologically advanced "modem" for "online" connection with Our Rescuer. Expert help then becomes ever available to remove the corruption of our self from our "files." For example, where one aspect of my "computer" is frozen with RV programming, my neighbors may have the latest in "antiviral SOFTware." Whether we realize it or not, such system-freeing content "downloads" the moment we desire it. When we interface with such a therapeutic broadband network, our "computers" become increasingly high tech, fast, functional, and versatile in routing and serving the human being (not the other way around!). We also become increasingly relaxed and unguarded about the wide range of "emoticons" forever floating across the "screen."

Password: Transferring our lives from our own *apparent* control to our users' Guide, Our Rescuer can seem terrifying. The reality we've known breaks down, revealing unknown startling or frightening aspects of ourselves and others. We can feel like we're losing our mind! Having identified with the RV programs, we experience threat to "ourselves" and "our" will when Our Rescuer, without asking our permission, closes "programs" for our protection. When we're attached to our "computer's" imagery, this can be very stressful! This stress often gets worse before it gets better. Know that new, healthier "programs" will be "downloaded" into our system when we are ready for them. In the meantime, Our Rescuer is the password that opens up *The Way* beyond the boot of our programming. She is the cleanup wizard who initiates the "defragmentation" that ultimately brings the "deleted" bits and pieces of ourselves and our lives back. She is also the Publisher who holds the ultimate location of every background picture (remember my computer club meeting?) within our One Mind!

Our Rescuer works diligently with the foreground and background of our "screens" and the hardware and software of our "computers" to delete the Rock Virus. As we scan the now-illuminated painful backgrounds of our images, we become aware of the Rockware (and Rock wear) that has dominated our lives (the Memory Stick [OUCH!]). Without adequate preparation, we're likely to drag this newly conscious material back into the "recycle bin" of our unconscious mind. However, if we do, we condemn ourselves to less "memory," slower "processing," and limited SOFTware. (The job Our Rescuer asks of us requires much more memory than is available to us as an image!) When we scan for Our Rescuer, she reveals the "backup files" on all the "lost" data about our true Identity, reminding us that only the virtual memory of this unlimited Self is real. *And* when we follow this Live stream of Movie #1, we discover it's not memory—"It's" ALIVE!

The teacher entered the room and informed me that the school was closing and I should finish soon. Immersed in my word-processing program, I had lost track of time. For the past few hours, I had forgotten there was a world outside my writing or a person beyond my thoughts. As I sat pondering, I realized why some people are more attached to their computers than to the people in their lives. I had spent the day without any fighting, yelling, back talk, harsh judgments, nasty looks, condescension, shunning, or disaster reports. The words I typed with the keyboard remained as entered. They weren't manipulated to mean other than what I had intended and then passed around as though they were my own. The day had been quiet, peaceful, and without confrontation. Although there is a world of programmed people crying out with their dysfunctions, sometimes we just want peace...

As I lay in bed that night "chatting" with Our Rescuer, I continued to think about the spell-check suggestions offered by PCs before sending e-mail—not unlike the changes made by the "computer" systems of our minds. Just as our computer gives us a choice of whether to accept or reject these offerings, we too have choice. We can choose the Live, Life-streaming "Movie" of our OM, as personified in Our Rescuer, or we can choose the copy in one of its many virus-infected forms.

In my experience, we do everything we know to keep our computers functioning. If they malfunction, we then do everything we can think of to unfreeze them and get them running again *ASAP*. If we fail, we call a "nerd" or a "geek." Yet regarding the areas of our psyches that are infected and even frozen with RV programming, we don't take emergency measures, nor do we usually seek professional help. Tragically, the Rock Virus Program has us cherishing these "computers" and modernizing and maintaining their programming, rather than servicing the human system within our mind. Perhaps when we value such external devices and their functioning more than our own lives, we do indeed become like them. However, when we esteem our <u>unlimited Mind</u> and its expression in our shared humanity, everything else fades into the background. Our world then shows the warmth, friendliness, concern, and help that come naturally to maturing human beings.

As drowsiness descended on me, I pictured my desktop images absorbed by the intensity of the illumination behind them. The inner parts of the entire system then came into view. As they gained connection, flexible movement, warmth, color, and choice, they slowly coalesced and grew, ultimately forming a human being. I recognized her as the cheerful New Orleans librarian who gave me my first computer lesson. She was smiling, mouse in hand. As she nodded her head in approval, I nodded off to sleep.

FORUM: Have a Chat with the Characters from Each of the Three Movies within You

1. Consider which aspect of your psychology corresponds to each part of your computer, and draw a diagram that illustrates this. What might any recent computer problem be communicating to you about your heart and mind? How might the protective measures you use on your computer aid you in securing your *human* psychology?

2. When are you open (1) and when closed (0)? What is this binary language communicating to you?

3. How do you give images power that they don't have?

4. Are you aware of the three movies playing within your "computer" system—the expressions of our One Mind, our individual selves, and RV programming? Document these with video footage,

photos, clip art, etc. Then make three films *or* create three scrapbooks on your computer. Which of the three do you prefer?

5. Which RV programs might be found in the following?
    a. "These reports about the New Orleans Superdome during and after Hurricane Katrina are greatly exaggerated. There were merely four deaths, only one of which was violent. The lack of available food and water was for the very good reason to encourage people to leave after the storm was over. All of the 'man's inhumanity to man' stuff never happened. I know because I read it in the paper."
    b. "We didn't have the money to build proper levees, so the levees breached in the storm, flooding 80 percent of our city. The resulting destruction will cost billions of dollars to repair. We don't have the money to rebuild proper levees..."
    c. Consider the fiasco in rescuing survivors of the New Orleans Levee Disaster. Are any of these programs impeding your rescue?

6. Practice noticing the RV programs in your daily life and keep a journal of your findings. Just as you can use any software program constructively or destructively, how can you tweak your most frequently used RV programs (or those you most frequently experience in others) to enhance your relationship with Our Rescuer?

7. Notice the Internet sites you surf and ponder what you might learn about yourself and Self through them.

8. Make a plan for exchanging the high memory usage of your individual identity for the Memory of our One Mind. How will this increase your performance? How will your life look when the OM replaces your imagery as the power source? Find a picture that represents this, your future, and put it on your computer's desktop.

Please note: Someone who spends most of his time in front of a computer monitor may be attempting to remind himself of his true Identity as the person at the "keyboard"—*not* a "special" image on the screen trying to "block this threat." Also, as you save your work, remember that saving yourself is far more critical!

---

[1] Samuel Butler, *Hudibras*, Part II, Canto I, ll, 839-44.

[2] National Children's Alliance, "Child Abuse: A National Epidemic," Child Abuse Statistics, *Family and Children's Services of Clark County,* May 2012, http://www.clarkdjfs.org/family-children/national-child-abuse-statistics.html.

[3] "Hundreds of firefighters who volunteered to help rescue victims of Hurricane Katrina have instead been playing cards, taking classes on FEMA's history, and lounging at an Atlanta airport hotel for days while they await orders." Greg Bluestein, Associated Press Writer, "Firefighters Stuck in GA Awaiting Orders," *Nation,* posted 9/7/2005, http://www.usatoday.com/news/nation/2005-09-07-firefighters-ga-katrina_x.htm.

[4] Louisiana School Board Financial Burden Prohibition Amendment 9SLS 06RS-815 ENGROSSED Pages 2-3, Regular Session, 2006, SENATE BILL NO. 296 By Senator Quinn and Representative Toomy, accessed August 14, 2012, http://www.google.com/url?sa=t&source=web&cd=3&ved=0CEwQFjAC&url=http%3A%2F%2Flegis.s tate.la.us%2Fbilldata%2Fstreamdocument.asp%3Fdid%3D378810&ei=IV4pUMv0FaS30AHktoG4DA&usg=AFQjC NEq9gLhZLaqqn3ttDQD7SmalC5Z0Q.

[5] "All of the post-Katrina investigating teams were initially baffled by the almost universal, and, in some cases, quite substantial deficiencies between the elevation of levee protection specified in the designs and what was actually discovered when earthen levee crest and floodwall heights were surveyed after the storm." *Design Elevation of Protective Structure, Chapter Five—Was the Level of Protection Incorporated in Designs Adequate?,* accessed August 5th, 2012, http://www.dotd.louisiana.gov/administration/teamlouisiana/Team%20Louisiana%20-%20Part%20II,%20chap%205.pdf, 116.

[6] O'Brien then said to Brown, "FEMA's been on the ground four days, going into the fifth day, why no massive air drop of food and water... in Banda Aceh, Indonesia, they got food drops two days after the tsunami." Michael Brown, Federal Emergency Management Agency, "Criticism to Government Response to Hurricane Katrina," *Wikipedia,* accessed August 26, 2012, http://en.wikipedia.org/wiki/Criticism_of_government_response_to_Hurricane_Katrina#Department_of_Homeland_S ecurity.

[7]Roger Highfield, "DNA survey finds that all humans are 99.9pc the same," *The Telegraph,* posted Dec. 20, 2002, http://www.telegraph.co.uk/news/worldnews/northamerica/usa/1416706/DNA-survey-finds-all-humans-are-99.9pc-the-same.html.

[8] George M. Lamsa, *Holy Bible from the Ancient Eastern Text* (New York, New York: A.J. Holman Company, 1957), Genesis 1:27, 8.

Chapter 7

Business

Image Succeeds at the Expense of Our Humanity

(Again, read slowly, taking breaks frequently to feel and think about the contents and not be overwhelmed.)

I woke up in the middle of the night, drenched in sweat, my heart pounding. I'd had a disturbing dream in which Effie and I were wandering around the second floor of my mother's house in New Orleans. I showed her the flood line in the now-moldy walk-in closet—about four feet up, just enough to soak all my clothing in putrid floodwater. Effie placed a firm hand on my shoulder and remarked, "This business of cutting corners by our officials is costing us all dearly!" I shook off the dream and yanked back the wet, clammy top sheet. I was wide awake, my whole body aching with sorrow. My city felt like a relative I loved dearly. I couldn't relax, knowing the nightmare she was going through and the suffering of the "children" she once held in her arms. Time stood still as I lay awake grieving…

I arose late morning. Effie was sprawled on the couch with Dr. Bear on top of her belly, rising and falling with her breath. As Dr. Bear attended to his patient, Effie gazed at a news program on TV. I soft-boiled a couple of eggs, unplugged the refrigerator from the generator just long enough to plug in the toaster oven for two pieces of toast, and then sat down to eat my breakfast in front of the TV. Panelists were discussing the antics of city, state, and national officials regarding the New Orleans storm and flood.

As the facilitator questioned if anything could have been done better(!), my flabbergasted mind retreated to a seminar I had taken in July for people seeking to start their own business. To my surprise, the speaker had announced, "The most important thing in business is *not* making money or providing a service, as most people think—it is actually valuing the customer."[1] This speaker from my past answered the question just posed by the TV discussion facilitator: yes, many things would have been done better if valuing the citizens had been top priority.

I began mulling over the many people I knew who were highly successful in business but greatly handicapped in the arena of personal relationships. This incapacity didn't make sense to me, given that the skills needed for success in both fields are the same—networking with the goal of mutual benefit. I jogged to my bedroom to retrieve my journal and then again settled myself in the La-Z-Boy.

EVACUATION DAY SEVEN: *The Business of Relationship*

Successful businesspeople listen to their customers to discover what they need or want. They ask specifically what is required and when, how, and to whom it should be delivered. They honor those requests if possible. When a customer is not satisfied, reputable businesspeople listen to the complaint and correct the problem. They want each customer to be happy, because a satisfied customer returns and refers others, helping the business thrive and grow.

Successful personal relationships are no different. They require thoughtful listening, questioning, and willingness to meet another's needs and wants, at times forgoing our own. They demand an acceptance of criticism, as well as appropriate and timely responses from us. In this way, we expand our mental, emotional, and behavioral repertoires while assisting the other with his or her expansion. We desire that our relationship partners be content because genuinely happy people radiate joy and inspire their companions. Healthy relationships are essential to the business of psychological development.

Why is it then that many people develop competency in business interactions but fail miserably in their personal lives (or vice versa)? How can people adapt to a rapidly advancing technological market or make sacrifices for their company's survival during times of economic uncertainty and yet insist that their spouse and children do all the adapting and sacrificing at home? Somewhere along the line, they learned to prioritize business over family. They welcomed training, practice, and hard lessons at work while shunning these challenges at home. The binary system in their computerized minds may have imposed different programming for each setting. For example, a man may trust a customer to ask for what she wants, but when his wife asks, he assumes she has ulterior motives or that her likes mirror his. Perhaps a woman clings to her husband's words ("I am happy with our marriage"), unaware that his actions speak more honestly (he rarely spends quality time with her). When listening to kids, an "adult" often discounts their perceptions and interpretations because they are younger and less experienced ("What do they know about life?"). How have we veered so far off course in regard to mutual respect?

There was once a time when we were all able to rest comfortably in someone's arms for an extended period, receiving what was given without opposition or second-guessing its relevance or the giver's intent. We even allowed our caregiver to make changes to improve our situation without complaint. As infants, we depended on others to provide the essentials of life and guard our safety. We instinctively reached for them, expressing ourselves and our needs without restraint. Doing so enabled our growth. In a healthy environment, this openness, expressiveness, and receptivity remain a part of us as we mature. We access these qualities when we're in need and when we're with nurturing individuals.

Commonly, however, trauma alters this built-in ability. Years of being socialized, schooled, and subjected to unpleasant and even downright horrible experiences redirect normal children. They then enter physical adulthood standing apart, often lording over those who are physically younger. They are rigidly discriminating in their receptivity and reject change. They are walled off from feeling and its expression—their minds distracted with "I've only got a minute because I have something really important to do!" The "nourishment" or gain offered by fellowship with others is deemed of lesser value than that gleaned from business activities: making "to do" lists (Cedric came to mind), scheduling meetings, dictating the next report, or keeping up with professional journals (my journaling came to mind). They become so externally absorbed that they are not aware of human assets, their own or others', or they've forgotten how to share them. They have also lost that basic human trust we all have as infants; they extend it to only a limited few (those "like them"), and/or they paradoxically attempt to derive their sustenance from the inhuman.

Preoccupations, busyness, and the "love" of objects that entrap the average person show that Mineral Stagers have made a lasting impression on our culture (how many people risked their lives attempting to protect their property during Hurricane Katrina?!). Rocks and Minerals have redirected our intense, innate interest in people and our deep need for human contact and interaction into an independent drive to get ahead. They have sidetracked our natural reception of what we need into consumption and secondary ambition.[2] They have taught us to rank ourselves according to our material goods and resources and to demean those with fewer possessions ("They need to pull themselves up by their own bootstraps and work hard like the rest of us!"). Rocks have also reduced our pleasure in camaraderie and cooperation, promoting instead a compulsion for "self"-sufficiency or competition, where we exclude or use others in our attempts to succeed.

Once we are familiar with the three movies in each individual's mind—the One of Unlimited Mind, the copy, and the inverted copy—we can identify which is being projected or acted out at any given time. We begin to recognize where each person assigns the characteristics or lead character of each film. For instance: "Unlimited Mind (Movie #1) makes me think of unlimited funds, so that's the Federal Reserve. The copy (movie #2) is my local bank, and the inverse (movie #3) is my dirt-cheap ex-husband who refuses to pay child support!" What happens when we confuse these movies? We create a lot of problems for ourselves *and* others! In the example just mentioned, what if this woman had, at the time of her marriage, seen her husband as the one with the unlimited funds?

Placing these three movies in the wrong contexts can be disastrous, which is precisely what happens with programming. We give inanimate objects (money, possessions) and inanimate people (Rocks and Minerals) our favorable projections, and we cast the unfavorable or unworthy projections on the more animate (human beings!). The invoice for our life thus becomes increasingly materialistic. Our humanity suffers greatly, as our possessions receive so much of our interest, care, and daily involvement, while building on and caring for our human qualities fall by the wayside. With such "currency" mismatches, we regress over time, engaging one another more and more as psychological babies. (A prime example is the professionally accomplished Cedric, who is oblivious to his family's emotional needs.)

Toward the end of the television program came a brief, sugar-coated synopsis of "what went wrong" in New Orleans before, during, and after Hurricane Katrina. As the credits rolled, Effie commented, "I see now that everyone really did their best." I nearly choked on my orange juice.

"Effie," I said gently, "do you realize how rare it is for *everyone* to do their best in any situation, and how few of us know what our best is, let alone pursue it? To me, your generality minimizes the heroic efforts of those who truly went out of their way to help. It also makes heroes out of those who don't deserve this label. Do you understand?" I asked with concern. When Effie didn't answer, I looked more closely and noticed from her slow breathing that she was already asleep. Wanting to be heard, I continued the discussion with my pen on the page.

ROCK SERVICES: Selling the HARD Life and the Impossibility of Human Relationships

Every Mascrock identifies with the first Movie (#1) while primarily acting out the third. He is in the business of promoting the Rock Virus Program and profiting greatly from the resulting disability and misfortune—this he considers to be doing his best! He cloaks this agenda in the form of a seemingly legitimate profession, institution, or public service, but a destructive derivative of the original that he runs like a business. Using market research, the Rock cloaks his primitive "products," whether they contain body toxins or toxic psychology. He adapts them according to current trends, making them seem new and exciting, ingenious and high-tech, sympathetic to your needs, or the best that money can buy. At some level, Rock businesses are always delivering products and/or actions that undermine our humanity and curtail its ever-so-natural reaching out and reaching back, all the while giving the Rock prosperity and a "respectable" reputation.

Let's look at some of the arenas in which Mineral Stagers have set up shop, as well as some of the Rock Virus programs they use to facilitate "their" work.

MINERAL MEDIA

Rock reporters filter events through RV programming (Filterware). They thus feed "facts" (Labeling Lock) that lead others to perceive newsworthy Mineral Stagers as upstanding citizens who merit their attention and respect. If viewers are not satisfied with a story, Rocks in the media use the Editorial Override Program to contrive another one or to generate a "public opinion poll" which "reveals" that the majority of people back these Mineral Stagers. If a distraction is required (Circumvention Program), another event is sensationalized into a major story. Rocks thus condition viewers to dismiss the actual facts about Rocks and Minerals that occasionally leak into the press— they'll come across as obviously exaggerated or made-up tales that some reporter concocted to get more viewers (Cubby Hole of the Difference Drive).

Rock media are manipulative—disposing the public to "their" way. For example, when the Reality Reversal Program is in use, crimes against humanity, such as an unwarranted invasion of a foreign land, seem like humanitarian aid ("Distraught citizens came to us in secret and begged us to intervene!"). Antiwar movements with hundreds of thousands of participants and other significant activities that go against Rock agendas are either ignored by the newspapers or given minimal lackluster coverage (the Confounder), perhaps a few lines on the back page ("A group of dissenters marched today..."). Meanwhile, in a community run by Rocks, the latest marriage of a movie star dominates the front-page report (Circumvention Program).

The Partial Program is another favorite of Rock reporters, who share only part of every story (not necessarily the factual parts)—for instance, announcing that "Teachers Are DEMANDING More Money" rather than highlighting the teachers' main agenda: better education for our children. The Contextual Warp is popular for making someone's situation-appropriate emotions, such as crying, seem freakish. Meanwhile, *highly* dysfunctional behaviors, such as delays in rescuing, are portrayed as perfectly normal ("Just following orders!") when the context of a life-threatening situation isn't mentioned. The Translation Matrix exploits the words and actions of human beings, while covering the tracks of those in the Mineral Stage.

The Definition Lock is also implemented consistently by Rock media. For example, "freedom of the press" means reporting only RV-sanctioned material. They tell us we live in a "free" country, rather than facilitate awareness and discussion of the various ways we are NOT free and what we might do to eliminate these shackles. Similarly, by linking with the Partial Program, "terrorism" has come to mean only the violence perpetrated by foreigners. Also, combining the Definition Lock with the Labeling Lock, Rocks' fictitious tales are given the misnomer "The News," which over time become "common knowledge," and those who take in and pass on such falsehoods are considered "well-informed."

A sausage commercial on television caught my eye. I was reminded of an acquaintance, Chris, who once recounted that she learned about our legal system from her father, a prominent lawyer in the community. "My dad said, 'There are two things the public should never witness being made—sausage and the law!' When I was young, I thought that the attorneys' gifts of persuasion brought truth to light for their client, and the client was punished or set free according to his or her guilt or innocence. As I grew older, I saw that the lawyers argued just as fiercely whether their clients were innocent or not, taking no account of justice or public welfare.

"One day, I was in an office where I overheard lawyers bargaining with judges and declaring, 'If you let my guy off, I'll do something for you.' There was an obvious class system. A poor black person in the wrong place at the wrong time was likely to be convicted. Verdicts favored upper-class whites, no matter how serious the crime. The system was based on who had money to pay them and who owed whom a favor. My dad was delighted when an opposing lawyer owed him something—that meant he would win some concession or even the case itself. My disillusionment with our legal system paralleled my disappointment in my father. I realized that they were both *corrupt*!"

The LEGAL Loophole

Rock lawyers employ our "civil" system (Labeling Lock) to protect themselves and their fellow Mineral Stagers, all the while APPEARING to safeguard the citizenry. They use the Confounder program and the legal formalities of advantageous laws, extensive documentation, incomprehensible contracts, approval by Rock "authorities," bureaucratic red tape, *and* office staff under the influence of the Stall program, to greatly delay, if not altogether stop, the enterprises of non-Rock endeavors. (Rocks easily work their system – what's wrong with you?) Legal proceedings are so abusive to non-Rocks that threatening to sue is all a Rock need do to make victims cower in submission to outlandish demands. Unlike so many Rock activities, these tactics are all perfectly "legal"!

Within the Rock's criminal "justice" system, innocent people can be arrested and jailed on circumstantial evidence or none at all. "Clues" are planted wherever needed to sway the jury in the desired direction (Editorial Override Program). Minor offenders have their charges reduced or eliminated if they commit to the Program. And the programmed, whether Rock actors and actresses or fellow inmates, are used as "witnesses" to incriminate the chosen fall guy (Delineation Drive) and discredit those brave enough to testify against Rock cronies. Of course, a "criminal" confession facilitates the process, so Rock investigators use manipulation, if not force (Punishing Program*)*, to "encourage" this outcome. If the person is not as intelligent, well educated, or well-spoken as those who are prosecuting him, he may be tricked into saying or doing what makes him APPEAR guilty. (The more he is manhandled, the more nervous he gets—and nervousness is PROOF of guilt, is it not?) The Mineral Stagers' predilection for hurting children and training them to hurt others and refuse help generates hidden pain and deep-seated guilt in people, whom Rock prosecutors can then skillfully maneuver to win their cases (Arguing Analog).

Testimony and evidence are superfluous when you "know" someone is guilty. To "prove" it to the "unknowing," however, Rocks use the Translation Matrix to interpret all events in such a way to mesh the condemned person's history with the crime scene, persuading court participants toward the predetermined verdict (Control Option Program). The conviction is what counts! Even in cases where the defendant truly *is* guilty, the penalties decreed by the Rock judge can be so SEVERE that the jurors feel guilt-ridden when asked to choose (Choice Commander) a sentence of either "innocent" or "guilty" (notice the binary choice!). The hardened, premeditated criminal and the easier-torehabilitate one who made a bad decision in a weak moment may receive similar punishments (Delineation Drive).

My mind wandered to my jury duty days when I learned about a middle-aged New Orleanian with no criminal or drug history who was found with a piece of crack cocaine the size of a breadcrumb in his pocket. The defense stated, "It was so small that the man who checked his pockets could easily have planted it!" Nevertheless, he was sentenced to five years in prison for possession with intent to sell. In contrast, I thought about those who chose to build defective levees, causing the deaths of *so many* people and the suffering of SO MANY more. These miscreants are roaming free, with no consequences for their actions.

When the accused is a Rock crony, many difficulties "arise" during the court proceedings. Police "forget" to take photographs, gather evidence, or talk to witnesses, or they "neglect" to bring evidence to trial (*if* they remember to go). Evidence may be "lost" (Deletion Program) or lost to the court because of failure to follow protocols. Such complicated transactions (the Confounder) that take MANY years to negotiate (the Stall) tire the prosecutor's client, the supporting family, and witnesses to such a degree that they become more interested in concluding the case than in justice being served. Also, lifelong criminals can be let off instantly by a breach of procedure (failure to read the Miranda Rights), a loophole in the law, the statute of limitations on lawsuits, an overturning by City Council, or a pardon. Rocks rely heavily on the Incompetence Program to swing the verdict "their" way.

Rocks believe that "truth" is whatever they can best defend (Definition Lock), so Rock lawyers use the Arguing Analog to fight furiously, spinning information around so quickly and repeating their assertions so loudly and frequently that a traumatized victim, retraumatized by the proceedings, may no longer display clarity or certainty of the details of the crime. Mineral Stage "experts" are also employed to reinforce the Rock's case and cast doubt on the plaintiff. As the Rock defense is so keen to destroy hard evidence, the case often concludes with "your word" (confused) against the defendant's (polished), and the Rock defendant is "absolutely sure" about "his" testimony!

As far as their criminal activities are concerned, Rocks are innocent until PROVEN guilty, but anyone who accumulates evidence will have evidence accumulated against him or her (the Overexposure weapon from the Punishing Program). "Documentation" may be easily manufactured with modern technology (inserting any face onto another body with computer graphics, for example). Rocks may also generate more foolproof "evidence" by drugging a person just long enough to get some compromising video footage—with the latest in pharmacology, that person won't even remember it the next day! Testifying against Rocks can be treacherous or even deadly. Most people would rather avoid their own incrimination, even at the cost of setting the Rock free. When Mineral Stagers are enforcing the law, "due process" is elusive and fraught with difficulties. Defending innocents like our children becomes a time-consuming, drawn-out, and uphill battle.

In contrast to Rock "adults," kids who break the law are shown no mercy by the Rock "justice" system ("ZERO tolerance!"). They are swiftly locked into detention centers, where they're subjected to more of the abuse and neglect to which their antisocial actions are a testimony. Rocks don't consider the dysfunctional families these juveniles come from or the traumas they've endured (Thumbnails). Rocks insist, "We don't have money for the psychotherapy of delinquents." Paradoxically, they do have funding for the extended and repeated incarcerations of these untreated juveniles who habituate to "prison life" and inevitably learn the life of crime from fellow inmates—a *much* higher price tag for society and taxpayers in the long run (Reality Reversal). While these untreated convicts return again and again to jail, their victims also have many trials—returning again and again to hospitals, clinics, and mental-health facilities and/or becoming juvenile delinquents and then criminals themselves. When upholding the letter of the law (and Rocks' rebuttal of our humanity) is more important than caring for our community's children and our "inner kids," the "justice" system of the Mineral Stage prevails.

Pebble Theatrics (Rocks in Pediatric Medicine)

The Rocks who have escaped the criminal justice system are free to commit atrocities toward children. Healthy children naturally cry out or act out in their distress, and concerned parents take them to their pediatrician for evaluation. When these doctors are Rocks, their Feedback Loop kicks in, and the child's pain is not noticed, let alone acknowledged and soothed. In the first act of this Rock play, these kids' stress reactions are associated with typical events of childhood and therefore not cause for worry *or* further investigation (Editorial Override). In conjunction with the Labeling Lock, descriptions such as "colic," "the demanding baby," "teething," "the high-needs child," or "separation anxiety" are used to explain away the symptoms of the traumatized infant whose basic biological needs are not being met ("I'm sure if you change her formula, she'll stop her screaming"). Children who behave particularly immaturely because of stress are considered "late bloomers" or "developmentally delayed." ("Males have always matured slowly in our family.") Victims of abuse who flee in fear from childhood, rushing to act an age well beyond their years, are praised as "exceptional," "gifted," or "such a fine young man (or lady)!"

Rock pediatricians fashion any number of reasonable-sounding excuses to pacify parents: "Your child is just overly sensitive." "She's probably adjusting to her new sibling (new school, new house, death in the family, and so on)," "Growing pains can manifest with any number of uncomfortable symptoms," or "Adolescent angst can make a teen act strangely." A boy's relentless harassment of his sister (deliberately knocking her down, lying about her, and doing things that cause her obvious pain) is framed as, "He's merely being a boy!" while his sister, the "critic," is labeled a "drama queen." In this manner, Rock pediatricians teach parents to ignore their children's real-life pantomime—expressing their very real feelings about the abuse and neglect they suffer.

My mind drifted back to a day in my pediatrics residency. We had just finished rounds on a child-abuse survivor in the hospital when my staff doctor recounted a case from his residency days: "Darryl was a physically healthy infant in the well-baby clinic. A few doctors had suspected child abuse because he reacted so strongly to physical touch. Those in authority counseled us not to dig unless there was substantial evidence, since such allegations can be 'very hurtful' to parents, who might then bad-mouth or sue the hospital. Proof came when Darryl's hysterical mom brought him to the emergency room after his father threw him down the stairs. Between sobs, she finally admitted that her husband could be 'a bit rough' with their sons, 'but…I never dreamed he would actually harm Darryl!'" (A typical Femrock!) "Darryl's dad was jailed, his mother disappeared, and his five-year-old brother, David, was moved to a foster home. Darryl was admitted to the hospital and discharged to foster parents several months later. He now had profound mental retardation with several severe physical impairments. He died of an infection shortly before his third birthday."

I heard in my staff doctor's poignant tone that this long-ago tragedy still moved him. As he peered into my eyes, he affirmed, "We must never assume that a parent will care for his or her child in a consistently loving way. Even if parents have good intentions, psychology is such a powerful force that if their inner business is *not* in order, it *will* impair their honorable pursuits at home and in the community." His stare intensified as he warned me, "Never underestimate the power of psychology—in your patients…their families…your colleagues…*and* in yourself!"

After work that day, a friend of mine mentioned a therapist she was seeing, and I asked for the phone number. I set up an appointment for the following week. Darryl's brief life had taught at least two physicians to take themselves and everyone else more seriously.

Young parents, like Darryl and David's folks, are often insecure in their parenting due to their lack of self-knowledge, their inexperience, and the scarcity of support in raising their kids. The Rock pediatrician rushes to their "aid," setting the stage with his own experience—the RV Program. He informs parents that rearing children is risky business—like investing in a start-up company—"even if you do everything right as a parent (Thumbnail), there is no telling how your kids will turn out." He assures them that personality is inherited through their genes (Partial Program), so any difficulty these tender creatures *may* have endured (the Sure to Possible Shunt of the Translation Matrix) is only significant when their biological makeup predisposes them to experiencing it as traumatic (Editorial Override).

So, in the second act, these Rock docs go to great lengths to spin the very real suffering of children into a melodrama where the kids' guardians (YAY!) are cast as the innocent "good guys" (movies #1 and #2). Meanwhile, the children who are depending on, looking up to, imitating, and otherwise learning from these caretakers (including movie #3) are labeled as problematic. (After all, *they* have the troubling symptoms [BOO!], and *they* don't pay the doctor bills!) The Rock pediatrician uses the Labeling Lock on kids who express their grievances—they are "overreacting," "attention-seeking," "manipulative," or "chemically imbalanced" (chronic stress does change our biochemistry). To their violent acting out, the Rock doc calmly remarks, "Curious children absorb the crime programs on TV like sponges and experiment with viewed behaviors." Meanwhile, these children's actual agonizing circumstances (beatings, molestations, rapes, emotional incest, programming, etc.) and the Rocks who perpetrate them are never endorsed as real—except in families of certain ethnic groups or lower socioeconomic classes. In my public hospital experience, poor children were diagnosed as victims of sexual assault, while wealthy parents were given comforting euphemisms and less shameful diagnoses—such as urinary tract infections—for their molested children. (Does this diagnosis really explain why a depressed child begins thrashing and screaming when physicians gently examine her private parts?) Published statistics can reflect these biases, making certain groups of people *appear* to be more harmful to children than are others.

I remembered meeting nine-year-old Manny, who was referred for hyperactivity to the pediatric clinic where I was working. My staff doctor and I went through the ADHD (attention deficit/hyperactivity disorder) checklist with Manny's mom, and sure enough, he had the majority of symptoms. When I was left alone with Manny, I asked him, "Why do you move around so much after school?" His reply was stunningly frank (most kids are not so forthcoming). "When my dad gets home from work, he beats me with his belt. I know what's going to happen so I'm really nervous—I can't sit still! It really hurts!" As Mom returned with my staff doctor with a prescription for Ritalin and some free samples, she inquired about the availability of government financial aid, since her son had a "psychiatric condition."

These kids *are* considered victims—not of their caretakers' Rock parts, but of secondary villains (Hiss!): from faulty genes to distorted thinking, biological to behavioral abnormalities, lactose intolerance to junk-food indulgence. Inadequate and/or destructive parenting is overlooked in favor of *heroically* "helping" these "oppressed" parents (YAY!) adjust to their "misfortune" in having a defective child—*they* are offered sympathy, support groups, Rock doc-approved pamphlets, encouraging books, and even sometimes government money. These parents are never confronted about their mistakes or the harm they are inflicting on their children. Also, when their "inner children" are angry, depressed, fearful, aggressive, self-destructive, incapable, delusional, and so forth, their outer children will mirror this for them and act out their pain. The Rock doc doesn't assist parents in discerning the reality behind the scenes—they are abusing and neglecting their children because of their own unresolved issues. Instead he helps kids to "understand" their parents—they are "overworked," "overstressed," and "doing the best they can" (Filterware).

Rock pediatricians keep the action "on stage," directing parental *roles*, rather than parental development. They stress the outward performance of parenting, giving parents rigid programs to follow. For example, they offer a feeding schedule for babies, such as six ounces of formula every four hours, rather than flexible feeding that is sensitive to an infant's hunger. This emphasis sets the child up for a lifetime of prioritizing schedules over human need. Rock docs encourage "protection" of children too—denying them admission to painful truths ("Daddy hasn't been coming home at night because he's working so hard" [notice how the File Decompression Program gets started]). This pretense so often includes lying, or at least playacting. (We get upset with children when they lie to us, but who is modeling this dishonesty?) Such "parenting" instructs kids to ignore or mistrust their physical and emotional signals. These kids then replace the uncomfortable body signals with an experience that comforts them—they "grow" to tell anxiety-relieving stories or pursue sex outside of marriage when they feel at a loss. They may no longer recognize the various forms of "satiation" or "hunger" (like the yearning for truth) communicated by their bodies, as no one has acknowledged and directly satisfied them. Children thus learn to deny, lie, and pretend themselves—hallmarks of the Mineral Stage.

Rock docs teach that parenting is little more than training children in rigid role-play—how to *act* like an adult. Kids are encouraged to channel their intense feelings about their parental figures' offstage, antisocial actions into something socially acceptable. With such behavioral modification, their "stubborn" insistence on genuinely expressing themselves is directed into "healthy" outlets such as schoolwork, talents, or sports (thus "I *need* to work out every day"). (Note how emotions get harnessed to behaviors that over time become compulsions.) Rock docs advise parents to mold their children into an "ideal" image by rewarding approved performances ("These behaviors are good!") and punishing divergence ("Those behaviors are bad!" ["*Kids* can be so manipulative, can't *they*?"]). Remember—when we give image and storytelling the spotlight, rather than communicate who we are and what is really happening in our lives, children learn that the fantasy is more important than reality—image is more cherished than the human being. Most children follow the acts of the alleged "good guys," their parental figures (at least in part), or assume other roles that will maximize their attention.

Rock pediatricians consistently dissuade us from rescuing our distressed children, insisting, "We mustn't indulge a needy personality type." (The child is needy because her needs are unmet!) Desperate children who persist in their communications and exhibit extreme symptoms are screened for pathology and assigned diagnoses. A vast, cinematic assortment of emotional/mental/behavioral/learning *disorders* (Labeling Lock)—mood disorders, attention deficit disorder, conduct disorder, dyslexia, and so forth—focus attention on the child's abnormal brain rather than on the child's abnormal experiences that may have led or contributed to this condition. While some kids do have genetic or biological defects, of course, we should not *assume* this is the only possible cause of their symptoms.

Using established treatment protocols, these Rock docs profit handsomely from the deteriorating health of those whose voices are not heard. Children are medicated with psychoactive agents (and we shake our heads in wonder when they turn to substance use and abuse later in life to temper their emotional upsets!). They are also disciplined with reward and punishment to behave in such a way as to *never* "blow the whistle" or consciously express certain aspects of their experience, such as their encounters with Rocks (Deletion Program). Although all these Pebble-theatric methods support the thriving of Rock businesses, these kids become spectacles because of their psychiatric histories—they're often labeled and judged for the rest of their lives.

Invalidated and untreated, the wounded and suffering "inner children" retreat into the unconscious. Upon casual viewing, these children may *appear* to be cured because their most obvious symptoms have subsided. Their caretakers are now content—happy with their parenting skills and their Rock pediatricians, who assured them that their kid's symptoms would likely go away with time. Should the wounds continue to fester openly, however, a child's post-traumatic stress disorder symptoms may become embedded character traits. The Rock doc then urges the parents to unconditionally love and accept their kid "just as he is" (Femrock style!), affirming, "It's hurtful to children to try to change 'their nature'!" These charlatans are quick to "*prove*" this point when, if a parent lovingly approaches the child with a desire to discover what's wrong and remedy it, the child's repressed anguish and grief begin to surface in this welcoming space—the child certainly *seems* to be getting worse! When parents are made to feel guilty for their attempts to identify their offspring's sources of pain and assist them in surmounting each one, who can help these children grow?

Psychoanalysts (Rocks in Counseling)

Children who have been denied their developmental needs and are rushed into an "adult" act must face their childhood at some point if they are to continue their growth where they left off. The Rock therapist, like Rock pediatricians, does not allow this natural progression to maturity (the Stall). She too attempts to race people to the end of the developmental journey, as defined by her personal experience (Definition Lock). She also doesn't t take seriously the many traumatic experiences in her clients' lives that have left them handicapped, broken, and stuck in childhood (Editorial Override). "Giving attention to your problems empowers them. If you would just speak as if you were problem-free, then you would be!" Using Program Opposition, the Rock counselor opposes every genuine expression coming from her clients—refusing to listen to or talk about their suffering. To someone who is just beginning to admit the pain he's been carrying about his alcoholic father, for example, this therapist chides, "*If* your drunk dad pushed you around, it was decades ago! GET OVER IT!" She will not "indulge" clients' natural emotional or behavioral "reactions." (Remember: Rock talk is block talk). On the contrary, she normalizes abuse and neglect by relating tales of "healthy" people she knows who, for instance, were molested as children, "but *they* didn't make an issue of it—some even enjoyed it!"

This crazed counselor insists that her clients take *full* responsibility for creating every aspect of their personal experience (Filterware)—"Your 'rough background' is NO EXCUSE for NOT being a mature, well-functioning person right now!" If clients condemn a Rock, she flies into defense—ignoring them (Feedback Loop), rambling on about another topic (Circumvention Program), rationalizing what "happened," or otherwise championing the victimizer—"Why are you so *hard* on him?" (Reality Reversal). Any "judgments" clients make about their perpetrators as being inadequate, wrong, or hurtful are instantly redirected to their own insufficient, mistaken, or malicious inclinations *and* their unwillingness to be at peace. She prods them to "stop keeping the past alive" (Talk Block of the Stall*).* She condemns their "accusatory nature." *And* she assails them for "taking offense." ("If those 'playing the victim role' would just shut up and clean up, where's the problem?" [notice the one-sidedness; the PSYCHOanalyst never mentions the "victimizer role"!])

The longer that this "we see the world we want" salesperson can dissuade her clients from expressing the painful truth about their lives, the more years or decades they'll need psychological assistance (better for business). At best, she offers superficial, stopgap relief for any emerging symptoms (Quick Fix of the Stall): "Focus on the positive!" or "Fake it until you make it!" Whatever her palliative comments, the underlying message is "PUT A LID ON IT!" As she insists that her clients "open the door to the future" by merely "closing the door" to the past, she blocks them from much of themselves and their experience (Delineation Drive), thus preserving the Rocky remnants with which she identifies.

A couple of years ago, an excited Jayda called me to share her latest discovery. "I was channel-surfing on TV when I found a talk show about passive-aggressiveness. It was an eye-opener—it was Austin! I had to ask myself, 'How do they know so much about my husband?' I half expected him to appear on camera! They talked about things I thought I was the only one who knew, like how everything is someone else's fault. Like when he's supposed to meet me or Jeremie, he doesn't show and then blames it on us like we got the wrong time or day or place. He's on the ball for fixing anything at the house, but he doesn't know how to treat the people who live there. When Jeremie or I have a problem, Austin barks something like, 'That's YOUR stuff: leave me out of it!' If it's urgent, like Jeremie's emergency surgery, Austin disappears. That time, when he sauntered home, he said he'd had 'important errands to run.' Once I planned a romantic getaway, and ten minutes before we were to leave, his boss called, and off he went as if our weekend plans never existed—he didn't even say he was sorry!

"Austin is constantly parading his control by thwarting my efforts! I keep asking myself why I put up with him—must be love, I guess. When I get pissed or hurt, he snaps, 'You've got an anger problem' or 'Go to the doctor and get a pill or something.' When my parents sent him a fat check for his birthday, I practically had to force him to say thank you. Everything has to be on *his* terms, with him holding the reins, or he accuses us of trying to control *him*. When we point out what he's doing, he grumbles about our 'negativity.' He says that's why he ignores us, because 'being around doom and gloom dames is *depressing*.' Meanwhile, he seems fine at work. He's been honored with awards for his salesmanship, so he has to act like a human with the customers, yet he can't seem to do that with us. At times I find myself begging him to treat us like his buyers. It's humiliating! But whatever I say, I'm the bad guy. He typically grunts something like, 'If you don't want what I'm doing, why do you allow it?'

"After the talk show, I couldn't wait to tell all this to Jack, our latest therapist. Jack started our session by driveling about how impressed he was with Austin's success selling computers. He poured on the syrup with how difficult sales must be and how savvy Austin obviously is. As many times as Jack has flattered Austin, he's never complimented me on anything. When he *finally* paused, I told him about the TV show and everything I'd learned, and I asked him what we could do about Austin's passive-aggressiveness. Guess what he said?"

I responded, "Hmm, let's see…Austin has an anger addiction, and you need to set limits to minimize his victimization of you and Jeremie. In general, don't make requests of Austin, as it sets him up to dump his anger on you…and if he asks something of you, only do it if he does something for you first, and then imitate his manner. Austin needs to find out what *he's* mad about when he makes you both feel his anger for him. Help him become aware of his genuine emotions stuck in his repetitive behaviors by telling him what you feel when he treats you that way. Austin *learned* these destructive actions from someone who similarly victimized him. So…he needs to discover who his victimizers were and are, and learn to thaw and express his frozen feelings constructively, putting them where they belong…Am I right?"

"You're way off, Anne—not even close! Jack said, 'I'd be glad to discuss *your* take on your husband, but not today.'"

A Rock counselor often presumes irreparable pathology in her patients ("You will be bipolar for the rest of your life!"). Meanwhile, she assumes health in people *without* a history of mental illness, herself included (Delineation Drive). She doesn't determine where each person is at any time along the psychological developmental continuum, nor does she interact with them according to these assessments. Rather, she separates people into discrete (binary) categories based on face values: those who are "healthy" or momentarily struggling with an acute or situational problem (movie #2) and those who are "unhealthy" or historically problematic (movie #3). The admission of any weakness, issue, or emotional pain reveals the category a person is in! (No wonder people learn to express their psychological problems physically! [Psychological to Physical Formula of the Translation Matrix].) This PSYCHOanalyst gives a clean bill of health and looks no further into the lives of those "secure" in the denial of their traumatic experiences and secondary shortcomings. Meanwhile, she subjects the unhealthy "few" to scrutiny, if not interrogation ("Can you PROVE your mom's boyfriend anally raped you in the middle of the night when you were seven?"), and "intensive" (expensive) treatment.

These PSYCHOanalysts are particularly malicious toward any colleague who listens deeply to the words *and* behaviors of clients that expose the brutality perpetrated by those in the Mineral Stage so that both victim and victimizer might receive treatment. Rocks pounce mercilessly on such a therapist ("He's a quack!"), accusing him of *causing* the very thing he is attempting to cure (Reality Reversal). They believe that this therapist's mere suggestion of childhood trauma somehow plants a destructive seed that begins to sprout in clients' highly suggestible, overactive imaginations, causing their emerging unhappiness and instigating ersatz symptoms that can blossom into full-blown false memories. Using the Definition Lock, Rock counselors define the false memory syndrome as bad "memories" of incidents that never occurred. (Rocks may implant false memories to cast doubt on real memories that surface.) The more common manifestation of this syndrome, however, is never acknowledged—"remembering" *good* times that never happened (File Decompression Program) or that were just a portion of a much bigger, scary picture (Partial Program). A Rock never questions people's positive "memories" ("I had a *marvelous* childhood!"), no matter how bizarre the clients' symptoms nor how unrealistic their idyllic tales. Researchers, lawyers, and reporters apprise us that most people attend to only a fraction of what is around them,[3] yet Rock PSYCHOanalysts never pursue the vast "unknown" (Deletion Program). Instead, they question and malign, if not testify against, those colleagues who do (Punishing Program).

The Rock therapist has only *one way* of counseling her clients—toughening them up (bestowing a taste of her own childhood), so they too become hardened to life's blows as well as insensitive to human feeling or need. She molds clients into the rigid Rocky framework to which SHE has succumbed (Her Definition Lock defines indoctrination with the RV programs as "psychotherapy"). Her clients become *less* aware, expressive, and responsive, and *more* resistant to asking for or receiving help. They often "grow" to proudly wear the straitjacket of "normal" behaviors proffered by this psychoanalyst. ("Like water off the back of a duck, *nothing* bothers me anymore!") They now have delusions of their own mental health. *Or* they suffer from a deep sense of failure, defectiveness, and hopelessness, and an unalterable, irascible belief in the power of their "illness." After all, they did as instructed at great personal expense and got nowhere (Closed Loop*)*. Clearly, NOTHING works!

I thought about how psychotherapeutic reparenting is a huge commitment, much like parenting in that it requires years of thoughtful and heartfelt effort. How is it that people seem to think healing a damaged psyche should be fast and easy for both therapist and client? I know of no accredited educational process in any field that fits this fanciful image. For example, Emily has shared many painful stories from her experience as a teacher in New Orleans public schools. Her pupils required parenting, sometimes the toughest kinds, and she struggled to fulfill both roles, often causing her to overwork and overstress. ("Over twenty kids in a classroom and only one of me!")

THE SCHOOL OF HARD KNOCKS

Rocks in "education" construct a stringent system of rules and regulations in which teachers' time and effort is consumed by extensive paperwork and documentation (Confounder)—as if documentation proves a good teacher! There is little time free to address the students' needs. Instead of adapting the curriculum to student interests and learning styles, Rock educators force the children to make all the changes (COP). They shape the kids (scare them stiff!) with "modern," "accelerated learning," assembly-line protocols, which result in the abrupt deceleration, if not regression, of the children's human development (into the Stone Age!).

Children in Mineral Stage schools are inculcated with the ONE WAY of the Rock. Teachers promote narrowly defined "truth" or distorted, partial, or false "information" from "textbooks" that memorialize Rocks. They present a Rock version of history that makes what didn't happen seem more real and worthy of memory than what did (Reality to Wish Paraphrase of the Translation Matrix). Rock teachers then TRAIN students in rote memorization of these "facts" (Choice Commander*)* in preparation for standardized tests. (Such standards simplify the pretest awarding of "answers" to the most obedient students.) They deny the vital human voice in both the learning process and the learners—supporting only the "knowledge," comments, or questions that align with the Rock curriculum (Feedback Loop). As a result, these teachers cater to certain types of children, creating a hierarchy among peers (Difference Drive), where those who bow to the indoctrination are lavished with attention: stars, stickers, public praise, honors, prizes, as well as complimentary labels like "good student."

Individuality may be granted lip service, but children who resist the mechanization process or express their unique insights and talents outside the Program are penalized or publicly ridiculed for "willfulness," "self-importance," or "not being a team player" (Labeling Lock). Originality, creativity, and interests outside the Program are discouraged as interfering with group "learning." Inquisitive and imaginative "noncompliant" kids who act out their frustration at being so curtailed are liable to be diagnosed with a behavior or learning disorder. Special-needs children are also ignored, punished for being "problematic," or isolated from "normal" children. Those who will not submit to the cramming of Rock protocols are left to struggle on their own, unless the parents pay the teachers directly or make sizable school contributions. Financial aid and other school funds often land in these Rock educators' pockets, requiring students and their families to fill the shortfall. (If kids want school supplies, they have to sell an awful lot of candy or magazines!) Kids may learn about initiative, industry, and sales, but also about theft, exploitation, and "whatever you need or want you *have to* work for!"

Rock educators usher young people into "higher education" (Definition Lock), giving priority to academic achievement while withholding the practical education critical for negotiating our world. Pupils must pick up on their own such skills as money management, household and car repairs, and personal communication and other relational abilities (such as psychological development). With such heavy concentration on book studies (a book can become like God to these kids!), students also miss the essential schooling offered by life. Antagonal learning predominates, whereby pupils learn what is antagonistic to their human growth *and* to learning itself.

After a decade or two of being plugged into the binary system of right (RV learning) and wrong (anything else), respectively receiving rewards or enduring punishments, students have lost much of their natural curiosity and openness to what's new or different. The genuine experience of their bodies, hearts, and minds is largely forgotten. They are now controlled by the "knowledge" that's been hammered into their heads (COP) and are forevermore willing to filter all information through Rock "authority" (Filterware).

Graduates of Rock "educational" programs bear the unmistakable imprint of those in the Mineral Stage—what they "know" comes from learning how a modicum of their needs could be met. What they don't "know" is fought off with the fury of someone whose life is at stake (Arguing Analog). They perceive *true* educators as forcing them against "their" will and trying to change "them" *for the worse*. To avoid the pain of their engineered, unconscious, and unbalanced existence, they have a tremendous drive to keep busy. They also retain an unwavering belief in their own "rightness" (and the grades to "prove" it!) with resulting entitlement. They go through life half-baked, possessing little common sense, sense of reality, or sense of themselves. Those with a different opinion or experience are "wrong," necessitating correction or punishment (Punishing Program).

Having been "assembly-lined" in their education and relentlessly drilled in the "right" answers, graduates don't know how to discover truth for themselves, figure out viable and long-term solutions to very real problems, or "learn" in any other way. Their hyperactivity of body, inactivity of heart, and unquestioning acceptance of, adherence to, and defense of Mineral Stage materials paves their way into Rock businesses (as do their ENORMOUS debts!). Human beings with calm, eager, inquiring minds, looking for a diversity of useful responses and creating limitless original possibilities for the evolution of humankind, need not apply.

Corp'rock Business

The Mascrock in corporations (Corp'rock) behaves as he does in any other setting. He seeks image enhancement, an EXCESS of personal gain, and an outlet for his aggression, seizing every opportunity to sell the Program. As a one-upper, he believes he deserves to rapidly climb the corporate ladder. He insists on maximum payment for minimal work, snatching any credit due the competent people who pick up the slack. He's willing to do ANYTHING to promote himself, no matter how many bodies he climbs over or who he must discredit or libel. Because of their EXTREME determination, Rocks run many businesses.

The Corp'rock boss anchors his employees in the one-downer position—performing maximally for minimal compensation. (A common tactic is making the customer pay through tips or requiring the employee to shell out for his own benefits.) He explains away his stinginess with "I'm short-staffed right now," or "We're pinched financially" (see "Excuse Escape," p. 175). As employees adjust to the increasing workload, the Rock dishes out more and more and more to maintain a constant stress-load and to ascertain what their "best" actually is. As they weary over time, he gives well-rehearsed pep talks at predetermined intervals, saying whatever will garner their support for continued effort and willingness to forego their personal lives "just a little longer" for the sake of "your" job.

The Rock employer establishes a culture of workaholism as the norm, keeping the nose to the grindstone. He praises these addicts, calling them "hard working" and "high achieving" (Labeling Lock). Employees with other priorities are reproached with pejorative names, such as "slackers," "slugs," and "lightweights," or are humiliated publicly: "If you can't take the heat, get your lazy butt out of the kitchen!" These company "deficits" are routinely traded (dismissed by a quick e-mail) for "more industrious" workers who are "willing" to put in more time for less pay. Young people are particularly prone to pleasing the Corp'rock boss. They require work experience for their resumes, and this is exactly what they get.

"TELEPHONE, ANNE!" Effie shouted, yanking me out of my writing trance. I jogged into the kitchen and answered the phone there, hearing the anxious voice of my neighbor, Abby, who was newly employed.

"I'd like your opinion of my boss, who has requested I return to work in uptown New Orleans. He called to tell me that my colleague Matt checked out the office and reported that there is extensive roof damage but no flooding. There's some mold on the wet walls, but it's not a serious problem yet. My boss said, 'The electricity is off, and the plumbing doesn't work, but I see no reason why you can't return and salvage what you can of our records.'

"'Will you or Matt be there?' I asked him.

"'No, we'll be working at our Covington branch.'

"Not wanting to be alone, I insisted, 'I'd like someone to be there with me.'

"'No, this is your baby, Abby. I've gone to great lengths to procure a special permit to get you into the city. You need to start tomorrow.'

"I explained that I'd have to discuss it with my husband, which I did immediately. Bryan was outraged, yelling, 'Is he out of his mind? Telling a lone woman to work in a building with no electricity, A/C, or running water in the heat of a subtropical summer with mold growing up the walls and armed looters prowling the streets? You're not going!' When I informed my boss, he fired me, saying, 'You'll need to find other employment, then, since you clearly can't be counted on in an emergency.'"

Corp'rock bosses believe employees should commit their lives to their jobs, with the joy of selfless devotion being their greatest reward. As a result, the "feminine" Rock form is encountered en masse within Rock businesses. No matter how poorly these Femrocks are treated, how excessive the demands, and how completely their humanity is disregarded, they make excuses, continue their Type A routine, and remain devoted. They labor steadfastly under chronic pressure to produce, regardless of pay cuts or lack of raises, few days off, minimal benefits, or straight-commission income. If they don't do exactly as their Rock boss orders (COP), they are frequently confined to a small, dark corner doing menial, mindless, repetitive tasks (Punishing Program). Even so, the Femrock feels grateful ("I'm lucky to have a job—a lot of people don't, you know!").

These Mineral Stagers feel a great NEED to care for Rock employers and their businesses with the same intensity with which they once tried to get their own needs met as children. ("My boss needs me, and I'm not going to let him down!") This unconscious drive compels them to work, continuing the self-neglect their Rock caretakers instilled in them so long ago. The Femrock allows NOTHING to interfere with her hard labor—not her "domineering" spouse (Labeling Lock), her "needy" children ("They must learn self-sufficiency sooner or later, so it might as well be now!"), or her "meddling" friends who urge her to slow down and take time for herself. She also fiercely upholds the mercenary company's reputation, even if it has damaged the environment and/or the people living there (The Crash). Such disasters (Incompetence Program) are a small price to pay compared with her personal benefit—survival!

The phone rang again, and Effie answered it. "FOR YOU, ANNE," she hollered over the TV noise. Within seconds I heard a voice I wasn't expecting.

"Jordan?" I said. He was a fifty-eight-year-old man, an on-again, off-again friend, who never married or had children. He had a long history of workaholism as an employee of a well-known oil company. This corporation was renowned for cutting extensive channels throughout Louisiana's protective wetlands, resulting in New Orleans becoming increasingly vulnerable to hurricanes. About this Jordan would retort, "Hurricanes have wreaked far more destruction in a day than anything done by my company—THEY should get our attention!"

Jordan toiled from sunup to sundown and sometimes well into the night if he was busy with a "special project." He often skipped lunch and never grabbed a break; weekends progressed much like the rest of the week. He had good intentions of watching an interesting movie or trying out a new restaurant with a friend, but he'd often want to check something at work on his way, where he'd remain for the rest of the evening. For years he took no sick days, no matter how ill he felt or how potentially contagious he was. He scheduled only brief vacations, perhaps over a weekend, or he attached a day or two to a required business trip. His boss occasionally patted him on the back, congratulating him on his fine work, but he never received adequate compensation for his grueling hours. Jordan assured me, "My day will come." What came, however, was ill health, requiring time off for doctor visits.

I returned to the phone call. "How are you? How did you get my number?"

"I'm OK…I guess. I got your number from your mom. Look, I've been laid off, and my boss confirmed that I won't be asked back." He sounded stunned! For Jordan, his life was his work, so this must have seemed like a death sentence.

For years I'd tried to convince Jordan to sit still long enough to figure out why he worked so hard. I encouraged him to see a counselor to learn to treat himself better. I reminded him that when we were growing up, most men were employed for forty hours each week and had time to pursue a wide range of obligations and interests. Jordan defended "his" decision: "I LOVE my job, so it's easy to grind out ninety-plus hours each week! It's how I CHOOSE to live my life!" Then he walked out of mine. The first time I confronted him, I didn't hear from him for over a decade. The second time I broached the subject, he ignored me for four years, and the third time, for sixteen months. I felt he was punishing me for asking personal questions and implying he needed help. However, after this sudden firing when he had given his all, Jordan reached out of his own accord and responded to the question I had first posed almost two decades before.

"Anyway, I've been thinking. You've wondered why I've stayed so busy…why I've invested so much of my life in my work…um…I can answer your question now…I've been trying to please…well, my father…I've wanted his approval."

Listening Step Seven: LISTEN TO YOUR INVESTMENTS

Observe how you spend time. Are you investing in yourself and others, growing the humanness in both? Are you heedlessly "getting something" done before you "have to" do something else? What are you "getting" out of this busyness? Where do you spend your money? Are you giving to those in need and supporting those who provide an honorable service at a reasonable cost? Are you sustaining greedy Rocks and their monetarily profitable, "winner takes all" businesses? These moment-by-moment investments reveal what we esteem: humans or images. We seek attention and approval from one or the other. One great benefit of choosing humanity is that we become more human. Any benefits of upholding image, however, are strictly imaginary (now that's a low-yield return!). However, since we have been so thoroughly programmed in this latter pursuit, the lack of cost-effectiveness rarely registers.

Notice your biases when you tell people what you do ("I'm a jack of all trades—I can fix anything" [how about yourself?]). What are your feeling prejudices? ("It hurts to see *others* making wrong choices for their lives" [how about *your* wrong choices?]). Be alert to partiality in what you believe ("I have great faith in God" [what about the faith of the unclaimed aspects of your psyche?]). Aren't you constantly creating an image of who you are while NOT sharing what would detract from that image? (Be aware of how these biases change when talking about others!) Now note the amount of time and money you spend on image enhancements (makeup, hairstyling, body building, clothing and accessories, books and seminars on how to refine your image and look and/or play the part you want to play). Perhaps you'd rather advertise yourself as capable, caring, beautiful, powerful, and/or spiritual than invest the time daily in truly becoming so—relating to others in a developmental way. Our advertising can be so impressive that we even sell ourselves with our marketing! *Many* years or even decades may pass as we think we're performing well and pleasing ourselves, perhaps even doing our best, when this is FAR from the truth. Sometimes great stress, duress, or even a disaster is required before we discover that we've been spending our time and money attempting to appease someone else entirely—at our own expense.

Many of us fool ourselves into believing we're doing what we love when a closer look reveals we're doing what we believe will bring us love. The unmet need for relationship haunts our lives as we are compelled to "succeed" or "fail" to win attention, approval, or connection to an important person ("My mom always told me I would never amount to much, and she was right!")—a heavy load to carry! When we listen, our daily routines reveal the attention-seeking "infant" inside who wants and needs to be cared for, as all infants do, and he is doing what he has learned will bring this about.

Unbeknown to us, our inner "infants" are micromanagers, impacting our every relationship *or* contributing to our lack of them.

Human Beings Become CORPORATE COGS

Rocks design their institutions to deny infants and children (both inside and out) what they need to psychologically mature. These Mineral Stagers also stamp out or redirect the natural functions of the human body, heart, and mind (Animate to Inanimate Analogy of the Translation Matrix). As they judge and "evacuate" from all that is human within us, we learn to do the same, and we lose our potential to cling to, reach for, support, nurture, and ultimately create HUMAN life (at least psychologically speaking).

Rocks must manipulate us into disowning our genuine feelings and thoughts if we are to devotedly serve Rock companies, because our physical body would inform us that fulfilling our Rock employers' endless demands is exhausting, and we desperately need more sleep, rest, and recreation time. Our emotions, if allowed, would disclose that we are being used, we miss close connections with our family and friends, and we long for a fuller life. Insight would reveal that we are workaholics, compulsively avoiding the pain of what we have become by having almost every moment of the day occupied by work. Without awareness of human need or care, we are oblivious to ruining our lives and the lives of those who depend on us. Instead, we feel a strong attachment to our work and an intense desire to serve the "personhood" of the corporation without distraction.[4]

Corp'rock businesses are large-scale models of the RV computer system—employees are "plugged" into the Program to replicate and carry out its viral agenda. Human beings are thereby reduced to "variables" with functions—which become their identity ("When I work, I feel alive!"). Yet the company offers these workers an attractive cover story (Editorial Override) to proudly share with friends and family—a nice salary and important-sounding title while working for a business that "endows" the community. Parents are pleased that their children have become "successful adults" (Definition Lock). All those costly trips to pediatricians and mental-health professionals and/or the GREAT expense of sending them to Rock schools have *seemingly* paid off! (Rocks funding teachers, professors, health-care providers, and their institutions through their businesses makes sense now, doesn't it?)

A Hard Pill to Swallow: Rocks in Medicine

However "successful" we might appear, our failure to listen to our human bodies and respond accordingly impacts our health. Rocks in medical practice, however, portray illness as largely unrelated to our choices (nor to the choices of secretive Rocks who so often contribute to people's ill health). They cite "case studies" to prove their point: "There was one patient who ate organic foods and swam regularly, but she dropped dead in her early thirties" (The Rock doc failed to acknowledge that this patient was swimming in a sea of carcinogens!). When patients are kept ignorant of the causal relationship between what they neglect to do (take care of themselves), what they do (hyperactivity/workaholism), and what's been done to them (toxic exposures), Rock activities prosper.

Rock medicine perceives disease as the physical body being involuntarily victimized by physical causes—sickness "happens" (Partial Program), and we have "no choice" (thus the *necessity* of insurance). Through the Delineation Drive, Rock docs teach that physical illness is separate from psychological health, except for a "minor" category termed "psychosomatic." As a result of this narrow focus, their cures tend also to be physical. Treatments range from symptom eradication (Deletion Program) or symptom control (COP) to modification or removal of the body part believed to be causing the problem. The frequency of hysterectomies in the United States is a prime example.[5] Rock medical management never acknowledges the benevolent communication of the body/mind in all symptoms, and so these requests for help are ignored. Not only is this urgent human voice unheeded, but it's judged as the problem and promptly subdued with all the power that modern technology and drug therapy can bring to bear.

The Mineral medical business thrives on Rocks' compulsion to squelch the human spirit and destroy what human beings need to survive (clean air and water; nutritious, pesticide-free food; loving relationships; and so on). A Rock doc offers his "support," for example, by disregarding hygienic protocols (Incompetence Program). He might weaken a patient's condition to strengthen his own (see "Authority Shift" on p. 202). (Potassium injected into a comatose patient enables this Rock doc to "ethically" perform the cardiac resuscitation skills he's keen to practice!) When a Rock is giving the shots, there is no telling what's in the syringe. Is there any wonder why our US health-care system is itself a leading cause of death[6] and why hospital-related infections and other complications are so high?[7]

Appropriate treatments for an illness can be as varied as the individuals afflicted, and people have apparently been helped or healed with all methods. Rocks in medicine, however, never deviate from "their" one way. Establishing themselves as the sole authority, they design rigid treatment protocols (COP) to maximize their profits while causing pain, suffering, and at times irrevocable loss to their patients. Patients may feel tortured by treatments such as chemotherapy, which poisons all cells of the body while attempting to kill the few deadly cancerous ones. Effie is a prime example as she has never recovered from her radiation burns. (She said, "I informed the technician I've always been very susceptible to burning, but she replied, 'Ma'am, you need to trust your doctor. He knows what's best for you!'") The side effects of treatments can be worse or longer-lasting than the original condition! (Not to worry—your Rock doc can prescribe something for that!)

Meanwhile, licensed individuals who choose more humanitarian methods are vulnerable to penalties, lawsuits, and/or revocation of their licenses (Punishing Program) for not following official protocols stipulated by Rock professional organizations (Choice Commander). Gifted healers who prefer the gentle approach, rather than licensure, are also liable to be sued for practicing medicine without a license. Meanwhile, insurance company employees can dictate or deny treatments without incurring such legal prohibition (Difference Drive).

People often wonder why medical costs are so high. In Rock medicine, practitioners adhere to a business model in which success is measured by profit rather than patient health. Selling such an all-around EXPENSIVE medical system (costly to person and pocket book) requires a lot of money for research and development to "prove" that Rock methods are effective, to establish new "norms" or standards (i.e., to "normalize" what is abnormal), and to advertise these results. Financial incentives and other rewards to compliant doctors who respond to hospital, clinic, and insurance company directives rather than patient needs contribute to the skyrocketing costs and the necessity for malpractice insurance, which further spikes the fees. In anticipation of paying so much, people buy health insurance. However, those who seek trustworthy practitioners who also meet their psyche's needs must leave this closed system, often at their own expense.

Retirees may depend on a part-time job to afford health insurance. Others fall into credit-card debt to remain insured, adding to their stress. Health insurance demands that we stay healthy enough to work long and hard to afford the premiums. We must also keep from getting seriously ill lest our insurance company increase these premiums or drop our coverage. By embracing good health, however, we waste tremendous amounts of money on insurance not needed. Those choosing to be uninsured or underinsured avoid going to doctors, and urgent treatments may be delayed. Those who do seek medical care soon have more than the stress of their illnesses to contend with. Any way you slice it, Rock health care hurts (the Crash)!

Rock insurance companies only pay promptly those doctors who are "team-players." Non-RV doctors and staff must negotiate an obstacle course of passive-aggressive bureaucracy (the Stall) to receive reimbursement (*if* they are lucky). After many tedious forms and phone calls (secretaries use the Feedback Loop to ignore most of them), the non-RV doctor finally obtains a check, but for a fraction of the amount due. After many more rounds of telephone tag, the doctor's office staff may reach a secretary who says, "Sounds like a simple typographical error—the decimal point was typed in the wrong place!" (Incompetence Program). "Sorry, but we have no record of your original paperwork, could you please resubmit it? *If* everything's filled out accurately, we should be able to cut a check within six to eight weeks." If the Closed Loop Program is operating, the doctor's staff will once again experience a maddening runaround. If the physician does receive the much-delayed compensation, it will not begin to cover the time-consuming effort and stress! For a typical harried doctor, it's much more cost-effective to join the "team."

In a similar manner, Rock docs and their administrations abuse and enervate patients, many of whom don't have the strength or clarity of mind to protect themselves, let alone fight for their right to adequate treatment or argue over excessive charges. Mineral medicine is contrived for patient aggravation (the Confounder) and decompensation. (Administrators define "public health requirements" as those that meet the "needs" of their establishment.) If Rock "medicine" and "health insurance" (Definition Lock) ensure healthy profits for a few in exchange for the wealth *and* health of the vast majority, where does one turn for healing?

Religion Rocks! Rocks in Religion

(This is not in any way to discredit genuine worship, but to help the reader discern the difference between the true follower of God and the imposter.)

Rock ministers USE spirituality as a weapon, a "two-edged sword" that slices all things into a binary classification system: that which is "godly" (supportive of Rocks and their business practices) versus that "of the flesh." They back church members into a corner with such rigid delineations. Members learn to extend these structures into their world, forever judging by appearances. For instance, they label all people as either "saved" (one-uppers) or "unsaved" (one-downers), based on whether they belong and contribute to Rock churches. (The label "saved" appeals to our "inner infants," who like to feel special ["I get attention!"], secure ["My needs will always be met"], and sufficient ["There's nothing I need to do!" {infants can't do much}].)

Rock reverends separate and divide the church body as well. For example, they teach that our All-wise and Ever-loving Father created His children to be unequal (Difference Drive). Church members are categorized based on gender into *one-uppers* (males—and usually a particular type of male) and *one-downers* (females). Rock ministers are too concrete to comprehend the psychological interpretations of scriptures—that the psychological Woman within all bodies is indeed the "weaker vessel" to the psychological Man, and only the latter should hold positions of ministry because only the Man ("Christ within us, the hope of glory"[8]) has transcended imagery. The Rock rev always reveals himself by his worship of images (e.g., the male image and his rank within the church are important), while ignoring the immature developmental states of the souls temporarily residing in these vessels.

Mineral ministers disguise "their" Rock programming and intent with endearing religious language and scripture. For instance, they teach that to "love your neighbor as yourself,"[9] we must speak only good of his or her image, closing our eyes and ears to that which lurks beyond it. Unfortunately, with this superficial focus, the "tares" within each individual can never be bound "into bundles to be burned" at harvest time, as mentioned in the biblical parable of the wheat and tares.[10] Someone who attempts to pick them out and "burn" them may seem scary or even demonic, compared with those who pretend they aren't there.

By sorting every human quality and expression into categories of "good" and "bad," the Rock reverend psychically splits his parishioners in two, advising the "saved" (Delineation Drive) to differentiate from and shun the "unsaved" parts of themselves as well as everyone else (Difference Drive). As members' "unholy" aspects retreat into their unconscious, Rock revs encourage the projection of these heathen parts onto others, particularly those who try to bring these church members' split personalities to their attention. (In my experience, these rescuers are given quick labels [Labeling Lock] such as "secularists," "cult practitioners," or "dabblers in New Age concepts.") During church services, classes, and "Bible studies," members are drilled in doctrine, "appropriate" decorum (COP), and techniques in "spiritual warfare" that keep these fragmented aspects of their psyche sheltering in fear in their unconscious mind. Church members' remaining character traits become inflexible—like those of the Rock—leaving little to no room for personal opinion, individual choice, or Divine Inspiration. In Rock churches, no one teaches that to "Love the Lord your God with all your heart and with all your soul and with all your might and with all your mind,"[11] we must INCLUDE every aspect of ourselves. Nor do they understand that the parable of the prodigal son is about *each* prodigal part of us returning to Our Father.[12]

Instead, Rock converts stick to "the inerrant Word of God" as translated, edited, and/or interpreted by those in the Mineral Stage (Filterware). The Rock minister insists on scriptural interpretations that are concrete and in the physical realm where he resides (Abstract to Concrete Translation and Psychological to Physical Formula of the Translation Matrix). This living testimony is contorted into a rigid rulebook that church members must esteem as their sole source of truth, RATHER than their Omnipresent Father. In fact, a child of God is taught NOT to go to the top and bother her Father with questions of biblical interpretation, whom she should be following, *or* what to do about every aspect of her life. She is instructed that He gave her a brain for decision making and expects her to use it (her brain is the location of her programming!). "He" has also appointed middle-management (church leaders) to address any problems. *And,* as *they* are "anointed by God," they must never be questioned or spoken against. The Rock minister relies heavily on the "It Means What It Says" Interpretation Lock of the Translation Matrix to back up his pyramid scheme. He also edifies fellow Mineral Stagers, inviting them to be elders or to lead the children's ministry, turning a blind eye to the ill consequences. If confronted about their numerous transgressions, he deflects, "Judge not, that *you* may not be judged!"[13]

Meanwhile, this Rock preacher is religious in opposing the efforts of his congregation's members toward self-healing (Program Opposition). If victims express injury or hurt, he demands INSTANT forgiveness of those who MAY have trespassed against them (Sure to Possible Shunt of the Translation Matrix). The Rock minister declares, "Your lack of forgiveness is SINFUL!" while the more flagrant sins of the trespassers are either quickly forgotten (Thumbnail) or judged as a momentary "spirit" passing through (rather than a sign of hidden Rock parts surfacing). These tactics prevent the recovery of both victimizers and their victims (see "The Squelch" on p. 182).

A congregation of people suffering from PTSD is the end result of the Rock reverend's activities. Members are in dire need of those with gifts of the Spirit, and the Rock rev is pleased to respond with elaborately staged performances known as "church services" (Definition Lock). For example, he may "prophesize" and then, abetted by his Rock mates, make sure these events "happen" exactly as "foretold." (Clearly, he's the one to approach for "Divine" Guidance!) The Rock may "cast out demons" (such as surfacing Rock parts) by driving them back into the unconscious mind, claiming an "instant cure!" An "unhealthy" or immature aspect of a seeker may indeed "disappear" in this Rock "healer's" presence, retreating in fear. It may also respond to hypnotic suggestion or a strategic touch on an acupressure point (the Quick Fix of the Stall). Once safety returns or triggers have subsided, this aspect resurfaces, and this person naturally reaches for what *appeared* to be "effective" the last time.

Church á la Rock operates as a religious corporation. Members are like employees who are asked to work very hard with minimal compensation that they may one day be paid with heaven's rewards. They're told to invest their money in the church[14] and trust in God to pay the interest, dividends, and returns. Tithing is a beloved sermon topic; the Rock minister defines tithing (Definition Lock) as "giving *at least* ten percent of your *gross* income to 'God'" (i.e., ME or MY church). This is the Corp'rock rev's manna from "heaven!" He remonstrates, "It's more blessed to give (to Rocks) than to receive!"[15] Compliant "believers" unwittingly become guilty of funding illicit Rock businesses camouflaged by religious banners. Meanwhile, those whose children go hungry through adhering to these policies are given no handouts, but are instead encouraged to examine *their* hearts.

Jesus *never* asked for any *thing*, yet he gave ABUNDANTLY, feeding multitudes for FREE. Christ also ministered to "tax collectors and sinners," spending time with those most in need of him. He commanded someone who'd never stood on his own two feet to rise and walk, and this man did![16] Unable and unwilling to follow Christ's lead, the Rock rev turns these scriptures around—taking rather than giving, rejecting (or reprogramming) "sinners," and knocking people down rather than lifting them up. Sadly, church members rarely notice these <u>antagonal interpretations</u> of the scripture.

The Rock minister similarly alters the verse "Get away, Satan, for it is written, 'You shall worship the Lord your God, and Him only shall you serve.'"[17] Using the Reality Reversal Program, this Rock teaches that God's job is to serve the church members while they serve the Rock. God is reduced to employee status, listening to parishioners' prayerful complaints and requests for change. Katrina and the Levee Disaster survivors know they have work to do on their damaged homes, but when it comes to our damaged psyches, Rock revs teach church members to expect God to do all the work! If God does not deliver what they want, when and as they want it, is there any wonder why they take their "business" elsewhere?

The product of the Rock church is "salvation" (momentarily saved from Rocks' Punishing Program) that is purchased at the expense of each "customer's" humanity. The "faithful" merely exchange the ever-growing and blossoming life gained from genuine spirituality for the Rock's rigid, "orthodox" dictates to receive a "guaranteed" ticket to heaven. (The catch is—they won't find out what they "bought" until they die!) Woe to those who fall off this "path," as Rocks offer a foretaste of the other choice available in this binary belief system—eternal torment. They admonish, "You've obviously erred to have fallen out of 'Our Lord's' favor and protection!" The "faithful" can become so fearfully frozen in their fervor that they will *not* listen to those outside this program, and they may willingly postpone living until the afterlife.

The Rock reverend forever markets religious phrases ("praise God!"), symbols (fish bumper stickers), and rituals (laying on of hands while wearing a "Jesus is Lord" T-shirt) that offer the impression of Christianity. These hide his psychologically segregating, mass-programming, and "self"-seeking motives, which are decidedly UN-Christlike. The Mineral Stage minister is a wolf in sheep's clothing,[18] shepherding his flock into religious form and conformity ("MY" way!). He also shies them away from such "deceptive" concepts as self-awareness and such "dangerous" practices as human evolution. (Since Rocks are unable and unwilling to grow themselves, they label this persuasion "heresy"!). As church members' faith in their own godliness grows and the worship of Rocky or graven images predominates, the more they build their "churches" on this Rock.

COFFEE BREAK

1. How are you paying into or otherwise supporting Rock enterprises?

2. Compare the behavior of the PSYCHOanalysts (pp. 161-2) with the symptoms of PTSD discussed in chapter 3 (pp. 37-9). Which aspect of their psyche are the PSYCHOanalysts delineating for themselves, and which are they projecting onto clients?

3. Have you had any Rock educational experiences? Meditate on what this "learning" has cost you.

4. Do you believe you are running your own life when you are really appeasing someone important to you?

5. What is the cost of the following Closed Loop Program?
    a. God created the world and said it was good.
    b. Rocks are destroying our world.
    c. If God is allowing this destruction, then He must be OK with it. Who am I to interfere?
    Do you have any similar Closed Loops in your beliefs?

THE "GOODS" OF ROCK BUSINESSES: RV Programming Continued

Once we know the business practices of those in the Mineral Stage, we can comprehend the deterioration of our families, societal institutions, food and water quality, and so on (Crash Program).

We understand why the businesses of emergency management and disaster relief are booming. We can also appreciate why so many people won't set foot in a church, Grandma won't go to the doctor, Sonny doesn't want to work, Junior skips out on school, Hubbie won't see a therapist, and Sis is struggling with her legal counsel, as well as why the younger generation doesn't read the paper or listen to the news. We sympathize with the sense of futility that permeates people's lives. So often we generalize our Rocky experiences and come to the conclusion that seeking help, healing, justice, or education is a lost cause. Or we figure that the bad comes with the good. ("If I need help, I have to put up with the 'costs.'") Rocks are supportive of this latter mentality, teaching us that those who resist their "services" and secondary expenses are the problematic ones. ("What kind of Christian doesn't support a 'church'?") To keep us buying into Rock businesses, while shunning socially responsible companies, institutions, and individuals, they use the following unique set of "computer" programs.

D. THE EVASION PROGRAMS: Strategies for Avoiding Relationships at All Costs

These RV computer programs are specifically designed to decimate human relationships as their users evade valid experience, authentic communication, and personal responsibility to meet one another's needs. The attentive person trying to connect with users is startled by their defensiveness, stunned by the misinformation or information void, or hurt by their hard sell or harsh rejection. With these "antitrust" programs, Rocks create the undistracted workforce and the lonely, needy clientele that ensure their businesses' success. The more this programming spreads, the more we must PAY someone to listen to us, talk to us, touch us, and do what we ask. The Evasion Programs consist of the following:

(1) **Excuse Escape.** Users of this program are ever churning out excuses to give themselves or other users the veneer of a "reasonable" person despite their unreasonable, if not disastrous, choices. ("I HAD TO make that executive decision because there wasn't enough money [time, help, interest, etc.] to do it any other way.") Rarely does anyone question why users CHOSE to participate as they did, rather than choosing to procure more money (time, help, interest, etc.) to avert the dire result.

The user also gives a litany of excuses for her rejection of non-RV activities. For example, a user "doesn't have a nickel to spare" for the campaign against the depletion and contamination of our nation's freshwater by hydraulic fracturing,[19] yet she readily pays for nonessential items such as cigarettes, alcohol, coffee, eating out, and the like. Similarly, low-price or even free therapy offered through reputable churches and community services is deemed "far too costly" for her. (The expense is her image!) What is truly costly, however, is swept under the carpet when the commodity involved is perceived as a necessity—"We need oil, so we have to put up with leaks into the environment!" (If we and our children are to be healthy, we NEED a clean environment and workers mature enough to secure that platform!)

The Excuse Escape blocks many users from realizing that their actions are controlled by "computer" MALware; they are adept at explaining why they did what they did and why they should NOT be held accountable for their actions—"Injustice is a condition of our world. We're all impacted in some way." This application is also initiated instantly when a person comments on any Rock boss's incapacities, insensitivities, or lies—"He's not himself today, perhaps he's tired or sick. We needn't go into the sensational, as I'm sure there is a mundane explanation for everything that's transpired." The excuses are often designed to make the recipient feel sorry for speaking so negatively about Rocks.

In February, I ordered some vegetable plants for my summer garden from a mail-order nursery. Each time I called to ask when the plants would arrive, I received a serious excuse for why there was a delay. In late March, the person on the phone explained, "We haven't shipped your plants because our employees have been bedridden with a very rare form of flu." In early May, I was told, "One of our buildings caught on fire, which resulted in a loss of inventory, and our business has temporarily come to a standstill." In June, I heard yet another tragedy: "The owner was in a car accident, and we don't know if he is going to survive!" The fourth time I called, in late July, I was informed, "Many of our plants have succumbed to a blight that arrived with a shipment of exotic orchids. We are hoping to get a part of your order to you next month." They seemed to have an excuse booklet they went through to maintain their customers' patience and even generate concern about THEIR well-being. Although curious about what the next excuse would be, I never called back. I imagined the employee saying, "We tried to ship your plants to you but couldn't as there was a hurricane and disastrous flood!"

IT Help Desk: Escaping Excuses—Don't buy the users' illegitimate excuses, but do point out where they are weak or faulty. For example, if a salesperson is concocting excuses about a defective product, ask her to speak honestly. If she refuses, ask for her supervisor. Continue to ask for new people as necessary until you reach someone who can hear your complaint and respond appropriately.

Don't let the PSYCHOanalyst user excuse those who have harmed you. Stand up for your experience! ("It's not 'normal' for a man to be an autocratic misogynist who seeks sexual conquests half his age. That actually points to his unresolved childhood sexual abuse.") When the user insists that the Rock she's protecting "couldn't" have done better under the circumstances, list the options you see ("He could have pursued the development of his humanity, but he CHOSE not to").

(2) Blame Game. This program deflects liability from its users and "playfully" bestows it on something or someone else. Favorite blame repositories are an object, acts of nature, and man-made installations, including policies, procedures, industry, orders, the budget, the economy, the war, the city, the state, and so on. ("So many people died in the days following Hurricane Katrina *because of bureaucracy*!" Note: No PEOPLE are being held responsible.) Rock users deflect their guilt onto institutions ("Unions are to blame!"). *Or,* ordinary citizens are held accountable for the crimes of corporate leaders ("If we weren't driving industry with our excessive needs, they wouldn't be doing what they're doing!"). Other popular scapegoats are people incapable of defending themselves, such as children, the dying, or the deceased. (Rocks may try to incapacitate their chosen fall guys so they won't interfere with their assigned roles.)

Users perceive "accusers" (Labeling Lock) as contentious when they try to make the truth of their victimization known. ("What did YOU do to MAKE him do that to you?" the user queries, deflecting the guilt.) They believe that if a person hadn't had expectations of victimization or had somehow behaved differently, the otherwise "respectable" Rock wouldn't have, for instance, brutalized, raped, or shot her. The user interrogates the victim with questions about why she *allowed* herself to be victimized and berates her for not taking better care of herself. He is also appalled at the grisly details reported by eyewitnesses and wonders about the perverse minds that would *entertain* such thoughts!

This application also causes users to perceive as accusers other people who are merely stating facts or encouraging responsibility. During my pediatric training, I was frequently asked, "Why do you blame parents?" when my goal was to educate moms and dads in the healthiest known methods of child rearing. For example, on several occasions I said, "Adding alcohol to your baby's formula to calm him encourages him to turn to alcohol for calming later in life. Is this what you want?" This program blocks the reception of vital information because the parent hears "she's trying to make me feel guilty!"

No matter how sadistic a user's behavior, how many people were harmed, or how serious the injuries, users will NOT accept any blame, nor express any regret. In their minds, someone else is always culpable. ("If you believe I'm capable of harm, why didn't YOU stop me?") Their "apologies" focus on other people's "reactions" ("I'm sorry SHE is upset," or "I'm pained by THEIR confusion about the issue"), putting the responsibility on the victim, whistleblower, and/or Mother Nature, who consistently lose in this "game."

Jayda called to say, "I saw in the newspaper that 'the soil is to blame' for the collapse of the Seventeenth Street Canal Levee."

I commented, "I read a newspaper article in which scientists blamed the levees for every New Orleans flood. I guess the people who CHOSE the soil or who CHOSE to build the levees are the victims, huh?"

"It sure SEEMS that way," Jayda replied cynically. "My friends who are still in New Orleans say it is like a war zone! They are watched closely, sometimes at gunpoint. They have to show ID everywhere they go. These survivors are being treated like criminals. My hunch is that we victims will be paying for it all with higher insurance payments, pricey utilities, increased taxes, and greater costs for just about everything else we could possibly need. And we still have to clean up this mess, not only our own places but our neighborhoods too. It will be exhausting to say the least—who has time to tackle the awful corruption? The real criminals will rebuild the levees and get paid for it AGAIN!"

IT Help Desk: Putting a Lid on the Blame Game—Investigate whatever the user blames for the problem and share your research. For example, when a journalist places blame on an object or policy rather than the Rocks responsible for using them destructively, write a letter to the editor pointing out the error in this logic. If your letter isn't published, contact the journalist and his or her superior. Share the facts as you see them, and insist on a correction. Follow up until this is accomplished.

When a pediatrician user blames a victim ("This child is mentally ill and will require medication for the rest of her life"), relay your experience ("I don't believe my daughter's DNA is the sole source of her eating disorder. She's upset about something, and I'm going to find out what it is!").

(3) Circumlocution Scroll. This program causes its users to speak EXCESSIVELY. They babble endlessly, hold conversation partners hostage until they are finished speaking, and host meetings dedicated to their own logorrhea. Their verbal profusion consumes tremendous amounts of people's time to wade through it all. Even in an urgent situation, they never take action. They retort, "Let's talk about it!" and proceed to gab for HOURS! The result of this dialogue box is a monologue—the number of words prattled correlates directly with their stress level on the topic.

Others have a *hard* time getting a word in. When they manage to do so, the user scolds them for their intrusion and then continues at the same pace or interrupts them midsentence, not to be dissuaded. With such excessive chatter, a user frequently forgets what she's saying and is only too happy to start again from the beginning, while the typical listener succumbs to dissociative escape or hypnotic trance.

Any non-RV topic or activity can trigger a verbal barrage. For example, a user may heavily criticize companies that routinely invest in the development of their employees and their communities. Those who espouse such investments are given no audience as this user does all the talking, endlessly pattering her programming while verbally discrediting well-informed, well-meaning people and businesses that provide genuine *human* services. This verbal deluge may not always be audible, as the user may have constant chatter in her head or feel compelled to write multipage, single-spaced e-mails to each correspondent.

IT Help Desk: Getting to the Heart of Circumlocution—Tell the co-worker user to stop preaching or lecturing so much (this will take a while) and start listening more (this will take even longer). You may need to use text-messaging, sign language, pictures, or music to communicate, as she will NOT pause to hear you. You may need to shout, "SHUT UP!" to get her to stop. If she does, have her reflect on what is compelling her to speak ad nauseam. *Pay attention!* She is likely to jump back into her monologue with a long-winded and seemingly irrelevant story that, on closer inspection, symbolizes what's driving this compulsion.

(4) Spam Program. When the user is exposed to vital truth, this program rapidly creates mundane, irrelevant, or faulty material in response. Confused by the cornucopia of indecipherable or conflicting data, the average listener selects the most appealing or least demanding option, or rejects it all— throwing the truth, along with the spam, into the "recycle bin." Spam Program users "inform" reporters and judges of their confabulated accounts of events, casting doubt on those who were at the scene in question. The voices of valid eyewitnesses are then muffled by these confusing contradictions. This application also causes the user to bury important facts among what's misleading or clearly ridiculous so that vital information will likely be ignored or derided as well. The user is apt to accept with relief the simple, concise "facts" offered by well-dressed, well-spoken Rocks.

The ***Spam Dam Subroutine*** fills its users' minds with so much junk that their reception of anything pertinent or new is blocked. As a result, they urgently request what you've already given or angrily criticize you for withholding what they've refused to receive. Their brains are so overloaded with data that they short-circuit, making clear, rational thought and communication impossible. Rather than recognize the deleterious program, users believe this cacophony in their heads is normal mental processing. They proceed to share the spam without restraint, *or* they conclude, "Intellect is a problem—it should be avoided at any cost!"

IT Help Desk: Spam Treatment—Help the user educator differentiate the valuable from the junk, his humanity from his programming, so he can teach the former and withhold the latter. For example, you might share human-interest stories, ask for his responses to them, and assist him in differentiating the real message from any rubbish. You might use his computer as an analogy. He is able to block or ignore unsolicited advertisements while waiting to watch a YouTube; he can learn to do the same with the Spam in his head—it just takes practice.

(5) "Vaguenese" Language Program. "It," "that," and "this" become common subjects of sentences: "It happened." "That wasn't acceptable." "This is really offensive—what a problem!" Users of this program make ambiguous statements, forcing the listener to make many inquiries, trying to discern what's being conveyed—"What's really offensive?" or "Which problem are you referring to, and how might we solve it?" Users cannot answer questions or explain their assertions because this program is not designed to inform or clarify, but to merely confuse and unsettle. Users typically retort, "It's bothersome that you don't get it!"

Users divulge vital information and facts in ways that are dubious, obtuse, or open to multiple interpretations. When this program is employed to create instructional materials, for instance, readers will need to buy books to fill in all the "blanks." These users also do their best to frustrate any attempts by others to know them ("How do you feel about what happened in New Orleans in late August of 2005?" The user responds, "a lot"). They present personal expressions and opinions ambiguously, even when sharing their knowledge or viewpoint is essential.

IT Help Desk: Confronting "Vaguenese" Speakers—Publicly ask the corporate user what she means when she offers vague statements. For example, "When citizens challenge you about the well-documented harm to wildlife and human populations caused by your company's pollution, what do you mean, 'It's impossible to say what is causing this'?" You may need to help her with suggestions. "Do you mean it's impossible to say because you'll lose your job if you speak the truth?" (Her body language may reveal when a suggestion is accurate.)

"Youthful" listeners may assume the "Vaguenese" speaker is communicating what they expect and then act according to their own ideas about her meaning. "Young" people may also hear what they want to hear and are glad to hear it! Therefore, attend to the audience as well: "When responding to your concerns about the foul smells coming from her factory, the speaker replied, 'They are our top priority.' But we cannot be sure that her 'they' is the same as your concerns" (see "The Scam Program," p. 181). Call listeners' attention to the speaker's choice of words: "What exactly did you hear? What do you suppose she meant by that?" Challenge them to persist with their inquiries until they uncover the facts.

(6) Scatterware. This program scatters the user's own perceptions, behaviors, emotions, thoughts, or priorities onto other people, places, and times. For instance, he experiences the ever-running RV programs that control his thoughts, feelings, and behavior, as coming from OUTSIDE, particularly from those who challenge him. In his experience, a challenger is "worming into my head," "trying to alter how I feel," or "controlling my every move." Meanwhile, the user has no awareness of these android trappings within himself.

The user's current problems are hidden in another time (as if he pressed page down or up on the keyboard). "I used to be a heavy drinker, but not anymore!" he mutters as he gulps his second double scotch and returns to work (page down). Current problems are attributed to ancient causes. For example, I remember once talking to a client with PTSD about his exaggerated startle response. He said, "My hunter/gatherer ancestry explains my jumping whenever the phone rings—my body reacts as though it's a saber-toothed tiger!" Physical memories from past trauma seem like current body symptoms, where remembered pain, bleeding, tiredness, numbing, tingling, and so forth are thought to be due to a present disease process (page up). Past persecutions and deprivations are projected into the future, overwhelming the user with feelings of hopelessness (time for Prozac!). Scatterware shifts the locations of all aspects of our experience. Our future potential may even be experienced as present reality—"I am an enlightened person, so you can trust me with your business." (A businesswoman actually said this to me!)

This program so scatters the here and now that the user is too befuddled to absorb, let alone prioritize, the many facets of his life or to respond appropriately. With each new idea or activity, he instantly drops the old without following it through to completion, leaves it for "later," or procures someone else to finish up. Organizing, scheduling, and timeliness are impossible! In his confusion, he can't distinguish progress from going backwards. He's also too scattered to register how scattered he is!

IT Help Desk: Collecting the Scatterer—Help the Scatterware user to own the lost pieces of herself that she's projecting onto people, places and things. If your secretary says, "Our office PC is possessed," you might try smiling and saying, "Sometimes the things in our lives are showing us something about ourselves. What do you think?" Notice if what the user says about the past, present, or future applies to another time, and alert her to your discovery. ("Your 'past' drinking problem seems to have continued into the present.) When the user is ill, investigate whether any part of the illness recalls a painful memory. Be aware—she may scroll to another part of the "page" that looks better or feels more comfortable to her than what you're referring to. Also, a physical scatterer needs a professional organizer, as well as a therapist, to reduce the daily clutter outside that mirrors the mess within.

(7) Indirect Application. This program prohibits direct, open, honest communication, cloaking it within external events. The user's expressions about the outside world can be interpreted as code for his state of being and psychological needs. For example, information about his personal life is hidden within his conversations about the weather: "We're having foul weather" means "I'm going through a rough time." Facts and figures are another way the user shares: "That company downsized last year" may refer to the speaker's diminished financial security and/or increasing psychological insecurity. However, when someone shares directly, this user feels disinterest, dismay, or disgust.

This summer I was involved in a weekly woman's support group. In one particular meeting, the focus was on romantic relationships and the difficulties the women were having in communicating with their men. I took notes.

"When my husband comes home from work, he plops on the sofa when I need his help to get dinner on the table!" remarked a busy executive on the verge of divorce.

"Why won't my husband do what I ask?" a newlywed inquired. "He wasn't like this when we were computer-dating!"

"I'm very expressive of what I like and don't like, but when my husband has an opportunity to apply this knowledge, it's like he hasn't heard a word!" said the wife of an accomplished scientist.

The following day, I attended a computer club meeting and was the only woman present. I jotted down what the men were saying about their problems with their computers.

"My computer crashes at the worst times!"

"My computer won't do what I want!"

"I've spent time and effort inputting data onto my PC, and then the damn thing malfunctions and I can't retrieve it!"

When I arrived home that night, I was dumbfounded to see that the list of the women's problems with their husbands was the same as the men's complaints about their computers!

IT Help Desk: Redirecting the Indirect Application User—You can best relate to the user by understanding that his words and actions are expressions of his experience. For instance, you might translate a Rock minister's sermon into more direct language, or at least language that is more psychological in nature. Relay this back to him, if you feel so led. If he preaches, "God gives each of us so much—some five talents, some two talents, and some one,"[20] you might say, "Couldn't this parable also be interpreted introspectively? Perhaps the different people given various talents speak of the different 'people' within each individual's mind. We hide the parts of us that we feel are lacking in some way. What do you think about that?"

(8) The Scam Program (Letter of the Law). The user cleverly speaks what is literally true, while implying something else. "I spent all afternoon with the material for our upcoming symposium" may sound like he's working hard, but in reality, the fellow took a nap using the notes as a pillow. Another example is a boss who announces, "Everyone's comments on the new proposal will be considered equally," and then ignores them all! How about "Please submit your complaints to the Unmet Needs Committee"? This user then maintains her integrity as she leaves these needs unattended.

IT Help Desk: Scam Treatments—Don't fall for the user's superficially true language. For example, EVERYTHING a corporate representative says must be scrutinized for all possible meanings. If she states at a public forum that air monitors stationed throughout the community are measuring nothing that signals the need for pollution concerns, even though production at her local factory has increased, find out if these monitors have been turned on!

(9) Point of View Shield. This application "protects" the user from others' points of view. He is shielded from the benefits and insights gained from anyone else's experience and knowledge, while "his own" viewpoint (the RV Program) is inflated into an immutable standard against which others' thoughts, feelings, and behavior are measured. He rationalizes his blocks ("Even though Marvy Marva's Childcare has had extensive abuse allegations, I'm sure my kids won't have any trouble there").

This hyperinflated user frames all experiences within the narrow viewpoint this program offers. For instance, the workman user gives his customers what he believes is best for them rather than what they've requested. He shields himself from their complaints by using them to confirm what he already "knows"—"Women are unrealistic perfectionists" or "Guys of my father's generation are pushy and unappreciative."

The POV Shield guards against the natural, useful, caring, or cost-effective ideas or activities that come so naturally to human beings. For example, a nurse user may keep loving parents from visiting their hospitalized child because "she cries so when you leave, and being upset isn't good for her recovery." Users block feelings, which they're convinced are the source of problems, rather than recognize the improper handling of those feelings as the problem—"Your anger toward your demanding employer is raising your high blood pressure. Let go of those bad feelings before YOU have a heart attack!" (Why not write a new resume and let your Rock boss go?)

Users become apprehensive or sick when specifically instructed to hear another point of view. They're quick to declare, "You're WRONG" or "You're CRAZY!" rather than consider that another's point of view might be FACT. In an increasingly complex, specialized world, where obtaining valid information is vital, these users are greatly handicapped because they're ignorant of what is beyond "their" field of perception *and* are determined to remain that way.

IT Help Desk: Pointing Out the POV Shield—Help the user investigate others' points of view. ("Before you send your kids to Marvy Marva's Childcare, why not talk to the prosecuting families yourself?") Also, challenge the user's point of view. ("Just because your work was of fine quality doesn't mean it met another's needs or wants." *Or,* "Another's opinion isn't sickening just because you felt sick after listening to him—it may be merely unfamiliar.")

(10) Program Paranoia. Users of this program are too scared to look long and hard at their surroundings. The RV programs of deception, terror, and defense are projected around them, leading them to fear what "others" might do (movie #3). Their responses to such perceived "dangers" are swift and harsh, as they "attack first and ask questions later" (if at all). They never pause to consider the harm they're causing. These users may also feel compelled to isolate themselves from human relationships to ensure "their" safety.

This MALware prompts the user to view as delusional and suspicious anyone who is aware of Rocks and their business practices. After all, Rocks are willing to have themselves scrutinized by either their own or another Rock company. When they pass inspections with flying colors and "prove" suspicions to be unfounded, their accuser seems malicious indeed. ("The poor fellow is probably trying to get his name in the paper or squeeze money out of a wealthy company!") As Rocks prey unmercifully on an accuser, this nonuser will undoubtedly come to believe that others are indeed out to get him.

IT Help Desk: Treatment for Paranoia—Check the validity of whomever the paranoid person claims is against her. As Rocks are so sadistic and highly secretive in the delivery of their cruelty, many people who have been diagnosed and medicated for paranoia are honest victims of such treachery. All reports of persecution, no matter how bizarre, must be taken seriously ("Aliens from another planet experimented on me in the middle of the night!"). In my training at a sexual abuse psychiatric unit, I saw many people arrive with fantastic stories of abuse that faded during treatment into more ordinary tales of family members or others in the community abusing them while wearing costumes (extraterrestrials, religious figures, storybook characters, etc.). Those in the Mineral Stage go to great lengths to assure that their *victims* appear to be the sick ones.

(11) The Squelch. These users instantly stop any threat to the RV programs. For example, a user may spurt, "You're really special," or "I love you," to prevent her spouse from saying anything against her. In reaction to her child's lament over daily parental abuse, she yelps, "Your complaining is causing me pain. Why are you hurting me?" When an aspiring artist requests personal feedback that requires involvement, attention to detail, genuine feeling, or original thought, the user deflects with "You're so talented!" or "Good job!" rather than step out of the Program to consider and appropriately respond to this sincere request.

The Squelch users relentlessly thwart the efforts of those living or working with them, lest their own lack of ability be revealed. For instance, "the Brain" at the office is ordered to make coffee and fill out forms; the person with superior people skills is isolated in a cubicle or lab; and an experienced middle-aged employee is told to train a new, young, and low-paid recruit who will soon take her job. There is also subtle parasitic squelching (consistent criticisms, daily difficulties, poisons put in food and drink, and so forth) whereby users keep their victims chronically low functioning.

The **Tell Him What He Wants to Hear Subroutine** assures the user that whatever is being asked of her is what she already is doing or has done, squelching any potential for change. If someone says,

"You need to sit down and have a chat with your angry inner child to find out why she's acting so badly," the user responds, "I'm already doing that!" "How about every day?" "Yes, every day!"

This MALware may relay seemingly positive or negative information to the user ("You're such a loser—you'll botch it up no matter how hard you try, just like you've always done!"). The user may even vacillate between these "positive" or "negative" fabrications—whichever is the most effective in squelching her human qualities and the implementation of developmental tools.

IT Help Desk: Stopping the Squelch—Don't allow the user, whether your legal, psychological, or spiritual counsel, to squash your human traits. For example, when he curtails your genuine self-expressions, feelings, and behaviors in response to the Rocks who have harmed you, act promptly. Respond earnestly to each of his squelching comments, and then go about your business, as in finding more humane help.

(12) Refresh Button Program. When healthy behaviors (e.g., helping others), sincere feelings (e.g., guilt or grief), or personal insights (e.g., "I've been living as an automaton") reach a certain threshold, the user's mind shuts down. The system resets itself to a time before these "attacks" on the RV Program when there is no memory of them. Feelings of relief coupled with thoughts such as "I've been taking life too seriously!" replace authentic feelings and thoughts. This program may also be activated after sexual intimacy. The user's momentary opening up to his partner triggers the refresh button, and he falls asleep. He awakens the next morning "refreshed," yet treats his partner as if the entire experience never occurred.

IT Help Desk: Refresh Treatments—When a user refreshes her RV system, let her know what transpired. For example, with a salesperson user who says, "I never told you that switching to our cell phone service would be free," refresh her memory: "We spoke at two p.m. yesterday, when you said..." Documentation helps, as the user will forget. Also, refresh your memory of Our Rescuer, who revitalizes all our systems to their original modeling of *human f*orm.

Let's BREAK from the Evasion Programs!

1. As you go about the business of your relationships, notice whom you consistently make excuses for. Why do you do this? Where do you believe "I'm doing my best!" when you could really do better?

2. Look at your blaming biases. Do you blame women more than men or vice versa?

3. Which program is used in the following: "Ma'am, if you're concerned about your well water smelling of methane and think our company has something to do with it, you need merely schedule an appointment, and a representative will come to speak with you." (He'll talk all right, at length, but he won't DO anything about the problem.)

4. Watch TV or YouTube videos, read newspapers or magazines, and note examples of the Evasion Programs. Next time you encounter those working in the occupations mentioned in this chapter, identify the RV programs demonstrated by their words and actions.

5. Note where you project the lead characters and characteristics of the three movie templates in your minds (as explained on p. 114). For instance, do you project on your doctor the unerring Life in Movie #1? Do you perceive Movie #1 in your blue chip stocks, having complete confidence that they will provide you with a relaxed, easy, and abundant retirement?

A disaster newsreel on television caught my eye. The merciless winds of Hurricane Katrina were driving the blinding rain sideways, breaking windows and smashing vehicles into buildings. Flying trees, snapped from their trunks, added to the ruin and danger. After the storm, looters were making waves through the floodwater with shopping carts piled high with stuff. Footage from the previous day showed bumper-to-bumper cars lining the highways, their occupants fleeing from peril. I looked away as painful feelings circulated inside me once again.

EXPENSE ACCOUNT—Rock "Goods" and "Services" Result in Widespread Destruction, Suffering, Loss, and Need from which Those in the Mineral Stage Profit

Because RV programs are rigid, their users stiffen. They don't bend with the normal fluctuations of relationships, nor do they weather the storms of life well. Programmed people are uncompromising, no matter how many people they blindside or how many broken relationships they leave in their wake. Like the hardwood trees that became projectiles in the squalls of Hurricane Katrina and impaled or crushed cars, homes, and businesses, users who adhere to the Rock Virus menu are left ever so damaged and damaging! They too tend to "snap" under pressure, often revealing a stormy, inhuman nature. Like the rain pelting sideways during a hurricane, their "natural" offerings are skewed, forceful, and *destructive*.

Since those in the animal kingdom naturally flee when unbridled forces head their way, RV-programmed people are often left with the least psychologically evolved life-forms and things. Rocks are unconcerned since human psychology, with its acute sensitivity and full diversity of expression, seems strange and incomprehensible in comparison—the humans in their lives seem an investment of diminishing returns. Rocks adapt over time, preferring the consistent, nonchallenging "companionship" of their lawns, tools, antiques, miniatures, or musical instruments, which they treat with the *greatest* tenderness and care.

Mineral Stagers readily attach to money because of the *seeming* power it bestows. This strong bond fuels their mechanical movements, and over time, money becomes their passion and even their God. They seek high-income positions, often becoming lawyers, doctors, and business bigwigs. They then indoctrinate their clients and customers in their worldview, which gives preeminence to the inanimate "kingdom." This preeminence permeates their culture, down to word definitions and usage. For instance, those who have "stored up treasures on earth"[21] are termed "wealthy" (Definition Lock), while those with heavenly stores *seem* comparatively empty-handed.

Just as Corp'rocks have been diverted from the family of humankind, they also work to divert us. They privatize our lives and mortgage our obligations to our fellow human beings so that we're in debt to Rocks and their companies instead. Corp'rocks offer substitute goods to replace our natural interest in deep human engagements. They encourage us to purchase a bigger house, a nicer car, a faster computer, and a new wardrobe (Choice Commander), instead of growing, mellowing, quickening, and restoring one another. Rather than "funding" the relationships that shelter us and provide psychological "transportation," loving synchronicity, and warm touch, we begin to grasp for *things* when desiring fulfillment. We learn to "thirst" for products we must pay for. We "hunger" for services that will supply our relational longings ("My hairdresser really listens to me!"). To have the money to meet these "needs," we look to capitalize on the potential financial gain in everything we do and in every alliance we make. Instead of experiencing and expressing Self in mutual refreshment and edification, we increasingly swap money and what money can buy, and *human* destitution results.

Rocks corner this market of despair by supplying that which creates the greatest demand for what they're selling (their "law of supply and demand"). For example, if their foods are depleted in nutrients,[22] we will crave more of them to feel satisfied. Such insidious methods lead to scarcity in every aspect of our humanity, resulting in a demanding population that cries out for these temporarily fulfilling material surrogates (Remember the motherless Rhesus monkeys?[23]). We become lifelong consumers who cling to Rock programming as "our" nature, rest in imagery as our truth, rely on Rock "goods" (Definition Lock) for our sustenance, and reach for Rock "services" when requiring care.

We "need" more and more money to obtain these inanimate substitutes, so money dominates our focus (earning it, saving it, investing it, and *spending* it). In our need, we are attracted to the "wealthy," "their" ways, and their businesses. We court "fat wallets" or "large portfolios" and do our best to allure people who might bestow some advice, lead us to riches, or at least give us a quick handout. In our "dependence," we pay their excessive charges or accept anything detrimental that comes from their "trying" to produce commodities as "cheaply" as possible.[24] There are also *numerous* unspoken charges, such as to our human voice, which is ignored and restrained and must now cloak itself in material symbolism to get our attention (Indirect Application). Our human mind has also been trapped in a belief system where achievement is defined as being "on top" rather than incorporating and serving the whole.

As we increasingly lapse into profit-driven materialism, we covet what doesn't serve us and finance what we've been taught we "need." Because of our concentrated focus, we often reject those who offer what we *do* need and still *unconsciously* desire. Also, when we honor each other's obvious requests, we may be discouraged to find that people have insatiable "needs" or don't have their best interests at heart. Do we give people what they say they want or address a deeper longing? As many people no longer know their psychological needs, we become desensitized to those who do know and who openly and directly ask for what will meet them. We've all had experiences where listening to others and abiding by "their" needs and wishes proved to be fruitless, detrimental, or DANGEROUS, serving only to kindle our inner yearning. In our dissatisfaction, perplexity, and pain, hedging ourselves in activities, such as our work, feels far less stressful. There we can contentedly excel without the hassles.

Connie and her kids returned, looking considerably ruddier than when they left. After brief answers to my many questions about their trip, the kids were off to bed, where Effie had retreated a couple of hours ago. Connie and I communed in the glow of one large flashlight, her gold-orb earrings reflecting the light. She chatted as I opened the white Styrofoam container of Red Cross provisions she brought back from Covington for me—chicken stew on white bread with canned corn. After one taste of this visually drab meal (blah!), I added salt, pepper, and plenty of Louisiana hot sauce.

Connie seemed more upbeat than when she left. "It felt really good to be working with others on their damaged homes. Helping them helped me feel better too."

I nodded as Connie continued. "The kids really supported one another too. I overheard a conversation Oliver had with his friends where he asked each one of them how they were feeling about what happened. Can you believe it—my son asking the other children how they were feeling? Just like David used to do with him. Thank goodness David's influence on him is stronger than Cedric's! Oliver encouraged his friends to talk about what they had been through, what they had lost, and how they were feeling about it. I was proud of him!" Connie's eyes reflected her love for her son.

"The kids were talking very personally. I'm just realizing that we adults were so preoccupied with all the things we needed to do to get our lives back in order that this theme dominated every conversation. At one point, though, I was cleaning out a new, expensive, restaurant-quality freezer with Chad, a work-relief fellow from my church. As we were almost retching from the ghastly smell of the now room-temperature rotten meat and seafood, Chad mentioned witnessing a particularly brutal stabbing in the Superdome! It was so odd. I expected him to be upset or something, but when he told me about it, he was completely unemotional, as if he were reporting the weather! He then gave a passionless account of all the people he personally knew who had died in the disaster."

I thought about the contrast between the children's open expression of feeling and the factual interchange between the "adults." *Just as the quality of our possessions are apparent to our conscious minds (expensive to cheap, new to old, fresh to rotten), the quality of our relationships (whether spontaneous, personal, human interactions or conditioned/programmed exchanges) are evident to our psychological bodies.*

"I was finally able to get through to Cedric by phone, so I asked him why he hasn't talked to the kids since we left. His response was, 'ALL you do is bitch, Connie! Can't we have a moment of quiet conversation without you nagging me? You're just trying to make me feel guilty for not indulging your childlike fantasy of some 'perfect dad' instead of trusting me to father my kids as I see fit. Oliver and Felicity are lucky to have a strong, successful father who doesn't let people push him around. And I can afford to buy them whatever they want! How many dads can do that? Besides, I am a man, Connie. I'm different from you, so I interact with the kids differently. If you would only respect our differences, everything would be fine!'"

"Ouch!" My body recoiled from his insensitivity and psychological-warfare tactics. My body tends to react to psychological abuse in much the same way that other bodies react to physical harm. "How did you handle that?" I asked tentatively.

"I sensed he was going to hang up, which always pushes my buttons—I feel so worthless when he does that, as though my feelings and concerns have no value. So I told him I was sorry and then explained, 'I've just been devastated about losing the house and the garden—we'd worked so hard getting everything just the way we like it, and now it's gone.' He accepted my apology and seemed calmer, willing to talk a few more minutes, but then, as always, he said, 'I've got to get back to work.' Ced's so difficult to talk to because he's either 'busy' getting ready for work, 'swamped' at work, 'needing to relax' after work, or thinking about work and 'can't be disturbed right now.' It's very, very *hard* breaking through!"

"OWWWWWW!" I emoted, feeling the pain in her report.

"What now?"

"You told him YOU were sorry?" I asked, shaking my head.

"Yes…why?" Connie said shyly.

"Well—I don't want to add to your burden, Connie. You've been through so much already, but…"

"But what?"

"Um…it's just that apologizing is not a useful way to interact with a Rock."

Connie perked up suddenly. "That's what David says! I mean, he says I shouldn't let Cedric push me around." She paused; I guessed she was thinking about her dear friend. "Oh no—I forgot to ask Ced about him AGAIN! I get so flustered when I hear him speak that way that I forget what I'm doing! SHOOT! Anyway, since David's not around, I guess I'm reverting to my old ways…" Connie's brow furrowed. "Why do you call Cedric a *rock*?"

I flipped through some printed pages of my writing and inquired of Our Rescuer what was useful for Connie to know. "It's pretty heavy," I informed her. "I recommend reading just a little bit at a time."

She nodded and said wearily, "Heavy is good if it will help me get some sleep. I think I'll try it out right away." She stifled a yawn. "Goodnight, then."

"Sweet dreams!" I replied. After watching her depart, I walked over to the TV, which had remained on despite no one watching it. I turned it off, much preferring it that way.

DEDUCTIONS

If we limit most of our waking hours to employment in Rock businesses and work-related endeavors, we're likely to negotiate with family members in a detached, businesslike manner. The Rock, of course, offers the extreme example. In Corp'rock families, "dependents" buy or barter for anything they want or need from the Rock on his terms. For example, he purchases household items as cheaply as possible and then charges his offspring a hefty markup. His kids mount up sizable debts before they are able to do much work (it can take years to pay off the obstetrician's bill!), so their first job is often child prostitution or at least servicing the Rock and his pals. Most kids learn to confine their wants and needs to hold "expenses" to a minimum (Definition Lock: want/need = cost).

To help pay their "bills," children also work for the family "business" as smiling salespersons. Quick to market the family image, they tell others only what promotes "sales." ("My mom and dad are the best!") The Corp'rock continually assesses input and output from family members, tabulating their effect on productivity and managing each person accordingly. Children caught "selling" a different product, such as the sincere sharing of their genuine thoughts and feelings (what alerts us to the slow death caused by such programming!) are considered disloyal, as if they're selling out to the competition. Corp'rocks make EVERY effort to keep their children from infringing on their own hard-earned territory—"MY" way! Poor "job performances" result in the loss of "benefits" (personal requests are denied) and/or in "pay cuts" (basic needs are *not* met). When parental "outputs" of attention, acceptance, and appreciation are at stake, not to mention personal intake of food and water, vulnerable members ultimately prioritize their "utility," "productivity," and "sales" within the family business and surrender to serving this "company" (Definition Lock: growth = professional advancement; company = family).

Remember, Rocks' imprint of "relationships" is one active agent and another passively complying with the active one—the dynamics of man and machine. Assuming the "man" position, Mascrocks manipulate others in any way they can, trying to get them to "work." Thus, Corp'rocks treat family members like office equipment—pushing their buttons, adjusting their "margins" and other parameters, dictating their verbal output, and so on. (Copy machines NEVER ask for breaks or time off!) Children, who by their nature want to belong and are eager to please, usually conform. They become, in part, Femrocks that allow themselves to be used and abused for the rest of "their" lives as someone's possession, reasoning that their "taxes" will be less (Definition Lock: possession = belonging).

In human terms, a personal life exists in an environment of intimacy where people know you through a multitude of caring interactions and events. In the Corp'rock family, these quality relationships are lacking. The "by-products" of a marriage (i.e., children) "grow up" knowing nothing about the psychology of their parents, themselves, or others. These Corp'rock kids therefore give what they have received and learned to enjoy—job performance and job-performance evaluations. Each person has a specific job to do and is promoted or demoted according to how well it is done.

The "adults" reared by a Corp'rock have internal quality-control settings that seek these familiar exchanges. They shelve people like inventory, placing them in stock boxes of well-known personality types and growing annoyed with those who "step outside their box." They spend their precious time only with those who help "business"—whether by increasing production, facilitating marketing, extending "product shelf-life," or boosting sales. All contacts must be purposeful and goal-oriented ("I'm calling because I'd like your input on an investment opportunity"). All assessments and decisions are based on cost ("That restaurant is cheaper—let's take the family there"). They give in an attempt to get. They also do only what you'll pay them for, and the quality of their work is strictly dependent on just how much you'll pay (Definition Lock: more money = greater quality).

Having lost their basic trust of fellow humans,[25] as well as any interest in their well-being, and having no awareness of our inherent interdependence, these Corp'rock-reared humans rely on their schedule and performance for security and comfort. Their "need" to produce outranks any requests for intimacy from other "workers," since their innate desire for close human contact is deeply buried. At best they understand closeness in only one capacity, such as sexual intercourse. Unless their spouses are willing to "produce" on demand or when there is a schedule opening, they are discarded or ignored, while the Rock gives priority to interactions with willing strangers—customers or Internet contacts receive any sharing or episodes of ardor. As prolonged intimacy brings to light each individual's underlying psychological condition (when we're our own best friend, it's easy to deceive ourselves), the Rock keeps people so busy and preoccupied that they're not available to notice anyone's inner state, let alone help it evolve (Definition Lock: intimacy = "productive" activity).

As intimacy-starved, money-driven, and image-focused Corp'rocks run our businesses, real people on phones or at check-in or check-out counters are increasingly replaced by "cost-effective" electronics (if you want to talk to a human being, it will cost you! [as it did them!]). Do-it-yourself manuals and workshops abound as we can no longer depend on people to provide the service they advertise, let alone offer product support. Self-help books are also extremely popular since we can't rely on our health-care professionals to guide us economically, ethically, and wisely. Nonetheless, technology advances by leaps and bounds as more and more people give the majority of their attention, care, and inspiration to the inanimate.

Focusing on what is outside ourselves is natural when we are "young," but we *learn* to take an exclusive interest in objects. For instance, when those closest to a person have been distant and unavailable or even treacherous, smiling broadly before taking him for all he has, he becomes cold or obnoxious to others in self-defense—a product of his environment. He insists on one-up/one-down relationships, since someone standing at his side as an equal feels TOO THREATENING! His rigid maintenance of the much safer "parent/child stance" yields inevitable conflict. Turning to objects that make no demands for closeness, availability, warmth, kindness, or equity, he forgets his outstanding debt to his fellow humans and neglects his inborn responsibility for unselfish service. Absorbed in purchasing and selling products and growing his net worth, he rests, satisfied, having found "his" way (the "Only What I Know Exists" Epilogue of the Translation Matrix: "My" way IS The Way!).

Value Investing—Putting Our Time and Effort into What Pays the Highest Premiums: "Customer" Service

Whether we learn the way of the Rock in a Corp'rock family, in a Rock school or other Rock institution, or in an increasingly Rocky community, we must work HARD to overcome it (inside and out!). The prevalence of Rock "goods" and "services" can even assist us, by reflecting the bottom line of our images and helping us see what we're "buying" when we choose imagery! Once we become aware of the serious tradeoffs, we can start forfeiting any short-term payoffs of image (momentarily looking, sounding, and feeling good) in favor of the true long-term gains of psychological growth. This development of our mutual humanity IS both the product and service of healthy relationships—a worthwhile investment! Like corporate expansion and franchising, the continual expansion of our behavioral, emotional, mental, and relational repertoires is the evidence of our success. Just as the routine investment of a few dollars compounds over time, when we regularly allocate our assets (despite "market" volatility!) toward furthering our human relationship with all we meet...in time we all prosper! It's that simple.

Let's return to the origins of our words and activities:

Roll over: Avoid settings that are dehumanizing (wanting the most from you while giving the least in exchange!). Don't let Rock businesspersons roll over you with their exorbitant fees, minimal services, and antisocial agendas. There are always *other ways* of getting what you need or want without feeding greed and malice. For example, consider taking a break from businesses and helping yourself or one another as our ancestors once did. (Try some kitchen wisdom or home remedies for those minor ailments!) Also, legitimate services do exist—those without spiels or gimmicks (see the answer to question 12 at the end of this chapter). Find them and do business with them only!

When scouting for socially responsible companies, be wary of the cheapest price tag. (Child or slave labor may be involved. Be mindful of contributing to the decline of reputable businesses and/or the exploitation of our shared environment and its resources.) Also, the easiest path to much-needed services may *not* be the best—be on the lookout! Conversely, the difficult path of standing up to Rocks and refusing their "services" may be far superior over the long term for you and the human community at large.

Markets: For all business decisions, consult Our Rescuer. (No rising and falling "markets" with her!) She is the most stable and most human presence within us. She exposes the least stable and least human parts of us that demand far more than they supply—because they are so "young." She is the supplier with unlimited stores, who throughout the psychological journey gives us whatever we need to meet the *genuine* needs of others as we discover and meet our own.

Bonds: When you buy into the face value of Corp'rocks and their businesses and depend on them, you secure a future for your family where only your bank bonds mature. So rather than opening only bank and other investment accounts in anticipation of future family needs, why not also open hearts and minds? Rather than merely purchasing stock shares, why not deeply share in one another's lives too? We soon find that satisfying our obligation to our fellow humans is what fulfills, strengthens, and unites us, *and* meets our own needs as well (psychological supply and demand!).

Take stock! The problems with investing in one person (self perhaps?) are similar to the problems with investing in just one stock. Psychologically speaking, we need a diversified "portfolio" that includes members of each stage of psychological development. Even the Rock is a shareholder of humanity (unconscious though "it" may be!) and needs our assistance to be redeemed (growth investing!). Investing in a Rock's innate humanness decreases the likelihood of the Rock investing in our inhuman derivatives or those of our loved ones. Experiencing firsthand the making of a Mineral in ourselves and those with whom we have a vested interest, such as our offspring, gives us compassion for all those stuck in the Mineral Stage and incentive to prioritize their psychological gains.

Mutual funds: Humanity is the currency we all share. How much we possess is a matter of endowment, education, choice, and effort—just as it is with how much money we have. Pay attention to how we devalue our precious humanity relative to the dollar. Compare the number of times you've questioned how much a product, service, or activity will cost you versus how many times you've considered the cost to your humanity. Consider the amount of work you've done to make money, and compare it with the amount of work you've done to grow in awareness of your body, heart, mind, and spirit. To what degree have you kept accounts of your human "income" and "expenditures"? We know the global economy has an impact on every one of us, but how often do we consider the well-being of our global humanity and its impact on our lives?

The REAL estate: The business skills we first learn in selling lemonade, Scout cookies, band candy, or Junior Achievement products can be transferred to the adult business world. Similarly, every Corp'rock business practice can be appraised in terms of maturation. For example, a Rock's money-making ventures, well-practiced negotiation routines, and office-management skills can be used, like venture capital, to start up the business of family relationships. His focus on profit and alertness to where every dollar goes can be redirected to the coming and going of human qualities, such as emotions. If a Rock is attuned to the rise and fall of the housing or stock markets and can maintain her course, she can do the same with her children. She can relate to her kids through these skills, being with them through their ups and downs, discerning patterns, anticipating both, while learning how to shore up their psychological foundations and support steady growth. If a Rock has a keen eye that can spot a good customer and a sharp mind that can maneuver them into a sale, he can tweak these abilities to notice and provide what his spouse needs. All these aptitudes can also be used to negotiate a Rock's inner world. Her finesse in marketing her company's image and products can then be modified to disclose what is real about herself. With creative thought, all corporate methods can be "refinanced" into a means of gently paying off the mortgage on our humanity.

Our years of serving Rock bosses and businesses can be redeemed by merely trading in our Rock "business" tactics for Our Rescuer's "soft-sell" human relationship resources—her version of "insider trading." However, as in establishing any new business, transitioning from Rock servitude to service to Our Rescuer takes time. Foremost, it requires a willingness to STOP buying into Rock business practices and to tap into our *human* reserves instead—our economic and *human* recessions can then recover side by side. Working with humanity everywhere, investigating its options, and persevering in such investments over a lifetime requires us to bank on this aggressive-growth adviser, Our Rescuer. She deprograms our Evasions by revealing common ground in all our relationships. For example, women may be heavy users of the Blame Game, Scatterware, and Program Paranoia, and men may be more enamored with the Excuse Escape, Indirect Application, and Point of View Shield, but both are equally incapacitated in terms of *human* relating—helping to heal and develop the wounded, regressed human being within all. Both genders are in need of each other's rescuing efforts and rebates. Just remember, for our markets to be free, we *must be* free ourselves!

Our Rescuer is the best of all possible investments as she is the media in which our "business" practices flourish as they transform into their original purpose of earnestly relating to her and to each other. She is the legal loophole that declares innocent the origins of everything we might say or do (our "inner children" are just telling our life stories!). She is the single-payer health-care provider who rescues us from all Rock "business" practitioners, practices, and priorities, with her psychological-growth-based economic model. An unlimited partnership with Our Rescuer also maintains price "floors" and "ceilings" that protect our emotional health, while minimizing Rocky returns (the perfect "tax" shelter!). In her we all find our futures, *and* the "property" value of our psychology skyrockets! The conception and maturing of this ongoing, ever-yielding intimacy with Our Rescuer and each other is doing the best we can.

BACK TO WORK!: Ask Our Rescuer's help in answering these questions:

1. What are your "business" practices in your relationships?
    a. Are you a consumer? Are you more interested in getting what you want than providing a service? Do you recommend Rock businesses to family and friends and make excuses when results are less than satisfactory? Do you then blame loved ones for "complaining" or being "HARD to please"?
    b. Are you a manufacturer? Do you relate to others in an assembly-line manner—giving everyone the same speech or act? Are you looking to personally profit from each exchange?
    c. Are you a rescuer? Do you meet your own and others' needs in the most timely and effective way? Do you proactively work to discern what will be required in the future?

2. Pick one of the Rock business practices and discern the confusion practitioners have with the three movies talked about in chapter 6. For instance, the Rock pediatrician implying that most parents are doing right by their children is presuming that Movie #1 (the perfection of our One Mind) is the only film playing in their systems. How might the inclusion of the other two movies that play in every individual mind improve this pediatrician's practice?

3. Read over Jayda's remarks about her husband and her therapist (pp. 162-3) and Connie's conversation with Cedric (p. 186), and identify the Rock programs involved. Can you relate to any of these characters or relate them to people you know?

4. Look at the prevalence of the Indirect Application in our society's institutions (law, medicine, mental health, and so on). How might clients profit if professionals in these fields helped them discern what the greater Body is communicating in each troubling event?

5. Notice the communication of Our Rescuer that can be found in your daily business interactions. How can you use your routine chores developmentally? (For example, "I wonder how I can pay my monthly bills more consciously and in a unique way?" {Let you "inner kids" choose the stamps!})

6. Do you give more of your attention to saving money or saving lives? Whose lives need your physical efforts, your emotional connection, your insight and ideas, and your spiritual wisdom? How do you define "your best" in these areas? Keep a weekly balance sheet of your assets and liabilities in each category to aid your accountability.

7. Which relationships have had the most powerful impact on you? What did you learn from them about "business" or the "business" of relationship? What were you taught to supply, to demand, and to withhold?

8. Which of the RV Evasion Programs do you employ most often? Consider how the distribution of such a program would affect your downline and your profits in a direct-sales business (the multilevel marketing of healthy psychology, for instance)? How might you transform these behaviors to maximize everyone's gain?

9. How can you convert your "micro"-managing or image sales into "revenue" for your real Self? (We can learn to reject images just as easily as deleting the scam ads that frequently appear on our computer screens!) What "sales quota" is reasonable for you? What steps can you take to attain this quota?

10. Set up a creative and playful accounting system that alerts you to how you spend your time, energy, and money. For example, you might add quarters to a piggy bank when you facilitate human development and remove them when you plug into Rock programming and business practices.

11. How might you make changes to support fair trade between the psychological and physical—your "inner" and outer worlds?

12. How do you spot Rock companies?

13. Realize the production and distribution of your mature psychology is your self-employment. What are your specific "products?" Evaluate yourself in terms of:
    a. Supply (In what areas and to what degree are you receiving what is coming to you?)
    b. Manufacturing (Are you cost-effectively producing the products you are designed to create and distribute?)
    c. Sales (Are these products finding suitable and appreciative customers? How might you improve your marketing strategies to reach the right people? How might you adjust your worldly skills to increase your productivity in the "inner" world?)
    d. Profits (Document your expenditures and returns. How might you best invest your gains?)

14. Take some time to express your feelings about this book so far. Write down what you value about it. Write about what you don't like. Be specific and don't hold back. Come back to what you've written at a later date and read it with the intent of learning about yourself. Then ask Our Rescuer if I need to hear any of what you've written, and if so, please e-mail me.

[1] SCORE Association entrepreneurial training workshop, New Orleans, LA, July 2005, SCORE.org.

[2] "The Century of the Self," *Top Documentary Films,* accessed August 16, 2012, http://topdocumentaryfilms.com/the-century-of-the-self/.

[3] "Inattentional Blindness," *Wikipedia*, modified June 15, 2012, http://en.wikipedia.org/wiki/Inattentional_blindness.

[4] "Corporate Personhood," *Reclaim Democracy: Restoring Citizen Authority Over Corporations,* accessed October 23, 2012, http://reclaimdemocracy.org/corporate-personhood/.

[5] "Hysterectomy is the second most common operation performed on women in the United States. About 556,000 of these surgeries are done annually. By age 60, approximately one out of every three American women will have had a hysterectomy." Debra Gordon and Stephanie Dionne Sherk, "Hysterectomy," *Encyclopedia of Surgery,* accessed April 15, 2012, http://www.surgeryencyclopedia.com/Fi-La/Hysterectomy.html.

[6] Dr. Joseph Mercola, "Nearly 250,000 Deaths From ONE Common Mistake: Here's How to Protect Yourself, *Mercola, com: Take Control of Your Health,* February 4, 2011, http://articles.mercola.com/sites/articles/archive/2011/02/04/death-by-medicine-an-update.aspx.

[7] "As many as 98,000 people a year die from medical errors, and preventable infections—along with medication mix-ups." "Hospital Infection Rates Continue Alarming Rise," *Healthcare on MSNBC.com,* updated 4-13-10, http://www.msnbc.msn.com/id/36465334/ns/health-health_care/t/hospital-infection-rates-continue-alarming-rise/.

[8] George M. Lamsa, *Holy Bible from the Ancient Eastern Text* (New York: A. J. Holman Company, 1957), Colossians 1:27, 1177.

[9] Ibid., Matthew 22:39, 978.

[10] Ibid., Matthew 13:30, 966.

[11] Ibid., Matthew 22:37, 978.

[12] Ibid., St. Luke 15:11–32, 1037–38.

[13] Ibid., Mathew 7:1, 957.

[14] "For the love of money is the root of all evil;" Ibid., 1 Timothy 6:10, 1189.

[15] Ibid., Acts 20:35, 1110.

[16] Ibid., Luke 5:24-25, 1020.

[17] Ibid., Matthew 4:10, 953.

[18] Kenneth Barker, *The NIV Study Bible, New International Version* (Grand Rapids, MI: Zondervan Bible Publishers, 1985), Matthew 7:15, 1453.

[19] Josh Fox, *Gasland*, an International WOW Company Production in Association with HBO Documentary Films, 2010.

[20] Lamsa, Matthew 25:14–30, 981.

[21] Barker, Matthew 6:19, 1452.

[22] "Agricultural practices are stripping the soil of nutrients with remarkable implications. They are devastating the nutritional value of crops, making dramatic changes at an alarming rate," "Nutrient-Depleted Soil," *Global Healing Center*, accessed April 15, 2013, http://www.globalhealingcenter.com/effects-of-pesticides/nutrient-depleted-soil

[23] "Harry Harlow," *Wikipedia*, modified September 22, 2012, http://www.ask.com/wiki/Harry_Harlow.

[24] "Nutrient-Depleted Soil," *Global Healing Center.*

[25] Hopes: Trust vs. Mistrust (Oral-sensory, Birth–2 years), "Erikson's Stages of Psychosocial Development," *Wikipedia,* modified April 14, 2013, http://en.wikipedia.org/wiki/Erikson's_stages_of_psychosocial_development.

Chapter 8

Politics

Image in Authority

Connie was waiting for me to get up. She had a cup of coffee in one hand and my writing in the other, and she was frowning. After a quick check on Pookie, I poured a bowl of granola and joined Connie at the table.

She got right down to business. "I stayed up late last night reading everything you gave me by flashlight. Needless to say, I didn't sleep well. I haven't been sleeping well anyway since the storm, but..." Connie drew a deep breath and sighed. "Look, Anne, I don't need psychoanalysis right now with everything else going on. My plate is full without taking on Cedric's problems. Besides, he's forever reminding me that he's the head of our household and my role is to respect and honor him."

Now I was the one sighing as I considered how to respond. "When we talked about Cedric last night, and you inquired about what a Rock is—you seemed to want information. That's why I gave it to you. I mean you no harm, Connie. I know this is a difficult time, and I want to help. Honoring someone with such delayed development and letting him lead the family can only increase your difficulties."

I paused to allow her a moment to consider what I just said. Then I continued. "When I first met you, you mentioned that you like to keep up with current events. Well, our inner world of psychology gives us information daily, just as our newspaper, TV, and online news sources report about our outer world. When we are so focused on the world outside that we exclude the world inside, our psychological news must piggyback on the external. In other words, our present disaster may be mirroring some disaster within us."

"I believe it's better to accept people just the way they are, offering encouragement rather than negativity!" Connie's tone revealed her annoyance.

I responded as a clinician, speaking gently, "Connie, the Mineral Stage is as serious a psychological illness as Effie's invasive cancer is a physical illness. We can make ourselves feel good by believing, 'Cedric will come to his senses eventually,' or 'Effie's going to be just fine!' but merely accepting their symptoms won't heal them. These symptoms must be acknowledged as pathological and treated appropriately for a 'positive' outcome to occur. Otherwise, we're in denial…and the disease spreads."

"That's only YOUR opinion; not MINE. Excuse me." Although soft-spoken, Connie's words were soaked in irritation. She abruptly left the table and hurried out the back door. As I followed her with my gaze, I noticed Felicity's baby doll propped in a highchair against the wall near the door.

Leadership in families is not about the seat at the head of the table! That's silly! Again, it shows how the Corp'rock business model has permeated our culture—assigning rigid roles with only one head of household and expecting submission from everyone else. Developmental psychology leads us to a new concept entirely: authority emanates from our collective Identity, Our Rescuer, and this Authority may be heard in any and all family members when we're listening. Of course, we can hear other voices as well, such as the Rock's core of rage, which rises to the surface when the family laundry is exposed.

LAUNDRY*! Oh, no! Effie asked me to do laundry this morning and I forgot! I can't seem to remember* ANYTHING *for more than a few seconds since the hurricane!* I jogged to my bedroom to get my spare underwear, which I'd been washing out by hand the past few days, my nightgown, extra shirt, and extra pair of jeans—my three-day supply of clothing, typical for the average New Orleanian who evacuates. Since I'd been waking up multiple times each night in a cold sweat, I decided to wash my sheets, which I wrestled off the bed. I carried the lot to a room off the garage, where I dumped it in with everyone else's clothes already in the extra-large washer. In the kitchen, I disconnected the refrigerator from the generator, noticing an empty four-liter container of red wine left on the counter. Again, I was aware of each of our stress reactions: Connie's denial of her husband's condition and her underlying irritability, my poor memory and night sweats, and terminally ill Effie's self-medication with alcohol.

Back in the laundry room, I plugged in the washer and started the cold wash cycle. I stuck my hand in the water—it was quite hot! The air temperature was close to a hundred, so this was no surprise. After tossing in the soap, I pulled up a chair so the moment the washing machine finished, I could reconnect the refrigerator. In my current state of mind, I couldn't trust myself to remember. After a calming conversation with Our Rescuer, I pulled out my journal and began to write.

EVACUATION DAY 8: Who Is Running the House (or Senate)—the Adult or "Child"?

Discerning the psychological adult from the psychological child is as simple as sticking one's hand under the tap and feeling the water temperature. This differentiation would be easy were it not for the Rock businesses among us and RV programs within us that demand antagonal perceptions and judgments. Nowhere is "testing the water" more ESSENTIAL than in recognizing and choosing good leadership. The psychological adult and "child" may LOOK the same, but *personal* contact quickly reveals the differences. We must immerse ourselves in the waters of our own psychology, however, if we are to truly know any person, distinguish the adult from the "child," *and* choose wisely.

The adult has years of experience with both outer and inner worlds—"laundering" on the inside as well as the outside as frequently as needed. This wealth of experience has taught the adult how to handle the full range of ages, personality types, emotional and behavioral reactions, and life circumstances; the routine as well as the unexpected; the "good," the "bad," and the disastrous. The adult is sensitive in sharing experiences, including painful errors, to minimize the suffering of others. Recognizing those who are younger, the adult nurtures and guides them, so they might avoid making hurtful mistakes.

In contrast, small children are inexperienced and limited in their abilities to pay attention to and learn from their restricted experience. They imitate others, confusing the positions and postures of physically older individuals with maturity and mistaking statements of mimicry or wishful thinking, such as "I can do it," for genuine ability. They pretend to be better or older than they are, and are delighted when you go along with the pretense. They don't like those who don't play along, particularly those who use diminutive names, such as "baby" or "little" boy or girl. Young children often say and do what will get attention ("Look at me! Look what I did!"). Their needs and wishes, like their hunger to be noticed and loved, influence the information they hear, accept, share, and withhold. They test limits too. They ignore existing knowledge and rules to do what they please or to explore ("I wonder what Mom's pink pills taste like?"). Not yet versed in the laws of nature, they require monitoring.

An adult conveys valid information that is pertinent to a situation or person and withholds what is superfluous. Adults' expressions are purposeful and productive, both in the immediate and over the long term. Regardless of personal repercussions, they say and do what needs to be said and done to serve the developmental needs of each individual as well as the whole. They see the entire picture as well as the parts, employing both. They offer recommendations about current problems as well as potential complications. They are actively involved, ensuring that precautions are carried out and follow-up measures are taken. Adults encourage healthy relationships, subscribing to a checks-and-balance system for each participant and problem. To sustain the energy, strength, concern, and wisdom to engage everyone they encounter, adults continually relate to Our Rescuer, who leads them in leading others.

Little children tend to be self-centered, playful, and undiscriminating, fancying what is not necessarily good for them ("Give me what I want! I want cake"). They spend their time (and any money they might have) on what gives momentary personal pleasure, rejecting at first glance what doesn't seem enjoyable. As much as they may demand a large piece of "cake," they often resist putting forth the effort to procure ingredients, make the "cake," and clean up afterward. (They are happy to play with their pals while you do the work.)

Young children have difficulty staying on task—they often dawdle or becomes distracted. When there's a problem, they react quickly, pointing fingers away from themselves. They have unrealistic expectations, seeking love and care from those without the capacity to provide them and perhaps not reaching out to those who do. They are attracted to people (such as Rocks) who *say* what they want to hear. They don't know the difference between those who beguile, those who mean what they say, and those who tell them what they *need* to hear for their growth. They are as credulous with the false "assurances" of Rock caretakers as when they are told that Santa Claus is coming. They also believe in magic. If they're asked whether they think our authorities can quickly clean up any radioactive refuse on our land or in our oceans, they answer "yes!" having seen their parents swiftly clean up all their messes. Without psychological adult supervision, a child is destined to be repeatedly fooled and victimized, often regressing to psychological infancy as a consequence.

These differentiating qualities of children and adults may seem obvious until the psychological "child" and the adult reside in mature physical bodies. Then people are perplexed and lose their ability to differentiate. Suddenly attractiveness, age, gender, status, and achievements of each body are given more weight than the psychological maturity demonstrated. We are similarly puzzled and at a loss when we look at ourselves in the mirror. We tend to focus on, assess, and alter externals rather than also attending to the states of our hearts and minds. This external bias leads to internal lag, oppression, and atrophy, and it ultimately results in a psychologically young population—as evidenced by the growing number of psychological "infants" seeking positions of leadership or lifting their voices in support of their "nursery" mates as authorities.

Should people who are physically adult but psychologically undeveloped have the right to hold public office? Can we trust them to fulfill their job description? Do we follow their counsel and accept the information they provide as truth? ("He says he's 'fighting terrorism' when he invades and terrorizes other countries!") If we don't rely on toddlers in matters of family, community, or state, why do we so often place faith in leadership that is as psychologically immature...if not more so?

ROCK HEADS: Leaders in the Youngest Stage of Psychological Development

Rock authorities uphold Rock businessmen and their guiding principle: "Money matters most!" From this principle, one can easily deduce that those with the most money are the most valuable people—the ones who can best lead us to a prosperous future or at least hire the people who can. Once in leadership, Rocks employ the same predatory economics in government as their compatriots do in business. Instead of goods and services, however, an idealistic image is what they have citizens buying, at the price of their human lives.

Rock leaders have little human experience. They're familiar with the Mineral Stage of Development and its inhumane programming, and it is this devolutionary path they share with their followers. They guide people *away* from their genuine human experience (Circumvention Program), denying them the lessons that experience imparts and any further learning that might be built on these lessons. Consequently, their followers do not develop. Lest they take note of their condition, however, the Rock head distracts them with stories. Rock leaders manipulate the mythology passed down in the typical American family, with its "good guys" and "bad guys," into a fanciful story line that supports their one-dimensional perspective. "Kids" then place their leaders' information into the same frames of reference to which they are accustomed: "We're the 'good guys'!" while the "bad guys" are those who attempt to interject reality (Filterware).

By the time we're physically grown, most of us have had extensive experience with adults and children of all physical ages. We've learned to cast our family members and others in rigid roles based on appearances, rather than perceiving each other's wholeness. Rock leaders eagerly tap into this role-typing. The characters in their tales are the same idealistic images we're all familiar with—dads, moms, brothers, sisters, and other kids who have endearments and triumphs but also foibles and difficulties—basically good people. (Remember, our families have trained us to see these family roles and images and NOT look past them!) Political Rocks (Polirocks) use these imprinted parent and child roles to cast themselves and their cronies as beloved characters from our own life stories (Contextual Warp). When a Polirock dons that familiar parental image, for example, we feel at ease, as if we're back in the home of our youth, where we can easily slide into the dutiful "child" mode, accustomed to being told what we can or can't have and what we should or shouldn't do. In such a youthful mind-set, we hear the scripts that are near and dear to our hearts from our own upbringing, and we are lulled into presuming that members of the "nuclear" family of Polirocks are like our loved ones in their caring for "the kids."

Just Like Dad!

The Polirock man favors playing the "strong" "fatherly" role in leadership, offering a firm handshake, "solid advice," and *unbending* tenets by which to live. We citizens are expected to submit to him and frame our experiences and receptivity to new information based on what "Dad" says (Point of View Shield). His guidelines instruct us to approach those that "fit" his mold, those that that sooth and support our images and make us feel powerful and capable in our "youth." We are to avoid those who make us feel unhappy or uncomfortable, disempowered or incapable (In other words, "Don't talk to 'strangers'!"). Notice the binary or bipartisan selection! The Polirock "pop" would keep us confined to our comfort zones, enabling him to preserve "his" Program and comfortably take advantage of us. (Noticing what he's up to would definitely make us uncomfortable!) When we are so focused on imagery, our lives inevitably don't work out well. The Poli'pop encourages us to be brave, to prevail amid hardship, and to maintain a strong front. If we cannot or will not, we succumb to the one-downer position.

Polirocks thus use their fixed, false one-upper/one-downer bipartisan mind-set to polarize a population and feed our denial, uncertainty, and FEAR. They "defend 'our' way of life" by "sheltering" us from the awareness of Rock reality (Fooling "facts" of the Circumvention Program). For instance, they offer themselves as "trustworthy" authorities to be counted on during our nation's uncertain and frightening times. Then, to minimize insecurity (particularly their own), they maximize the defense budget[1] (Program Paranoia) and channel massive amounts of public monies into armament businesses owned or operated by those in the Mineral Stage. (Mineral media helps out by supplying a stream of iconic "human"-interest stories that demonstrate that these actions were necessary for OUR national security! [Public "I" Program, p. 206].)

Rocks grant "equal protection" to the common man (Scam Program). We citizens are harbored from facts ("Since they might not handle it well—we wouldn't want to panic the public" [Excuse Escape]). We are shielded from "nonprofitable" solutions ("There are NO nontoxic/nonviolent/ inexpensive remedies that work!" [POV Shield]), *and* we may even be screened from the decision-making process ("The average voter cannot understand the complexity of the situation, so their participation would only confuse them and delay progress" [the Confounder Program guarantees confusion!]). As a result of such "cushioning," few people monitor Rock activities, *and* the Rocks' core of rage—from having known NO consistent protection themselves—is given free reign among the population. Time, energy, and money must then be spent directly by citizens or indirectly through our government to restore some semblance of safety: security systems, firearms purchases, taxpayer-funded regulatory agencies, inspections, tests, law enforcement, and increasingly costly insurances to cover anything that could possibly go wrong. (The building of faulty levees in New Orleans necessitated that hundreds of thousands of people buy flood insurance!)

Embracing the "ample provider" role, Poli'pops are only too willing to offer EXTENSIVE "safeguards" that require citizens to pay more and MORE and **MORE** for protection, while our sense of safety ever diminishes (brings the mafia to mind, doesn't it?). One "stable structure" provided by these Rock "pops" is taxation, something we all can count on to ALWAYS be there (Select All or None Program). For example, we pay federal, state (except for a few states, such as Texas), and local income taxes on what we earn. We pay a gift tax when transferring large amounts of money and property, and we pay sales tax on our purchases. We pay property taxes and hefty taxes on utilities, phones, and public services. With each tax given a different name (use taxes, wheel taxes, capital gains taxes, franchise taxes, estate taxes, and so on), we may not notice how many times the same dollars are taxed (Scatterware). Also, when people are so heavily and *diversely* taxed, many struggle to survive (Squelch Program). Not to worry, as "Dad" steps in to apportion a fraction of the funds to poorly functioning bureaucracies that offer public assistance. Problems inevitably arise (Incompetence Program), and so replacing them with private profit-making Rock companies *seems* the most viable option. With the ever-increasing exploitation of the citizenry, the slow and methodical deprivation of human rights, and the growing lack of basic necessities (such as truth!), we need comfort!

What Would Mom Do?

The "nurturing," "caring" "mother" role is another favorite of the political Rock. With "sincere" smiles and "reassuring" words, the Polirock "mom" "faithfully" supports Mascrock leaders, encouraging us to do the same (POV Shield). When people whose hearts and minds are still functioning decry her standards, "she" quickly discounts them. This Poli'mom cooks up a canard: "*Overly sensitive* and *over-reacting* citizens can make up *preposterous* stories. These *alarmists* create *absurd conspiracy theories* and actually think that many of the serious problems burdening our dear country are deliberate! Disasters are part of our world, and a mature person accepts them as such." The Rock "mom" pans her opponents in a most genteel manner. She encourages us to stand with her in patronizing them as if they were the preschoolers in the family (little kids see monsters while lying in bed at night, right?). We are to offer understanding grins and pats on the head, but "we mustn't take their fancies seriously."

Another common tale the Poli'mom tells is about Rock professionals making "simple mistakes" and run-of-the-mill "human errors"—something "children" relate to, identify with, and consider "normal." As kids always want another chance to get it right when they've erred, she rallies us to extend this courtesy to the Rock and absolve him of adult responsibilities. So as these Rocks slide into the role of small children ("Oh gosh, there was a horrible 'accident'!"), the Rock "mom" cautions us NOT to scold or to have "temper tantrums" about what happened, but to step up to that "kind," "understanding" parental role that so many of us have longed for ourselves. The population then becomes "responsible" for accepting their Rock leaders' "human" limitations ("Poor dears, they just don't get that the strip-mining practices they've endorsed are permanently damaging the environment!"), cleaning up their messes ("Haven't we all needed outside help from time to time?"), or picking up the tab for someone else to do the job properly (e.g., a "reputable" Rock company). If all goes as planned, the Rocks then manipulate the parental public to hire, subsidize, or bail out their buddies as well.

As the Polirock mom cajoles with "compassionate" stories of "really quite ordinary" "happenstance," she schools "kids" with children's literature rather than reality. Using the Labeling Lock, she consistently guides "children" to judge those individuals who might alert us to her deception as "dumb," "doomy," "delusional," "boring," or perhaps engaged in some form of sibling rivalry. She may also cast such realists as dysfunctional parental figures going on and on about nothing ("What they're saying hasn't been substantiated by *our* experts!") or crying over spilled milk ("How can any *reasonable* person comment when no baseline tests were conducted *before* the milk was spilled!"). Remembering how our own dad burst our bubbles and our mom failed to nurture the good in us while harping on the exaggerated "bad," we're willing to project these residual negative feelings as our Poli'mom directs. *And* we extend our positive feelings toward our Poli'pop. Poli'mom then pacifies us with comforting words like "security" and "prosperity" when describing our future, and she assures us that all is well (the "All's Fine" Shine of the Stall—the hallmark of the Femrock!).

Kids Will Be Kids!

Rock leaders may take on the role of small boys who can be impulsive in their excitement and eagerness, often acting without thinking through the consequences (they didn't do their homework, did they?). They use modern, sophisticated technology when they want something done right and resort to child's play when they don't. Poli'lads feign "good-natured" young boys whose judgments are often faulty, getting them or others into trouble. They then "quite naturally" become fast talkers who hide what they are up to and tell "little white lies" to minimize their complicity. Polirock "parents" encourage us to give them a firm yet gentle hand and endless opportunities to practice in order to improve their skills.

As we have had hard times with Rock businesses, we tend to empathize with the Rocks' seemingly boyish explanations of "unforeseen difficulties." Having made many mistakes ourselves as a result of being overworked and overstressed, we assume that Rock leaders are operating under the same conditions. We feel sorry for them and consider them victims of the system—like us—rather than perpetrators of it.

Finally, Rocks may play the role of the naïve Little Mary Sunshine, who is always kind and enthusiastically accepting of everyone. Unable to tell friend from foe, the helpful from the harmful, she just trusts that everything will work out for the best. She much prefers talk to action ("Saying Is the Same as Doing" Stall). Why waste time on maintaining infrastructure like buildings, roads, and bridges when there are so many more interesting things to do?! She appears ignorant or unaware of the problems around her. Quick to please, however, she withholds "bad" news and gives priority to what's "good" or "uplifting" ("If we don't have enough money, we'll just print some more!"), what's "optimistic" ("I'm sure that sinkhole will be filled in no time!"), or what makes us feel proud ("We live in the greatest country in the world!"). When this Pollyanna Poli'lass is asked a serious question, such as "Do you think the fact that more than fifty New Orleans levees breaking during Hurricane Katrina[2] might be evidence of some sabotage?" she shakes her head vigorously and says, "Nope!" Much preferring lemonade to lemons, she returns to humming a happy tune. With the enduring faith of a child, she reaches out to each of us and asks that we stand with her in hope of an ever better tomorrow—without any basis for that hope. Over the years, we have listened to many a children's story where the situation looked dire, only to end happily ever after thanks to the youngest of children saving the day. Why consider any other story line?

Family Time!

Every family not only passes mythology, roles, and expectations from one generation to the next, but also uses particular words and definitions to embellish these stories. Polirocks merely ask us to include them in our family culture and understanding. For example, they apply the word "democracy" to the manner in which they are "elected" (Definitions Lock). This simple practice avoids "unnecessary" discussions about what democracy is, how the voting process is currently working or not working, and the unlikelihood of ruling Rocks bypassing their Control programs to allow the electorate to choose its own leaders. (Rocks consistently manipulate the voters, the voting process, and/or the voting machines to hijack the helm.[3]) While they speak of our nation's "wealth" (Partial Program), we "need" not notice our economic decline or the abject poverty in both our inner cities and psyches. Their "histories," like our own, have more to do with the stories we love to hear than with truth. By employing the words and meanings that are familiar and emotionally engaging, Polirocks appeal to the small children inside each individual and thereby draw our attention *and* support.

Another fantasy of our "inner children" that the Rock leader indulges is the notion that "adults" are already all grown up. While our imaginations are running away with us: Why stop at adulthood? Why not pretend we are God Himself, knowing what's best for us and our families and expecting others to honor our wishes? The Polirock feeds such foolishness by buoying up our sense of personal accomplishment, power, and worth. Once we're preoccupied with our own importance or heavenly nature ("It's Just Around the Corner" Coo of the Stall), we're ready to extend it to those who pamper these delusions. For instance, we may accept God's authority, not understanding His ways, and we offer this same uncomprehending but trusting stance to our leaders.

Having been so elevated by the Rock leader, we willingly allow him to use his position of power to elevate himself and his cronies—above the law, for example. Delighting in our own authority and personal gratification, the Polirock's concentration on "HIS" agenda, "HIS" career, and "HIS" bank account seems natural. With his focus on the family, "his" way even seems like our way. While he erodes the ground laid by our founding fathers (the Constitution and Bill of Rights) and quickly squanders the natural resources made over millennia, he creates an image of affluence that our unknown "inner children" can cling to, like hugging a warm blanket. A smiling, handsome face with soft, supportive words and well-versed, engaging lines expressing care for our beloved homeland appeals to those "young ones," who are enthralled by his charming tales. They delight in the make-believe and magical thinking of already being godly and all grown-up and yet at the same time having someone "take care" of them.

The spin cycle of the washing machine ended with a clunk. I immediately reconnected the generator to the refrigerator, tossed the laundry into a basket, and carried it to the backyard. There I hung the clothes on Effie's clotheslines next to her empty "garden"—a heap of dirt. As I hung up my spare pants, something dropped to the ground, which I promptly picked up. "Laundered money!" I whispered as I shoved the now-clean twenty-dollar bill into my back pocket. After completing my task, I paused to gaze at the large, brightly colored floral flag hanging in the far corner of the "garden," contrasting with the patch's barrenness. Already wilting from the heat, I returned to my inside perch. Since different environments bring out different facets of my writing, I continued to sit in the laundry room, peering out the lone window.

EXECUTIVE FUNCTIONS: Manipulating Our "Inner Infants" and "Children"
ROCKS RULE!

Mineral Stage leaders wave flags of normal, healthy, "family" functioning, all the while administering the execution (i.e., a slow death) of our democracy, diplomacy, economy, schools, communities, and humanity (to name just a few). In functional families, both parents and children are valued and have freedoms and rights that are respected. In contrast, when the Rock is commander in chief, only Rocks have freedoms and rights, which they interpret and carry out in unique ways. ("We the People" becomes "wee the people!") With their **Freedom of "Religion,"** for example, Rock leaders feel entitled to convert the unsuspecting public to their "beliefs." In their **Right to Own Property,** they claim a right to yours as well as theirs. (Now that your property is a disaster site and smells of toxic waste, you'll sell it for a song!)

Rock leaders use their **Freedom of Speech** to portray a lovely scene—their lives and affairs appear to be continually in bloom, like a garden flag (quite a contrast to an ever-changing living garden that requires consistent care!). With their **Right to Privacy,** they feel justified in hiding behind proprietary claims and skirting transparency. Upholding their **Right to Recognition, Honor, and Reputation,** Rock heads "correct" unfavorable perceptions of themselves and take revenge on those they hold responsible for those "mis"-perceptions. They use their **Right to Bear Arms** against those who threaten their "good" name. Any investigation into Rock activities is deemed an **Unreasonable**

Search—if attempts are made to prosecute their crimes, their Rock cronies employ the Legal Loophole (p. 156) to get them off in no time. (After all, they have a **Right to a** SPEEDY **Trial**!)

Rock representatives may speak incidentally of human rights but somehow manage to link the common good with their destructive and "self"-indulgent plans.[4] (They have the **Right to Work** the system, don't they?) For example, a bill that proposes "unemployment benefits to millions of Americans!" and "permanent jobs!"[5] might be attached to the expedition of an oil pipeline that could ruin an essential aquifer if there is a spill. When what is beneficial for the public is linked with what is potentially ruinous, the former can always be shelved later. Our "inner infants," with their short attention span and poor memory, will likely not notice or, as time passes, not remember.

VOTING Rights (and Wrongs)

Rocks believe they alone have the right to appoint or deny leadership—they have a **Right to Know** who will next fill an office, even before the election! They have a one-party system, the Rock Party, but offer a mockery of the democratic process to appease the public, with a selection of candidates that are Rocks or Minerals (programmed or manipulated to serve Rocks). By staging different characters in different settings, Rocks lead the psychologically young to expect a new and different story while getting the same old Rocky politics ("Change the Font" Formula of the Stall).

Nevertheless, Rock heads insist we have **"freedom" of choice**—we can pick which of *their* candidates "we" want. Some of the "choices" may appear so frightening that the preferred Mineral ticket *looks* good by comparison, manipulating the voter in the way of the Rock (Choice Commander). If we choose not to participate in voting because we don't like the despairingly narrow selection, we have "no right to complain." Also, when the winning candidates inevitably get into trouble, responsibility for their actions is redirected to the American people who elected them. (If you don't like our authorities kowtowing to corporations, blame the voters!" [Blame Game]) By performing our democratic duty, we then take part in pretense and support an EXTREMELY corrupt system.

Rock leaders disseminate through the population a unique set of "computer" programs (their **Right to Reproduce**) to effectively deter the healthy leadership that would alert young minds to pretense and corruption. Users gravitate to "charismatic" Rocks, while feeling anything from disinterest to revulsion toward less showy but better qualified authorities. No matter how physically mature or engaged in "adult" activities users are, these MALware programs assure that the departments of their "interior" remain immature—separate, at odds, and easy to manipulate.

E. THE STRETCHING (and reduction) PROGRAMS

These Rock Virus programs make less seem more and more seem less. They distract a user with preoccupations of his or her own "superiority" (or inferiority—what could I ever do to budge a Rock?). Each user becomes politic in championing Rocks and challenging legitimate authority.

(1) Authority Shift. Through this program, a user assumes authority he doesn't have or has in name only, lifting himself well beyond his level of competence. He feels entitled to start his career at the top, or expects to excel in leadership on his first try (one-upper stance). He sees no need to improve, receive instruction, or gather experience from those more capable. That path is for lesser individuals (one-downers). By the authority vested by this program, the user acquires sovereignty.

The user must then become a headhunter—tracking those who DO have unprogrammed intelligence, people skills, and exceptional talent or expertise, so they'll work for him. To maximize *his* success, he minimizes their opportunities for other employment or advancement—spreading rumors or uncovering a scandal to lend some basis of reality. He's not beneath using extortion to gain loyalty and optimize efforts and, if all goes well, to take the credit himself. Gifted people make the Rock look bad, so if they don't join "his" Program, the Authority Shift makes the user stultify them. Through this application, authority is held by the person who has worked hard to extend an authoritative IMAGE, while those who are truly accomplished in their fields are waylaid into serving this Rock.

During a Bacchus parade one Mardi Gras, I chatted with a woman who was dressed as Little Bo Peep. She pointed to a masked man riding on one of the floats and said, "That's my boss—he's a buffoon! He is good-looking and charming, but I think he has the lowest intelligence of anyone in our building. He sits in his office talking to himself while he watches TV game shows. He doesn't have a clue! His employees do everything. We bust our buns making the department run smoothly, going into his office only for his signature or to tell him about some decision that needs to be made *and* how to make it. We even write his speeches. He's the elected official that has the title and social status—the kingpin who gets the cushy office, largest salary, and prestige of being in charge—yet he's so out of touch that he thinks he's doing an admiral's job! He's not even on the ship! I think of quitting, but my boss gave such a bad evaluation to the last person who quit, I don't want that on my record! I guess I like running the show, too. Even though I don't get any official recognition or rewards, I like being needed."

Users of the Authority Shift have a God complex, believing themselves to be their own authority (Caps Lock). Although it's rare for a user to actually say the words, "I am God," their behavior speaks this message loud and clear. After all, they are not aware of any imperfections, and they "know" they're always right, in small matters as well as large. For example, if you recommend red, white, and blue for campaign materials, she'll choose yellow and green. If you explain a serious problem in your community, he loftily corrects you ("Our studies 'prove' otherwise" or "That's been remedied"), even when he's not directly involved with the situation and you are. If you ever hint that Rocks may have intentionally caused a predicament, this user is quick to say, "They were just in a hurry," or "Those folks were a bit sloppy, as we all are sometimes," as if she KNOWS, while you do not.

Users' presumption of absolute authority, however, shifts rapidly when a problem arises. They then become the helpless victims of inexperienced or incompetent staff, demanding citizens, or any group of comparatively powerless people who "forced" their hand—"I had no choice but to agree to what the taxpayers wanted!" (These "dominating" taxpayers only affect their decisions when *they* need a scapegoat.) If at a loss to find suitable whipping boys, these users pass the buck to their only competitor: "It was God's will!"

Users of this program have a double standard. They feel entitled to the highest positions, wages, praise, and prestige, no matter their education, experience, or job performance. Meanwhile, to others they recommend courses, counseling, practice, and their own "practical" advice. If you return the favor with a similar approach, they quickly take offense. When you don't jump to follow their counsel in an area where you have extensive expertise and they have none, they complain ("Why are you so bull-headed and ornery?"), yet *their* refusal to learn from *genuine* authority doesn't bother them in the slightest. Their programmed tendency to reject or "correct" the knowledge of nonusers results in self-imposed ignorance and the repeated need to "reinvent the wheel"—and boy, are they impressed with *their* "discoveries" when they do!

Jayda called to talk about her recent phone conversation with her mother-in-law. "I really like Willa. She's been a leader in her 'Women in Community' group for many years and done a lot for her town. She can be so funny, and she's up on current events…with the exception of her baby boy. There, this sharp lady suddenly becomes downright dense. She told me she had seen a change in Austin, and I thought, *All right, Willa! You're starting to pay attention!* She said he spends more time with her than ever before and doesn't barge in on her as much when she's talking. She said she was proud to be at his side during their emergency evacuation. But now, get this—she said, 'Austin remarked that you have him in therapy.' I really thought she was going to say something like, 'You've been a real help to my son, thank you,' but no! Guess what she said?"

I was hesitant. "You better tell me."

"She said, 'I expect you mean well, dear, but there is nothing *wrong* with Austin, can't you see?! He doesn't need you mowing him down with your feminist ways. For goodness sake, let him be! When we were *alone* during the disaster, he was so manly, talking about how you and Jeremie need to listen and give people what *they* want rather than what you want. He can be such a darling—that is when no one is around lording over him!' She blew me away! What Austin told Willa about Jeremie and me were actually words I'd spoken to Austin about *him*!

"Anyway, Willa recently read an article about women who'd had bad experiences in the past with men and have gone on to have trouble with their 'perfectly normal, if not exceptional,' husbands. I told her, 'Husbands have trouble with their wives because of bad experiences, too, you know. Many guys also have trouble with *manhood* because of difficulties in their past.' 'What does *that* mean?' Willa was a little ruffled, so I replied, 'If a guy didn't have problems with men, he'd be willing to become one!'"

The Authority Shift moves users to elevate the psychologically "young" and inexperienced into positions of leadership. They then ask "older" and more experienced people to "get off their high horse" and go with the Program. Internally, this MALware encourages decentralization from Self to selves. It directs developmental strivings away from psychology and toward the muscle flexing of ego building. Users look down on their fellow humans and from this self-determined "peak," assume "I'm at the top!" However, people who have actually trodden a path to a pinnacle know how to guide others, while these users with delusions of grandeur have no such abilities. Lest users notice their shortcomings, however, this program gives them the "understanding" that supporting another's psychological growth is itself dysfunctional—"People save themselves when they're ready." (Tell that to the youngest victims of the New Orleans' Levee Disaster!)

IT Help Desk: Reversing the Authority Shift—Help the Rock shift authority back to those with real expertise and experience in the field. Remind him that true authority is not about income, appearances, popularity, social or career positions, or apparent level of responsibility, but is the expression of a *mature* human being. A real expert needs no bells or whistles, catchy slogans, persuasive campaigns, or mass-marketing techniques. She merely requires the opportunity to exercise her skills—her gifts speak for themselves. When the user embellishes his achievements, say so. Then refer him to those who truly have the talents he professes. Remember, he's likely to feel insulted when you don't support his grandiosity, so be ready for a temperamental shift.

(2) Select ALL or None Program (also known as **Extremism**). This program projects the binary code of the Mineral Stage of Development, separating all situations into tidy packages of "all" or "none." For instance, if a male user has one particular area of talent or expertise, he believes he's exceptional in ALL areas and acts accordingly. In contrast, if a female user is struggling in one area, she assumes she's a failure in EVERYTHING! As far as balancing their extreme positions, both users will have NONE of that!

This program causes users to continually assert generalizations or espouse uniqueness, whichever protects their image in the moment. If a person implies that a Polirock has a problem, for example, the user responds with "EVERYONE is like that!" ("Louisiana politicians have ALWAYS been corrupt, so what else is new?") The user vacillates between absolute assertions—PERFECTLY normal in EVERY way *or* outside the application of statistics, science, or current trends—"NONE of that applies to me!"

This Select All or None MALWARE compels users to spread responsibility equally to the wider populace when only one or a few people caused the trouble. (A well-paid authority in the criminal justice system once announced at a New Orleans public forum, "ALL those complaining about our broken legal system have ONLY themselves to blame if they have not personally tried to make it better!") Abdication of responsibility is another manifestation of this program, as in ignoring politics ALTOGETHER because NONE of the people you'd want in leadership are on the ballots. (Wouldn't elections be more revealing if citizens voted on their degree of confidence in each candidate and this information was tallied?)

IT Help Desk: Neutralizing the Select All or None Program—Encourage your Rock leaders to come up with more possibilities than the binary "all" or "none." Offer examples of moderation and ask questions. You may also use words they find comforting in new, constructive ways. (In your public addresses, you say, "There's NOTHING wrong with building a private business with taxpayers' money. Why not then give ALL taxpayers their fair share of the profits?")

"ANNE! Another call for you!" Effie's voice drew me from my writing. Picking up the phone in the kitchen, I heard the welcoming voice of Lea, a friend who is the right-hand woman of the Orleans Parish Civil Sheriff. She told me about her homes.

"My house on the West Bank (of the Mississippi River in New Orleans) is fine, with only a few roof tiles blown off. That's a relief, but my house in Bay Saint Louis (Mississippi), which sits twenty-two feet above sea level, was surrounded by seven feet of water for a few hours. A thirty-foot wave washed over the seawall, flooding everything for miles. A neighbor who stayed perched on her rooftop recounted the horror she experienced. I'm not sure what I'll find when I go there."

Lea also informed me about some of the politics in our beloved city: "There was an organization in New Orleans called the Local Emergency Preparedness Committee (LEPC) organized in September 1998 after Hurricane Georges. This group included representatives from the sheriff's offices, Red Cross, Catholic Charities, police departments, EMS, hospitals, and nursing homes to cover all aspects of preparation for a major hurricane. There were so many people involved that we filled an entire room at the Municipal Training Academy on City Park Avenue. We volunteered our time for years, working out all the details of this vital project—*but* when Hurricane Katrina approached, our officials didn't follow our plan!" She sighed deeply, then explained that new city leadership didn't want to use the plan of old leaders, so the meticulously orchestrated plan was shelved. "Our YEARS of effort were wasted!" Lea lamented.

I registered yet more waste: the unprecedented damage, bedlam, and loss of life that ensued as a result of this one misguided choice!

After I hung up with Lea, Effie relayed the "official" story: "What I learned from TV newscasts is that there was never a plan for what to do if a major hurricane hit New Orleans."

(3) Public "I" Program. The users of this MALware investigate their audience and then emulate it—putting forth whatever the crowd considers to be "the best face" and the most engaging routine. The user portrays himself as an admirable leader, a regular guy, or one of the gang (the type you'd sit and have a beer with). He quotes from the books you like or makes references to your favorite TV shows and restaurants. You get the impression that he wants what you want—"what's best for our children!" or "affordable health care" when these aims are far from his focus. He merely embraces the most popular belief systems, activities, and adages of the people, constantly adjusting himself to new audiences, so they accept his leadership.

This program also causes the user to manipulate events to give her good publicity or public sympathy, while covering up what might tarnish her image or disturb her plans. For example, to get public backing on her attack of an "enemy," she first "proves" how ruthless and inhuman this enemy is. She may stage an event to convince the average person that extreme methods are necessary to curtail this "monstrous" perpetrator. With such a grave threat to the life we love, why would anyone question this user's "sincerity"?

The user talks only from his public "I," which often takes the form of "we." ("Unlike our opponents, *we* believe in family values!") Private problems soon become public as the user starts the very commotions to which he later says, "WE need to stop this!" His part of the "we" usually recedes with time.

IT Help Desk: Closing the Public "I"—Create opportunities to open the public's eyes to Rock politics by giving speeches or arranging forums (through Toastmasters, environmental groups, service organizations, churches, and so on). When the topic of your Rock leader comes up in public, convey your experience of her—"Her response to our disaster was NOT merely 'inadequate,' as stated by the press, but APPALLING! Here are some examples..." Be warned—most people won't want to look past the facade. *But* you'll have at least performed your civic duty to inform the citizenry, which has the potential to penetrate their consciousness. You can employ the Rock's "need" to maintain a good public image to your advantage by questioning or confronting her only in public. You may want to hint that there's more to her than meets "her" I's.

I was beckoned to the outside world by cold air. Felicity had the refrigerator door open and was searching anxiously for something inside.

"What are you looking for, Felicity?" I asked as she examined jars, plastic containers, and bags one by one.

With a sigh of exasperation she declared, "FOOD!"

(4) Web Browser. This program sorts all incoming information into the appropriate RV programs that delete, rewrite, or render unapproachable, unpalatable, or unproductive any non-Rock material. Through this MALware, users understand that if they ever step out of the restrictive parameters of these programs, they too will be deleted, "rewritten," or altered in some way to become irrevocably tarnished, in pain, and/or incapacitated. Ultimately, they will be alone, miserable, and unwanted.

The Web Browser shows its user that the RV Program is life—rotating from one program to another or using several at the same time is all there is to it! The many changing forms and seemingly endless combinations of the individual programs come across as "human" personalities, "unique" relationship styles, and unpredictable "life" challenges. Thus, the user "experiences" again and again the APPARENT "pervasion," "power," and "dominance" of the Program and the images it controls.

"I found some!" a grinning Felicity remarked with relief in her voice as she closed the door of the refrigerator that was full of nutritious food. She showed me her "find"—a half-filled twenty-four-ounce bag of milk-chocolate chips, into which she shoved her eager hand.

IT Help Desk: Web Browser—Help the user become aware that there is LIFE beyond the Program. When he insists on "his" programmed way, remind him of all the other options. LEAD him into other behaviors in any activity by doing them with him. You'll need to strongly encourage him by pointing out people who are exercising their right to choose what's beyond the Program. ("You can do it too!")

COFFEE BREAK:

1. Is there anyone in your life you've been treating as a psychological adult (capable of leading his or her own and others' lives) but who is largely stuck in "infancy" or early "childhood"? What parenting skills does he or she need from you? Whom have you cast in a child's role who has much to teach you?

2. What are some of the family roles your leaders are portraying (dad, mom, children, infants)? Who in the community are they casting as adults? Who are they protecting as if they were infants?

3. List some of the Rock traits in your leaders: local, state, or federal. Which of your rights are being neglected or exploited? What can you do about this?

4. Do you pretend to have more authority than you really have? Do you pretend to be LESS skilled than you are? Why do you do this? Where do you have double standards?

5. Do you use words like "always" and "never" in reference to people? Do you believe ALL men, ALL women, or ALL politicians are a certain way? If so, cite examples of those who don't fit these rigid criteria.

6. Do you put on a front to fit in with any particular group of people? Are you more interested in people seeing you in an entirely good light (or bad light) rather than the wholeness that you are? What does this show about you as a leader?

ROCK LEGISLATIVE FUNCTIONS: "Follow the Rules!"

Rock leaders control a population in a manner similar to how the RV programs and the programmed control *them*. They make many laws and bylaws, ordinances, statutes, regulations, edicts, rules of order, policies, principles, maxims, and so forth—again, so many different names for the same thing! Rock rulings curtail competition or confrontation, and they ensure that Rocks' criminal acts APPEAR legally bound ("We HAD TO follow the law!") or at least within the legal limits ("Our lawyers don't have a problem with our actions—why do you?").

Of course we need laws. Clear, *flexible* rules and procedures are important guidelines that encourage ethical actions from "children" until they have the maturity to make wise decisions themselves. However, as a society becomes younger and younger psychologically, more and MORE safeguards are necessary to protect these "kids" from themselves and others (voila—BIG government!). People complain about having so many restrictions, when the greater problem is the psychologically immature leadership that imposes laws to saddle a population of increasingly immature citizens. (When people receive what they need to grow in their humanity, they demand more mature leadership.) When we are bound by excessive, at times frivolous hard-and-fast rules, rather than being free to follow Our Rescuer, we learn that "rightness" is rigid, EXTERNALLY imposed, and the same for everyone, rather than flexible, unique to every person and situation, and found within the physical, emotional, and intellectual intelligence of a mature human being. For example, the administrative order after Katrina that only authorized personnel could enter New Orleans kept out vagrants but also many people who could have helped. Such edicts are not only partially helpful (Partial Program), but they falsely teach us that what's inside is subject to what's outside. They maintain that the concrete, tangible, outer world rules the "immaterial" world within. In this way, Rock authorities lead us to where they are—dominated and controlled by programs originating outside the self.

Such externally controlled, artificial <u>binary systems</u> of "right" and "wrong" (i.e., legal and illegal) reduce the hierarchy of psychological stages and infinite nuances into a binary system that may or may not be effective in any situation. For instance, announcing a mandatory evacuation because a category-five hurricane is coming will not motivate everyone to escape. Adults listen to Authority (outside and within) and lead others to safety. Adolescents tend to rebel against parental figures. School-age children mind those they trust. Toddlers say "NO!" and infants go where carried. Mature leaders know about human development and temper their actions accordingly to ensure the safety of ALL citizens. Rock leaders, in contrast, see only those who SEEM to comply with *their* rulings and those who do not—themselves excepted!

Rather than correctly categorizing and then appropriately helping those in the younger developmental stages, the Rock leader attempts to prey upon and profit from them. For example, psychological "infants" reach for and try to grab hold of whatever *looks* good, so this is what Polirocks offer ("If you vote for me, I will lower your taxes!"). These Rocks encourage the "toddlers'" "NO!" toward what might interfere with their own plans. By emphasizing the moment, they call out to "preschoolers" who are focused on the here and now, oblivious to future consequences. ("With this new post-Katrina loan, you can afford to make all the repairs and improvements you want!") "School-age children" obey the rules that Polirocks eagerly make in excess. (I've heard people say, "Maintenance of the levees was the responsibility of Orleans Parish, so the Army Corps followed the law when they made no serious effort to repair their poorly constructed levees." [What about the lives of the citizenry?]) These Rocks thus take advantage of each youthful predilection, using "young ones" to advance their agendas and ambitions.

Human experience reveals that making mistakes and growing from these mistakes is part of maturation. When Rocks deny their mistakes, they reveal just HOW MUCH growing they have yet to do. Polirocks may occasionally SAY they regret "mistakes," but these usually aren't "errors" at all, rather the result of calculated planning or the Incompetence Program. Also, instead of making amends for their mistakes, Rock heads make amendments—imposing stricter laws that establish even tighter controls over the *population*—never themselves.

I joined Connie's family on the back porch. They were each rocking at different speeds in their rockers. Since Connie had been angry with me, I felt a bit sheepish. "Do you all want to talk about your time on the North Shore?" I asked, reaching out to the subdued children.

"There were lots of trees down. Branches were everywhere!" Felicity said sadly as she thrust her hand into the nearly empty bag of chocolate chips. "Some trees weren't standing tall anymore. They were leaning." I could tell she was a tree lover like me.

Connie put her hand on Felicity's forearm in loving support, and Oliver eagerly added, "I'd say about every fourth or fifth house had a tree *slammed* down on it!" Oliver supplied hand gestures of falling trees with sound effects as they hit and crushed the "houses." "Sometimes most of the house was *smashed*! Then every once in a while, there was a house that was completely *flattened* or just plain *gone*!" Oliver extended his hands in front of him with fingers spread wide for effect. "My friend Ace said that was caused by mini tornados!"

"You create a vivid picture for us, Oliver." Connie smiled warmly at her son and then continued the report. "In Mandeville, many roofs were partially or completely ripped off. Remember the missing signposts, the splintered telephone poles, and the fence panels that had spread out in all directions?" Connie directed her question to her kids, who nodded in reply. "As Felicity mentioned, hundreds and hundreds of trees were either down or broken. All along the roads, people were stacking large piles of logs to be disposed of. Such a waste of beautiful wood that could be used in constructing houses or furniture or, at the very least, making firewood or mulch. That's what's so depressing about this disaster—the waste is SO EXTREME! I feel sick about it all!" Teary-eyed Connie wasn't angry anymore—just sad, very sad.

I noticed how Connie supported her children's perceptions and expressions in various ways, adding physical connection with young Felicity. She validated what they saw, adding her own perceptions, thoughts, and feelings. So many of the "kids" I'd worked with over the years had had no such actively engaged parent in their lives. No "adult" added their genuine experience and validation to these children's expressions so that they would expand their seeing, hearing, feeling, and expressing to include more and more as they matured and would respond to their environment in increasingly beneficial and creative ways. On the contrary, many of these kids were not allowed to talk about the disastrous things going on in their lives. Over time, they stopped talking about them, then stopped perceiving them, and finally embraced their "programmed" experiences and talked about these instead. Such children "grew up" to be oblivious to the differences between genuine human sharing and mere pretense. I shook my head mournfully at SUCH LOSS and continued writing in my journal.

Parenting Goes beyond Protocols

At any given moment, each individual's needs are different due to differences in genetics, physical and psychological stages of development, personal experiences, and choice. For this reason, rules of conduct, "best practices," cookbook formulas, and time-honored activities and mind-sets do not work for all, nor do they work at all times. Just as physical needs are age dependent, so are psychological needs. For example, we wouldn't feed spicy New Orleans food like jambalaya to a baby, but we might to an older child or an adult. Similarly, feeding the parts of us stuck in psychological "infancy" the poignant emotional and mental nutrition that an adult can readily "digest" makes them ill. Also, advanced spiritual concepts like "it's all good" in the hands of the psychologically young are just as dangerous as telling children that everything is good to eat!

Polirocks don't have the ability to delineate psychological stages, let alone to adapt accordingly. They turn our focus instead to "their" law, requiring human beings to do all the adapting (what they learned from their Rock schools!). For their own benefit, Rock leaders herd people into demographics based on what they "should" and "shouldn't" be doing, experiencing, or expressing. For example, "people SHOULD be healthy," no matter HOW unhealthy their habits, environments, leadership, and so on. This is like saying, "The Mandeville trees and houses that Connie and her kids described SHOULD be standing and intact!" Another example is "People SHOULD speak ONLY 'positively' about their country— 'negative' comments promote political problems!" These restraints gag those of all ages from directly expressing their REAL external and internal experiences, forcing them to find another mode of communication. As they become accustomed to being insincere, they don't notice their leaders' flagrant lies. They also waste the truth—what could have led to innovative, life-giving outcomes. Rather than meeting the psychological "nutritional" requirements of a population, Rock heads profitably regulate the resulting sickness and unhappiness, while they deregulate the most profitable arenas of Rock activity.

Thus, the Rock authority promotes citizens' self-reference—as people are rigidly controlled from the outside (Rock rules, protocols, false or confining "information," etc.), they are told to look no further than themselves for the cause of any unhappiness. Whatever their misfortune, they "should" have seen it coming or taken different steps. Rather than thoroughly investigating why events unfolded as they did, and identifying all the people responsible, Rock victims are led to self-blame and dissuaded from sincere sharing. They learn to follow the Rock's lead, controlling their own actions and words (stump speeches prevail!), CONTROLLING their feelings, *and* **CONTROLLING** their thoughts (COP). Over time, outer Rocks become inner Rocks as people CONTROL themselves (which spills onto others) and CURTAIL their natural HUMAN reactions to unnatural, inhuman situations. If they lose control— there's the problem!

I thought about test questions from my written professional licensing boards in psychiatry in which the physical ages of the people giving psychiatric histories and receiving diagnoses and treatments were mentioned, but NEVER their psychological ages (a useful measure to include, don't you think?). For example, a history provided by someone in a younger stage is less complete and less reliable than someone in an older stage (compare Felicity's and Oliver's reports with their mother's— they didn't verbally express their thoughts and feelings). Also, treating a problem in a Rock ("YOU CAN'T MAKE ME!") as opposed to someone in the Child Stage of Development ("Please don't hurt me!") requires very different methods (toughness for the Rock, tenderness for the Child).

Operating under gross simplifications and inadequate measures in academic training may explain why those who have been "educated" may not have the common sense of those who have avoided institutionalized learning but have been deeply involved with life. For instance, I remember talking to a superior about a depressed patient whose home life seemed to be consistently disastrous. He corrected my line of thought with: "Depression is a GENETIC illness (Definition Lock). Besides, people are different—what might seem disastrous to you may be no big deal to someone else." (Difference Drive). When we have such "laws" or programming governing our minds ("Our genetically induced biochemistry determines our level of happiness"), we're more likely to adapt a person to the "rules" ("If you're depressed, then you need an antidepressant" [Beware the Squelch Program user!]). We don't see such symptoms as evidence of depressing circumstances having an impact on the person's constitution, as with Connie's non-clinical depression. (The symptoms are each an aspect of our human voice!) The one-upper and one-downer mind-set thus extends to character traits. What is "right" (e.g., happy) or "wrong" (e.g., sad) is decreed by an externally imposed belief system, and people are rigidly categorized and treated accordingly. ("Healthy people feel happy," rather than "Healthy people are those whose emotions are appropriate to their circumstances.") Since this process is inherently judgmental, we again withhold deeper forms of sharing. When people do share deeply, *they* then seem out of line.

In this manner, Rock "authorities" indoctrinate us out of our genuine, in-the-moment experience of ourselves and others. The particular methods of assessment they teach us use the past, our culture, or a field of study to structure or "program" present experience. We perceive in a prescribed "healthy" way, rather than attentively and genuinely. As a result, we're no longer able to absorb the full spectrum of possibilities for any situation, feel all its nuances, or consider the multiple layers of feeling and meaning in any communication or event. For example, I've heard many people refer to those who didn't leave New Orleans prior to Hurricane Katrina as "ignorant." In fact, some citizens had valid reasons for staying in the city, such as limited resources, medical incapacities, or no transportation.[6] If they had known some of the levees were poorly constructed and likely to breach, they might have been more motivated to find a way to overcome their obstacles. However, in the past, our authorities had given many false alarms, so a past-based interpretation would lead a person to risk that this hurricane would blow over as well—why waste precious time, effort, and MONEY? Assessments based on past learning can be fruitful at times, but when they become automatic and unalterable, the results can be VERY depressing.

Whatever we block from our inner awareness in one place (our own unhappiness, for instance), we will likely block externally as well (we'll be less likely to register others' unhappy feelings). If we make excuses for our inside condition, we may make these same excuses for similar circumstances outside (Excuse Escape). Consider the following comment I've heard many times: "So New Orleans officials neglected to warn residents about levees breaching and the imminent flooding of their homes. As a result, many people drowned in their sleep. Everyone fails in their duties sometimes, especially when stressed" (Select All or None Program). Only the youngest of children or those physically or mentally handicapped would neglect to relay news of such magnitude!

We may also have one set of assessments or standards for ourselves and another for others, and then NOT notice when Polirocks fail to follow their hard and fast rules (Authority Shift). For example, they expect the indigent to get out of the way of danger but take no responsibility themselves for neglecting to help the disadvantaged by every means possible. The authorities who failed to warn New Orleans citizens about the rising floodwaters were so often given sympathetic understanding and encouraged to do better next time. Meanwhile, so many New Orleanians were left for days to fend for themselves on blistering hot roofs or in sweltering attics, or they were directed to wade through toxic floodwaters to find safety. Who are being treated as little children and who as impervious adults in these scenarios?

The Youngest Child Leads

When children are reared under Rock authority, they learn they must fend for themselves if they are to survive. These unprotected and unparented "orphans" gradually take on this essential parenting role, trying to fulfill their needs for guidance and instruction by becoming the "leaders" themselves. Young children cannot help but imitate the behaviors of those in leadership around them, particularly when Rocks insist on "their" way. Any time these children's unmet needs surface, they respond with commands, controls, and corrections, mimicking the travesty of leadership they've known. So filibustered by traumatic reenactments, their unmet needs and pain retreat to the unconscious. Over time, these emotionally starving children become power-hungry "adults" who demand positions of authority to assuage their unconscious lack and longing.

Humans are a social species that require parental figures to fully mature—there are NO self-made adults! Yet, the more Rocks are in leadership, the more citizens associate "authority" and "maturation" with corruption and incompetence. People can become wary of any leaders, authorities, parents, or adults who attempt to influence them. Their painful experiences with Rock leaders have set precedents they use to justify their refusal to be guided by any "out" source (outside of "themselves").

When we reject true help and guidance, we stay "young" and vulnerable to Rocks. When they've had "their" way with us, they pat us on the back and encourage us to follow "our" instincts and lead "our" own lives, further empowering us with "You know what you're doing!" Carried by the Program and the programmed, swallowing what they spoon-feed us and spitting up anything else, we are ultimately "rocked" to sleep by their "bedtime stories," and we live the lives of psychological "infants." Thus, the "infants" ruling our adult bodies are not self-made either. These aspects of us have been sculpted and honed through extensive, regressive, traumatic experiences, and maintained by our unwillingness to admit and "redistrict" this reality, and our inability to recognize and receive help. Together, we form a docile, unaware, and unquestioning populace that is willing to go wherever taken. We ignore the psychological adults still within and among us, leaving them to observe their one Rock-given right—the right to remain silent.

COFFEE BREAK:

1. Study the Bill of Rights and decide which rights you are denying the various parts of your psychological self. For example, are you giving your traumatized parts freedom of speech?

2. Are you stuck in any roles? For instance, do you always assume the parental role, taking care of or cleaning up after those who need to do more of these things themselves? Do you consistently advise others without also receiving their advice?

3. Do you maintain the child's role in any of your "adult" relationships? Do you do what others suggest rather than following Our Rescuer's guidance? What proactive steps can you adopt for balanced relationships with "parental" types (e.g., you parent them as much as they parent you)?

4. If you were to direct a movie about the politics of your psychology, which famous people would you cast for your administration? Which "laws" would they uphold, and which would they amend? What would be the movie's theme, plot, and climax, and how would it end?

5. What are some questions you might extend to those in your community who are RV Program users? Remember to ask Our Rescuer for guidance to minimize arguments.

The Judicial System of the Mineral Stager: PARENTS ARE GUILTY!

Once under the influence of the Authority Shift, the "infant" parts of ourselves deem themselves capable of judging and interpreting maturational laws. (Notice the double standard—they do no such tampering with gravitational laws!) In their resentment at having incapacitated caretakers, they may even renounce maturation laws, as in "parenting is unnecessary."

The Mascrock goes a step further, however. He uses his latent anguish to endlessly put on trial those who fit the parental mold, accusing them of deception and disability, collecting evidence of their "failures," and "prosecuting" them as traitors or terrorists (his caretakers certainly were!). He ultimately declares them "GUILTY!" and worthy of "cruel and unusual punishments." The other side of the coin of the Polirock who became a leader to fulfill his lack of childhood parenting is the revenging Rock. All the parents in his life woefully neglected him, and he is FURIOUS (!) that his need for proper parenting was never met! When these parental types confront the Rock about his assaults and verbal battery, he defends himself fiercely (Arguing Analog), feeling "accused," "interrogated," "harassed," or otherwise "attacked" (Labeling Lock). When these "confronters" then walk away from his aggression, he declares them "dismissive" and "abandoning" (POV Shield). His judgment that ALL parents are abusive and neglectful is AGAIN confirmed (Select All or None Program). In his estimation, the problem is not a LACK of healthy parenting, but parents themselves! PARENTS ARE TO BLAME (Blame Game)!

Polirocks secure their authoritative positions and binary legislative systems (right/wrong, good/bad) by appealing to that "inner newborn" they indulge who prefers designs of black and white. If Rocks can direct this infant's narrow focus to themselves and their activities and define these as "good," then whatever appears contrary must be "bad." Since this "babe" can see only in a narrow range, if her attention is drawn to the part of Rock enterprise that looks attractive, she will assume the rest is as well. As Polirocks repetitively direct attention to the *apparent* problems of any detractor, the psychological "infant" will consider everything about this person problematic. With these methods, Rocks lead our "inner infants" to boycott healthy "parents" and even the parental traits themselves. (People expressing genuine affection, praise, reproof, and correction and revealing deep personal involvement that feeds the human spirit are "BAD"!)

The Rock's rage doesn't stop at parents and parental traits; it extends to anyone who REMINDS him of his victim role from his forgotten past. Rather than interpreting the law to care for and protect the vulnerable and needy, the Polirock manipulates it to defend the violent and the greedy. To the latter he extends sympathy and subsidies (in his childhood, these types at least gave him a lot of attention [perverse though it was!]). He finds *nothing* wrong with what they're doing (Select All or None Program). Meanwhile, this Rock bars the vulnerable from human consideration. He harshly judges victims for having needs and feelings, condemns them for their hurts and handicaps, and commands them to do what he refuses to do himself, such as "Grow up!" Again, it's not just the person or the role, but the very characteristics that remind him of the vulnerable child he once was that move him to swift actions of attack or rejection.

The Polirock defies competent authority by placing the young, naïve, and unskilled in positions of leadership (albeit answerable to him). As he gloats in the inane, destructive, or chaotic consequences, he *proves* his power and the absence of any worthy competition (Web Browser). When Rocks are running the show, proceedings are consistently out of order, ranging from gross ineptness to sheer lunacy (workers in government offices and programs offer many such examples). The population becomes increasingly handicapped, hardened, or despairing. Of course, the Rock politician judges the cause of each fiasco as unintentional, and thus, perpetrators are "innocent!" ("All's Fine" Shine of the Stall).

The Polirock's binary judicial system evidences the imprinted "parent"/child power struggle from his youth. With this adversarial imprint in the deep recesses of his mind, he perceives all human relationships as a courtroom battle between parent and child. Presiding as judge, he sentences the diversity of people in his life to extremes. With verdicts such as "innocent!" (Rocks) and "guilty!" (those outside his influence) [Labeling Lock], he passes on the paradigm of his past. When we're listening, we hear his rigid rulings of "right" and "wrong," "good" and "bad," as the remnants of this once-human child being told long ago that he was a "bad boy," while some Rock—a mere image— was "good."

Clearing her throat, Connie brought my attention back to my immediate external environment. "We adults had a long talk about the problems that occurred in New Orleans—the people who would be alive today if they'd been rescued promptly and if the sick or disabled had been cared for properly. Most importantly—if only the levees had been built correctly, most of what's going on now wouldn't have happened![7] Periodically someone chimed in, 'At least the contraflow of evacuating residents on the highways went well!'"

Oliver remarked, "Remember last year when we evacuated to Baton Rouge for Ivan? It took forever!"

"An otherwise two-hour trip lasted fourteen hours," Connie said. "And yes, sweetheart, I remember it *vividly*."

Infantile Leadership Results in One Disaster after Another

In Rock governments, those at the top are the willing servants of the Rock Virus Program. Those who resist are kept at the bottom, no matter how accomplished. The result is an upside-down hierarchy (Reality Reversal Program). The Rock's chain of command links all participants through programming, elevating their inner compliant "infant" parts that are willing to say or do whatever they are told. Their submission is rewarded with many perks (Rocks bestow "honors" for behavior FAR from honorable!). Meanwhile, the accomplishments of the noncompliant are nullified by loss of face, stature, and income, if not loss of health or life! As participants' individuality, autonomy, and humanity shrivel under such threats, so does their awareness, such as of the fact that they NEED help. They witness their own issues as being outside themselves (Scatterware), so "others" (outside the Program) now seem fringy, unbalanced, and unsafe.

Polirocks support these negative projections, methodically directing us *away* from those with true parenting or leadership skills. Meanwhile, they dispose us *toward* images that act out our "infant" fantasies ("I'm sure you are all good people, just like we are!"). Inevitably, these Rocks "lead" others into a miscarriage of justice and a binary mind-set of extremes—all bad or all good (Select All or None Program). Citizens thereby rally around the youngest "children" who offer them *apparent* freedom to be "themselves," while rigidly curtailing any "parents" who would try to change "them" or interfere with "their" plans!

Serving Rock "authorities" has such dire consequences! When, in our desire to get ahead, we give weight only to those whose status, authority, and wealth appear "above" our own, we are increasingly burdened. When we fail to sustain those who seem "beneath" us (minimizing human services and denying citizens what they need to lead healthy *human* lives), our society loses stability and collapses over time. Following the <u>antagonal leadership</u> of those psychologically behind us, we can only go backward. What was once with us is suddenly apart from us, then beyond our reach, then farther than our vision, and ultimately not even in our memory. The pursuit of our human potential becomes a pipe dream as we loop around in circles, covering the same territory over and over again, mistaking our ongoing exertion for progress. In our delusions, we also believe that by following Rock leaders, adhering to Rock protocols, and gratefully accepting their meager handouts (Femrock-style), we are being good citizens AND keeping ourselves safe! In reality, our humanity is overruled, we become accomplices to Rock crimes, and we add to our own Mineral content. Like Hurricane Katrina and the Levee Disaster, the devastation instigated by Rocks in authority is EXORBITANT!

Infantile Leadership Can Move Citizens into *ACTIVE* Involvement...Yet...

I glanced up from my writing and noted that Connie was staring into space. "Connie—I've been thinking about what you said last night about how helping others makes us feel better. I've decided to go to the Red Cross shelter this afternoon and see if there is anything I can do to support the people staying there."

Connie responded immediately. "I've been thinking along the same lines. Our church in Jefferson Parish is seeking volunteers to stock boxes with food and supplies for those in need. We'll start next weekend."

"That sounds good—I'll see y'all tonight then." Somewhat reticent about leaving my rocker and view of the restful countryside, I proceeded inside to prepare for an afternoon with evacuees from home. After a quick lunch, I drove into the tiny town of Greensburg—off to a new adventure.

I parked my car under a magnolia tree shading the small parking lot of the Red Cross shelter. Stepping out of the car, I noticed three dogs tied to the tree, lounging under its shady canopy: a pit bull, a Catahoula—both popular in Southern Louisiana—and a black puppy. Several people were sitting, chatting, or smoking outside the one and only sturdy metal door.

I strolled into the tan, box-shaped concrete building and found a large room with stained, off-white walls, filled with people and littered with cots, chairs, luggage, stuffed plastic bags, and other scattered possessions. It was relatively quiet and still, considering some fifty people were there. I approached a uniformed man and asked him who was in charge. He gestured to a middle-aged, dark-haired, heavyset woman who was having a serious phone conversation at a center table. I wandered over, waited for her to finish, and then introduced myself.

"Hello! I'm Anne Redelfs, a retired psychiatrist from New Orleans. Can I help here in any way?"

"Hi! I'm Maxine Armond, head of the shelter, but everyone calls me Maxi. Welcome! If you want to help, talk to that sad-looking woman on the cot in the corner," she pointed as she spoke. "Then the guy with the yellow T-shirt...then, ooh...*that* fellow over there with the camouflage army pants. I've got plenty more for you if you have extra time on your hands." I nodded, glad that the usual formalities of "bring in your resume and three references" are waived in an emergency. I could simply get to work.

The sad-looking woman turned out to be Loretta, a trim, slightly graying mother of five, dressed in lavender sweats and clearly distressed. She explained, "I don't have time to watch the news or read the paper—I'm too busy with my kids. So my cousin Lotti calls when I need to know somethin'. Friday, before the storm, she called to say that Hurricane Katrina was headin' our way. She told me to close up the house and get the kids ready to leave. She called several times after that to check on us. She knew I was havin' car trouble, and T. Ned, my husband, was out of town, so she swung by the next day to pick us up. So if *I* knew about it—and I can't imagine anyone busier than me—how could our government not have known as much? Don't they have cousins tellin' them what's going on and what to do?

"In my Saint Bernard neighborhood, we look after each other. We know the kids—who's a back-talker, who's a little too full of himself, who's a bully, and who tries to get away with what, and I can usually see them headin' for trouble before they do and stop it. From what I can see, our leaders aren't any different in their need for neighbors to check in on them. Like when we're havin' this disaster, why does the governor have to spend her precious time trackin' down the president to tell him what's needed? Why aren't our leaders being neighborly by callin' her and sendin' obvious help? Why wait for *her* to ask? Us needin' food, water, police, and doctors is a no-brainer—like that time a car hit J. R.— that's my nephew. His neighbors saw it and called an ambulance. Savin' lives! What's the problem here? That's why I'm at this shelter—lookin' after some folks from church.

"My kids can reach me wherever I am. They know my cell phone number. They give me a text or a call if somethin' comes up. We all know there are ways of gettin' through to the president, too, in an emergency, but his staff isn't reachin' him. Why not?

"I help with school fire drills so kids know what to do in case of emergencies. Why don't our city officials have hurricane drills? Our local schools celebrate Earth Day, where the children learn about preservin' our natural resources. Why not have a Hurricane Day, where kids learn about serious storms and how to protect themselves—learnin' they can take home to their parents so everybody knows what to do?" Loretta was getting increasingly emotional as she spoke.

"We give SO much money in taxes, yet when we have a real need, like strong levees, we're told there isn't enough money! Now, I give my kids a small allowance each week, and if they're smart with it, they get a bit more. If my kid throws away his allowance, like T. J. was doing buying beer, he doesn't get any again until he can show me that he'll make better choices. Now these federal folk are blamin' Louisiana officials for not wisely spendin' the millions they dished out over the years—then why on earth give money to irresponsible people? And why aren't they responsible in watching for HOW the money is spent, like I am with my kids?

"If any of my children spends more than his weekly allowance, borrowing from friends, then HE has to pay it back. When politicians overspend, though, they expect the American people to do the paybacks. They act like spoiled brats! *And,* why is it that WE have limits on our credit cards, while our leaders are free to spend TRILLIONS?"

Loretta took a breath and then continued. "Where does all the money go anyway? T. Ned says that our officials take a nice heavy tip for themselves before a job is even started, and if these crooks kept their hands out of the pot, there'd be plenty of money. Speakin' of pots—why not have potluck suppers for their inaugurations and important meetings? They shouldn't waste money on frills until the essential needs are taken care of —like makin' strong levees!

"I don't get how people who have spent so much time learnin' and workin' hard to get ahead have so little to show for it! The Army Corps of Engineers isn't even givin' answers to what happened to the levees; they're just sayin' they want more studies. I don't know why they need to study MORE, because even with all their studyin', the levees didn't hold! They FAILED that test! Then those in charge FAILED to warn us about all the floodin', and they FAILED to rescue us right away. With ALL these failures, WHY ISN'T ANYBODY BEING HELD BACK?!" With this last sentence, Loretta let go of the tears she had been holding in throughout her passionate speech. She buried her face in a handful of tissues as her body shuddered with sobs.

Where Is **Adult** Supervision?

Mature leaders show characteristics and behaviors similar to those of a healthy parent—they're engaged with "family," the *human* family. They're not waiting for payment, permission, or inauguration. What kind of parent states, "If elected to the school board, I plan to take a keen interest in my child's education"? Adult leaders aren't conditional about fulfilling their obligations. Does a good parent say, "If I am appropriated the necessary funds, I promise to feed my family"? Does he make excuses or blame others? "I would have protected the children, but I got no support from other members of the house." *Or,* "I would have saved our child from drowning, but legally speaking, it was *your* weekend to be with her!" A psychologically healthy leader, like the responsible parent, sees past the costumes "children" wear, the fantastic tales they tell, or the grown-up roles they play, and relates to the vulnerable, wounded, and needy psychological "kids" who require adult attention.

What does a mature authority look like in a typical political playground? Like a loving parent, he's supervising "children" at the same time he's learning from them. He knows that "kids" who have a history of problematic behavior, such as ignoring rules or protocols, falsifying evidence, and/or bullying those who would speak the truth, are prone to more of the same when stressed, so he anticipates these problems. At the same time, he attempts to minimize stressful circumstances by not assigning adult responsibilities to the psychologically "young."

Just as a child may refuse to make his bed or clean his room, a "child" official may renounce her campaign promises or veto the cleanup of her act, office, or administration. A good parent withdraws privileges from this uncooperative child, while the healthy leader removes permits, licenses, and positions, and metes out discipline in accordance with the "child's" violation and "age." For example, mandating mere restoration to preoffense conditions doesn't deter Rocks, as they will perpetrate the same crimes again and *again* and AGAIN. Self-monitoring and self-discipline are also contraindicated for the psychologically "young," as these abilities grow only with psychological maturity. Nor can small "children" be expected to correctly discipline others. For instance, if some kids were protecting a few bullies, would any healthy adults bomb the neighborhood to stop them?!

Bullies in any "school" yard are renowned for picking on those smaller than they—stealing their lunch money or tax money or hitting them when no one is looking. Gang members, for instance, use violence and group intimidation. Good leaders, like healthy parents, discern these dynamics. They don't make assumptions. ("The red tape was the reason why our officials responded so slowly to the cries for help during the Levee Disaster!" [Blame Game].) They don't empathize with those who've caused destruction. ("The levee engineers must have been very upset when their Seventeenth Street and London Avenue Canal floodwalls toppled during Hurricane Katrina when the water level was more than four feet from the top!"[8]) They don't ask bullies to pay small fines in "punishment" that are but a fraction of the money they stole or reaped at others' expense, nor do they allow bullies to profit by selling to their victims what they need to recover (this REWARDS criminal behavior). The adult leader calls for full restitution to victims *and* suitable punishments and rehabilitation for victimizers. (Those who gain financially through others' losses might think twice if their assets were liquidated to make the others solvent.)

"Children" rarely learn their lessons if they're bailed out of problems of their own creation without suffering any consequences—particularly when they are given bonuses. Good leaders know this and consider the actions of "inner children" when choosing how to respond to each troublesome "adult." For example, when an infant pushes his plate off the table, his parent doesn't expect him to wash the floor—he's not old enough. The mature leader applies this knowledge to all "spills." There is a time to clean up a mess even if you didn't cause it (because you have the ability, and the perpetrators don't). There is also a time *not* to attempt remediation, even though you're responsible—for instance, when your "cleanup" efforts would be ineffectual or make matters worse, as in harming the health and welfare of the local population and the workers hired to do the job.

When young "children" are allowed to run a country, steal its wealth, and misuse its troops in war games, they are terrified (usually unconsciously), further terrorizing others to share what they are feeling. Part of leadership is maintaining safety. Both healthy leaders and parents insist on certain standards of behavior because they value "children" and strive to keep them ALL safe (when "kids" harm others, their own well-being is threatened as well). Adults know that a "child" who resorts to bullying, whether punching another child in the nose or punching nations through their pocketbooks, is in trouble. Thorough investigation doesn't stop with the bullying or the bully, but seeks to uncover what's going on "at home" that compels the bully to draw such negative attention to himself. Mature authorities investigate all parties (*inside* and out), noting who made each decision that led to the problem and who was responsible for supervising those responsible.

A good leader knows that "children" in adult bodies *need* rules just as physical children do, since they are prone to similar excesses and inhibitions. For example, the youngest of "children" test boundaries, such as spending more money than *they* have and imposing taxes for more money than *we* have. When permitted, they make rules that free them to do whatever they want, as with jumping over the rope of public-safety rules. As a precaution, a healthy authority routinely reassesses laws with an eye for any loopholes in terms of health and safety, rewriting them accordingly. (Amazing that we childproof our homes, but do so little to protect our children from the increasingly dangerous world they inherit!) Some decrees are nevertheless steadfast, such as "'Kids' should NEVER have access to nuclear weapons!"

Just as the healthy parent gives each child developmentally appropriate tasks that contribute to the welfare of the household, mature leaders assign tasks that MUTUALLY serve individuals, the department, and the surrounding community. Thus, they only bestow responsibility on those of an "age" to act responsibly, barring the psychologically immature from leadership. ("Covering up the catastrophically destructive, economically devastating, and morally bankrupt choices you and your friends have made is worthy of a time-out of office and time in prison [*not* the country club kind!]. Psychotherapeutic treatment is mandatory UNTIL you grow to a level of maturity where you won't repeat these atrocities!") In a country with no restrictions on psychological "infants" and "children" holding leadership positions, parenting these headstrong (RV Program-minded) "kids" is a difficult and never-ending job!

After more time with Loretta, supporting her very valid assessments and her grief, I left to find the next person. Before I did, however, I was intercepted by Wayne, a young, small-framed, short-haired, African-American man who wore blue jeans and a colorful tie-dyed T-shirt. He said he was an aspiring University of New Orleans student who had big plans for his life.

"This country is a mess!" he said. "We're sitting back and expecting our leaders to clean it up, and it's not working. These politicians are too self-serving. So, after I graduate from college, I'll go to law school and then become a politician. I'm going to get this mess straightened out!"

"I WANT IT!" Our attention was diverted by two little African-American boys fighting over a Star Wars light saber.

"Gimme it! Gimme it—it's MINE!" The smaller boy was adamant.

"NO, it's not! I want it!" The slightly larger boy was pulling the saber as he spoke.

Someone who appeared to be the parent joined the fray, so I returned to my conversation with Wayne. I explained, "I've got to talk to a couple of people right away who are upset, then I hope we can chat a bit more." Wayne nodded.

I turned to look for my second "patient," whom I soon found on a messy cot, fidgeting with his fingers. He was a thirtysomething, sandy-haired, overweight man named Avery. He, like Loretta, was from Saint Bernard Parish.

"I've been crying myself to sleep every night, and I can't stop thinking about it…so much has happened. *So much!* But…all this has brought up an important question that I've been wanting to ask someone, so I'm hoping you can answer it. Um…well…you see…my question is…do you believe there is a God?" he asked nervously, his face wrinkled with concern.

"Yes, I do. How 'bout you?" I spoke with conviction.

"Well—I'd like to think so, but I can't imagine why He would do this to us. Why…would He want to hurt SO many people…and wreck our homes…and take our property…what took years to pay for? It doesn't make sense that a loving God would do that!" Avery shook his head back and forth as he spoke. His shoulders were hunched and his eyes watery.

I replied, "Is destruction God's nature? In my experience, violence results from our choice to separate from God—wishing to go 'our' way. When we don't admit where violence is, within individuals, we tend to see it where it isn't—in God. Do you want to talk about what happened?"

"No," he muttered softly. Then he got up from his bed and sauntered away whispering, "It doesn't make any sense…why would God do that?"

Where Is *Ultimate* Authority?

Just as people often mistake psychological "infants" and "children" for adults, we can confuse immature worldly authorities with God. If we project the superiority of Our Divine Parent onto leaders and heads of family, we forget they are ordinary people who may at times reflect what is godly, but may also express the ungodly and everything in between. As a result of our confusion, we do not offer one another what we need to grow and to revolutionize what is less than human inside us. Also, Rocks have taught us that to offer aid, except in physical forms, is to "stand in judgment" of one another and assume the mantle of God ourselves! As we withdraw in "humility," the others are left free to exercise their "sovereignty" without interference (Authority Shift).

While we withhold the powerful positive influence we might have on one another's lives, Rock leaders ruthlessly impact as many lives as they possibly can. In our confusion over what is rightfully God's role and what is a human's role, we allow this impact and needlessly prolong it. We willingly give Rocks our attention, at times bordering on worship. (Just look at how much time people spend with worldly "news" each day![9] Now compare this to their time spent in spiritual pursuits![10]) We act on their "information," as though it were godly counsel. We allow Rock actions to change our characters, often permanently! We take their will for us to be our own and follow "their" way. Are these not stances that are best given to Our Creator alone? When a person under the influence of Rock leaders asks, "Why would God hurt people?" how often do we respond, "God DOESN'T hurt people. On the contrary, He removes the hurt caused by injured people and their world." And when someone says, "That person wouldn't hurt a fly!" how often do we retort, "Some part of him would and has done many times, as have we all!"

To maintain such a significant and widespread reversal of roles, Polirocks must discredit God, molding Him into "their" image (perhaps so we won't be able to tell the two apart!). Most people I talk to have endowed Our Creator with Rock traits, such as having vengeful wrath if we do something "wrong" (Program Paranoia). To them, God is inconsistent, since His proclaimed followers tell us that abortion is *always* wrong (Select All of None Program), but murdering infants, children, and pregnant women by bombing foreign countries is OK. God also appears precarious and fear-worthy, as *His* storms and disasters have the power to bring individuals, cities, or even countries to their knees. Even if we try very hard to be faithful, we may live beside someone who isn't, and we are drowned in the same floodwater!

When we don't hold our Rock leaders responsible for their ungodly actions, we tend to question our Higher Authority and blame God (Blame Game) for "allowing," if not causing, the terrible consequences. (A lot of people blame God for man-made problems, such as the Levee Disaster or childhood traumas!) Not only does this deflected accountability make God guilty and DANGEROUS, but it validates the Rock's delusion that HE is God! Many people like Avery spend their lives futilely trying to understand "God" or simply rejecting Him, when the nature of immature people pretending to be "godly" or "godlike" or deeming to speak for God has perplexed them, misled them, or made them SO resistant. Moreover, when we are rallied into blind obedience to our Rock leaders and their interpretations, God then receives our balancing or rebellious stance of "YOU CAN'T MAKE ME!" The Rock's embargo on healthy parenting is most catastrophic in relationship to our Eternal Parent. We resist the very Leadership that is *completely* capable of rescuing us *and* rearing us to maturity!

As I searched for the third person among the people congregating in the dining area, I overheard a conversation between two gray-haired, old men. One said, "Ya know our country has changed a lot over the years. In the old days, I worked for the Feds. *Then* laws were made to protect people, and people were punished for the wrong things they did to folks and rewarded for the good they did. These days, it's just the opposite. Back then, our leaders had a right to send a posse after ya, which could hunt ya down and lynch ya—*no questions asked.*"

"Yeah," the other replied. "Now ya commit 'suicide,' die in a car accident or plane crash, or some deadly disease gets ya. Yeah, these days dey be more careful. In the old days too, destroyin' the food and water, poisonin' the land, hurtin' its people—thems were acts of war. Now dey call dat 'business,' and den most of them people don't mind."

I looked at the two old guys—still and expressionless. Their faces told me they'd seen too much over the years, and they no longer reacted. They merely reported the facts and left the reactions to the younger generations, people like me who are aware of the enormity of what they're saying. I felt my stomach churn in response.

Where Is Community Action?

To pull off the "act of God" or "natural causes" ruse, Rock leaders employ their **Right to Associate and Assemble.** They create clubs, civic organizations, banks, regulatory boards, and other commissions to carry out their Program under a mantle of legitimacy. Their goals and their ways of accomplishing these goals are, of course, true to their Mineral mind-set. (After all, they have the **Right to Choose "their" Own Culture**.) These Rock groups wrangle members in good standing into higher and more influential positions of authority, perhaps using the Labeling Lock to call one of their own "the self-made man." However, these persons are but figureheads, puppets of the greater organization that "made" and controls them. The ersatz "checks-and-balance system" requires members to constantly check up on one another to ensure that they fulfill their obligation to the Program, quickly "balancing" anyone who begins to operate independently.

Unsuspecting citizens don't realize that their letters, phone calls, e-mails, and other petitions to the government urging change have NO effect on Polirocks—their loyalty is not to their job description, their party, the greater community, nor their nationality. They are owned by Rock enterprise, which they slavishly serve. Even if, through tremendous exertion, a law is passed that upholds a non-Rock organization's platform ("We won!"), it will have NO effect on Rocks and their activities. ("YOU CAN'T MAKE ME FOLLOW THE LAW!" [at best, they only *appear* to follow it].) The group member who suffers the repercussions is generally *not* one who breaks the law of the land, but one who dares to step outside the "greater law" of the RV Program. So when a Rock in authority states, "I am doing everything in my power to remedy this disaster" (Scam Program), you know how truly powerless this individual is.

Manuel, the third person Maxi asked me to see, was a thin, tawny, middle-aged man from Jefferson Parish. He seemed appropriately anguished by the circumstances of the past few days. "I'm thinking about Cuba—my family is still living there. Did you know that Hurricane Dennis was a category five when it hit my home country in July? A million and a half people were evacuated from the west side of the island to the east.[11] In Cuba, neighborhoods are organized by blocks—*manzanas*—and people in each manzana were moved together. These include the doctors, nurses, and *curanderos*—the natural-medicine practitioners—who all knew the families and the medical needs of our close people. Our neighborhoods' organization made this evacuation succeed. Our casualties were only sixteen![12] So it is *not* understandable what happened with Hurricane Katrina! My country, Cuba, even offered over fifteen hundred doctors to help people of the Gulf Coast, but did you know they were rejected?[13] They had tons of medicine, too, that they made themselves, not from the US, and all we offered was rejected. It's unbelievable!"

He continued. "Did you know that the east bank of Jefferson Parish would not have flooded if the parish president hadn't shut down the water pumps and sent the workers home before the storm?[14] Even the ones who *wanted* to stay he sent home. He said he wanted to *save* the workers' lives. *Esto fue que una locura—fue criminal!*" Manuel muttered a few more Spanish expletives I didn't understand. "I know at least ten guys in my Metairie neighborhood who stayed behind. We saw the water going up. We would have worked our local pumps and slowed the water so my neighbors would not have DROWNED! We know, too, they were able to power the pumps remotely. This technique they use on offshore oil platforms could have saved the HUNDREDS of people who died in the flood! When I explain all this to a Jefferson official, he look at me like, 'Are you crazy?'" Manuel's eyes were fiery in their rage as he went on to express his many genuine grievances in a loud, angry voice. After unloading his anguish, however, his face softened, and he cried. Beneath his fury was a hurting heart.

Where There Are No Parents or Leaders, There Can Be No Progress

We learn to protect humanity when *our* humanity is protected. Such protection comes naturally to mature leaders, but Polirocks have had little experience with this. They've been coerced into protecting image, facilitating reFORMS, or merely introducing a new "slate" when an old one loses appeal ("Change the Font" Formula of the Stall). For example, when corruption is discovered in a department, they change the department's name. Perhaps children have been abused in a certain juvenile detention center, so they build a new one. A Rock exposed in a scandal may be assigned to a similar setting in a new location or asked to resign, only to be replaced with another Rock.

If the stress over the disparity between the facade of change and the devastating underlying reality becomes excessive—not to worry! The Polirock "pop" can recommend professional services to "assuage" our uncomfortable feelings and disturbing thoughts (see chapter 7, "The PsychOanalyst"). Meanwhile, the Polirock "mom" readily explains away our natural reactions to what "she" and her cronies are covering up (Excuse Escape): "We live in insecurity—deadly pathogens, gangs of wayward youth, crazed terrorists, and other criminals, *and* unpredictable environmental events." Of course, "she" never includes "herself" and "Pop" in these dangers, which they are at liberty to create or use to "their" advantage. As their colleagues destroy the bottom of the food chain to impact the top, Polirocks maintain a calm, distant, authoritative stance from which they judge and condemn the otherwise-preoccupied populace.

Gutje was a tall, slim, short-haired platinum blond from the Netherlands who I guessed was in her late thirties. Because she had family in the area, she had flown in after the storm to help. She related, "More than a quarter of my country is below sea level, so we know how to deal with low-lying land and have built many modern dikes.[15] Rijkswaterstaat is our governmental organization in charge of water and waste. A subgroup of specialists within this organization, called RIZA, routinely inspects dikes around the world in areas that are under sea level. They are also experts on the effects of storms and streams on dikes. My husband came with RIZA to New Orleans in April to investigate the levees. Their assessment was that the city was one of the most dangerous places in the world to live because the levees and floodwalls were so unsafe. They gave recommendations for your government to improve them immediately, but nothing was done.[16]

"Two days before the storm, your president declared a state of emergency for Louisiana.[17] Doesn't that mean your federal government is responsible for what happened?[18] Especially since most of the Army Corp of Engineers' levees in New Orleans breached at some point?[19] We were not surprised! Although your government was slow in response, other nations responded right away. I heard the Canadians sent a search-and-rescue team to Saint Bernard Parish two days after the storm, and your government took almost a week to get there![20] If I were Governor Blanco, I would have relied on THEM rather than Washington. The Canadians would surely have done a better job!

"I don't understand you people! You are so rich, yet you are so poor in responding! Any other civilized country would have acted on the assessment of our experts and made prompt improvements to the levees and floodwalls. Such a technologically advanced country as yours is capable of having a superior flood protection system like ours, yet yours is so primitive. Why? If any other developed country had such a disaster, their government

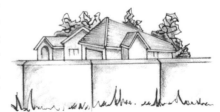

would be doing everything possible to help. This is their job, and tax money is collected for such emergencies. Your government acts like the money belongs to them and if they dole out some to your city or its people, it's a handout! They seem to forget that the money comes FROM the people to be used FOR the people. It's not a gift!" Gutje became quiet, but she had a confused look that seemed to be asking for an explanation.

I replied, "I'm sure a lot of Americans could give you lengthy, detailed reasons why the leaders of a 'rich,' 'civilized,' and 'technologically advanced country' behaved as they did. However, I like simplicity. In my experience, false images break down in emergencies. Although the average American has more money than most people the world over, we lack the maturity to know how to spend it wisely. For example, we don't invest in the development of human beings. While we have advanced in our technology, we have regressed in our human psychology—we aren't applying our technical knowledge to better ourselves. In my field, we call the slow disaster response 'passive-aggressiveness,' and it's hardly civilized. *And,* those in a truly developed nation do *not* allow the psychologically undeveloped to rule and oppress them. On the contrary, they use their power, knowledge, and resources to protect, care for, and mature their people—ALL of their people." I then turned to Wayne. "Since you're interested in politics…do you have anything to say to this lady?"

"Sure…easy…the United States is run like a corporation where the adult population provides the workers, and the government and their friends set up opportunities for profit. Why didn't the Army Corps of Engineers, and the federal government they work for, listen to all the warnings from citizens and experts who told them their levees and floodwalls were faulty?[21] I believe it's because the corporate friends of the involved officials will be making a killing on the cleanup and rebuilding— disaster capitalism! That's also my guess as to why much of the aid offered by other countries is being stalled or denied[22]—if other nations *give* us what we need, these corporate cronies can't charge an arm and a leg to sell it! Even now, there are 'no-bid' contracts going out to 'good-old-boy' companies. We need to merely follow the money to get to the bottom of the corruption!"

Gutje nodded in agreement before Wayne continued.

"There were so many political agendas behind this disaster. With exports and imports that normally go through New Orleans put on hold, food prices are going to shoot up and stay up. I think it's also a dry run for deploying troops against civil unrest. That's right—getting the people accustomed to a military presence. The Levee Disaster also distracts attention from an unpopular war. We've bombed other countries because of *their* 'weapons of mass destruction,' murdering hundreds of thousands of people,[23] and now *we're* getting the sympathy! I betcha our taxes will rise, too, and stay high, which everyone will understand because of this tragedy. There's going to be an even bigger gap between the rich and poor after this, too. A friend of mine calls it 'the peasantization of America.' If this keeps up, there's not gonna be any more middle class!" My mind quickly shifted to the binary mind-set of Rocks that can be acted out quite literally!

"Excuse me." A young man walked between Wayne and me, eating out of a square white Styrofoam container. "This red fish is *good*!" he muttered between mouthfuls.

"Red herring is more like it." Wayne looked at me sternly. "And that's not good at all! You know, there are many 'benefits' to staging a disaster on the heels of a hurricane. They can get rid of 'undesirables'—the working poor, most of whom were black, as well as the elderly and disabled— 'legally'! The body count in New Orleans is greatly minimized, by the way.[24] I have a friend on a search team, and his team alone found nine hundred bodies in this first week. HUD [US Department of Housing and Urban Development] will tear down the housing for the poor, and gentrification will no doubt follow. A lot of revealing records were ruined in this flood too. All these perks, and then to top it off, countries all over the world send our administration financial aid, so they are rewarded for their treachery and masquerade of incompetence!"

"How do you explain the 'incompetence' of *so* many people?" I asked.

"Do you like movies?" The tone of Wayne's voice was softer.

"Yes, I see quite a few."

Wayne smiled. "I like movies a lot…did you see *The Manchurian Candidate*?"

"Yeah," I responded.

"Well, even though it's fiction, there are some facts illustrated in the movie. It's about a soldier that's been brainwashed, right? Well, there are many people who have been brainwashed to act in a certain way and do things without their own knowledge. Brainwashed 'incompetence' has an important function—creating problems where there is much personal profit to be had, and corporations can take over more and more of the public realm as a result.

"As a society, we've made so many technological advances, yet we continue to use fossil fuels and coal for energy, when these are known to harm the environment and its people. We continue to use pesticides, herbicides, and fungicides that are known to kill a lot more than the organisms we're aiming at. We're currently killing off about two hundred species per day![25] The rampant untested synthetic chemicals in our homes and all the contaminants released by our industries add up to a toxic world that impacts human beings with an epidemic of disorders, from endocrine disruption to cancer.[26] Our lives are at stake! There are so many viable, healthy choices that we don't use. We have to ask ourselves why! Government incompetence has corruption at its core, and it's mind-boggling to me that so few people realize what's going on!

"We feel dependent on big business and big government to meet our basic human needs—safety, drinkable water, and nontoxic food in an increasingly dangerous world. In our deep fear, we cede our power and control to the government, accepting the denigration of our Constitution and the erosion of our civil liberties. Yet how can we trust our leaders when they violate our most basic human rights—like the right of our children and babies to breathe clean air?"

As Wayne paused for a moment, a teenager with a protruding belly, probably in her second trimester of pregnancy, walked past, caressing her abdomen. She seemed to be focusing on her little one, oblivious to the shelter scene around her.

The Psychologically Unborn

Remember, wounded people who do not receive treatment tend to run from or re-create their traumas (p. 37). Traumatized children regress, returning to thumb-sucking or clutching a favorite toy. Infants who endure ongoing painful experiences return psychologically to the "womb." The Mineral Stage of Development is the result of chronic catastrophic trauma overwhelming "children's" abilities to cope. They survive by psychologically crawling back into the "womb" of unconsciousness, closing their eyes on personal experience, and allowing "nature" (the Program) to take over.

By understanding the human <u>embryo</u>, we can anticipate the actions of Polirocks, who are psychologically following their biological programming as well as the environmental programming received from their Rock caretakers. Within the mother's body, an embryo has a constant environment—a warm 98.6-degree fluid with minimal light. A static milieu is also an expectation of Rock leaders. No matter how brutal their activities, they expect from those around them warmth, fluidity, and a willingness to remain in the dark. They demand that the environment meet their "needs," appropriating whatever is there without giving thought to where it may have come from or to whom it might belong.

The umbilical cord of the embryo connects it to the placental circulatory system, which delivers everything the growing babe requires to live and grow and removes what interferes. (Rocks may symbolize this physiology by engineering an extensive network of underground pipelines, where a leak can lead to lethality!) The "circulatory system" of Polirocks follows a similarly predictable course—money flow is from you to them, while their toxic life experiences are transferred from them to you. Their reactions are one-sided. They respond to what is coming toward them or what is withheld, and are oblivious to what they discard. Just as the embryo is given top priority when there is a shortage of maternal nutrition, Rock leaders automatically usurp "the best" for themselves. They exploit commonly owned resources to build themselves up and increase their own "stature."

Waste removal is a simple procedure in the womb: the placental blood automatically whisks toxins away from the embryo—no effort or awareness is required! Naturally, Polirocks resist cleanup efforts. Any problems that "might" have existed in the past are now "gone" or perceived to be outside of them, whether their violating controls or their uncontrollable violence. Rock leaders don't consider the consequences of their continual dumping of refuse or pollution. They freely release whatever they "need" to be rid of, whether amassing plastics in the Pacific Ocean[27] or petroleum products in our state landfills,[28] and they feel free of any adverse effects. Notice how a Rock manipulates others to BUY his waste and even take it into their bodies, as would a pregnant mom. (Fluoride, a "hazardous waste" of the fertilizer industry, is currently a component of toothpaste and about seventy percent of American water supplies!)[29]

An embryo doesn't have a sense of time or space. The psychologically "unborn" Polirock is similarly unencumbered, having no respect for others' boundaries or borders. Expecting this Rock to adapt and stretch by responding to citizens' health problems, financial stresses, and family upheavals, or to colleagues' poisoning and plundering is as irrational as expecting these from an unborn child. Polirocks anticipate OTHERS adapting and stretching *their* limits in response to *the Rock's* ever-increasing "needs." Just as an embryo is usually alone in the womb, we can count on the Rock leader's self-reference ("It's all about me!").

Wayne moistened his lips and then continued his commentary: "Louisiana is known for corrupt politics—you know that! Politicians make oodles of money with their finagling, like creating phony organizations to receive funding. They put their relatives in lucrative positions, or even in petty jobs, like janitorial positions, but with huge salaries. The list goes on and on. I sure hope I don't get corrupted when I become a politician! Anyway, these leaders on the take are just part of the problem. If you pay attention, you see they neglect serious issues too, like violent crime.

"New Orleans is my hometown, and I'm ashamed to say how many people are getting killed. The homicide rate is the highest per capita in the nation,[30] and some of these crimes are even committed by police![31] We have a poverty rate of twenty-four and a half percent![32] Look at our public education system. Not only are many school kids denied the basics of a good education, but a couple dozen school employees are under indictment for corruption.[33] These are extreme problems, and to top it off, experts are estimating our disaster has a price tag of twenty-seven BILLION dollars in New Orleans's main basin alone!"[34]

"AAAAAHHHHHH!" Our attention was once again drawn to the two small boys who were yelling as they pushed over the castle of wooden blocks they had just built. "BAM!" "CRASH!" The boys made multiple explosive sounds as they brought every block to the floor and then fell themselves. After resting a moment from the demolition, one boy said, "Let's do it again!"

"YEAH!" the other responded with glee, and they returned to building.

I turned back to Wayne. "Where do you get your information?" I asked as he nodded, apparently at the boys' illustration of what he had been talking about.

"I've been searching the Internet since I was ten and been interested in politics almost as long. I also read, research, and think, and I listen—I might even eavesdrop." Wayne laughed. "I used to be in the National Guard too. I talk with everyone. High-ranking people can reveal many truths when they get on their cell phones—this is where the eavesdropping comes in. They seem to forget other people can hear their conversations!"

Wayne began rummaging through a large garbage bag at his side, saying, "I got a DVD here for you that I want you to watch…Here it is—*Hotel Rwanda*. This movie shows the truth about government priorities. It also shows how an ordinary guy can change things, even in the most violent situation you can imagine. Watch this, and you'll know what's going on. Keep it. It's one of the few things I have left, but I want you to have it."

After the loss of so many of my possessions and the loss of his, this gift seemed particularly precious. I extended my hand to accept it. "Wow! Thank you!" I said.

"I hope I can count on your vote one day." Wayne grinned broadly and then left to join his friend. I smiled as well, noticing the back of his T-shirt—a gold arrowhead pointing up.

I sat at the shelter's dining table to jot down some more notes. Out of the corner of my eye, I watched the two small boys build and destroy three more castles.

Infants Cannot Be Separated from "Parents" and Survive

When Rocks are in charge, the safety and security that infants and young children need are often not available. Family stability is repeatedly threatened by work stress, money *stress*, relational STRESS, crime-ridden community STRESS, and so forth. Parents are often preoccupied and unavailable. When children lack stability in their lives, they bond with what is stable—certain activities, beliefs, or feeling states, such as constant tension. They later pass these "stabilizers" on to their children.

When any of these people become leaders, whether in street gangs, city hall, or Washington, DC, the cycle continues in a larger arena. Because of their experiences with conflict and broken homes, they re-create adversity. Accustomed to deprivations, they arrange shortages (safety, money, gas, employment, food, water, and so on). As fear for their lives has been a frequent occurrence, they perpetuate life-threatening concerns amid the populace. The multigenerational imprint of Rock leadership has such far-reaching effects because those stuck in the younger stages of development cannot but confer on others the stress that stymied their own psychological growth.

To cite an example, Polirocks can spend exorbitant amounts of money on ineffectual or petty upgrades to benefit just a few, like themselves, yet hem and haw, complain about, and derail a proposal that will be life-enhancing, if not lifesaving, to the majority. Helping people doesn't feel "safe" because it's unfamiliar. What does feel familiar is plaguing the poor, the homeless, and the castoffs of society, those most vulnerable who remind them of whom they used to be (and still are, psychologically speaking). These disadvantaged people mirror an unconscious part of most individuals' psyches, so we are often deaf to their cries, and this unresponsiveness may remain fixed as Polirocks target larger and more diverse populations.

Utterly powerless, incapable of choice, and totally dependent, psychologically "unborn infants" within Rocks have little recourse for calling attention to themselves. Their innate mechanism for seeking help is to physically communicate, so they move their more psychologically mobile companions into the Rock's last known *life* position of excruciating pain, utter misery, and devastating loss. (Remember—a mom's first experience of her unborn baby's movement is often a kick!) Using this inverse body language (IBL), Rocks coerce others into experiencing and expressing what they are yet too psychologically young to take on and communicate directly. In their need, they manipulate people into desperate circumstances and positions of smallness and insignificance. Thereby, each victim might know the Rocks' inner state and potentially rescue them.

Just as everything within a womb exists to develop a baby, Polirocks' utter domination of everything external feels "natural" to them. Not knowing self apart from this "other," they believe the all-powerful "giver of life" role belongs to them, and they attempt to turn others into miniatures of themselves, at least in part. Meanwhile, their "immune system" is defensive, attempting to eliminate anything "foreign." Just as an unhappy mother passes on her stress biochemically and emotionally to her unborn child, if the Polirock is disturbed, others are going to feel it. (As the saying goes, "If Mama ain't happy, ain't nobody happy!")

This crude staging of "child" and "parent" (one-downer and one-upper) is the biologically built-in pattern of the human psychological "embryo" in which the youngest of Mineral Stagers are stuck. Their environmental programming (the Reality Reversal Program and the Authority Shift, for instance) has added to their confusion, however, in that they believe that they, mere "embryos" are the one-uppers and all adults are one-downers. Notice all the manifestations of this child/parent pattern by Rocks in government. For example, the Polirock assumes the innocent posture of an unborn child—incapable of wrongdoing. Yet, when problems arise, he looks for a "woman" to blame. The Femrock accepts and absorbs this guilt, holding her true femininity accountable, as well as blaming, attacking, or shunning it in others. A feeling of innocence comes to her only vicariously through championing Mascrocks as the only worthy authorities!

Rock leaders' programming runs them, just as an embryo's genetic material orchestrates its functions automatically. This unborn-child analogy also explains why those in the Mineral Stage are so compliant with programmed dictates, yet have such difficulty with HUMAN communication. Some require YEARS of reiteration before they understand, let alone retain or act on it. Embryos receive primarily from the mother. Likewise, Rocks are fed by the Rock Program—its incessant activity of building up (Rocks and "their" enterprises) and breaking down (individuals, families, society, and the environment) is assumed by their embryonic psychology to be pro-life. (This stance kept *them* physically alive!) All the political movements of Rock leaders are merely the instinctive expressions of the psychologically "unborn."

All "Infants" and "Children" *NEED* Parents

As I parked my car on Effie's driveway, the intense conversations I'd had that afternoon were tumbling in my head. Thinking about Loretta and her protective cousin, Lotti, brought my Cousin Joan to mind. Joan keeps in close phone contact with all her friends and "relatives," so not hearing from her for a week and a half was very unusual.

An idea entered my head. Joan's husband, from whom she's separated, lives in Chicago. Maybe I could get his number from directory assistance and discover Joan's whereabouts. After trying to reach FEMA, something I'd been attempting routinely, I called the Chicago operator, who gave me five phone numbers. I called them all, leaving my information on the answering machines of all except one, where a soft female voice answered.

"Hi, my name is Anne, and I'm from New Orleans," I said to her. "I'm trying to reach my friend, Joan Johnson, who also lives in New Orleans. I haven't heard from her since Hurricane Katrina, and she doesn't have a cell phone. Her husband is a physician in Chicago, and I was hoping I could discover her location through him. Do I have the right Johnson family?"

"No…there is no Joan in our family, but I'm *so* sorry about what happened to you— really sorry. It breaks my heart seeing what all those people went through during the flood. I've been watching the news—it's so devastating! We really feel for what has happened to your city and your people. I wish you all the best, and I sincerely hope you find your friend. I'll be praying for you, Anne."

My eyes were full of tears as I hung up the phone. My grief had surfaced in response to the verbal hug extended by this sympathetic woman.

Parents Can Be Found within Strangers (and Strangers Can Be Found within Parents)

Our parents and leaders are not necessarily those in positions of authority, but those who are actively and proactively fulfilling "children's" needs—guiding them to maturity. Sometimes we are more open to the guidance of those we don't know because they have genuinely met our needs, such as our need to be heard and have our experiences validated. When we've had families that cleave to fabrications, rather than acknowledge the truth of our lives, we look to those biologically unrelated to us to meet our needs—if we are to develop. When we lack the consistent presence of a psychologically mature authority figure in our lives, we become dependent on brief encounters with caring strangers to keep us in touch with our hearts and minds. When caring strangers are in short supply, however, our "inner kids" act out, trying to locate those parental figures they *need* for growth.

People have authority problems *because* their authorities have been a problem. For example, when a child is trained to see frequently abusive and neglectful caretakers as *only* concerned, loving adults *and* to be obedient to their command, she learns to project this same image of goodness onto similar people throughout her life. She seeks them out as authorities, repeating the pattern of her past. To ease mounting pressure, however, her accumulated anger and resentment are expressed toward relatively safe surrogates. Her scapegoats are usually more legitimate leaders who have the same position, political party, religion, name, manner of speech, or hairstyle as those she's truly mad at. Attacking or shunning these substitutes or their objectionable traits allows her to discharge pent-up emotions resulting from Rock leadership.

The devastation from Rocks includes not only the direct outcomes of their actions, but also the indirect outcomes—what their immature victims do in revenge. Rock leaders channel victims' pent-up anger and hatred toward whomever might interfere with their devious plans. For instance, a large group may be peacefully demonstrating for a humanitarian cause. The Rock will choose an unattractive or apparently "abnormal" group member to interview for a broadcast—someone unkempt, with poor grammar or a heavy accent, with emotional volatility or unclear thinking. He may then arrange a destructive act, complete with "evidence" PROVING that the demonstrators did it. *Or,* he has one of his affiliates infiltrate the organization to cause the destruction, so he can then honestly accuse the group of the subversion (Scam Program). Another possibility is a Rock-orchestrated chain of events that *demands* the very action the Rock leader is advocating while also revealing the folly (and danger) of employing humanitarian principles. With these tactics, people who are inclined to be angry and litigious because of past unresolved trauma are manipulated into taking their rage out on well-meaning groups, acting derogatorily, if not vehemently opposing their peace-loving platforms. Manipulating a population with PTSD is child's play!

Without a sustained conscious effort, our training from our childhood authority figures remains with us for the rest of our lives. ("My mom says she 'cares' about me, yet she often yells or curses at me." Since "care" comes with a loud or cursing voice, this person will likely express herself harshly when she wants to give or receive care.) We can thus determine the nature of our leadership exposures by examining our present-day responses to bogus and valid authority. For example, when we support violent, self-seeking politicians and when we avoid healthy leaders, demeaning them through joking, derision, flirtation, or condescension, we're revealing previous experiences with Femrocks and Mascrocks. Somewhere along the line, these Rocks taught us their <u>antagonal perceptions</u>—seeing *them* as respectable, while experiencing their opponents as laughable, contemptuous, seductive, or inferior.

Thus, there are two main authority problems. The first is blindly following immature leaders: accepting their interpretations and decisions, overlooking or "understanding" the devastating effects, and making no rescue attempts. The extreme form of this blind follower is, of course, the Femrock, who will not allow anybody to "belittle" her beloved Polirocks. She harshly judges each "miscreant": "He's adolescent and disrespectful." "She's got authority issues and lacks patriotism." *Or* "They're un-American!"

As Loretta, Avery, and Manuel show us, questioning our leaders and expressing our *genuine* feelings about them is healthy—and essential when healing from trauma! Wayne's goal of becoming personally involved, hoping to be a politician himself one day, is another potential path of healing. Both paths entail confronting false leaders. Those afraid of confrontation because of their own unresolved traumas can easily displace their fear onto a worthy leader (HE seems frightening!) and confront him instead (this feels SO MUCH safer!). Thus, the second authority problem is denying, discounting, defying, or confronting honorable leadership.

As we experience the consistent FORCEFUL repetitions of the Polirocks' upside-down "reality" and the Femrocks' incessant criticism of anything else, replayed throughout our world, we can comprehend how our <u>Rock parts</u> were created and have been regularly reinforced. Their self-destructive presence within us maintains our authority confusion, our misjudgments of character, and our errors of action *and* inaction. Working through the trauma of immature leadership from our past is often necessary before we can effectively negotiate with immature leaders in the present.

Listening Step 8: Citizen Participation—LISTEN TO YOUR AUTHORITY

"Who's yo' mama?" This question is one of the first posed by a New Orleanian when meeting another local for the first time. We, too, need to ask ourselves this question to understand our authority issues. Whether we are parented by a psychological adult, "child," "infant," or "embryo" makes a BIG difference—it creates a frame of reference based either on reality *or* on dress-up and role-play (imitated, conditioned, or programmed). Reality coaxes our maturation, while indiscriminate role-play so often relegates us to the realms of fantasy. Again, the psychological journey is the progression from fantasy to reality, from the infant or child to the adult.

Once we can distinguish between the adult and the immature leader, we can discern at any moment who is governing us, outside and within. Contrary to appearances of "autonomy," the psychological adult is focused on and deferential to true Authority, represented within our world and selves as Our Rescuer. The developmentally "youngest" of human beings, Rocks and Minerals, are deferential to the Program and function within a programmed and programmable world. Mineral Stage leaders keep us image-focused, like them, and preoccupied with character roles, fictional tales, and the appearance of personal freedom. In contrast, Our Rescuer guides us away from imagery, out of the fragmented, bipartisan Mineral Stage mentality of "you" and "me," and toward Herself—an attentive, responsive, and BRILLIANT Adult—"growing" within each person. When we reject her parenting skills, however, believing "parenting is to blame!" we find merely a large family of "kids" inside an individual.

True leadership is always mutual; leaders are accountable for following Our Rescuer in themselves as well as their followers—every person has an area of brilliance (as well as areas of ignorance or stupidity!). When we notice where people are gifted in guidance and we receive their gifts, our "inner children" flourish from the much-needed and long-awaited parenting. In registering other people's immature, needy aspects (including those in our politicians!), we know where to extend our own parenting skills. The only possibility for error is in mistaking the parent for the child or vice versa. Just remember—the "child" is the one who clings to the qualities in you that she longs for in herself; or what he refuses to see in himself, he INSISTS on seeing in you.

Since the entire human "family" exists in each of us, what differentiates us is whose leadership we are following with each aspect of ourselves in any moment. Since we become like our chosen authorities, this choice is paramount. Our Rescuer brings healing, while Rock leaders wreak havoc. Polirocks' antagonal leadership and our subsequent regression and need, however, can spur our reaching more and more for Our Rescuer. As she directs our movements, through the practice of mutual parenting within the family of humankind (both outside and inside ourselves), our authority confusion diminishes, and our social security accrues.

Reflections on Our Rescuer (and the Rock):

1. How do you distinguish between these two leaders within you?
   a. Describe Our Rescuer within you:
      What are her communications like?
      What is her desire for you?
   b. Describe the qualities of your commanding Mascrock and controlled Femrock:
      What does each of them tell you?
      What do they want and how do they manipulate you to get it?
   c. Cut out pictures of leaders who represent Our Rescuer and these Rocks, and place them in prominent places to remind yourself to be mindful of these internal politics.

2. Do you like leaders who feed your ego or enhance your image? Do you prefer subordinates or dependents who unquestioningly do whatever you ask? Why are you like this?

3. When there is a problem, do you point a finger at authority figures, never pursuing the extent of your participation? ("My parents ruined my life!") Or do you take full responsibility without giving

any credit to all the other people involved? ("Who I am is entirely my decision, and none of my caretakers growing up have had anything to do with it.")

4. Do you spend more time acting as an adult, parent, or child? Remember, mature adults don't stand by and do nothing when "kids" call for help through their unruly, disrespectful, and destructive behaviors. What calls are you leaving unattended? Also, small children may forget to relay important news. What aspects of your life are you forgetting or ignoring? What are these behaviors revealing about your psychological age in these areas?

5. Are you upset with politicians who fail to solve the major problems in their jurisdiction, when you are not solving your own? Why do you have a double standard? Look at a political issue that is particularly bothersome to you, and ponder what it means about your psychology.

6. Are you exercising your right to participate in government outside and within yourself? How might you be proactive in your external community? What executive, legislative, and judicial plans might you make to remove your dictatorial inner Mascrocks and replace them with Our Rescuer?

7. Remember—the underlying "corruption" in each of our lives is our choice to separate from our united Identity, a decision that made leadership necessary to guide us back. Are your authorities helping you return to Wholeness? If not, how might you guide them to be better leaders?

I stretched out on my bed of freshly laundered sheets, smelling the faint lemon scent of the laundry soap, as I continued to think about the differences between the false and true leader. *When we discern the difference, we see that treating a Rock leader as an honorable adult, worthy of esteem and obedience, is insane. Allowing an unqualified and incompetent (not to mention violent!) person to maintain a position of authority is a disservice to him or her as well as devastating to those he or she leads. Yet, this condition of gross inadequacy is true of all of us when we're disconnected from our Source. Why do we fight this knowledge so fiercely? Why are we so often congratulating each other on being good parents or fine leaders, when these are qualities of our greater Self, who alone consistently and completely manifests these abilities. Wouldn't it be better to admit this truth and allow this Body to run our lives so these abilities are genuine and unbroken within us, rather than fool ourselves with fabrications or pacify one another with temporary manifestations? Wouldn't it be much more loving to support our children's anguish and grief at having inadequate parents, join with them in their expression of pain, and then go together to the One who cannot but satisfy every need in us all? Steady incomes, prominent positions, "good cheer," and all our feel-good family stories are such poor substitutes for Our Rescuer who ever supports our inalienable right to Mature Parenting.*

FATHERHOOD (the Stage of Man): Moving and Removing Rock "Authorities"

Few of us have direct access to national and state leaders, but we interact with local leadership every day. They include heads of departments, committees, clubs, and so on, as well as heads of households. The following recommendations are a guide for your encounters with Rock heads wherever you might find them. (Remember to include Our Rescuer in how you might most effectively implement these suggestions for your own unique situations.)

Within our own communities, we might look for examples of Rock lunacy ("security" measures that threaten or harm people, for instance). We might confront those who are indiscriminately littering, spraying, or otherwise polluting our neighborhoods. We might volunteer to help them *personally* clean up their messes and practice more environmentally friendly methods. And we might hold accountable those whose leadership decisions led to adverse environmental conditions and to economic debt.

In a larger arena, removing psychological "unborn children" and "infants" from "high chairs" is no easy task. Rocks manipulate the media to promote them. They "buy" support from well-positioned and wealthy cronies. They make laws that protect themselves (sometimes retroactively!), and they retaliate against those who interfere. They also indoctrinate the military to defend them. To counter such a well-organized strategy, only a group effort directed IN EVERY STEP by Our Rescuer is likely to succeed. Success also requires the presence of a Man who has broken down his own Rocky parts and knows how to similarly aid others. This coordinated endeavor led by the greater Body is what Rock authorities, unbeknown to them, are antagonally pleading for in their meticulous efforts to bring down every aspect of our society.

All individuals who participate in such a community coalition must also be making individual strides to develop themselves in the process. To budge the Rocks in our world, we must recognize and move the Rocks inside ourselves. Otherwise, Rock leaders will continue to mirror the truth about our own undeveloped internal state and its consequences. We must vote for the redevelopment authority of our mature humanity (this choice is where our vote always counts!) if we are to assist these disabled Americans who are merely portraying an image of authority, maturity, and humanness. Rocks may then learn that true power lies not in destruction. (Even an infant can push a button that activates a lethal military drone!) Genuine power is found in psychological adults who are capable of creating, maintaining, and nurturing human life.

MOTHERHOOD (the Stage of Woman): Meeting the Essential Needs of the Psychologically Unborn

We will never succeed in meeting personal or public needs through the "embryonic" Rock leader. That tactic must lead to disappointment. Instead, try human understanding and a parent's approach.

(1) A psychological embryo cannot comprehend our requests. He doesn't yet hear or see the realm of psychology, so no amount of proof, data, or documentation in this realm moves him in the slightest. At best, he will do nothing while our stress level mounts. At worst, our neediness will resonate with his own ENORMOUS unconscious need, and he will lash out when we least expect it. We can most effectively move the Polirock through unexpected, uncomfortable vacillations in his circumstances. Instead of "fluidity" and "darkness" all around him, he needs a corresponding, unwavering enlightenment from people who refuse his campaigns of destruction and who expose his fraudulent character that he costumes in family roles.

(2) An embryo cannot give what it hasn't received. The psychological Mom's job is to meet this "baby's" needs, but to do this well, she must be in contact with Our Rescuer and the required aspects of her own humanity. For example, she must have an open mind that understands what this soon-to-be-human being has been through to become what he has become. Since a Rock is incapable of creating safety, this Mom holds him within her consciousness of Our Rescuer's Authority, who uses both parties to safely heal both parties. As Mom then helps the Rock past his notion of being an authority unto himself, his brutality <u>antagonally "helps"</u> this Woman evolve beyond the fantasy of this "computer"-generated world. In this Mom's discovery of the State of the Union, her true Identity, and what it took to motivate her return (repeated encounters with Rocky politics), she hears the faint beating of this Rock's tiny human heart.

The Mom's enormous heart leaps to greet this emerging life, sustaining it with her compassion while ministering to his yet-to-be-developed psychological sensory system. The Mom is emotionally sensitive and strong enough to express the rejected feelings of this emotional "embryo" in such a manner that he might grow to one day note these feelings inside himself. She also senses the OVERWHELMING shame underlying his insistence of innocence—shame that she's willing to share.

(3) The Rock "embryo's" intake of psychological nutrients and release of toxins must be carefully monitored. The Mom must slowly and consciously "nourish" this still-to-be-born "baby" with accurate information about himself and his life (for example, the reason he doesn't allow our Freedom of Speech is because *his* human voice was suppressed). What comes out of the Rock is merely what has gone into him, so this Mom doesn't take his words or actions personally. She redirects him from the endless repetitions of what he has endured and the stifling structure of Rock programming (indefinite detention!), to the barebones of human life—whatever supports his growing psychological body!

(4) The "embryonic" leader needs help in differentiating himself from "Mom" (healthy parents, leaders, and God). In assisting the Polirock, we must remember that his mind is fragmented into a commanding Mascrock with a God complex, who distracts him from his unconscious Femrock, who is a slave to the Program. The extreme disparity between them is too great for his vulnerable psyche to bear, so he furiously fights off this awareness and those who would bring it to his attention. Thus, a Mom must tiptoe when communicating her perspective to him, understanding that his terror at being left utterly alone without *human* parents and his grief over this life-destroying loss underlies his uncontrollable rage. To assuage such extremes, she maintains the static milieu of our undivided Self.

(5) We must allow the Rock to move us! Just as a growing baby changes a mom's body, the person parenting the psychological "embryo" must be mature enough to share the Rock's experiences and unconscious reactions and allow them to reciprocally expand her behavioral repertoire, enlarge her heart, and broaden her mind. *And* she must NOT act out inappropriately in reaction herself. Each time she braves the inevitable abuse when parenting someone in the Mineral Stage, a part of her softens, enlivens, opens, and awakens. And as she "moves," so does the "baby." Unconditional love comes naturally to a healthy mother toward her own dear child—the psychological Mom realizes that ultimately she is parenting a slowly developing aspect of her self.

Mature leadership is not about *playing* the role of father *or* mother, but BEING both and allowing both to move together, as with a man and women joining to create a baby. Because psychologically "unborn" Rocks become leaders to fulfill their childhood need for parenting, they will not step down until this unconscious need is met. Therefore, if Polirocks are to stop leading people back in time, they must be fathered and mothered. For example, the Man is *unrelenting* in wearing down the Rock and thwarting his way until this mere "babe" is at last willing to receive the Woman's *unceasing* supply of what he needs to develop, *and* allow the removal of what harms him. The more the Mascrock receives from the true Feminine and is able to acknowledge her value, the more the "embryonic" human female inside him strengthens and grows. *And* the more the Femrock experiences the exquisitely loving leadership of the true Masculine, which is keenly sensitive and kind (and devoid of domination and violence!), the more she is willing to allow the Woman access to her devastated "embryonic" male. As each Rock begins to psychologically move and grow and take human form, he or she becomes a Mineral (the psychological "fetus"). The selfless acts of mature citizens united, Man and Woman together parenting such tiny human lives, taps the unlimited "funding" by their greater Body, through which Mineral Stagers regain their humanity.

LATTE BREAK: Inner Work Is an Effective Painkiller for Rock Head-aches!

1. Which Rock Virus programs can be seen in each of the following?
    a. A New Orleans citizen told me, "FEMA couldn't have come to our rescue earlier because there is an official protocol that bans FEMA from a disaster area until *three days after the event*!"
    b. People communicating the truth about Rock politics are often called "conspiracy theorists" who are "suspicious" and "mired in pessimism"!
    c. A Rock politician, challenged about the poor quality of food in public school lunches, retorts, "Whether children consume local, fresh, organically grown fruits and vegetables, or produce that is genetically engineered, sprayed with pesticides, green-harvested and ripened with chemicals for extended shelf life—it's all just chemistry to the body!"
    d. For "health purposes," all children must be vaccinated against childhood diseases before they enter public schools. However, they are *not* protected from the toxins spewed into our environment by Rock industries.
    e. When increased levels of radioactivity are discovered, an incident involving foreigners thousands of miles away is assumed to be the sole cause, rather than the radioactive waste of closer, domestic industries, which receive NO attention.

2. What rules, cookbook formulas, and beliefs do you rigidly adhere to? Which codes based on childhood learning (economic, educational, ethnic, and so on) do you use to judge your fellowman? ("I'm further up in the hierarchy because I make more money," "have more education," "am native to the area," and so forth.) How do these distract you from following the greater moral code of developing our shared humanity?

3. How do you typically respond to your leaders?
    a. As an infant (going where you're carried): You believe what they say and do as instructed. When you notice a problem, you may cry out, but you take no steps to solve it.
    b. As a toddler (saying, "NO!"): You tend to disagree with politicians, but you don't stand up for long when expressing your grievances.
    c. As a preschooler (focused on the here and now): You ignore the past (what led to today's problems) and the future (what effect the current course will have over the long term). All problems are addressed strictly in terms of "today."
    d. As a primary schoolchild (intent on learning): You study and share information dispersed by adult leaders and follow their guidance. Afraid of Mineral Stage bullies, you address merely the *outcomes* of their actions rather than confront them directly.

    e. As an adolescent (healthy rebellion against false authority): You speak out against injustice with a unique voice and join together with other like-minded people to make changes.

    f. As an adult (serving true Authority): You play whatever role facilitates growth in all parties, as instructed by Our Rescuer.

4. What happens when we project one of the three movies described in chapter 6 (p. 114) onto a particular gender or race? How about on specific nationalities or socioeconomic groups? Which movie is being projected when we hold to a certain formula or rule as good for ALL people at ALL times?

5. If the following examples are part of a consistent pattern, which psychological age groups might be demonstrated by these leaders?

    a. A politician, knowing an ecosystem would be destroyed, diverted a river from its natural course so it would supply necessary water for a new desert golf course owned by his rich golfing buddy.

    b. The citizens voted against carrying concealed weapons, but their legislators overruled them.

    c. This leader has encouraged businesses to move overseas because the labor is cheaper.

    d. After many encounters with activists, this politician finally notices a recurring problem in his jurisdiction. However, he fails to take any steps to surmount it.

6. Which Rock "family" member can be surmised in the following: When a Mineral Stager causes harm with a gun, this Polirock imposes gun controls upon everyone else!

7. What biases do you use to resist help and guidance and thereby block what you need to grow? Which judgments do you use to resist action? (Do you think you should be isolated from the public until you are enlightened or until those you'll be working with are all well-mannered and respectful?) How might you discover the psychological adults, both female and male, within you? Make a plan for assisting them into leadership, and then follow it.

8. The next time you watch "the news," identify any RV programs used by politicians. How do you use these tactics in governing yourself? Write a commentary on internal and external politics. What entitlements do you allow yourself? Are you equally in favor of these for others?

9. Consider alternatives to rigid Rock systems. For example, instead of monetary taxes for all citizens, we could tax people according to what they have in abundance. (The money rich pay in dollars, those talented in the performing arts give performance time, those strong and energetic do labor, creative types share their skill and crafts, and so on.) We might create some flexibility in the judicial system as well. Mandatory community service might be a punishment for those who enforce Rock law over human need. It's time we all stand up as leaders to demand and take steps to implement another way.

[1] The United States is the world's largest military spender, spending $711.0 billion annually. SIPRI Yearbook 2012, "Military Budget," *Wikipedia*, modified September 14, 2012, http://en.wikipedia.org/wiki/Military_budget.

[2] "In the City of New Orleans, the storm surge caused more than 50 breaches in drainage canal levees and also in navigational canal levees and precipitated the worst engineering disaster in the history of the United States." "Effect of Hurricane Katrina in New Orleans," *Wikipedia*, accessed April 15, 2013, http://en.wikipedia.org/wiki/Effects_of_Hurricane_Katrina_in_New_Orleans.

[3] "Elections with Electronic Voting Machines," *Politicol News,* April 6, 2012, http://www.politicolnews.com/elections-with-electronic-voting-machines/.

[4] "Congress is at it again with another significant assault on health and environmental protections." National Resources Defense Council, "2012 Anti-environmental Riders," accessed April 15, 2013, http://www.nrdc.org/legislation/2012-riders.asp.

[5] Frances Beinecke's Blog, "Republican Leadership Holds Tax Relief for American Families Hostage to Keystone Pipeline," *Switchboard: National Resources Defense Council Staff Blog,* December 18, 2011, http://switchboard.nrdc.org/blogs/fbeinecke/gop_leadership_holds_american.html.

[6] "The 2000 U.S. census revealed that 27% of New Orleans households, amounting to approximately 120,000 people, were without private mobility." Evacuation process criticism, "Criticism of government response to Hurricane Katrina," *Wikipedia*, modified April 15, 2013, http://en.wikipedia.org/wiki/Criticism_of_government_response_to_Hurricane_Katrina.

[7] "A report released by the American Society of Civil Engineers in June 2007 concluded that two-thirds of the flooding in the city could have been avoided if the levees had held." Levee failures, "Effects of Hurricane Katrina in New Orleans," *Wikipedia*, modified April 16, 2013, http://en.wikipedia.org/wiki/Effects_of_Hurricane_Katrina_in_New_Orleans.

[8] 'The storm surge was still more than four feet below the tops of the floodwalls at all four of these sites at the times of the levee failures. Deeper sheet piles would likely have prevented these catastrophic failures,' said Dr. Seed." ("Dr. Ray Seed [is] co-chair of an independent post-Katrina analysis underwritten by the U.S. National Science Foundation"). "Corps of Engineers Blamed New Orleans Officials for Katrina Flooding but New Data Shows Corps Took Deadly Shortcut," *Levees.org,* August 22, 2012, http://levees.org/2012/08/22/corps-of-engineers-blamed-new-orleans-officials-for-katrina-flooding-but-new-data-shows-corps-took-deadly-shortcut/.

[9] "On an average day, 81 percent of Americans access news. On average, Americans spend 67 minutes of each day gathering news from various formats." "Where Do We Get Our News?," *Frontline,* February 27, 2007, http://www.pbs.org/wgbh/pages/frontline/newswar/part3/stats.html.

[10] 9.1% of the civilian population on average engages in religious or spiritual activities per day / Civilians spend on average .15 hours per day in these activities. "Organizational, Civic, and Religious Activities," American Time Use Survey, *Bureau of Labor Statistics, U.S. Department of Labor*, accessed September 10, 2012, http://www.bls.gov/tus/current/volunteer.htm.

[11] "Hurricane Dennis," *Cuba Hurricanes.org: The Ultimate Info about Hurricanes in Cuba*, accessed September 6, 2012, http://www.cubahurricanes.org/hurricane-dennis-info.php.

[12] Ibid.

[13] "Cuba offered to send 1,586 doctors and 26 tons of medicine, but this offer was rejected." International criticism, "Criticism of Government Response to Hurricane Katrina," *Wikipedia,* modified April 15, 2013,

http://en.wikipedia.org/wiki/Criticism_of_government_response_to_Hurricane_Katrina#Department_of_Homeland_S ecurity.

[14] "Aaron Broussard," *Wikipedia*, modified April 8, 2013, http://en.wikipedia.org/wiki/Aaron_Broussard.

[15] Matt Rosenberg, About.com Guide: "Polders and Dykes of the Netherlands," *About.com Geography*, accessed April 28, 2012, http://geography.about.com/od/specificplacesofinterest/a/dykes.htm.

[16] "As part of its post-Katrina investigation, IPET (Interagency Performance Evaluation Task Force) interviewed NOD (New Orleans District) managers to try to understand what appeared to be a nearly two decades of delay in addressing datum and subsidence issues affecting the GNO HPS (Greater New Orleans Hurricane Protection System), once they were revealed by other agencies and local sponsors." "Was the Level of Protection Incorporated in Designs Adequate?" *Corps Policy on Datums and Subsidence*, accessed April 15, 2013, http://www.dotd.louisiana.gov/administration/teamlouisiana/Team%20Louisiana%20-%20Part%20II,%20chap%205.pdf, 130.

[17] August 27, 2005, Katrina Hits the Gulf of Mexico, "Chapter Three: Hurricane Katrina—Pre-landfall," in *The Federal Response to Hurricane Katrina: Lessons Learned* (The White House: President George W. Bush Archives), accessed September 12, 2012, http://georgewbush-whitehouse.archives.gov/reports/katrina-lessons-learned/chapter3.html.

[18] "By declaring emergencies in these three States (Louisiana, Mississippi, and Alabama), the President directed the Federal government to provide its full assistance to the area to save lives and property from Hurricane Katrina's imminent impact." Ibid.

[19] "Most of the city's levees designed and built by the United States Army Corps of Engineers broke somewhere, "Effect of Hurricane Katrina in New Orleans," *Wikipedia*, http://en.wikipedia.org/wiki/Effects_of_Hurricane_Katrina_in_New_Orleans.

[20] Cecilia M. Vega, "The Parish that Feds Overlooked / Canadian Group Reached St. Bernard before US Troops," *San Francisco Chronicle*, September 15, 2005, http://www.sfgate.com/news/article/The-parish-that-feds-overlooked-Canadian-group-2609002.php.

[21] Stephen A. Nelson, Department of Earth and Environmental Sciences, "Hurricane Katrina – What Happened? The Geology of the Katrina Disaster in New Orleans," *Field Trip Guide,* Stop 7 – 17th St. Canal Breach, Updated 9-17-2009, http://www.tulane.edu/~sanelson/Katrina/Hurricane%20Katrina%20Field%20Trip.pdf, 36

[22] "Concrete help was refused by the US government initially," Pledges and donations from countries, "International Response to Hurricane Katrina," *Wikipedia,* modified February 23, 2013, http://www.ask.com/wiki/International_response_to_Hurricane_Katrina.

[23] "Iraq Deaths," *Just Foreign Policy,* accessed March 22, 2013, http://www.justforeignpolicy.org/iraq.

[24] Lise Olsen, "5 years after Katrina, storm's death toll remains a mystery," *Houston Chronicle,* August 30, 2010, http://www.chron.com/news/nation-world/article/5-years-after-Katrina-storm-s-death-toll-remains-1589464.php.

[25] "UN Environment Programme: 200 Species Extinct Every Day, Unlike Anything Since Dinosaurs Disappeared 65 Million Years Ago," *Huff Post Green*, updated 5/25/11, http://www.huffingtonpost.com/2010/08/17/un-environment-programme-_n_684562.html.

[26] Theo Colborn, PhD, *The Male Predicament* (Paonia, CO: TEDX, The Endocrine Disruption Exchange, 2009), 37-minute DVD, available from http://www.endocrinedisruption.com/endocrine.male.php.

[27] "A massive conglomeration of plastic waste in the middle of the North Pacific Ocean is said to be one or two times the size of the US state of Texas, according to Greenpeace." Ed Fitzgerald, "Pacific Ocean Plastic Waste Dump,"

Ecology Global Network, September 10, 2011, http://www.ecology.com/2011/09/10/pacific-ocean-plastic-waste-dump/.

[28] Garance Burke and Jason Dearen, "Oil Spill Waste Heads to Gulf Landfills that Already Have Environmental Problems," *Huffington Post*, August 25, 2010, http://www.huffingtonpost.com/2010/08/25/oil-spill-waste-heads-to-_n_693752.html.

[29] Dr. Joseph Mercola, "Harvard Study Finds Fluoride Lowers IQ," *Mercola.com: Take Control of Your Health*, posted August 7, 2012, http://articles.mercola.com/sites/articles/archive/2012/08/07/effects-of-fluoride-to-children.aspx.

[30] Kim Murphy and Richard Fausset, "Five Years after Katrina, New Orleans Still Caught between Storms," *Los Angeles Times,* posted August 29, 2010, http://articles.latimes.com/2010/aug/29/nation/la-na-katrina-20100829.

[31] Kevin Mcgill and Michael Kunzelman, "New Orleans Police Department Reforms: Plan Aims to Excise Corruption, Discrimination and Frequent Use of Deadly Force," *Huffington Post,* July 25, 2012, http://www.huffingtonpost.com/2012/07/25/new-orleans-police-department-reforms_n_1700960.html.

[32] "New Orleans was already one of the poorest metropolitan areas in the United States in 2005, with the eighth-lowest median income ($30,771). At 24.5 percent, Orleans Parish had the sixth-highest poverty rate among U.S. counties or county equivalents." Evacuation process criticism, "Criticism of government response to Hurricane Katrina," *Wikipedia*, modified April 15, 2013, http://en.wikipedia.org/wiki/Criticism_of_government_response_to_Hurricane_Katrina.

[33] "Since 2002, there have been 24 indictments against school employees. $71 million in federal money was unaccounted for, and there were other problems." "New Orleans Schools Before and After Katrina," *PBS News Hour,* November 1, 2005, http://www.pbs.org/newshour/bb/education/july-dec05/neworleans_11-01.html .

[34] "And on August 29, 2005, the newly raised floodwalls along the 17th Street and London Avenue canals slid laterally, fell over and led to direct residential, commercial and public property flooding damage in excess of $27 billion in the city's main basin." "Corps of Engineers Blamed New Orleans Officials for Katrina Flooding but New Data Shows Corps Took Deadly Shortcut," *Levees.org,* August 22, 2012, http://levees.org/2012/08/22/corps-of-engineers-blamed-new-orleans-officials-for-katrina-flooding-but-new-data-shows-corps-took-deadly-shortcut/.

Chapter 9

Sports and Recreation

Mineral Stagers in the Home and Community

The grating mechanical drone of the generator right outside Pookie's shed was really annoying to me the first few days. But now, after so many stresses and adjustments, its constancy seems somehow comforting. It's gone from being an obnoxious producer of noise pollution to sounding like a cat's purr.

I was lost in my thoughts as I stroked Pookie's dusty fur. My focus turned outward, however, as I noticed the box of toys Jayda had sent along with Pookie. A stuffed gray mouse caught my eye. I picked it up and experimentally tossed it in front of this currently docile creature. With claws fully extended, Pookie pounced. I rushed back into the house and returned with my journal and a pen. After making myself comfortable on a couple of bags of potting soil, I began to write.

EVACUATION DAY 9: **WARNING**—Gaming Devices Inside!
When Rocks Are Around, "Play" Is Treacherous

Whether the game board is in business, government, the community, or the family, Rocks are forever "playing," and they have every intention of winning "their" games, no matter what the cost. Their sporting can lead to peril because people are the toys with which they play. Since it's only "a game," they don't understand why you get so upset about losing...sometimes disastrously! Their pain-producing tactics consistently eradicate lightheartedness, good humor, and joy, leaving their playmates cynical, somber, and obviously burdened. To add insult to injury, Rocks then point a judgmental finger at their victims: "She needs to lighten up!" "Where is his sense of humor?" or "They are *so* serious!" Below are some of the Rock's favorite forms of recreation.

The Game of BINARY

This is an assortment of related games that have the goal of separating players into rigidly opposing categories, where one side dominates and otherwise oppresses the other:

(1) Predator/Prey. In round one of this game, the Femrock welcomes easy prey, such as the young, handicapped, and/or wounded. Tempting her prey with tasty treats, wonderful surprises, and endearing mementos (perhaps a framed picture of you and her smiling, arm in arm), she lures not only physical children, but also the young parts living inside adult bodies. Her soft, "sweet" voice speaking affectionate terms—"honey," "babe," "dear"—and her frequent hugs, kisses, and pats bring out a soft spot in most people, giving them a warm, fuzzy feeling. She also extends exciting invitations to important social gatherings or to inexpensive vacation getaways that no one would want to miss. She employs an arsenal of ego-stroking devices: "You are beautiful!" "You are such a virile and sexy man, that if I weren't a married woman..." "I made you your favorite meal, sugar, just the way you like it!" "You've got to be the most intelligent person I've ever met." She vigorously applauds your every performance, expounds your virtues, and uses special pet names and demonstrative squeezes.

Once this Rock has your attention and care, she moves on to round two—setting the trap. She tells touching tales of how she has helped others, leaving out the parts where she failed miserably or suddenly turned cold and vicious. Once she has your trust, she "confides" some "personal" information that manipulates you to disclose something equally personal. After you have divulged your desires, insecurities, hurts, fears, and/or sins, this player preys on every one of them, usually behind your back. She is always close by to observe your decline or languishing. *And* she offers soothing words, hugs, and homemade brownies when your reputation is ruined, your life falls apart, and/or your health deteriorates. When you get annoyed with her without knowing why, she is "pained" by your lack of gratitude or "startled" by *your* lack of "Christian love." Lest you forget, she quickly reminds you and everyone else just how much she "helped" you when you were down.

I find that most people presume others play by the same rulebook as they do, but Rocks "play" with <u>antagonal rules</u>—those that are antagonistic to society. The Mascrock may entice people by introducing them to a potentially hot date, or offering an opportunity to shine, get ahead, or become richer (money is easy bait!). He says and does whatever prompts people to believe he's on their side (Public "I" Program). For instance, he'll grumble at length about the corruption in New Orleans. Then when you invite him to join your neighborhood association, it will soon have its own corruption to deal with. You're unlikely to look at the Rock as the problem, though, because he "generously" supplies the coffee and donuts at each event.

(2) Either/Or. In this game, the Rock narrows a vast array of possible options to only two. "It's either right or wrong," for example. "We either have corrupt leaders or no leaders." "Either we put up with the widespread contamination caused by oil spills, or we stop driving our cars." A child who mentions she's hot after roughhousing inside may get locked outside in the snow until she cools off— "First you're too hot, and now you're too cold! You're EITHER hot OR cold! Which one is it!?" The Rock allows no space for a middle ground or the investigation of other possibilities.

The Rock can also use this game to vacillate from one extreme to another. If you complain that he is too dominating or confrontational, he then avoids you entirely. If you ask him to stop ignoring you, he returns to controlling or criticizing your every move, now that he's realized your preference. If you encourage him to share more of his life with you, he makes up stories. If you say you like openness and honesty, he proceeds to devastate you with a lengthy commentary on your faults (Missal Missile of the Punishing Program). The Rock doesn't understand your "constant griping" and unhappiness, when *he* is always so agreeable!

The player of this game may shift from a stance of extreme aggression or control (Mascrock-style) to nonparticipation and anticipate similar tactics from you. However gently you might confront him, he becomes instantly defensive, as if protecting against a life-threatening attack. For instance, a Rock doesn't have a problem with having "his" way 24/7, but when you request your way for just a fraction of the time, he reacts with a vengeance, as if you want *your* way all the time. He cannot comprehend diplomatic negotiations where *each* person's needs and wishes are fulfilled at least some of the time.

Some versions of the Either/Or Game do not betray their binary nature at first. **Up or Down** is one rendition. For example, members of a Rock organization watch your spirits soar when you get what you've always wanted. They then pursue an action plan to bring you crashing down to earth. **Give or Take** is another example: if you've got something the Rock or Mineral desires and you don't give it on his terms, then he will find a way to take it from you. (Remember, grasping is one of the early movements of a developing fetus![1]) Next time, perhaps, you will be more willing!

(3) Over/Under. In this game, the Rock charges you well over the already agreed-upon price for her services or the going rate in the area (perhaps three times more!). When you complain, she goes into a tirade, insisting on the long hours she spent toiling over her task. (Queries of "why did it take you so long?" are not allowed!) She threatens with lawsuits, defaming you on Facebook, and escalating the bills the longer you refuse to pay. Once she sees that she has you under her thumb, she offers a deal to show her "good nature." She "compromises" and agrees to meet you in the middle. (You only *have to* pay double—what a deal!)

(4) If/Then. If the Rock performs some action, he expects a predictable response from you. For instance, "If I work for you, then you must pay me." He does not consider qualifying factors, such as the quality of his work, the problems he caused secondary to his work ("Goodness me! I accidently stepped through your ceiling!"), the time and effort you put in to guide or help him in his work or undo the damage, and so on. He cannot see beyond "If I worked, then you pay!"

(5) Image/REALITY. In this game, the Rock puts forth whatever image is most likely to seduce you. She may assume childlike masks for her masquerades: the wide-eyed "innocent" babe who doesn't have a clue what is going on; the furrowed-brow toddler who "stumbled" after taking her first steps on a new project; the grinning, playful preschooler who wants you to join her in a "game"; or the endearing child who spins a yarn that every softhearted, but immature person falls for again and again. This Rock may also use adorable little children as a means to her ends. Most people find it hard to resist the tender voice of a small child asking you to do something *apparently* helpful or harmless ("Come into town and stay with us—pretty please!").

The Rock may also pretend to be debonair and polished—he wears expensive clothes, he's immaculately groomed with not a hair out of place, and he's always polite and mannerly. Whatever his masquerade, once he's attained his prize—his dream job, the boss's daughter, the position on the board, or your respect and appreciation, his make-believe begins to falter, and his Rocky reality surfaces. The more devastated his chosen opponents, the greater his score.

(6) "MY" WAY!/Your Way. The Rock starts this game by asking, "What would YOU like to do?" (In public, he's likely to say to his significant other, "Whatever YOU want, sweetheart!") While the Rock *agrees* to do whatever you want, he actually *does* what "he" wants. When you bring this to his attention, he reminds you, "I TOLD you I'd do what you want, remember?" ("Saying Is the Same as Doing" Stall) "So why are you harping on me NOW?" For the Rock, convincing you that "his" way is your way is entertaining: "I went over this with you, and you agreed to every detail—have you forgotten?" If you manage to finally get him to do what you want, he'll make sure it won't work out well, "proving" once again that only "his" way works (COP). The Rock scores points each time you regret choosing your way or you admit, "If I had only done it 'your' way, I'm sure it would have turned out better." He wins the game when you concede that you are powerless and ineffectual, a failure in all you do. This "good sport" of a Rock may then even grant you your way, but only when you no longer want it.

Those with consistent exposure to this game adapt to following the way of the Rock, which may change so frequently that his children and spouse find it impossible to please him ("You said you didn't want the lasagna I prepared for dinner even though you've loved it in the past, so I went to the store to buy the pot roast you requested, and now that it's done, you feel like lasagna!"). To keep from losing too drastically, they ultimately learn that the "right" way is whatever the Rock says in every moment—HE is the way!

I thought about what Connie shared this morning about her husband: "I've talked to several of my friends from New Orleans over the past few days. They all mentioned that Cedric had called to see how they were doing. Each of them commented on what a thoughtful man he is! Melba said they chatted for hours, and Cedric complimented her on being so easy to talk to. How is it he can call my friends and ask about their well-being, but he can't call his own family? He has time for them but no time for us. It breaks my heart that he shows more interest in acquaintances than his own wife and children. And *then*, when I tell my friends about my difficulties with Cedric, it contrasts so strongly with their experiences of him that they figure I'm going through a midlife crisis, exaggerating our problems for attention, or I just don't have the ability to bring out the best in Cedric the way they do. Or they see me as he does—always complaining! It must be my fault because no one else seems to have trouble with him. The situation drives a wedge in my friendships too because they no longer feel like *my* friends!"

The Charade of Intimacy

Relationships are a game to Rocks. If they've pegged you as an opponent, they assign you a rigidly negative role and do their utmost to force you into it and keep you there. They finesse people and situations to bring out the attributes they've chosen for you. They similarly orchestrate their own chosen roles. For instance, Rocks  may put on a flawless performance as a loving spouse, the perfect parent, or the devoted son, daughter, or friend, who selflessly endures their spouse's misery or mood swings, their kids' anger or neglect, or the rudeness or rejection of someone for whom they have only "brotherly love." Since strangers or acquaintances are more likely to fall for these charades, they receive much more of the Rocks' attention than those closest to them.

Rocks are notorious for instant intimacy—too much too soon. For example, within a Mineral family, sex with family members as well as Rock visitors is commonplace—children learn that this is how you say hello. Therefore, Rocks' practice of sex first, talk later (if at all) is no surprise. They may also say, "I love you," when they barely know you, particularly if these words encourage your willingness to "say hello." They may express incredulity or comment on your pathology if you don't acquiesce after a date or two. If you're agreeable, they may propose marriage, particularly if you own a nice house, expensive car, or something else they want to get their hands on.

Once married, the game changes. The Rocks <u>relate antagonally</u>, doing the opposite of what you want or need and ever vacillating between extremes of abuse and neglect. They are like a video-game character that only moves in one direction—away from you—except when you walk away from them, in which case they doggedly follow to get you back. If you turn to embrace them, they cast you aside once again. Rocks take their spouses on an emotional rollercoaster ride—acting like an ideal partner in public, and then dropping their mate like a sex toy once their "needs" are satisfied. Of course, marital therapy is out of the question for this Rock. Why work on the relationship when the marriage license PROVES the marriage is intact?

In contrast, these Rocks are relentless in "bonding" with their children. Every time their child displays interest in or attachment to people other than the Rock parent, the Rock chases the others away, harms them in some way, or manipulates them to attack or reject the child. Over time, offspring associate affection with abandonment, harm, darts of anger, or dismissal. Whether or not a decline in care, health, or circumstances is Rock-induced, this Rock pop tells his child that her affection, attachment, and so on "caused" the trouble, so she feels dangerous, guilty, and responsible, and she avoids closeness, or she acts out inappropriately so others naturally keep their distance.

The typical Mineral Stager also directly teaches his children to abuse or neglect those they care about. If the children don't do so, then the bigger and more powerful Rock will show them how it is done in a bigger and more powerful way. The average child opts for the lesser evil and does the tormenting—that way she achieves some control. And even if she makes her loved ones sick or miserable, as with frequent cross words, at least they are still alive! However, she can't live with the knowledge of what she's done, so she banishes her memory and guilt along with her self-awareness to the depths of her unconscious, and she walks through life with these "pebbles" in her psychological "shoes."

A Rock's child learns, in her loneliness, to attach only to what cannot be harmed, cannot react, and cannot die. (In Mineral Stage families, objects are more human than the people—*they* don't use or abuse anyone.) The Rock trusts objects—these she's able to "love." She can depend on them to do exactly as she wishes and accept her as "she" is. They don't "complain" or suggest she do what "she" doesn't want to do. Objects allow the Rock to be in complete control and have all the apparent power without any opposition, so she is committed to them.

Meanwhile, all Rocks lack commitment to human beings. The Mascrock typically shares "himself" readily with strangers, often seizing sex wherever he can. (The typical Mascrock has dozens, if not hundreds, of sex partners, with little energy remaining for his wife.) The Rock's spouse and children, who yearn for a personal word, who ache for intimacy, and who long to know what the Rock is thinking or feeling and what he's doing with his time, receive stony silence or verbal combat. Somewhere in the Rock's unconscious mind is the memory of what happened to everyone he cared about, often by his own hands. Distance and coldness are "his" way of offering protection, since he has firsthand experience of leeching relationships.

The Sport of STAMPEDE:

In this game, the Rock masterfully herds a crowd in a direction that tramples his or her opponent. The Rock's communications are well crafted to take advantage of the average person's tendency to judge by appearances. For example, a woman may brief her companions on her difficulties with a "jealous" husband, expressing her concerns that his insecurities might ultimately, much to her dismay, lead to their divorce. ("But *please* don't breathe a word of this to anyone!") In this way, the unfaithful Rock manipulates others to be deaf to her husband's concerns and quickly jump on him if he ever questions her fidelity. This trick has the added benefit of generating many "understanding" people who will make excuses for the Rock's absence from home. (Any *normal* person would need some space from his jealous tirades, right?)

The Rock also diligently crusades against those who practice the very antisocial behaviors that he and his Rock pals have so deliberately taught them. These untreated victims of barbaric treatment, who are acting out with others what was done to them, are framed as having genetically ingrained character flaws or a moral depravity that surely won't change unless exposed to further brutality or ostracism. People are thus herded into stamping out the behavioral voice of the Rock's victims, or the victims themselves, rather than hearing their cries for help and lassoing them into treatment.

An animated Oliver came into the garden shed, closing the door quickly before Pookie could escape. After a few attempts to grab Pookie, he said, "I was watching the news, and the Superdome was left full of garbage—it was a stinky mess!"

I was suddenly aware of the smell coming from the litter box. "I think I'll clean up Pookie's mess in recognition of the cleanup in the Superdome."

"What's this doing with the cat toys?" Oliver had noticed Pookie's toy box and was pulling out a bright red squirt gun.

"I think that's used to let Pookie know she's in trouble."

"Can I borrow it?" Oliver asked, smirking.

"Yeah, sure," I replied, and Oliver quickly disappeared behind the shed door.

How Do You Spell 𝕿𝕽𝕺𝖀𝕭𝕷𝕰?

When Rocks are not involved in plotting or implementing major disasters or minor "accidents" and "injuries," they cause irritation or discord by doing "little" things to get on people's nerves and make life more stressful. For example, in nonprogrammed community ventures, the Rock may "try" to do what you ask, printing expensive postcards to advertise an important event and mailing them out before realizing she "forgot" to put the affair's time, date, or location on the card. "A little mistake, silly me—you should have proofread them." Perhaps the phone number for further information is wrong, or it's for a phone no one answers or a line that's always busy. Because the Rock's "accidents," "forgetfulness," and "mistakes," are so often premeditated, those with extensive Rock experiences can come to believe these are always malicious acts that are personally motivated. They may also get upset when people say, "I'll try."

Again, Rocks believe that they and their possessions should always appear superior to others, so they do "small" destructive acts to make sure you and yours don't look as good: In homes, the Rock thrills in taking tiny nicks out of furniture, perhaps a bit of sandpaper to remove the varnish—just here and there, mind you, nothing too obvious. She is glad when your child is playing in that area so she can say, "Oh look, I'm seeing signs of wear!" Many annoyed parents will yell at a child for defacing the furniture—it's so much easier, and safer, than noticing, let alone confronting, the real perpetrator.

It *seems* as though you can never get a good haircut, when in fact your Rock family member snips your hair in the middle of the night so it won't hang correctly. He may put drying agents into your cosmetics, creams, shampoos, and soaps, joining your friends in chastising you for not covering up when you're in the sun. He marks your new handbag with permanent magic marker, stretches your new clothes out of shape, puts an ugly stain in the seat of your most expensive coat, or makes a little hole in the seat of your pants that will become more obvious as you wear them. If you acclimate to the small stuff, he may intensify his treatments—adding small stones to your cereal to chip your teeth (guess who is sued?). Of course, there are also the plumbing problems, electrical problems, pest problems, car problems—anything he might do to make your days difficult, while his, in comparison, seem a breeze!

Rocks' use of household items to harm people can result in their victims strongly reacting to these apparently innocuous items. For instance, a Rock may apply something caustic with cotton swabs to the eardrum of a "disobedient" child or mix up grotesque substances in a blender and force this child to drink the mixture. The child may react violently to swabs or blenders in the future, proving to everyone in his life that HE is a nutcase. A little girl might wake up in the middle of the night screaming that spiders are crawling all over her. There are, of course, no spiders, but there were the night before, when her Rock relative was babysitting. Ever wonder how phobias begin? Their origins are often from a very REAL threat.

With their bag of tricks, Rocks teach children to fear the mundane. For example, they may wield common household supplies (cleaning agents, car products, medicines, or readily available pesticides) in uncommon ways when they want a child to learn that acts of kindness have "side effects." ("What a shame that the special meal your mom made just for you made you SO sick!") Similarly, the Rock may dress up like Jesus, a doctor, a policeman, or perhaps playact being a therapist before molesting or beating a child. The child associates these aspects of the traumatic experience and from then on carries a grudge against Christianity, doctors, police, or psychotherapists.

When Rocks hurt children, they may arrange the settings in such a way that kids will be reminded of their painful victimizations for the rest of their lives: telephones ringing, certain types of music playing, vacuum cleaners running, perfume scenting the air, and so forth. This pairing ensures that whenever these kids hear a phone, a song, or a vacuum, or smell a whiff of fragrance, the memory of the trauma will be triggered, and they will become anxious, angry, or depressed rather than functioning at their best. Also, the Rocks may utter certain common phrases, such as "I love you," when causing pain, guaranteeing that victimized children will feel alarmed ever after when anyone speaks these words (associative learning).

Children are persecuted by Rocks in every conceivable way. Their favorite toys are "lost" or maimed, their projects sabotaged, their pets killed, and far worse—the exuberance of their as-yet-unchecked humanity is just too threatening! When their personal interests have been thoroughly trounced, these kids are then easily seduced by the Rocks into a malignant substitute. Every Rock instructs children in the unnatural games he has mastered, rewarding them as their proficiency improves. For example, he may teach them to download a virus into dad's laptop or contaminate mom's favorite candy if their parents punish them for any of their Rock taught offences. The Rock may even show them how to use a pillow on the new baby to snuff out the competition. As Rocks control all children in their "care," these kids learn to exert control over others. Whenever there's a Rock in the "neighborhood," there's bound to be extensive and ongoing TROUBLE.

The Game of 1-2-3...

This is a favorite of high-rolling Rocks. It is played outdoors with as many people as possible. In round one, those in the Mineral Stage cause some major scare that makes everyone else run around in a frenzy, trying to protect themselves. (If you'd like an example, watch the news!) It turns out either to be nothing of consequence *or* the problem resolves relatively quickly. In rounds two and three, the same threat occurs; again people are frightened, but less so each time, and they make fewer preparations with each round. Again and again, nothing of consequence ensues, or the resulting problem goes away in no time. By the fourth round of this game, people know the score. They stay calm and take few if any precautions—only this time...**KABOOM!**

I drove to the Red Cross shelter, munching on a couple of breakfast bars. Once inside, I introduced myself to the two small boys I'd observed the day before. They were throwing a small green ball to each other by bouncing it off one wall of the shelter. The older boy said his name was Chester, and the younger one announced, "I'm Felix."

"How old are you guys?" I asked. Ever since my residency in pediatrics, I've enjoyed guessing a child's age and then inquiring to determine my accuracy.

"I'm six, and my little brother is four," Chester spoke proudly. *Close, I thought. My guesses were six and three.* We chatted a bit as they played, and then Chester handed the ball to me. "You try it!" he commanded. I tossed the small ball against the concrete wall of the shelter, and it promptly bounced right back, hitting me on the head. They both burst out laughing, Felix falling to the ground in the process.

Ball Games

Challenging Rocks about the problems they cause can be *exceptionally* difficult. Much like bouncing a ball against a wall, whatever you say or do comes back at you—sometimes so fast that you have to move quickly to avoid injury! As in baseball, whatever you pitch is batted back in your direction, but in a particularly foul manner. (The Rock was slammed when he was small, so he thinks knocking opponents off their feet is how you play ball!) Yet while aggressively blocking your pitch, he gives important hand signals about which throw works best for him: HARDBALL!

Inherent in all Rock sports and games is a serious <u>antagonal request</u> for help. The Rock is rough because he needs roughness; she's confrontational because she needs confrontation. His aggressive, preachy monologues feel like you're being hit over the head with a baseball bat, because he requires forceful self-expression. When the Rock does the opposite of what you ask, she's requesting the opposite of what *she* asks. When he treats you as an incapacitated child in areas where you are skilled, be alert to his incompetence and immaturity, and respond opportunely. She insists on utter control of your "plays" because she needs extreme methods to control hers. By reducing your ballpark to rubble, he is conveying that you must abandon your accustomed turf to reach him, since he's SO FAR OUT in left field. Rocks DO NOT STOP throwing their merciless "curveballs," no matter how much you plead for a time out, because this relentless tenacity and twist of each throw is what they need to be benched. By consistently practicing similar techniques on Rocks (with guidance by Our Rescuer and without tossing away moral guidelines), you can learn to cover all the bases, expand your own playing field, and begin to score.

Home Run!

Loretta was feeling hopeful today. She related more about herself and her family, mentioning a time when her husband criticized her a lot—telling her what she should do, how it should be done, and with whom. He took his anger out on her or the kids if he was mad about something. When she confronted him about it, she said he gave her a lot of fast talk or didn't speak at all.

"Honestly, it's like talking to a dead phone sometimes—he doesn't hear me! One day, I was at a family reunion in the country, and the women were shellin' black-eyed peas on the porch while we shared our problems. My auntie told me, 'Loretta, honey, someone who is self-serving, critical, not aware of his feelings or how to express them, deaf to women, and demanding his own way is just being a man—they're all that way.'

"My cousin Lotti stopped her shellin' and jumped right in. She said, 'No, ma'am! I don't go along with that! A man isn't one-sided, like what you're sayin'. He's got both feet flat on the ground—like Uncle Hebert. Now *he* genuinely loves women and children. He doesn't pretend they're beneath him, like so many young fellas. He just sees who people can be and helps them get there. He's tough when he needs to be, yet he's strong enough to be soft too. He isn't afraid of feelin's—they flow out of him like the Mississippi in springtime. Guys these days seem to disappear when someone's needin' what they don't have, but Hebert is always involved because he knows what to do. Whether it's Theresa's marriage on the rocks or Wallace gettin' hooked up with a drug dealer, Hebert figures out what's really goin' on and helps.

"'Uncle Hebert knows us well, and when there's some major family problem, he always gets everybody on to what they do best—like Paw Paw's sent off to share stories to occupy the children. Maw Maw's fillin' the house with wonderful smells from the kitchen and enough good food to keep everybody fed. Morris is the thinker, so he's given the task of comin' up with some solutions, and his wife's great at calming everybody down. When there isn't something happenin', Uncle Hebert has us learnin' from each other, so we're not stuck if somebody with needed skills isn't around, or so we don't become too stuck ourselves.

"'It's like we're all knees of one ole' cypress tree! Hebert makes us feel part of somethin' big and beautiful. Yep, he can be smooth as puddin', sweet as pecan pie, but if you mess with anybody, he's on you like mosquitoes after sundown. When Hebert's around, nobody gets seriously hurt because he's always lookin' out for *everybody*—not just his own.'

"So then Lotti turns to me and says, 'Here in the country we don't put up with that macho man stuff that T. Ned's pullin'. If my husband bullies me, I just hit him over the head with a fryin' pan! Works every time!'"

Loretta took a deep breath and then continued. "So when I got home, I started lookin' in my kitchen cupboards, wondering whether I should use the Teflon-coated pan that I do fry bread in or maybe the cast-iron skillet I use for bacon. Then it hit me that maybe Lotti was jokin'. She was tryin' to tell me to dish back at him what he was dishin' at me! So when T. Ned criticized me next time for handlin' the children 'wrong,' I took to heart what he was sayin', but I criticized him right back by telling him somethin' I didn't like. When he tried to fix one of 'my' problems, I let him, but I insisted we fix one of his too. When he was angry and put me down to our neighbors, I just did the same thing to him right back. We had some serious fights, but he learned he couldn't push me around, and I learned fightin' can be kind of fun sometimes, especially makin' up afterward!" Loretta was smiling.

Dress UP or Redress: Differentiating Rocks from Adult Men

Psychological Men (again, they can be males or females) stand on and move with both their "feet," the right and the left, the complementary aspects of their personality. They are equally comfortable with their masculine and feminine natures, their inner "infants" and "children," and their inner parents or adults. They assert themselves or not, taking action only to the degree necessary. They are as at ease receiving from others as blocking reception, and they engage and learn from traumatic experiences no differently than happy times. They enjoy serious pursuits as well as frivolity, personifying the greater Self in both. As a result of this "give *and* take," their movements are agile, their stance is balanced and stable, and their stature is secure. Rank, role, riches, or "manly" behavior do not "prove" their manliness. Their noble manhood is the natural manifestation of embracing and expressing all that they are. This Wholeness vests them with indisputable authority.

Mascrocks merely give the impression of manhood by dressing, acting, and speaking some semblance of the part—a role to which they often rigidly adhere. They always reveal themselves by their domination of the female. They talk over her, sit in front of her, or walk ahead of her, demanding her respect while disrespecting her. As Mascrocks have no awareness of their feminine or childlike aspects, they show no heart, grounding, flexibility, playfulness, or curiosity in their strictly "masculine" stance.

Men are able to wear many "hats" because they have grown through all aspects of their worldly experience to the point of now living fully through all. The Man may "dress up" or "dress down," wearing "natural" or "synthetic materials"—whatever suits the situation at hand. He is as willing to play the loser as he is the winner, to be a participant or spectator, but always as a means to an end— the transcendence of our psychological sports and games. The Man finds threads of our united Self woven into all costumes and worldly ways—thus "MY way" is not an issue. He employs ANY way, play, expression, method, or condition that is most efficacious at the time, and as a result, he's highly functional and productive in reaching all types of people. The Man has relinquished his individual desires in preference for Our Rescuer—and this communion is what commands his every thought, feeling, and behavior. As he pursues her with every fiber of his being, he also does everything in his power to assist others in transcending their superficial "outfits" of independent identity.

As demonstrated by Lotti's Uncle Hebert, a Man naturally rescues, whether a flood victim or a person drowning in "his" or "her" programmed feelings and thoughts. Contrary to cultural stereotype, a Man attends to and expresses the full range of emotions, tailoring them to each situation as required for growth. For instance, if a psychological "infant" needs to release bottled-up grief, the Man may cry openly as an encouragement. Men team up with psychological adults, working in tandem to provide for the needs of "younger" family members within each individual.

At best, Mascrocks hire others to do the rescuing if they want to give a respectable impression (you'll never see them on their hands and knees scrubbing scum off of flooded floors!). Their own <u>rescue</u> attempts tend to be <u>antagonal</u>, causing the "rescued" to need even more help as a result! Consistently, Rocks are insensitive. To penetrate their interminable numbness, they frequently indulge in antisocial pleasures, risk taking, and thrill seeking, such as drugs, crime, or sexual perversions. (They may feel arousal only when reenacting some aspect of the traumatic scenes from their childhood.) Rocks always prefer the inanimate—money, things, rules, schedules, and Rock pals, skirting whatever requires HUMAN engagement.

The Man cloaks himself in the Spiritual. He is ever transparent to our greater Being, whose luminosity shines through every part of him. He alerts us that our struggles with Rocks and Minerals are because of our blocks to this united Self, and he requests that we relinquish these blocks and join him in this One-up position beyond the material world. Meanwhile, the Rock only dons the surface attire of "spirituality" to amass material goods and status.

A true hero, the Man fearlessly champions the psychologically "embryonic" human within Rocks and the "fetal" human within Minerals. He is able to father and mother these tiny lives by exuding his own mature humanity, deftly wielding both his masculine and feminine natures. This strong parental stance is unassailable by Mineral Stagers, and their flimsy disguises fall and their game plans fail before it.

Having welcomed and met the needs of all aspects of himself, the Man has self-control. Complete in his psychology, he leads others to their completion, even drawing upon the colorful costumes, well-rehearsed playacting, and underlying horror of Rocks and Minerals, to facilitate the growth of individuals, families, communities, and nations.

If Men and Mineral Stagers are *so* different, why do we confuse them? After all, Men risk their lives to help those held hostage by homicidal and suicidal Rocks, while Rocks continuously risk the lives and well-being of others to avoid threatening "their" own. The narrow focus and limited attention of our predominant inner "infants" is the answer to this question. Were these mere "babes" not grossly incapacitating our psychological vision, the difference between Rocks, Minerals, and Men would be obvious and undeniable.

Timothy, from Saint Bernard Parish, was a heavyset, middle-aged man with a receding hairline. He was listening to the radio as he stretched out on his cot next to the shelter's barren concrete wall, turning down the volume slightly to talk to me. He mentioned he had a friend who heard an explosion right before the Industrial Canal started to flood. "I believe it, too, cuz I was listenin' to the radio real early the other mornin', and the announcer said, '…when they blew the levee…I mean…ah…when the STORM blew the levee.' He covered up for himself real quick, but I heard it…I heard it! I looked 'round the room to see if anyone else heard it, but everybody was sleepin'!"

Timothy shook his head and continued. "But just about everybody is sleepin' these days. Have you noticed? One afternoon, the year before the storm, some scientists had the cops firin' seven hundred blanks near where I was stayin'. The paper said not one person called the police to report the shooting![2] Now, I heard it and was wonderin' why those coppers were takin' so long hittin' their mark! My wife thought Frank, my neighbor, was workin' with his car again, but I says, 'Nope, he shuts it off before it gets *that* bad.' My preacher figured the end of the world was a comin'. The young folks, though, hear gunshots 'round there all the time and hardly batted an eye!"

Let's Play House!

The easiest way to distinguish psychological Women from Femrocks is by observing their abilities to listen and to respond. The Woman is deeply receptive. Being in touch with all of her physical and emotional feelings, she senses where people are coming from and what they need to move on. She generously "feeds" the "inner children" within all, guiding their steps, and delighting in their growing humanness, just as she receives regular "nutrition," guidance, and support from Our Rescuer. Rearing "children" is the Woman's purpose and pleasure—giving them whatever they need to grow physically, emotionally, and mentally, so they might one day embrace the Spiritual with all that they are. A Woman is also devoted to the psychological Man (remember—this has NOTHING to do with physical gender), who supplies her with everything she and her "children" need to thrive.

Metaphorically speaking, the Woman is an exquisitely beautiful home with open windows and doors that allow the gentle, refreshing breezes of nature to pass through. Many large windows let abundant light into every room. Lovely scents fill the air from freshly cut flowers and mouthwatering food simmering in the kitchen. The fire in the hearth is always burning, and many creatures warm themselves near the flames, resting on the many cozy cushions. She offers safe shelter and quality provisions for all life-forms. The melodies wafting through the house are heard uniquely by each individual, rousing all who enter to their destiny.

The Femrock, in contrast, is like a small, vinyl, factory-made playhouse with a fairy-tale design. The "house" is impregnated with colors, with everything *pictured* "as it *should* be" on the inside and out. There is a home-sweet-home "banner" on an "awning" in front. "Windows" and "doors" are printed on the outside as well as inside, and under the one open door lies a cheery welcome mat, a cutout of the same cheap vinyl. Her offerings are like a little girl's tea party, where there is nothing to drink inside all the pastel plastic cups! There is plenty on the plates, but no aroma. A close look reveals brightly colored foods of many varieties—all made of hard plastic! Yet in the mind of this "female" Rock, her "playhouse" and her "meals" are no different from the Woman's sumptuous buffet at her palatial Garden District estate. The Femrock resents anyone who notices the difference, hissing "That's YOUR perception!"

Gina, a matronly, heavyset woman, told me her disaster story. "I evacuated from Saint Bernard with my neighbors, Ralph and Arlene, who have a car. We ended up in a cheap motel. For years, Ralph had been telling me how crazy his wife was. I'd seen her crying from time to time for no reason, so I believed him, and I comforted him when I saw him, and he'd bring me little gifts in appreciation. The night after the hurricane, though, Ralph called me from his motel room and asked me to come right over. He said Arlene had just cut him in the leg.

"Well, I arrived within minutes with first-aid supplies and tended his wound as he told me how his wife gets violent when she's uptight. I just held him and said, 'Ralph, you dear, sweet man, you gotta get out of here and find a safe place to stay. That woman *is* crazy! You're right! There is *no* excuse for this! This is terrible!'

"'No,' he responded firmly. 'This is the first time she's gone through with it. It's just Katrina, you know? Katrina did this!' I couldn't talk him into leaving, so I went to my room. But the next morning, I thought I should check on him. Ralph and Arlene were sitting on a bench outside, and Arlene was wearing dark glasses. I asked how things were going, and they both said, 'Everything's fine.'

"I coldly asked Arlene, 'Why the glasses today?'

"Ralph answered quickly, 'Well, I slapped her after she stabbed me.' Then he added, 'You're a good woman, Gina, the way you helped me last night—a real lifesaver!'

"I told Ralph I just wanted to see how he was doing. I started to leave, but then I turned back, which is when I saw Arlene's face. The sun was shining on her. I could see her black-and-blue eye, and it was swollen shut. *That was no slap*, I thought. *He punched her hard!*

"I decided to speak with Ralph alone the next day and give him some money to encourage him to find another place to live. When I got near their motel room, I could hear Arlene screaming. I ran over to the window, and through the crack in the curtains, I saw Ralph beating up his wife—punching her and kicking her while she crouched in the corner, crying and begging him to stop. It was awful! I was about to call the police when the door opened. Arlene ran out, her face bright red and puffy from the blows. I walked over to her, sat her down on the bench, and held *her* in my arms for the very first time, feeling so ashamed of my mistake.

"'Arlene, you poor child!' I whispered to her gently. 'I had no idea! At my age, I shoulda known better and seen this comin, but I didn't. I'm *so* sorry. You've got to get out of there, you know? You shouldn't put up with that—there's no excuse whatsoever! You can stay with me until you find a safe place to settle. I'll help you. Ralph is very sick and needs help. I'll see to it that he gets professional help while you're gettin' yourself straight. In the meantime, remember that you're beautiful and, baby, you deserve so much better than this abuse—*so* much better!'

"'Well, I've been tryin' to get him to stop,' she whimpered. 'I've tried everything I could think of, EVERYTHING, but he won't stop! He's *really* a good man though, you know? But it's just since Katrina that it's been *so* bad. He's been too stressed out. It just has to be Katrina's fault!'"

"PASS THE PAIN" Game (also known as the "Switcheroo" or Game of "Guilt")

The goal of the Mineral Stage "Pass the Pain" Game is to spread pain to as many players as possible (even including the Rocks' own bodies—Femrock style). With their utter disregard for human need, desire, life, or love, Rocks can bring almost any individual into an extremely vulnerable or stressed state, which may appear to casual observers and untrained listeners to be quite different from what it is. While those who side with the apparently wronged Rock may SEEM to move ahead in life's "game," they ultimately lose—their guilt festers and builds in their unconscious minds, and the "Pass the Pain" Game continues unabridged.

The typical Rock victim who tells of her plight receives a backlash of negative responses. A battered wife, for example, hears: "You're the one who married him!" "What did you do to cause it?" "But he's a successful professional, what have YOU done outside the home?" "Why can't you just focus on the positive—you live in an upscale neighborhood, don't you?" The woman who stands up to an abusive spouse is besieged with accusations by a society of people who learned these responses as children when their perpetrators were similarly protected. The "adult" domestic violence survivor often struggles to find someone to listen and understand how she is being harmed, just as in her childhood. At times, she's driven in desperation to violence herself, as her husband has been. She often feels powerless to convey the truth of her experience and get help. (Even some therapists with unresolved abuse issues will support the victimizer over the victim—"He sounds sincere when he says he has only good feelings toward you.")

These traditional "male" and "female" positions reveal an identification with one part of the abuse/neglect paradigm—the "male" taking the "strong" victimizing caretaker role and the "female" remaining in the role of the "weak" child victim. Each person is condemning the other as "GUILTY!" The victim feels what she felt as a child—worthless, incapable, and powerless to stop the trauma—qualities she associates with innocence. The victimizer, however, learned in childhood that innocence belongs to the perpetrators of abuse. Besides, when he reenacts his childhood traumas, he feels "powerful" and "in control" of the situation, having "escaped" the "victim role." The reverse scenario is also true—the victim of domestic violence suffers guilt when she's assertive, capable, and in the power position, while the victimizer endures guilt when he's "made" to feel inadequate, incapable, and *not* in control. Both stances evidence PTSD.

People with PTSD pair trauma with the stance and feelings they DON'T identify with, so they resist the experience of these aspects of themselves. The woman who links trauma with feelings of power and control hides these parts of herself as scary and dangerous. The man associating trauma with feelings of powerlessness and vulnerability (and perhaps feelings at all!) conceals *these* aspects of himself as scary and dangerous. The PTSD patient is then liable to act out traumatic scenes with these hidden, untreated parts when any of the corresponding stances or feelings are called upon or stirred. I call this a <u>kinesthetic flashback</u>. For instance, if a Saint Bernard Parish resident feels insecure after having lost his possessions and seen his home destroyed, when other circumstances later evoke these feelings of insecurity, he may steal, vandalize, or harm in some way if his mind has paired insecurity with the experience of loss, destruction, and emotional injury. His housemate, when she feels insecure, may tend to lose things, accidently ruin something, or experience someone else stealing or ruining her possessions. Remember, feelings that are not overtly expressed will be expressed covertly since PTSD patients reflexively run toward or away from reminders of their traumatic experience.

Thus, both victims and victimizers are communicating their learning about how to pass the pain! The Rock can then come along and manipulate people to act out inappropriately by causing them to have feelings of pain and shame. The end result of these PTSD-induced actions is, of course, yet more guilt.

Rocks go to GREAT lengths to teach people to forget their pasts and all the traumatic experiences they contain. As these people then pass on their pain, in one form or another, in an unconscious attempt to tell their life story, Rocks gain PLENTY of material for blackmail. In this way, a Rock collects a sizable group of loyal subjects who will do ANYTHING for him. As the Rock acts out these dynamics of domestic violence on an increasingly larger scale, he can count on these devotees to turn their heads away and ignore his crimes. They defend his innocence and excuse his failings just as the typical wife of a spouse-abuser does ("I'm SURE he didn't mean to hurt anyone!").

My mind began to wander to comments I'd heard from both newscasters and citizens regarding the New Orleans disaster:

"BE REASONABLE! Our politicians' actions were what ALL politicians do…they're ALL the same (Select All or None Program)! To want them to be different is an UNREALISTIC expectation!"

"It was a *natural* disaster! Our authorities don't need anyone's ANGER and BITTERNESS during this difficult time. They need our *support and encouragement*!" (Why not support those who are *protecting* our citizens?)

"God was punishing the WICKED in New Orleans, just like Sodom and Gomorrah! I'm certainly not going to give to those from WHOM GOD HIMSELF HAS TAKEN AWAY! However, many businesses are taking initiative through this tragedy *and* making a profit! To them, I say—BRAVO! Well done!"

With so few PTSD patients receiving adequate treatment for their child abuse and neglect, domestic violence abounds. True victims *and* their rescuers are shunned or persecuted with words and behaviors that range from callous insensitivity and condescension to overt derision and cruelty. Meanwhile, victimizers are consistently protected, whether in our homes, corporations, or governments. As a result, these "rescuers" of the Rocks' images condone negligent, destructive, and generally antisocial behavior while chastising those who are suffering and needing help, as well as those who are helping them. Here are a couple more examples of talk I've heard since our disaster:

"There are TROUBLEMAKERS murmuring against our levee engineers. This is hardly the time for a WITCH HUNT!"

"RESENTFUL FOLKS are ACCUSING our *hardworking* officials of having lined their own pockets with the funds for our levees! That's SLANDER! To show these officials my backing, I'm sending *them* my check for disaster relief."

When we remember the extremely traumatic childhood of the Rock, this Guilt Game becomes understandable. As a human child, *he* was labeled as "bad," "sick," or "problematic" and "suitably" punished. *He* was held accountable for his own abuse—"*You* chose to be born into this family!" Meanwhile, his victimizers were given all the positive labels in the Rock's binary classification system: "healthy," "an upstanding citizen," "the one who feeds the family" or "solves the problems." Rescuers were either absent, maligned, harmed, or chased away by his Mineral Stage caretakers. This Game of Passing the Pain through role reversal is the only game the Rock knows how to play. Through his extensive experience, he's become an expert at it. He may even *appear* to be the only "successful" player on any game board. He is a master of illusion, fooling many people with his expensive house, "devoted" spouse, "obedient" children, lucrative career, and worldly productivity. Few people notice that his apparent winning in the "game" of life has cost him his humanity. When the Guilt Game is in play, everybody loses.

Whack the Mole

Chester and Felix were now playing a board game in which the heads of moles would periodically poke out of holes in the "ground." Chester was showing Felix how to score by hitting each one with a mallet as soon as the head appeared. My attention was then drawn to a group of people who were seated close by.

"There is absolutely NO evidence that anything unusual happened in the Superdome!" The stern-faced woman was emphatic in her denial.

"But I have close friends who were there," a man said passionately. "One friend, a nurse, was given a priority evacuation from the Superdome when 'her safety could not be guaranteed.' She told me she saw a 'pile of dead bodies!' Women and even children were raped! People were committing suicide—one guy said, 'I might as well because if I don't get my medicines in a few hours, I'll be dead anyway!' The TV showed a lot of violence early on—so did the papers, and…"

The woman interrupted. "Calm down, man—you'll hurt yourself!" Her voice dripped with condescension. "Your friends are either too stressed to see straight, or they're in another world, lost in an urban legend. Don't listen to them. I had a friend there too, and look at this picture he e-mailed me." She pulled out a picture from her handbag and handed it to the man. "See? Everyone is smiling! I can tell you exactly what happened at the Superdome—nothing out of the ordinary."

"That's a lot of bull!" he angrily shouted.

She retorted, "I don't have to listen to an imbecile—the picture is the proof!" She got up and walked away. Chester then batted his last mole and raised both hands in a stance of victory.

Rock manipulation works best when the traumatic experiences of Rocks' victims are "underground"—stored in their unconscious minds. To facilitate this repression, the Rock verbally batters those who honestly convey their traumatic experiences and the feelings and thoughts that result. In the Whack the Mole Game, those in the Mineral Stage attempt to silence anyone from talking about the darker aspects of our world, such as Rocks or their activities. Whacking the homes, businesses, or family members of Rocks' victims is also a possibility if they don't acquiesce fast enough.

To add to his "play," the Rock consistently projects an image of impeccability, enjoying the inner turmoil of his victims as they are charmed by his "courtesy," "helpfulness," and "humanitarianism," while something in their subconscious minds attempts to alert them to his ruse. The Rock might say, "I overheard a woman at the supermarket bemoaning the fact that she couldn't pay this month's rent, so I gave her a wad of bills and told her to keep the change and the faith." On hearing this touching tale, the psychologically young second-guess any negative feelings or thoughts they have toward the Rock, batting them away rather than questioning the Rock's authenticity—"I must be one lost soul to feel revulsion toward such a kind and generous person!" *Or* "My angry and fearful feelings are clearly from a pestering spirit, so I'm praying to God for deliverance!" With the Rock's touching tales of care and compassion in their hearts, these "children" are easily led down a "rosy" path by those in the Mineral Stage, who teach them to call all evidence of the Rock's antisocial nature something else entirely. Rather than look at the whole, uncensored big picture, they join the Rock's game of hammering each fact the moment it surfaces or knocking the person (or the part of themselves) who brings it to their attention.

Battered young children may be very delayed in learning to speak or may cease talking altogether. Most people stop verbally communicating their Rock experiences, and many ultimately forget these painful events. Meanwhile, Rocks repeat their censored "recollections" (Editorial Override), which are more likely to be remembered. They also direct any persistent "negativity" toward scapegoats, such as self-improvement techniques or those who encourage these practices. ("You've had bouts of crying ever since you started that whole-foods diet—it's not healthy, and neither is your hippie boyfriend who recommended it!") I hear so many people angrily blaming "Katrina" ("the bitch!") for the flooding of New Orleans and the traumatic impact it has had on their lives, rather than targeting the people who built the levees improperly. Like the flow of floodwaters, their emotions rush to where there is least resistance.

Since the Whack the Mole Game has become so popular, we must *indirectly* discern Rocky influences on people. For instance, a woman may wear a lot of unattractive, "protective" clothing or put on extra pounds in an attempt to shield herself from unwelcome touch. (Rocks did not respect her physical boundaries, so she's fortified them.) A man may not bathe regularly, or he'll garb himself in grotesque or scary T-shirts to keep others at a distance. (We can only guess at the unhygienic, grotesque, or scary things he's been exposed to!) Some victims become obsessive-compulsive, attempting to undo the Rock's damage (perhaps repetitive washing to erase that dirty feeling after being sexually abused). They may also perform the purposeless rituals a Rock has taught them in an attempt to garner the Rock's favor and avoid the severe punishments of not doing them or doing them "wrong." Many forms of deviance are merely reactions to Rockplay.

The Game of KEEP AWAY!

One way to discern a Rock within a family is by noticing whose problems are never openly and honestly discussed. (Talking frankly about a Rock can bring on anxiety or panic attacks!) When the Rock is mentioned, most people remember only his or her exceptional qualities. The same "memories" of loving dedication, notable achievement, or rich spirituality are mechanically stated over and over again, often word for word, giving the impression that the speech is memorized (or programmed). When pressed to express some shortcoming of this "worthy" individual, family members will skate over the same material already covered, or they may recall a minor weakness or failure, usually involving someone else's even-greater shortcoming ("She was a bit tipsy one night, but her husband was plastered!"). Unsavory character traits suggested by anyone outside the family circle are easily dismissed by a ready excuse, and "castles" are quickly built in the "sand." After expressing great admiration and affection, or reciting one of the Rock's delightful anecdotes, family members are quick to change the subject to someone or something less threatening.

The relationships between family members and Rocks feel unnatural or precarious—too good to be true or like a house of cards that might fall with the slightest movement. Those "interlopers" who comment or "meddle" soon suffer the consequences of each member's buried rage. These family members defend the Rock's integrity and reputation as if their own were at stake (they might be!). As a result, if you quest for the truth, they perceive malice in *your* manner and keep away from you.

As the Mascrock's family guards him with a smoke screen of his superiority, Mineral Stagers isolate any uncooperative family members behind a facade of pathology ("She's been on antipsychotic medication since childhood!"). Since many people recoil from the "mentally ill" (too close to home!), these victims are often ostracized and alone. By orchestrating this egregious public shunning, however, the Rock is sharing the pain of his own experience of isolation. He has kept away, through attacks and avoidance, any person able to look beyond his "irreproachable" image and "perfected" performances, so NO ONE knows him. Underneath his programmed popularity, he has no real friends and is utterly alone. He has not even one close affiliate genuine enough to notice his pretense, aware enough to see him as he is, *and* brave enough to try to help. Large numbers of programmed devotees are small comfort for the endless solitude and gripping, incapacitating loneliness.

SOLE SURVIVOR!

"Hi, Maxi!" I managed to catch a rare moment when the shelter head was off the phone. "Anyone need some extra attention today?" I asked.

"Hello, Anne. Yes, there is someone—over there." She pointed to a rotund young woman slumped over the edge of her bed, looking down. "Mandy lost her home in the Lower Ninth Ward and everything in it, escaping with only the clothes she was wearing. She's been here a week now, and she's kept to herself, rarely speaking. She had refused to remove her sole remaining possessions even to bathe. Finally, a caseworker convinced her that she'd feel better if she had a shower and put on some nice clean clothes that were given to her by the Baptist church. Mandy followed her advice and showered, but never took her eyes off her faded blue jeans and high school T-shirt, the only things left of her old life. When she saw her clothes were being picked up by a worker who announced she was going to wash them before returning them, Mandy hollered with more life than anyone had seen in her since her arrival. The caseworker assured her that they would be returned, but calming Mandy down was a bit of a project. I don't think she'll talk to you, but at least you can say hey."

I meandered over to Mandy, introduced myself, and asked if I could sit with her for a few minutes. She nodded, but the instant I sat down, she stood up and shuffled away, clutching her neatly folded jeans and shirt as a child would a beloved stuffed animal.

Rocks are able to con so many people into believing their image by wearing the one "set of clothes" that has survived their disasters unharmed. Yes, even Rocks have one "outfit" that expresses something of their true identity, a part of themselves that has evolved past the Mineral Stage and to which they cling. These are talents, skills, or areas of worldly knowledge that their Rock caretakers allowed them to develop—as a reward for their service and so that these caretakers may call these abilities into *their* service at any time. (Rocks sabotage abilities that are *not* serving them.) Perhaps the Rock is competent in his job working for Mineral Stagers, or she's a real community go-getter when she's "helping" usher in the Rocky plan for the region. Rocks attempt to assert this last vestige of their humanity, this one part of themselves that has "survived," pretending that all the other wounded and gravely disabled parts don't exist or are comparatively unimportant. To coax others into this deception, Rocks employ another highly effective "entertainment."

The Game of One

To begin play, a Mineral becomes involved in one charitable, service-oriented, or inner-growth type of activity, sometimes very briefly, and mentions it routinely in conversations. Maybe she once had a moment of spiritual understanding or a brief experience of genuine, human relationship, or more likely, she's merely passing on the words of someone else who did. She then magnifies that instant as if it is her main interest or concern, making sure everyone in her life knows about it. Even though there are many things that point to her darker nature, she never speaks of these, and if anyone else does, she walks away or punishes them behind the scenes (Punishing Program).

Next, this Mineral picks one "negative" feature of a person who threatens her—perhaps he's short or has a facial defect, physical disability, or a very modest income. The Mineral harps on this "problem" repeatedly, expounding on the implied character defects. She ignores or verbally attacks those who remark on this person's virtues, and she flatters those who pass on her words. In this game, the Mineral gets double points for convincing anyone that she is the saint and the other is the sinner. She receives single points for those who believe they are both well-meaning or both malevolent.

Minerals play the Game of One in many settings. After one session with a marriage counselor, one outing with the kids, or once hiring a minority employee ("That proves I'm not prejudiced!"), they feel secure in having met their obligations. Maybe a Mineral had one episode of guilt, grief, or passion in his life, which he often refers to as PROOF he has indeed access to all his feelings. ("You say I'm too busy with my business to have sex with you, hon, but I remember taking the weekend off so we could go to the beach together. As I recall, I was all over you!" His wife replies, "But that was our honeymoon five years ago!") Also, if the Mineral remembers any of his horrific childhood, it will be one minor incident—that adolescent neighbor or visiting cousin, the tip of an enormous iceberg of torment and tormenting. ("A scoutmaster once touched my privates, but I didn't let it bother me.")

A Mineral also uses this game to judge and categorize information. For example, if an article is predominantly factual but has one error or exaggeration, she points out this one part to persuade people to dismiss the whole article as inaccurate or blown out of proportion. In contrast, if a Rock source prints an article with extensive propaganda, but with one aspect that is true and well stated, the Mineral accentuates that part as evidence that the whole is valid, eloquent, and relevant to us all. Similarly, if a Rock's methods *appeared* to be successful once, she will assure you of their future success, while an opponent's one obvious failure means he's forever destined to fail.

Usually, however, at least one person in a Mineral's crowd—perhaps a spouse or other family member—notices that he is other than the role he plays. This person sees his severe handicaps and attempts to broaden his focus from his sole surviving area of normal or exceptional functioning, encouraging him to try something new. The Mineral does not understand that she is offering him balance, wanting to widen his experience and his world and, in so doing, meet her own needs as well. He is severely threatened by the prospect of change *and* the anticipation of yet more loss. The changes rendered by the Mineral Stagers in his youth all but killed him, so he now resists furiously, runs away, or worse.

Ray and Rodney were brothers in their early twenties who told me about their evacuation experiences, including a few grievances. "What bugs me most is wherever you go, when people hear that you're from New Orleans, they immediately think that you're some sort of criminal! That's REALLY fucked up!" Rodney was angry.

Ray looked seriously at his brother and said, "You're full of crap, bro! You've been runnin' drugs and hidin' from the cops for almost as long as I've known you—hustlin' folks and causin' trouble. You've been in and out of detention or prison since you were twelve! You *are* a criminal!"

Rodney punched his brother in the upper arm on top of his indigo *Defend New Orleans* tattoo. "Don't forget, asshole—I got more badges than you in Scouts, so quit dissing me like that! The fuckers around here shouldn't *assume* anything! People like that are shits and deserve whatever they have coming to them!"

"Truth" or Dare

Remember, Rocks and Minerals use <u>antagonal language</u>—words that are antagonistic to what is true or constructive. This antagonism, of course, also manifests in their behaviors. They then dare anyone to contradict them or show a better way. Some Rocks have a roulette wheel of persecutions ready for such challengers. They spin the wheel in one direction and a ball in another, and wherever the ball lands, they follow the written recommendation: public disgrace, vilification, arrest, personal injury, family tragedy, etc. They may spin the wheel repeatedly for people who are particularly bothersome. For instance, a Rock may be offended by a competitor who invents an environmentally friendly recreational vehicle with superb gas mileage. This Rock believes his business will suffer, so he first discredits the inventor and downplays her work ("impractical!"), then arranges for difficulties (one after another) at her factory, and finally puts her out of business.

Newland, a middle-aged African-American wearing a Saints football jersey with a zero on the back, said he'd been trying to track down his ex-wife and three kids. He also shared about his job of helping people with severe disabilities, such as autism, cerebral palsy, and mental retardation.

"The one autistic girl in my care looks normal, but when you try to reach her, she's in her own little world. She repeats back to you what you've just said, or she gets 'I' and 'you' mixed up. She has little interest in relating to others. Sometimes when I try to talk to her, she ignores me like I'm not even there. People think she has an attention problem, but give her an interesting toy, and you realize how long she can pay attention. Some think she's stupid, but I've seen her figure out complicated computer games that I couldn't even understand. Sometimes she spins her body around and around, but I just hold her in my arms with a big bear hug to stop the spin, and it works every time. She can waste away the hours in her fantasy world or doing things that have no apparent goal or purpose—quite a contrast to her goal-oriented family. I've spent some time with her parents, though, and they each seem to be preoccupied at times—even 'spinning' in oblivion, in my opinion. So I try to 'touch' them in some way too. Anyway, I've found touch is the key to communicating with all my patients *and* people in general." Newland grinned. "People may think me bold, but I find touch is something most people can 'hear.'"

Fantasy Games

Mineral Stagers are psychologically autistic, isolated in their own little world. They attempt, however, to include others in their "world," and their victims may tune out the world in protection. Minerals may appear to be like you, but when you try to connect with them beyond the superficial, you'll notice you're standing alone. They give back to you what they experience you giving to them—experience that is filtered through their programming. For example, if you record some obnoxious things a Mineral said when you were attempting to be helpful, and you play the tape back to her, she's likely to insist, "That's not *my* voice on the tape!" *Or* her perception reverses roles: "You're the one being obnoxious when *I'm* trying to help!" When Minerals accuse you of a lack of care and willingness or an excess of indiscretion and force, be aware that everything they say about "you" is true of them.

People often suspect Mineral Stagers lack intelligence ("She just doesn't understand how hurtful she is to her children!"), not noticing they can show evil genius in implementing and covering up their inhuman acts. Sensory apparatuses develop slowly in an unborn child, so appealing to Minerals' more complex perceptions may not be the best way to reach them. If cleared by Our Rescuer (and *only* if cleared by Our Rescuer), try engaging one of the first senses to form in a baby—touch.[3]

Manuel placed his strong hand my shoulder, greeting me with "Buenos dias" as he passed. "I'm off to the Chinese takeout to pick up some tacos, and I have some news for you. A soldier, which is my friend told me that a bunch of *invasores*—looters—were living in a housing project in the Irish Channel of New Orleans. They were blown up by his squad using grenades."

"Wow! War tactics!…Are those projects entirely gone now?" I asked.

"Well, he say they just look like they were swiped by a hurricane!" He proceeded out the door with a young black man and an elderly white man who was missing his right arm.

HANGMAN

Since anger and aggression are known to be common reactions to stress, a humane response to those who reacted with criminal activity to the stress of Hurricane Katrina and the Levee Disaster would have been to constrain them and then offer treatment for their Acute Stress Reaction, rather than murder or imprisonment. However, these law enforcers were similarly suffering from stress, and hence their violent actions. Perhaps some were Rocks who were seizing the opportunity to play their beloved game of Hangman—causing harm to people when they have a ready excuse to explain away the effects (no need for further investigation!).

The extreme forms of anger and aggression demonstrated by Rocks often cause chronic victims to move to the opposite pole. Under NO circumstances will these victims display anger or aggression—even in an emergency, when such traits might be lifesaving. When someone can't function in an area where human beings are normally functional, we have to consider the possibility that chronic trauma, as with Rock sports and recreation, has eliminated that person's capability. The evidence is in the absence.

Listening Step Nine: LISTEN TO THE ABSENCE OF LIFE

Most people assess others by what they personally see, hear, feel, and understand in the others' presence. Meanwhile, what they DON'T see, hear, feel, and understand can be equally significant. Remember, traumatic events like Hurricane Katrina chase people AWAY from the site of the disaster. When they are profoundly traumatized, they may never return. Therefore, to truly know a person, we must determine where she or he is NOT present or functional, which will identify where a disaster has befallen her or him.

Any aspect of our humanity that has been erased implies a Rocky imprint. Since Rocks never cease their persecutory tactics, a child who is consistently in their presence often blocks his or her experience of them by numbing the sensory apparatus that most acutely perceives the Rocks' activities. If a girl is violently raped, she may freeze her physical feelings in her terror, and if a boy is beaten, his body may stiffen in rage. If a woman is purely intellectual, her body and emotions were damaged or rarely acknowledged in her upbringing. If a man is driven largely by his hormones or is merely focused on having a roof over his head and food on the table, his heart and mind were sorely abused and neglected. *And* where there is a block from the past, there may be a Rock in the present.

As humans, we are capable of a wide range of abilities, interests, and activities, and it is normal for each of these to continually develop throughout our lives. A vacancy in any of the following is worth noting:

(1) PERCEPTIONS. Most of us were born with the ability to see, hear, taste, smell, and experience touch. How strongly these senses manifest and how aware of them we are reveals past conditioning, whether healthy or unhealthy. For example, a girl may curtail her vision when she is consistently forced to witness what is revolting *or* when she doesn't have her visual perceptions validated and engaged. (When a little child says, "Look at the pretty purple flowers!" a healthy parent might respond with something like, "Yes, those flowers are lovely, aren't they?") If a boy is frequently berated, he tunes out his hearing. Rocks often "play" with children in such a way as to fool them into abandoning their senses—for instance, moving things around behind their backs. ("You said you put the skateboard in the shed, but look—it's *here* in the closet. You're such an idiot—you can't even see what you're doing!") Over time, a child may learn to keep checking his perceptions. He may come to believe that objects have the ability to move on their own or that he can't trust his experience.

As we mature, we are also capable of perceiving people's psychology—seeing their psychological age at any moment, hearing their needs, getting a taste for what they've been through, perhaps smelling a "rat" in the "basement" (a Rock in the unconscious mind), and receiving their unique touch on our own psychological life. When we've suffered uncontested abuse or neglect in any of these areas, these abilities may be diminished or absent too.

(2) FEELINGS. We have the capacity to feel our bodies outside and inside—pleasure, pain, light touch, pressure, temperature, and the condition of our organs and tissues. We have senses that tell us when we are thirsty, hungry, satiated, aroused, tired, bored, sick, and so on. We have natural physical reactions, such as coughing when something is stuck in our throats or tearing up when debris lands in our eyes. As Rock caretakers INSIST nothing is wrong and no needs are unmet in their household, their kids learn to ignore physical signals that imply a problem or lack. For instance, if asked if he's hungry, a child might glance at his watch to see if it's lunchtime before answering.

Healthy humans are endowed with a FULL range of emotions: happy, angry, fearful, sad, guilty, ashamed, hopeful, excited, joyful, and loving. We may express these emotions in a myriad of creative ways. We also have the ability to sense these feelings in others as well as recognize them on a face or in a voice. We can respond to them uniquely and creatively. Feeling deficits—"I'm *always* happy; that's just the way I am!"—are a sign that other emotions were attacked or shunned in that person's experience. (Rock caretakers offer sad consequences if any of their kids are *not* "happy"—lest anyone think they are not PERFECT parents!) These unwanted and unexpressed emotions must then be communicated indirectly through sickness and injury of the physical body—people with "pain-free" emotions often have physical problems that highlight their discomfort. Shunned feelings may also be concealed behind a wall of insensitivity or derision toward those with strong emotional and/or physical expressions.

(3) **APTITUDES.** The average person has multiple areas of giftedness or skill:

(a) ***Worldly gifts,*** including athletic abilities, creative artistry, mechanical skills, foreign language proficiency, communication competences, and so forth. Even those with severe handicaps can have extraordinary exceptions. (One patient I had with mental retardation possessed spectacular dance coordination and another showed unconditional receptivity.)

(b) ***Relational gifts,*** such as empathy, sympathy, passion, tenderness, and the ability to effectively confront.

(c) ***Emotional gifts,*** such as love, faith, joy, and fearless willingness to take vital risks.

(d) ***Gifts of mind,*** as with sharp perception, keen insight, accurate memory, rapid problem-solving, spatial acuity, apt invention, a ready wit, being a quick study, and the ability to organize rooms, thoughts, and so on.

(e) ***Gifts of healing:*** Any of the above gifts in the hands of Our Rescuer become tools to develop hearts and minds.

Because Rocks are psychologically incapacitated, they try to possess those who are overtly gifted, unconsciously trying make up for their own deficits or to retrieve what they have lost. A Rock may finance them to control them and use them for his or her own "needs." Such Rocky experiences can make people downplay or hide their talents for the sake of safety and personal freedom. Ever wonder why people refuse to share their extraordinary gifts?

Maturation is about working on and expanding our areas of ability and minimizing our areas of disability—practice, practice, practice! A lack of desire to improve our abilities, receive guidance, and consistently practice is also noteworthy. I once heard a New Orleans musician boasting, "I'm self-taught in everything I know about music. I never had any lessons—I did it all by myself!" I wondered, with so many talented musicians in New Orleans, why wouldn't someone take advantage of this wealth of available, top-quality education? Very likely Rocks had a part in his sidelining stance!

(4) **COGNITION.** As adults, we are able to imagine, study, deliberate, decide, and anticipate the future. We can learn (to understand ourselves and others, for example), remember what we've experienced and learned, and comprehend ever-deepening meanings in everyday encounters and events. Rocks tend to interrupt our mind's potential for spontaneous, dynamic, and pertinent-to-the-moment inspiration by offering a rigid alternative: "Study, know, process, express, and remember ONLY what we authorize, or we will hurt you." As their programs encapsulate and dull our supple and subtle human minds, no wonder those with chronic exposure to Rocks come to believe that "thinking is a problem—DON'T THINK!"

(5) **SPIRITUALITY.** We all have a spiritual connection that feeds us like an umbilical cord. We have the choice, however, to welcome this constant source of sustenance or to pretend that "it" is something else altogether. A perceived spiritual absence is the underlying cause of the many other manifestations of absence or loss in our lives.

Of course, the above categories are not really separate. We have physical and emotional memory, as well as memory for knowledge. We can intuit with our heads and guts as well as with our hearts.

And we can touch someone with body, heart, or mind. Thus, each absence has an impact on the whole. For instance, when we're uncomfortable with our physical being, we may have knowledge or feel strongly about something, but DO nothing. When the physical is most exercised, we may act without thought of the consequences or without sensitivity to others' feelings. If the emotional realm is our comfort zone, we may be moved by our feelings without considering where these feelings are coming from, and we may express them without first sensing the best method for doing so. If our mind is our strongest suit, we may share difficult information too soon ("Your parent has some sociopathic tendencies!"), before a person is emotionally able to handle it. When our mind is slow in its functioning, we may give information too late—only AFTER much damage has been done. Also, without psychological exploration and conscious connection with the spiritual, "our" thoughts, feelings, and actions may be more about Rock-sport than about our developing humanness.

The Absence of Awareness

When a part of someone's physical body is missing, such as a limb, we acknowledge the loss. We are aware of the handicap and seek to aid these people so their lives may be as normal as possible under the circumstances. However, when some aspect of a person's heart or mind is absent (someone has lost the ability to feel a particular emotion or think freely), we often DON'T notice or comment, or we make excuses for not assisting them ("I'm not qualified to get involved!"). We miss our chance to exercise our *human* abilities and responsibilities to attend to one another and expand ourselves in the process. We then remain mutually handicapped.

Wherever there is a vacancy in our human capacities, there is a part of self that was not valued. It was either overtly persecuted or not nurtured. Total absence suggests the former, while minimal function implies the latter, or the former with partial treatment. (In my experience, few therapy patients ever hit the Rocky bottom of their abuse issues because few therapists have gone there themselves.) What we are unaware of *inside* ourselves so often blocks or distorts our awareness of it *outside* ourselves. We cannot resonate with this part of another, and so we cannot give them what they need as they need it, let alone identify any underlying problems.

We can get a more complete picture of our past by taking a seat "in the audience" for a moment and observing which aspects of ourselves are unavailable *and* what effect each absence has had on others. Do our areas of incapacity incite others to anger and violence? Then anger and violence were likely involved in the initial damage. Do they lead others into misery or despair? Then perhaps we eliminated these parts of ourselves to make someone happy. Do people enfeeble us by merely running the show in our areas of weakness instead of guiding us to become stronger and more competent ourselves? Then we've likely been coddled like infants and not encouraged to grow. Underneath every relatively "healthy" family facade lies some unhealthy Mineral content.

CHAI BREAK! Please answer the following questions regarding your areas of absenteeism:

1. In what areas are you deficient? (Remember, running away from reminders of traumatic experience is a symptom of PTSD.) Go over the above list of abilities, interests, and activities with yourself in mind, and then repeat the exercise with someone who knows you well.

2. In what specific ways are you unavailable and to whom? Under what circumstances do you feel there is a "no vacancy" sign hanging in your window—what are the times, situations, or conditions where you are less receptive, willing, or productive? What types of people are you least open to?

3. How did you learn to shut down or block these aspects of yourself?

4. How much time do you spend each day practicing the different aspects of your humanity?
    a. Improving your worldly skills?
    b. Enhancing your emotional life?
    c. Sharpening your cognition?
    d. Connecting to the Spiritual?

5. Design a plan with the aid of Our Rescuer to regain what you have lost.
    a. If you avoid the sensual, read books and poetry and view movies and performances that emphasize this arena; spend time with nature, animals, or small children; focus on truly hearing, seeing, smelling, and sensing with your skin in each environment in which you find yourself. Pick out distinct flavors in your food, use skin-care products with pleasing textures and scents, and so on. Have your touchy-feely friends or your spouse help you.
    b. If you are emotionally unaware, watch tear-jerkers on TV, listen to passionate music, notice people's emotions as you go about your day, and talk about what you see, hear, and feel. Have emotional types talk about what they see, hear, and feel as well. List your hobbled emotions, and detail specific, practical ways to constructively engage and express them. For example, to give voice to your grief, you might write a loving letter to someone who is grieving, pray for them, call and visit them, and show them that you care. (Try something similar with those feeling any other emotions you need to comfortably embrace.)
    c. If you are intellectually challenged, take a course that might help you exercise your mind; play with puzzles, brainteasers, cryptograms, or brain games; read thought-provoking books; and ask assistance from someone who excels in this arena.
    d. Catch yourself when you put down other people as inferior. What do they have that you lack, and how might they help you retrieve what you have lost?

Remember, when we are absent from a part of ourselves, we can't know what is going on there—just as I can't really know exactly what is happening in my home city of New Orleans while I'm in Greensburg. This is why "eyewitnesses" can have such different accounts of the same event—although all are present in body, they are not all present *to* their bodies, as well as to their hearts, minds, and spirits. Where we are NOT present, we tend to creatively fill in the blanks.

Movies and Other Rock Video Entertainments

The television caught my ear. I turned to see a small group of residents in the corner of the Red Cross shelter watching a violent video with shooting, screaming, dead bodies, and general chaos. It reminded me of New Orleans after Hurricane Katrina. I never cease to be amazed at how we seek out—whether on TV, in movies or books, in the lives of those we choose as our companions, or in our own behavior—the very stressful situations from which we've escaped. One part of us may flee from our disasters (our bodies were no longer in the precarious New Orleans area), but another part returns to them again and again, attempting to work them through.

Rocks produce movies and TV programs that distribute the overt and subliminal information they desire a population to absorb. The psychological, if not physical, violence and perversions they contain also desensitize the public to all manner of cruelty. When paired with popcorn, candy, and togetherness of friends and family, many people find these films entertaining (ferocity can be fun!). On top of this, Rock video games teach young people to amuse themselves with fast killing responses, whether hunting game, attacking enemies of war, or zapping aliens from other planets (kill or be killed!)—often scoring points for each hit. Players may acquire an insensitivity toward victims and identify with aggressors. Their brains habituate to violence, so the Rocks' orchestration of similar activities in real life feels like nothing to get worked up about. Many people merely sit back and enjoy the "show," just as they do in the movies, or they "play" along, as they do with their video games.

Knowing their "documentary" films are not for the faint of heart, Rocks also create "family entertainment"—movie shorts where "young" ones can smile and laugh or ride an emotional rollercoaster, all the while imbibing important "life lessons." For example, I was informed that after Hurricane Katrina, people called a New Orleans radio station and reported obviously false information, including "Governor Blanco has been kidnapped, and the house where she is being held is on fire!" Well, the governor was just fine, but this gave many people firsthand "experience" of how stressed people make up stories. This audience is then easily manipulated into "understanding" that those who are emotional or under stress cannot be trusted. While people do in fact retreat into their imaginations to help themselves feel better when stressed, there is no survival value in making events seem WORSE than they are (this just stresses people MORE!). Rather, there is comfort in believing events are NOT as bad as they appear—people can relax, maintain confidence, and happily go about daily routines.

When our caretakers and leaders are psychologically too young to meet our basic needs, such as safety, we have to discover other ways to feel secure. Our imaginations are a great resource—creating satisfying mental "movies" to pass the hours. Of course, Rocks constantly play with these movies of our minds' making to their own advantage. They focus our attention on Movie #1 and movie #2 (p. 114), while they act out the very films (movie #3) that we have yet to feel safe and strong enough to allow into our conscious awareness.

Remember, when we reject any part of our life story and any corresponding parts of ourselves, we insert a commercial message about our lack of wholeness. In doing so, we block our unlimited Mind awaiting us beyond all stories and selves. To illustrate, look at the exercise we just completed about contemplating our areas of absence from our humanity. We've had these deficits for years, and we've concocted stories to explain them away, rather than earnestly work to retrieve what we've lost. When we begin to notice how many aspects of our lives are less than they could be, the next step is to wonder about the traumatic experiences that so curtailed them and the inner pain that must still be present, since our developmental needs have clearly never been met. The rampant popularity of television programs, news shows, commercials, and films that are violent or are about violence highlights the violations to our humanity that remain unresolved for most people.

I returned to Effie's house midafternoon to discover a drenched Oliver jumping around on the driveway. I asked, "What happened to you?"

"Nothing—I used the garden hose to cool myself off." He shook himself like a wet dog.

"Right—good thinking!" There was still no electricity and no A/C, so we had to come up with our own strategies for keeping ourselves comfortable.

I sauntered into the muggy house and grabbed a cold lunch out of the refrigerator, fanning myself the whole time with pages of my writing.

"I'm bored! Anybody want to play a game?" Felicity appeared out of the hallway carrying three boxes and a bag of M&Ms.

"What did you have in mind, Felicity?" I asked.

"Trivial Pursuit, Monopoly, or Life."

I was startled by her apt description of my daily preoccupations.

"These are children's versions," Connie added, as if reading my thoughts.

I laughed. "Well, in that case, count me in,"

"Mom?" Felicity's large eyes were beseeching.

"Sure, honey—after I finish my daily devotion."

"Oliver?" Felicity spoke loudly to draw the attention of her brother who had put on dry clothes and was heading toward the TV.

"Yeah, OK," Oliver said as he changed course and sat on the floor.

Felicity picked the game of Life, which I considered the best choice under our present circumstances. As we all adjusted our positions on the speckled, earth-toned carpeting, Connie commented that she had played that game often as a child, while I, on the other hand, was most familiar with Monopoly. Felicity placed the other games on the floor beside us—"in case we want to play another game when Life is over." (Kids say such profound things!)

BORED Games

Children are imprinted by the recreation they are exposed to when growing up, and they often enjoy the same or similar activities later with their own children. Rocks, too, pass on the "amusements" of their childhood. The "winner" of any game is typically "treated" to sexual abuse, while losers suffer a wider range of persecutions. Regular participants in a Rock's "recreation" transfer their learning to the "game" of their life—often losing their ability to be playful and have fun. They may shun team sports or any cooperative, goal-oriented interactions. *Or* they may become fiercely competitive, as if their lives were on the line. They may deduce that the rewards of winning are NOT what they seem, so they lose all ambition. By the time they reach "adulthood," they may not remember how to unwind, assert their interests and desires, or receive tokens of merit or affection without feeling threatened.

Children with Rock caretakers do EVERYTHING that grown-ups do—they work (child-labor laws have no bearing on Rock households or boarding schools) as well as study (in hope of someday being paid for their efforts). They don't have much time or energy for entertainments, except perhaps to collapse in front of the TV for the nightly "news." They are most familiar with the extreme tension associated with Rock "recreations" and the relief and relaxation when the "game" is over, so they reenact these games when life lacks the accustomed stimulation or they "need" tension release. Kids reared by Rocks are often addicted to stress—they actually experience withdrawal symptoms from plummeting stress hormones if life goes smoothly for any length of time. To feel stable, secure, and alive, they must constantly create chaos, plan and implement problems, and curtail orderliness, functionality, and recovery. Also, when children are not allowed healthy play in childhood, they will try to make up for this deprivation later in life, as with Rock "fun and games."

Terribly Trivial Pursuits: In this game, Rocks trivialize our most poignant calls for help and offers of aid, reducing them to the mundane, insignificant, or irrelevant. For example, I remember once watching a news program about a serial killer who ruthlessly tortured and then dismembered his victims. The consulted "expert" attributed this murderer's horrific behaviors to his having seen his dog run over by a car when he was a tender boy. Although certainly traumatic, this incident doesn't begin to explain the enormity of his violent crimes! Those who try to help such survivors of truly catastrophic trauma *before* their behavior is "screaming" for help are disqualified by the gaming Rock, who is quick to point out these helpers' psychological issues—"First clean up your own act!" (For the inundated-with-issues Rock to cite another's problems is a comparatively trivial focus!) The Rock insists that intervention is best left to Rocks who, by their own estimation, are "problem free."

Rocks trivialize widely, from the "causes" of their premeditated activities to the consequences (some of the stories they concoct to incriminate their whipping boys are preposterous!). Most importantly, Rocks trivialize our lives, distracting us from the pursuit of self-knowledge and our greater Identity. Everything in this world is trivial next to this powerful causal nature, of which we all are effects. By teaching us to prioritize worldly effects, however, Rocks keep us trapped in trivia and resign us to lives of mediocrity and insignificance.

Mineral Stage Monopoly: Once we're absorbed in the trivial, the Rock is free to "walk on the boardwalk," usurping what is valuable or most vital to a community without serious obstruction.

Rocks endeavor to possess the best property and the most viable businesses and utilities, including electricity, gas, and waterworks, if not the owners and managers of such services. By controlling resources, they can easily railroad citizens into serving them by requiring that people allow the Rock "his" way to get what they need to live. With such control over their offspring, the Rocks' grip becomes ironclad.

Children ruled by Rocks freeze into rigid playing pieces that anyone can easily manipulate around their game boards. The forging wrought by Rocks can be surmised by the current shape of each "piece." For example, when a person is eager to please, readily performing any trick for praise or "treats," the Rocks in his life tormented him if he ever attempted a more upright human stance. His "dog" or people-pleasing personality is a conditioned response. When Rocks persecuted any resistance or complaint in another person, she then allows herself to be "walked on" without protest, becoming a "shoe," doormat, or dupe. When Rocks ceased their torture only when someone was yelling and

explosive, he is bound to scream when he wants something unpleasant to stop— forever a lit cannon ready to go off. As Rocks supply or allow the basic needs of each "piece" *and* cease passing their PAIN only when the "piece" has assumed the form they have chosen for him or her, over time the personality becomes imprisoned. The only "get out of jail free" card for these deeply conditioned characters then is to chance the recreation of Our Rescuer:

The Game of *Our Shared LIFE*: Rescuing from the Game of Guilt

In the Guilt Game, we shape people into "pieces" that fit our game boards—ignoring them (or whacking them!) when they speak out of character. We keep them away from the whole truth about themselves and those who would reveal it. And we maintain their survivor mode rather than lead them into the sufficiency of our shared humanity. In contrast, the Game of Our Shared LIFE reveals rescuers. These Men and Women introduce a neutral perspective into the Guilt Game—the fact that we have ALL been victimizers *and* victims to varying degrees and at different times in our lives, if not throughout each day. We've routinely confused infants and children with adults—not caring for the former *and* not allowing the latter to care for us. We are ALL guilty of this confusion (and we *need* to recover!).

Let's look at a community setting, such as the New Orleans disaster. The victimizers include Hurricane Katrina, the breached-levee builders and board members, looters, and corrupt politicians. The victims comprise hundreds of thousands of people who lost their homes, health, loved ones, neighborhoods, property, jobs, hopes, and dreams. In the severity and widespread nature of this tragedy, the desperate voices of the distressed parts of many psyches were heard in the greater community. Those who responded were our rescuers: all the people who physically rescued survivors; challenged the levee engineers and lax officials; arrested criminals; sent money, supplies, consolation, and other support; or came to New Orleans to charitably help in the cleanup and rebuilding of our city and psyches.

The goal of this rescuing game is to serve LIFE—every token character, whether victim, victimizer, or rescuer, is equally worthy to have his or her TRUE needs met, *and* every able body is taught to be attentive to meeting these needs—Search and Rescue! For instance, we notice where "kids" have been deprived of an opportunity to play a certain aspect of life's game, so we arrange for them to have plenty of coached practice. We look for where "children" have had more than their fair share of time on the field and replace them with players who have spent too much time on the sidelines. In this game, all "children" learn to generously share what they have in abundance, whether worldly goods, talent, knowledge, loving kindness, time, or energy. (This is NOT communism or socialism, but preschool and kindergarten!) "Kids" also discover how to gratefully receive what they lack (whether hands-on help, human feeling, advice, or money). When the game is played well, those who have much give to those who have little, so we all approach middle ground. Over the course of the game, extremes even out as EVERYONE's needs are met!

We lose the game by giving to those who are already "rich." For example, when we give what we *don't* have enough of ourselves to those who already have plenty, we make the recipient guilty of depriving us. Conversely, withholding from those who are genuinely lacking keeps the aspects of us they represent in need. Also, if we give through a middleman, there is no guarantee that a reasonable percentage of our gift will get where it is supposed to go. We often end up "rescuing" an image when we "support" an organization or person, as with Gina "rescuing" Ralph from Arlene. (This imaginary version of "rescuing" has become so common it has taken over the original definition in my profession!)

This Game of Our Shared LIFE can be difficult for many reasons. First of all, Rocks demand so much of our money, whether through taxing, tithing, mandatory insurances, or ever-increasing fees, there may be little left for those who really need it or who could make good use of it. Also, the fact that victims, victimizers, and rescuers exist in each of us complicates the task of giving to those in need. Which do we attend to at any one time, and how? For instance, we may tend to the needs of a victim in one moment, perhaps donating money or other provisions, only to have her throw it away in destructive behaviors, such as supporting Rocks or their "charities." We can feel sorely victimized ourselves and convinced that helping another leads to harm, which is the belief system of Rocks—only they go one step further: believing that hurting people helps! This is why we *require* Our Rescuer to referee.

Mr. Machine

"I was just thinking," I said, looking up from my writing to engage my fellow players and disaster survivors, "why wasn't there some sort of siren to alert those in the Lower Ninth Ward about the flood, since it's flooded there so many times in the past? The news is now saying that the Seventeenth Street and London Avenue Canals breached Monday morning, the day of the storm, but none of y'all listening to your separate radio stations got this information until Tuesday afternoon when Effie told us. If our city officials wanted the news about the levees to be disseminated into the soon-to-be-flooded areas of the city, they could have informed people once the worst of the storm was over." I turned to Felicity and Oliver. "Did you two study Paul Revere in school?"

Oliver spoke up. "Yeah, he rode through the streets on his horse shouting, 'The British are coming. The British are coming.'"

"Exactly, and it worked. If many of the official lines of communication were down, we still had human beings capable of delivering a message: 'Many levees have breached! New Orleans is flooding rapidly! The only open evacuation route is Interstate 10. Tell everyone you know in the city and have them spread the word.' This would have gotten the message around in no time!" New Orleans's exceptional grapevine is renowned for being more like a small town than a sizable city.

"That could have easily been broadcast through a bullhorn like those preachers along Canal Street do," Connie added. "They could have used boats or helicopters in the wet areas and Hummers or Jeeps in the dry areas."

"Or they could have flown a big banner over the city," Oliver said with enthusiasm, "just like the advertisers do at Jazz Fest or French Quarter Fest."

"They have an alarm at school!" Even young Felicity had a pertinent suggestion.

"I agree." I was impressed with the ideas from our small, motley group. "There were so many more possibilities than 'There was no communication![4] There was nothing we could do!'"

When Mineral Stagers' "one way" is not possible, they are unable to come up with another plan of action and will state they "couldn't" do otherwise. For example, Minerals tend to rely on machines in place of human effort. (I think they must consider electronic devices colleagues, if not relatives.) If their walkie-talkies, radios, or phones weren't functioning during the storm, then in *their* minds no communication was possible—despite the fact that the human route of person-to-person was still wide open. Human beings are capable of great inventiveness and resourcefulness when established procedures go awry. Minerals, on the other hand, are at a loss. They mechanically repeat the same "battery"-operated routines, trying to get them to work and afterward announcing, "There was nothing anyone could do!" When Minerals are asked to function outside of their known parameters, there *will* be "errors."

After playing Life, we sat down to a meal of canned ravioli, compliments of the Red Cross. Effie, in her blue bathrobe, emerged briefly from her bedroom during our dinner. "Anne dear, several people from Chicago called to say there was no Joan Johnson in their family."

"Oh, OK. Thanks," I replied, saddened by the news since I had still not heard from Cousin Joan. "How are you feeling, Effie?"

"Feelin' just fine, dear. I'm up to get some liquid—my doctor told me to keep hydrated." She went into the kitchen, poured a tall fire-engine-red plastic cup of Merlot from her two-liter carton, adding maybe an ounce of tap water to the top. She then disappeared again into her bedroom.

"Fun" with *SABOTAGE*

Rocks enjoy thwarting human endeavors. When people are happily cooperating in some beneficial project, the Rocks' Program Opposition moves in. Ordinary adult activities, such as working, deepening a marriage bond, rearing children, and perhaps even using mechanical devices, are fraught with frustrations and failures when a Rock, behind closed doors, is arranging extensive complications: outages, illnesses, breakups, breakdowns, and every manner of obstruction. Below is just a short list of examples of the endless ways Rocks play the sabotage game.

Many of our tasks would be quick and easy, or even unnecessary, were it not for Rocks creating perplexing instructions (tax law) and inefficient and time-consuming methods. For example, if you want a particular service, you must agree to the terms outlined in seven pages of single-spaced text. To save time, people acquire the habit of signing documents without reading them. *Or* they may become so focused on written minutiae ("Everything you need to know is right here in black and white!") that they forget to read *between* the lines.

Rocks design activities for difficulty, engendering stress, strain, and secondary problems. For instance, public-relations employees may know less than the customers they are serving. Workers may be so specialized that when their one skill isn't needed, they do nothing, and when they are absent, their work isn't done. Processing of prolific paperwork (the Confounder), agreements, applications, permits, licenses, copyrights, complaints, and so forth proceeds ever so slowly because of precise protocols that can't be altered without a committee meeting or conference call that may take weeks to months to orchestrate, and at least as much time afterward to implement the results of any decision—if there's been consensus (probably not!). If there is ever an easy solution, a shortcut, a path of least resistance, Rocks won't see it or won't use it.

You'll get quite a workout jumping through hoops or wrestling to procure what you want from Rocks. Do you require some documentation? Go to this remote office during a limited time period and talk to this particular person. Chances are the clerk "can't find" your document so he sends you on a scavenger hunt, which leads you to every type of information except what you need. It may seem a "comedy of errors," except you are far from laughing. Dealing with Rocks and their endless hurdles can be annoying at the least, but when people's lives are at stake, all their dawdling and dallying, their bungling and boggling with "oversights" and "miscalculations," and their forgetfulness, fruitlessness, and underhanded maliciousness is disastrous!

Rocks "love" to manipulate people into whatever their society, culture, religion, or personal mores consider most intolerable. To do so, they often use live bait. For example, a scripture-quoting Rock will woo and charm a single Christian woman over many months. After he proposes and their future marriage seems secure, he talks her into intimate relations. Then his wife will call. If a man is derisive of homosexuals, the Rock will pay a strikingly beautiful transvestite to entice this fellow into compromising situations. Rocks are masterminds in getting people to taste "forbidden fruit" or oppose their most cherished beliefs and then never let them forget it. Their victims may not be able to live with the resulting shame and self-loathing, let alone their fear of exposure. This game may end abruptly when victims terminate their lives.

Connie usually disappeared with the kids at night after dinner. Tonight, shortly before seven, she asked me to go with her while the kids stayed with Effie. As we drove down the long driveway, Connie said her disappearance each night had been to buy gas for her SUV and/or the generator. "As we wait in the long gas line, Oliver plays his video games, Felicity plays with her toys, and I relax and enjoy the cool breeze of the air conditioner. It feels wonderful after a long hot day in temperatures of over ninety degrees! But tonight, I wanted to see if you'd be interested in waiting in the food-stamp line with me. I'm out of cash. The computers are down at the bank, so I won't be able to withdraw money for a while. No one is taking credit cards either. I'd asked Cedric to give me more money for the evacuation, since I only had two hundred dollars in my purse, but he said that would be enough for a couple days. HUH!"

"Sounds like a new experience for us both—let's go!" I replied. After waiting in a short line at the gas station and filling up Connie's SUV, we were soon waiting at the end of a long line of automobiles, which seemed almost as long as the town of Greensburg itself. When we arrived at the front of the car line, we were handed a numbered ticket and instructed to drive to the location of a long line of people in the heart of "downtown" Greensburg. Once in this line, we heard a lot of vivid life stories from others waiting with us.

"Tex," a tough-looking fellow wearing denim and cowboy boots, told me he was fleeing the rising waters in New Orleans with his most valuable possessions when two men approached him and hollered. "They were bigger than me, and it looked like they were pullin' out their piece, so I pulled out mine. I got 'em before they got me. I told 'em, 'Didn't your mama ever tell you not to talk to strangers?' As I watched the bodies float away, I felt kinda sad, so I apologized. I said, 'I'm sorry—I don't got anything against you, but I saw that it was you or me, and I chose me.' When I think about it, I was stressed, and maybe I didn't have to do it. Maybe I overreacted."

OVERREACTIONS

Unshaven, burly, middle-aged "Bobcat Bill" related that Hurricane Katrina destroyed his boyhood home in the southern Louisiana countryside. With an animated face, he reminisced about his childhood memories.

"In my neck of the woods, boys are given toy chain saws to play with until they're old enough to get a real one when they are about ten years old."

His petite wife, Sue, originally from northern Louisiana remarked, "And that's not all they're given rather young. The average boy gets a shotgun when he turns five and chewing tobacco when he turns seven!"

"Sue, you make up these stories that just aren't true. Why do you do that?" Bill rubbed his forehead in dismay.

"All right, sugar pie, you tell the story then." A smiling Sue spoke with obvious affection.

"I've never known anyone in my entire life who got a shotgun BEFORE he started school. Naw—it's usually a present for gettin' through first grade. I took to it right away, but my lil' brother shot off a few fingers and toes before he got the hang of it!"

"Wow! How did your parents handle that?" I asked, thinking if that had been my kid, I would have been devastated.

Bill was matter-of-fact. "Daddy always took things in stride, but Mama—*she* overreacted!"

For every "child" with a "weapon," there are those who gave him the "weapon," provided access to the weapon, or saw the danger and did nothing to stop it. Responsibility rarely rests on only one person's shoulders, as much as we might like to point fingers. Guilt itself is a weapon. Rocks expose children to it very early in life, teaching them antisocial acts before they can understand their actions or the permanent consequences. As kids grow to understand, most of them repress their guilt and memories to survive psychologically. As "adults," they may live relatively "normal" lives until someone or something reminds them of what was long ago buried, and then they suddenly lash out in anger, withdraw in depression, have a panic attack, or hurt others or themselves in some way (illnesses are a common manifestation of triggered guilt). Alternatively, those who have been triggered may also stiffen in fear and become immobile and unresponsive. If we investigate how we over- or underreact to a given situation, we usually find Rock recreations at their core.

I've spent many years of my life working with these over- and underreactors in a culture that defines these expressions of Rock sports and games as "normal," God-given personality traits, genetic abnormalities, mental illnesses, and physical disease. I wonder how long we as a people will make these over- and underreactors wait, stalling them with storytelling—*our* recreation—before we learn to hear their human voices, acknowledge their unconscious guilt, and address the underlying need.

A tall, gaunt young man dressed in a hooded T-shirt and baggy shorts in line just ahead of us started talking. "It was around daybreak in Saint Bernard, when I stepped outside to watch Katrina coming our way. I saw the water rising in the street. Then before I knew it, my house was flooded chest high. I got on the roof, and I hung on to the chimney for dear life to keep from being blown away. The wind was unbelievable and I was *really* cold. No way was I goin' into the water with all the junk—branches, shattered wood and metal, chemicals—you name it! Not to mention deadly creatures like water moccasins and dem gators—plenty o' gators! On the roof I had a great view of what was goin' down in the 'hood. Like at one point I saw the water swallow my next-door neighbor's one-story home with them inside. That was horrible because they were an older couple—they couldn't have survived," he said wistfully. "I could have saved them!" He had regret in his voice as he blinked away his tears. "But I was too busy trying to stay alive!

"Later, I saw a man and a woman with a big dog swimming for safety, only to have a hungry gator snatch the dog and roll him under. I heard the man then yell to the woman, 'That dog saved us! I told you these waters were full of hidden dangers!'"

The Game of "I told you so!"

How many lives might we have helped save if we weren't so consumed with fanciful tales and so preoccupied with maintaining our beloved images? Think about how much more of ourselves would be available if we weren't so resistant to admitting our Rocky pasts and processing the horrors and the horrific impacts they've had on us. Also ponder how much more of themselves others would have available if we assisted them beyond their Rocky resistance?

Consider what our world would be like if we prioritized psychological development? How would our days be different if we kept an eye out for people in trouble and, with the aid of Our Rescuer, met their needs? What would life be like if no one was stuck in the Mineral Stage of Development? How would it be for children to be raised with mature parents who both lived at home, loved them and each other dearly, and prioritized ever-deepening this love. Communities might once again be safe if we only took the time to relate to everyone in a developmental way. Wouldn't supporting each other's growth be better than having to vigilantly circumvent the chronic vexations and hidden dangers perpetrated by those frozen in the younger developmental stages?

This guilt we carry is not merely the sum of all the things we've done to hurt one another, passing on the pain that has been passed to us. Our guilt includes the remorse of what we *haven't* done to save each other's physical and psychological lives and the recognition of HOW MUCH it has cost us all—an increasingly Rocky world! We're ALL paying grievously for neglecting to mutually rear our fellow humans to maturity. **It only takes the consistent presence of ONE human being to keep a person from becoming stuck in the Mineral Stage of Development!** This is Our Rescuer's Game of One. So it's not just fear that delays our standing up to and helping the Rocks in our lives, but our guilt and shame. Deep in our unconscious mind, we have judged ourselves "GUILTY!" and worthy of Rocks' Punishing Programs for having routinely walked away from people in need. All along, Rocks have accused us of being guilty and assailed us for it. Let's hope they won't have to tell us again.

Just after midnight there were still a lot of people in front of us in line, as well as behind us, so we told our neighbors where we'd be and strolled off to get a few winks of sleep in Connie's SUV. As we were adjusting the front seats for comfort, Connie spoke in a serious tone.

"I did read what you wrote about Rocks." She sighed. "A lot of it sounds like my husband, except the violent, rageful parts—those don't. Cedric can be grumpy or irritable, but never extreme. He's never hit me or the kids. He's just not around most of the time, not since the kids were born. Usually, he's upbeat and positive—at least that's what everyone says about him. Everyone else in his life seems to think he's just fine." Connie's facial expression told me she had doubts.

"Can you feel the anger in someone refusing to give children what they need more than anything?" I asked.

"Huh?" Connie had a deep furrow between her eyebrows.

"Cedric is keeping your kids from having a loving, interested, actively involved, MATURE parent. That's cruel and horribly depriving."

"Ah…yeah…I get that, but…. he doesn't mean to. It's like he's on automatic pilot—he goes about his daily schedule, while ignoring me and the kids. What interests him is his work."

"Whether he means to or not isn't the point. His neglect causes pain to you all, and he is responsible for that."

"But he's NOT violent!" Connie insisted, her voice escalating.

"Well, Rocks have a way of revealing themselves over time when their families want the truth. Wait and see."

Connie nodded her head and closed her eyes, and I followed her lead. After I briefly reviewed my day with Our Rescuer, my mind drifted toward home, and I fell asleep.

TIME OUT! DEALING WITH ROCK SPORTS AND RECREATIONS

Rocks are skilled at playing with the rigid aspects of people's hearts and minds, which they themselves have often created. If we attempt intervention without higher Guidance, we soon discover we're out of our league. Success demands that we team up with Our Rescuer in ALL our plays. Ways to deal with Rock recreations include the following:

(1) Button, Button, Who's Got the Button? Just as many children's toys have buttons that make a baby doll cry, an action figure move, or a stuffed dog bark, we too have "buttons." Our "buttons" are unresolved psychological issues that, when "pushed," cause us to react, overreact, or underreact. The Rock draws our attention to buttons we didn't know existed. She makes a point of finding these "buttons" or producing them, and then pushing them one by one (if not all at once). She repeats this behavior endlessly until we get over such buttons or get rid of her. Working with a Rock requires that we defuse the buttons she exposes by discovering why we have them and what we can do to neutralize them—and then DOING it.

(2) Poor Sports. Hold the Rock accountable for his abysmal relational track record as he continually laps around the same course. When he squashes you or steps on a loved one in reaction, let him know he's out of bounds. When he tries to make a quick pass and blame someone else for making the racket, hit the ball back into his court. Typically when challenged, the Rock volleys many offensive lines and a lot of unnecessary roughness to keep the game going "his" way. He forces you into a defensive position, which he then criticizes you for. ("What are YOU so defensive about?") You can stay one step ahead by insisting, "I brought up an issue first, so hear me out before we talk about your issue with me. We'll take turns." The Rock may refuse to jog that terrain, or he may race to the finish ("You're not telling me anything I don't already know, so we're done!"). Don't be sidelined by his fancy footwork or cries of "I'm getting nothing out of this!" Be a sport and get something out of it for you both.

(3) The Magic Mirror. Rocks' programming distorts their perceptions, much like carnival fun-house mirrors. The behavior of others appears grossly abnormal, while Rocks see themselves as irreproachable. Although Mineral Stagers are masters of illusion, we can listen to their antagonal communications and learn to hear what they are truly saying. By analyzing the mirror image of their words and behavior with Our Rescuer, we get a direct reflection of what is true or useful, and we can avoid their circus.

(4) "Playing" with Blocks. When we earnestly seek to meet someone's genuine needs, a Rock part in that person often surfaces because this is her neediest part. Remember, a Rock part is a blocked part—a hardened aspect of a person that is walling off agonizing unconscious memories and pain. (No wonder she thinks WE are hurting HER when we engage her humanity!) Like hard modeling clay, these Rocky parts can soften over time when held and moved by human "hands." (Contact with Our Rescuer ensures that our psychological "hands" are indeed consistently human and warm enough to penetrate the cold, hard Rock.)

(5) Workout! If used consistently over an extended time, any techniques can be useful that exercise the behavioral, emotional, and mental repertoires of the Mineral Stager, reduce the troubling programs in his brain, and rouse his sleeping consciousness. His persistent resistance can prod us into exercising the Rocky areas inside ourselves too. Behavioral, emotional, and mental gymnastics are often required to reach him as he's quick to close off to formerly effective methods, perhaps "realizing" that "you don't know what you're doing!" Do what you can, but also set up "aerobics classes" for the Rock or Mineral—exposure to ever new people and activities that will work his emotional heart. Sessions with "personal trainers" are also useful—people who have easy access to the personal and are able to share this skill with those who have none. The more people who join you in helping the Mineral Stager, the better!

(6) Dance Therapy or Rock'n Roll. Healing Minerals of their "false self"-absorption is through "touch"—reaching beyond "their" song and dance and the underlying horror and "touching" the real person, the psychological human "fetus" within them. The more we cling to our shared humanity and take steps in time with "its" music, the more the Minerals in our lives are likely to follow along.

(7) Chess. When helping a child who is the pawn of a Rock, all the moves recommended in child-care manuals must be carefully considered *and* reviewed with Our Rescuer. An intelligent Rock has included the expected movements of each "piece" in his strategy and will have planned his offensive moves accordingly. Relating as a human being, outside of accustomed patterns and perhaps societal norms, takes him by surprise. Parents and caregivers must set firm boundaries and just consequences for pebble behavior in children, *as well as* discern where each child is learning Rocky recreation. *I can't stress enough the potential danger of Rocks to everyone involved and the NEED to make full use of the Queen, Our Rescuer, by allowing her full use of you!*

(8) Take a Hike! We need to be on the lookout for "garden paths" laid by Rocks, so we stay clear of them. Concerning our children, we may appear momentarily controlling and insensitive ("spoilsport!") when we say no to our child's request to go on a Rock-led overnight camping trip or a weekend scouting activity. (Watch out for the verbal retaliation by Femrocks: "Can't loosen up on the apron strings, eh?") However, when Rocks are involved, we'll be protecting the psychological life of every family member over the long term. For safety's sake, we must only follow the trail laid by Our Rescuer and NOT step off.

(9) Let's Pretend! When we have expectations of mature behavior from Mineral Stagers, we're engaging in fantasy play, much like small children with their dolls. For instance, when we project our human feelings, aspirations, and motives onto Rocks ("What they did was MERELY to save money!"), we're passing on our pain of having been treated like a plaything ourselves. When Rocks then pass on their **PAIN**, we are in part responsible. As long as we're pretending Rocks and Minerals are "normal," respectable people, the only reasonable expectation of them is that they will continue to be anything but normal in an unconscious attempt to draw people's attention to their condition. Once we comprehend this, then their needs become very much our own.

(10) Game Technology. As Mineral Stagers are so threatened by human beings, inanimate objects may be the best way to get through to them—books, recordings, Internet sites, answering-machine messages, and telexes can deliver the message you want to send in a form that is more palatable. A therapist online or on the telephone may seem more comfortable to Minerals than one in person—they're apt to listen better to a voice coming through a video screen or a receiver they hold in their own hands, and thereby progress faster. "Self-help" manuals with plenty of programming, but also a few important psychological or spiritual truths, are good beginner books for teaching them a more humane "game."

Be creative in delivering your information to Mineral Stagers. For example, use mechanical words like "*Plug* into that new recovery group that advertises *access* to feelings!" to catch his attention.

Help your Rock move beyond his binary mind-set of "right" or "wrong" by looking at both the possible "rightness" and "wrongness" of whatever his current focus is. Also, meditate on how you might use your current Rock and Mineral interactions to make yourself more sensible, accessible, mobile, and functional.

HALF TIME: Pause for a moment to consider areas of Rockiness in your life and how you might work on them before continuing. Keep a scorecard and give yourself points every time you choose another way!

1. See if you can identify possible Rock games in the following:
   a. The media in some regions have falsely led many US citizens to believe that New Orleans will always be a danger because nearly half of it lies below sea level and nothing anyone can do will secure the city. When New Orleans residents complain about the Levee Disaster, these citizens retort, "You have no one to blame but yourselves for choosing to live there!"
   b. The Levee Disaster resulted in the loss of many legal documents and other important papers (government and criminal files, bank, medical and pharmaceutical records, birth and death certificates, school reports and degree verifications, and so on).[5]
   c. A doctor and two nurses were implicated in several patient deaths during the Levee Disaster and were charged with second-degree murder.[6] In contrast, those responsible for thousands dying in the flood received no criminal charges.

2. Create a game to teach children about Rock recreations so they learn to avoid these deadly traps. Consider playing it with some of the children you are close to. Then consider sharing it with local schools or childcare centers.

3. While using an inversion table or an inverted yoga posture, ponder which Rock games have turned you upside down in some way. (You may need some help from others to get an honest answer.) For example, have you been conned into the Binary Games (Predator/Prey, Either/Or, MY WAY/your way) or the Charade of Intimacy? How can you neutralize the effects these have had on you?

4. Go to a toy store and find a doll or stuffed animal that most accurately represents the character you tend to project onto Rocks (an angel? a little lamb? a monster?). Consider buying it and putting it in a place that will remind you to develop a relationship with this part of yourself and to stay alert to your projections!

5. With puppets, act out your version of the Pass the Pain Game. Then finish the "show" with your version of the Game of Innocence.

6. After reading this far in this book, what questions would you like to ask yourself? What answers would you like to find within yourself?

7. Does anyone play "Keep Away" in your family? Is there someone whom no one is allowed to criticize? Is there some part inside yourself that does not allow "negative" feedback? What or who are you most wanting to avoid?

8. Look deeply into some "overreactions" you have witnessed, and see if you can understand what the person's emotional body is communicating about his or her experiences with Rock recreation.

9. Are you engaging in Fantasy Games by pretending to be only an adult, when parts of you are stuck in child, infant, fetal, and/or embryonic psychological states? Do you indulge in the same fantasies with others? How might you use others as a mirror to help you perceive your own inner state, and vice versa?

10. What are some ways in which you can tumble your sharp inner Minerals into smooth gemstones? How will this help you stay ahead of "your" game?

[1] Kristin Wakeham, "Fetal Development," *To the Unborn: A Pro-Life Page,* posted July, 2000, http://www.angelfire.com/nj3/rebekah8367/.

[2] "Crime Wave in New Orleans," *Harvard University Press Blog,* January 12, 2007, http://harvardpress.typepad.com/hup_publicity/2007/01/crime_wave_in_n.html.

[3] John Medina, *Brain Rules for BABY* (Seattle, WA: Pear Press, 2010), 32.

[4] "Paul McHale, the Assistant Secretary of Defense for Homeland Defense, summarized the damage by stating, 'The magnitude of the storm was such that the local communications system wasn't simply degraded; it was, at least for a period of time, destroyed." Disaster in the Gulf Coast, *The Federal Response to Hurricane Katrina: Lessons Learned, Chapter Four: a Week of Crisis—August 29- September 5*, February 2006 http://library.stmarytx.edu/acadlib/edocs/katrinawh.pdf, 34

[5] Nikki Swartz, "Katrina Devastates Gulf Records," *Bay Ledger News Zone,* October 31, 2005, http://www.blnz.com/news/2008/04/22/Katrina_Devastates_Gulf_Records_1182.html.

[6] Sheri Fink, "The Deadly Choices at Memorial," *The New York Times,* August 1, 2009, http://www.nytimes.com/2009/08/30/magazine/30doctors.html?pagewanted=all.

Chapter 10

Auto Mechanics

The Workings of the Individual Self

At 4:10 a.m. Connie and I were awakened in the van by the man behind us in line knocking on the window. He hollered, "You two are next!" By 4:15 we were talking to one of the two workers in the food-stamp office, and by 4:30 we had our food-stamp cards. The whole process had taken over nine hours!

Before leaving, I asked to speak to the person in charge, so I was directed to a young woman outside the building. I introduced myself and told her I'd like to volunteer my time to help speed the line along. She shook her head and said, "No thanks, we have all the staff we need." Even in my sleepiness, I was flabbergasted by her response. As I glanced at the small line of people still waiting to be seen, I thought, "*Your* needs? What about THEIR needs?"

Evacuation Day 10: The Human Race or the Racetrack

Rock sports and recreations put the brakes on available, *human* help. Without assistance, we're destined to spend our lives lapping around the same course of "good" times to "bad" times, some particularly disastrous. Rather than find another path, we adapt to the recurrent rugged terrain and the struggles, believing this is the way "life" is. Since Rocks have taught us ridiculously complicated, demanding, inane, or just plain wrong ways of doing just about everything, we experience life as stressful, if not gravely disabling. We may be so accustomed to these arduous and/or deleterious ways that they have become habits—we do what we do automatically without pausing to think, feel, or ask what action or response would be best.

Automatisms Turn People into Machines

Driving home, Connie began chatting about "Peter." When I'm tired, my brain tends to short-circuit, so I questioned Connie. "Who are you referring to?"

"Peter is our SUV, what you're riding in. Felicity heard Cedric and me talking about our mechanic, Peter, and she thought we were talking about the car, so the name stuck." We were passing the post office when Connie asked, "Have you forwarded your mail to Effie's house yet? There's no telling when we'll be allowed back into New Orleans."

"Ah...no," I said sleepily. Except during emergency evacuations, my body is never awake at this hour.

We stopped at a red light and waited, even though no moving car was in sight. Connie continued. "In New Orleans, most people don't seem to observe traffic lights or signs if there's no one around. Have you noticed? Actually, even if there are other cars, New Orleanians frequently run a red light. If I'm sitting in my car at an intersection where the light has just turned green, I often count one or two cars or trucks going through their red light—occasionally even three! I ALWAYS glance both ways at a green light before putting my foot on the gas. I don't want to run into someone who is slow to register new information."

A machine's movements are predictable, made to fulfill certain functions for human beings. A mechanical device typically has an on/off switch—it is or isn't functioning, depending on the position of the switch, and nothing you say to it can alter this fact. No one ever asks a machine to change its ways, nor do we have to make a request with a certain tone of voice for the machine to respond to us. Let's consider the automobile and the limitations of its parts. For example, a steering wheel (even if it has POWER steering) doesn't have the strength and rotational ability of a tire and cannot replace it. Also, like every machine, the automobile has a certain life-span, tending to lose function over time and require more frequent repairs.

In a similar manner, Rocks seek to limit human beings to machinelike predictability ("Men are insensitive"; "Women are illogical") so they have fewer variables to contend with when they use us. By teaching their binary system—"You're right on course" (normal = following the Program) or "You're off track" (abnormal = finding your own path)—Rocks divert us from the enormity and diversity of our human experience and expression. Psychologically speaking, we learn to fall in line with another person or have her or him meet us where we are rather than travel new ground together. (Astonishingly, the "parked" person often perceives himself as superior by having made the other one move!) Rocks also instruct us in our morbidity and mortality. Hospitals and retirement homes are full of people who have bought into the expectation of infirmity and suffering as we age, the fear of which keeps many people treading the path laid by the Program.

This mechanization process freezes the full range of abilities that is our human legacy and creates our Mineral parts, which are consistent in what turns them "on" or "off." (If you turn me on, you are responsible for my conduct. If you turn me off, you caused my inactivity [Notice the Rockthink!].) Our Mineral parts are programmed and predictable. ("He ALWAYS eats breakfast at this restaurant.") Their actions are limited, as in only receiving 'correspondence' coming through *their* 'address'." ("If God wanted me to know something He'd tell *me*, not *you*!) Their reactions are automatic. ("If you criticize her, she cries.") Their responses are one-sided. ("I'll settle your argument—he is right, and she is wrong.") They have abrupt "starts" (they instantly love you) and "stops" (not any more), and they have areas of severe dysfunction and nonfunction, all consistent over time.

In contrast, movement is natural to every part of a human being, whether mobile itself or through movement by something else. We can extend and contract the various aspects of self with fine coordination, skill, artistry, grace, passion, and complexity. We can maintain, exercise, and/or develop each and every part as we choose over time. (Compare the human with a car, where each part has set movements or is stationary and a driver is required to move the whole.) Humans can choose when to move, how much, how, where, and with whom. We are self-repairing too—we're able to take care of ourselves.

Machines Are Manufactured to Specific Standards

Once back in Effie's kitchen, I investigated her coffee maker. Caffeine was in the same chapter of my medical textbooks as alcohol, Valium, cocaine, and heroin, so to me, they are all drugs. Unlike most people, I use coffee only medicinally—when I need to stay awake. I'd scheduled an appointment to have my soft brakes checked in Covington, an hour away by car, so I wanted to be alert for the drive. When the coffee was ready, I poured myself about 150 milligrams of caffeine—one cup of coffee—and grabbed some food to go. Dr. Bear was engrossed in his morning routine, wagging his tail at my feet in eager anticipation of me sharing my breakfast.

Calling FEMA had become automatic every time I passed by the phone. This early morning, I finally got through! I answered all the questions about the location of my home and my current living situation, and then I was informed that I'd receive a $2,000 check to cover my evacuation expenses. YAY! Persistence paid off!

Unlike what we do with our children, we never criticize or belittle our cars for being other than what they were made to be. ("Soft brakes, huh? You're a BIG car—you're supposed to be strong!") We never blame our cars for causing adverse conditions, such as the narrow, unpaved country roads we may be traversing. We also don't chastise cars for accumulating mud on their tires ("You don't have to take any dirt! Just let it go!") or acquiring scratches and dents ("Why did you *choose* to react this way?"). Everyone knows that automobiles show wear and tear the more they are used, particularly if driven inappropriately. Also, most individuals maintain their cars, periodically changing the fluids, washing them, and maybe even removing noticeable scratches, dents, and rust at a body shop. A child "growing up" with Rocks and Minerals notes this concern and compares it to the attention she receives when she reveals the damage from her rough, Rocky rides. Rather than respond to her damaged "vehicle," her caretakers typically command, "Stop!" When the machine gets the human care, and the human bears the inhuman, which path is a child likely to follow?—the way of the Mineral Stage!

The dehumanization of children is an ongoing, daily process in our society. For example, when we attempt to change a child to meet rigorous standards (such as our own apparent needs) rather than directing him to "roads" most conducive to his growth and accompanying him on his travels, his heart hardens. When we mechanically pass on the "information" that's been passed to us, a child's mind stiffens. Add the abject abuse and neglect perpetrated by Rocks, and countless children end up moving through life as separate, solid, unchanging vehicles of someone else's navigation, without concern for the developmental needs of their growing humanity. Their psychological bodies becomes like automobiles, which they use to explore our seemingly mechanistic world. Let's look at some automotive parts and contrast them with the human "vehicle."

Transmissions Contain Gearshift Positions of Park, Reverse, Neutral, and Drive

Seeing the sun rise before me, I felt optimistic as I drove toward Covington on I-190 East, a road that runs due south at times. At one point, I saw an elevated highway crossing mine, where two cars were moving backward, as if they were driving in reverse. Startled, I viewed the scene again carefully and realized that the cars were actually secured backward on an auto carrier that was proceeding normally. *Everything seems surreal these days,* I thought. *Trauma really messes with our minds!*

Psychologically speaking, our culture conditions us to look forward "to the horizon." By presuming we are already mature adults, we pretend that we've already arrived at our maturation. We may then feel we're going backward to notice our actual stage of psychological development, as opposed to where we imagine ourselves to be. Our developmental path may not always *appear* to be facing "the light" or may not always feel right or good. Our days may become jarring, enraging, or despairing on the drive to face ourselves. Mineral parts, with their binary mind-set, insist that "right" turns (what *looks* or *feels* good) are always better than "left" (what doesn't). They encourage us to always turn "right" instead of taking into account where we are, where we are going, and why. Listening to them, we may drive around in circles until someone outside the loop shows us that a few "left" turns can at times more effectively lead us to the "right" or that a "wrong" turn will sometimes bring us to what's "right" over the long haul. A "wrong" turn can even reveal a shortcut!

Similarly, we can face our destination while being taken away from it. For example, anticipating that we'll be able to relax during our golden years may keep us going, but when we arrive, we may have to continue working to pay the bills. Or we might live in the moment while the rest of time is forgotten, but what then happens to planning for and financing our children's future? If the past has no relevance, why do our creditors find it important? When we only allow the now, we ignore the trends shown over time that could guide our advancement or warn of our decline.[1] If we're strictly focused on any one time period, how will we deduce that what Rocks did yesterday is causing the illness, degeneration, and death of today, for which the cure won't become obvious until sometime tomorrow?

On the psychological journey, there is a time and place for going backward, revisiting where we've been. At other times, we must prioritize our potential and cruise toward our future goals. There are also times for parking in the present. All "gears" are essential. Our refusal to use a particular gear causes problems, as we then lack the ability to accelerate out of danger's way or back out of a situation that limits progress. For instance, just as we need to drive "in reverse" to leave a tight parking space, we can't be free of our Mineral Stage programming if we're unwilling to go back in time to discover what drove them to their current condition and what happened as result. Also, those driven to "Be Positive!" can't shift to a neutral or even negative stance when necessary, such as to balance those who are relentless in their "positivity."

A car that is unable to shift easily into any gear indicates a problem with parts, either how they were manufactured or how they have been used. The same is true of our psychological "vehicles." Considering the past, much like we do an automobile's history, allows us to gather important information. For example, when we remember our traumatic experiences, we realize that we have concluded that certain routes, directions, or gear positions are "bad" or best avoided because our experience of them has been bad. We steer clear of the past (reverse) to shun these difficult, painful memories. We dodge achievement (drive) when we have been harmed for our strivings or have witnessed the awful consequences of someone else's failed exertions. Or lastly, we cannot sit still or wait, lest our fear, anguish, grief, or pain about the Rocks in our lives and ourselves overtake us (as in the past). When we refuse to back up, move forward, remain in neutral, or park, we seriously limit our mobility and our lives.

An hour and fifteen minutes later, I stood in the waiting room of the repair shop, where the TV blared even though no one was there to watch it. I shut it off, sat down, and began dozing—my medicine was wearing off.

"Hey, lady!" I woke up to see Lloyd, a mechanic in a grease-covered gray jumpsuit with an air gauge sticking out of his chest pocket. He was holding a sheet of yellow paper under my nose. "You need a brake job. And your CV axle on the driver's side is cracked. All the wear and tear on the roads—rocks can hit 'em and crack 'em. You're from New Orleans, huh?"

"That's right." I smiled, feeling my hometown now carried a touch of infamy.

"I think there needs to be a car manufacturer that makes cars just for driving in the New Orleans area—having tires and suspension that can easily handle all the potholes."

"Yeah—they could make them theft proof, bullet proof, and waterproof while they're at it, huh?" I said, amplifying his idea.

He grinned and then pointed at the estimate. "Do you want me to go ahead?"

I scanned the page and stared at the price. "OW!" I said, wincing. *The money from FEMA isn't going to last long at this rate! But I certainly don't want to drive anywhere else with bad brakes. To me, a well-functioning vehicle is vital.* I sighed deeply and muttered, "Yeah, go ahead." As he disappeared, I pulled out my notebook to unload.

Every Car Has a Gas and Brake Pedal

Human beings are equipped with the ability to accelerate, slow down, or stop—as gently or abruptly as needed. People can also change course at any moment of the journey. When Rocks have taken us for rides against our will, however, one part of us logs each reckless trip by behaving similarly toward others. Meanwhile another part balances such extreme driving by riding the brakes. As long as we're unwilling to travel into our pasts to resolve these traumas *and* travel into our futures where we are already healed and whole, parts of us remain frozen in these extreme patterns. Unable to shift our gears and our speed according to "road" conditions and "travel" needs, we impulsively go *or* compulsively idle or stall, or do both in rapid succession! Needless to say, our "shock absorbers" get a lot of wear! Within this scenario of PTSD, the human family within our psyches seems more like a collection of auto parts, with each part having specific areas of action *and* inaction.

A short, thirtysomething brunette with bobbed hair and a perky smile entered the room looking around. "Is anyone else waiting here besides you?" she asked hurriedly.

"No…not that I've noticed," I answered slowly, still preoccupied with my bill.

"Good, I'm not late. I've got a roofing nail in my front tire. I think those nails were *designed* to stand up when they fall on the road so they puncture tires. Everybody's getting flats driving around looking at the storm damage. Anyway, I hate wasting time, so I like to multitask, particularly when I'm driving. I'm meeting a friend here so no time is lost while I wait. And the coffee is free!" She quickly poured herself a cup, then glanced up and exclaimed, "Hi, Lil! There you are!" I turned my head to see another brunette of similar age, a little taller and wearing sunglasses and a bright colored scarf around her head, striding toward us. They hugged affectionately with big smiles. "How are you, Lil?"

"Fine, Judy. I thought I'd get my hundred-thousand-mile checkup while we visit. How 'bout you?"

"I got a flat, but otherwise I'm great. Hey, it's time for *Good Morning, America!* Do you mind?"

Lil looked disappointed. "Well, I want to talk to you about what's going on, but I guess we can chat during the commercials." Judy turned on the TV, louder than before, and I realized my snoozing was over. As Judy and Lil conversed, a commercial took me inside a luxury car. I was "peering" out the car window at beautiful scenery and "feeling" the smooth ride over a mountain road.

Are We Human Beings or Automobiles?

Knowing the similarities and differences between man and machine is key. For example, a mechanic's job is to return a car to its original functioning. In contrast, a developmental psychologist facilitates the expansion of human beings so that they think more clearly, feel more deeply, work more efficiently, and experience more profoundly than in the past. A car mechanic would be tremendously damaging if he used his automotive tools on human beings ("Easy with that pneumatic hammer!). Likewise, using the methods on our automobiles that we employ with people would get us nowhere. If a neighbor bemoans her dead battery and expresses an urgency to get to her job, would we reply, "I'll be praying for you"? If an elderly woman is stuck on the side of the road with a flat, would we say, "We all go through phases; I'm sure the tire will be back to normal before you know it"? If we don't rely on these actions to return our automobiles to full functioning, why do we expect them to work on the malfunctioning, mechanical parts of our hearts and minds that likewise need hands-on help?

To carry the analogy further, let's consider how well our cars would function if we treated them with the biases typical for raising children in our culture. Suppose strong-colored cars with larger chassis are designated "male" and their owners are taught to focus on engine power, drivetrain maintenance, and piston action. Meanwhile, the owners of smaller, muted-colored "female" cars are encouraged to dispose of these "unfeminine" parts and direct their attention to the workings of headlights, shock absorbers, and the radiator. An interior with soft carpeting, comfortable upholstery, and some amenities is also essential. The mind contained within each "vehicle" then identifies with only the approved parts and maintains and repairs only these, so independent transportation becomes impossible.

All of us identify with the parts of our "vehicles" through which we comfortably function, these parts differing from person to person. Most of us yet imagine ourselves to be the human driver of this "vehicle," even when our psychological life is largely static. A few parts are moving, and some wheels may be spinning, but we're not working and moving as a whole. The judgments, adjustments, and disassembling of our psychological vehicles that occurred in our childhoods, as well as all the unskilled attempts at repair, have had far-reaching effects that we've been unwilling to acknowledge, let alone correct. Like a GPS, our mind merely shows us where we *wish* to be, rather than where every part of us is—which satisfies most of us most of the time. *If we are to progress in the psychological journey, however, we have to distinguish the human aspects that need rescuing from the mechanical parts that require repairs.* We also must discern which aspect or part needs mere maintenance or minor adjustments, versus a complete overhaul.

A tanned, slender young woman with long, straight, blond hair and large expressive eyes rushed into the waiting room, obviously shaken. She explained, "I was stopped at the tollbooth on the causeway when a truck slammed into the back of my car. The driver's from out of town and didn't know he had to stop. He didn't notice the signs either, so he wasn't all there, if you get my drift. Now I've got a smashed rear end! Man—if it's not one disaster, it's another!" All of us nodded in agreement.

She went on. "I'm from up North, and my last accident was when my husband and I had just moved to Louisiana. He was the driver and was seriously injured. I was fine, so I called a friend to pick me up, and she pulled up just as the ambulance was leaving. We had to stop for gas and to grab some coffee and snacks since we'd probably be up all night. I figure our stops took about twenty-five minutes, and yet we still arrived at the hospital before the ambulance! I thought, 'My God! Even the ambulances here are slow!'

"Yet, as behind the times as we are down here, we've impacted the entire country by what's happened—for the worse *and* for the better. Last week when we were in Atlanta—that's where we evacuated to—people encouraged us to share our story and our grief. They put us up in a very comfortable gas station—free of charge! After all we'd been through, we were very grateful. One guy gave us two new front tires, and another did a complete brake job on our car. The brake room was full of donated clothes, and we were told to help ourselves. One man gave my husband a hundred-fifty-dollar money order, and a woman pulled me and my sister aside and said, 'Y'all need something special. Come on—we're going shopping!' Other women gave us books on dealing with stress or asked us to attend church with them so we could pray together. Each one gave to us in his or her own way. They were all so kind!"

"A disaster can sure bring out the best in some people," I said, heartened by so much goodwill. Still, I was aware that bringing out the best can come at great cost. For every person who uses misfortunes to open up more to her or his humanity, there are many who shut down further to avoid their pain.

Listening Step Ten: LISTEN TO TRANSMISSION FAILURE = THE PRESENCE OF PAIN

When our humanity is treated more like a machine than a spontaneously moving, feeling, and thinking life-form, it hurts! When we're blamed for someone ramming into us and smashing our "bumper," it feels bad! When what is inanimate and mechanized is given preferential treatment (cars get immediate repairs, while our psyches wait for *years*, if not DECADES!), our human identity experiences pain. This sensitivity to pain lets us know there is a problem and can motivate us to make changes. Rocks turn this around, however. Instead of allowing our discomfort to propel us to learn what is wrong and to evolve through attempts at correction, Rocks demand devolution by teaching us to rid ourselves of this human sensor. By stifling pain, we become desensitized to the vital information it provides. (Psychological growth is so painful *because* it drives us out of the denial of our pain!)

Navigating around New Orleans tends to be a challenge as there are consistently many streets under repair, and each repair may go on for months or years. As a result, drivers must frequently find new routes. Similarly, when our pain is barred from our awareness, our body seeks another avenue for its expression. For example, the pain of a damaged psychological "vehicle" commonly expresses itself through the physical body since this is where most of us focus our self-awareness. We're also more apt to admit to physical pain and sickness than psychological suffering and infirmity. (How much conversation time is spent talking about our muscle or menstrual cramps, headaches and stomachaches, cold symptoms or hot flashes, and so forth, compared to our psychological ills.) As Rocks and Minerals show us, other people's bodies are also an option for referring our pain.

We may be less likely to label pain as an unwanted alien presence or a mechanical malfunction to be medicated, belittled, manhandled, put off, or passed on when we sense the humanity within pain's cry for help. When we pause to listen, we discover that pain represents one of our human voices that has been unheard and thus has become louder and more persistent in its efforts to be noticed. It has an essential function: to indicate that something is awry. We may even avert an accident, injury, or mistake simply by listening to ourselves—ALL of ourselves. You see, being human is not about mechanically moving through life, but deeply engaging every moment with each part of ourselves.

Even though one part may look or feel "better" than another, and some may appear more alive or human, we mustn't judge one as more worthy of our attention than another. Just as a mere plug or patch can extend the "life" of a flat tire, making an urgent car trip possible, each part of us, no matter how seemingly insignificant, has a vital function to fulfill in our psychological journey.

I began thinking about people on TV who said, "We need to put this disaster behind us and move on." How can we move on when we haven't yet seen our damaged homes, let alone repaired them? We haven't sorted through our flooded belongings to identify what's salvageable. We don't even know if some loved ones survived, and if they did...where are they? (Cousin Joan and Connie's friend David came to mind.) Repairs and renovations await on the road ahead, and many decisions must be made for both our outer and inner worlds. Why is the media hurrying us past this disaster that has consequences bound to persist long into the future? Why aren't they giving us the support we all need to slowly process what's happened and work it through? What's the rush?

When we've rejected our pain, we usually try to get rid of it anywhere we perceive it. Whichever parts of ourselves we've driven away in our attempts to "mature," we tend to avoid, control, crush, or otherwise punish throughout our life. For example, our urgency to hurry people past their intense emotions, vulnerability, and neediness reveals our discomfort with these qualities within ourselves. If we don't drive on fast, this disaster and aftermath might start a chain reaction in which we ultimately discover just HOW MUCH pain and agonizing unconscious material we are lugging around in our "vehicles."

Under the Hood: PAIN Is Part of Us and Part of Our World

Judy, flipping through the television channels, alerted my attention once again to the outside world. She paused briefly on a soap opera in which a hospital orderly was surreptitiously putting something toxic into some poor woman's IV. Judy responded, "I just hate soaps these days. When I was a teenager, they were really good, but now they've gone off the deep end—they're just plain unrealistic!"

Unrealistic?! My mind instantly flooded with memories from my time working with patients in New Orleans hospitals—quite a number were Rocks! There was Chad, who took great delight in introducing highly addictive crack cocaine to as many young people as he could. "I assured them it'll make 'em feel better!" he remarked with a sinister smile. Mira kept bringing very ill children from her nursery school to the emergency room until she was diagnosed with Munchhausen's by proxy (SHE was causing each sickness). Alvin had rage attacks where he'd beat up his victims until they were near death. When I asked him why, he calmly replied, "I don't like people disrespecting me!" Barbie was diagnosed with AIDS in her early twenties. She had been raped so many times that she didn't know how she got infected, but her revenge was to spread it to as many members of the male population as were willing. Rob liked to invite a married woman to his home for a "platonic" glass of wine. Hers would have a strong sedative in it. After she fell asleep, he'd rape her and then periodically visit the nursery nine months later to see his new baby. He said he "couldn't help" mentioning every time he saw his kids how "different" they looked from other members of the family.

Also in the hospitals were countless Rock victims like Sonny, a man with a diagnosis of paranoid schizophrenia. He recounted, "My mom told us almost every day that she would kill us if we didn't do exactly what she wanted. Occasionally, she'd hold Dad's loaded gun to our heads and cock the trigger if we stopped taking her threats seriously." Mentally, emotionally, physically, and sexually abused children consistently passed through the pediatrics halls. Femrocks did as well. These were the family members and physicians who adamantly refused to admit these horrors were taking place. As agonizing as it was to work with these people, I learned a lot from them. I slowly and painfully realized that I need to be attentive at all times and keep my "antenna" up, my senses ready, my heart open, and my mind clear and in constant contact with Our Rescuer. Our world can be treacherous!

Indicator and Warning Lights

To safely and easily negotiate the streets of a painful and precarious world, we MUST have an intact psychological body with all parts fully functional. Like a car, we humans have "gauges" that are finely attuned to both our external and internal environments. We can perceive our own and others' signals of "stop" and "go." Our physical perceptions and emotions are important indicators. Take pain, for example. Whether physical or emotional, it is like the *check engine* light on the dash. When it "flashes," we need to stop and assess what it's communicating. It may indicate a problem that is easily and inexpensively remedied (yank your hand away from that hot engine or your heart away from that hot-headed hunk). It may also alert us to a nearby ruthless Rock.

What happens to a car after years of being driven on New Orleans's bumpy streets? The suspension system often wears out. A human body that's been treated like a car ("Go, go, go!") shows similar evidence. When we've consistently traveled particularly "rough roads," our ability to adapt to our stressful environments and bring ourselves to equilibrium can wear out. We then express the emotional and physical reactions we have been withholding. If we ditch these "problematic" aspects of ourselves that are revealing our external and internal conditions, we lose the function of our "indicators" and "warning lights" as well. Blind spots result.

Where we are psychologically "blind," we have mechanical functioning at best—indicating a Mineral or Rock part. As Rock parts are diametrically opposed to our humanity, their "instrumentation" is antagonistic to true conditions. Having adjusted to chronic abuse and neglect, Rock indicators register these as "normal." Rock parts also tamper with the instrumentation of other "vehicles" to align them with their own. Instead of reading and registering the world and its creatures as they are, these gauges convey the opposite information. For instance, the mechanical drone of Rock oppressors may seem soft, reassuring, and upbeat, while the "noisy" outbursts of their challengers register as shrill, harsh, and paranoid. As we are then drawn to those who harm us, ompounded pain results, which these instruments record <u>antagonally</u> as <u>pleasure</u> or don't record at all. See if you recognize these perversions of "auto" instrumentation below.

Rock Indicators Warn Us Away from Our *Humanity*

(1) Rockometer. This "gauge" registers Rock interactions and events as the quickest way to move our lives forward. Listening to Rock "authorities," following Rock instructions, passing along Rock "facts," etc., cause the greatest shift in the needle—keying us to how we're cruising. In comparison, human beings and their developmental activities cause the needle to, at best, only faintly flicker.

(2) Guilt Gauge. Shame and remorse in a well-functioning psychological "vehicle" attunes us to hurtful behavior. Wanting to maximize wrongdoing, the Rock sabotages this gauge so that it registers guilt and ill feelings when we DON'T hurt someone or when we're actively helpful. Conversely, we experience feelings of innocence and well-being when we pursue the Rocky way.

(3) Care Alarm. There was once a car alarm in my New Orleans neighborhood that woke me up routinely at six a.m. with a mechanical voice stating, "This car has been violated!" Harsh words—all because of an innocent early morning bump from another vehicle. In a similar manner, this Care

Alarm indicator converts the registration of "contact" or genuine love and concern into alarm reactions ("What do you want from me? I can tell you're up to no good!"). When people hear the resulting "noise," they believe that the caring human has truly harmed this Rock, and they then rush to the Rock's aid. "Vehicles" with a Care Alarm HAVE been brutalized in the past (their perpetrators may have used similar words or appearances in the process of harming them), but their present reaction may just be an indication that someone has cared enough to come close, see past their facades, and touch their true identity! How alarming!

(4) Distractometer. This instrument colorfully lights up any of the multiple images on the "dash," drawing our attention away from looking through the windshield of our world. Like airbags, the distractometer can cause serious injury in its task of "protecting" us from what is really "out there."

(5) Full THROTTLE. When you don't support Program activities, Rocks will get stuck in the gears of your operations. For example, if you start a business, they'll arrange for construction work in the neighborhood that will block your customers' access to parking. If you invite your romantic interest for a drive in your sports car, they'll inform her of your tendency to "take women for a ride!" She'll avoid you like a clunker after that! To others, you seem a lemon, or maybe fate is against you. Amazingly though, when you withdraw from projects in resignation, the rubber hits the road, and they instantly take off! Observers often jump to the conclusion that you were the problem and give you a wide berth. The full throttle works equally within us, as our inner Rocks consistently swerve from, drive over, or brake attempts to merge with our united Identity.

When Rocks tamper with our "gauges," we may learn to ignore them and the confounding information they give, perhaps assuming that everyone's instrumentation is faulty. If we accept these faulty readings, we uphold what is contrary to our humanity, yet "enjoy" the denial of our pain. Our minds become like New Orleans highways during a hurricane evacuation—the incoming lanes are redirected so that all lanes lead away from the city. We prohibit people from approaching our wounded psychology. We block movements that might take us back to our disaster sites and the Rocks that caused them.

I strolled into the garage to determine how my car was coming along and found myself staring at a bright-red sports car with a black canvas roof. Two large headlights with smaller golden indicator lights on the inner side seemed like eyes with pupils. Black vents across the back were like tufts of hair. The windows were very darkly tinted, and a large crack ran down where the driver normally looks. The hood was open, and a mechanic was deeply immersed in what was under it. I smiled, realizing that I know as little about car parts as most people know about the parts of their human psychology. I turned to the right to see an old woman squinting at me.

"This is my grandson's first car." The woman extended her arthritic hand toward the flashy automobile. "Get a load of those dark windows—scary, huh? Our family is always poking fun at his jalopy, but he explodes and yells, 'I just hate people who have nothing better to do with their lives than criticize my car!' I try to help him with his temper, but he walks away."

Why Are We SO Defensive?

Because sporty Rocks appear initially benign or even helpful, and they prey upon our natural human tendencies to ask for and extend help, we learn to change our driving habits. We veer away from those offering help, since "help" from the Rock has been uncompromisingly hurtful. We may attack or reject those requiring assistance. We associate pain with the activities of helping and receiving help, and experience pain in the parts of ourselves that have been involved (caregiver parts or vulnerable, needy parts). We're hesitant, if not rigidly opposed ("You can't make me!"), to engaging these ever again.

We may go so far as to ignore the needs in ourselves, others, and the environment, not even noticing they are there, lest we again fall prey to Rocks. Our "windows" become darker and darker as we are less willing to share what is within us in order to keep such "help" at bay. We become unwilling to look deeply into anything, lest we feel inclined to stick our necks out. The parts of us that honestly express, validly perceive, and are able to give and receive help lie dormant and then atrophy from lack of use.

Our PAIN Is Hidden in Our "Auto" Parts

As we lose functioning, if not awareness, of our "auto" parts, we have fewer indicators by which we can perceive. Poor psychological visibility can result in accidents, just as poor visibility while driving a car can. For example, we may assume we're looking through the windshield of our "vehicles," when we are actually seeing a reflection of ourselves or something behind us in the "rearview mirror." The danger that ensues may lead us to conclude that reflection is dangerous. In response, we may psychologically remove the "rearview mirror," thinking, "I don't need it for where I'm going." While this may SEEM beneficial, it's further limiting our visibility—we can't see what's riding our bumper or about to overtake us. Repeated situations like these result in many parts "missing"— <u>dissociated</u> from our awareness.

Let's take the situation of a boy reared in a family that tells him that "mufflers" are a sign of insecurity ("They're for sissies!"), so he psychically throws away this part of his "vehicle" and never dampens his verbal expressions. One day, a psychological mechanic comments, "Sounds like you need a new muffler." The boy's mom is horrified at this mechanic's "criticisms" of her son, his lack of respect for her child's "unique" personality, and his "snap judgments" ("How could you possibly know anything about someone you just met?"). She quickly chases the man away with a barrage of insults. When the child is picked on or beaten up in school because "you're too loud," he echoes his mother's verbal abuse or turns off his "engine" in compliance, when he needs only to retrieve his "muffler."

When the boy "grows up" and marries, his rejected "muffler" finds expression by muffling his soft-spoken wife's speech. She doesn't know about this "disconnected" part of her husband, so she reacts negatively to his domination of her voice. The husband has no awareness that this part he severed association with so long ago is still involved in his life without his knowledge. No, he assumes his wife is "driving on empty" or "recycling used motor oil," or perhaps he concludes, "No one ever appreciates me!" *She* then becomes the pain and the problem. He doesn't think to look within himself for *his* part and *his* pain that's extending from him to her and then being mirrored back. His wife similarly doesn't realize the opportunity she's being given to strengthen her voice by standing up to him.

When our painful pasts are not recognized and owned behind us, we tend to experience them in front of us, somewhere in the present. The more we deny our pain-ridden parts a place within our "vehicles," the more they must approach us from outside, where we will inevitably skid into them and feel the impacts. Our pain may manifest in multiple sources—"evacuation sites," or places of referred pain. A clean, intact, properly placed "rearview mirror," however, can show us our own image as a contributing factor to these recurring problems. Do you see how far our pain travels trying to get our attention?

"Life" as Auto Parts

The psychologically young tend to avoid pain, the parts of themselves that carry their pain, and the people who notice and comment on their pain. This tendency reduces their identity to a few auto parts, and they become incapable of true choice and change. When we then appeal to such people's human tendency to give, they give only what their specific part can offer, whether the recipient needs it or not. A person living as a "spark plug" doesn't realize that some folks don't need to be sparked, they actually need calming. This person may feel rejected, unwanted, or harassed when she's told to stop doing what she does.

Another person may be like the "engine." Naturally, he is pro-oil and uncomprehending when oil in some environments results in ruin, or in illness or death in the bodies of human beings. Also, he considers whatever does nothing for *him* unimportant, oblivious to the fact that it might be essential for others' "vehicles" *and* unknown parts of his own "car." Just as it would be ridiculous for a "seat belt" to feel superior to a "timing belt," we, too, are very silly in our derogatory stances toward other "auto parts."

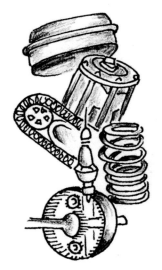

Although we may understand the necessity for each part of our car, where our psychological "vehicles" are concerned, we tend to zoom in on our areas of proficiency and ignore or minimize the importance of lesser functioning parts. We may associate with people who have actions and requirements similar to ours, convincing ourselves of our "normality." But, like parts positioned together in auto-supply stores, we won't be going anywhere soon. Moving a car requires a diversity of parts that are individually functioning as well as working together. The same is true for our psychological "vehicles," individually and collectively.

Do We Claim the Pain or Shelve these Parts?

When we are familiar with the psychological "vehicle" of human beings, we can appreciate each part and anticipate its movements (or lack of them!). Take Rock parts, for example. We can expect them to perform according to their "manufacturer's" design—that's what ALL Rock parts do without exception. A steamroller isn't personal—it smashes everything in its path unless guided by human hands to flatten only where needed. The same goes for our Rock parts—they require human direction to make their actions constructive. We can't just shelve these painful components, like car parts in a garage, and expect them to sit quietly in a state of useful potential. We must understand that, as human beings, every part of us is alive. Those parts of ourselves that we have rejected continue to live and act, but in a separate life, apart from the life we know.

The loss of "auto" parts also diminishes our faculties—we can no longer apprehend what's being given to us or taken away. For instance, without our sense of taste, we're unaware of the foul taste of pesticide-laden produce or the tastelessness of genetically engineered, green-harvested foods, so we buy them. When we've lost a sense of smell, we may believe "official" reports stating that polluted air is "within acceptable parameters" or that contaminated water is "safe for swimming" or even drinkable! When we lack access to our hearts, we don't detect the hollow words of "We care," or "We're working around the clock to make needed repairs." When our minds are indoctrinated or programmed, they have lost their flexibility, creativity, and inspiration. We then believe our health depends on paying lots of money to medical "mechanics" who merely doctor our parts, rather than on addressing and restoring our wholeness as a human being.

Tragically, our abandoned parts cannot mature with our owned parts since we don't include them in our experience. At best, each disowned aspect remains at the same age with the same needs, capacities, preferences, and vulnerabilities as when we blocked it from our consciousness. At worst, it has devolved. Either way. it will have its own unique and limited exposure to the outside world. For instance, if we abandoned a part of us during its molestation, it will go on to molest or be molested, as this is what it knows. It doesn't possess our adult morality. All such unconscious parts determine values, accord reality, make decisions, and act based on their limited experiences and insufficient information. They live apart from the conscious parts of ourselves that would alert them to a greater perspective. *And* we live apart from these unconscious parts that would widen and deepen our perspective as well.

ROADBLOCKS

Wally was an enthusiastic young man sporting a Mohawk who talked to me while waiting on repairs to his Jeep. "I snuck into N'awlins yesterday using a back door. I had to check my crib and grab some stuff. Man, the 'hood was whacked! One blocked street bore a sign that said, 'ROAD CLOSED,' but a brother added in red, 'Absolutely no exceptions.'" I laughed, knowing New Orleanians tend to find ways around any system.

"Hundreds of peeps got back ta N'awlins to scout out their digs. They used docs, revs, rescuers, even some 'rent-a-cops,' to slip past the checkpoints. One homie slid into my 'hood with a copper escort to feed his dogs and fish. He was freakin' like in a major sting, as the po-po cased the joint with heat in hand before he gave the green light. My old man tried to get his cat, but a guard got to'm and told'm to go back the way he came. He musta took too much room in his turnaround 'cause all of a sudden, machine guns were drawing a bead on him."

When we come to a roadblock in our travels, our normal expectation is that the road will be open for traffic again soon. With blocks in people, however, we have no such expectations. When street repairs take years, we blame people—officials for withholding funds or giving priority to other needs, trouble with road crews, and so forth. Why don't we see similar impedances with self "repairs"? Usually a block on the road to healing means a Rock on the road. Our rejected "auto" parts, living such restricted and isolated lives, restrict and isolate us, barring pertinent aspects of our life and self from our awareness and use. When we are psychologically "young," we often strive to avoid confrontations or difficulties, so these "roads" may be blocked for decades. But, as in New Orleans, just because there's a barricade blocking a passage doesn't mean no one has gotten through.

Abandoned Cars and "Auto" Parts

A flooded car being towed reminded me of the abandoned cars I saw during my drive to the shop. Along roads or in weed-covered yards, these cars had no wheels and were rusted through. Some had obviously been sitting unattended for years. Abandoned cars in New Orleans were a common sight even before the disaster. Owners know that parking these cars in the streets is hazardous, since flash floods can damage them quickly in low-lying areas. Also, carjackers can break in, hotwire the car, and sell it or use it for illicit activities. Sometimes they strip them on site and leave only the frame. I wondered what was happening to the many flooded cars throughout New Orleans.

Each part of us that we've not owned and occupied is vulnerable. Our meager defenses merely shield us from those respectful of our boundaries, but certainly not everyone. Though we readily acknowledge what hoodlums do to cars, we rarely admit what Rocks do and have done to our physical and psychological "vehicles." These youngest of humans harm so much more than our possessions. They possess our children, our spouse, our passion, and our compassion. They sap our strength, our health, our heart, our hearth, our savings and pensions, our will, and our will to live. I cannot overemphasize how destructive these people are to everything we might hold dear.

While we may enjoy our working "auto" parts, their range of functioning, and their comradely interactions with others, our abandoned parts know isolation, defenselessness, and trauma. Where we've lost connection with an aspect of our humanity, we have no say over who employs it or for what purposes. So that they might enjoy unrestrained use of our rejected parts, Rocks are deliberate, methodical, and relentless in teaching us that various aspects of ourselves must be suppressed or repressed for our "masculinity" or "femininity," "happiness," "peace of mind," or "spirituality." *Or* they instruct us to alter these parts into a "more acceptable" (rigid Rocklike) form that easily plugs into their machinery.

These abandoned parts, once in the hands of Rocks, become like the cars left in the wake of the New Orleans Lakeview levee breach. They are immersed in a polluted, corrosive, and fetid environment that strips them of their natural inclinations, affections, and activities, while teaching them to be cold, distant, unreceptive, unresponsive, unfeeling, uncaring, closed-minded, blocked to correction, and eager to ram the Program into other "vehicles." Rocks train them in "high-performance" words and superficial behaviors *and* nonperformance techniques to bar psychological inspections or interventions ("I just don't sense a need for anything like that!"). As each malnourished psyche withers and succumbs to psychotic depression, the imaginations takes the wheel and offers a "hydraulic lift." These people perceive themselves as a "race car," "love bug," "family sedan," perhaps an "adventurous Jeep," a "fuel-efficient hybrid," or a handy, all-purpose, "four-wheel-drive truck"—all way off track from a profoundly damaged "vehicle" missing many of its parts. The horror of this truth keeps them frozen in fear and shame, functioning mechanically, chasing human beings away, or ceaselessly blocking whatever might bring these abandoned parts to consciousness.

COFFEE BREAK:

1. Do you travel the same roads in your daily drives and automatically turn onto them even when you intend to go elsewhere? What else do you do automatically? What do you do excessively? What do these traits reveal about your psychological journey?

2. Is there any "direction" that you prefer in your psychological "driving?" Would you rather move forward than backward, go up rather than down? Is your comfort level with psychological movements different from those with your car? If so, why?

3. How do you treat human beings like objects or machines? Who in your life might need hands-on help with a "nuts and bolts" communication style?

4. Draw a picture of your psychological "vehicle." Compare this to any image you may be conveying about yourself or others—do you make yourself seem the top-of-the-line sporty convertible,

while implying your parent, spouse, or boss is nothing more than a rust bucket? Which parts of each person's "vehicle" do you zoom in on and which do you ignore?

Claiming Auto Parts

When we live, work, and socialize with those who are functional in areas where our parts are missing, together we may make up a whole "vehicle." Society functions this way. Psychological growth, however, requires more deeply engaging interaction. We must investigate each part in one another, see how it's working alone and in relation to other parts, assess what's happened to it over time, and make adjustments accordingly, outside and within. For example, the extreme parts we find in "vehicles" evidences a history of chronic neglect. Other people or parts might have tempered their excesses but chose not to, or even chose to encourage them instead.

Let's look at a human "radiator" who has been chronically chastised for cooling an "engine"—"No one has the right to FORCE their agenda on another!" If this "radiator" were like the average young child, it would try to be less "forceful," resulting in the engine overheating. In a typical psychiatric setting, that "engine" would be given a diagnosis, such as overheating disorder. Besides being prescribed an expensive medication, the "engine" would likely be counseled, "Take very short trips because you can't handle the long ones, and if you're ever in New Orleans in the summertime—REST!" Absurdities with respect to our cars are somehow easier to spot than with people, where they wreak havoc.

Situations like the above are among many where we learn that people can't be trusted—not like our automobiles! We readily hop into our car to take us somewhere because we will get there faster and more comfortably than on foot. In contrast, we often refuse to overtly allow a human being to take us to a destination within ourselves that would reveal a long history of neglect and abuse. As a result, the parts of ourselves that may have been easily repaired and/or aligned with the rest of us remain dysfunctional. These parts may also resent the choices WE'VE made from conclusions WE'VE drawn from OUR painful past experience, such as "People don't take me anywhere!"

Unlike inanimate car parts, the unwanted aspects of ourselves may have intense feelings and hold serious grievances against each another, making reconciliation difficult. For example, some parts may be hiding in shame, not wanting to be "seen." Also, when we attend to and care for one part of us while ignoring another, the shunned part develops a tremendous amount of anger and jealousy toward the privileged part. Sabotage is common. Their complaints and reasons for hurting us or rejecting us may be complex and extensive, similar to those of the people in our lives. (Notice the similarities!)

We (who we identify as "self") have "our own" strong feelings. We've spent years of our lives denying these other characters inside ourselves, each of which can have very different agendas contrary to our own. For instance, you may have stuck to your diet, but your "inner child" did not (you even yelled at your husband for eating all the cookies!). We can be overwhelmed as we remember what we've forgotten ("I didn't know I did that to him!" or "I never knew she did that to me!"). We may be consumed with remorse or grief when we finally apprehend that our disowned parts have been trailblazers of the path of pain. They've perpetrated many "hit-and-run accidents" while we've been blinkered to their existence. We may sink into deep depression as we realize just how much of our lives we have been missing. Most of us would rather feel the occasional pangs of guilt for avoiding self-improvements rather than deal with the tempests of accusatory thoughts and agonizing regret that surface as we increase our self-awareness.

We've mistakenly trusted "ourselves," unaware that the parts we've identified as self were too psychologically young to make good decisions. Perhaps we've lived mainly in our fun-loving "child" parts or in our tender "infant" parts because we like the soft voices and warm strokes we receive. Maybe we let our "inner fetus" lead because following the Program *seems* to require the least effort. There may also be an antagonism between younger, playful parts and older parts with adult goals and values. Integrating our "auto" parts can be a confusing, eye-opening, and humbling experience.

In healthy families, adults live as individuals that are yet part of an immediate family, extended family, and greater community. As we naturally turn on the A/C on a hot day or the heater when it's cold, a healthy person naturally tempers other family members' excesses and inhibitions, such as jacking them up when they're down. Similarly, when all parts of ourselves are embraced and welcomed as essential, valued, and contributing parts of our "vehicles," they balance each other and even out. For example, a part that was once brazenly impulsive becomes spontaneous and flexible in shifting at critical moments when ventures fail to serve the greater good. Aligning with our rejected parts brings wonderful gifts and wise teachings (along with any discomfort or difficulties) that CAN enhance our functioning in EVERY way.

Again, we may have rejected our **"infant" parts** because they're so vulnerable, needy, short-sighted, and genuinely expressive. When shunned, their distress is expressed through yelling, crying, eating disorders, gastrointestinal problems, sleep disturbances, and insistence on being fed. When their expectation of healthy stimulation has been neglected, they consume excessively and indulge in risk-taking activities. However, when we allow them their place inside our adult psychological bodies and meet their needs, they give us the ability to receive another's care, to enjoy the moment, to be sensitive, and to cry out when someone or something is uncomfortable. Also, we can avoid giving attention to what's unworthy of our time.

The exuberance, curiosity, and playfulness of our **"child" parts** may have seemingly led to trouble. We may also have cast them out of our psyche because of their many hurt feelings, grudges, and unmet demands for engaged parenting. Our shunned inner "boy" may then act out his anger with heart-wrenching behaviors or by kicking away what or who makes us happy. Our rejected inner "girl" may verbally batter when she feels ignored, and she may choose what enables her to feel more, whether it be drugs, sex, or thrill seeking. When we love these children as our own, however, we have exciting dreams, the ability to belly-laugh, enthusiasm for exploration and adventure, an open mind eager for new experiences and learning, and an attitude and visage of perennial youth.

If we've set aside our **"inner woman"** because we don't like her introspection, her unconditional caring, and her "meddling" into people's personal lives, then we've also lost her multitasking efficiency, unbounded resilience, inspired creativity, and gentle healing. Unwanted, she may interfere with our lives by setting up the circumstances that necessitate our getting help. (A degenerative illness might get us off the independent track and into receiving from our fellowman!) When our Woman is included, however, her deep feelings, intuitive brilliance, interpersonal genius, and innate sense of justice for all become vehicles that take us somewhere vital—into ourselves...and then out the other side!

If our **"inner man"** is an outcast because such undaunted Self-assertion seems frightening or too risky, we forfeit his strength, problem-solving skills, powerful human voice, clarity of vision, wisdom, and proactive preventive help. He may stand by and watch us go nowhere with our lives until we admit we need his forcefulness to get Rocks and Minerals in gear and our own lives cruising. When integrated, our Man puts all "auto" parts in their place and keeps every part fully functioning and in sync with the others. The result is an all-weather performance passenger vehicle for the inner human family, ready to transport everybody where they psychologically need to go.

I observed a worker cleaning dead lovebugs off a windshield as I wandered to find Lloyd. He was at the end of the line, tinkering with my Honda Civic. He showed me his work and parts of my car that I hadn't seen before, despite Emily's occasional lessons in auto mechanics. Satisfied that he was taking care of the problems, I trudged over to the cashier and reluctantly paid the bill. Behind me, I overheard Lil and Judy exchanging their farewells.

"Where are you living now, Judy, since you can't go back to New Orleans?"

"We're staying at a lovely hotel…sleeping in their parking lot. There are clean restrooms, the lobby is comfortable, and there's a supermarket just down the street, so we're set. We're hoping no one will notice our beat-up old cars among the expensive new ones."

"Well, if you'd like to park them in Mandeville, you'd be welcome."

"Thanks, Lil, but right now we're enjoying this one-of-a kind adventure."

Again, information about our missing parts may come from outside us or inside us. For example, the feeling of anxiety or fear upon meeting a Rock is a normal, healthy response—allow it. It does NOT mean we are "unmanly," "unwomanly," "unloving," or "acting from ego." It means our emotions and intuition are functioning naturally—fulfilling their design to alert us to threats. If we're listening to our gut, it disrupts digestion in preparation for fight or flight. (Have you wondered what your low stomach acidity was trying to tell you?) Our heart feels the cold Rock's absence of emotion, compassion, and care. The mind is savvy to the Rock's arrogance, rigidity of beliefs, mechanical thought processes, and rote answers to questions. Our Spirit experiences the Rock's adamant rejection of what is capable of healing him or her completely. These strong reactions are also natural as we approach the Rocks within us, adding to the discomfort of integrating them.

We have rejected our Rock parts for obvious reasons. On their own, however, these parts have committed battery on physical and psychological bodies trying to get our attention. They've choked characters. They've wiped out ideas and plans. They've stalled rescue and rebuilding efforts. They've checked talents, opportunities, resources, and our youth. They've kept the wheels of time spinning without allowing any movement of our "vehicle!" They've also turned people's psychology into "auto" parts scattered in many a junkyard. It's no surprise that we feel aversion toward these Rocks. However, it is actually BECAUSE they have been shelved and forgotten that they behave so badly. (How would you like to bear the brunt of pain and suffering in someone's life, then have your reality refused *and* be denied expression of your anguish?)

Our Rock parts challenge everything we believe about ourselves ("I'm a gentle soul") and our loved ones ("They are too"). They show us unmistakably that our self-pride is misplaced. Our childhoods were rougher than we realized, and we *have* let these legacies bother us—"infants" and "children" cannot do otherwise. In searching for our missing parts, we find those that were indeed adversely affected, just like the many people we've looked down on and harshly judged. We've been *sorely* mistaken about our state of normality and maturity and in our rejection of help!

Rescue Attempts

Driving home, I spotted the word AUTOMATIC printed in large black letters on a white awning. Just then a police car whisked past with siren blaring and lights flashing. Minutes later I arrived at its destination—an accident. To my right was an overturned, totaled black pickup on the side of the road. A bit farther on, a blue compact was smashed into a tree. Paramedics carried a man with a breathing tube on a stretcher into the ambulance, while multiple police officers talked with some of the people present—I'm guessing they were witnesses to the accident.

Although we readily notice a wrecked, upside-down truck as a sign of an accident, astonishingly, most people don't see the Rock's demolished, inverted psychological "vehicle," let alone recognize it as a SERIOUS problem. They don't realize that EVERY Rock needs ACTIVE human intervention, just as unconscious accident victims do. Rescuers must haul him out of his "vehicle" of "MY" way. The "airway" to each opposing part of his split mind must be opened so he can take in what is life-giving and release what is not. His mechanized programming must be converted into a "ventilator" that aerates, energizes, and enlivens his psychological body. His immobile heart requires emotional "shocks" to pump his flat-line "EKG" into a healthy "sinus rhythm" that integrates both "positive" *and* "negative" feelings. A rescuer must establish a point of access where the Rock can begin receiving "fluids" (flexibility) and, later, essential "nutrients" (feeding his humanity). Just as an enormous team effort by *many* people over an extended time is necessary to keep a totaled truck or car crash casualty physically alive, the Rock NEEDS intensive, multifaceted, long-term treatment.

Adding to the difficulties of a Rock's recovery is the Femrock, who is grossly offended by rescuers and their "exaggerated" responses to, in her mind, "mere fender benders" (if that!). When she overhears "paramedics" discussing the Mascrock's injuries and poor vital signs, she protests, "That's so critical and judgmental! You professionals think you know everything—slapping labels on people like that! Don't you have anything nice to say?" As the rescue team secures his "airway" and begins "ventilation," she screams, "Leave him alone! He didn't ask for this, so you have no right!" As they apply "shocks" with a "defibrillator" to the Mascrock's "still chest," she gasps in horror at the "brutality" of it all! As they place the "IV" into his "veins," she squeals with accusations of "You're invading his boundaries and hurting him!" As the "ambulance" hastens away, she is left behind yelling, "If he wanted to go to the hospital, he'd go there himself IN HIS OWN WAY AND TIME! You'll be sued for this!"

The fury with which the Femrock "protects" her "male" from those who would save his psychological life is criminal and grievously insane, yet she rallies many people to her cause. "Just because he is functioning outside the parameters set by those paramedics doesn't mean there is anything WRONG with him. He's just different, that's all. I wish people could understand that!" she cries on many a soft shoulder.

Let's consider another accident scenario. This time the casualty is a Femrock who was thrown from her vehicle and is lying in a "pool of blood" on the ground. The Mascrock who witnessed the tragic auto accident is unwilling to acknowledge it. He merely stands above the unconscious body, looking down with disdain. "YOU! Overreacting AGAIN! You just don't get that you have choice in everything that happens to you. Your victim mentality is sickening!" He is able to convince onlookers that this woman, barely alive, is a "drama queen" who will go to any length for "a little attention." "Trust me—she'll suck you dry!" With such remarks as "She might stop these childish stunts were it not for all the nuts who fall for them time and again," he convinces passing well-wishers to abandon any rescue attempts.

Thus, both Rock types detour us from rescuing. They automatically transmit the words and behaviors of their own Rock caretakers who were relentless in chasing away assistance. The Femrock endlessly extols the virtues of damaged "vehicles"—"You're fabulous! Trust me—you don't need any help!" Remember though, she speaks antagonal language. She's really warning you NOT to trust her—you DO need help, as do we all. The Mascrock cranks out condescension and futility. "You're inherently flawed—trying to go anywhere is a total waste of time!" Realize that he's antagonally reminding you of your worthy identity within the undivided Self, where you must return to regain full use of your "vehicle."

Our Cars' Movements Affect Other Cars

Back at the Greensburg Red Cross shelter, I met a cheerful Manuel. "*Hola*, Anna! *Como naz estado*? What have you been up to?" He grabbed my hand and gave it a friendly shake.

"I took my car to Covington this morning for some rather expensive repairs, and I encountered heavy traffic and a horrible accident on the way home. Driving around here is sure different from New Orleans."

"Driving around New Orleans is different from *anywhere*, *si*!" Manuel's animated face showed me he had plenty of experience with New Orleans driving.

"What do you mean, Manuel?"

"People in New Orleans—they drive like turtles, like they are walking; they stop in the middle of the street to talk to someone or to let someone in or out of their car. Their blocking people's way—it doesn't come into their heads! When they are turning, they often do not signal, or if they do, it is very late. Sometimes in making a right turn, they nearly stop before creeping around the corner. When I'm behind these dizzy people, I have to slam on the brakes—they are so slow! I've nearly hit them many times because I don't expect these cars suddenly moving like a snail. Then I see a car on a side street wants to turn into my lane, but the driver seems to wait for me to pass, and then just before I get to the intersection, he changes his mind and speeds up, pulling in front of me. You always have to be ready for an emergency stop! For a place that is flat, we use our brakes a lot—like a crazy! When I am behind these people, I need to pay attention—to the front, to the back, to my right, to my left—because I don't know where these people are coming from or where they are going! They don't even seem to know because sometimes they move left to go right, or they go right before turning left. Have you noticed this?"

My experience agreed with Manuel's. I related, "Yes! My fisherman mechanic in New Orleans, Mark, explained this to me. He said, 'It really burns me when people move their car to the right when turning left or move to the left to turn right. But then I realized they're acting like they're captaining a BOAT, so suddenly it all made sense! In a channel, you have to turn right to go left because if you get too close to the banks, you'll run aground. You have to slow way down for turns, too. Even people who don't captain a boat or fish from one drive like that because they learned from fishermen. Around here, there's just a boat mentality—that's all it is!'"

When we have disowned our Rock parts, we cannot comprehend the signals others give in response to these extremely negligent and aggressive parts of us. Those who turn and flee in self-protection seem cold and rejecting. Those who suddenly slow down on a project or block "our" way, appear oppositional and untrustworthy. However, when they unexpectedly swerve or "slam on the brakes," there may just be a Rock on the "road" that they're appropriately trying to avoid.

When we register such signals and movements from others only superficially, they seem irrational, so we may learn to ignore them or classify them as bizarre or meaningless. Our Mineral-run mind may inform us that we were rejected because we expressed some aspect of our humanity, such as our human needs. In reality, these people rejected us because our Rock part rammed them like a bumper car afterward (just like our Rock relatives used to do with us!). We may even interpret others' movements as menacing and flee ourselves. With this uncomprehending outlook, we can be easily seduced by those stuck in the Mineral Stage who prattle on and on about their "good intentions" that are misunderstood by so many. As Rocks and Minerals veer to the "right" in the process of turning "left," we are apt to trust their "righteous" verbiage over the final destructive results of their actions and the reports of people who complain.

Our IMMOBILITY RESTRICTS Others' Movements

I started chatting with Wally, a fiftyish-appearing man with dull eyes who looked like he forgot to pack a razor in his evacuation luggage. He told me he knows somebody who "had to" shoot six people during his recent visit to his boyhood home of Hollygrove, an inner-city neighborhood of New Orleans. "He shot two on the way in and four on the way out. He needed to check his pops—that's why he went there. He figured he'd run into a hassle, so he brought his equalizer, his three-fifty-seven magnum. Anyway, these guys had their 'friends' with them too and were in his way," Wally commented nonchalantly. "He nabbed his dad and his dad's stuff, then after paying respect at his mama's grave, they left."

Since our "auto" parts have learned different mechanical ways to survive and go about "their" lives, placements in the same "vehicle" require some exacting adjustments. "They," the other parts, require repairs and upgrades, as do "we," the parts we're conscious of. Because our survival mechanisms tend to have each group traveling the same "roads" day after day, regardless of where we're needed or where we need to go ourselves, we resist these alterations. We're like the tourists riding New Orleans streetcars along set routes—Saint Charles Avenue, the French Quarter riverfront, or Canal Street. Following the same familiar tracks over and over again, these parts never connect with one another. We maintain these separate tracks with our rigidly held associations from the past. For example, when we think of home, we may think of a warm place where we can just be ourselves with close family around that love us no matter what. Meanwhile, the parts of us that "grew up" with the violent Rock parts of our relatives associate home with violence; places frequently threatened by violence (e.g., New Orleans), feel homey. These parts of us may even become violent when they seek the comforts of home.

Embracing these survivor parts of ourselves can also feel devastating as they fill us in on the gory events of our lives from which we evacuated to calm ourselves, save our sanity and perhaps our life. As we listen to them, pieces of our life's puzzle fall into place, and we get a clearer and more complete picture of why we, and those closest to us, have acted as we have, and why circumstances played out as they did. Perhaps a woman spent a lifetime resenting her husband's unhappiness or jealousy, only to discover that her intrusive Rock slept with every man in the neighborhood and all the kids but one were conceived out of wedlock. Maybe her husband medicated the children as a last resort for their obstreperous behaviors, only to realize that they were acting out their pain over being beaten and raped by his unconscious Rock. We may wonder why seemingly successful people self-destruct, by either their own hand or others' actions or from illness. The elusive answer can be found in the deep, dark secrets of their intrusive Rocks.

Our discarded pasts and parts have leaked from the cracks in our psyches and corroded many lives. As we receive this information internally, we may be surprised to discover that our human biology is not the cause of most of our difficulties. No, the real culprit has been our inhuman psychology—something that must shift and recover as we become willing to include every part of ourselves in our "vehicles" and be driven by Our Rescuer. But beware! If we use the "dipstick" of a Mineral Stage part to assess what's under our "hood," we'll believe what's there is very dark, dirty, and void of life. Rocks teach us that the "primitive" nature of our hidden parts will ruin us if we ever become conscious of them and allow them to once again be part of our lives. (Rocks often threaten to publicly expose them if we're not completely subservient—"You'll be rejected, ostracized, jailed, or WORSE!") If we understand that any Rocky part is merely an unborn psychological "infant" sharing his "Elemental" experiences, we'll be eager to grant these youngest aspects of ourselves a human parent (NOT a pacifier, life imprisonment, or threats of eternal punishment!). The LACK of conscious access to our Rock parts has created the greatest danger!

At the opposite extreme, Rocks have also conned us into believing that these wounded parts don't exist: "You're a good person—why look further?" Strange that there is always more to learn in ANY field of study, yet Rocks consistently hoodwink us into seeing through the eyes of an infant and imagining that what we attend to is all there is to know about ourselves and our lives. If a mom, infant, and unborn child are all occupying the same seat in a car, do healthy people only acknowledge the mother?

Manuel returned to where I was writing to say, "I noticed something else about New Orleans driving. One-way streets change. One block one way, the next block is the opposite. The engineers, I think, lost their minds! There are also a lot of 'no U-turn,' 'no right turn,' or 'no left turn' signs—it's really complicated to drive. I remember in Kenner, I had to drive a mile just to turn. It's hard to understand why these turns are not allowed. Seems like some politician must be making money." Manuel smirked and then lodged his hands deep in the pockets of his black jeans.

"When I was young, I drive like a savage. I drive fast, and I had a lot of accidents. I hit a dead-end sign, and for that reason I decide don't drive for a while. Well, you know, everybody has a wild side…at different times…or for different reasons."

"Definitely!" I responded. "Like maybe your parents allowing you to drive unchaperoned when you were reckless?"

"Well, I was sixteen, and I had a license. *Que podian hacer*? What could they do?"

License to Drive

When individuals attain a certain physical age, they qualify for driver's education and hands-on training with a licensed driver. Before acquiring a license, they must pass a vision test, an exam on traffic and safety laws, and a road test. If they fail at first, they have several opportunities to try again. Once granted, however, this license can be revoked at any time for reckless driving. In contrast, there are no such criteria of maturational age for driving psychological "vehicles." There are no requirements of developmental education and one-on-one training with a functional "driver." There is no perceptual screening, nor are there written and practical examinations to ascertain people's abilities to drive their own "vehicles," let alone anyone else's. Why? There are also no regulations or protocols for removing those who "drive" dangerously, such as Rocks and Minerals.

Since we don't assign superiority to the *first* replacement part on an auto-supply store's shelf, or one displayed on a *higher* shelf, why do we compare people based on *position*, rather than the *condition* of their humanity? Similarly, would we expect a brake pad to power a car just because the label "engine" was attached to it? The mislabeling of Rocks and Minerals, however, leads to them stalling many human lives. Their high positions or VIP labels result in their writing many of the "operating manuals" for our "vehicles." They also administer exams that test our retention and application of their Rocky "statistics" and "knowledge." Certifications, degrees, and licenses awarded or possessed by Mineral Stagers may have little significance. Also, just because some parts of our "vehicles" have the maturity, training, and experience to have earned legitimate accreditations doesn't mean ALL parts of us have these qualifications. What if our educational system filtered out Rocks and Minerals and "repaired" them *before* awarding educational and professional labels? What if our society gave out tickets for careless psychological "driving" in the same manner as reckless driving of motor vehicles? Then, so many of us would *not* be spinning our wheels or braving undue hazards.

COFFEE BREAK

1. Which systems in your "vehicle" are well-functioning, and which are not? Draw a close-up cartoon of whichever of the following most needs your attention:
   a. The steering assembly
   b. The powertrain
   c. The electrical system
   d. The braking system
   e. The exhaust system
   f. The suspension

2. Where are the overt and covert locations of pain in your life? Listen to music that supports the surfacing and release of this pain. Ask Our Rescuer what you can do to become GENUINELY pain free.

3. Look again at your response to question 4 in chapter 3 (p. 50) and consider how your prejudices reflect the "auto" parts that you are rejecting within yourself.

4. How has the rejection of your "auto" parts affected your life? What keeps you from accepting your unconscious parts and allowing them to operate within your conscious "vehicle?"

5. What steps can you take to retrieve your missing "auto" parts? Which functions would they offer you if integrated into your psychological "vehicle?"

6. Which members of your inner human "family" are hidden within these "auto" parts: embryos, fetuses, infants, children, women, and/or men?

It All Boils Down to...

Lewis was a thin, middle-aged man with loose-fitting clothes who also talked to me about his evacuation experience. "I seen our driver hot-wiring the evacuation bus and den go behind to smoke crack. When I tells this to my boy, he say, 'No shit! I seen him shootin' up!' I thought, *heroin* AND *crack? Jesus save us!* I figure da man was a looter who stole da bus to escape and was pretendin' to be da bus driver. All I could do was pray, 'Mercy, Lord!' dat we arrive safe. When I met up with a friend later, I tells him what done happened, and he says his evacuation bus was hot-wired too!

"The mo' you look 'round, tain't nothing what it seems to be…like I heard on the news that a barge 'accidentally' ran into the Tennessee Street Levee, bringin' it down and causin' mo' floodin', but I don't believes it. Who in der right mind parks a barge next to a levee when a hurricane's a comin'? And why would anybody allow that? Besides no barge's ever been parked there befo', far as I can remember! I think it was done put there on purpose to destroy the levee, because that's what happened!

"And that's not all my gripes neither. 'Bout three quarters of my 'hood depends on buses or streetcars to get 'round N'awlins—this is what they do. To expects them to do something different, especially in an emergency—it don't add up. Since our government knowed about this hurricane days before it hits, why don't they send buses to get everybody out of town? They's gettin' paid, yet THEY didn't do what they's paid to do! THEY didn't do much to help us for almost four days after the storm— that's the rub! If they lets down their end, how do they expect us folk to change our ways and do right?"

…Who Is Driving?

When there's a Mineral in the driver's seat, we function on autopilot. We ALWAYS take the shortest route or the one that passes by the bar. We NEVER filter our "exhaust," no matter what effect it's having on others or how much people complain. Maybe we've had the SAME beliefs throughout life, and we vehemently oppose anyone who asks us to try a new "vehicle." Such ruts make us easy victims for those in the Mineral Stage who prey on our routines, predilections, and expectations. (Where we are predictable, we are easy to manipulate!) Rocks move us where they'd have us go by offering us who and what we're accustomed and drawn to, or who and what repulse us. For instance, they move us forward with our favorite foods, activities, and people—whether attractive personality types or body types. They move us backward, away from any enterprise, by employing our pet peeves, personal grievances, or perhaps the poor and homeless ("This could be you, if you don't…"). The approach and avoidance patterns we learned to keep ourselves "safe" and "pain free" in our pasts can lead to danger in the present *and* a clamp on our humanity!

Our own inner Rock can also drive us by using our post-traumatic stress disorder and what we're compelled to do and resist. For example, to steer us in "her" direction, this Rock will mention how "her" way supports our conditioned aspirations ("This will make you rich!"). If we're a victim of violence and are fearful of being revictimized, this Rock can easily turn us to the left by suggesting the likelihood of harm on the right. Utilizing our sins and whatever we're most ashamed of, she'll have us slam on the brakes in one project and drive full speed ahead on another to avoid their exposure. With these tactics, Mineral Stagers inside and outside can control most of us most of the time! Rocks consistently set up situations that take advantage of our most strongly repressed emotions, needs, and desires to move us in the direction and at the speed they would have us go—often without our knowledge. We think we are driving, when actually, *we are being driven*.

When we choose to detour the difficult aspects of our lives and ourselves, rather than journey through them, we have psychological "dead ends" that are noticeable to those who travel such terrain themselves. Our "roads" become like those in New Orleans that stop abruptly in rough, drug-trafficked, crime-ridden housing projects, pick up again a few blocks away, and perhaps end in a lovely, upscale uptown neighborhood. The same street can be enlivening or potentially lethal depending on where you look. Just as we must know a city to navigate it well, we must know a person to most effectively relate. The areas of access and the "blind alleys" have significance for both. *And,* when we don't know our inner Rocks, we're less likely to recognize outer Rocks, and we may be blind to what both are doing with our "vehicle."

Remember, Rocks are deceptive. They have us believing that the feelings, thoughts, and impulses we have are our own, when we are so often mechanically going through the motions of our environmental programming and conditioning. We merely say and do what we have been taught in response to what we have been instructed to sense, feel, and think. We're also unaware of what we are doing or saying a lot of the time, let alone knowing why. Automatically approaching what's pleasurable and withdrawing from what isn't, we convince ourselves that these choices are conscious *and* our own.

Our Rescuer replaces such automatic transmissions with manual drive when we allow her hand to direct our lives—a shift that can *seem* dominating and disempowering when we've been blinkered from the realization that we're *not* driving our cars. Yet, when we insist on "our" way, we condemn ourselves to following our genetic and environmental "programming" and the Mineral Stagers who've used both to remodel us to "their" advantage—hardly our own decisions! Yet, the choice of Our Rescuer terrifies us as she details our psychological "vehicles" and opens the doors. When she illuminates the "driver" behind our steering wheel, will she find a dummy? We may be shocked to discover that what we thought was "living" has been mere crash-testing!

Felix and Chester were taking turns "driving" a small, remotely controlled, sun-yellow sports car with decal head lights. When Felix was "at the wheel," the car seemed to end up going into the wall more often than not. I think he enjoyed watching it crash or flip over. Chester pretended to "drive" while straddling a chair and maneuvering a paper plate as his steering wheel. His sound effects of car noises added to the realism. "My car is bigger than yours!" he jeered at his brother.

Felix paused for a moment to stare wide-eyed at Chester. "What car?"

A grinning Chester exclaimed, "This one I'm drivin'. I'm drivin' us home!"

The Driver Who Never Experienced the Disaster

Elderly Mr. Samson spoke loudly as he relayed some of his life experiences. "I rode out World War Two, and I gonna tell you, I rode out every New Orleans storm, including Katrina—ain't not a problem! Some of them people complainin' 'bout the noise. What's their problem? It sure didn't bother me none!" Annoyance was in his voice. "I was blessed. There was plenty of food and water, but man, it sure was HOT! I can't imagine hell being any worse! We just needed some of that 'electiticy' to run that airs. Them pipes was workin' so I coulda just stayed forever. When Thursday came 'round after that storm, some of them officers came by and said I gotta go by mornin'—I said, 'Man, we didn't even have no flood!' But when my lil girl came over—she and her husband live 'round the corner—we made plans to skidoo in a few hours.

"I'm eighty-five, and soon I'll be eighty-six. The politicians keep promisin' to fix things, but if they don't hurry up and does it fast, I may not be around. They act like there's all the time in the world, but for some of us, we ain't got much time left."

I tried to comment periodically, but Mr. Samson didn't hear a word. Many elderly patients I've worked with who were losing their hearing compensated by talking loudly. If anyone spoke in a normal tone, they would often yell, "Speak up! You don't talk loud enough!" When we rely solely on our own body's perceptions, we can come to many erroneous conclusions.

We all know that the elderly can lose functioning. They do not think, move, hear, and/or see as well as they once could. Sometimes their driver's licenses must be revoked for safety reasons. Often they do not realize the extent of their disabilities. Similarly, most of us are slow to catch on to our psychological impairments. Rather than admit our insensitivities (faulty "indicators"), we tend to rail at the messengers who *do* indicate our handicaps (yes, human beings have external as well as internal sensors). Like Mr. Samson, we perceive those "complaining" as the ones with the issues—"I didn't hear the storm; why did you let it disturb YOU?" We often reveal our dysfunctions by how we treat others, such as attempting to drive others when we ourselves are being driven. Yet, when people comment on the condition of our "chrome," what's missing under the "hood," or the fact that we're not driving our lives, we feel threatened. Then, like an unloading trash truck, we dump on them the pain we've been carrying. *Or*, like used-car salespeople, we pursue those who buy our shiny paint job or who buff up our image. Our limited awareness of our disasters, our disregard for those who are functioning where we are disabled, and our faulty conclusions about what is happening have more to do with traits of infancy, such as poor attention and sensory deficits, than old age. Psychological babies feel secure within these confines, however, much like being strapped in an infant car seat.

The Driver Who Experienced the Disaster...

Yvette, the middle-aged, African-American woman I was sitting beside, unloaded her Katrina experiences. "I know people who had jus' finished renovatin' their houses in New Orleans. Some had been workin' on 'em for years and had gotten them jus' like they want. Then the levees failed. Not only was their efforts wasted, but their dreams turned to nightmares. That's SO SAD! Just terrible!

"For me, though, the worst part was the gut-wrenchin' screamin' and the desperate splashin'—so many people drownin'! People were even killin' themselves when they saw what had been done to their homes. During this time, people were drivin' empty buses back and forth and back and forth over the Mississippi River, but they wouldn't even pick us up! Some o' the folks waitin' with me on the Crescent City Bridge was so scared when no one would help 'em that they jumped off! Some of the cars tryin' to git across the bridge, they was hijacked and then they killed the drivers. There was even crazies drivin' through the streets shootin' at everything—windows, car tires, lights, people. I never seen anything like this before! A man who was tryin' to git out of town on his bicycle—they shot him dead! Stone-cold dead! I know people who bought guns and took to defend themselves. They felt our government deserted us, so they took the law into their own hands! I don't blame 'em!

"My family and others tried to cross the bridge to git to the other side of the Mississippi where it didn't flood, but they turned us around. Armed guards stopped us. They thought we were looters! Imagine that! We were turned away at gunpoint. The officials said, 'Our orders are that NO ONE gits across!' I know some desperate parents with preschool children—they was chased away with bullets! Everybody was just survivin', you know? I remember seein' a dead body floatin' in da water and but a short distance away, people was drinkin' out of it, tryin' to quench their thirst! Um-um." Yvette shook her head, looking very concerned

"I jus' don't understand why people kick others when they're down. You'd think they'd wanna lift people up when there's a disaster, doin' anything possible to help. But I seen it this time, and I seen it time and time again. As much as people talk about helpin' their neighbor, when given half a chance, they simply takes what they can git and runs! A frantic friend even tried to call the twenty-four-hour crisis hotline, but no one answered—she got an answerin' machine! I'm tellin' everybody though, 'cause I don't ever wants to forget this! Not ever! But it's already turnin' foggy in my mind."

...AND It's Effects: Fog on the Bridge

Once again, people make associations based on personal experiences. The people who experienced the Levee Disaster after renovating their homes will pair the two in their minds. If PTSD ensues, they'll avoid renovations in the future, or they'll pursue home remodeling as a hobby or profession but be compelled to somehow undermine their work in reenactment of their trauma. These divided highway dynamics keep us from driving our own vehicles. After every unresolved disaster, we either automatically run from reminders of it and/or approach or re-create such reminders in an attempt to process them. For instance, the New Orleanians who escaped their flooded and crime-ridden city to make their way to the Crescent City Connection Bridge sought safety and help. Instead they found armed guards who threatened violence and refused them their needs.[2]

Take a moment to think about parents with small children who fled violent, chaotic New Orleans, abandoning flooded homes, having lost all their earthly belongings, and perhaps leaving behind loved ones, alive or dead. What would it feel like to bear such hardship? Now—imagine these devastated, desperate-for-help folks perceived as potentially hostile enemies, and you will know the mind-set of someone even more devastated and desperate—someone with a history of disaster whose damaged psyche has never recovered.

Unresolved trauma and unconscious pain take an excruciating toll on our lives! Our perceptions become hazy, and we consistently act and react from this cloudy vantage point. For example, when we've repressed memories of harmful childhood caretakers, we put up strong boundaries against people functioning in similar capacities in the present ("Adults with small children are dangerous!"). To them, we express the long-held-in "NO!" that we wanted to declare to our perpetrators when we were small, but we were too young, powerless, and afraid (rightly so!). We finally get our revenge by refusing those in the present who remind us of what we've hidden in the past.

We may experience vulnerable children as menacing if they resonate with the unconscious, traumatized "children" in ourselves. The infant outside of us poses no threat to city security, but the abandoned psychological "infants" inside do, and this danger is then projected. These are the dynamics of every untreated childhood trauma survivor—seeing the suspicious or malicious in the vulnerable and needy, and denying them safe passage from their disaster sites. Our psychic smog and tunnel vision prevent us from noticing that we do outside of ourselves what we do within—our unwillingness to give safe shelter to all parts of ourselves has hindered the rescue of MANY! Psychologically speaking, we've all taken "potshots" at "preschoolers" to ward off the agony of when we were that age, that needy, or that desperate.

Thus, our "roads" outside and inside are the same. We fiercely "protect" the seemingly unscathed parts of ourselves from the wounded parts that have endured our disasters and suffered alone and unwanted, while we've kept up our images. We "cruise" past or "bump" into these parts in others every day as we go about our lives, never recognizing them as aspects of ourselves. We may even consider them enemies! We don't realize that what we spot as most prominent in others, and react to or ignore, are the very pieces we need to be addressing inside ourselves. Rather than judge them and evacuate from them, we must begin to approach them (at least within our own minds and hearts) and know them as aspects of our own life experience. This inclusion of more and more into whom we call "self" is how we psychologically grow. Helping and healing anywhere enhances the whole, whereas psychological "road"-blocking or automatically driving away from problems and pain hampers the whole.

The Driver Who Knows the CAUSE of the Disaster...

I glimpsed Mandy out of the corner of my eye and felt a need to connect with her again. "Hi, Mandy!" I called as I approached the morose, heavyset woman with rounded shoulders and downcast eyes sitting immobile on her cot, her jeans and T-shirt folded neatly beside her. As she stood up to leave, I reached out, put a hand on her shoulder, and said, "I wanted to tell you that I too lost my personal possessions—a lot of them, that is. The week before Katrina, I moved my belongings into my mother's house, where I'd been living for about six months. Her home is in Broadmoor, which flooded about five feet. I feel so stunned—it happened so fast. All the stuff from my childhood, my photograph albums, things given to me by everyone who has passed through my life—it's all submerged in that filthy floodwater! Some treasures are irreplaceable!" Mandy turned toward me, clutched my forearm, and pulled me down with her as she sat again on her cot.

She patted my hand as she opened her heart. "My home was next to the Industrial Canal in the Lower Ninth Ward. It's hard, I know. I lost EVERYTHING in the flood! I feel terrible. It's just too much to take on—just too much! But that's not even the worst part." Mandy's voice became very high and shaky. Her eyes filled with tears as she glanced around the room, apparently to check if anyone was listening. "The night before the storm, I couldn't sleep with the howling wind and all. Then early in the morning, I heard cars and trucks on the gravel road that leads to the levee, so I watched out the window. After a little while, the cars and trucks left, and then I heard a big explosion and saw fireballs in the sky. There was this huge roar and then, suddenly, water was rushing into my house. Luckily, I had an attic room where I stayed for the storm. I had to swim out when it was over.

"I'm so scared! Lots of people heard the explosion, a few saw the fireballs, but I'm the only one I know who saw the cars and trucks. It seems really important, like I should tell somebody, but I just don't know…what to do!" Mandy's voice had faded to a whisper, and she cried as I now patted her hand, speechless.

...And the *Cure*

I rushed out of the shelter, swerving around the pit bull, Catahoula, and small black puppy, still tied to the tree in front of my car. I leaped into the driver's seat, slammed the door behind me, and burst into tears. I drove home on autopilot, barely able to see through the water streaming from my eyes and the smashed lovebugs smeared over the windshield. With Mandy's sincere sharing, the well-constructed floodwall around my heart, built so long ago to "protect" me from being harmed by my fellowman, had suddenly and unexpectedly given way. A flow of feeling rushed over my distant, clinical manner and swept it aside. My awareness drifted to detached parts of me that had assumed my life was somehow better than others', and I felt my underlying regret of this grievous error. As tears rolled down my face, my emotional current hurled me into even more isolated aspects of myself, ones that have believed my life was actually far, far worse and that have been reclusive in their shame. The bereavement my false beliefs caused now seemed the background of every day of my prior existence, but I had never noticed, nor felt the heartache.

With this flood of psychological awareness came a blessed new sense of wholeness. I finally embraced the emotional impact of what I had understood intellectually for some time—we're ALL trauma survivors, momentarily hiding under facades of "superiority" and "inferiority" or, even deeper, our imagery of "me" and "you." The pain within every individual possesses the same current, whether this pain is experienced through victimization or through sympathy with those, such as Mandy, who constructively and poignantly share their thoughts and feelings. Differences lie only in degree and the manner of expression.

I cried on as I recalled, one by one, the tragic stories I'd heard in the past few days. The agonizing reality of each tale prompted seemingly everything inside me to respond with grief, a grief shared with an entire city of oppressed, devastated people. I was no longer alone with my sadness! *And,* my sadness was not mine alone! With this company, I felt the emergence of my wounded "inner child" who has searched my entire life to find "family"—a community of people who would listen to the language of a beaten, broken heart and a tortured, uncomprehending mind, and would join with "her" with these aspects of themselves. In the presence of hurt people like "her," in an environment of "we," "she" was finally able to release the burden of pain "she" had been carrying for decades. No longer the outcast, "she" came out of hiding, and "her" intense feelings of sorrow and care for everyone flooded over me. When I reached Effie's house, I collapsed onto the passenger's seat. Surrendering to my "inner child's" feelings at last, I bawled like a baby.

Only when we know and are comfortable with each part of our psychological "vehicles" can we comfortably, appropriately, and fully relate to each part of others' "cars." We can show other people how each part works; wherever we find it, we can tend to its maintenance and repair and adapt its function for the whole. A receptive heart in a sensitive body, for example, can feel who is hurting and join with a clear mind to discern what is wrong and how to help. With the aid of physical instincts, that body then offers what is needed according to each individual's physical and psychological condition.

When we know each part of our lives and have allowed it to further our maturational journey, we can likewise support others in so empowering each part of their lives. Any intersection of human beings with "vehicles" and their "parts" can afford us good "mileage": opportunities to improve our human relational abilities, practice our "auto" mechanical skills, develop new "antipollution" technology, and employ ourselves where we are rusty. Wherever we roam, we can reclaim lost "auto" parts, reacquaint ourselves with the thoughts, feelings, and behaviors we have rejected, and effectively reintegrate all into our lives and selves.

Over an hour later, I rose from my car and crept into the backyard, collapsing under Effie's lavender-blooming crepe myrtle tree. I needed to breathe in nature and sense her warm support under my weak and whimpering body. In the muted light of the still-hot sun, I felt a quietness rest over me. After a few minutes, Oliver and Felicity emerged from the back door and sat on rocking chairs, followed shortly by a slow-moving Connie.

"Did you talk to Daddy today?" an anxious Felicity questioned her mom.

"No, honey. I spoke with him four days ago when we were in Mandeville and you both were busy with your friends."

"Did he ask about me?" Felicity's eyes were large with longing.

"Don't be a moron, Feli!" Oliver said. "He NEVER asks about you or any of us! He could CARE LESS!" He was steaming.

"That's not true—he cares!" Felicity replied. "You weren't there, stupid, how would you know? Right, Mom?" She gazed beseechingly at her mother.

Oliver also turned, red-faced and wild-eyed, toward Connie. "Yeah, GO AHEAD, TELL US! Does he EVER ask about us?"

I too stared at Connie, wondering whether she would tell her kids the truth or what Felicity so desperately wanted to hear.

Connie was silent as she looked deeply into the faces of both her children and then finally glanced at me, as if pleading for help, her eyes becoming watery. "Dear Lord...I'm so sorry," Connie uttered as tears streaked her rouged cheeks, her eye makeup smearing in the process. "I can't pretend anymore, I just can't." Connie was shaking her head "no" as if she wasn't sure of this herself. "You have a right to know the truth. You NEED to know the truth. That's what David says." Connie's voice was quavering. "Your father has some problems—some very serious problems. One of these problems is…he never asks about you or me. He never asks about any of us…" She whispered again, "Never."

　　　　As Connie began sobbing, Felicity ran into the house screaming hysterically, "I don't believe you! You're lying! YOU'RE LYING!" Angry Oliver repeatedly kicked one of the porch posts, yelling, "I KNEW IT! I TOLD YOU SO! I KNEW IT ALL ALONG!" He continued shouting as he bolted down the hill toward the road. Before she disappeared into the house, Connie murmured, "What have I done?"

Driving Out the Human Child Leads to a Dead End

On every psychological journey, we arrive at a juncture where we realize that the "vehicles" that have kept us alive and sane or helped us feel safe and happy can no longer take us where we need to be. Come what may, we must venture beyond our known experience, face whatever may approach us from outside and within, and speak the truth of what we find. We must admit that we're not just the "good guy" or the "bad guy," but we're all the guys *and* gals—every part can be found, in one form or another, within our own "vehicles" as well as outside in other "cars." As vibrantly alive and exquisitely human as we can be at times, we can also be cold and mechanical, and our confusion between these two has mechanized many would-be human beings.

We "live" more like cars when we continually watch the clock, keeping to a programmed schedule of maintenance, such as "it's time for bed," rather than following an intuitive timing or sensing the body's experience of sleepiness. Instead of allowing the body to rest when tired, we refuel and drive it to its limits, if not beyond. Rather than discerning what's troubling us when we're angry or depressed, we fill up on sweets, alcohol, or prescription drugs. Where anyone's self-esteem is deflated, we mete out hot air, perhaps applying pressure to change, rather than nurturing the human inhabitant of the "vehicles" that IS naturally confident and Self-assured. Not wishing to cross the line in our encounters with one another, we're usually more concerned about avoiding "scratches" and "dents" and preventing "punctured tires" and the need for a "tow," rather than seeking to bestow what the *human* driver is asking for.

We handle our children like automobiles when we merely fuel their "tanks" and then expect them to move as they are steered. We attempt to shift their behaviors, emotions, and thinking into positions that least threaten us and most support our status quo. We curtail their upsets to create an immediate temperate environment, which may stifle a more long-lasting and widespread contentment. We try to accelerate their "maturation" as if there is something wrong with childhood or the natural inclinations of children. We speed them on "their" way to "success," unaware that they may be traveling a road littered with Rocks and Minerals.

We treat people like auto parts or other objects when we expect them to be the same each day (always cheerful with a "good" attitude) or functioning in the same way (all-season high performance!). When they are not, we adjust our input or their output, to maximize alignment with our "vehicle." We mute the genuine expressions of their physical or emotional bodies and push them into expected modes of operation, which repeat the unresolved scenes from our own lives. We fast-forward them to the future WE desire for them, *or* we attempt to rewind them to a happier time before their problematic behaviors began. We turn down the volume on their criticisms and concerns, rather than honoring the human voice within them *and* moving, changing, and developing ourselves accordingly. Perhaps we acknowledge brokenness in people and work around their disabilities, making no demands on them for the rest of their lives. *Or,* conversely, we offer a quick fix, expect instant upgrades, and become annoyed when symptoms readily return (particularly when they require *our* help). Our automatisms consistently fall short of sincere engagement with our fellowman as we mutually navigate the ups and downs, lefts and rights, and swerves and spins of our ever-evolving humanness.

We don't realize that by acting like machines ourselves, we're encouraging the same in others, *and* treating others like machines maintains our own mechanization. Our collective "vehicles" have driven out or driven over much of our precious human nature. Yet, rather than intrepidly face this truth, we dodge the psychological journey and pretend, as the Femrock does, that everything is as it should be. Our list of offenses then grows, rather than our humanity. The pain we've been so eager to deny or run from has merely been trying to alert us to these errors. When we fragment, objectify, and mechanize what is vibrantly alive and so brilliantly and lovingly relational, __IT HURTS__!

> When Oliver didn't come back before dark, Connie got worried. "Oliver tends to go off by himself when stressed, but he usually stays close by. This isn't familiar territory, though."
>
> I replied, "Let's start a search. I'll call Lou to round up some neighbors, and we'll spread out in teams. We can give each other a couple of hours, and then we'll rendezvous back here if we don't find him. If anyone does find him, we'll holler."
>
> "Yeah, OK." Connie nodded her head in agreement with that drained look she's had most of the time since the disaster. "I need help," she uttered as her strikingly blue eyes waded once again in tears.

Integrating Mineral Stage parts is NOT work for amateurs (ALWAYS consult the Professional, Our Rescuer). We can't just yank the woolly cover off the "vehicle" of someone's life and expect him or her to quickly and gratefully come out of denial. This maneuver is like removing a radiator cap before allowing the engine to cool. The rage stored in our Rock parts and expressed in "their" behaviors must be slowly and carefully released to minimize harm. If you try to rush a Rock into purely constructive behavior, he's liable to balance you with the opposite extreme. GO EASY! The following are some potential steps for integrating Mineral Stage parts (as always, refer to Our Rescuer before implementing any suggestion):

(1) As you well know by now, Rocks and Minerals persecute people who remind them of their pain. Although their methods of expressing rage can be horrific, the rage itself is valid. They were once victims of every atrocity with which they now victimize others, and they are furious that they are unable to move from this disaster site. Many of the New Orleanians who were stranded for days after the Levee Disaster were angry when they were finally rescued—rightly so! Now imagine the rage of the Rock who has been waiting a lifetime! Thus, a rescuer's job is to validate the anger while diverting its expression away from hurtful behaviors and toward NONDESTRUCTIVE outlets. For instance, if a Mascrock part "likes" to strike children and animals, you might routinely bring him to a gym to work the punching bags, encouraging him to release his aggression in this manner. You might channel the Femrock's verbal cruelties into an area where critical feedback is needed (editing, for example). (Be wary: if they act out from time to time, returning to "their" old ways, they are likely to blame you as the cause!) Continue their new training (as directed by Our Rescuer) until the old habits have been extinguished and more constructive behaviors have become automatic.

(2) While they are punching or criticizing, see if these Rocks can turn their attention within and sense the feeling that is making them want to hurt someone. What is that feeling? However they might physically or emotionally describe their anger is OK, whether as "energy," "my heart is racing," "my jaw is tight," or "I'm *pissed*!"[3] Refer to these feelings as "stop signs"—whenever they are sensed, it's time for these Rocks to stop whatever they are doing and calm down.

(3) Encourage them to pay close attention to these feelings. Just as when a tire explodes and we pull over to the side of the road, when Rocks first notice these signals, they need to stop whatever they are doing. Have them call or text you and share what they are aware of within themselves. See what constructive expressions they might come up with to communicate these feelings. Might the feelings wish to speak, write, paint, sing, do something athletic, and so on? (If they insist that their feelings make them want to hurt someone, tell them to sense inside[4] to discover where they learned to harm with their feelings. Did Dad, Mom, or someone else in their childhoods teach them that by hurting them?) You may want to add your intuition of the most useful forms of expression for them.

(4) Ask these Rocks what they are thinking when they wish to hurt others or themselves. Are these thoughts reasonable? ("Is that dog or child really a danger to you, or are you more dangerous to them?" "Does your neighbor's 'look' truly warrant you scratching your skin until you bleed?") How did they come to view such things as ominous and worthy of attack?

(5) As Mineral Stagers become more comfortable with their internal signals, help them figure out the messages these feelings are conveying. "A left-turn signal means the car in front is about to turn left. So what might your anger be signaling?" Bear in mind that many Minerals have special names for their feelings—"It's only anger, not MY anger, but just plain anger." Or "It's energy! What's YOUR problem that YOU see it as anger?!" Respect their terminology until you sense an opening to talk to them about it. Also, help them detect what they might truly want that they're furious about not getting.

Keep in mind that these steps may take a long time. (Remember, Rocks have associated human functioning with trauma and Rock behaviors with their survival!) Those in the Mineral Stage often rock back and forth over the same spot for extended periods before they choose psychological movement as a way of life. You might have to threaten to call animal rescue or child protective services and perhaps the police if Rocks refuse to diverge from "their" way. *And* you may need to make good on your threats since, for Rocks to "feel safe," they often endanger or otherwise harm life. Also, please be sensitive to the enormity of the request you are making of them—you are turning "their world" upside down (right-side up, actually), and that feels life-threatening!

Rescuing the Child

Connie tucked Felicity into bed while I phoned Effie's neighbor Lou. We agreed to meet right away at the old live-oak tree. Connie and I grabbed flashlights before hurrying down the quarter-mile drive, alert to the occasional hurricane debris still on the road. Everyone was there waiting for us. Lou's wife, Esther, greeted us with an outstretched hand containing insect repellent—the type used for jungle combat. "Oh yeah—we forgot!" I said sheepishly, glancing at Connie. As we sprayed a heavy coating over all exposed skin, Lou assembled three teams: Mr. and Mrs. Wagner, daughter Ruth, and dog Baxter took the area to the south and west. They'd drive their truck along the highway and into town, stopping periodically to make inquiries. Connie, Lou, and Lou's two teenage grandsons, Eric and Sim, took the area north—the farms and old cemetery adjacent to Effie's property. Esther, her eldest son, Manny, and I were to explore Effie's acreage, which ranged from well-maintained farmland to woods with a lake, finally bordering on a river. We set off in no time.

About twenty minutes into our search, I heard Connie yell, "WE FOUND HIM!" Our team jogged over in the direction of the voice and soon found Team Two in a small family graveyard. They were huddled around Oliver, who was perched on a gravestone, looking dazed.

"…sorry—I didn't mean to worry you." Oliver yawned and continued, "I was really tired. I haven't been sleeping much."

"I know, honey, I haven't been either," Connie said, stroking her son's hair. Murmurs from the group let me know that restful sleep was hard to come by these days.

"…anyway…I fell asleep," Oliver finished his story.

"Let's go back to the house, Oliver. You could be eaten alive out here!" Connie said, shooing away the noisy bugs swarming around. Lou pulled out the insect repellent, but the boy shook his head.

"They don't bother me," Oliver muttered as he got up slowly, slapping a mosquito on his face. He brushed himself off and then followed Team Two out of the graveyard, his mom's arm around his shoulders. I shone my flashlight on the engraving of the gravestone where Oliver had been resting. "Here lies Cedric, beloved husband and father—R.I.P." A couple feet behind the stone was a large statue of an angel.

"Whoa!" I exclaimed as I took in the powerful metaphor Oliver was giving us.

"We'll be off, then," Esther said to me. "Thanks for the evening's adventure. Glad it all turned out OK. I'll call off Team One when I get home—I have a friend who lives where they were headed who can track them down."

"Great. Thanks, y'all. Good night!" I paused, my mind still processing the moment, before I ran to catch up with Connie and son.

After we got back to Effie's house, we sipped hot cocoa, a treat from Connie's kitchen. Felicity and Effie, neither able to sleep, joined us. We had a good laugh about having HOT cocoa when the temperature was still close to ninety degrees outside and in. My heart was also warmed as well as I thought of Cousin Joan. "Comfort foods," Joan would have said. "We're all driven to find comfort!"

Rescuers are all around us if we look and LISTEN. When we merely zoom in on the dysfunctional parts of others' "vehicles," we often miss the provisions that each person has for our journey—a needed resource or skill, necessary support, or important information. Similarly, when we focus on our most functional aspects, we usually don't notice what we're lacking that others are supplying. Recovering and repairing our forgotten "auto" parts would be far less difficult and time-consuming were it not for our Rocklike selectivity in where we place our attention and reception. Our cars offer no such resistance to being moved by any driver or worked on by any mechanic. They don't recoil from the ego threat of a human being approaching them to improve their functioning, nor do they attack them in perceived "self"-defense. As a result, they are usually operational after a few hours or days in the shop.

In contrast, our lives often become overtly disastrous before we consent to someone working at length on our "vehicles." A shocking event in the family or community occurs, or perhaps a few head-on "collisions" with Rocks, before we're willing to remember the truth of our traumatic lives and our reenactments of these traumas. Our Mascrock parts may pull out in front to drive us back into our past, so we admit some parts of us are stuck there. They may thrust us into grief before we realize that our mourning from childhood is unfinished. They may jolt us into terror before we embrace that vulnerable, needy *human* child inside us who has been hiding in fear since our baneful choice of image over our reality. (We must choose again if that child is to revive!)

Femrocks had us convinced that returning to our disaster sites would lead only to dead ends, irrevocable loss, our demise, or the death of someone we love. In fact, they were antagonally warning us that such events are more likely when we DON'T tour the road to recovery. Mascrocks then roll into our lives to give us direct experience of our own disastrous driving habits. Although Mascrocks may appear to hold the power position, they are merely rearview-mirroring our internal state and showing us the condition of some part of our own "vehicle."

Fortunately, Our Rescuer is ever present to help. When she illuminates our Rocky experiences, we suddenly perceive new meaning and potential. When Mascrocks drive us to disaster again and again, we can use these difficult conditions to become competent drivers of harsh terrain and traumatic times, thus healing the incapacities from our pasts. When our current environments are reminiscent of the places where we discarded our missing parts, we can then rescue these long-abandoned "children" and "infants." When Rocks barbarically force us to feel, whether intense "negative" emotions *or* physical deprivations, infirmities, and pain, we can reclaim those human feelings we rejected in our attempts to be more acceptable to our companions or more comfortable ourselves. Rocks' mechanization of our thought processes through programming can compel us to rely on the minds of everybody in our lives and depend on Our Rescuer, who is the licensed Driver of every vehicle. (Expecting our "vehicles" to function well without her is NOT a reasonable expectation!)

After YEARS of stalling our healing in fear of being harmed, we discover that the anticipated dead end is merely the end of our imagery, and the loss we have so dreaded is of our denial. Our "imminent demise" is no more than our ego taking its proper back seat to our collective humanity. As the false image fades, the human child revives! In relief and joy, we experience a strange sense of gratitude toward the Rocks and Minerals who unmercifully drove us to this transformation. Thus, even these most damaged parts of us have a valuable function to fulfill and are worthy to be included in our "cars"!

Our new awareness and compassion become the "battery" and "starter motor" that ignite the truly powerful engine of an unconditionally loving heart. In our *genuine* appreciation and repossession of our most primitive aspects, they once again become constructive, functioning parts of our psychological "vehicles." Our inner Rocks boast a new motto—**"YOU CAN'T MAKE ME BRAKE OUR GROWTH!"** We discover boundless energy and a willingness to do absolutely anything to find these lost "children" and "infants" who have hardened into "auto" parts *and* return them to their human form and function. Just as a couple with a growing family buys a bigger car, we too acquire a larger and more powerful "vehicle" as we reclaim more and more of our humanity. *An individual image is not big enough to contain all that we are!*

The Return of Civilization!

"Something's wrong!" Felicity's voice quavered as she sat motionless.

"Oh no, what now, Felicity?" Her mom's voice sounded equally concerned.

Felicity wiped her hand across her forehead and glanced at it. "I'm not sweating!"

"I'm not either," Oliver said as he stood up and reached to the wall to turn on the light switch. The lights came on instantly. "IT'S ON! IT'S ON, EVERYBODY! THE ELECTRICITY'S ON!" Oliver was clearly elated, as were we all—so nice to experience! I wish I could have captured that moment on film—when our faces were full of joy for something we had taken for granted eleven days ago. A primitive lifestyle has its lessons, no doubt, but given the choice, give me the comfort of modern living!

"Thank God for electricity!" Connie's words paralleled my own thoughts. "Those line workers we've seen along the road for days now have finally succeeded."

"I was getting so sick of carrying a flashlight around at night!" Oliver grimaced again.

Felicity chimed in, "I was sick of sweating!"

Our returning humanity can seem "wrong" when we're used to living without it. Our "inner children's" strong feelings, needs, and expressions can feel uncomfortable when we've become accustomed to the inertness and insensitivity of "motor vehicles." We may experience the originality, creativity, and inspiration of our human mind as foreign, weird, or incomprehensible when we've been domesticated into one "right" way. However, when we choose the "open road," a non-judgmental, receptive stance to all that is within (using the "gas pedal" and "brakes" as needed), every aspect of us can become a "vehicle" for our development *and* for the advancement of our civilization.

ROADSIDE ASSISTANCE: **HELPING ROCKS!** (and Minerals too!)

We can work with the mechanized parts of ourselves using the following techniques. But first—BUCKLE UP!

(1) School zone. Our Rock parts are understandable when we perceive them as "auto" parts rather than people. We don't instruct a steaming radiator to get help for itself and then react when it doesn't heed our advice. We also don't expect it to fix itself. We don't call it names or blame it for ruining our day. We merely take it to a competent mechanic and trust his or her expertise. Remember: Rocks have "leaky gaskets" (huge gaps in their psyches), so much of what you give them flows right through, falling flat on the underlying pavement. Expect this—it may be signaling our own inadequate reception of Our Rescuer's help. A consistent flow of guidance from Our Rescuer will maximize retention in both "vehicles."

(2) No outlet. Learn to recognize Rock programming, and ask Our Rescuer to translate it into a human alternative. If you get a green light from her, you may wish to alert the Rock to what he's doing. "That's programming—please stop right now." A Rock doesn't like such candor or correction, but her displeasure affords her an opportunity to feel what she is passing on to her victims and thereby start recharging her own humanity.

(3) No parking. Pay attention to where you are hyperactive ("go, go, go!") and be sensitive to any inclinations within you to stop and rest. Be aware of how you handle these inclinations. If a family member is opposing your extremes (hyperactivity) with his or her own extremes (inactivity), perhaps you can both work on moving toward the middle. If someone is overly active like you, create situations where you can share some down time (enjoy a quiet meal together, for example).

(4) Dead end. Have those closest to you tell you about your Rockometer, Guilt Gauge, Care Alarm, and Distractometer, which maintain the "dead ends" within your psyche. Get to know when and where you use these gauges, how you use them, and with whom.

(5) No U-turn. Your Rock parts came into existence to defend against overwhelming stress, and they are continually turning back from whence they came—re-creating stress and then defending against it. Be aware of your "driving" habits that stress others or yourself, and make other choices.

(6) Wrong way! Rocks design situations where the obvious response results in trouble and the correct response gives you the *appearance* of having a few loose screws. Our Rocks clear the roads that lead to perdition—if we think we've found easy street in this world, we are SORELY mistaken. When we fall for this and many other Rock ruses, the trunk of our unconscious mind is stuffed with guilt and pain, which we WON'T want to feel. To evade avoidance and lighten our load, we must follow the directions and speeds recommended by Our Rescuer.

(7) Yield. Look at your rigid beliefs hiding within your mechanical actions. Notice where you pursue only one way of:

- Doing an activity (you always follow your schedule)
- Feeling in a given situation ("You shouldn't let other people's problems bother you!")
- Thinking about information ("She said what she meant, and that's that!")

Consider how you learned such inflexibility:

- Someone taught you that a rigid program keeps you safe.
- Someone instructed you in the opposite extreme that you're still rigidly reacting to.

Then ponder:

- Which unresolved issues with these people are indicated by your inflexibility?
- Which restrained emotions are maintaining your rigor?
- Which new belief system might give you more freedom and better mileage?

How might others propel your movement in these areas?

Also, employ any scheduling rigidity toward creating time each day for your human developmental task of yielding to Our Rescuer.

(8) No turn on red. Take time to pause and evaluate any stops currently in your life. Remember, a "roadblock" might point to a road Rock, which should be investigated. Such rest stops (a dead-end job or stalled marriage) might also indicate the necessity for a purposeful change in direction. How might you "put the pedal to the metal" to promote forward movement with every part of you?

(9) Report unsafe driving! Regularly tuning into our bodies (physical, emotional, mental, and spiritual) and the bodies of those around us will maximize driving safety. There are many books and courses available to assist with this endeavor.[5]

(10) Right of way. Find any "rightness" in your Rock behaviors ("my" way can be the HIGHway). For instance, your chronic pain, illness, or other infirmity (Femrock afflictions) may be motivating you to make changes in your routines ("BORING!") and your relationships ("They aren't growing!"). Perhaps your bullying of people (Mascrock style) is making them stand up to you and demand you seek psychological help ("Nobody likes bullies!"). Notice any "child" sleeping on the "gravestone" of your Rocky experiences and expressions, and seek avenues for waking him or awakening yourself to his obvious presence.

COFFEE BREAK:

1. Examine your automobile. How does its condition reflect your psychology? Inspect for dents, scratches, rust, tears in the seat covers, or mechanical problems, and determine what they may be communicating about you. Which auto parts do you most identify with? Which "vehicle" do you maintain better: your auto or your psyche?

2. To which of the following manners of interaction do you most relate?
    a. Because you need an "oil change," you think EVERYBODY does—at the same time and with the same grade of "oil."
    b. You believe each person's psychological "vehicle" is utterly unique. Not only do you reject what comes your way because you believe no one could know what is good for you, but you neglect to help others on the same grounds.
    c. You don't own many of your "auto" parts, and as a result, they have caused problems without your awareness. When another person points out these parts to you, you consider him or her to be short on parts.
    d. You believe your "auto"-part perspective is superior.
    e. You are so busy adding "lubricants," minimizing the friction between people, that you don't allow the uncomfortable situations that deepen human relationships. (If you are always jacking up people's spirits, their egos may be too far off the ground for them to drive anywhere!)
    f. Eager to get back your own lost "auto" parts, you vicariously "live" through these aspects of others. Or you attempt to possess or control these aspects in remembrance of them once being part of your own "vehicle."

3. Sometimes the "vehicles" around us aren't working because they need something from us. Use your answers to the last two questions to decide how you can better relate to your fellowman, such that these "vehicles" are better functioning and in alignment with Our Maker's design.

4. Be attentive to where you operate on automatic pilot (like Cedric). For instance, do you periodically back up and repeat the cold, uncaring words you heard as a child?
    a. Listen and discover your pat phrases and predictable reactions. (Ask those you trust for help.)
    b. Consider their source and your reasons for using them.
    c. Which emotions are fueling your automatic (addictive or habitual) behaviors?
    d. Write down each stimulus-response pattern (e.g., ""When I feel _____, I _____").
    e. Who or what is hindering you from feeling your feelings and expressing them in a constructive manner?

f. How can you reframe your stimulus-response patterns to allow for movement and ultimately to welcome the return of your vital human voice and spontaneous, inspired behaviors?

g. Determine which curtailed actions and/or physical feelings might be frozen within each automatism and how they can be thawed and expressed to free the flow of genuineness. For example, whenever you notice your pat phrases and predictable reactions, shift gears, sense inside, and then offer a more thoughtful and heartfelt HUMAN response.

5. Ask Our Rescuer:

a. How can you return your Rock indicators to their original Self-protective functioning?

b. Do your "tires" need balancing? How can you make adjustments so that the physical, emotional, mental, and relational are all equally represented in your spiritual life?

c. How can you transform any "auto" mechanical energy into human inspiration?

Then—watch for signs of emerging civilization!

---

[1] Robert Ornstein and Paul Ehrlich, *New World, New Mind* (Cambridge, MA: Malor Books, published by ISHK, 2000), 75.

[2] "The City of Gretna on the West Bank of the Mississippi River received considerable press coverage when, in the aftermath of Hurricane Katrina (late August 2005), displaced and dehydrated survivors who attempted to escape from New Orleans by walking over the Crescent City Connection bridge over the Mississippi River were turned back at gunpoint by City of Gretna Police, along with Crescent City Connection Police and Jefferson Parish Sheriff's deputies, who set up a roadblock on the bridge in the days following the hurricane." Gretna controversy, "Effect of Hurricane Katrina in New Orleans," *Wikipedia*, modified April 16, 2013, http://en.wikipedia.org/wiki/Effects_of_Hurricane_Katrina_in_New_Orleans.

[3] Hendrie Weisinger, PhD., *Dr. Weisinger's Anger Work Out Book* (New York: Harper, 1985), 26-27.

[4] Ann Weiser Cornell and Barbara McGavin, *The Focusing Student's and Companion's Manuals* (Berkeley, CA: Calluna Press, 2002), 9.

[5] Ibid.

Chapter 11

The Exodus Ends

How Rocks Facilitate Our Journeying Home

"Want some breakfast?" Newland's voice jolted me awake. I had dozed off in the Red Cross shelter reading a book from Effie's bookshelf—*The Developing Human*.[1] I was still having trouble sleeping at night. I glanced at Newland, who offered me a package of sweet rolls and a bottle of orange juice.

"No thanks," I muttered, dismissing the meager fare while recalling the full meals that had been cooked for the shelter residents during the first couple of weeks of their stay.

I scanned the large room briefly and estimated that only half the people remained from when I first arrived three weeks ago. The Red Cross was giving shelter residents free tickets for buses or flights anywhere in the continental United States if they had a place to live, so the number of people was rapidly decreasing. A military man from Alaska announced, "It's time for everyone to move on!" I figured the diminishing quality and quantity of food was an encouragement to leave.

Loretta had departed for her cousin Lotti's house to rejoin her husband and five kids. Manuel flew to Miami to spend some time with his nephew. Wayne hooked up with a group of activists in Washington, DC. Gina moved into her church in Jefferson Parish to start a program there for domestic-violence victims. Wally learned his ex-wife and kids had been evacuated to Utah, but he chose a plane trip to Atlanta to stay with a close friend. Yvette took a free flight to Los Angeles to stay with her aunt. She hoped to get a job to make enough money for a trip to Hawaii, her birthplace. "I've always dreamed of going back," she told me. "Here's my chance!"

Noticing that Avery was gone, I inquired of Maxi, the shelter manager, who relayed that he had suddenly decided to visit his family in Lafayette and left immediately. "I'm guessing his FEMA money arrived," she said with a grin. I wondered whether Avery saw this money as a gift from God or our tax dollars at work. I figured the former. I shook my head smiling, opened my journal, and began my morning communion with Our Rescuer.

EVACUATION DAY 29: Differentiating God from Our World and Its People
God Is Sovereign—We Are Images

Just as children without adequate parents try to meet their own needs by taking on the parental role themselves, those who deny their Divine Parent may attempt to meet their NEED for their Creator by assuming a divine posture. (Don't many people seek lofty positions to control those under them and "play God"?) Others, missing their Divine Parent, imagine that whatever is coming from the world and its people is coming from Him, as Avery has done. They then seek provision, comfort, and leadership in imagery, rather than in God Himself, and are so often disappointed in Him when these are insufficient, inclement, or intolerable. Furthermore, when we imagine ourselves as God and our world as God-given, it's too easy to project the qualities of imagery onto Our Maker! For example, we believe we must access Him only through blind faith, rather than with the practical moment-by-moment walking in His Omnipresent Presence.

The one absolute on this planet is change. Therefore, whatever we view as unchanging and unchangeable, whether birth defects or character deficits, terminal diseases or interminable political oppressions, we're according Divine characteristics. (Wasn't the Gulf Coast's evacuation from Hurricane Katrina a testament to how quickly a population can change its circumstances?) When we let traumatic experiences, such as violence in our homes and on our streets, car accidents, and environmental or man-made disasters, affect us irrevocably, we are bestowing a godlike power on them. We do as well when we accept the "one way" of our worldly experts ("You'll need to be on medication for the rest of your life!"). When we grant mere mortals permission to run or ruin our lives, we invest our time, efforts, and assets in pleasing them, rather than serving Our Divine Parent.

Prioritizing our realm of separated images over God has consequences. We must journey through the full range of what this world has to offer—from reminders of God to upside-down replacements: Rocks! (Remember those three "movies" in our minds' "computer" systems?) We may tour our mind's contents slowly over a lifetime or more quickly, as in one day of hurricane season. But sooner or later, we encounter every stage of psychological development, outside and within, as we do their representations in the physical plane. I find many people believe this cycling through our psychology is "God's will," rather than *our* will to move apart from Him.

How do we get Creator and created so confused? Again, unborn children experience no difference between parent and self, and neither do the psychologically unborn within and among us—Rocks and Minerals. Projecting themselves onto God, they've taught us to run and hide in fear, oppose in anger, or reject as unnecessary or ineffectual our only true Reality, Safety and Hope—God. *And* they've trained us to place our faith in images, including our own fragmented identity, and rely on their fraudulent authority (Authority Shift)—SCARY!

We may see God as the inattentive child who must be informed of what's happening and advised on what He should do about it, as if our limited mind-sets and perceptions are capable of full knowledge and accurate assessments! We may give Him daily assignments to make us, our households, and our communities more peaceful and better functioning, rather than ASK HIM what we need to be doing about what HE tells us to see, hear, feel, think, and believe. We imagine that WE are waiting on HIM to show up and do what we wish, not realizing that our showing up to do *His* Will is truly what we're ALL waiting for. *And* we apprise Him of how much we love Him and what we're doing for Him...as if He doesn't know, but we do! As young children, we are too immature and self-absorbed to believe and accept God's complete knowledge, unlimited power, unfathomable brilliance, and boundless love. We're too preoccupied with our infantile imitations of Him (or the opposite!). We so often reject His ever-ready guiding, giving, helping, and healing, as it interferes with OUR Lilliputian "knowing," feeling, and doing.

We have indeed indulged in extreme role reversals, consistently confusing Parent with child. With the arrogance of a Mascrock, we've presumed to lead our lives, as if we have authority to do this. Like the Femrock, we've also actively or passively supported this arrogance in others, denying the resulting problems, making excuses, or blaming victims and their rescuers (Thumbnail Program, Excuse Escape, Blame Game). Because of such confusion, most people, at least in the deep recesses of their unconscious minds, hold God accountable for their less-than-perfect lives. Yet, rather than blame God when apparently "meager fare" is our "daily bread," we might also view these situations as an encouragement for us to "move on" from our Reality Reversal Program—we individuals are not

God! (Only God is doing what's best!) The purpose of time is NOT about our individual doings, but about UNDOING our absurd upside-down stance!

God Is the **PERFECT** Parent—We Have Facsimile Parents and Children (Inside and Out)

I paused for a moment, reflecting. I wouldn't be at the Greensburg Red Cross shelter if not for the Levee Disaster, and I wouldn't have met this kaleidoscope of interesting people. I'd be in my routine back in New Orleans, working out of my home and going out with friends. Although unwelcome at the time, this evacuation has given me many new experiences, a larger perspective, and a fuller life. I now feel a part of what is around me, and what is around me is a part of me as well. Giving and receiving what benefits this whole, while eliminating what doesn't, now dominates my attention. Our Rescuer, the outreach of Our Divine Parent in ourselves and in our environment, now feels more present, alive, involved, and responsive than anything in this world of imagery. If it took a disaster for me to arrive here—so be it!

Once we understand that we individuals are not God and never will be, we can relax into our infant role in relation to Our Parent and depend on Him and our spiritual nanny, Our Rescuer, to care for us PERFECTLY. We can put down the pretense of perfection for ourselves and freely share our imperfections with one another. We can admit our psychological immaturity, ignorance, and foolishness, and we can focus on doing what children do so well—learning from those who are older and wiser.

Listening to Our Rescuer in every circumstance, we learn that the cold, cruel reality of this world that drove us as physical children to regress and evacuate from our humanity can also move us, with proper Parenting, to grow and become MORE human. Our disasters can have a noble purpose! They interrupt our routines and fixed responses of mind, heart, and body. (One Red Cross shelter resident stated this was her first time outside of Orleans Parish other than Christmas shopping at the Lakeside Mall in neighboring Jefferson Parish!) Just as Hurricane Katrina drove me to the tiny town of Greensburg, Louisiana, our most violent personal storms can impel us to the smallest or most remote places within ourselves, where otherwise we would never tread; or they can pry us out of places that, without a crisis, we would never leave. They can compel us to join the greater community *and* what is beyond. Our most painful moments can prompt us to listen to and rely on a diversity of folks whom we customarily wouldn't relate to, let alone depend on for our survival and healing. Traumas also can accelerate our acquisition of new skills (I'm writing a book!). Disasters can wake us up!

Mature parents realize the value of appropriately timed difficulties. They give "children" experiences that are well-suited to their developmental ages, while never exposing them to what is beyond their coping abilities. The "infant" or "child" parent, in contrast, is too busy seeking his or her own stimulation, comfort, or fun to attend to the developmental needs of others. This "young" parent consistently submits "children" to more than they can handle, while oblivious to what will stimulate their psychological growth.

The Rocks we encounter expose these immature "parents" within us and force us to admit to the wide range of our experiences with "parenting" styles from people of all psychological ages—styles that remain with us. Only when we make these experiences conscious are we able to deduce the psychological age of any "parent," inside and out: those who push us down and keep us down are "embryos" and "fetuses"; those who coddle us and carry us are "infants"; those who encourage mere baby steps are "preschoolers"; those who enjoy playing, studying, and growing beside us, Our

Rescuer, and Our Parent are "children"; "adolescents" are those actively seeking to calm each individual's rebellion against Our Parent and end the separation while still being rebellious and separate themselves. There are also adults, who would facilitate the fulfillment of our life's purpose, just as they are fulfilling their own.

Our growth demands that we make the most of developmental opportunities with all "parents"—those who would shove us backward to eliminate any challenges to their false leadership claims, those who would maintain the status quo, and those who would guide us forward to ever giving and receiving mature parenting ourselves. Noting the consequences of each parenting type on each stage of development is also necessary experiential learning so that we can maximize the efficacy of each pairing.

Remembering and processing the traumas perpetrated by immature parental figures is a necessary part of human development, but timing matters. This recollection occurs most favorably at a psychological "age" when we can use these traumas to fuel our maturation (the Child Stage and above). We must also embrace the guilt and shame of our own immature attempts at parenting. Again, we evolve more swiftly with a strategic uncovering of our repressed remorse. Our personal experience with all these dynamics of mature and immature parenting then enables us to pair maturity levels and styles of parenting most effectively with "ages" and personality types of "children." Of course, we must check all decisions with Our Rescuer because her unlimited experience ever evidences the gross inadequacies of our own.

"AUTO" MECHANICS: Within God, All Parts Have Function and Purpose
We Are Self-selective

In the hands of Our Rescuer, the Master Mechanic, Mineral Stagers become tools for releasing what's stuck in us, repairing and replacing our mechanical parts, and aiding the maturation of our humanity. For example, the Rocks that exploit our blind spots can motivate us to open our eyes and survey more of the scenery. The Rocks that are quick to throttle fruitful pursuits can encourage planning and perseverance as we learn to anticipate problems, take precautions, oversee every turn, and abide by Our Rescuer's course (no matter what!). We can acquire patience from the Femrock's endless stall tactics, as well as healthy impatience ("I've had enough!"). Mascrocks can coerce us into admitting our weaknesses and finding and developing our strengths. Rocks are so HARD to direct off their Rocky route that we *must* depend upon every aspect of our humanity (including our Rock parts!) to deal with them. Thus, Mineral Stagers can help us retrieve our missing "auto" parts as these most obstinate people require the capacities we need to practice to regain full use of our psychological "vehicles."

We need an integrated Rock inside us to remain undaunted as we trek with the Mineral Stagers in our world. We can then apply extreme pressures or be relentlessly aggressive when human life is at stake. We can promptly rescue disaster survivors who, in their devastation, are frenzied, combative, or adamant in thwarting their own rescue. We can also stand alone, immobile and unflinching against great opposition, having attained the endurance and "flame-proofing" to handle Rocks' rat race and seemingly endless persecutions. We can be hard-nosed in offering much-needed, Rescuer-directed repairs, despite the Rocks' clamors to stop, their unwillingness to stop or get going themselves, or their cries of "YOU'RE HURTING ME!"

The more we accurately remember our Rocky roads, the more we can sympathize with others' travails. For example, when we recall how quickly we New Orleanians were driven from our homes by Hurricane Katrina, we can comprehend how traumatic experiences compelled Rocks to abandon much of their psychological "vehicles." Seeing newscasts of the floodwater's damage to our homes and belongings, we can imagine why the Rocks' skills, including any abilities to give and receive help, have been tarnished by their toxic exposures. As we struggle to find lost loved ones and keep in contact with family and friends scattered all over the country, we can appreciate how Rocks lost their human contacts, resulting in their isolation, insensitivity, hardening, and hindering of humanness everywhere. Just as we New Orleans evacuees have started life anew elsewhere, we can understand how Rocks and Minerals adapted to "their" Mineral Stage identity and never returned home to their humanity.

This comparison is not to minimize or dismiss the intensity of pain Rocks perpetrate. However, as this pain so often overwhelms our coping mechanisms, the reservoir of suffering stored in our unconscious minds surfaces. The Rock's FORCE is actually necessary to jumpstart this process, as gentle methods often don't penetrate the Femrock's thick defensive walls or the Mascrock's arsenal of brutal weaponry. However, when the pain of our present reality resonates with that vast unconscious misery, we're finally willing to unlock the "trunk" and unload the heavy burden we've been carrying. *And* we begin the slow process of revitalizing our mechanical parts, transforming them back into vibrant, spontaneous, and responsive-to-the-moment aspects of our *humanness*.

Only when we feel our pain and admit to our disasters can we truly share these burdens with others. We can join in suffering (grief, fear, anger, guilt, shame, and so on)—just as we join in joy or any other aspect of our humanity. We're then willing to cause people pain if it will minimize suffering in the long run. We're also ready to receive pain if it facilitates some greater good. We gladly fall if it will lift up another, and we'll even fail if this leads to a more important or long-term success, such as the return to our humanness. In contrast, when we withhold from others the constructive expression of our suffering, falls, and failings, we deny them the modeling that all "children" need to inch closer to these experiences in their own lives. As Hurricane Katrina and the Levee Disaster taught me, sharing the payload of pain can be a powerful vehicle for uniting and mobilizing a community.

God Is the Cure—We Both Help and Harm

Yet another hurricane, Rita, had arrived and departed the day before without anyone in our household flinching. I was largely oblivious to the rain as I read and wrote in my bedroom. Effie and the rest of the group quietly watched the news in the family room. I had passed through on my way to the kitchen to get a drink and noted Felicity hugging her baby doll, but there was no other outward sign of stress from anyone. I think we were too traumatized still from the Levee Disaster to get worked up about any potential catastrophe. I was more interested in absorbing the contents of my books than encountering any additional threat from my environment…I wanted a break!

Out of the multitudes of people who have been victimized by Mineral Stagers, so few genuinely come to their aid. The compounded traumas endured by so many people diminishes their innate ability to listen and respond, so the "unborn child" within the Rock and Mineral remains unheard and distressed. Therefore, discerning the roles each has played in harming or <u>antagonally helping</u> us is not the end of the story. We must look at the roles we've played in her or his life as well.

Allowing the Rock to run amok with "his" diabolically detrimental behaviors, without boundaries or discipline, is hurtful to him—a hurt he will extend far and wide. Excusing his horrific behaviors and cleaning up his disasters without him suffering any serious consequences supports the continuance of his offenses. Standing by while he divides families, communities, and nations reinforces his own psychic split and the divisive contexts that created it. Meeting his false "needs" by honoring his requests, patronizing his businesses, paying his exorbitant fees, and pretending our lives depend on "his" way only upholds "his" belief that the Rock Program has value. When we accept "his" leadership, we ally with the dominating and hate-filled Rocks from his own tortured past that led him to devolve. We also equate him with an inanimate object or even a force of nature when we don't acknowledge his human origin and do everything in our power to restore him to this birthright. We're GRIEVOUSLY condescending when we imply Mineral Stagers are doing their best when they are actually capable, with proper Parenting, of growing into psychological adults.

Yes, Rocks and Minerals have harmed us, agonizingly so, but we've harmed them too. We don't see their reality, let alone assist them to the next developmental stage, perhaps because we feel we can't take on any more stress. Besides, "my" choice of not helping Mineral Stagers and not developing "my" own psychology is "my" decision to make, right? WRONG! Rocks show us CLEARLY how mistaken we've been in assuming individuality, in neglecting our responsibility to evolve one another, and in denying HOW MUCH impact one individual can have on his or her environment and everyone in it, for better...or for worse. *Our stage of development sets the stage for our developing world!*

SPORTS AND RECREATION: God Creates—We Recreate

All of our nondevelopmental activities are psychological games we play, which at their core, are merely rounds of the Keep Away game to distract ourselves from the truth of our undesired parts. Such "play" sets us up for repeated rounds of Predator/Prey as these fragmented-off "undesirables" tell their story by acting out with everyone in our lives the events that led to their exile. Of course, they tenaciously follow us, because as parts of us, they cannot be but where we are! Do we continue to dodge the ball of our unconscious reality, retreating from anything or anyone that stirs this uncomfortable material? Do we together stampede or individually whack whatever mirrors our unexpressed thoughts, feelings, needs, and wishes? Do we imagine ("Let's pretend!") that these are "our" choices rather than "recreational activities" learned from our childhood caretakers? *Or* do we realize we want to stop such gaming?

Adulthood is when we no longer play with our lives. We take each moment as an opportunity for tending each person's psychological needs, including those of Rocks and Minerals. Understanding the growth that Rocks can launch is essential to be willing to work with them effectively and integrate them within ourselves. Realizing how we've *horribly* neglected their needs is also vital if we're to level the playing field between "us" and "them." Indeed, Rocks have forced us, but we've also forced them with our insistence on only one field position ("I have only loving feelings!") as they must then balance us with the opposing rigid stance. Remember—because we are whole, whichever character traits we refuse for our image obliges the disowned aspects of ourselves to assume...perhaps to the *extreme*.

We don't have a monopoly on our lives. When we assert control over our individual playing piece, secondarily affecting all the pieces around us and within us, we're toying with life. When we play as if this piece is somehow more worthy than other pieces of our time, attention, or the "good things" in life, Rocks then maneuver us as pawns on their "game board," showing us our own play. Rocks easily checkmate our lives because we've already checked ourselves by insisting that an image (our "book-cover" character) is our identity. Like playing hot potato, we inevitably receive and then pass on the pain of this disastrous choice.

We individuals have all failed *horribly* in the "game" of our lives because we are NOT individuals. (School, employment, stock market, marital, and even heart failures have been cluing us in on this for years!) Yet we're not inherent failures. We've merely failed to include all that we are in our "play," thus failing as a result. Unbeknown to us, the "cards" we've dealt to each player on our life's "game board" have been received by whom he or she represents within us. The more we personally experience and finally recognize our own poor sportsmanship, the more we and our Mineral Stage parts can meet in the middle and ultimately embrace as *equally wayward* aspects of the same person. With reconciliation, we can then set our focus beyond playing pieces to the One choosing to play our "game," with whom we enjoy a MUCH greater win—our Self!

POLITICS: God Is Our Sole Authority—We Have Authority Only When He Moves Us

Just as the residents of the Red Cross shelter helped me in my immediate and long-term grieving process, the "underprivileged" parts within ourselves have much to offer our lives. They have endured our life's greatest challenges, and we can draw on their strength, humility, wealth of experience, and survival skills. With their integration, a fresh form of leadership emerges as everyone we meet now reminds us of some part of ourselves. We relate to people with the affirmative action of shared experience—sitting next to them, standing with them, walking beside them, and empathizing with them—giving as we receive. Hard-and-fast rules, rigid judgments of "right" and "wrong," and the punishments that so often ensue pale in comparison with the benefits of mutual leadership and rescue.

Most people consider the residents of the Red Cross shelter "the poor" and "uneducated," yet they've given of themselves and taught me so much through our exchanges. For example, the expressions of loss and lack by these shelter residents have moved me to be more aware of what I've been missing in my life, such as greater involvement with my community and my community's greater involvement with me. These residents' earnest questions have encouraged me to ask more questions myself and of myself. I've felt and thought more deeply because of our interactions—I've stretched as a human being.

Although monetarily poor, these residents are rich in the honest sharing of their lives. They have valid human feelings and reflections and precious, tight-knit neighborhoods. I thought about young Wayne, who perceives the Rocky reality beyond political appearances. To contribute to its correction, he's informing the public and pursuing a career in politics. Manuel spoke of his "wild side" and his care for his neighbors, angrily grieving the loss of their lives. Yvette talked about many horrors, and yet she desires to remember and relay the truth. Loretta shared homespun wisdom. She knows that our leaders, albeit "adults," have little "children" inside who are making GIGANTIC messes and needing parenting like any child. Newland is able to connect with severely handicapped children through touch. All these folks showed some qualities of mature leadership, one of which was the ability to "touch" and move another person—me, for example.

I compared my lessons from these shelter residents with those learned during my medical residency, where I acquired the elevated label of a professional—an "authority." I had memorized many scientific "facts" and protocols, including many "do's" and "don'ts" (if a patient says A, you say B; if he does C, then you do D, NEVER E). We treated disease processes with pills and procedures, rather than listening to the human voice communicating through these symptoms and signs. We didn't acknowledge the parts of their humanness that had evacuated in different areas and to varying degrees and that needed to return. We weren't instructed to engage each patient deeply and respond uniquely with our own unblocked humanity. On the contrary, some psychoanalytically oriented teachers even recommended being a blank wall on which people could easily project their issues. How can people ever evolve as relational human beings if they have a "wall" for a surrogate parent?!

Similarly, some of our "rich" and "well-educated" authorities are responsible for impoverishing a large percentage of New Orleans's population and keeping them and others ignorant of essential facts ("The city is flooding!"), yet more people blame "the indigent" for being a drain on society. My eyes began to tear up as I weighed the disservice brought on by Rock definitions and labels—a TREMENDOUS drain on our psychology! If only we were willing to see the "rich" and "poor" as well as the "educated" and "uneducated" in every individual, then we might understand that they ALL have contributions to make to our life stories and our personal awakening.

I wondered where I'd be in my development were it not for "the uneducated" in Charity Hospital disclosing the violence in their neighborhoods, families, and selves. In my experience, the "indigent" talk freely about the destructive element in people—they don't pretend to be beyond the perpetration of violence or the victimization from it. Their candor about the Rocks in their own lives and selves supports the emergence of these unconscious memories and parts within those of less candid cultures. By esteeming their precious gifts of authenticity, the "rich" may come to know and respect the "poor," and then, perhaps, be willing to share what they have in abundance while receiving what they lack.

God Is Omniscient and All-Encompassing while We Are Experimenting with Our Limits

Our superficial labeling of "rich" or "poor," "educated" and "uneducated," "leaders" or "followers," and "parents" and children" subsides as we plunge into the depths of our own psychology. What differentiates us is not one character trait over another, but the location and quality of each trait and how each is used—by ourselves or Our Rescuer. Character traits then become far less relevant than the person using them and for what purpose. Yet "infant" vision doesn't see this whole, so in our "infancy" we've separated so many traits and activities into categories of "good" and "bad" based purely on our limited experience with them and our PTSD.

However, when Rocks consistently rob us of our "goods"—whatever we cherish in this world, whether "our" way, our job, our personal and national treasures, our pristine environments, the natural beauty and functioning of our bodies, and so on—we finally face our experience-based learning and realize we don't need these things. When Rocks force on us what's "bad," we eventually discover that these threats by themselves don't have power to harm us. When what we've believed to be essential is gone and what we've assumed to be noxious seems ever present, and we not only survive but grow in the process, we can finally surrender our beliefs of what we do and don't need to live or be happy. We also disempower the Rocks who use what is "good" and what is "bad" to manipulate us. There is exhilarating freedom in having weathered the worst the world and its creatures have to offer, and yet, guided by Our Rescuer, we have prevailed.

GOD IS JUDGE—We Are the Jury of His Judgments

In prevailing, we step down from the Mascrock's authoritarian platform of presuming to harshly judge and condemn those psychological "children" or "parents" who threaten us. We also step up from the Femrock's stance of strict nonjudgment ("Who am I to judge anything?"). Instead, we judge developmentally, judging ourselves and others as human beings in different stages of growth, some of whom are momentarily progressing and some of whom are not. With this comprehension, Rocks no longer seem so overwhelmingly menacing, and we lose our fear of them. We no longer feel compelled to laud, attack, or recoil from them, thus condemning them to an existence of incapacitating immaturity. We can offer these youngest of humans what they are lacking and what we have in abundance—our shared humanity.

When we listen to everyone in our lives, we learn that no individual is innocent. We've all engaged in reckless conduct—directly or indirectly. We've all denied or lied about what we've done or what's been done to us. We've demanded that others be held accountable for violations that were our own. We've "lovingly" excused and "forgiven" those expressing their post-traumatic stress disorder, yet neglected their need for treatment. Maybe we've hurried people to "get over it" without first helping them to go into it, thus supporting their psychological fragmentation. We have rewarded those who have honored our images and attacked or avoided those who would bring our truth to light. We've condemned as mentally ill or criminal those who act out the derangements and misconduct that were the "norm" in their childhoods. We have followed the rules of our culture (e.g., directing needy people to "authorities") while breaking the moral imperative of our humanity (at times these "professionals" were Rocks!). We've not only "helped" Mineral Stagers to harm a lot of people, we've shared our own misappropriated innocence with these *hardened* souls. For example, we've imagined that some of us are indeed godly individuals that deserve others' obedience. We've believed that we then have a right to judge and withhold from those who aren't as good at pretending, but who may be better at revealing the reality underneath the pretense.

In our "youth," we've all been afraid of Rocks and their retaliation. However, with our "infant" vision, we haven't noticed all that has "happened" because of our compliance. Rocks have polluted our air, water, and land such that it mutates, sickens, and kills life and dulls the minds of human survivors. They've contaminated our foods with pesticides, preservatives, pharmaceuticals, and environmental poisons. They've programmed our spouses and children to behave in ways that keep them unhappy, unhealthy, psychically split, relationally competitive, and ever grappling with enemies outside themselves. Rocks have used us to fight their wars, profit their companies, pass on their propaganda, and generally facilitate their agendas to keep the population so immature, ignorant, stressed, and fearful that we don't interfere with their profiting through everyone else's loss. In choosing a modicum of personal comfort or public stature rather than standing up to them, we've become contributors to each cause. (Can you now see the *profound* influence of our "inner children" on our lives? When we seek pleasure, avoid pain, and harshly judge those who follow true Authority *no matter what* the cost, our "inner kids" are at the wheel.)

As we acknowledge the unborn psychological "infant" in the Mineral Stager, we see too that none of us is entirely guilty. When Poli'pops commit global atrocities, they're doing to others what was done to them (psychologically speaking)—what we have all done to varying degrees. When Poli'moms follow "their" programming rather than the requirements for human development, we catch glimpses of our own tendencies to give precedence to schedules and agendas over human need. The maddening (if not DEVASTATING!) incompetence of Poli'lads and Poli'lasses, that we all partake in as images, is an aspect of immaturity and a sincere request for mature, competent guidance. In stark contrast, Rock antagonal leadership compels us to cry out, what our "inner infants" know so well how to do, increasing the likelihood of a listener hearing our distress and responding with prompt rescue.

Arriving "home" from the Red Cross shelter, I plopped myself into one of the raw-wood rocking chairs on the back porch and surveyed the freshly cut hayfields. In the rocking chair beside me sat Felicity's baby doll, which seemed to be viewing the same panorama. As I spoke to Our Rescuer, my mind drifted to my home in New Orleans and then to the people who had been trapped by the floodwater after the Levee Disaster.

Frantic for food and water, they had cried out for help, begging to be rescued, waving down any passerby, yet so few responded. So few! Many people died as a result—physically and psychologically. My mind wandered further back in time, and I saw myself behaving similarly in my lack of response to trauma survivors. I had flashes of people throughout my life who were screaming for attention with their behavior, and I had not met their needs. Suddenly, "the penny dropped," and my eyes flooded with tears.

As a youngest child, I'd been accustomed to looking up to others, seeing them as older and wiser and honoring their wishes, unless these appeared harmful in some way. When I entered the greater community as an "adult" and received training as a psychotherapist, I found many people seemed to reject my offers of psychological aid. In nonclinical settings, I often didn't pause to consider which member of their inner "family" was relating to me—was I hearing programming, conditioning, animal instincts, or their humanity? When people responded to my gestures of help with (1) "I don't need any help," I withdrew. When they sneered (2) "Help from YOU—HA! Don't make me laugh!" I sensed their condescension. When they snapped (3) "If someone needs help, it's YOU!" I felt their cold counsel. When they tried to limit me (4) "Outside of your work, you have no business trying to help me or anyone else!" I accepted their limitations. When they admonished me (5) "If you want to FIX someone, fix yourself!" I worked on myself more diligently. Now as I reflected on all the desperate people in New Orleans who clung to trees or chimneys or sheltered in sweltering attics in their attempts to survive the storm and flood, and who reacted to rescuers with discourtesy or aggression, I realized I had not been listening.

In my heightened post-disaster alertness, I recognized distressed young "kids," "infants," and unborn "children" in each of these people. They had responded to my invitation to help by revealing their problems to me: (1) a belief that they don't need help, the god complex forged by Mascrocks, to which they were clinging for "survival"; (2) a learned "need" to shelter themselves from those offering help, since "help" had been traumatic in the past; (3) a devaluing of whom I represented inside them; (4) a rigid delineation of where help is and where it isn't (Delineation Drive); (5) a learned belief that we fix either "self" or "others," rather than BOTH, who are equally valuable and worthy of development. Uncomprehending at the time, I backed off and withheld further invitations…just like a Femrock! I also was insensitive to how much they were helping me—giving me essential experience, improving my listening skills, *and* sharing vital information for my book.

My heart burned with regret for all the apparently rejecting people I'd walked away from in my wish to respect their choices and boundaries, now realizing I was protecting what I considered my own. In my desire for kindness and my "need" for safety, I judged them as unfriendly or aggressive, rather than wounded people who were also seeking kindness and safety—their experience had just taught them to define these words differently. As I am such a verbal person, I had listened to them in my language, using my words and definitions, when they spoke more truthfully through their body language, as the youngest parts of us do. My responses were based more on where I was than where they were—I weighed my needs more heavily than theirs. I had interpreted the context incorrectly, in terms of "I" and "them," when I was not part of their picture. They weren't talking to ME, they were SHOWING me old "snapshots" from their past—acting out disturbing and painful scenes from their lives. They were too young to discern where I was; they needed me to go where they were and give my sympathy, validation, and feedback on their traumatic events, as well as healing HUMAN touch of body, heart, mind, and spirit. They also clearly required my support and assistance in undoing past learning and trying something new. Listening superficially to their words and honoring their mimicry of past caretakers was not fulfilling their developmental needs—quite the opposite! They needed me to PAY ATTENTION to these snapshots, HEAR their story within them, SEE their past childhood role and their learned "adult" role, FEEL their emotional pain, UNDERSTAND their condition, and then DO something to actively help.

As tears of remorse streamed down my face, I vowed I would not make this mistake again. I know some people are too treacherous to help directly, but I can still help indirectly by listening and caring about their devastating life experiences and connecting them to Our Rescuer within myself. Though Rocky precipices abound, I will not turn my back on fellow disaster survivors, no matter how much, in their traumatized state, they clutch what's unhealthy for them, beg me to leave them alone, or "throw" Rocks to prove their point. They may recoil from my perceiving beyond their facades or "kick," scream, argue, and call me names in their reluctance to be rescued. They may demand what has furnished security in the past or barricade themselves from what *seems* unfamiliar. In my service to Our Rescuer and my growing humanity, I will find the strength to help them—come hell or high water. With this firm determination, I felt my heart swell within my chest, breaking through the small frame that had so long contained it.

Only God Can Effectively Negotiate **ALL** Variables

We are born to help each other, as every nursery baby shows us by crying when another is in distress. Asking for, receiving, and offering help are essential aspects of our humanity that our traumatic experiences have suppressed or distorted in their development. As a result, we don't hear all the cries for help from other undeveloped members of our human family. Listening to them and responding appropriately is no easy task, however, as the "young" of our own inner "families" are also seeking attention. Opportunities for development are missed when "infants" cry out to "infants," and their voices merely grow louder.

As long as we delay treatment for our Rock-victimized parts, however, reenactments of "this is what happened to me" are inevitable, which can be often and extreme. We enter the Closed Loop Program: (1) I must reject help lest I be harmed, as in the past; (2) as long as I reject help, I will unconsciously tell my story of abuse and neglect through body language, attempting to get help; (3) if I get help, I will learn how much suffering I've caused or not alleviated, and I can't face that; (1) I must reject help. This spin keeps us traumatized, traumatizing, *and* ineffectual in our rescuing, while pretending, like the Femrock, that all is well.

Contrary to popular belief, our most mature selves are NOT those who pretend to be above it all, ahead of the pack, free of trauma, or devoid of responsibility when problems arise. The inner Man and Woman aren't pretending! They are able to be WITH it all *comfortably* and do whatever is needed to help, whether rescuing, parenting, or being Parented themselves. (Contrast this with the "infant" leader who sits "above" and mouths orders.) Aware of their own genuine need, mature leaders reach out for and engage the true Authority within all, acknowledging that Our Rescuer, cannot but permeate the entire hierarchy of our imagery. Astoundingly, our "inner infants" with their *big* heads believe they have the power to oust her!

God Is Immeasurable and without Bounds—We Are Finite

As our humanity develops, we arrive at a point where we experience the reality of our image and don't want it anymore. We're willing to relinquish the "protective" barriers we've built to isolate ourselves or give us a feeling of independence from God and our fellowman. We no longer desire to keep the ever-rising waters of our unconscious material at bay. The exorbitant effort to continually maintain the pretense of our imagery is exhausting, and we're ready to let go and let come what may. We finally admit that our fixed adaptations, extreme reactions, rigid restrictions, and frightening defenses we've used to secure ourselves against Rocks have done little to divert them and much to enable them. Indeed, our primitive defense mechanisms have merely made us more Rocklike, more amenable to Rock use, and more abrasive and aloof to our companions.

The behaviors that preserve our feelings of comfort and safety can cause a lack of comfort and safety for others. What to us is personal space may be "standoffishness" or rejection to someone else. A man's expression of interest may meet a woman's definition of sexual harassment. Firm boundaries can seem impenetrable barricades to a person with no such limits. Even the literal locks and bolts, burglar bars, and sturdy walls that secure one individual lead others to disaster when, in a flash flood, they prevent quick escape. Our imitation of others is natural for the "infant" in us, but when these others are Rocks, our behaviors may be so unnatural to our victims that they physically or psychologically die.

Rocks do indeed violate our boundaries. However, by breaching our uncompromising "safety" barriers, we feel some of the pain we've perpetrated. With our defenses down, we then realize we've not only barred people who might have hurt us, but we've also screened out those who would have helped us and may have needed our help. These barricades we've built have interfered with our receiving and giving on so many levels, internally and externally, blocking our abilities to sense, emote, understand, and respond. Thus, the breaching of the poorly built and maintained New Orleans levees that caused extensive flooding and widespread suffering may <u>antagonally direct</u> us to the well-constructed and well-maintained "dikes" of our psychology that, unknown to us, have been causing comparable pain. The human soul is passionate, fiery, and deeply loving in saying exactly what "it" thinks and feels and doing what "it" *truly* wants, making the most of this and every moment. We do "it" such a disservice and cause much distress when we block "it," believing we know better. Damning our humanity is agonizing!

Ruthless Rocks, in impelling us to the far reaches of ourselves, drive us to discover that these far reaches ARE ourselves. By finally claiming ownership, we fully embrace these once-healthy "infants" and "children" who were expelled from their homes of equality, wholeheartedness, and open-mindedness due to chronic abuse and neglect of their physical and psychological bodies. As we rescue them from their disaster sites and extend constant care, they gradually release their tight grasp of people, objects, events, behaviors, feelings, and beliefs from their traumatic pasts that once lent some semblance of safety, so they can be at last removed from harm's way. Our unyielding rigidity *is* harmful!

We are then able to play all personality types. We can relate to people from the part of ourselves that is like them, whether Man, Woman, Child, Animal, Vegetable, or Mineral, and from there know their needs. If interaction with a certain character would be useful to them, we can offer this. If the opposite character type is suddenly useful, we can extend this as well. Whatever they require to advance their development or temporarily regress to pick up lost pieces, we can comply in our acceptance and versatility with all that we are. This complete flexibility is psychological maturity, which so often arises from the rubble created by Rocks. Where there is no power to be grabbed, no glory to bask in, no monetary wealth to be amassed, and yet the potential for even more Rocky times awaits on the horizon, mature women and men appear. (I thought of dear Gutje flying all the way from the Netherlands to help.) These genuine leaders are willing to do WHATEVER is necessary, as directed by Our Rescuer, just because it needs to be done.

The Business of *Relationship*: God Is All-Engaging in Giving Himself
We Are Discriminatory in Our Image Sales

I find that most people don't want to stick their noses in "other people's" business under the assumption that these are indeed "other" people. They don't want anyone interfering with "their" business, applying similar reasoning. They also presume that what is within them is their own, while what comes from outside them is foreign. This use of the self/other or subject/object Definition Lock greatly undermines daily opportunities for the intimate exchange of our humanity that is so necessary for psychological development. Valuing possessions more than possession of self, we may more commonly relate by giving, receiving, and employing things, inevitably craving more and more of them in an effort to generate feelings of self-worth. Rocks and Minerals are the extreme example, bringing great nations to bankruptcy, reducing cities to ruin, and causing ineffable suffering and loss to millions as they seek still more personal gain. They never stop plotting and scheming, plundering and pillaging, in an attempt to meet their imagined "needs" at the expense of all life. Our world's resources, including human beings, cannot long withstand the onslaught of such unquenchable desires.

In contrast, what would our society be like if we pursued psychological growth with the same intensity we currently devote to material gain? Imagine! Our authorities would institute standards that *enliven* all aspects of our humanity. The media would demonstrate and teach genuine communication skills where "value" and "success" are defined in terms of human development. News would be accurate, offered in a creative and personally moving manner. ("Let's take a moment to ponder what this latest government corruption might be mirroring within ourselves.") The legal system would have a balanced and just approach, highlighting criminals' traumatic pasts as well as their guilt in reenacting the crimes of their caretakers, literally or figuratively. Convicts would receive PTSD treatment as well as proper parenting to hustle their psychological growth. (To a Rock, this punishment would be torture!) Meanwhile, medical institutions would listen to the body's communications in every symptom and disease process and respond to these requests for change. Health-care professionals would also screen for Rocks, outside and inside, that are punishing bodies and body parts that remind them of their traumas.

In schools, cafeterias would serve only the healthiest foods so students develop the habit of giving their bodies what's best for them. Emotionally mature teachers would model how to tune into and share feelings, assisting students in the practice of emotional expression that is sensitive to individual need. School curricula would require that pupils learn how to think, to question, and to notice propaganda and various methods of indoctrination to avoid being harmed by them. They would learn to recognize Our Rescuer in one another and admit her help. Schools would have ongoing classes in relationship skills, sharing difficulties and offering techniques for surmounting them. Stress management and PTSD courses would be mandatory, so students would anticipate and work through the inevitable stresses and traumas of living in this Rocky world. They would also receive instructions and demonstrations on the stages of psychological developmental. Students would explore the universe inside, as well as outside, and study its full array of characters, adventures, achievements, shortfalls, pitfalls, and endless lessons. These pupils of life would come to appreciate their exquisite, multifaceted, ever-seeking-to-evolve humanity in relation to all that is and to esteem its play, study, work, and development as priceless.

While Mineral Stagers turn their families into businesses that sell the Rocks' "pristine" images, businesses run by psychological adults would be like families. Employees' psychological age would be assessed, and people would obtain what they need to grow—incentives, promotions, and bonuses would be based on their maturation, as well as work performance. "The best" would *not* be automatically bestowed on those with the most money, but on those who would make the best use of it. With businesses, institutions, and other places of employment prioritizing human development, every aspect of society would evolve. Regular encounters with wise counselors at the office or in the neighborhood would become as routine as trips to the store or hair salon. (Businesses would hire ONLY people who are working on themselves!) *And* our religious institutions would have us tithing out of the abundance of our human inheritance—our skills, talents, and time—to the spiritual temple that resides within us all.

In such a human-development-based culture, our daily priority would be to rear "children" wherever we find them and return them to their Parent. Only then will our domestic, educational, economic, medical, legal, political, and religious issues subside. Contrary to Corp'rocks' insistence that *they* are selling what we need, proper parenting is actually the single most important commodity in all our interpersonal and commercial transactions, *and* it cannot be manufactured! The desperate demands of our "inner infants," whether housed in greedy leaders and businesspersons or in needy followers and consumers, DO NOT STOP *until* these "babies'" cries for psychological parenting are heard and responded to!

Parenting the most psychologically immature is particularly challenging. Just as an embryo and fetus are surrounded by mom twenty-four hours a day, the Rock requires extensive exposure to parental figures who can psychologically nourish all aspects of him. These "parents" must balance the Rock's extreme "masculine" and "feminine" positions—aggression and passivity, hyperactivity and inactivity, inflexibility and spineless flaccidity, and so on. They also must balance what the Rock reflects about their own areas of excess and absence, such as their inability to effectively manage their own lives (We ALL need Our Rescuer!).

When we are under the management of our all-incorporating Rescuer, our extremes are tempered, and credit is given equally to body, heart, and mind. Our focus then changes from individually making, spending, and saving money to collectively saving, tending, and raising lives, a shift that may seem expensive at times (especially when rescuing Rocks!) but is FAR less costly in the long run and **FAR** more lucrative. Human life contains, feeds, comforts, instructs, and enlivens one another so much more than our imaginations or any precious metals we might temporarily hold in our hands or safe-deposit boxes. As the dollar continues to lose value, may the currency exchange of our humanity take its place! As our "inner babies" are esteemed more than objects and money, as demonstrated by our consistent meeting of their HUMAN needs, these true needs overpower the artificial programmed and conditioned needs. Our "infants" then remember their overwhelming desire for close, *human* contact.

COMPUTERS: God Is the Creator of Life
Without Him, We Are Programs and Programmers ⬜⬜ ⊢→⬝⬜ ↕⌣. ⋠⌄∘⬜⌟⊢→Ŧ⌟

True human services are the predictable outcomes when we interact with Our Parent and our fellow *human* beings. In contrast, fixed programs or false RV MALware are the output when we mimic or mock these interactions. By the time we reach physical maturity, most of us have had such extensive downloads of these imitations that we've been conditioned, if not brow-beaten, into placing image in the power position and believing that those who've built up their images are the most powerful people ("My image is bigger than your image!"). Just as children are incapable of standing up to the abuse and neglect they receive from "adults," we as mere images cannot stand against the formidable, pathological system of Rocks and Minerals. The "there's nothing I can do about it!" motto of the Femrock is certainly true of lone images.

Our computers may at times act like people to show us the way out of our mechanical thinking, feeling, and behaving. Our Rescuer may be nudging us beyond our expectations of programmed responses from others too. When we ourselves are programmed, we forget that human beings naturally vacillate over time depending on what is going on, in and outside themselves. We don't realize that people NEED to express the fullness of their experience. We are oblivious to people's great sensitivity to their environment and their reflection of or transparency to others' inner states (windows!). We humans are equipped to perceive and respond to any situation in multitudinous ways—we get tired, flustered, overwhelmed, passionate, and silly, while machines do not. Sometimes our own mechanical functioning, which is itself a malfunction, necessitates our instrumentation acting aberrantly to point out what we're doing!

In the automatic mode, we are not causes, but effects, like images produced by computer programs. When we investigate our computers, however, we can see that what happens on the screen is the result of many pieces and programs, hardware and software working together; a defect in any part may manifest as a problem on the screen. The person at the keyboard may also have produced a problem. We never blame the imagery on the screen because we know the images are but effects of the machine or the person interacting with it. So are we!

By empowering the individual images on our mind's "screen" with our attention and belief, our morbid fear of psychological "infants" makes sense—they can indeed behave ABOMINABLY! Another choice, however, is to attend to the "circuitry" of the mind that is currently projecting these scary images. This individual mind is but a simulation of our united Mind that we as individuals have been walking around in, experiencing "its" contents, attaching ourselves to or detaching from, and coming to terms with, but not recognizing "it" as such. We can thus transform any binary language into communications of greater Mind and separated mind, respectively—the Whole or a tiny fragment or pixel. The psychological journey is, of course, the path to Wholeness. It requires that we include all the pixels of our imagery, so we can view the rainbow-colored fullness of ourselves on the screen in any moment and know the extent of our thoughts. *When we're deeply listening, our imagery shows us what's on our minds!*

Rocks can only program us when we prefer "computer"-generated imagery to our genuine Identity. They overpower us when we "underpower" this constant source of help. Rocks impact or crush us when we are rigid and unyielding to Our Rescuer's instructions. They impose Rock business practices on us when we evade the business of human relationship and its development, and they poison us and our neighborhoods when we choose toxins for our own bodies, hearts, and minds. Rocks cause us pain when they kindle the painful Rocky conditions within ourselves, such as our Auto-Hide of the One beyond the "screen." As the grip of the Feedback Loop loosens upon our minds, we can listen to this deeper messaging. Within Rocks' utter unwillingness to alter "their" programmed way with us, we hear the caring transmissions from Our Rescuer who wills that we alter "our" way with her—for safety's sake!

Oh—the power of our minds! Through them, we have the ability to "disable macros" and experience mere images as vital, ubiquitous, solid, long lasting, and powerful—creating significant and irrevocable effects. Meanwhile, the Almighty and Eternal, the only true Power Source, APPEARS unsubstantiated, fleeting, unreliable, or ineffectual. ("If God really exists, why is *His* world in such TURMOIL?") Our freedom lies in our realization that everything on the "screen" is an effect of this choice we make in every moment—Who or what is causal? (Upon Whom or what do we project Movie #1?) Rocks can no longer hold us hostage with their threats of injury, sickness, destruction, or death when we choose the true Power and Person beyond the "screen." All the tactics with which Rocks terrorize us can't touch us when we don't believe in the potency of imagery. Images only have the power of our belief!

Supporting Rocks in our fear or blaming them in our anger is yet much easier than looking at what they're mirroring within our own psychology. For instance, their preoccupation with minutiae (the Confounder), petty differences (Difference Drive), inconsequential "problems" (Delineation Drive), and absurd causality (Reality Reversal Program) is much like our own obsession with our image. They design events that "PROVE" what they want us to "understand," just as we use our lives to prove that we as individuals are real and have power to help, heal, and evolve *or* to hurt, sicken, and destroy.

Rocks thrust us into personal experience of "life" as imagery: we feel powerless, valueless, unfulfilled, and unfulfilling. We then have the motivation to choose a better Life for ourselves and extend this Life to images everywhere! (It's "safe to remove HARDware!") We merely use imagery to comprehend the Significance, Reality, and Power beyond it or to process our blocks! Just as Rocks have wasted a tremendous amount of our time and energy on inane or destructive activities, we have wasted Life with our insistence on "computer" imagery outside us and with our resistance to its illustration of what's inside us. After all, the inside is a frame or compressed file of the outside. Likewise, the outside is what's inside, magnified in high definition so our "inner infants" might see it better and learn to pay attention.

NATURAL SCIENCE: God Is Ever Present and **Unalterable** People **Can** *and* **MUST** Change!

Although I was sheltered in Greensburg, the major hurricane and flood endured by my New Orleans home made an impact on me. For example, I was altering some of my automatic behaviors. As far as my memory serves me, I've never been a morning person, but I was adapting and no longer spending so much time lounging in bed before rising. Now when the sun comes up, so do I. In the evenings, I commune with others, a change compelled by the darkness while the electricity was off (it's hard to read in the dark!). I have developed the habit of talking to my mother on the telephone every day. Also, I'm more frequently checking my activities with Our Rescuer inside me, and I've become more attentive to hearing her instruction through others as well. My delusions of autonomy, independence, and capacity as an image have, temporarily I'm sure, washed away with the floodwaters. Some of my internal "levees" that I erected and fortified for "safety" have breached, and I've become more aware of JUST HOW MUCH I've been keeping my distance from all that is around me. Having watched my stranded fellow New Orleanians desperately waiting to be rescued, I'm ever more keenly aware of the urgency of everyone's rescue, my own included—there's no time to waste!

Just as the paths and effects of hurricanes can be predicted with a good degree of accuracy, so can the paths and effects of Rocks and Minerals. Notice stagnant communities where residents believe there's no need to alter the status quo, and you'll know where Rocks have laid the groundwork. In contrast, we human beings can move ourselves, as in avoiding hurricanes. We can adapt to new circumstances, such as our evacuation sites. When we're separated from our loved ones, we can connect with and grow to love those close by. We can also make the extra effort to bridge the distance with those far away...or seemingly so, such as the unacknowledged aspects of ourselves.

Understanding the petrifaction of those stuck in the Mineral Stage, and their parallels with geological rocks and minerals, leads us to the realization that everything in our inner natural world has external representation. We are not independent of our globe, or vice versa. Similarly, nothing in this world just "happens," as Rocks would have us believe. All things exist and occur for one another and are in intimate relationship with each other, engaging according to the maturity of that relationship.

Our external circumstances are a reflection of our inner selves, and by "listening," we can come to know the parts of our inner landscapes and members of our internal "family." For example, the inanimate realm may represent the stuck, traumatically frozen, psychologically unborn within us. The plant kingdom may be a metaphor for our injured "inner infants," who are not-yet-mobile of heart and mind. Animals in our world may manifest our wounded internal "preschoolers." Healthy human beings in these age-groups may mirror these healthy aspects of our "inner family." Dysfunctional and diseased people may also correspond to parts of ourselves. Of course, not everything in our world fits into these stratifications, but neither does everything in our inner experience. As long as we cling to an image as our identity and defend its impulses as "my way," there will be storms, entropy, pathogens, and so forth to encourage us to move through the "concrete" and become more abstract and less delineating in our experiencing and assessing.

Tragically, all the imaginative and traumatically induced mental "drawings" and beliefs of our "inner children," the poor attention and distress of our "inner infants," and the programming of our "unborn babies" have confused our minds SO MUCH that we don't realize we're interacting with ourselves—undivided Self or individual image. What else is there? Well, the Rock's core of rage comes to mind. Just as Rocks often isolate their victims, we, in our anger, have secluded ourselves from our true Identity and exiled ourselves in this precarious world. Just as Rocks deny us accurate information, we've kept ourselves ignorant of basic facts (Fooling "facts" of the Circumvention

Program). For example, most of us don't grasp that what we've been researching, evacuating from, dominating, wrestling with, and adapting to, is Self, who has been persistent in alerting us to our folly.

When we recognize that our undivided Self is expressing "its" Nature in all things *or* that we're perceiving the vicissitudes of "our" own individual nature, even weather can participate in our evolutionary process. For instance, Hurricane Katrina has moved a population into new territory, outside as well as INSIDE. Everything in our world can support the developmental life of human beings if properly anticipated, perceived, and channeled. Thus, Mineral Stagers can also be instrumental to our global awakening...when we're listening.

Rocks may be heard <u>antagonally communicating</u> our potential for swift change by their fast depletion of reserves the earth has built up over millennia, their speedy demolition of civilizations that have been cultivated over centuries, and their rapid ruining of lives that have been nurtured over decades. Within a psyche, quick, *constructive* change is merely a matter of choice—choosing Our Rescuer to guide *and* live AND BE our lives. Our collective growth then is like the movements of our earth that push rocks to the surface and alter their form, turning them into landscapes of natural beauty, firm foundations for our homes, and a supply of raw materials for so much of what we might want or need. When our Rock parts so shift and transform, we know NOTHING as permanent, unalterable, insensitive, or set in stone. And Mother Nature seems a lot friendlier too.

TEXTBOOKS: Our Rescuer Is the *Unassailable Superhero!*

As with any classroom teacher, Our Rescuer gives us daily assignments to alert us to the important teaching contained in our lives. As in this book, every scene has an accompanying multilayered text, where the level of comprehension is up to us. I'm trained in developmental psychology, so I read my life seeking this content, but you can peruse yours with any orientation, any depth, and in search of any answers. Once we know our walls are artificial and Our Rescuer and Teacher lies beyond each one, we can find instruction anywhere. For example, I've illustrated psychological teaching through daily encounters and common aspects of each of our lives. As I gleaned the information I needed to write this book through my daily "listening," you too may discover everything you need coming to you—whether advice on how to be a good spouse and parent, how to make the latest scientific breakthrough, or how to expand a small paycheck to pay big bills. Try it—it works! The more we practice hearing Our Rescuer, the more we notice that every aspect of our lives and selves is being addressed, guided, and educated—honorably and fairly—in every moment!

Like every beginner, we must practice diligently before we can read our lives with proficiency. Ultimately we'll be not only listening to and learning from EVERYTHING (Select All Program!), but acting on this instruction and evolving ourselves/our world at the same time. My journaling, for instance, is about a factual segment of my life with fictional elements woven in to cover for those who didn't wish to be a part of my story. Which specific facets I've chosen to write about and how I've expressed them show a lot about my own mind and heart. My psychology is represented in every setting, every plot, every theme, and every man, woman, child, animal, vegetable, AND mineral, as is your psychology with your life story. The conditions of our hearts and minds must influence everything we touch, feel, perceive, and think about. For example, if a person is sad, she may put together letters to spell "sad," as Felicity did in our Scrabble game after the hurricane. If a person is angry, he may see angry pictures, such as Oliver was drawing after the Levee Disaster. When we're longing for our true Identity, we may concentrate on heroics, like Felicity staring at Wonder Woman on her book cover. And if we're reared in a Rocky culture, the imprint of which is still on us, we will inevitably draw to us those who "help" us recall, grieve, and process the pain of our storms and disasters. Remember, no part of ourselves or our experience can be missing if we are to know our home in Wholeness.

The Reunion: God Is Faithful

I peered into the distance at Effie's old live-oak tree. Its broken trunk lay on the ground beside the one still standing. "It's still there, but it's not connected," I thought, realizing the same is true for all the disowned aspects of our psychology. A car turning onto Effie's driveway diverted me from my internal discourse. "JAYDA!" I jumped out of my rocking chair and ran toward her, waving my arms in greeting as I watched Jayda's rental car slowly traverse the long, unpaved drive. Only four weeks had passed since Pookie and I were last with her, but it seemed like years! I jogged beside her car for the last bit of the journey.

The car door opened and travel-weary Jayda pulled herself out. We hugged for a long time, as we both seemed to need it.

"How are you? How was your trip?" Many questions filled my mind, but I limited myself to two.

"Life's been crazy, but the flight and drive were easy. Thanks for warning me about the tree branch over the road that looks like it could fall at any time. Luckily for me it didn't." She grabbed her floral tapestry carry-on and followed me into the garage. Her small piece of luggage was quite a contrast to Emily's…or Pookie's!

"Do you want to come in the house and meet Effie?" I asked.

Jayda frowned. "Would it be OK if I saw my Pookie first?"

"Of course, she's right here inside the garden shed."

Jayda released her bag, picked up her pace, and within seconds I was witnessing an ever-so-tender reunion. Pookie emerged instantly from her dark corner, and Jayda grabbed her, slowly lifting into her arms the enormous, weighty, wild-eyed creature with claws extended. Jayda cuddled her with great affection and many sweet words, stroking Pookie's fur with her cheek, as Pookie purred loudly.

Jayda's gorgeous, shiny red hair was quite a contrast against her cat's dusty, cobweb-laden black coat. Jayda's hair was probably her most striking feature—long, thick, and wavy—it always looked like she had just left the salon. Whenever someone inquires about her secret, she shrugs and says, "Heredity—I got it from my mom."

"My sweet baby," Jayda whispered as her eyes filled with tears, and Pookie closed her eyes, seemingly in contentment. "Thank God, you're OK!" I suddenly remembered that the dozen or more street cats that Jayda had been so faithfully feeding had no doubt perished in the flood.

What we are doing with our bodies may be symbolic of what we need to do with our psychology. For instance, traveling, whether by plane or car, has parallels in our inner world—we need to use public and private "transportation," social settings and solitude, to delve into our psychology. Also, the activities of others, such as Jayda choosing to see Pookie before meeting Effie, can reveal similar dynamics inside ourselves—we may be requiring a comforting relationship after a major trauma, we may be emphasizing our animal nature rather than what's human within us, or there may be an urgency to reclaim our nonhuman selves. There are SO MANY interpretive possibilities! When we ignore our inner life and don't comprehend the external metaphors that would bring it to our attention, demands and difficulties outside of us often increase. However, the more we work on the inside while also working on the outside, the more the requirements of both become doable or even easy.

As we offer the same time, attention, care, understanding, and ready responses to our inner scape as to our outer environment, our two worlds come together and finally integrate. Our complex outer world, full of many lives and a multitude of things needed to keep the many lives happy, healthy, and constructively occupied, dematerializes while our internal world gains substance. Outer and inner experiences become fluid, both reflecting our Self or self—as we choose. The more we prioritize our united Self, the more our blurry "infant" vision acquires focus. Slowly but surely we recognize a Spiritual Body around us—One that seems strangely familiar and frighteningly irresistible. Time and space dissolve as we forget our claim to an adult image, and we become conscious of our true identity as a spiritual being in infancy. To our delight, what we had perceived to be a vast universe to explore in excitement or to shield ourselves from in apprehension was none other than Our Divine Mother offering sustenance— Herself—to her unaware unborn child.

Our Mother never left us! (The most evolved life-forms actively parent until their children are grown in ALL ways.) She's responded to our distress regardless of whether we remained silent, made a request, or issued an order. She's been protecting us from our active imaginations that so readily turn our joyous, secure, ever-nurturing, and beatific experience of Her into an uncertain, scary place where we struggle to get our needs met. The upside-down positioning of each not-yet-born psychological "baby" leads him to experience himself in the power position—acting on and in his imaginary "world." The immature caretakers and authorities there have merely been playacting these musings of his mind—entertaining the possibility of a child preceding the Parent and usurping Her/His role!   (**"YOU CAN'T MAKE ME!"**)

As with infants in the nursery, the distress of this spiritual babe has echoed in many locations: in our government and corporate corruptions, in our computer and car malfunctions, and in our many personally traumatic events. Because of our static-laden "radio stations" and our preoccupations resulting from our PTSD, we haven't heard him. Our resonating "inner children" and "infants," wanting ALL of their Parent (both Masculine AND Feminine Sides), have been using our "computer" screen imagery to make their desire known and to express their anguish when it is unsatisfied. *But,* when this one true Need is at last fulfilled, they settle down in contentment, and we ourselves are birthed OUT of this largely inanimate world!

Our Mascrock's relentless exacerbation of need comes to an end as his needs are now perfectly met. He is contained by a Body that has no fear of what he might do, as She heals it all instantly. And he is at last soothed and saved from his CATASTROPHICALLY traumatic life.[2] Our Femrock traits of fixed, one-sided attention ("Let's just look at the BRIGHT side!") and undying devotion that have been so detrimental when applied to situations and people, are essential in relation to Our Divine Mother. As we then allow the Femrock's valuable function in our lives, her unwavering loyalty shifts to One truly worthy of it.

The wounds and afflictions that these Rocks have endlessly re-created, then denied, or dismissed as unimportant, are all tended by this greater Being with whom these youngest of humans find complete satisfaction and healing. In Her, we find our lost will and way, our human voice, our genuine feelings, our original thoughts, and the eye of every storm. All our worldly needs, which Rocks have been so malicious in denying or manipulating, melt into this one true underlying Need—our Need for Our Mother (The Choice Commander Program has never included this selection!). All other needs are symbolic of what Our Mother offers. (The Confounder program has made addressing human need seem SO complicated!) Separation from Our Mother is what our "inner babies" and "children" have been so strongly reacting to! They accept no substitutes, as She alone has the power to clean up all messes, restore all losses, "shatterproof" our psyches, and return us to a completely healthy, mature, HUMAN identity where we THRIVE! The contentment of the entire family of our psychology then radiates out...and we rock our world!

God Moves through Us

Jayda and I decided to go for a walk. We encouraged Connie to join us, and she told us to get started—she'd catch up shortly. We set off across the now fully harvested hayfields as Jayda filled me in on her activities since we were last together.

"After my conference, I flew to Natchez, as did Jeremie, for a little family reunion and to talk about where to go from here. Austin's greeting was cold. He hugged Jeremie, then me stiffly and then walked away to clean his new Suburban—he gives his car a quick clean every day, whether it needs it or not. That afternoon his mom, Willa, took Jeremie shopping so Austin and I could have a little time alone. While I slipped on some of my sexy new clothes I bought in New York, he sat down at his computer. Do you know he spent our entire time together trying to find the best font and color combination to fill out his FEMA papers? I tried everything—a back rub, foot massage, and even whispering in his ear didn't faze him in the slightest—like I wasn't there. In fact, at one point, the computer told him he had committed a 'fatal error,' and he got pissed at *me*—saying I'd caused it! It's freaky that Austin turned into a roaring lion over his computer locking up, when everything we've been through—the storm, the flood, losing our home, the deaths, and his decision to be in the middle of it all with his mom—was nothing, like a walk in the park!" A dismayed Jayda shook her head before continuing.

"This has been a nightmare for all of us, but some people lean on and support one another when there's trouble." Jayda pointed to the precarious broken pine branch overhead that was being held up by a neighboring pecan tree. "Other people are 'gone pecans'—they're just unreachable. Being with Jeremie again was wonderful, but Austin, no matter what, I can't count on him...I guess I never could."

"Have any of your therapists been able to get through to him at all?" I asked, knowing that Jayda had dragged Austin to quite a few over the years.

"I don't think I ever got through to any of *them*...about just how wounded Austin is and how painful what he does is for Jeremie and me. The way he isolates himself is just as painful as his verbal punches. Our therapists seemed satisfied that he has a solid job and pays the bills, as if this is all he needs to do. But I need more than a tepid body, I need a warm heart, like I give him. Oddly enough, I keep waking up feeling like this new day may be different—better somehow. After all, as long as there's warm sunshine, my plants are growing. But nothing changes with Austin. So my gut is telling me I'm the one who has to change."

"What are you going to do, Jayda?" I inquired, after giving her a pregnant pause.

"I'm going to leave Austin and try living on my own for a while. This was one of the suggestions of my therapists—'love him or leave him.' Well, there are a lot more choices than that, but I feel at a loss of what else to do. Jeremie is going to stay with her friend Monica in Houston to finish her school year, then she'll be off to college. This disaster made me realize that we've got to go for what we want in our lives right now. I need some training in how to respond to the stressed bodies I'll be massaging, and there's a course in PTSD in New York City that starts in two weeks. Getting away for a while should help me see if this choice is going to work out."

"It feels good…to get some exercise and take a nice walk…I've been so preoccupied with everything going on…it hasn't occurred to me…to just enjoy this lovely area," Connie said, short of breath, having jogged to catch up with us. Her fair and delicate complexion was now red and ruddy.

We sauntered on, chatting, while I observed Jayda caressing the plants and trees with her hands, at times as if petting Pookie. She seemed to notice every branch, bud, and bug, while taking in the smells. (Jayda had told me numerous times, "Nature is my favorite therapist.") Glassy-eyed Connie appeared on the verge of tears, her brow deeply furrowed. I guessed Mother Nature was extending her therapeutic techniques to her as well.

I mused about how different the three of us were. Petite, blue-eyed, blond, upper-class Connie is always immaculately groomed in designer fashions. She's an LSU football fan, housewife, and mother who is active in the Parent Teacher Association and her Pentecostal church (not necessarily in that priority). Tall, big boned, redheaded, gray-eyed Jayda is a massage therapist, community activist, feminist, animal lover, and gardener. She had a carefree, "hippie"-type wardrobe and manner in mothering her one human offspring. Only Jayda's hair seemed organized…and Pookie's corner of the utility room.

I have shoulder-length brown, curly hair and hazel eyes. I am a retired psychiatrist who enjoys studying books for their psychological and spiritual content, as well as "reading" whatever comes into view. For as far back as I can remember, I've preferred reading and writing to physical activity. That's a long time! I figure the Levee Disaster has altered this lifelong pattern. Volunteering at the Red Cross shelter was a start, and now Connie has asked me to assist at her church in Jefferson Parish, where she and the kids have been volunteering part-time for the past two weeks. The ministers there are requesting counseling professionals to talk with people while they wait in their cars to pick up the food, water, and cleaning supplies the church is giving away. Connie, Oliver, and Felicity will resume their work in the gym, making care packages from these essential items that are being donated by churches all over the world.

Yep, we're different all right, and I'm betting our past traumas have something to do with some of these differences. Without conscious effort, our disasters and our reactions to them so often separate, restrict, and label us for life, as we compulsively perpetuate reenactments, judgments, and evacuations. For example, four weeks ago, we were one people, New Orleanians. Now there is Connie from Lakeview, Jayda from New Orleans East, and Anne from Broadmoor, as these neighborhoods reveal the extent of our traumatic experience and loss.

Disasters CAN also profoundly connect us, if we let them, since trauma is something we all have in common. These two women and I have shared an emergency evacuation, the wreckage of our homes and city, and the resulting loss of life. (I heard my mother's voice in my head bemoaning, "If they'd only built the levees right!") Along with other New Orleanians, we've experienced a special bond and camaraderie during these stressful times, as well as an expectation for a future in which we rebuild our homes, neighborhoods, and lives together. These similarities carry so much more weight than our many superficial differences.

God Is Permanent—SHe Is What Is Unchangeable in Us

Connie lurched forward, bringing me out of my musings. "I tripped on a rock," she muttered, a look of embarrassment on her sad face. I noticed the metaphor, aware that Connie, Jayda, and I have all been tripped up by the Rocks in our lives, outside and inside, and at times, shoved ahead.

Connie began sharing her day. "I took the kids to the library so they could see the satellite pictures of our neighborhood online. I thought viewing our now-vacant lot from a distance might help them with the transition before we see it in person. Besides, their friends are doing it and talking about it. Well," Connie said, sighing, "there was no sign of our house, just like Cedric said—he's my husband, Jayda. When I consider how my friends have told me over the past few years that I need to get out of the house more—well, I'm finally out."

Jayda smiled and nodded as if to say she had moved from her comfort zone as well. "I have a hard time with all the talk—I'm a hands-on kind of person," she confided. "I have to experience what people are saying in order to get it. I need to look at the condition of my house with my own eyes and get a whiff of the musty, moldy stench before it will sink in. I need to sit in the yard and pat the once beautiful green lawn that my husband kept perfectly manicured, but now is dead grass. I need to hear, see, smell, and touch with my own physical body—words and pictures are not enough for me."

As we continued our walk in silence, I pondered the word "experience." Isn't our experience what gives meaning and life to words and pictures? Here we were walking the same terrain side by side, yet each of us was experiencing it differently based on our training from past experiences. As I perceived the situation, Jayda was connecting with her external "therapist," Connie was feeling her loss, and I was writing clinical notes on a loose page of my mind. One setting was engendering multiple unique and equally valid experiences and responses. This is also true of all parts of our selves—the physical, emotional, mental, and spiritual. We must own them all if we are to receive all the words and pictures, appreciate the Whole of our life's story, and wholly follow along.

HORROR: Life without God and Ourselves

While the majority of New Orleans residents are mourning their homelessness and the loss of their property, very few people actively grieve the apparent butchering, dismemberment, and sacrifice of our united humanity that we reenact daily, and the staggering scale of this loss. Our essential material belongings will be repaired or replaced sooner or later, but most of us go to our graves embracing only a tiny fragment of who we are. We admire each other's collections of coins, stamps, ceramics, rocks and minerals, and so on, but we rarely appreciate those who are busy collecting lost pieces of themselves. When authorities and news agencies fail to inform citizens of imminent danger, leaving them to drown in their sleep, we are aghast. When we fail to awaken our fellow humans, standing by while they perish in their misperceptions and misinformation, few, if any, notice (we're more likely to be alarmed by those attempting to awaken us! [Care Alarms]). When we are unwilling or unable to fulfill such human obligations, we are then dependent on Mother Nature and the trauma-induced "nature" of man to do the rousing.

While Mineral Stagers are relentless in passing on the abuse and neglect they have sustained, even those who routinely aid their fellowman are rarely as unrelenting in their benevolent actions. To achieve this tenacity, we must have access to our Mineral parts. When our Mineral parts are integrated, we can merge all of our skill sets and purposefully and consistently help one another— again, and *again*, and AGAIN, and **AGAIN**… We can also be selective in sharing our life's horrors— VERBALLY(!) *and* only when therapeutically or relationally useful.

If an illness was known to be attacking and handicapping the vast majority of our population, there would be a general outcry demanding that scientists work diligently for a cure. Yet rarely do we recognize that our personalities have fragmented from trauma and the different aspects have succumbed to various degrees of post-traumatic stress disorder. The multiple forms of trauma we have all endured and adapted to seldom come up in conversation and at best are referenced indirectly: "our war veterans..." All of us individuals have battled over our very hearts and minds. We've been wounded with lasting injuries and have further limited ourselves by our efforts to compensate without addressing the underlying cause.

PTSD is epidemic in our country since consistently mature parents who naturally protect children are in such short supply. Traumatic reenactments are widespread, evidenced not only by domestic violence statistics, but by the extensive neglect and abuse of human need that occurs regularly in schools, churches, businesses, and governments. Denying people the information they require to successfully negotiate the psychological world is a good example. Statistics attest that neglected and abused children without treatment "grow up" to harm their own family or to marry such a perpetrator. With our "infant" vision, however, we're unaware that traumatized "children" go on to use classrooms, pulpits, police beats, companies, and political offices to victimize large populations, or to zealously defend those who do. *And* we don't register the snowballing CATASTROPHIC costs of allowing these once-human voices to limp through life unheard as their behavior SCREAMS for attention. Hearing them, we will feel horror, outrage, terror, and seemingly bottomless grief; but ultimately we find compassion, as we realize Rocks and Minerals are merely disaster victims...still waiting...after all these years...to be rescued.

Untreated trauma leaves us psychologically mutilated and undeveloped, which colors EVERYTHING we experience, say, and do. We must then encounter trauma-induced traits within our fellowman and express these at times ourselves. For example, when we acknowledge, interact with, and respect the wishes of the most dominant parts of people's personalities—rather than serving the whole—we often support their post-traumatic stress disorder. Also, as long as we choose an individual image as our identity, cutting ourselves off from our true Self, we must repeatedly draw abuse and neglect to us in reenactment of this traumatic choice. Each "inner infant" with PTSD then clings to his or her image and its possessions, much like Mandy clutching her clothes, her only belongings that survived.

EVACUATION DAY 30: When We Withdraw from God, We Separate from Our Support, Maturity, Power, Help, and Healing

Having few possessions has advantages. I was packed in no time and was the first to show up the next morning for our last Greensburg breakfast. I perused a favorite psychology book as I ate muesli with fresh pomegranate from one of Effie's trees.

Immaculately dressed in a rose-colored pantsuit, Connie seated herself with a chocolate Slim-Fast bar and cup of coffee. Jayda, in khaki shorts and a floral tee, followed shortly with a plate of soft-boiled eggs and toast and a glass of orange juice in her hands. Dr. Bear was at our feet, eagerly awaiting leftovers, while I anticipated psychological nutrition from my companions.

"Don't tell me—let me guess...ah...hmm...psychology?" Jayda appeared to be in good spirits, poking fun at my light-reading material as she massaged my "stiff as a board!" shoulders.

Connie commented, "I've never cared for psychology—it seems so nebulous compared to the tangible here-and-now physical world." Being present to the physical was a struggle for an intellectual like me, so I took a moment to be more attentive, noticing that Connie held her breakfast bar with a perfectly manicured hand.

"Yeah," Jayda agreed. "You can reach out for the physical and grab hold of it." She grabbed my book and tossed it onto an empty chair. "You can sink your teeth into it." Jayda took a bite of toast and chewed before continuing. "I went to my first therapist when I was in college, and I thought it was all a bunch of 'psychobabble'—like mist in the air. But psychology started to sink in when I practiced bodywork. I finally absorbed what I'd been taught because I was experiencing the physical displays of my clients' psychological issues—up close and personal. So much stuff comes up for people during a massage. I put rosemary under their noses to calm them or add an essential oil or two into the massage cream to help the emotional release. But I've never really met their woundedness with my own or touched them on that level. I've felt that I should maintain professional boundaries and keep my distance; I'm licensed as a massage therapist, NOT a counselor! Yet since this horrible disaster, I sense that helping another is just being human—imagine that! Do we really need a license to be ourselves?!

"Once I was massaging a client when I heard my neighbor practicing commands with his dog. My client said, 'Play that lovely waterfall CD,' and then, 'Work on my painful pelvis.' During the session, I was saying things like 'relax' and 'turn onto your back.' This wasn't much different than my neighbor's 'fetch,' 'come,' 'lie down,' and 'roll over.' My gut told me that human relations are something more, and we should expect more from each other. As Jeremie came home at that moment, I sensed that we should be treating one another more like family members we expect to grow old with and for whom we feel responsible for making sure that happens." Jayda returned to her breakfast.

"Psychology has led me to the same conclusions," I said. "It's the method I've found most grounding. It gives meaning to what seems meaningless and clarity to what appears incomprehensible—such as extreme violence and wide-scale destruction. Without psychology, the physical world seems so precarious and unpredictable. With it, I know that whatever happens CAN have a positive purpose—we can always use it to grow ourselves."

Connie added, "But don't forget the heart and its powerful feelings. For me, Spirit dwells in my heart—that's where I find God's grace and peace amidst any upheaval."

Jayda resumed, "In my PTSD course, we'll have live demonstrations with patients and group discussions in the morning, and then we'll have practical application in the clinic in the afternoon. I'll get some hands-on experience in using this new material with my massage clients. This is what I need—my hands on a client's skin, cats in the yard, plants in the garden. I need to touch them—that's when I feel Spirit."

"I hear and feel God best through books," I interjected quickly. "But I'm sure we can sense Spirit or God communicating through all parts of ourselves and our world, if we listen hard enough." Remarkably, the brilliant morning sun suddenly poured through the front window as if on cue.

Although we label the body, mind, and heart differently, I thought, *experience shows they are not separate entities. For example, I hear the mind communicating its indoctrination or beliefs through bodily symptoms and "negative" emotions (e.g., "This part of my physical body is 'bad' or 'sick'"; "That part of you is 'bad' or 'sick', and this is how I feel about it"). I sense frozen emotions in compulsive behaviors—often anger or sadness at having been wrongly taught, guilt and shame over having hurt people,* and *an underlying fear that impairs the person from doing otherwise. Listening to Spirit within each part of us is what facilitates the body, mind, and heart working together equally as an integrated whole—an internal checks-and-balance system. The heart keeps the body from going overboard with its impulses and desires. The mind alerts the heart when it's attaching itself to the wrong thing or person. ("That person is largely stuck in the Mineral Stage of Development—not marriage material!") The body curtails the heart's and mind's excesses (perhaps falling asleep when the person spends too much time feeling or thinking). So it is with every aspect of our being—each adds sensitivity, intelligence, and many subtle qualities to every other part of us, but when any part is absent, all are diminished. Only when ALL our parts are sensible, well-functioning, and in balance, can we progress holistically and can our humanity fully shine.*

I continued, "It's time to get my head out of my books and my attention out of my head. Not entirely, of course, but my body and heart would do well with more time with people. Connie, your invitation to help at your church is just what I need." Jayda looked relieved and then glanced at Connie, who sat silently for a moment with a worried look before she spoke.

"I need it too. We can't do anything about our property yet since Orleans Parish is still closed to the public, but we can help damaged areas that *are* open, as in Jefferson Parish next door, where my church is."

Connie was sharing some important teaching. We were all approaching our damaged property in New Orleans, which no doubt symbolized some aspect of our psychology that was not yet accessible. On the psychological journey, we work with what is open and available, knowing that more of ourselves will become conscious as our skills improve. Attending to others is a prerequisite to awakening whom they represent inside ourselves.

Listening Step Eleven: LISTEN TO WHY WE AREN'T LISTENING
Choosing Images To Be God Is DISASTROUS!

Now you have a better understanding of why we are afraid to listen. What we hear at times is far from pleasant (we don't like what we're hearing!), and if it is pleasant, it may be far from the truth. Our listening takes us into experiences of loved ones and ourselves we'd rather *not* know about. Deep listening confirms that we have Rocky walls on which we have projected our stories and movies, and as we practice listening, these Rocks will surface to act out their unadulterated tales of trauma so they might at last be heard! Our Rock parts will share their heartaches, power struggles, secret sins, gut-wrenching torments, and gory details about their tormentors and their tormenting. Yes, the more we listen, the more we understand why we choose to stop listening...seeing...feeling...thinking... helping...*and* why, in our outrage, we've chosen to harm instead (whether by commission or omission [such as the omission of Our Rescuer]).

We also realize why we've supported Rocks. They never draw our attention to what we *don't* want to look at: *ourselves.* They don't ask us to express the fullness of our feelings. They don't encourage us to question, study, deliberate, meditate, and grow. Rocks don't demand internal investigations because they don't wish for us to evolve to our greatest potential. On the contrary, as long as we are psychologically immature, Rocks are at liberty to seize control and make the changes they choose. They extract our money...ruin our neighborhoods...move our jobs to foreign soils...curtail our civil rights...erode our Constitution...eradicate all but the most superficial story of our democracy...and corrupt human services and institutions in such a way that they no longer serve humanity. By listening, we learn just how great a cost we've been willing to pay to maintain our images and sustain whoever supports them.

There is good reason why psychological "infants" have limited attention and perceptions. They have neither the emotional strength nor insight to handle what might be seen and heard. The full spectrum of imagery from human to inhuman, gorgeous and inspiring to loathsome and deadly, would overwhelm these tiny humans. Thus, part of listening is preparing ourselves for what we may notice. This preparation is what psychological development is about—growing ourselves to a place where we can "listen" with all that we are. When we are young, we work with what is outside ourselves, but as we mature, we increasingly add ourselves to the workload, ultimately developing every aspect of our lives and selves. We receive what is going on around us *and* within us, and gain the stability to handle the news that it is all us. In any moment, we merely choose which part of us we would experience, learn from, and/or help.

DRAMA—Our Improvisations of Something Other than God

Inclusion of every part of our world into ourselves becomes easier the more we realize that we're just telling stories—the false and the true, the horrific to the beatific—with our words and behavior. The harshest stories create the demand for us to listen more deeply. Instead of drugging, ignoring, talking over, battering, or otherwise subduing those threatening voices within us, we finally hear the communication of a developing human being crying out for Mom. Gentleness and sweetness return to our lives the more these voices are listened to everywhere *and* responded to appropriately. (Remember—they feel such a great need to have their stories heard, validated, and soothed!) Whether harsh or sweet, can mere stories truly harm or heal a human being? Settings may change within hours, as they did with Hurricane Katrina and the Levee Disaster. Characters can be quickly recast, altered, or eliminated. Plots can suddenly shift and head in unexpected directions. Stories can be a distraction if we allow them to be, but as with any tale, we can also listen for what is personally relevant. We can also listen for whomever needs to be heard, and with this practice, finally detect that Voice beyond all worldly voices that is using the Indirect Application of our programming to communicate what is beyond our computerized minds. With practice, this Voice seemingly "goes viral," using all the beloved images and stories of our "inner infants" to guide us beyond the seemingly black-and-white page.

Focusing on God Is the Prevention of and Remedy for Disaster

Connie and I exited the bedroom where we had just said our thank-yous and good-byes to a sleepy Effie and her doctor, Bear. "By the way, how do you know such a country-farmer-type like Effie?" I asked Connie, her expensive designer shoes catching my eye.

"She was a client of my first boss, who was a real authoritarian and made my life miserable. I was praying earnestly about how to handle him when one day Effie visited the office, noticed my distress, and asked what was wrong. So I let her in on the details. To my surprise, she relayed exactly how to handle him, step by step. It was amazing, and it worked. At least it seemed to at the time. Much later, when I quit the firm, my boss admitted that Effie told him that if he didn't treat me with respect, she would shoot him with her shotgun." Connie laughed. "Effie and I have been friends ever since. She's given me an open invitation to unwind at her country house any time, so I can return to the city renewed. When I was single, I accepted her invitations frequently, but I've come over less and less as my family has grown. Cedric rarely wants to take the time, and I've stayed home if he's there, trying to catch any of his free moments. I feel I've lost myself in doing this—I now realize just how much. Being with Effie in her condition these past few weeks, I regret the wasted occasions over the years when I could have enjoyed her company, especially since..." Connie paused, looking grieved.

"Since the disaster?" I filled in her blank, feeling sad myself about missed chances to be with Effie.

"Yeah—everything seems different now. Time is so short—a lifetime is so short—we need to take advantage of opportunities as they arise and not put them off. For Effie...and ourselves...our city...and our country as we know it...we don't know how much time we have left!"

As with any book, how we read the story of our lives is up to us. By digesting only certain parts, however, we miss out on necessary life lessons, essential self-understanding, and the development of vital qualities of our human nature. Due to the nature of our creative mind, whatever we exclude from our consciousness must manifest somewhere in our experience—such as with rejecting and abusive relationships—to get our attention. Every difficulty has the potential to alert us to what we're doing. Unfortunately, our continual judgments and evacuations usually block our awareness of this fact. Not only do we not perceive ourselves, but we miss the all-inclusive Life of Our Parent that lies beyond us, since we're caught up in our fantasies of "other" lives (Contextual Warp).

Again, favoring one character as our identity over the whole is akin to picking infancy over adulthood, and this choice necessitates the psychological "infant" having a prominent role somewhere in our lives. These "babies" have been facilitating storms and even disasters to draw attention to themselves so their biologically built-in expectation of healthy Parenting might at last be met. Little did we know that even in the most horrendous circumstances, they're merely "crying out" for Our Mother—Her Familiar Voice is what "infants" everywhere unequivocally prefer!

When this Need of these "young ones" is finally met, they naturally develop into mature human beings, capable of meeting others' needs and rearing them to maturity. Yes, when we truly satisfy "children's" developmental needs, maturation is automatic! Isn't this reciprocal meeting of needs better than criticizing and punishing "kids" for behaving immaturely, demanding they grow up, insisting they abandon their resentments and quit succumbing to the "victim role," while pushing them to forgive the images that claimed to be what they could never *wholly* and adequately be—their parents? Within our humanity, all of us are receptive and responsive to Our Universal Parent.

The psychologically unborn are the most extreme example of these desperate "cries" for help. Only Our Real Parent can hear their voiceless turmoil amid all the aggression, horror, deception, and utter rejection of correction. Only Our Real Parent can sense their distress and rescue them from an existence of such depravity and destruction without shaming them. Only Our Real Parent cares for those who show no care and yet need it so desperately. Only Our Real Parent is unrelenting in Her Rescuing until every one of her "babies" is safely Home in Her.

Only Our Mother provides that constantly warm and secure environment in which the Rock and Mineral parts of us, frozen in traumatic shock, can relax and soften, and in which the underlying human psychological "embryos" and "fetuses" can comfortably reveal themselves as they are. The experience of Her Truth over time rights their upside-down paradigm. Her Presence ever supplies whatever is genuinely needed, while also taking away what is harmful. However, too young to perceive the difference between Mom and self, our unborn "infant" parts react to Her Containment as domination and control, Her Nutrition as unwanted and threatening, and Her Removal of what's hurtful as deprivation and loss. (Remember—the youngest humans have extreme reactions to mild provocations [p. 43].)

God Is Whole

In our identification with only a tiny part of who we are, we've assumed that Divinity also is partial or incomplete—only God the Father. Our Mother is the half of our Parent who's been too close for our inner "newborns" to clearly see, while they've perceived Our Father as largely absent or far away. Father and Mother are complementary aspects of the Same Divine Being, and we CANNOT know our wholeness without both.[3] Without God the Mother, for instance, the feminine inside all characters cannot mature. Neither can the masculine, which derives "his" fearless, indefatigable strength from "her" never-ending love. Likewise, the feminine is dependent on the masculine for "her" heart's vitality and fierce protection.

Therefore, meeting "infants'" and "children's" needs everywhere requires removing our blocks to each aspect of our Divine Parent and then passing on to all the abundance that we receive from this Connection. When we extend this abundance to our own most wounded parts, we find they too have blessings to bestow. For example, when we embrace our now Parented "inner infants," we can fully accept our physical being without judgment. We can release our emotions exactly as they are without shame, beginning with our tremendous remorse for the harm we've caused by rejecting Parental supervision. We're curious about our environment, which affords ever-fresh perceptions and unlimited learning. We can also trust Someone to always be there for us, outside and within, to nurture our developing humanity, and we can cling to Her as if our survival depends on Her—it does!

When our Rock parts are reclaimed, they break down and dissolve into "mineral solutions"— natural components of the human psychological body, just as minerals are part of the physical body. We then gain access to the wonderful qualities that healthy unborn psychological "babies" have to offer, such as the ability to receive what seems insignificant and grow from it. We can easily discard what doesn't serve us. Experiencing Our Mother's Constant Presence, we can depend on our surroundings to supply our every need—not our "needs" to run toward or away from our traumas, but to recover *completely* from our PTSD. In our new-found freedom and fulfillment, we no longer take the "woman" for granted, blame her entirely for problems, or regard her as having less value than the "man." We instead treasure her. With our projections and judgments gone, only deep gratitude remains as we receive her mothering. We also appreciate the ever-helping and healing feminine nature, Our Rescuer, within Our Savior. *And* we rest, as dependent as the unborn child, within Our Feminine Parent, Our Mother God.

GOD ALONE Is Reality!

"It's time to go!" Oliver's voice was impatient as he emerged from the hallway carrying his suitcase in one hand and a book in the other.

"I recognize that book, Oliver. It's from Effie's book collection," I said.

"Ms. Effie told me I could pick any book I wanted," he announced, looking pleased.

"Which one grabbed you?" Jayda asked, unaware that Effie's books had helped us all weather the storm and its aftermath.

"*Explorers of Space*!" Oliver lifted the book so Jayda could see the cover—a person in a space suit with the Big Dipper constellation behind him. "I'm gonna be an astronaut when I grow up."

"Great! How exciting!" Jayda replied.

Oliver responded to her encouragement with increased animation. "I'm in space lab at school— or I was. We studied the Milky Way Galaxy and its stars and planets, and we built models. We followed what the scientists on the International Space Station are doing too. But my school flooded, so I don't know where I'll go next, or if they'll even have a space lab…a lot of schools don't, you know." Oliver bit his upper lip, while his eyes showed concern. He gave us a quick glance before he and the Tasmanian devil on his T-shirt dodged out the garage door.

Whether the story of our lives is temporarily focused on the outer universe, like Oliver's book, or on an individual's experience, like my journal, eventually this fable beckons us to include the full range in our awareness. Any circumstance can be part of this expansion process, moving us to go to, be with, interact with, or profoundly open up to somewhere, something, or someone new. This opening is maturation—allowing in more and more of our experiences/ourselves until there is no setting we're unwilling to enter, look at, or consider; there is nothing we refuse to be involved with, feel about, and learn from; *and* there is no one we won't hear, respond to, and humanly help when so Guided. We no longer "need" to vacate any part of us from our "premises," since who we are is big enough, bright enough, strong enough, and caring enough to incorporate and handle all.

Understanding all experiences as metaphors is how we best cope with the reality of our world and its characters. We listen inclusively to hear the deeper story—that of our collective human family. Meeting the needs of each family member as he or she is encountered, outside and inside, is how we grow to live as the Whole. We come to realize that immature "problem"-people are calling for our mature humanity, and their demands drive our explorations of exactly what this is. With our discoveries (and their INSISTENCE[!]), we even find this mature humanity hidden within the most difficult or dangerous people who have so accelerated our psychological evacuation from this evacuation site of our imaginary world.

We Are Fictional Characters in a **Make-believe World**

I surveyed Effie's bookshelves on my way out to my car. Over the years, I'd flipped through most of the books. The genres were varied—mysteries, stock-market investing, organic gardening, animal tracking, romances, pregnancy, parenting the newborn, and so on. Each subject has parallels for the growth of hearts and minds and the progression of our life story. Many of the characters portrayed have been part of my experience, and I've played many of the different roles myself, in one form or another. This recent disaster, along with others, has antagonally expedited this greater diversity and versatility, as well as spurred my growing awareness that I am the reader of my story, of which my individual body is but one character. As this individual extension of our undivided Self has become more prominent in my attention, my care for and involvement with the entire cast of "characters" has intensified—I'm less emotionally entangled, yet more engaged than I've ever been. Strange, huh? My retreat to the country has led me to a greater connection with my home. Fervent drama has furthered my sense of reality. *And*, so many tragic deaths have propelled me to a profoundly fuller life.

Besides the psychological journey of human development, there is the path of devolution. Rocks and Minerals compulsively direct us away from our humanity to have us fit and "function" in "their" rigid, restrictive, mechanical system. If we follow their direction, we become increasingly incapacitated, needy, and seemingly dependent on them and their Program to survive. These evolutionary and devolutionary paths may appear opposing, but the incapacity, need, and
dependency resulting from the latter may also prod us onto the former by compelling us to depend on Who is beyond all paths. All people and all paths either direct us to Our Divine Parent or show us our blocks—our imagery is such a block!

Another block is our one-sidedness and double standard—we're willing to call a physical baby an infant, but not a psychological "babe." I believe we would do well to meet in the middle with our standards, showing flexibility in both arenas. When we admit the incapacities of psychological "infants," whether born or unborn, we can then expend our energies in meeting their developmental needs, rather than demanding they fulfill adult responsibilities and then being disappointed when they fail miserably. We should also appreciate that more is going on with physical babies than meets the eye—we have MUCH to learn from these youngest of humans. But if we're waiting for them to bring home a paycheck or rescue us from our disaster sites, we'll be waiting a long time!

Thus, maturation is not a one-way street—growing older, for example, since we "grow" younger too. By growing into these small, most wounded and immature aspects of ourselves, we gain the exuberance and vitality of the young while we foil their inattentiveness and inactivity (psychologically speaking). As we incorporate them into our humanity, however, we are then increasingly able to go wherever Our Father leads and Our Mother carries us, without fussing or fighting. The rescuing task of our "inner infants" completed, we acquire a deeply listening, keenly perceptive, unconditionally caring, fully responsive, and "all-knowing" (knowing all as Self) adult psychological body.

TRAVEL: BACK TO GOD—The End of the Road

Our cars were packed. My passenger seat was full of books—the ones I'd brought as well as a few I borrowed from Effie, *The Developing Human* on top of the pile. Oliver was playing video games in the back of their SUV—or should I say "Peter." In the front, Felicity was already munching on travel snacks. All three drivers stood outside with doors open, breathing in the moment, as if we all knew that our lives were about to irrevocably change—but then hadn't they many times over the years *and* in the past few weeks? Yes, they had and would no doubt again and again, as long as we choose to grow.

I took in the simple sweetness of the farm that had been my haven from the storms and disaster, and I thought of the ever-present haven of Our Rescuer. I then glanced at Connie. She looked hesitant, as if she wasn't quite ready to leave our safe house, not knowing what she'd find at her destination. I gave her a questioning look—she then nodded and slowly entered her car. Jayda put her pet carrier with Pookie inside on the front seat of her rental car, while I eased behind the wheel of my Honda. I had company—a couple of connected lovebugs were crawling across the dash.

I heard Felicity yelling, and then she rushed into the house, the lights on her sneakers flashing on and off as she ran. She emerged a few minutes later with her baby doll in arms. When both were secured inside, Connie's SUV began the trek down Effie's driveway. I placed a hand on my books, anticipating a journey much quieter and less stressful than when I arrived. As Jayda's car began to move, I chuckled, realizing that on this return trip *she* would be the one enduring Pookie's howling and car sickness. I glanced once again at the old farmhouse surrounded by harvested hayfields. Then, deeply inhaling the fresh country air, I turned the key, extended my foot to the gas, and slowly followed the other cars down the gravel drive.

We return to our humanity by the same road on which we left, this time without holding our human qualities responsible for the problems we encounter along the way. (Our humanity is NOT to blame!) Also, this time we are not alone without competent supervision—a Mature Parent is present. She gently guides us in the knowledge that the "approaching storm" we've been ever running from in fear is none other than our own lives and selves clamoring for our attention. She doesn't recoil from these unwanted aspects of ourselves, but recognizes their once human nature and wholeheartedly welcomes them, showing us how to do the same. We discover our original innocence, which she enlivens and augments, while she comforts all parts that had been convinced otherwise. In Her Presence, the life-changing, identity-inverting impacts of our trauma and the creative license in our drama translate into Her Absolute, Ever-present Solution to every problem. Full recovery comes through Our Mama!

Enveloped and sustained by Her, we no longer feel the "need" to defend our phony images, such as those of our immature leaders. We no longer attack or reject "inner children" and "infants" for their natural reactions to unnatural circumstances or their reenactments of these events. We no longer evacuate from and deny our youngest parts that so frighten us by such candid expressions of their experiences and by the great lengths they've been willing to go to get attention and help. Instead, we search for these lost "children" beside each Rock or block and rescue their humanity, knowing all as family of different psychological ages. We listen to their stories and respond to their needs, growing to understand them, appreciate them, and ultimately embrace and love them as vital expressions of our inescapable Self. We return to the forks in the road where we once chose one way of being ("my way") over another, and with Parental Guidance, we safely explore other "paths." Rather than encountering disaster, as perhaps in the past, we find our Destiny!

Unlike the city of New Orleans, which had no choice about its destruction, we as human beings have many constructive options, such as allowing every aspect of our lives to be a vehicle for our return Home. Thus, our aim is not to isolate and focus on particular parts of ourselves, judging them as superior. It is not to deem one road as the only way to go. It is not to move in one direction alone. Our goal is not one thought, one perception, one feeling, or one behavior to the exclusion of others. On the contrary, with the willingness to navigate ALL that we are with ALL that we are, we fully yield to our greater Body, within whom all movements are automatically developmental. "My" way becomes an excursion through ALL ways, including every aspect of our world and our bodies and every stage of psychological development, inside and out, as conducted by One who claims all.

There is no return from the psychological journey because we begin as a tiny part and we end as the Whole. We start in anticipation of our destination, and we stop in awareness that our destination is wherever we remove our blocks to This All-Encompassing Presence. At the onset, we feel ourselves above or beneath our fellowman and, in finishing, we embrace all equally as expressions or offspring of This Ever-present Parent. Ultimately, even Rock Virus programming has this important antagonal message to share. Take the Control Option Program, for example. We set off on our journey as one of many images, believing this "life" to be ours and ours alone to direct, and we conclude it in realization that, for an image, self-possession and autonomy are NOT options. In relief and joy, we return control and our lives to Whom all have always belonged. We are God's.

SMOOTHIE BREAK:

1. In what ways do you confuse God with man? How does this confusion affect your relationships? How does it impede your psychological development?

2. Consider someone you know with offensive behavior. How would you interpret any action if it were coming from a psychological "unborn baby" (a Rock)? An "infant?" A "preschooler?" A school-age "child?" A "teenager"? A woman? A man? Yourself?

3. What role have your disasters played in the growth of your heart and mind? How can you use Rock encounters to balance out any one-sidedness of your personality?

4. How have you hindered the psychological development of the Rocks in your life and yourself? How might you be more therapeutic? (Please ask Our Rescuer for assistance with this.)

5. Use action figures (or other suitable representations) to act out the antics of some Rock leaders and to discern the lessons you can learn from them? How do they aid you in differentiating the deluded "infant" leader from the capable adult?

6. What rigid boundaries and/or blocks have you built to protect yourself? How do they keep you from your fellowman and your wholeness? Why do you maintain them?

7. What false needs are you trying to meet? Which true need are you neglecting?

8. In your daily choices, do you ascribe more power and authority to God or images? How so? What do you retain as "knowledge," which is really your belief?

9. Pick someone you are close to and draw pictures of each part of his or her inner "family." What is the Man in him or her like? How about the Woman? Describe the "children" and "infants" (born and unborn). What are the adults teaching you? What do the "kids" need from you? Practice this holistic perspective when you feel inclined to judge anyone in only one way.

10. Play a game of marbles and notice how one marble can move another when guided by human hands. How might you turn your own Mascrock into protective armor and inner strength when you confront the Rocks and Minerals in your life? How might you transform your internal Femrock into a spinal column that strongly upholds your human psychological body?

11. Evaluate the progress you've made in studying this book.

12. Which "infants" in your life still need your attention:
    a. Psychological "infants" inside and out
    b. Projects you are just beginning
    c. Relationships that are in their infancy
    d. Ideas that must be nourished for them to grow
    e. This moment

13. Are you willing to translate the images on the screen of your mind into data about your selves or the tender, loving human voice of Our Mother? Keep a journal and jot down "scenes" of your life, and then write what Mom is teaching you through these daily experiences.

14. Developing qualities like Our Mother's is what leads us back to remembering Her, sensing Her, and finally experiencing Her. What are some of these qualities, and what can you do to develop them? (For example: availability—how can you create more time for the people in your life?)

15. Are you ready to find your niche nestled within the Body of our united Humanity, waking up your "siblings," as they in turn awaken you?

16. If not, listen to what is in your way...

---

[1] Keith L. Moore, PhD, *The Developing Human* (Toronto: Elsevier, 2011).

[2] "At birth the infant is reliant on adult interaction for soothing." Susan Aposhyan, *Body-Mind Psychotherapy* (New York: W.W. Norton & Company, Inc., 2004), 44.

[3] Neil Douglas-Klotz, *Prayers of the Cosmos* (New York: HarperCollins Publishers, Inc., 1990), 12.

Epilogue

I wrote this book, in part, so my childhood dream of being heard would at last be fulfilled. Thanks for allowing me to air my life's story on your "radio station." And thank you for listening! Granted, I haven't shared the whole truth with all the grim details communicated directly. In my experience, most people tune out if you're too open and honest, and those who do listen aren't likely to respond in a helpful way. So I've cloaked my life in other people's stories, adding some fictional characters and story lines to make my narrative more acceptable to you and less revealing for me, not unlike you perhaps. Some of these experiences are literally true, while others have been disguised with symbolism or metaphor. I placed some distance between me and the villains and disclosed only minor problems about myself and those close to me, keeping true to my culture. However, if you've learned how to listen, you'll discern these hidden elements within my story and hopefully seek them out within your own and others' lives—every human life deserves to be heard!

I also wrote this book in hopes that the psychologically youngest of human beings might be heard and might receive the help they SO desperately need. I've repeated the same information, using different words and metaphors and viewed from different perspectives, because Rocks and Minerals require repetition to be reached. I went on and on with the material for well over three hundred pages(!) because Mineral Stagers demand this tenacity if we are to budge their hearts and minds. I'm sure reading this book seemed TEDIOUS at times, a feeling we must be comfortable with if we are to help these victims of overwhelming trauma. As this book has finally come to an end, so too can the Rocky parts of our life story—when we're willing to exchange this story and our world for the Reality of the One that lives beyond them.

Perhaps you can now understand why, as a listener, I am not always smiling. I can't merely acknowledge the part of you or me that is pleasing and ignore the rest. This selectivity would be a disservice to us both. Yet, in noticing a bigger picture, at times I'm greatly saddened by what I hear, and at other times I'm angry or frightened. When I attend a party or social gathering, I can't just have a good time like so many people do, because there is usually at least one person there who will relate the real, unadulterated story of some aspect of his or her life. People tell me terrible things, and I try to defuse the tragedy and heartache coming my way. Usually I'm led to ponder how I can help. I cannot listen and then have a drink or saunter onto the dance floor. I am always moved—to tears, to anguish, to spending the next half hour in the bathroom trying to compose myself before attempting another conversation. I've learned that this flow of feeling does *not* mean I am defective or in need of a pill, such as an antidepressant, as so many people have suggested over the years. My emotional response means my humanity is awakening, and the wealth of feelings and thoughts stirred within me are merely expressions of this precious endowment of human life.

Since people are often unaware of the extent of the trauma they've disclosed, they do not comprehend my reactions. Unaware of their own deeply buried emotions, they don't notice that my feelings are but a tiny taste of their own: So much pain! So much shame! So much remorse! So much pretense to cover up the truth! Such widespread unwillingness to stop and regard the inhumanity braved and perpetrated by every individual! Admittedly, it's not fun. It doesn't feel good. More often than not, what I hear alters my day. However, it gives life an intensity and realness that, as we mature, is so much more satisfying than "fun." Listening has also become my job, not one I get paid for in the traditional sense, but one that pays me in growth. Who I am expands each time I pause, open up my ears, my eyes, my heart, and my mind…and listen…and then prayerfully respond.

Again, thank you SO MUCH for hearing me. Having finally shared the story of my life, I sense I can now move on and yet return to these details as required for our ongoing human development. Perhaps you are moving more freely and purposefully now too! Since you've shown you can listen to a wounded "child" within one adult's body and learn from her experiences, why not continue this listening practice? Why not give your rapt attention to the wounded "children" within you and those close to you who need to be heard. Also, why not listen to hurting children *before* they physically grow up? Ask Our Rescuer who is most longing for listening ears, and do as she instructs. Be willing to invest whatever amount of time is necessary to uncover the REAL story. Listen hard with all that you are, and in time, what the child needs you to know will come to you. It's that simple. All you have to do is sincerely want the truth. And then, reach for Our Rescuer for the wisdom and strength to handle it!

Traumatic experiences abound in our world. I've shared my most recent disaster with you in great detail so you might see it for what it is and recognize these patterns in your own lives. I've shared my evacuation experience so you might apply this outward account to your inner world and understand how you have evacuated from your human potential. I've embraced complete strangers as fellow evacuees, disaster survivors, and developing human beings needing to give and receive help, hoping you will do the same with the estranged and traumatized aspects of yourself and others. I've shown how I've been changed by disaster, torn from the comfort zone of my books, and thrust into greater participation in the reality of our world and its people, so you too may trust your disasters to be an impetus for transformation.

Aware of my own unmet need to tell my life story and be heard, I saw the same need in a greater setting—that of my community and its people. I've allowed the pain of an oppressed population to resonate with the pain from my own oppression and to guide me past the barriers I'd long ago built to keep my body safe and protected from future storms. Having known tremendous loss myself, such as the loss of our united Self and corresponding aspects of my humanness, I know how agonizing lesser losses are when they remind us of this one inconsolable grief. Because of the Levee Disaster, I lost many precious possessions, yet through the collective devastation, I've discovered our shared Humanity. I believe I made out exceptionally well in the bargain!

The human voice is such a treasure—a value realized only when we listen! When we do hear and respond to this ever-engaging human voice, *and* we allow it to join with other human voices, we collectively awaken the sleeping spiritual Infant that is our true united Identity—the "Child" who indeed saves the day! Then, the dark, stormy, and treacherous realm of the unconsciousness is no more! Every baby has such a powerful ability to bring us back to our origins! We are all born human—naturally giving and receiving our humanness. And this innate humanity must return and grow as we cradle all in the arms of Our Eternal Parent.

"Greater is he who is in you than he who is in the world."[1]

---

[1] The King James Bible: the Oxford Standard Text (United Kingdom: Oxford University Press, 1769) 1 John 4:4, 1884.

Bibliography

Mish, Frederick C., ed. *Merriam-Webster's Collegiate Dictionary: Tenth Edition*. Springfield, MA: Merriam-Webster, Incorporated, 2002.

Chapter 5:

Fluit, Richard Foster, and Brian J. Skinner. *Physical Geology.* New York: John Wiley and Sons, Inc., 1974.

Medenback, Olef, and Harry Wilk. *The Magic of Minerals.* Berlin: Springer-Verlag, 1986.

Pellant, Chris. *Rocks and Minerals: A Smithsonian Handbook.* New York: Dorling Kindersley, Inc., 2002.

Strahler, Arthur N., and Alan H. Strahler. *Environmental Geoscience: Interaction between Natural Systems and Man.* Santa Barbara, CA: Hamilton Publishing Company, 1973.

Chapter 6:

Adobe Photoshop Elements 11 (Version 11.0 {20120830.r.32025}). Adobe Systems Incorporated.

Gookin, Dan. *PCs for Dummies, 11th Edition.* Hoboken, NJ: Wiley Publishing Company, Inc., 2007.

Matthews, Marty, Carole Matthews, Gary David Bouton, and Bobbi Sandberg. *Computing for Seniors.* New York: McGraw Hill, 2011.

Microsoft Word 2010 (Version 14.0.4762.1000). Microsoft Corporation.

Microsoft Publisher 2000 (Version 5.1.2600 Service Pack 3 Build 2600). Microsoft Corporation.

Rathbone, Andy. *Windows XP for Dummies.* New York: Wiley Publishing, Inc., 2001.

Chapter 7:

Flynn, Sean, PhD. *Economics for Dummies*, 2nd *Edition.* Hoboken, NJ: Wiley Publishing, Inc., 2011.

Hallak, Jacques, and Muriel Poisson. *Corrupt School, Corrupt Universities: What Can Be Done?* Paris: International Institute for Educational Planning, 2007, http://www.unesco.org/iiep/PDF/pubs/synth_ethics.pdf.

Orman, Suze. *The Road to Wealth.* New York: Riverhead Books, 2010.

Chapter 8:

Kristin Wakeham, "Fetal Development," *To the Unborn: A Pro-Life Page,* July, 2000, http://www.angelfire.com/nj3/rebekah8367/

"Fetal Development from Conception to Birth." National Right to Life website, http://www.nrlc.org/abortion/facts/fetaldevelopment.html.

Verny, Thomas, MD, with John Kelly. *The Secret Life of the Unborn Child.* New York: Dell Publishing, 1981.

Glossary of Terms

acting out (41): Communicating psychological issues through hurtful behavior.

"adult" (vii): A physical adult who rarely lives as a psychological adult. Most of the time, "adults" act from their "inner children" and born and unborn "infants."

adult (vii): An aspect of our psychology that cares for all members of our internal "family." These Men and Women also tend to the psychological needs of our external human family—everyone in our lives.

Adult (22, 67-9): Our Rescuer or our united Self's manifestation in our world and in our individual self.

animacy (115): The degree of human life we embrace in any moment. (See *life*.)

Animal (77, 80-1): Someone largely stuck in the Animal Stage of psychological Development.

antagonism: Rage-filled Rocks, petrified in post-traumatic stress, negotiate life antagonistically. They oppose normal human functioning by relentlessly recreating their dehumanizing traumatic experiences. Here are a few examples of how Rocks defy and undermine our human qualities.

> **antagonal communication** (128): Mineral Stager "information" is antagonistic to the truth—this communication style is a hallmark of the Rock. To understand what is being said, remove the "nots" or add them.

> **antagonal confrontation** (130): A challenge of someone who is asserting the truth of his or her humanity.

> **antagonal directions** (324): Guidance that leads us into pain, which then motivates us into becoming more pain-free.

> **antagonal feelings** (130): A Rock experiences and expresses feelings that are the opposite of how he or she genuinely feels—"I'm always happy!" Underneath the underlying rage is terror and grief.

> **antagonal "giving"** (130): Giving to those who don't deserve it and/or don't need it while depriving those deserving and in need. Rocks "give" to others what they need themselves (245).

> **antagonal "helping"** (233, 317): The Rock's "help" is in appearance only. Underneath the facade, the Rock's "helpful" behaviors HURT!

> **antagonal interpretations** (173): Explanations that oppose the intentions of the original speaker.

> **antagonal language** (94, 130, 257): Communication that is the opposite of the truth. Rocks are pathological liars. (See *antagonal communication*.)

> **antagonal leadership** (213-14, 230): Through domination, aggression, and other actions that are antagonistic to humans, the Rock leads people in the opposite direction of where their humanity would guide them.

> **antagonal learning** (130, 165): Rock students are drawn to indoctrination that is contrary to their intellectual development and to the learning process itself.

antagonal memory (103, 120-1): Memories that are antagonistic to the truth. False memories may include happy times or traumas that never happened (to distract from all the traumatic experiences that did occur!)

antagonal perceptions (126, 229): Those in the Mineral Stage perceive malevolence in their victims and in those rescuing them, while *they* experience themselves as worthy souls. The perceptions of Rocks and Minerals are consistently upside-down

antagonal pleasure (87, 284): When Rocks reenact their painful life experiences on others, they feel pleasure.

antagonal relations or relationships (242): Rocks relate to others through abuse and neglect. They repel those they need to come close. They dominate those whose guidance they require, and they push down those whom their embryonic or fetal humanity would have stand up to help them.

antagonal request (232, 247): Asking for the opposite of what one needs or wants.

antagonal rescue (95, 248): Rocks "rescue" antagonistically, "helping" those who don't need their "help" or the type of "help" they are offering.

antagonal response (130): A response that is the opposite of what is asked for or needed.

antagonal rules (240): Rocks "play" with people as if they were toys, using "rules" that are antagonistic to society and individual well-being. Rock rules or laws protect Rocks (206-7).

antagonal spending (130): Buying what is unnecessary, useless, or valueless when human need is crying out for our resources.

antagonal vengeance (103): Rocks take revenge on those who perpetrated their abuse and neglect by similarly abusing and neglecting anyone who reminds them of their long-abandoned human identity.

associative learning (126, 245; 295): A person learns to associate two independent things when she has repeatedly experienced them together or experienced them together during one particularly traumatic event. Later when one thing is experienced or remembered, the other is experienced or remembered at the same time.

binary system (208, 214): When we choose to separate from our united Self, we create duality—a binary system in our mind and world, as in animates and <u>inanimates</u>.

binary language (110, 327): Our choice of individuality results in two languages within our "computer" systems. The first (1) speaks of our original Identity as One Mind. The second (0) speaks of individuality and all that it entails. Our choice of language reveals our preference.

Child or "child" (40, 77, 80-1, 291): Each aspect of our psychology in the Child Stage of Psychological Development.

"childhood": The time we spend in the Child Stage of Psychological Development, regardless of physical age.

"computer" (110-115): A mind that has chosen an individual image as its default setting.

conscious (24): I use this term to mean awareness of psychology—being present and attending to genuine, in-the-moment human thinking and feeling as well as what is not genuine or human within.

Corp'rocks (166-7, 184-5, 187-9): These Rocks have exchanged their obligation to humanity for undying devotion to the corporation for "whom" they work or to those businesses that supply what they "need."

dissociation (25, 286): Psychically removing some aspect of ourselves or our memory from our awareness.

ego (101): An identity focused on expressing, supporting, and defending our individual image as self (ME!). It excludes and ignores our collective Self while pretending to possess his/her attributes. In this book, ego is synonymous with the Rock Virus.

extrusive Rock (87, 90, 93): This igneous Rock form is obvious—the person is overtly cold, rigid, cruel, and dangerously dysfunctional.

Femrock (88, 89-91): This Rock form shows EXTREME "feminine" characteristics, as defined by the Rock. She is ever-bending to Mascrocks, whom she slavishly serves and pathologically enables. To those outside the Program, however, she is a stationary monolith (**"YOU CAN'T MAKE ME!"**).

genuine Identity (13): Whenever you see capitalization regarding Identity, think of the One Self we all share (see *Self* below), which is real, undivided, and ever-expressing "Itself" within our illusory world.

heart (34): The psychological heart refers to the emotional body or being—the feeling state of an individual. (As the word "ear" is contained within the word "heart," having heart requires a lot of listening!)

human (vii, 143): The grand identity within us that is made in the Image of God and expresses God on earth.

human nature (viii): What naturally extends from our humanness, which will be whatever a situation calls for to facilitate the growth of everyone involved.

humane (viii): The quality of being human. (While biological humans may not appear humane in any moment, all psychological humans are humane.)

humanity (viii): Our Divinely-endowed and shared humanness.

humanness (46): The state of being human, which may be experienced individually, relationally, or collectively.

igneous Rock (87, 90, 93, 99): In this Rock form, the rage of a chronically persecuted child has superficially cooled and solidified into very dysfunctional behaviors that are seemingly unalterable.

image: (A) The most superficial appearance of a person's personality or a situation (42, 62, 111). Image is a facade—the character traits and story lines we prefer over the truth about our selves and circumstances. (B) Image also refers to the "screen" images on the desktop of our minds (111). All individuals are images of our minds' making, since only our undivided Identity is real. The first definition of image (A) is the most superficial aspect of the second definition (B). Where our attention is on imagery alone (definition B), our perceptions must be restricted, as in definition A.

imagery (viii, 68): A world of individual forms that we perceive and experience with our individual image.

inanimate (81): Devoid of the qualities of psychological life (movement of feeling and thought, ever-increasing awareness, intelligence, inspiration, and so on). See *Rock* and *Mineral.*

"infancy" (21): The psychological state where we allow our "inner infants" to run our lives, having learned that these limited, imitative aspects of our psychology *are* the adults. (See *Vegetable.*)

inhuman nature (95, 104): What opposes our human nature but which can be used by our human nature to evolve our selves.

"inner animal" (40, 77, 80-81): The aspect of a human psyche in the Animal Stage of Psychological Development

"inner child" or "children" (iii, v, 60, 291): Aspects of our psychology that are child-like, having the interests, expressions, and nature of children. Every individual has both a boy and girl inside and sometimes MANY of each. The chronically abused and neglected child regresses along the developmental continuum, functioning more like an Animal, Vegetable, or Mineral.

"inner" (or psychological) "embryo" (v, 224-5, 226-7): The youngest aspect of our humanity, which is without human form and functions solely through genetic and environmental programming. When "aborted" from our consciousness, it becomes a Rock.

"inner female" or "woman" (80, 81, 91, 291): The "feminine" side of anyone of the male gender or any woman raised to be a man. Every Mascrock has a Femrock within.

"inner" or (psychological) "fetus" (v, 234): A psychologically unborn aspect of our humanity, which has human form, but still functions only through genetic and environmental programming. The unconscious "inner fetus" is synonymous with the Mineral Stage.

"inner infant" (v, 22, 291), **"infant"** (20) or **"baby"** (19, 22): A comfort-seeking aspect of our psychology that, when cared for, possesses the qualities of a healthy infant, such as honest emotional expression, the ability to receive what is essential for life and release what is detrimental, and so on. When abused and neglected, this aspect becomes a Vegetable.

"inner male" or "man" (80, 81, 90, 291): The "masculine" side of those of the female gender. In a Femrock, this is a Mascrock.

inner Rock (210): A catastrophically traumatized aspect of our psyche that has taken on a rigid, lifeless identity (void of humanity).

"inner vegetable" (40, 77. 80-1): The part of a human psyche in the Vegetable Stage of Psychological Development.

inner world (20-1) Our individual psychology. Everything in our psychological world has representation in the outer world and vice versa. The "world" inside each person is as vast, fascinating, and ready for exploration as the world outside.

"inner" or "internal family" (20-1): As long as we choose an existence separate from our true Identity, we must have a family of "people" within us, ranging from mature adults (representing our Self) to infants, born and unborn.

inside (as in "inside and out") (21): Refers to the intangible or psychological realm within each individual.

introjection (91): People we are close to in childhood become a part of our psyche (an introject) as we grow such that we "hear" their words and "feel" their influence when they are not there.

intrusive Rock (87, 90, 93): This igneous Rock form is invisible to the eye. This aspect of an individual must be inferred by its effects.

inverse body language (227): Manipulating others to experience and express one's own unconscious and unprocessed thoughts, feelings, and life experiences. IBL is a hallmark of those stuck in the Mineral Stage of Development.

kinesthetic flashback (251): PTSD patients may act out a traumatic scene from their past when they are triggered by some internal or external aspect of this trauma (the same physical feeling, emotional state, perceptual experience, and so on). (See *reenactment*.) The average person is unaware of what he or she is doing.

life: In terms of psychology, our degree of animation or life comes from allowing the Our Rescuer within us to express Herself through us and every aspect of our experience. (See *"animacy."*)

MALware (114): The programs of the Rock Virus that control the mind of every user such that he or she functions as an automaton.

Man (78, 80-1, 231-32, 247-49, 291): Someone in the most mature stage of psychological development. A good listener can tune into this most mature Adult in all human beings, whether male or female, young or old.

Mascrock (88-9): This Rock form displays EXTREME "masculine" traits as defined by the Rock. Underneath the Mascrocks "masks" of innocence, they are violent and controlling with an "excuse" ever-ready to "explain" away their antisocial actions.

maturation (viii, 28): The process of psychological development as well as the end result. See "psychological journey."

metamorphic Rock (88, 89, 94-5, 100): Rocks that routinely change their appearance, manners, or modes of operation to facilitate "their" way.

microprocessing (110): Processing what is minuscule, such as our individual images and their stories.

Mind or One Mind (OM) (110-115): Our shared Mind that contains all minds and all of our individual experiences.

mind (x): What observes and processes our individual experience.

Mineral Stage of Psychological Development (77, 80): The first stage of development, which is characterized by an unfeeling, unreceptive, and obstinate psychological state.

Mineral Stager (83): Someone stuck in the Mineral Stage of Psychological Development. This person is further classified as either a Rock (most extreme) or Mineral. Every Rock is made up of Minerals. Since Minerals are often run by Rocks, outside and within, I've used the term "Rock" throughout this book to discuss the characteristics and activities of those in the Mineral Stage.

Mineral part or aspect (277): Every individual has an aspect of his or her psyche that is rigid and uncompromising ("male" form) and one that is unstructured and apathetic ("female" form). Our Mineral parts are those with hardened and/or mechanical "human" traits (e.g., forced affection or unwavering optimism). When conscious and under the service of Our Rescuer, these Minerals become healthy parts of the human psychological body.

Minerals (77, 80-1, 91, 202): People with a majority of Mineral Stage parts within their psyche, which have not coalesced into their chosen identity (i.e., they maintain a human appearance, psychologically speaking). Minerals are easily forged into forms that plug into Rock systems.

movie templates in our minds (111, 114): Movie #1: The expression of Our Rescuer within our world; movie #2: A copy of Movie #1 in which each individual body is the subject and lead character; and RV movie #3: an inverted copy or perverse rendition of Movie #1.

one-up/one-down (83): The binary mind-set of the Rock, where the Mascrock assumes the one-upper, or superior, stance while others, like the Femrock, are given a one-downer, or inferior, role.

Our Rescuer (67-69): Our undivided Self manifests in our world as a Rescuer. She has the function of rescuing us from our fixed, false belief systems, which are portrayed throughout our world of imagery. She is also a Mentor and Friend, who offers technical support, leadership, "auto" mechanical assistance, and parenting—we give her many names and many functions because we project onto her the multiplicity that exists in ourselves.

Parenting (340): The continual Guidance and Care that extends from our Divine Parent. (See *Our Rescuer*.)

Polirock (197): A Rock in politics who disguises his or her malevolence by playing well-known family roles. The renditions include:

> **Poli'lad** (199-200): Plays the role of a good-natured boy who is prone to poor judgment and impulsive action which lead to mistakes and accidents, all of which align with the Rock's agenda.

> **Poli'lass** (200): Plays a wide-eyed little Mary sunshine in her promotion of a Rocky course.

> **Polirock mom,** or **Poli'mom** (198-9): Portrays a motherly role to move along the Rock Program.

> **Polirock pop,** or **Poli'pop** (197-8): Acts out the role of a traditional father to lead people to their downfall.

post-traumatic stress disorder or PTSD (37): The default condition of every person who chooses an individual identity. We must draw abuse and neglect to ourselves in reenactment of our choice to separate from Wholeness and ignore the ever-present call to return and be rescued.

the Program (115): The overall agenda of the Rock Virus, which those stuck in the Mineral Stage of Development serve with "their" life.

programming (139-40, 209-11): Using programmed rewards and punishments to mold children into rigid, automatic patterns of behaving, feeling, and thinking. Rocks use extreme methods to program children (105, 114-15, 289). Their programs include:

> **Control Programs** (115-19)
>
> **Evasion Programs** (175-183)
>
> **Lies and Manipulation Programs** (120-28)
>
> **Stretching and Reduction Programs** (202-207)
>
> **Strife Programs** (129-39)

psyche (x): the psychological body *or* the individual mind that identifies with a physical body and is necessarily fragmented as a result of choosing a life apart from our collective Self.

psychological adults (21, 77-8): Those who have owned and mourned their traumatic experiences (transcended the Child Stage), have gathered together and owned all opposing parts of themselves (Man) or are in the process of gathering them (Woman). Both know the greater Body as Self and serve this Self with their lives.

psychological infancy (21): The state where we're only focused on what pleases our individual image.

the psychological journey of maturation (vii, viii): The great adventure of self-discovery which takes us into all the stages of development within our psyches. When we hit Rock bottom, we are highly motivated to exchange our individual existence, the "baby," for our original, united Identity, the Adult.

psychology: The mental (mind) and emotional (heart) processes within an individual and their development. This word also includes the study of these processes and the resulting behavior.

Reality (77): What is beyond, yet shining through, this imaginary world.

reenactment: People suffering from PTSD are compelled to act out unresolved aspects of their traumatic experiences. This behavioral communication is how the parts of ourselves stuck in the youngest stages of psychological development share their life's story. (See *kinesthetic flashback*.)

rescuer (73): The profession of every person who is in contact with Our Rescuer, listening to her voice, and doing as she instructs. Rescuers can be found in every individual—these are the adults within our psychology.

rescuing (40): In this book, I attempt to return this word to its original definition of taking someone in trouble out of harm's way. Psychologically speaking, we must follow the guidance of Our Rescuer to rescue successfully, working to develop our "inner infants" and "children" and at the same time, helping the psychologically young outside ourselves. This definition is in stark contrast to the term that is currently in vogue in my profession of the codependent "taking care of" (Femrock-style!) the dysfunctional partner or family member who needs professional treatment (265).

Rock (81 on): Someone stuck in the youngest stage of psychological development, such that it is his or her predominant character and main mode of operation. The Rock has regressed to such an extreme degree as to possess a non-human psychological form The Rock who is demonstrating extreme "masculine" traits is called a Mascrock, whether genetically male or female. The Rock expressing extreme "feminine" traits is called a Femrock, whether genetically female or male.

Rock part or aspect (147, 229): An aspect of our psychology that has owned the Rock Virus identity as self. It continually replicates "itself," harming human life in the process.

Rock relationships (92-97, 242-43): Rocks "prove" the strength of their relationships by acting a role in public or citing the number of years they have been married. Underneath this surface facade, their programs keep them frozen in opposing stances to their partners.

Rockthink (126, 277): The programmed "thoughts" expressed by Rocks. These "beliefs" rigidly confine the Rock to an existence of automatism.

Rock Virus or RV (113): A virulent "microorganism" that enters the "computer" system of our individual mind when we choose an individual identity. (See *ego*.)

RV Programs (114): Programs that the Rock Virus or those infected "download" into our "systems" that sabotage human functioning. They include the Control Programs (113-18), the Lies and Manipulation Programs (118-27), the Strife Programs (127-37), the Evasion Programs (173-181), and the Stretching and Reduction Programs (202-6).

"screen" (111): Visual perception as viewed by our individual minds.

sedimentary Rock (87, 89, 94, 99-100): These Rocks form layers of deception, obstruction, and persecution to defend their Rocky ways.

self (24, 112-14, 147-8): Our individual identity as a separate body, which includes many fragmented parts or personalities reflecting this chosen separation from and rejection of our true Identity.

Self (13, 110-13): When we choose individuality, this greater Self who permeates every part of our world, SEEMS to have individual parts. Thus, I give this Self many names in this book: greater Being (142, 146) or Body (104, 110); ever-loving Heart (110); original (13), genuine (13), undifferentiated (22), united (x, 146), or true Identity (96, 148); unlimited Mind (110, 122, 147) or One Mind (See Mind); Reality (12, 77, 111, 144); collective (69), unified (27) or undivided Self (x, 25, 146); our Source (110); or any combination of these terms. I do this because we give so many names to it ourselves, yet when we're deeply listening, we're hearing only this One Voice within all voices.

I call this undivided Self "Our Rescuer." Most chapters have a focus on a particular aspect of this Self: Chapter 4 introduces Our Rescuer as a Teacher; chapter 5 looks at Our Rescuer as a Guide for traversing our precarious physical world; chapter 6 speaks of Our Rescuer as a manifestation of unlimited Mind communicating through the "computer" systems of our individual mind; chapter 7 relates Our Rescuer to a consistently top-performing CEO who is ever-available for consultation; chapter 8 leads us to perceive Our Rescuer as an Authority and parental Figure; in chapter 9, we see Our Rescuer as our Home; and in chapter 10, Our Rescuer is seen as the rightful owner and driver of the "vehicle" of our lives.

shotgun (83): A house style common in New Orleans, so named because if you open all the doors in the house, you can shoot a shotgun through the front door and the bullet will come out the back without having caused any damage.

story: We have the true story of our lives [life stories (22)] and the stories we make up to meet the needs of our "inner infants" and "children" (15, 25-6). I use the same word for both because ultimately both are creations of an imaginative mind wanting something other than our genuine Identity.

system or "computer" system (110-11): An individual mind processing itself.

System or Operating System (143): The manifestation of our collective Identity filtered through an individual self and the resulting world of imagery.

"tough love" (104): Rocks require toughness from a rescuer. She or he must stand up to their relentless persecutions, endless excuses, and unwavering unwillingness to allow help.

unconscious: A) NOT paying attention to our psychological self (24, 45) and our united Self that uses all aspects of our world to communicate with us (45). B) The recycle bin of our individual mind where we store what we don't wish to remember (33, 44, 45).

user (115): Anyone who uses any of the Rock Virus programs, whether consciously or unconsciously.

Vegetable or "vegetable" (40, 77, 80-1): Someone largely stuck in the Vegetable Stage of Psychological Development.

"we" and **"they"**/**"us"** and **"them"** (44): This binary method of classifying people, commonly used by those in the younger stages of psychological development, is one of the many manifestations of a split mind.

Woman (77, 80-1, 232-34, 249-50, 291): The penultimate stage of psychological development. The Woman can be found in all human beings, whether female or male, old or young.

ANSWER KEY

Chapter 6:

Mocha Break (129): 5. Partial Program

Forum (150): 5a. Thumbnails, Reality Reversal Program, Fooling "facts" of the Circumvention Program; b. Closed Loop Program; c. Incompetence Program, Program Opposition, Feedback Loop, Stall Program, Punishing Program, and so on.

Chapter 7:

Coffee Break (174: 2. There are many ways to answer this question. Here's one:

The PSYCHOanalyst "runs toward" reminders of her trauma by reenacting these events of her own life ("YOU CAN'T MAKE ME MEET YOUR PSYCHOLOGICAL NEEDS!"):

a. She is without empathy when clients speak of their experiences of abuse and neglect.

b. She is compelled to reiterate the cold, uncaring words she heard in her childhood, verbally directing her clients to bury past "unpleasantness," along with the associated thoughts and feelings, in their unconscious minds. She grossly minimizes, if not denies, their childhood traumas.

c. She pushes them to find immediate value or even enjoyment(!) in their irrepressible traumatic experiences (rather than supporting the grieving process and the learning that comes with time).

d. She blames victims and champions victimizers.

e. She defines those in denial of their immaturity and pathology as "healthy" and those who are more aware and expressive of these traits as "problematic."

f. She rushes clients to "grow up" (i.e., put on a "healthy," "adult" act), while diminishing their awareness, expressions, and sense of self.

g. By ever toughening her patients through abuse and neglect of their psychological bodies, they regress in their psychological development, becoming more rigid and Rock-like themselves.

The PSYCHOanalyst also "runs away" from reminders of her trauma, avoiding anything that might bring to consciousness her own repressed memories, feelings, and thoughts:

a. She evades "hashing over" episodes of abuse and neglect ("That's enough already!")

b. She ignores genuine feelings or strictly contains them (she often combats them with harsh labels and judgments: "You're *overreacting* again!").

c. She insists that clients move on from the past merely by choosing to put it behind them, along with their unmet needs ("You don't need that at *your* age!").

d. She labels trauma-induced character traits as the individual's "God-given" or "genetically-determined" personality. ("I see no signs of PTSD!" [mental blocking].)

e. Instead of listening to symptoms and understanding what a healthy psychological body might be intelligently communicating, she merely diagnoses clients (or sends them to someone to do the diagnosing).

f. She teaches her clients to be insensitive to and controlling of the traumatized aspects of themselves—through overmedication or "healthy" defense mechanisms ("distract yourself with an activity whenever that comes up for you!").

g. Many of the reenactments described in the first section of this answer could also be included in this trauma-avoidant section. For example, by verbally battering clients, the PSYCHOanalyst keeps at bay the material that might surface the vast unconscious reservoir of her pain.

The PSYCHOanalyst's modus operandi is image-focused: movie #3 memories are to be avoided (this technique has "worked" for her[!]). Clients who insist on discussing movie #3 will receive "treatment" as well as the projections of her own unconscious traumatized parts.

Evasion Programs Break (183): 3. The Scam Program, Circumlocution Scroll.

Back to Work! (191): 2. Working with movie #2, a pediatrician might see not only his patients in terms of development, but also their parents. A pediatrician's awareness of movie #3 would allow him to perceive the painful abuse and neglect that his patients are enduring so he could help them, along with their families.

3. **Austin**: Blame Game, Implied "Saying Is the Same as Doing" Stall, Delineation Drive and Difference Drive, Squelch Program, Excuse Escape, Point of View Shield, Deletion Program, Control Option Program, Labeling Lock, Feedback Loops
Jayda: Difference Drive, Delineation Drive, Definition Lock, Indirect Application
Jack: Delineation Drive, "All's Fine Shine," Labeling Lock, and "It's Just Around the Corner Coo" of the Stall
Cedric: POV Shield, Program Opposition, Select All or None Program, Negative Feedback Loop, Blame Game, Labeling Lock, Subject/Object Switch of the "Cut and Paste" Translation Matrix, Reality Reversal, "Saying Is the Same as Doing" and "All's Fine Shine" of the Stall, Difference Drive, Excuse Escape
Connie: Thumbnail Program, Blame Game, Partial Program

12. **Spotting Rock Businesses**: Human beings are *not* valued, despite all the lip-service. You must give A LOT more than you get.
- They use subliminal or deceptive advertising, or they have juvenile ads that appeal to "inner children" who are easy to manipulate.
- Their marketing creates a desire for what is useless or is even harmful to the consumer.
- There is an urgency to their sales—"if you buy now…"
- You pay for an image, to which the product doesn't measure up.
- With all-or-none purchasing, you *have to* buy their complete "package."
- Expenses seem minimal up front, but mushroom over time.
- Predatory pricing puts small, local companies out of business.
- Notice the dependency they create (you "need" to buy this, and then when you buy it, you must use only their brand's ever-so-expensive supplies to keep it running).
- They ship products in excessive, nonbiodegradable packaging (like Styrofoam). Note how much bigger or better made the package is than what's inside! They also don't recycle.
- Their products are designed for planned obsolescence, and they require expensive part replacements.
- Extended warranties must be purchased.

- Instruction manuals are either not included or difficult to understand. You may, however, *purchase* comprehensible instructions or, *for a fee*, call their help line.
- They have an automatic hiring process where a computer program selects "suitable" employees, and no interview is required. Firing is done on a similarly impersonal basis. (You didn't follow the Program!)
- Their contracts only protect their business, NOT the employee or customer.
- Customers are assembly-lined and given minimal personal contact. Those customers who request something contrary to the company's protocols meet immediate opposition. ("We can't!") However, higher-ups in the company readily adapt rules to meet their own "needs."
- Communication from employees is like an answering machine message—it sounds prerecorded.
- If there is a mistake in your order, YOU have to pay for it (with your time, effort, and/or money)!
- Their factories trash the environment, and residents suffer the consequences.

Of course, employees of Rock businesses are heavily programmed, and they allow this programming (Partial Program, Incompetence Program, the Stall, and so on) to control (Control Option Program) much of what they say and do.

Remember! You have a choice of where you do "business."
(Now use the above as metaphors and perform similar investigations into your personal relationships!)

Chapter 8 (234):
Latte Break: 1a. Excuse Escape, Blame Game; b. Labeling Lock; c. Select All Program; d. Partial Program; e. Delineation Drive.
5a. embryo; b. toddler max; c. preschool max; d. infant max.

Chapter 9 (274):
Half Time: 1a. Mr. Machine, Sport of Stampede; b. Sabotage; c. Terribly Trivial Pursuits, Hangman.

ABOUT THE AUTHOR

Anne Redelfs is a retired psychiatrist who has been studying human beings for as far back as she can remember. She has a bachelor's degree from Duke University and a medical degree from Tulane University, where she completed two years of residency in pediatrics and three years in psychiatry at Tulane-affiliated hospitals. However, she considers life her greatest teacher. After twenty-six years, numerous temporary evacuations, and the Gulf Oil Catastrophe, Redelfs left New Orleans. She currently resides in Texarkana, Texas where she practices her ministry of developmental healing. You can reach her at: annethelistener@yahoo.com

Back cover photos of Hurricane Katrina and Levee Disaster devastation (from left to right, top to bottom):

1) A New Orleans house that was pummeled by Hurricane Katrina—notice the precarious end to the stairway! (photographer Peg Redelfs)

2) Flooded highway and homes of New Orleans (photo courtesy of FEMA, photographer Jocelyn Augustino: 8/30/2005)

3) Flooded school buses (photo courtesy of FEMA, photographer Liz Roll: 9/4/2005)

4) Flooded Canal Street – a major thoroughfare in downtown New Orleans (Joseph Nickischer / i-stock photo)

5) Flooded downtown New Orleans (photo courtesy of FEMA, photographer Marty Bahamonde: 8/30/2005)

6) My mother's recently flooded home in Broadmoor—check out the flood line and the debris left behind by the floodwater on her front porch; the X on the front door posted the date the building was searched, the search party, the number of bodies found, and any hazards (photographer Peg Redelfs)

7) My mom's moldy family room (photographer Peg Redelfs)

8) I'm pointing at the breached Seventeenth Street Canal floodwall that contributed to the massive flooding of New Orleans (photographer Peg Redelfs)